MOVIES OF THE 70s

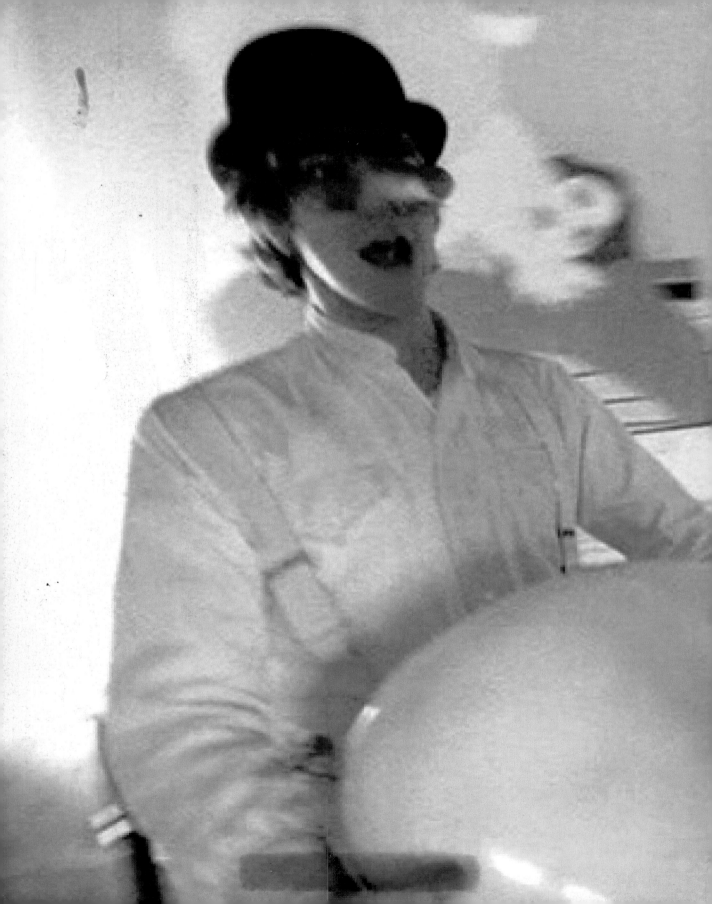

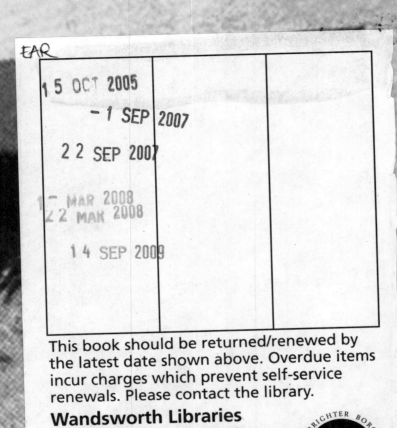

JÜRGEN MÜLLER (ED.)

MOVIES OF THE 70s

IN COLLABORATION WITH
defd AND CINEMA, HAMBURG
BRITISH FILM INSTITUTE, LONDON

TASCHEN

KÖLN LONDON LOS ANGELES MADRID

THE SKEPTICAL EYE
Notes on the Cinema of the 70s

"Municipal Flatblock 18a, Linear North. This was where I lived with my dadda and mum," says Alex (Malcolm McDowell), as he strolls home whistling between the houses of a suburban housing development somewhere in the middle of nowhere. The place is like a labyrinth. Lights burn in a few windows, weakly illuminating the protagonist's path. There's something strangely static about the camera that accompanies him through these streets in a single parallel tracking shot. The dramatic impression is not created by Hollywood's standard techniques – shot/reverse shot – but by a camera that glides like a ghost through dilapidated flowerbeds full of discarded junk.

In this dismal environment, the film's young hero is the only sign of life, and he's just enjoyed a good night out. Alex and his droogs have tolchocked an old tramp and a writer, raped a devotchka, stolen a car, and forced a respectable number of fellow-drivers into the roadside ditch. Horrorshow.

Alex is in a splendid mood. Accompanying him homewards, we become highly aware of the camera's presence. We're waiting for a cut, but the camera does not blink, staring persistently at Alex as it slides along at his side. What we see here is more than a happily whistling hoodlum; we're seeing the fact that we see him.

Stanley Kubrick's *A Clockwork Orange* (1971, p. 62) is one of the key cult movies of the 70s, and certainly the most controversial. It might be described as the hinge that links the 60s with the 70s, for Kubrick's film may well be seen as a skeptical critique of the ideals formulated by the 60s student movement. Yet although the movie makes constant allusions to the progressive optimism of that decade, its purview includes the entire century and the inhuman ideologies that marked it out.

It's hard to think of another film that assigns us the role of voyeur so effectively. In a shocking way, *A Clockwork Orange* makes all of share responsibility for the things it shows. Thus the eloquent off-screen narrator who tells us his story never doubts for a second that he has our sympathy – and our consent. Again and again, he addresses us as "brothers." Still, the risk remains that we might have to see things from another perspective; and once, indeed, we find ourselves in the role of the victim – with Alex insisting we take a *veddy* good look… In this respect, Kubrick plays with the viewer's expectations. The film insists on breaking the bounds of fiction and assigning a series of different roles to us, the spectators. It's as if the director wanted to demonstrate his awareness of the pleasure we take in voyeurism, while also demanding that we see the world through Alex's eyes.

But Kubrick takes possession of us to an even greater extent than this, using all cinematic means available to give an authentic representation of Alex's world. We don't just see through Alex's eyes; we hear through his ears; and the music that accompanies his atrocities "allows" us to share his visceral pleasure in cruelty. As we watch a vicious brawl in a disused cinema, we hear Rossini's *La gazza ladra*; but this doesn't mean that Kubrick is trivializing violence.

On the contrary; the fighters' fun is simply being made plain to us. Kubrick is attempting to show – to make us *feel* – what violence looks like from the inside. Here, violence is presented as a creative principle. It signifies lust, intoxication, as described by Nietzsche in the "The Birth of Tragedy." The film sketches a theory of ecstasy as the true fulfillment experienced by any human being who escapes the limits of his individuality. One scene shows this with particular vividness: like a satyr of the ancient world, Alex embraces a stone phallus – life petrified into art – and reawakens it in a grotesque balletic dance.

As we accompanied Alex back to the flat, we got so close to him that we almost entered his Holy of Holies – home itself, with dadda and mum. In the entrance hall of his apartment block, the camera blinks; and now we're gliding along in front of a mural. Once again, the director has flouted our expectations. Naturally, we interpret this tracking shot as if we see what we're seeing through Alex's eyes, or as if we had just escorted him into the foyer; yet now, to our surprise, we see him enter the frame from the opposite direction. And while we wait for him to arrive, there's time to ex-

amine the heaps of garbage, the parched and trampled lawns. With the passage of time, this once impressive stairwell, with its murals and its potted plants, has adapted itself to the forbidding and inhospitable concrete jungle that surrounds it. The tenants' rage is directed at the "beautifications" – and especially at the mural, which is now disfigured by paint smears and obscene graffiti. The building's inhabitants, waiting in vain for the broken-down elevator, can only have taken pleasure in this fresco for a very short period. For they've "improved" it by adding enormous male sex organs, along with some helpful advice: "Suck it and see," says a boy bearing a narrow barrel, as he gazes down on his beholders from the painting on the wall.

Yet even without the obscenities, these heroic images of the working class don't really fit into their grim concrete environs. We see men and women of all ages united in their praise of skilled labor, agriculture and industry, an assurance of the happy future awaiting mankind. Here, careful planning and conscientious work are two sides of the same coin. Thinkers and doers, young and old, farmers, laborers and craftsmen, all striving together in the service of a better life, a new world forged by a vigorous humanity. At the center of the painting stands a man whose physique and headgear mark him out as a leader; brave and strong, he gazes heroically towards the future.

The fresco in the foyer of Alex's parents' apartment block seems very familiar – as if we had encountered it all over Europe in course of the 20th century. We know this kind of agitprop art; we've seen it in Berlin and

Rome, in Bucharest and Moscow. It's as if Kubrick wished to comment, in passing, on a century marked by totalitarian systems. But this director doesn't make it easy for the audience; for he's set us a trap by asking us to sympathize with this apparently peaceful world, now defiled by vandalism. But who in fact are the vandals? The kids who've desecrated the artwork with filthy graffiti? Or the state technocrats who think they know the fate of humanity, and who paint a rosy future to conceal the inhumanity of the present?

Alex and his droogs counter moralists of all colors with the growled refrain, "If it moves, kiss it," while attaching outsized phalli to the heroes of classical antiquity. The droogs are shamelessly, indeed proudly, evil, and they're clearly convinced that work is for jerks.

Commentators who have written about this film have so far failed to notice that the mural in question is based on designs by Fritz Erler, a German painter and Hitler portraitist who readily adopted the themes of National Socialist art. Kubrick confronts us with two separate examples of state-ordained schemes to improve the world – modern urban architecture and the painted image of a utopian society – before letting loose their anarchistic adversaries. For the patently starry-eyed idealism debunks itself, leading inexorably as it does to a world in which the only choices left are between violence or boredom, hurting or being hurt; a world inhabited solely by brainless conformists and evil geniuses.

"Viddy well"

Alex, the hoodlum, is pure literature. His language is a bizarre patois invented by Anthony Burgess, a potpourri of adolescent slang, onomatopoeia and Russian. In Kubrick's apocalyptic vision, Alex mutates into a creature of cinema whose "Gulliver" is haunted by the dreams and nightmares of 60s movies, from Warhol's *Vinyl* (1965) via Hammer's *Dracula* (1958, 1960, 1965; further productions of the same subject were realized by the Hammer Studios in 1968, 1970, 1972 and 1974) to Antonioni's *Zabriskie Point* (1969). We all have the freedom to worship our own personal graven images; and in Alex's case, these happen to be Beethoven, manslaughter, rape, and the products of the Deutsche Grammophon record label.

The paradoxical truth of Kubrick's film consists in the assessment that there can be no morality as long as human beings are not free to flout it – even if the upshot is the collapse of civilization while Free Will stands by and applauds. *A Clockwork Orange* aestheticizes violence in order to express the autonomy of creativity; indeed, this is one of the film's central theses. Implicitly, the American director Kubrick is narrating the Fall of Man in the 20th century. He is showing us how the dictators – Hitler first and foremost – became conscious of the power of film and realized that the medium could do much more than merely tell stories and deliver snapshots of reality. In the 20th century, the camera became a perpetrator of violence. What's more, the camera is the viewers' ally, and it presupposes they will acquiescence – and relish

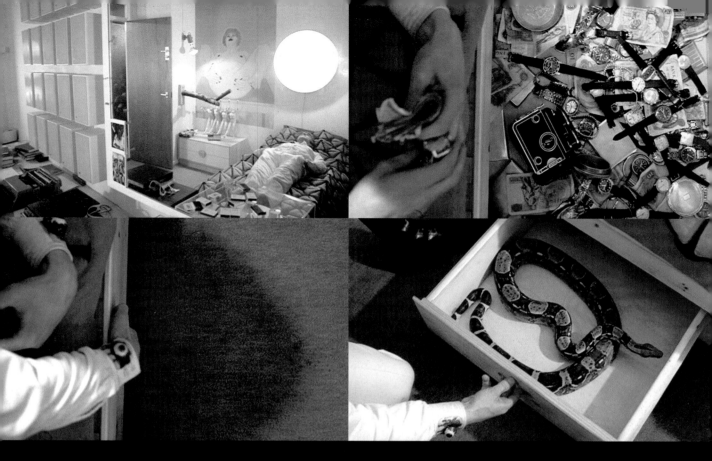

the experience – when it shows them images of brutality. "Viddy well, little brother. Viddy well," says Alex, getting ready to rape, as he stares into the camera and makes direct contact with the viewer

In *A Clockwork Orange*, the camera does not move enquiringly through cinematic space: instead, the camera's large-scale movements constitute and confirm this space's right to exist. It forms the stage on which the camera operates with icy precision, putting the beloved protagonist through his paces; first with pathos, later with pity, the camera follows its hero, bending the cinematic space to its will, so that Alex may bestride it like a king. When he struts through the record store, it's his spatial environment that seems to adjust to his trajectory, rather than vice-versa.

The few scenes we have described are enough to make it clear that *seeing* constitutes one of the major themes of *A Clockwork Orange*. The film sketches seeing as a sensual pleasure, if not an instinctual drive, and shows us as no more than its agents: cheerful voyeurs and accomplices, gourmets of the violence displayed with such narcissistic vanity. Thus it's no surprise that we even continue watching as Alex pisses blissfully in the toilet bowl.

Only a few films in the history of cinema have provoked such varying reactions. The legendary Pauline Kael, for example, was one film critic who despised this movie, and it inspired her to pen a veritable tirade: *A Clockwork Orange*, said Kael, "might be the work of a strict and exacting German professor who set out to make a porno-violent sci-fi comedy." Well, Alex would probably be delighted by this judgment; but why, one wonders, a "German" professor...?

In any case, the peasants and proletarians in the foyer mosaic do seem to be German; and this grandiloquent glorification of social upheaval is lost in the midst of an urban landscape that has now buried Utopia in a concrete crypt. Though Anthony Burgess tells us that the story takes place "somewhere in Europe," the location could as easily be anywhere else in the world.

Yet there's even more German in Kubrick's film: the uniforms sported by Billy Boy's gang, for instance; and of course the music of Ludwig van Beethoven, which fills Alex's head with magnificent dreams of death and destruction. (In this respect at least, he may well resemble some German professors before him...) In the conglomerate of qualities regarded as "typically Teutonic," Kubrick finds a paradigmatic relationship between genius and madness, high art and barbarism, the creative powers of genius and the horror of mass murder.

A Clockwork Orange is also, and not least, a film about the power of music. Though the book describes a lover of classical music in general, Kubrick makes him a fanatical fan of Beethoven in particular. Alex describes his auditory experiences with his usual inimitable eloquence: "Oh bliss! Bliss and heaven! Oh, it was gorgeousness and gorgeousity made flesh. It was like a bird of rarest-spun heaven metal or like silvery wine flowing in a spaceship, gravity all nonsense now. As I slooshied, I knew such lovely pictures!"

The second movement of Beethoven's Ninth Symphony (*Molto vivace*) is accompanied by a wild carnival of images; this associative montage does not balk at mocking Jesus as a naked, quadrupled, porcelain Messiah, flinging his arms around to the strains of the glorious Ninth. In this world, there is

no inconsistency between the outer limits of blasphemy and the adulation of the Most Sacred – though in this case, of course, the latter is represented by Beethoven. Kubrick is attempting nothing less than to show, without losing his ironic distance, the ecstasy of a human being whose individuality dissolves in the experience of music. Alex loses himself deliberately in order to find refuge in the sublime. Images of Beethoven's portrait and Alex's face are repeatedly intercut. For Alex, the German composer is a kind of *Übermensch*, an ideal representation of creative genius; and above all, he's the source of inspiration for Alex's explosions of violence.

This is one of the most absurd sequences in film history: the prostrate Pop Art goddess, the Jesus can-can, the designer nightmare of the parental apartment… These images overwhelm us and capture our sympathies for these slick-talking sadists. The pictures we see are indistinguishable from Alex's narcissistic view of himself: Alex *is* the camera, and he has his eye on us, his "brothers and only friends." Anyone who observes participates; and why should we of all people, the audience in the cinema, not be seduced by the pleasures of violence and sly blasphemy?

Pavlov's Dog

Seeing is always a deliberate act, as Kubrick makes clear in a variety of ways. Most clearly perhaps, when he decorates Alex's cufflinks with a set of artificial eyeballs; every criminal act committed by his hands is witnessed by these symbolic onlookers. There's a similarly suggestive connection between the eye and the phallus in the sequence where Alex kills "Cat Woman" (Miriam Karlin). First of all, we see this elderly woman performing her gymnastic exercises. She is presented in a vulgar and somewhat indecent manner, which already places any male viewer in the position of a Peeping Tom. At the climax of the struggle between her and Alex, he beats her to death with an outsized sculpture of a penis. The killing itself creates a parallel between the camera and the phallus, so that seeing itself becomes an act of homicide. For as Alex raises his arms to work up the momentum for the fatal blow, we find we are watching from the viewpoint of the phallus. The camera must be located at its tip. Kubrick makes much of this scene, showing us twice in quick succession how Alex hoists the statue aloft.

Seeing as a starting-point for profound manipulations: this is a theme examined by the director in other sequences too, as when Alex is committed to the care of Dr. Brodsky (Carl Duering) and forced to sample his methods of treatment. "The ineluctable modality of the visible" (James Joyce) is misused in the interest of the state: Alex, his head immobilized and his eyes prised open, is forced to watch images of the Second World War while the "therapists" play the works of his beloved "Ludwig Van."

Dr. Brodsky's methods are reminiscent of the experiments of Ivan Pavlov, the famous Russian behavioral scientist who conducted experiments on dogs at the beginning of the 20th century. He succeeded in conditioning his animals to salivate at the mere sound of a bell. The tests carried out on Alex after his therapy demonstrate Dr. Brodsky's success: for Alex, the very

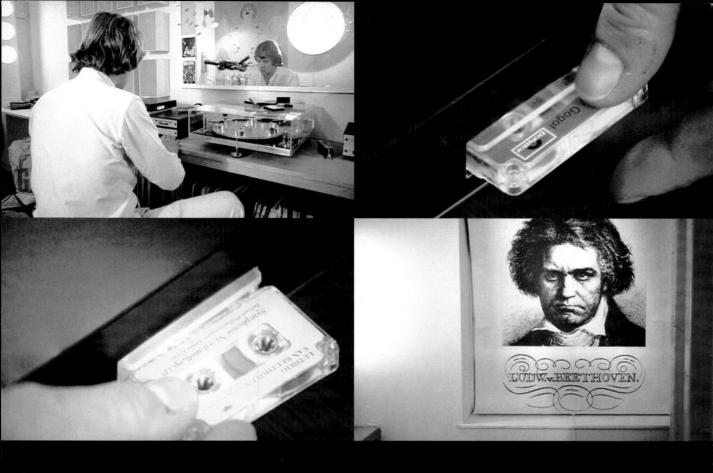

thought of violence has become equivalent to the violent act itself. The image has replaced the deed.

A Clockwork Orange conveys a significant and pervasive mood in the cinema of the 70s. With this film, an American director expresses his skepticism about the emancipatory potential of technology, science and morality. Kubrick doubts whether any of these can ever lead humanity, driven as it by fears and instincts, onto the right path – whatever that may be. At the same time, the director is providing a commentary on the 20th century, which began with unparalleled aspirations to improve the world, and soon led to the most dreadful catastrophes. In the 20th century, the cinema became an important artistic medium; and at the same time, it turned out to be the most effective method of manipulation (as with the propaganda of the totalitarian systems). But Kubrick is not content to leave it at that. For it's significant that two of Alex's droogs have become policemen in the second half of the movie. Although his former friends have now changed sides, they haven't had to give up their passion for brutality. Humankind, whatever it does, is always stuck with violence.

The Wunderkinder

Even today, the films of the 70s have an astonishing potency. This applies not least to the American cinema of the decade, which experienced an unprecedented renewal that few would have considered possible. It was a time of unparalleled freedoms, and many felt they were living through a kind of revolution.

By exploiting the possibilities of commercial cinema with a new vigor, and by examining the myths as critically as the social realities, cinematography achieved a new truthfulness, which emancipated it once more from the pre-eminence of TV. Though the monumental Cinemascope epics of the 60s may have paraded the silver screen's superiority to the box, the cinema only realized its true strength when it began to fill that screen with new subject matter. In America, there were particularly good reasons to do so, for the USA was a deeply traumatized and divided nation. The war in Vietnam continued to drag on unbearably, consuming more and more victims; and the political justification for the military intervention was in any case more than questionable. What little trust was left in the political administration was destroyed by the Watergate scandal. America had lost its credibility as a moral instance, and U.S. cinema traced the causes and effects of this trauma in a series of memorable films. The basic skepticism of 70s cinema is balanced by the filmmakers' huge enthusiasm for their medium. Their curiosity, creative will and refusal to compromise now seem more fascinating than ever, for we live in an age in which Hollywood seems ever more rationalized and conformist.

At the end of the 60s, a period described by Hans C. Blumenberg as "the most dismal and boring decade" in American cinema history, Hollywood was on the ropes, both economically and artistically. In the face of the prevalent societal crisis, the cinema had lost its power to form identity; and for anyone

after mere distraction, the TV was clearly the simpler and cheaper alternative. As the movies declined in importance, the old studio system was doomed to collapse, for it had been showing signs of sickness since the early 1950s. The last of the old-style Hollywood moguls stepped down, and a younger generation took over the management of the studios, which were now almost all owned by major corporations. By this time, the studios were barely developing a single project themselves.

Such was the situation as the 60s drew to a close; until a few small movies, most of them produced independently, turned out to be surprise hits – simply by encapsulating the rebellious spirit of the age. In *Bonnie and Clyde* (1967), for example, Warren Beatty and Faye Dunaway blaze an anarchic trail through the mid-West, each bank heist and shoot-out a token of their mutual love and a gesture of defiant revolt. In *Easy Rider* (1969), Peter Fonda and Dennis Hopper transverse the vastness of America, ostensibly to sell drugs, but in fact quite simply for the hell of it – to be on the road, to be free. These new heroes were not just excitingly beautiful and cool; they also embodied a truth irreconcilable with the truth of their elders. And this is what the young wanted to see at the movies: actors who gave a face to their yearnings.

These films gave a decisive impulse to the New Hollywood. From now on, the studios would give young filmmakers a chance. And they knew how to use it; with Francis Ford Coppola, Brian De Palma, George Lucas, Steven Spielberg, Peter Bogdanovich, William Friedkin, Paul Schrader and Martin Scorsese, the 70s produced a generation of "child prodigies," who defined a new kind of Hollywood cinema. These young movie-maniacs helped the American film industry to make an unexpected and lasting commercial comeback. For their films included some of the biggest box-office hits of the decade – *The Godfather*, (1972, p. 108; Part II, 1974, p. 256), *The Exorcist* (1973, p. 214), *Jaws* (1975, p. 306), *Close Encounters of the Third Kind* (1977, p. 476) and *Star Wars* (1977, p. 456).

Naturally, one has to be careful when comparing the *Wunderkinder* with European *auteurs* in the tradition of the *Nouvelle Vague*, but the influence of the latter on the New Hollywood is readily apparent. In the 70s, American directors enjoyed a stronger position than any of their predecessors since the days of Griffith – and this in a film industry characterized by specialization. The decade marked a highpoint of directorial independence. Having begun with the death of the old Dream Factory, it ended with the invention of the blockbuster: an "event-movie" swaddled in a tailor-made marketing strategy, with which today's Hollywood continues to rule the commercial cinema practically worldwide.

The Back Doors of Power

The most important American director of the decade is Francis Ford Coppola. He is also the one who most radically upheld his position as a "film author." As the first director of the New Hollywood, he scored a major triumph. *The Godfather* was an artistic and commercial success, and he even managed to

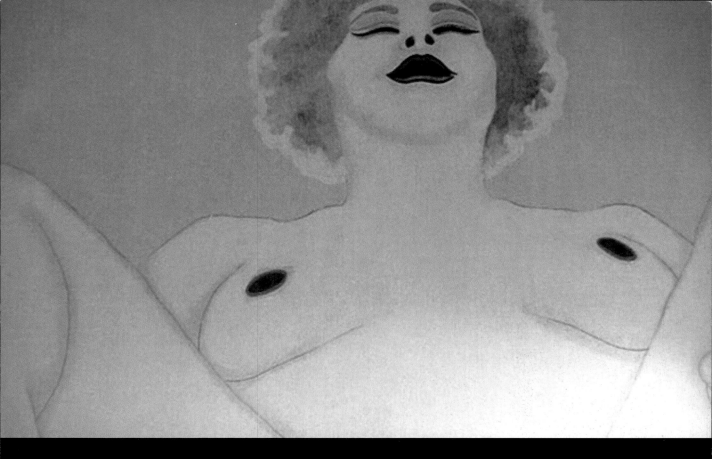

top this with the second part. Marlon Brando, the one-time embodiment of rebellious youth, was an indubitable sensation as Don Vito Corleone, the massive patriarch with the rasping voice. There were, however, other reasons for the film's enormous popularity.

The epic tale of the Corleone Mafia clan marked the first cinematic treatment of a non-WASP American family history. Until this film appeared, the white Anglo-Saxon protestant majority had enjoyed uncontested cultural dominance. *The Godfather* shows how the Corleones succeed in transplanting their Sicilian ideas of family and business onto American soil, where they take root and flourish.

Thus, *The Godfather* corrects the traditional and long-established Hollywood image of the birth of modern America. Its methods include the positively Mediterranean flair of the opulent wedding scene at the start of the film, an effective contrast to the gloomy rooms where the men settle their business matters. What's more, the sedate, almost operatic tempo of Coppola's film stands in stark contrast to the feverish dynamics of the American gangster movie, which celebrates the apparently boundless power and freedom of the individual. In *The Godfather*, events proceed with fatal inevitability, while brilliant editing emphasizes how strongly each figure is bound to the family system. Thus there seems no way for the sensitive Michael Corleone (Al Pacino) to avoid being transformed into the unscrupulous Don. The law of the Family insists on it.

Coppola's film revealed the existence of a parallel world alongside "official" America. The average decent citizen, however, knew no more of it than

he read in the newspaper. Coppola showed us insulated centers of power, impervious to external influence. In the terrifying final scene of Part I, Kay (Diane Keaton) realizes that her husband Michael is the new Godfather. The door is ajar, and she sees him greeting his accomplices; as a sign of deference, they kiss his hands. Then the door closes before Kay's eyes, and the picture fades to black. This film's pessimism captured the mood of an entire nation.

God's lonely man

Martin Scorsese was the second great Italian-American director to make a breakthrough. In contrast to Coppola, the son of established middle-class parents, Scorsese came from a poor family of Sicilian immigrants to New York. He grew up in Little Italy and had first-hand experience of life on the mean streets: the claustrophobic narrowness, the co-existence of the Catholic Church and the Mafia, the open and repressed aggression. All of this can be seen clearly in Scorsese's films. *Mean Streets* (1973) and *Raging Bull* (1980, p. 660) convey the atmosphere of Little Italy with such intensity that they permit no doubt of the therapeutic function of film-making. This personal aspect was an excitingly new development in the commercial merican cinema. Scorsese filmed the sexual frustrations, the eruptions of violence, with a brutal directness that was quite unprecedented in the history of film – and in Robert De Niro, he found an ideal partner. Like

Scorsese, De Niro immersed himself in the filmmaking process with an almost fanatical intensity; and he, too, wanted to explore the depths of his own psyche.

The most spectacular film Scorsese made in the 70s was *Taxi Driver* (1975, p. 346). As the flipped-out Vietnam Vet Travis Bickle, De Niro gave definitive, threatening form to the existential nausea, frustration and blocked-up aggression of the lonely city-dweller. It was all the more disturbing because the film allowed us the opportunity to identify with Bickle. The scene in which De Niro, armed to the teeth, poses in front of the mirror must be one of the most frequently quoted in film history.

Taxi Driver shows New York through the eyes of its psychotic protagonist. Night after night, he drives his yellow cab through a sick city that infects its inhabitants, a monstrous metropolis that mirrors the decadence of society. The film's atmosphere is dark and the use of color is disturbing, a typical example of how even non-political films gave expression to distrust of the American political system and showed the growing brutality of a society undergoing cataclysmic change. Certainly, the corruption of the political classes was directly addressed in various political dramas, such as Alan J. Pakula's Watergate thriller *All the President's Men* (1976, p. 414) or Sydney Pollack's *Three Days of the Condor* (1975, p. 362). But in the American cinema of the 70s, a general loss of confidence is perceptible almost everywhere – in disaster movies such as *The Towering Inferno* (1974, p. 240) and in countless paranoia thrillers. In such a situation, the return of the horror film is no surprise – and George A. Romero, Tobe Hooper, Wes Craven and John Car-

penter created some real classics, though William Friedkin's *The Exorcist* is probably the most notable example of the genre.

Towards the end of the 70s, the U.S. cinema began dealing explicitly with the Vietnam War. Here, too, Coppola was the pioneer. In *Apocalypse Now* (1979, p. 602), he attempted to grasp the nature of war. The film depicts a regression to an anti-humanist world in which good and evil have become indistinguishable. Here, Coppola made a radical break with the alleged realism of the war-film genre, by combining the greatest possible degree of authenticity – the film was made on location in the jungle – with a lurid, expressive artificiality.

Apocalypse Now is one of the most daring projects in cinematic history. It stands as proof of a passionate filmmaker's unbroken faith in himself, for Coppola was prepared to risk both his livelihood and his health in order to realize his vision. In retrospect, however, the project's very radicalism seems to presage the end of large-scale "authorial cinema" in the New Hollywood era. Soon after, Michael Cimino's box-office disaster *Heaven's Gate* (1980, p. 674) supplied the death certificate.

It took so long to complete *Apocalypse Now* – while the media speculated avidly about the project's impending collapse – that other Vietnam films reached the theaters sooner. Hal Ashby scored a considerable success with his melodrama *Coming Home* (1978, p. 490), the story of a soldier's wife (Jane Fonda) who falls in love with an invalid war veteran (Jon Voight). This was a relatively conventional tale, told in the best liberal Hollywood manner.

By contrast, Cimino's *The Deer Hunter* (1978, p. 500) was the source of considerable controversy, with the negative representation of the Vietcong arousing particular criticism. If truth be told, the film is completely uninterested in a balanced representation of events, and less interested in the conflict itself than in what the American film scholar Robin Wood called "the invasion of America by Vietnam" – the war's penetration of the American psyche. In Wood's reading of the film, Cimino is examining the myth of an ideal America at the moment of its dissolution. Vietnam initiated a process of increasing awareness, a terrible dawning. At the end of the film, the survivors join together in singing "God Bless America," and the song is heavy with grief. These people are in mourning, not just for their dead friend, but for a lost ideal.

The Comeback of the Classics

Following the lead of the French auteurs, young American cineasts discovered the great classics of U.S. cinema. For not a few of these new directors, the older movies were their declared models, and they paid tribute to them in their own films. Peter Bogdanovich began his career as a film journalist, interviewing Hollywood legends such as Orson Welles and John Ford. When he himself took up directing, most of his films were homages

to the Hollywood movies of the past. With *What's Up, Doc?* (1972, p. 150), he attempted to create a screwball comedy *à la* Howard Hawks. "Reclaiming" such classic genres was typical of the "Wunderkinder." In this case, the result was a splendidly exuberant film-buff's jamboree, packed full of movie quotations and amusing nods to past classics. Nonetheless, the film worked even for those who were less in the know, partly thanks to the comic talent of Barbra Streisand, one of the top female stars of the 70s.

New York, New York (1977) was Martin Scorsese's extravagant attempt to revive interest in the musical. To evoke the Golden Age of the genre, he placed all his bets on the glamour and star quality of a Broadway icon: Liza Minnelli. Although the daughter of Vincente Minnelli and Judy Garland had received a lot of attention for her lead role in Bob Fosse's *Cabaret* (1972, p. 102), *New York, New York* failed to attract a big audience. Instead, moviegoers flocked to pop musicals like *Hair* (1978) and the tongue-in-cheek *The Rocky Horror Picture Show* (1975, p. 368). These were two films that achieved remarkable cult status – yet ultimately, they too were isolated, one-off hits.

Of course, Neo-Noirs such as *Taxi Driver* were also modeled on classic films of the past; yet they reveal much more than the cinematic preferences of their creators. In the pessimistic perspective of Film Noir, it's obvious that these filmmakers saw clear parallels to their own take on American reality. And so they didn't merely adopt the dark visual style of 40s and 50s thrillers; they also facilitated the comeback of a genre with a supremely skeptical outlook on social mechanisms: the detective film.

Roman Polanski's *Chinatown* (1974, p. 294) is a masterpiece of the genre, and one of the best films of the decade. The Polish-born director created a magnificent portrait of universal corruption and violence, while also managing to conjure up the glory that was Hollywood. Nonetheless, his film was much more than a mere homage, thanks not least to some fabulous actors. Faye Dunaway perfectly embodied the mysterious erotic allure of a 30s film vamp, without ever seeming like a mere ghost from movies past. Jack Nicholson's private detective was also far more than yet another Bogart clone: J. J. Gittes is an authentic figure, a tough little gumshoe made of flesh and blood, who maintains his credibility even with a plaster on his nose. For a moralist like Gittes, a sliced nostril is just another hazard that goes with the job.

The U.S. cinema of the 70s took a skeptical and pessimistic attitude to the myths of the nation, and this had its effect on the most American film genre of them all – the Western. John Ford, Howard Hawks and John Wayne all died within a few years, and these were the personalities who had stamped the genre for decades. Ever since the late 50s, a process of demystification had been at work; and now the *content* of the Western was also taken to its logical conclusion.

The classical Western had always taken an optimistic attitude to history and progress. Sam Peckinpah's *Pat Garrett and Billy the Kid* (1973, p. 208) is a sorrowful elegy for the old Western, and a complete reversal of its basic worldview. As the film sees it, the growing influence of capital on social relationships meant the end of the utopia of freedom. Individuals can only succumb and conform to a corrupt society, or else they are doomed to perish, like Billy the Kid. Kris Kristofferson gave Billy the aura of a hippie idol – and with the outlaw's demise, the film also buried the hopes and ideals of the Woodstock generation.

It was clear that Western heroes would no longer serve as the icons of reactionary America. Their successors were "urban cowboys" like the protagonist of Don Siegel's controversial *Dirty Harry* (1971, p. 46): Clint Eastwood plays a cynical cop who takes the law into his own hands – because the legal system only serves crooks – and who makes no bones about despising the democratic legitimation of power. When Dirty Harry Callahan has completed his mission by killing the psychopath, he gazes down on the floating corpse – and throws his police badge in the water.

The primordial American yearning for freedom and the open road were now better expressed in road movies such as *Easy Rider*, Monte Hellman's *Two-Lane Blacktop* (1971) or even star vehicles like *Smokey and the Bandit* (1977), featuring Burt Reynolds. But as demonstrated by Steven Spielberg's feature-film debut *Duel* (1971), even the endless highway offered no refuge from the paranoid nightmares of the 70s.

The Triumph of the "Jedi Knights"

During the 1970s, Vietnam and Watergate cast their dark shadows across the cinema screens. The divisions in the national psyche came to expression in horror and paranoia movies as well as pessimistic thrillers, war films and do-it-yourself-justice potboilers. In the midst of the crisis, many people wanted one thing and one thing only from the cinema: a short vacation from real life. Hollywood was more than happy to cater for their needs. At the end of the decade, the science fiction genre boldly went where no films had gone before. The sensational success of George Lucas' *Star Wars* and Steven Spielberg's *Close Encounters of the Third Kind* laid the foundations for the blockbuster movies of the decades to come.

One reason for this triumph of these films was their sheer technical perfection, which made a substantial contribution to the credibility of their plots. In addition, Lucas and Spielberg succeeded in bringing together so many different elements of popular film so convincingly that these movies, however fantastic their premises, offered a huge potential for identification. *Close Encounters* and *Star Wars* are also remarkable for their overwhelming visual power. These were cinematic adventures that even adults could enjoy with childlike pleasure, and millions were happy to do so. The escapism of these films anticipated the cinema of the 80s.

The Return of German Film

The enlivening influence of the French *Nouvelle Vague* was felt not only in America. "New Waves" arose everywhere, including West Germany. Artistically, the 70s were the most interesting decade in German cinema since the Golden Age of the 20s and early 30s. Film authors such as Werner Herzog, Rainer Werner Fassbinder, Wim Wenders and Volker Schlöndorff drew the world's attention to the New German Cinema.

Many of these young filmmakers forged conscious links to the traditions of classic German cinema, seeing themselves as the legitimate heirs to a body of work supplanted by Nazism and forgotten ever since. In this respect, Werner Herzog's *Nosferatu* (*Nosferatu – Phantom der Nacht*, 1978, p. 544) seems almost programmatic, for it is a spectacular remake of a famous silent film by Friedrich Wilhelm Murnau.

Like most of Herzog's films, *Nosferatu* bears witness to the director's sympathy for outcasts, for lonely and eccentric personalities. Klaus Kinski provided the ideal embodiment of such figures, in this and in five other Herzog films. Artistically at least, the two men complemented each other perfectly: an obsessive director with a touch of genius, and a wildly eccentric actor who endowed each of his roles with all the strangeness and seemingly unrestrained intensity of his personality. In their jungle projects *Aguirre,*

Wrath of God (*Aguirre, der Zorn Gottes*, 1972) and *Fitzcarraldo* (1978–81), this was a constellation that almost led to catastrophe; but the final results were two utterly original film creations. As was *Nosferatu*, in which Kinski added a tragic dimension to the vampire's existential loneliness – an astonishing achievement when we consider the grotesque horror of the vampire's appearance. In a world of bourgeois businessmen, Kinski's Nosferatu is a creature crucified by despairing love.

The tragedy of an individual life is also the focus of each of the films made by the most productive German director of the time. In a tempo that can only be described as feverish, Rainer Werner Fassbinder made more than 40 films in the 13 years before his early death (in 1982). These included genre films, literary adaptations, melodramas, radically "committed" films, intimate character studies, and even movies with popular appeal, such as *The Marriage of Maria Braun* (*Die Ehe der Maria Braun*, 1978, p.526). Both in form and content, Fassbinder's films are uncompromising studies of society's brutality and emotional coldness. At the same time, they are also reflections on his work as a filmmaker and his personal demons. Fassbinder's fame is also founded on his genius as an actor-director; and the female members of his "film family" – first and foremost, Hanna Schygulla – stamped the image of the New German Cinema.

Volker Schlöndorff, by contrast, made his name by adapting works of literature. *The Tin Drum* (*Die Blechtrommel*, 1979, p.578), brought him the Oscar for Best Foreign Film, and he is the first German director to have won this award. (The second German is Caroline Link who won an Oscar for *Nir-*

gendwo in Afrika, 2001.) In the role of the little drummer boy Oskar Matzerath, David Bennent played a large part in assisting the New German Cinema to its greatest triumph. Only a few years later, however, Fassbinder's death marked the almost complete collapse of the German *Autorenfilm*. The sole director to preserve his status was Wim Wenders, whose films displayed a fascination for the American cinema. At that time, however, his enthrallment was also tempered by critical reflection.

An "authors' cinema," in spite of everything

By the time the 60s ended, most people in France regarded the *Nouvelle Vague* as essentially over. Not least under the impact of the student revolts of May 1968, the movement's former protagonists – Jean-Luc Godard, François Truffaut, Claude Chabrol, Eric Rohmer und Jacques Rivette – moved apart, or began to pursue their own ideas more assertively.

Since the mid-60s, Godard, the most important force for change in European cinema, had increasingly seen the film medium as an instrument of political dissent. Post-'68, he turned his back completely on the commercial cinema, devoting his time to experimental, political film-projects. The one exception was *Everything's Fine* (*Tout va bien / Crepa padrone, tutto va bene*, 1972). Only in 1980 did Godard return to the mainstream cinema with his

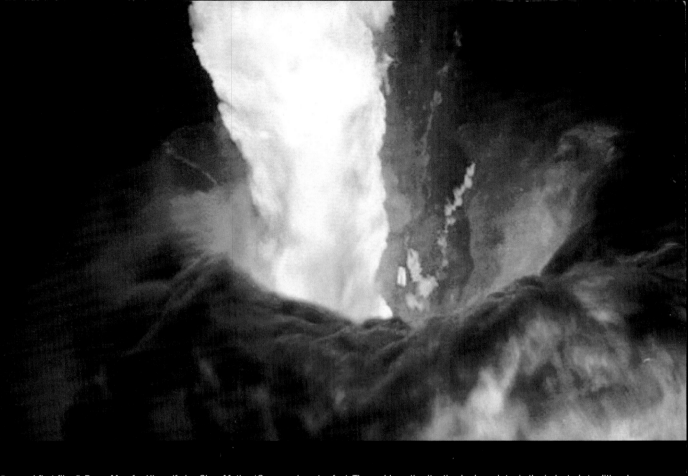

"second first film:" *Every Man for Himself* aka *Slow Motion* (*Sauve qui peut [la vie]*, p. 670) was a resigned, allegorical commentary on the state of cinema and society.

While Godard chose radical opposition to commerce, the 70s saw François Truffaut, Claude Chabrol and other French *auteurs* become increasingly established as popular filmmakers. With *Day for Night* (*La Nuit américaine*, 1973, p. 178), Truffaut achieved a considerable feat: this intelligent and entertaining movie tells the story of how a film is made, and managed to appeal both to cineasts and a broad movie-going public. In 1974, Truffaut's wonderful homage to filmmaking earned him the Oscar for the Best Foreign Film.

The Last Metro (*Le dernier métro*, 1980, p. 640) even succeeded in reconciling the art-cinema of the French *auteurs* with the perennial appeal of the stars. It tells the tale of a love triangle during the German occupation of Paris, and brought Truffaut an exceptional box-office success. As the woman beside Gérard Depardieu and Heinz Bennent, Catherine Deneuve gave a performance that established her reputation as the *grande dame* of French cinema. Some critics, though, were less than complimentary; to them, the film's classical brilliance exemplified the kind of sterile, workmanlike cinema that Truffaut had so doggedly opposed in his days as a film journalist. Despite his detractors' polemics, however, Truffaut remained one of the leading theorists and practitioners of the French cinema until his death in 1984. His influence on the European cinema can be felt even today.

For Britain's film industry, the 70s were a difficult decade and the continuing success of the James Bond films could do nothing to alter this fact. The problematic situation had much to do the industry's traditional economic dependency on foreign (especially American) film productions made in British studios. Though there had been many such productions in the past, their numbers were now in decline. In addition, the Free Cinema directors had by now lost their clout. Though they had initiated a renewal of the style and subject matter of British film from the late 50s onwards, the time of the Angry Young Men had clearly been and gone. The number of films produced in Britain sank rapidly, and even more English filmmakers than previously now felt forced to seek work in America. Many of them, indeed, remained on the other side of the Atlantic.

Nonetheless, pronounced individualists such as Nicolas Roeg continued to work frequently in Britain. Roeg's extravagant thriller *Don't Look Now* (1973, p. 222) was a British production that included a wonderfully sensuous love scene between Julie Christie and Donald Sutherland, a sequence unrivaled in any other U.S. production of the time.

The American Stanley Kubrick was another director who valued the freer production conditions outside Hollywood. He had emigrated to England in the 60s. With *Barry Lyndon* (1975, p. 352) he made an outstandingly beautiful costume drama that seemed gloriously indifferent to any kind of commercial consideration. Kubrick did return temporarily to the States to make his Steven King adaptation *The Shining* (1980, p. 696), but he shot the interiors of the Overlook Hotel in the time-honored Elstree Studios near London.

Sceptics in the Empire of the Senses

In Italy, the situation looked very different. At the beginning of the decade, many commercially successful films were being made. Spaghetti Westerns were still selling well abroad, but the genre had long since passed its artistic zenith, with Sergio Leone's *Once Upon a Time in the West* (*C'era una volta il West*, 1969). Directors such as Luchino Visconti, Michelangelo Antonioni and Federico Fellini, many of whom had their roots in the neo-realism of the 40s and early 50s, sustained the Italian cinema's international reputation.

But it was another director, one of the leading members of the intellectual avant-garde, who was responsible for the most ambitious Italian project of the decade: Bernardo Bertolucci's *1900* (Part I and II) (*Novecento*, 1975/76, p. 374) was a monumental two-part epic featuring a cast of international stars. It traced the history of Italy in the 20th century by following the lives of a few people from a single country estate – and might well have been entitled "Once Upon A Time In Italy."

Three years previously, Bernardo Bertolucci had caused a different kind of hullabaloo. His *Last Tango in Paris* (*Ultimo Tango a Parigi / Le dernier Tango à Paris*, 1972, p. 144) examined the self-destructive sexual relationship between a cynical, ageing American in Paris (Marlon Brando) and a

young Frenchwoman (Maria Schneider). The film's representation of sexuality was extreme for its time, and provoked a storm of protest. Attempts to ban screenings of the movie led to an avalanche of court cases in Italy.

The sexual revolution continued in the cinema. Particularly in European films, there was more and more sex on the screen. Nevertheless – or rather, for that very reason – the 70s were also a decade of "scandal films." Bertolucci's *Last Tango* was by no means an isolated exception. Many moviegoers were also outraged by Pier Paolo Pasolini's *Salo, or The 120 Days of Sodom* (*Salò o le 120 giornate di Sodoma*, 1975). A deeply pessimistic film that transferred the plot of a De Sade novel to the Italy of the Fascist era, it depicted the sadistic fantasies of a decadent *grande bourgeoisie* in images of icy perversion that are hard to watch even today. In many countries, the film was censored. Another movie to hit the headlines was Nagisa Oshima's Japanese-French co-production *Ai no corrida / L'Empire des sens* (1976, p. 436). A ballad of sexual dependency, the film tells the story of an *amour fou* that ends in physical mutilation. During Berlin's International Film festival in 1977, the German authorities temporarily confiscated the film, as it was suspected of being pornographic. Isolated actions such as these, however, did little to hinder the general tendency towards liberalization. Naturally, this was not entirely unconnected to the fact that sex sells.

Looking back at the movies of the 70s, it seems that the freedoms brought by the influence of the film authors are reflected in a highly heterogeneous range of visual styles. Quite clearly, the director's personality determined the look of a film much more strongly than in previous decades. There

was certainly a trend towards stylization apparent in many Neo-Noirs, SF and horror films. Yet the realistic elements and faith in a good storyline were just as new, and more significant. Movies shot on location increasingly supplanted those made on studio sets. In the 70s, films were made in real streets, real backyards, and real apartments.

The recording technology too developed an unprecedented, dynamic mobility. Nervous hand cameras were soon practically standard, and opened up new frontiers, even for the commercial movie business. The Steadycam made it possible to film smooth pans and tracking shots without laying down cumbersome tracks; and for the simulation of amateur film sequences in *Mean Streets* and *Raging Bull*, Martin Scorsese even used an 8mm camera. Clearly, many 1970s directors were looking for something closer to real life – which doesn't mean they were trying to slavishly reproduce the world around them. Though Coppola set up his cameras in the primeval jungle, what he produced was a war film that looked liked an acid trip: "This is not a movie about Vietnam. It is Vietnam."

In the 70s, it became clear at last that the old myths would no longer suffice. Vietnam and Watergate were only the most blatant symptoms justifying the terrible diagnosis of the decade's filmmakers: the Enlightenment had failed, and reports of humanity's progress had been premature. The American cinema of the period cast a strong light on the murky depths of American society. This was a country that felt recklessly secure in its possession of democracy and free speech. And the filmmakers were as skeptical about personal relationships as they were about politics. Predictions of sexual liberation, apparently as much of a myth as the Enlightenment itself, remained stubbornly unfulfilled.

If we turn our thoughts once again to Kubrick's *A Clockwork Orange*, the prophetic quality of the film becomes clear. For the American director is questioning nothing less than the idea of a world without violence. By postulating a future in which there is nothing but oppression, revolt and opportunism, he is rejecting the utopia of a conflict-free society. In Kubrick's film, sadism and ignorance are more than merely "lapses" by an individual, a group, or an institution.

The film takes its leave of the idea that humanity is perfectible. If the cinema nonetheless remains an instrument of enlightenment, then the main reason is this: it forces us to undergo a paradoxical experience. For film can only retain its integrity by refusing to shield us from the irrational nature of the world. But it's not only the filmmakers' findings that undermine rationality. Our simple desire to *look* sometimes makes the movies seem more real us to us than our own lives. As Alex remarks during the therapy inflicted on him by Dr. Brodsky: "It's funny how the colors of the real world only seem really real when you viddy them on a screen."

Jürgen Müller / Jörn Hetebrügge

STRAW DOGS

1971 - GREAT BRITAIN / USA - 118 MIN. - THRILLER

DIRECTOR SAM PECKINPAH (1926–1984)
SCREENPLAY DAVID ZELAG GOODMAN, SAM PECKINPAH, based on the novel *THE SIEGE OF TRENCHER'S FARM* by GORDON WILLIAMS DIRECTOR OF PHOTOGRAPHY JOHN COQUILLON EDITING PAUL DAVIES, TONY LAWSON, ROGER SPOTTISWOODE MUSIC JERRY FIELDING PRODUCTION DANIEL MELNICK for ABC PICTURES CORPORATION, AMERBROCO, TALENT ASSOCIATES LTD.

STARRING DUSTIN HOFFMAN (David Sumner), SUSAN GEORGE (Amy Sumner), PETER VAUGHAN (Tom Hedden), T. P. MCKENNA (Major John Scott), DEL HENNEY (Charlie Venner), JIM NORTON (Chris Cawsey), DONALD WEBSTER (Riddaway), KEN HUTCHISON (Norman Scutt), LEN JONES (Bobby Hedden), SALLY THOMSETT (Janice Hedden), ROBERT KEEGAN (Harry Ware), PETER ARNE (John Niles), DAVID WARNER (Henry Niles), CHERINA SCHAER (Louise Hood), COLIN WELLAND (Reverend).

"This is my house."

Young American mathematician David Sumner (Dustin Hoffman) has taken up residence with his wife Amy (Susan George) on an old farm in Cornwall, England. It is the house of Amy's parents, and David hopes to find peace and quiet for his work. But the opposite proves to be true. In the nearby village, the newcomers are greeted with suspicion. And the men whom David has hired to repair the garage roof of the farmhouse show their disdain for him with increasing audacity. David, who feels intellectually superior, tries to ignore this, as well as the growing dissatisfaction of his sensually lascivious wife, who is bored and feels bothered by the workers. But the tension gradually intensifies and ultimately the situation escalates.

After the frustrating bickering over *The Wild Bunch* (1969) – Warner Brothers released a heavily edited version – *Straw Dogs* presented Sam Peckinpah the welcome opportunity to shoot in Europe for the first time and more importantly, independence from the big Hollywood Studios. *Straw Dogs*, shot on location in the English countryside and in London's Twickenham Studios, was Peckinpah's first film outside of the Western genre. And perhaps it is this missing genre context that was one of the reasons why the violent scenes in *Straw Dogs* caused such unusually heavy indignation. Two scenes in particular provoked repugnance: Amy's rape by two villagers, which she seems to enjoy, and during which she is depicted anything but

3

1 How low can we go? In Sam Peckinpah's films, civilization is a thin sheet of ice over an abyss of brutality.

2 It's a man's world: One of the few significant women in Peckinpah's films is Amy (Susan George), whose naive sensuality provokes an escalation of violence.

3 The odd couple. The marriage of David (Dustin Hoffman), a mathematician, and his sensual wife Amy is increasingly dogged by frustration.

"The film is a provocation and a diagnosis. It takes the hysterical debate about the portrayal of violence in the media to new heights, thus questioning its own right to exist. Withdrawal treatments of this kind are vitally necessary." *Die Zeit*

nnocently. The second, more controversial still, was the bloody finale. David, Amy and the feeble-minded Henry Niles (David Warner) barricade themselves from a fanatical mob in the farmhouse and kill off one besieger after another with shocking brutality. This showdown inspired several polemical attacks by critics who accused Peckinpah of propagating fascist violence.

Straw Dogs is doubtlessly a highly provocative and upsetting film. From the beginning, an atmosphere of oppressive violence looms over the bucolic setting, and the apparent archaic simplicity of the villagers undeniably recalls

the notorious scenery of the Peckinpah Western. David, the rational man, seems to be the diametric opposite of the locals, though he is in no way a sympathetic figure. Hoffman's character is a far cry from the endearing helplessness of his Benjamin Braddock in *The Graduate* (1967). Contrary to Amy, David seems unable to decode the behavioral language of the locals and attempts to cover up his insecurity with cowardly servility. His frustration that he is unable to implement his intellectual superiority against the aggressive physicality of the villagers is expressed instead in his degrading conde-

4   Trouble brewing: The village pub in *Straw Dogs* is strikingly reminiscent of the Western saloons in other Peckinpah films.

5   Scandal. The brutal rape scene met with particular outrage – and for Peckinpah, a full-scale offensive from the censors.

6   Home sweet home: David and Amy's lifestyle contrasts strongly with that of the rough and ready villagers.

"I can think of no other film which screws violence up into so tight a knot of terror that one begins to feel that civilization is crumbling before one's eyes." *Tom Milne*

scension toward Amy. The deep-seated violence that lies beneath this culti-vated form of cruelty comes to the surface when David finally throws his habitual reservation overboard and allows his shocking aggression to burst forth, which is all the more effective for spectators as this is what they expect from the locals. Here Peckinpah expresses the same deeply pessimistic view of civilization that is evident in his Westerns: every man, the film posits, is ca-pable of bestial atrocities when he finds himself in the relevant situation. The observation by some critics that this commentary represents emancipation for David Sumner, placing his eruption in a positive light, seems questionable at best. In the end, David drives through the night with Niles, the supposedly harmless village idiot. "I don't know my way home," says Niles. "That's okay," responds David, "I don't either."   JH

SAM PECKINPAH   His rough manner was just as notorious as the violence in his films: Sam Peckinpah (born February 21, 1925 in Fresno, California, died December 28, 1984 in Inglewood, California) doubtlessly belongs to the most legendary Hollywood outsiders. After taking some acting courses, he began his career toward the beginning of the 1950s as a stage hand for television. Within a few years he rose to become the assistant for action specialist Don Siegel, and before long he was writing and dramatizing Western series for TV. And when the second-class script for the Western *The Deadly Companions* (1961) came across his desk, he took his chance without hesitation. His second feature film, *Ride the High Country* (1962), like most of his films a swan song to the old West, thrust him into the international limelight. But shortly thereafter, with his next project, the epic army Western *Major Dundee* (1964/65), Peckinpah's famed recurring problems with his producers began: the film was released in a heavily edited version. This fate also befell his subsequent film, *The Wild Bunch* (1969), considered his masterpiece, as well as his melancholic Western *Pat Garrett and Billy the Kid* (1973). After *The Wild Bunch* Peckinpah was repeatedly criticized for his extreme portrayal of violence, not least for *Straw Dogs* (1971), his first foray outside the Western format, which the critics blasted for its fascist undertones. Cynicism and pessimism aside, the fact that Sam Peckinpah was often able to reveal a tender depiction of the characters in his films – most notably in *The Ballad of Cable Hogue* (1970) and *Junior Bonner* (1972) – is seldom praised. Peckinpah is regarded as a brilliant stylist, though from the mid-70s onwards his films seldom achieved the same quality as his earlier works.

THE BEGUILED

1971 - USA - 105 MIN. - WESTERN

DIRECTOR DON SIEGEL (1912–1991)
SCREENPLAY JOHN B. SHERRY (= ALBERT MALTZ), GRIMES GRICE (= IRENE KAMP), based on the novel of the same name by THOMAS CULLINAN DIRECTOR OF PHOTOGRAPHY BRUCE SURTEES EDITING CARL PINGITORE MUSIC LALO SCHIFRIN PRODUCTION DON SIEGEL for JENNINGS LANG, THE MALPASO COMPANY.

STARRING CLINT EASTWOOD (Corporal John McBurney), GERALDINE PAGE (Martha Farnsworth), ELIZABETH HARTMAN (Edwina Dabney), JO ANN HARRIS (Carol), DARLEEN CARR (Doris), MAE MERCER (Hallie), PAMELYN FERDIN (Amy), MELODY THOMAS SCOTT (Abigail), PEGGY DRIER (Lizzie), PATTYE MATTICK (Janie).

"I'm going to have to watch you from now on. You might just decide to cut off my other leg."

The movie posters promised the kind of Eastwood film that in 1971 the general public could expect from their previous experiences: the unstoppable, victorious advance of a revolver-twirling, cigarillo-chewing Western hero. But it was not to be. Beneath the opening credits, sepia-brown photos from the U.S. Civil War flash across the screen. They are not nostalgic photos, but stark depictions of war atrocities, wounded, and dead bodies. Union Corporal John McBurney (Clint Eastwood) has had his share of hard times. Seriously wounded after an intense battle, he comes upon a remote boarding school for girls in the middle of enemy territory. Barely conscious, he is taken in and administered medical care by the school's students and principal, Martha Farnsworth (Geraldine Page).

His condition soon improves. Martha plans to hand him over to one of the frequent patrols at the first opportunity, which would seal the fate of the Northerner. Initially McBurney confronts this threat with considerable charm. He wins the affection of the 12-year-old Amy (Pamelyn Ferdin), gallantly captures the heart of the virginal teacher Edwina (Elizabeth Hartman), and even coaxes the overbearing Martha Farnsworth over to his side. The hardly demure, 17-year-old Carol (Jo Ann Harris) independently makes unmistakable advances toward him.

McBurney's presence stirs up emotions and needs, which he exploits with cold-blooded psychological cunning. Jealousy and disappointment are the logical consequences. McBurney believes that he has the upper hand, but his arrogance is to prove deadly. Caught by Edwina in Carol's room, he hurries out, falling down the stairs in the process. He lies unconscious at the foot of the stairs with multiple broken bones. Martha Farnsworth punishes him mercilessly, amputating his shattered leg.

"Don Siegel portrays life in a boarding school, where young ladies learn etiquette while war rages around them. The director has separated the school so radically from the world beyond it that the plot acquires a timeless quality. This is the story of a man who abuses the trust and the love of lonely women." *Film-Echo/Filmwoche*

2

1 The badly injured John McBurney (Clint Eastwood) receives some tender loving care at a girls' boarding school.

2 McBurney remains vigilant – enemy soldiers are on patrol in the woods.

3 A confidence game: McBurney attempts to find an ally in the slave girl Hallie (Mae Mercer).

4 Absent without leave… Amy (Pamelyn Ferdin) finds the bloodied corporal and sounds the alarm.

McBurney realizes what has happened when he awakens the following day. All friendliness dissolves and in his anger he ruins the sympathies he had previously won by confronting the women with several unpleasant truths. In spite of everything, Edwina still remains on his side – her sincere love ultimately calms and appeases him. But his conversion comes too late – the women have already served him poisonous mushrooms. Dying, he staggers into a side room while in the dining room the meal is peacefully finished.

Don Siegel created a gloomy, symbolically charged horror Western in the tradition of Edgar Allen Poe or Ambrose Bierce. In Bruce Surtees, who was known as a brilliant camera technician but had not yet worked as director of photography, he found the perfect cameraman to create the requisite atmosphere. Surtees' ability to work with a bare minimum of light eventually earned him the nickname "The Prince of Darkness."

It often appears as if the action is illuminated exclusively by candlelight, as in the horror scene in which McBurney's leg is removed – a process

"It's not only a different picture for Eastwood. In my opinion it's his best film."

Focus on Film

regarded by all participants as a symbolic castration. Siegel retains a certain distance here, showing Martha's bloody hands, the revolted faces of those standing around, and the shadow of the bone saw moving up and down – a nightmarish, sinister scenario, much more gruesome than it would have been had the amputation been shown in a more graphic manner.

Siegel and Eastwood would have liked to premiere their film at one of the big festivals, but Universal Studios decided on a quick release. The U.S. public, deceived by the adventurous themes of the marketing campaign, reacted with disdain. *The Beguiled* was a commercial flop. But opinions later changed and today this incomparable psycho horror Western enjoys true cult status.

HK

"A Southern Gothic horror story that is the most scarifying film since Rosemary birthed her satanic baby."

Time Magazine

5 Medley of a love-sick teen: It starts with "Love Me
Tender" and ends with "Break It to Me Gently."

6 Testing the waters: After the initial shock, Amy
and McBurney become good buddies – but Amy's
feelings run slightly deeper.

7 Carol (Jo Ann Harris) isn't shy about approaching
the stranger – and her feelings are not unrequited.

HERO DEATH   Audiences were used to seeing Clint Eastwood retaining the upper hand in his films. But in *The Beguiled* (1971) he is the victim of an inglorious
end – unusual for a star of Hollywood and even more extraordinary for an action movie star. John Wayne attempted something similar in his own
production *The Alamo* (1960), but his hero's death pandered to the hurrah patriotism that was the film's central message. In contrast, Eastwood
dies an un-heroic death, the victim of his own male arrogance.

Just how much Eastwood and Siegel went against the grain of the Hollywood traditions is indicated by the fact that Albert Maltz and Irene Kamp,
both responsible for versions of the screenplay, did not consider themselves able to write the negative end that corresponded to the literary
forerunner. The final version was written by Claude Traverse, the associate producer of the film. The death of a male lead is a rare exception in
Hollywood films. The only films that justify such a demise are martyrdom epics like *Braveheart* (1995), or nationalistic fodder like *The Alamo*.
Armageddon (1998) offers another variation: Bruce Willis sacrifices himself for the future of the Earth and as an anachronistic hero, makes way for
the younger generation, giving it the opportunity to correct the mistakes of those that went before.

GET CARTER

1971 - GREAT BRITAIN - 112 MIN. - GANGSTER FILM

DIRECTOR MIKE HODGES (*1932)
SCREENPLAY MIKE HODGES, based on the novel *JACK'S RETURN HOME* by TED LEWIS **SCREENPLAY** WOLFGANG SUSCHITZKY
EDITING John Trumper **MUSIC** ROY BUDD **PRODUCTION** MICHAEL KLINGER, MICHAEL CAINE for MGM.

STARRING MICHAEL CAINE (Jack Carter), IAN HENDRY (Eric Paice), BRITT EKLAND (Anna Fletcher), JOHN OSBORNE (Cyril Kinnear), TONY BECKLEY (Peter), GEORGE SEWELL (Con McCarty), GERALDINE MOFFAT (Glenda), DOROTHY WHITE (Margaret), ROSEMARIE DUNHAM (Edna), PETRA MARKHAM (Doreen).

"Remember, they are killers... Just like you."

Jack Carter (Michael Caine) is back in town. Against the will of his syndicate, the professional killer leaves London and returns to his home town of Newcastle, where his brother has died in a peculiar road accident. Carter suspects murder, and he wants to find the culprits; but his brother's friends, and girlfriend, are no help at all. Undeterred, and driven by a desire for vengeance, Carter becomes brutal in his persistence; and the king of the local underworld, Kinnear (John Osborne), is standing in his way.

Although many film buffs are fans of his work, the British director Mike Hodges has only made one movie that achieved real popular success: *Flash Gordon* (1980). *Get Carter* is no real exception to this rule. Although it eventually became a cult film in Britain – thanks in no small part to Michael Caine's performance – 30 years elapsed before its (re)discovery by the rest of the world, on the occasion of a Hollywood remake starring Sylvester Stallone.

"There is nobody to root but the smartly dressed sexual athlete and professional killer (Michael Caine) in this English gangland picture, which is so calculated cool and soulless and nastily erotic that it seems to belong to a new genre of virtuoso vicousness. What makes the movie unusual is the metallic elegance and the single-minded proficiency with which it adheres to its sadism-for-the-connoisseur formula." *Pauline Kael*

MICHAEL CAINE

Michael Caine once said that he and Harold Lloyd were the only bespectacled actors ever to have made a name for themselves. Indeed, the glasses were not the only disadvantage Caine had to contend with. The son of a cleaner and a fishmonger, Maurice Micklewhite (as he was then known) was born in a working-class area of London on March 14, 1933. From an early age, Caine wanted to become an actor; but although he made his cinematic debut in the mid-50s, his breakthrough as the laconic secret agent Harry Palmer in *The Ipcress File* (1965), directed by Sidney J. Furie, was still ten years away. He was equally successful in the film's two sequels. In *Alfie* (1966), Caine played a working-class Casanova. The film made him world-famous and earned him his first Oscar nomination. Since then, he has been one of the busiest stars in the English-speaking world. Michael Caine's trademarks are his understated acting style and his distinctive Cockney accent. In the course of his long career, he has won two Academy Awards as Best Supporting Actor for his performances in Woody Allen's *Hannah and Her Sisters* (1985) and in Lasse Hallström's *The Cider House Rules* (1999).

1   In the flesh: To this day, Caine excels at everything from rugged working class hero to demented doctor.

2   Local boy gone bad: Professional killer Jack Carter (Michael Caine) is back in his hometown to investigate the death of his brother.

3   Sex and Crime: Assassin Carter (Michael Caine) knocks 'em all dead.

4   Wherever Carter goes, violence, corruption and ruin are sure to follow.

Get Carter was Hodges' cinematic debut. Up till then, he had spent years working in television, making reports and documentaries. In 1969, he directed *Suspect*, his first TV drama, a thriller about a child murder that took a critical look behind the mask of British society. *Get Carter* is a film with equally few illusions. While charting the course of a private mission of revenge, it also depicts a nation grown squalid, amoral and violent. Carter cruises the city like a detective. Wherever he happens to land, from the elegant apartments and villas of the decadent élite to the bleak pubs and terraced houses of the working class, he encounters cunning, mistrust and naked greed. In Hodges' film, we hear the dying echoes of the Swinging Sixties, and all that remains in their wake is a riotous and unconscionable hedonism. Corruption and brutality rule; one rapid sequence combines fast sex and fast cars, but "liberation" is the last word that comes to mind… As if to demonstrate that he was dealing with reality and not just following the conventions of the genre, Hodges filmed on location in the grim and chilly North of England; and he did so with the beady eye of a trained documentary

"You know, I'd almost forgotten what your eyes looked like. Still the same. Pissholes in the snow."

Film quote: Jack Carter

5

5 Rolling with the times: Sex is just one more aspect of life that's ruled by greed and brutality.

6 A twisted latter-day *angry young man*: Carter rages against an amoral system that has long since corrupted him too.

"One man against an organization. The courage and naivety of an individual versus the overwhelming power and sophistication of a system – a perennial theme in the oeuvre of that underrated director, Mike Hodges." *Süddeutsche Zeitung*

filmmaker. In this, he is heir to the Free Cinema of the late 50s and early 60s, a period he pays tribute to by casting the dramatist John Osborne as the gangster boss Kinnear.

And in fact we may well see Carter as a twisted, latter-day "angry young man" – an armed proletarian criminal fighting the status quo. In a key scene, he discovers that his niece has been abused for a shabby porn film; as he watches the images on screen, he loses his distance and his icy façade melts into tears. The professional assassin runs amok, slaughtering men and women alike, driven by hatred and the pain of his own loss of innocence.

Even in his rage, Carter kills only the guilty; yet he knows he's no better than his victims. He too is part of the system. The film's inner logic can offer him no new beginning, merely a permanent ending. The final showdown takes place on the beach – one of the mythical places of the cinema. Death takes the form of a precision shot from the rifle of a contract killer. On the marksman's signet ring, we see the letter "J." Like Jack Carter, he's a master of his trade; but unlike Carter, he still has the necessary professional distance from the job he's paid to do.

JH

KLUTE

1971 - USA - 114 MIN. - THRILLER

DIRECTOR ALAN J. PAKULA (1928–1998)
SCREENPLAY ANDY LEWIS, DAVE LEWIS DIRECTOR OF PHOTOGRAPHY GORDON WILLIS EDITING CARL LERNER MUSIC MICHAEL SMALL
PRODUCTION ALAN J. PAKULA for WARNER BROS., GUS PRODUCTIONS.

STARRING JANE FONDA (Bree Daniels), DONALD SUTHERLAND (John Klute), CHARLES CIOFFI (Peter Cable), ROY SCHEIDER (Frank Ligourin), DOROTHY TRISTAN (Arlyn Page), RITA GAM (Trina), VIVIAN NATHAN (Psychiatrist), NATHAN GEORGE (Trask), MORRIS STRASSBERG (Mr. Goldfarb), BARRY SNIDER (Berger), ROBERT MILLI (Tom Gruneman).

ACADEMY AWARDS 1971 OSCAR for BEST ACTRESS (Jane Fonda).

"Tell me, Klute. Did we get you a little? Huh? Just a little bit? Us city folk? The sin, the glitter, the wickedness?"

A man has disappeared without trace… All efforts made at pinpointing the whereabouts of upstanding Pennsylvania family man Tom Gruneman (Robert Milli) have led nowhere. When the police declare the investigation closed, private detective and family friend, John Klute (Donald Sutherland), takes on the case.

He follows a lead to New York, as evidence suggests that Gruneman wrote obscene letters to call girl Bree Daniels (Jane Fonda) before he vanished. Klute tries to question the woman, but doesn't get very far. Highly suspicious of the snoop, Bree tells him to stick it to himself. Only after Klute taps her phone line and uses snippets of the conversations to pressure her does Bree agree to cooperate. Although she claims to have no recollection of Gruneman, she confides in Klute, telling him about an experience with a violent john – a dumper as she puts it – who might have something to do with a string of anonymous phone calls she has been receiving. Bree admits to being afraid, but finds her anxiety ridiculous. Klute, however, senses that Bree is truly in danger. His hunch is confirmed when one night he notices from inside Bree's apartment that the two of them are being watched.

Paranoia thrillers reached their zenith in the USA of the 70s. Vietnam and Watergate devastated the nation. The malignant state of emergency and the American people's growing distrust of the Nixon administration were magnified in films like Francis Ford Coppola's *The Conversation* (1974), Sydney Pollack's *Three Days of the Condor* (1975) along with Alan J. Pakula's so-called paranoia trilogy, which included *Klute* (1971) *The Parallax View* (1974) and *All the President's Men* (1976).

In *Klute*, Pakula paints a portrait of a relentless, invisible menace. Even during the picture's prolog, the seed of anxiety begins to take root, as the camera reveals a tape-recorder picking up the conversation at a serene holiday dinner at the Grunemans. The oppressive atmosphere gains momentum, eventually engulfing the entire film. Surveillance equipment seems to be planted in every crevice, in a private sphere wholly unprotected from unknown predators. The piece's shadowy images, lacking both depth and sharpness, seem to come from a hidden camera. The tinny audio track has a bugged sounding quality to it, giving us the impression that even life's most intimate moments do not go unobserved. Pakula thus forces his audience

"Jane Fonda dominates the film from her first to her last appearance. In a brilliant performance that almost bursts the confines of the character she plays, she combines subtle expressiveness with intelligence and feminine self-assurance. Yet she also shows the suffering and uncertainty of a lonely human being." *Stuttgarter Zeitung*

into the role of a conscious voyeur, an impression accentuated by frequent switches back and forth between the maniac's diabolical mousetrap and Bree's suffocating frenzy. The audience is left squirming in their seats, gasping as terror encroaches upon them. Pakula's direction suggests that the imminent danger he depicts is more than just a story, but a universal threat that extends far beyond the confines of his film.

Klute is, nonetheless, much more than just an example of a masterfully executed, claustrophobic thriller. Pakula's film is also a complex portrait of a woman. Contrary to what one might assume from both the film's title and premise, it is not the investigator who serves as this film's centerpiece but Bree Daniels. This can be attributed, without question, to Jane Fonda's incom-

parable, Oscar-winning performance. She portrays Bree as a prostitute but avoids the clichés. Neither the moral wreck, nor the hooker with a heart of gold, she is a young woman shielding herself behind a harsh and cynical suit of armor. Alone in the world, she has no illusions about the fickleness and egocentrism of human nature. The wary Bree is a woman full of contradictions who attempts to assert herself in a hostile, male-dominated society. Her greatest aspiration is to become an actress, claiming that her performance as a call girl already proves that that she ranks among the world's greatest. At the time, in the early days of the so-called New Hollywood, this assertion was no gentle poke at the chauvinist female images dominating the contemporary American cinema. It was nothing less than a slap in the face.   JH

1   Fond of Jane: In the early 70s, Jane Fonda was the premier personality among America's female movie stars. She was awarded her first Oscar for her role as call girl Bree Daniels in *Klute*.

2   Not just film partners: Jane Fonda and Donald Sutherland made the most of their fame and worked together to oppose America's military intervention in Vietnam.

3   Getting past their inhibitions (Donald Sutherland): *Klute* made a clean break with the clichés of the genre.

3

4   All talk? Bree mistrusts the world around her –
and she doesn't find it easy to open up to Klute.

5   A girl about town: The title "Klute" is misleading:
Jane Fonda is clearly the central focus of the film.
Her performance made Alan J. Pakula's thriller

one of the most gripping and sensitive portraits
of a woman in 70s cinema.

"This film belongs to Jane Fonda. She portrays a prostitute who is both the classic victim and the captain of her fate."

James Monaco, in: American Film Now

JANE FONDA   Prior to her 1960 screen debut in Joshua Logan's *Tall Story*, Jane Fonda (born December 21, 1937 in New York), daughter of Hollywood legend Henry Fonda, had already worked as both a fashion model and theatrical actress. She also successfully completed her formal studies at the Lee Strasberg Actor's Studio prior to her film career. Initially, Jane Fonda appeared in a number of romantic comedies. In the mid-60s, the young ingénue went to France – to "discover herself" as she put it – where she met her husband Roger Vadim, starring in several of his pictures, most notably *Barbarella: Queen of the Galaxy* (1968). Following her return to the United States, she garnered her first Academy Award nomination for her performance in Sydney Pollack's *They Shoot Horses, Don't They?* (1969). In 1972, Jane Fonda was recognized with the Best Actress Oscar for her stunning portrayal of a Manhattan call girl in Alan J. Pakula's thriller *Klute* (1971). In the years that followed, she used her fame and status to aid the human rights crusade. Fonda was a strongly opposed to the Vietnam War and the climax of her involvement in the anti-war effort took place when she visited American POWs in North Vietnam. Only towards the end of the 1970s did Jane Fonda begin to focus on her film career again, winning her second Best Actress Oscar for her role as a woman who volunteers at the local veterans' hospital in Hal Ashby's *Coming Home* (1978). Three further Academy Award nominations promptly followed. Ms. Fonda's career took yet another surprising turn in the 1980s, when she started her decade long reign as the nation's most prominent fitness guru thanks to her best selling series of workout videos. In 1989, she took a leave of absence from film and married media mogul Ted Turner two years later. They recently divorced.

DIRTY HARRY

1971 - USA - 102 MIN. - THRILLER

DIRECTOR DON SIEGEL (1912–1991)
SCREENPLAY HARRY JULIAN FINK, RITA M. FINK, DEAN REISNER DIRECTOR OF PHOTOGRAPHY BRUCE SURTEES EDITING CARL PINGITORE
MUSIC LALO SCHIFRIN PRODUCTION DON SIEGEL for THE MALPASO COMPANY, WARNER BROS.

STARRING CLINT EASTWOOD ("Dirty" Harry Callahan), HARRY GUARDINO (Bressler), RENI SANTONI (Chico Gonzalez), JOHN VERNON (Mayor), ANDREW ROBINSON (Scorpio, the Killer), JOHN LARCH (Chief), JOHN MITCHUM (Frank DiGiorgio), MAE MERCER (Mrs. Russell), LYN EDGINGTON (Norma), JOSEF SOMMER (Rothko).

"I think he's got a point."

A killer lurks on the rooftops of San Francisco. A young woman becomes his first victim. Sensuously following her movements through his telescopic lens, he watches her rise from her lounge chair on the top of a high-rise across the way and dive elegantly into a pool. The killer lets her swim a few laps, and then squeezes the trigger. The clear water in the light-blue pool turns dark red and the girl momentarily flails about, and then dies in a thick cloud of her own blood.

Some time later, police inspector Harry Callahan (Clint Eastwood) scrutinizes the crime scene from the killer's perspective – clearly a voyeuristic spot. But it is all too apparent that what had once been a pleasure in watching has now become a pleasure in killing. And the killer has just one objective: at the scene of the crime, Callahan finds a note from the mysterious man, who calls himself Scorpio (Andrew Robinson). If he does not receive $100,000 he will continue to kill one person a day – anyone from a "Catholic priest," to a "Nigger." The mayor (John Vernon) wants to agree to the demands. Callahan's advice, however, is to investigate and search for the suspect without further delay. Experience tells him that Scorpio will most definitely kill again – for the sheer fun of it. Callahan's prophecy turns out to be correct. Intensified surveillance of the high-rise buildings, including helicopter sorties, does not stop Scorpio from his murder spree. Soon, Callahan sets a trap for the killer and Scorpio is just a few steps away. But he eludes capture by shooting indiscriminately and killing a police officer.

"As suspense craftsmanship, the picture is trim, brutal, and exciting; it was directed in the sleekest style by the veteran urban-action director Don Siegel, and Lalo Schifrin's pulsating, jazzy electronic trickery drives the picture forward."

The New Yorker

LALO SCHIFRIN

Composer and director Lalo Schifrin, born in Buenos Aires in 1932, fundamentally shaped the sound of the 60s and 70s. His themes are immediately recognizable and consistently contemporary. The recognizable melody from *Bullitt* (1968) was used again decades later in a commercial, and the robust title music from the TV series *Mission: Impossible* (1966–1973) was rerecorded and used in 1988 for the new episodes of the series, as well as for the subsequent movie versions with Tom Cruise (1996, 2000). Schifrin's name is closely associated with Clint Eastwood's movies, which made him a regular composer for Don Siegel's police films like *Coogan's Bluff* (1968) and the *Dirty Harry* series (1971, 1973, 1983, 1988), with the exception of *Dirty Harry III – The Enforcer* (1976). A further classic is Schifrin's musical contribution to the Bruce Lee film *Enter the Dragon* (1973), its gentle grooves and symphonic jazz enriched by influences from the Far East.

Lalo Schifrin is a classically trained conductor. In Buenos Aires he studied with Enrique Barenboim, in Paris with Olivier Messiaen. But the gifted musical scholar fell out of favor with Messiaen because of his nightly appearances in Paris jazz clubs. He did this not only to earn money for his studies, but out of his passion for the music of Thelonious Monk and Art Tatum.

He studied both classical music and jazz simultaneously, and this mixture heavily influenced his later work for the cinema, which in addition to the typical Schifrin sound, also includes chamber music soundtracks like the one from Mark Rydell's D. H. Lawrence adaptation *The Fox* (1967).

3

1 "The most powerful handgun in the world:" Harry Callahan (Clint Eastwood) in action.

2 Moments later: Dirty Harry trashes the bank robbers' car.

3 Enemy of the people: "Scorpio" (Andrew Robinson) hijacks a school bus and takes the passengers hostage.

4 Chico (Reni Santoni) and the man: Harry's new Mexican partner finds that the tight-lipped cop can be one tough nut to crack.

Scorpio then changes his tactics. He kidnaps a 14-year-old girl, demanding $200,000 in ransom. Callahan takes control of the hand-over and begins a battle against the clock – the girl only has a limited supply of air to breathe. Callahan is able to confront Scorpio in an empty football stadium. The camera pulls back, ascending and allowing the action in the stadium to disappear behind a thick mist. What the audience can only suspect in this dramatic moment is proved true when the district attorney is seen harshly admonishing Callahan. Callahan tortured the suspect in order to find out where the girl was stashed and save her. But he failed: the girl is found dead. And because of Callahan's illegal methods, Scorpio is set free.

Upon his release, Scorpio devises a perfidious strategy to get rid of his stubborn adversary once and for all. He has not yet given up his original plan to blackmail the city for $200,000. This time he seizes a school bus. And Callahan, despite strict orders to the contrary, confronts Scorpio once again.

Dirty Harry was the fourth collaboration between director Don Siegel and Clint Eastwood. In their first project, *Coogan's Bluff* (1968), the two skillfully relocated Eastwood's successful Western image to the modern city.

With *Dirty Harry* – a project originally conceived for Frank Sinatra – they elaborated upon the idea. The Eastwood character has since become a man with a history: he was married and lost his wife in an accident. Years of police work hardened him and made him reckless toward both his partners and himself. When he inadvertently stumbles into the middle of a bank robbery, he marches toward the armed culprits with his pistol drawn, the thought of taking cover not even crossing his mind. Behavior that might seem heroic on Main Street in a Western here indicates a latent suicidal tendency.

Again and again, Siegel allows the ambivalence of the character to come to the fore, revealing a basic similarity with the rampant killer Scorpio: both indulge in voyeurism. Harry can't turn his eyes away when he observes a couple playing around amorously. His duty offers him a clandestine view: from above the high rises, from the helicopter, and from the police car that crawls the city streets. This underlying similarity to the killer allows him to get closer and closer to the criminal, but scares him deeply. When he throws away his badge in the end, we could put it down to frustration with bureaucracy. But perhaps it's also a rousing moment of self-perception. HK

SILENT RUNNING

1971 - USA - 89 MIN. - SCIENCE FICTION

DIRECTOR DOUGLAS TRUMBULL (*1942)
SCREENPLAY DERIC WASHBURN, MICHAEL CIMINO, STEVEN BOCHCO DIRECTOR OF PHOTOGRAPHY CHARLES F. WHEELER EDITING AARON STELL MUSIC PETER SCHICKELE, JOAN BAEZ (Songs) PRODUCTION MICHAEL GRUSKOFF, DOUGLAS TRUMBULL for MICHAEL GRUSKOFF PRODUCTIONS, UNIVERSAL PICTURES.

STARRING BRUCE DERN (Freeman Lowell), CLIFF POTTS (John Keenan), RON RIFKIN (Marty Barker), JESSE VINT (Andy Wolf), CHERYL SPARKS (Drone 1/Dewey), MARK PERSONS (Drone 2/Huey), STEVE BROWN (Drone).

"You don't think it's time somebody had a dream again?"

In March, 2001, in Cornwall, England, the "Eden Project" came into being: eight greenhouses standing in the middle of a stony landscape almost destroyed by mining. Combined, they are as big as 35 football fields and look like giant golf balls. Thousands of exotic plants grow underneath a skin of air cushions that are stretched into a steel construction. It is no coincidence that the futuristic aesthetic of these hot houses recalls a cult film of the 1970s. Architect Nicholas Grimshaw based his design on the contrast between nature and technology that is the subject of Douglas Trumbull's *Silent Running*.

Trumbull's film is set in 2008. After a nuclear catastrophe, the Earth is devoid of plants and animals. All that could be saved was shot into space and is on its way to the planet Saturn. The "Valley Forge" floats in space like a kind of Noah's Ark. It is one of numerous space ships that serve as greenhouses – a literal Garden of Eden with lush plants and cascading waterfalls in which deer, rabbits, turtles, and frogs can live without worry. Astro-botanist Freeman Lowell (Bruce Dern) and his crew colleagues make sure that the flora and fauna are well maintained and preserved until a time when suitable living conditions prevail once more on planet Earth.

Freeman Lowell longs for the news that the "Valley Forge" can finally return to Earth. But an unexpected order comes: the experiment is to be terminated, the artificial biospheres are to be destroyed and the man-made paradise abandoned. When ordered to destroy his beloved forests, Freeman goes mad. He kills his colleagues and attempts to flee in the space ship.

"Lowell is an old-fashioned, unreconstructed plant-freak, an organic food loon who keeps The Conservationist's Pledge pasted next to his bunk." *The New York Times*

1 Hug a tree: Galactic botanist Freeman Lowell's (Bruce Dern) love for nature can be smothering to humans…

2 Space, the final frontier: The model of the Valley Forge space cruiser included everything but actual jet propulsion. Compiled of wood, steel and plastic, the "compact" ship measured in at 60 feet.

3 Many hands make light work: Trumball kept production costs down by "employing" student interns to work on the special effects.

4 All heart: The robots prove to be Lowell's most cherished playmates and able guardians of the natural world.

Silent Running was Douglas Trumbull's directorial debut. He made his entrance into film a few years earlier with Stanley Kubrick's *2001: A Space Odyssey* (1968), to whose special effects he made a fundamental contribution. It is no coincidence that *Silent Running* seems like a direct descendant of Kubrick's *2001*. It takes place seven years later, and as in *2001*, the protagonist finds himself alone on a space ship without humans, surrounded by machines. But in contrast to the cool, collected Bowman of *2001*, Lowell is fragile and fallible, just like the small robots, Huey, Dewey, and Louie, who are more reminiscent of a Disney film than of Kubrick's super computer Hal. After Freeman reprograms them, they become almost human: not only can they play poker, they are also able to look after the Garden Eden entirely by themselves. All they lack is the ability to feel.

Michael Cimino and Steven Bochco joined Deric Washburn in producing the film's screenplay. The three authors concentrated entirely on their protagonist and the other characters remain mere sketches, with just enough contours to help emphasize Lowell's humanity.

Trumbull used the science fiction genre to call attention to contemporary ecological and social problems. This connects him with other films from the same period like Richard Fleischer's *Soylent Green* (1973) and Michael Campus' *ZPG – Zero Population Growth* (1972). But in contrast to these films, the "space ship Earth" from *Silent Running* has stood the test of time – not only in the hearts of its fans, but also as an ecological theme park in a man-made crater on the coast of Cornwall.

APO

BRUCE DERN

American actor Bruce Dern was born on June 4, 1936 in Winnetka, Illinois. Dern, who comes from a family of politicians and wealthy businessmen, dropped out of the University of Pennsylvania, to the displeasure of his parents, to study at Lee Strasberg's Actor's Studio in New York. During his acting debut on Broadway in 1960, he was discovered by Elia Kazan and given a role in *Wild River* (1960). After playing a psychopath in an episode of Alfred Hitchcock's television series, The *Alfred Hitchcock Hour* (1962–65), he was typecast as a villain for years to come, in films like *Marnie*, 1964, and *The Wild Angels*, 1966.

Only in the 70s was Dern able to establish himself as a character actor. Many of the films Bruce Dern appeared in over the course of his 40-plus years in the business are considered classics today. The long list includes *They Shoot Horses, Don't They?* (1969, Director: Sydney Pollack), *The Great Gatsby* (1974, Director: Jack Clayton), *Black Sunday* (1977, Director: John Frankenheimer), and *Coming Home* (1978, Director: Hal Ashby). Dern is married to Andrea Beckett, his third marriage. His daughter, Laura Dern, was born of his second marriage (1960–69) to the actress Diane Ladd.

SHAFT

1971 - USA - 100 MIN. - DETECTIVE FILM, THRILLER

DIRECTOR GORDON PARKS (*1912)
SCREENPLAY ERNEST TIDYMAN, JOHN D. F. BLACK, based on the novel of the same name by ERNEST TIDYMAN
DIRECTOR OF PHOTOGRAPHY URS FURRER **EDITING** HUGH A. ROBERTSON **MUSIC** ISAAC HAYES **PRODUCTION** JOEL FREEMAN for SHAFT PRODUCTIONS LTD., MGM.

STARRING RICHARD ROUNDTREE (John Shaft), MOSES GUNN (Bumpy Jonas), CHARLES CIOFFI (Vic Androzzi), CHRISTOPHER ST. JOHN (Ben Buford), GWENN MITCHELL (Ellie Moore), LAWRENCE PRESSMAN (Sergeant Tom Hannon), VICTOR ARNOLD (Charlie), SHERRI BREWER (Marcy), REX ROBBINS (Rollie), CAMILLE YARBROUGH (Diana Greene).

ACADEMY AWARDS 1971 OSCAR for BEST SONG: "THEME FROM SHAFT" (Isaac Hayes).

"He's a complicated man, no one understands him but his woman."

Now and again, a film comes along that strikes the nerve of its age with instinctive certainty. *Shaft*, developed as a technically simple, low-budget project with neither expensive stars nor a renowned director, became the surprise hit of 1971 and saved MGM Studios from looming bankruptcy. With *Shaft*, the multi-talented Gordon Parks Sr., a photographer, novelist, composer, and director, developed a unique language of images still referred to in the iconography of today's rap videos. And John Shaft (Richard Roundtree) became the embodiment of black self-confidence – at least for black males.

The first images of the film, underscored by Isaac Hayes' explosively sizzling title theme, immediately signal a character who follows his own rules. The camera aptly captures John Shaft as he emerges from a subway station – the depths of the underworld in more ways than one – and enters the lively scenery in and around New York's Times Square. He weaves through the traffic, lean, black, and self-confident. The themes of the opening sequence are sustained – protagonist John Shaft does not knuckle under to

anyone – white cops or black drug gangsters. He sympathizes with a militant black organization and refuses to tolerate demands made on him. He cannot be assigned to any form of male organization, instead enjoying the adulation of women, a privilege he savors to its fullest extent. But his sensually charged relationships have no master-slave dimension to them.

Even Bumpy Jonas (Moses Gunn), the black underworld boss who controls Harlem, must accept that Shaft is a truly independent character; one of Bumpy's handymen who is sent out with an associate to escort Shaft back to his boss doesn't survive the incursion. But Bumpy wants to avoid a quarrel at all costs, as he is pursuing a personal matter. Accordingly, he makes an exception to the norm, visiting Shaft in his office. He even sheds a few crocodile tears when he reveals that his daughter Marcy (Sherri Brewer) has been kidnapped. Shaft is to bring her back safely – and money is no object.

Shaft's investigations take him all through Harlem, through the milieu of hobos, pickpockets, and small-time crooks. He is searching for Ben Buford

"*Shaft* is the first picture to show a black man who leads a life free of racial torment. He is black and proud of it, but not obsessed with it..." *ESSENCE magazine*

1 Neighborhood watch: Ben Buford (Christopher St. John), leader of a black gang, supports Shaft in his investigations.

2 Movin' in on his turf: Bumpy Jonas (Moses Gunn) is king of the Harlem underworld – and white gangsters want what he's got.

3 Solid as a rock: John Shaft (Richard Roundtree) is his own man, and he won't knuckle under to the cops or the gangsters.

4 Outsourcing: The syndicate has flown in killers from elsewhere – and they take their work seriously.

2

3

4

ISAAC HAYES   The suspense-filled title track, perfectly fitting John Shaft's first appearance in the film (*Shaft*, 1971), immediately caught audiences in its spell. It was the work of Isaac Hayes, one of the most reliable hit makers of the preceding decade. In collaboration with songwriter David Porter, the autodidact wrote and produced a handful of successful songs for the Memphis-based Stax-Volt label, including "Soul Man," "Hold On, I'm Coming," "B-A-B-Y," and many more. Most of the tunes were performed by the soul duo Sam & Dave.

Only in 1967 did Hayes try his luck as a solo artist, and he soon created his own brand of symphonic soul, with a grand orchestra and an eccentric stage show. This was the determining sound of the double album *Shaft* Soundtrack. His enigmatic, physically driven appearances destined Hayes for a film career. Initially he appeared in *Shaft*-inspired "Blaxploitation" films like Duccio Tessari's *Three Tough Guys* (*Uomini duri*, 1973), and Jonathan Kaplan's *Truck Turner* (1974), naturally composing the music for the soundtracks as well. In later years, he appeared in films like John Carpenter's *Escape from New York* (1981) and Keenan Ivory Wayans' "Blaxploitation" parody, *I'm Gonna Git You Sucka* (1988), among several others. He made a guest appearance in the television series *The Rockford Files* (1974–1980) in 1977 with his occasional musical partner, Dionne Warwick.

(Christopher St. John), an earlier companion who is now the leader of a militant civil rights group. Shaft eventually meets him at a conspiratorial gathering. But their conversation is interrupted by an arson attack in which most of Ben's men are killed. Shaft pulls Buford from the danger zone and brings him to safety at a friend's house. It soon becomes clear that the Mafia is behind the attack, as well as the kidnapping, which was carried out in an attempt to force Bumpy from his territory. Shaft demands financial retribution for the death of Ben's men from Bumpy, who withheld the genuine background of the kidnapping from him. Bumpy pays up and Ben agrees to aid Shaft in the liberation mission.

Marcy is holed up in a small hotel guarded by numerous thugs. Shaft comes up with a spectacular rescue plan: while Ben's men act as hotel personnel and neutralize the guards, he will let himself down from the roof with a rope and jump through the closed window, directly into the gangsters' room.

Shaft is driven by the visual talents of long-time *Life* photographer, Gordon Parks, whose son Gordon Parks Jr. also delivered a black cinema sensation with *Superfly* (1972) before dying in 1979 in a plane crash. With cool images from wintry New York, specifically the sequences of Harlem at night, Parks Sr. gave the film an almost documentary-like veneer. This partially harsh realism is intensified by Isaac Hayes' soundtrack, which ranges from rebellious funk to atmospheric ballads. Just like the film, the theme song also had a sequel: Isaac Hayes' band, the Bar-Kays recorded the piece "The Son of Shaft," which was used in the concert film *Wattstax* (1972).   HK

A CLOCKWORK ORANGE

1971 - GREAT BRITAIN - 137 MIN. - LITERARY ADAPTATION, THRILLER

DIRECTOR STANLEY KUBRICK (1928–1999)
SCREENPLAY STANLEY KUBRICK, based on the novel of the same name by ANTHONY BURGESS DIRECTOR OF PHOTOGRAPHY JOHN ALCOTT
EDITING BILL BUTLER MUSIC WALTER CARLOS PRODUCTION STANLEY KUBRICK for POLARIS PRODUCTIONS, HAWK FILMS LTD.,
WARNER BROS.

STARRING MALCOLM MCDOWELL (Alex), PATRICK MAGEE (Frank Alexander), MICHAEL BATES (Chief Guard Barnes),
WARREN CLARKE (Dim), JOHN CLIVE (Stage Actor), PAUL FARRELL (Tramp), ADRIENNE CORRI (Mrs. Alexander),
CARL DUERING (Doktor Brodsky), CLIVE FRANCIS (Joe), MICHAEL GOVER (Prison Governor), MIRIAM KARLIN
(Miss Weatherly).

"Viddy well, little brother, viddy well."

A Clockwork Orange was banned in England until Stanley Kubrick's death in 1999. The director himself had withdrawn it in 1974, and the motivation for his self-censorship remains obscure. Perhaps he had simply grown tired of being blamed for glorifying violence, but it's possible he had actually been threatened. This is not as outlandish a suggestion as it may seem, for the film had occasioned a great deal of heated debate. No film before *A Clockwork Orange* had depicted violence in such an aestheticized manner, and with such a laconic refusal to justify itself. The critics accused Kubrick not merely of fomenting an appetite for extreme brutality, but of failing to challenge or even question that appetite. The violence on screen, they felt, was crying out to be imitated in real life. But Kubrick is no moralist, and no psychologist either; he doesn't explain what he shows. The audience is forced to decide for itself what it wants to see in his film, and the price we pay for this freedom includes accepting the risk that Nazi skinheads will love it.

Black bowler and bovver boots, white shirt and pants, tastefully topped off with an eyecatching, fortified codpiece: this is the uniform of Alex (Mal-colm McDowell) and his Droogs, a teenage gang in constant search of some real "horrorshow" action. On a particularly enjoyable night out, they start off with a few drinks in the Korova Milkbar before going on to kick a drunken bum to pulp, indulge in a rumble with a rival gang, and play "road hogs" in a stolen car. Having warmed up, they proceed to break into the country house of a successful author and take turns at raping his wife, making very sure that the elderly writer – bound and gagged – gets a first-class view of her lengthy ordeal. Back at the bar, "feeling a bit shagged and fagged and fashed," they chill out with a "moloko plus" (milk with a little something added) before heading "bedways."

It's not so much the brutality that makes *A Clockwork Orange* such a haunting experience: it's the choreography. Alex above all, adoring fan of Ludwig Van, celebrates and savors his own "appearances" like works of performance art. In the writer's villa, he parodies Gene Kelly in "Singin' In The Rain," keeping time to the music with a series of kicks to his victim's guts. In contrast to his three mates, who expect to pick up some booty on their raids, he has

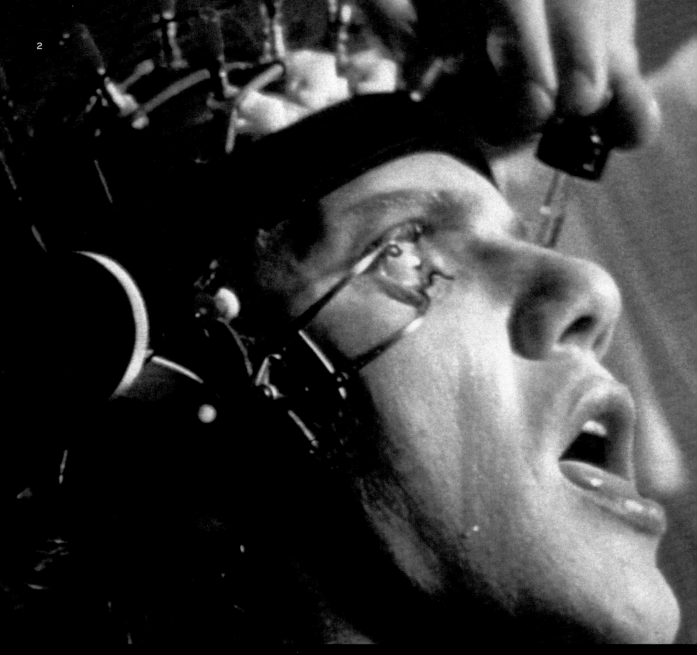

1 Here comes Alex (Malcolm McDowell) – the personification of brutality.

2 Doomed to look: Alex undergoes the Ludovico therapy.

3 Mmmm… milk plus vellocet (or is it synthemesc?): Dim (Warren Clarke) tanks up for a night of the old ultra-violence.

4 "That was me, that is Alex and my three droogs, that is Pete, Georgie and Dim. And we sat in the Kórova Milkbar, trying to make up our razudoks what to do with the evening."

"In my opinion, Kubrick has made a movie that exploits only the mystery and variety of human conduct. And because it refuses to use the emotions conventionally, demanding instead that we keep a constant, intellectual grip on things, it's a most unusual – and disorienting – movie experience."

The New York Times

little interest in money. To show them who's "Master and Leader," he beats them up. This will turn out to be a fateful difference of opinion. For later, when Alex inadvertently kills a woman with an *objet d'art* (a giant phallus), his disgruntled and mutinous droogs smash a bottle in his face and leave him to be found by the police. He is sentenced to 14 years in jail, but thanks to a new re-socialization program and a revolutionary therapeutic technique, he is granted an early release. From now on, Alex will be violently sick whenever he's tempted to indulge in "a bit of the old ultra-violence." But though he can't hurt a fly, his past is inescapable: the world is full of people who suffered under his rule, and who will now exact revenge on their helpless ex-tormentor.

    A Clockwork Orange is a complex discourse on the connections between violence, aesthetics and the media. The film gives no answers, it

---

MALCOLM MCDOWELL   *A Clockwork Orange* (1971) would not have been made without him. For Stanley Kubrick, Alex simply had to be Malcolm McDowell. At that time, the 27-year-old had almost nothing to show for himself. He had just made his very first major film, the impressive *If…* (1968), set in an English boarding school and directed by Lindsay Anderson. But Kubrick was convinced of the qualities of the young, unknown actor, for he saw in him the human being in a natural state. And so Malcolm McDowell became a star. His instant success was also a kind a curse, for his face came to stand for everything evil, incalculable and dangerous, and he has rarely been permitted to play anything but the villain.
Born in Leeds in 1943, McDowell worked as a coffee salesman before going to drama school in London. Later, he acted with the Royal Shakespeare Company. After *A Clockwork Orange*, he went on to make two more films with Lindsay Anderson, both of them intelligent satires: *O Lucky Man!* (1973) and *Britannia Hospital* (1982). In 1979, he caused another stir, this time as the notorious dictator in Tinto Brass' controversial *Caligula*. He then disappeared from view, showing up almost only in B-movies, although he did have some interesting supporting roles in movies such as Paul Schrader's *Cat People* (1982). In the 90s, however, MacDowell was a very busy man, making around 50 appearances in movies or TV series, for example in *Star Trek: Generations* (1994), where he faced off Captains Kirk and Picard, and in Paul McGuigan's *Gangster No. 1* (2000).

5 "A truly Satanic cinematic satire, made with almost unimaginable perfection," said *Der Spiegel*. In this scene, Kubrick himself operated the hand-held camera.

6 The writer Alexander (Patrick Magee), a victim of Alex and his droogs. But he'll wreak his revenge.

7 Pop art: Alex batters a woman to death with a giant phallus.

merely asks questions, and it calls some assumptions into doubt: for example, that violence in the cinema will inevitably lead to violence in the world. Alex's therapy consists of forced viewings of brutal films. The longer he's bound to his seat with his eyes propped open, the worse he feels – an effect reinforced by the drug he's been given. Alex the Doer is transformed into Alex the Watcher. For the former hoodlum, it's a terrible torture; for the average moviegoer, it's a regular delight: to become a mere seeing eye, with no obligation to act; to watch, entranced, happily "glued to the seat." Kubrick almost literally pulls the audience into the film. Alex often looks straight into the camera, apparently addressing the spectators. Before he rapes the writer's wife, he kneels down before her on the floor: "Viddy well," he says to the captive woman, and to the captivated audience in the argot of the droogs: "take a good look." The real scandal of *A Clockwork Orange* is that we catch ourselves looking forward with excitement to whatever is going to come next. It's not what Kubrick shows us that shocks, but how we react as spectators, fascinated by a masterly and unforgettable film. NM

"Objectively, it has to be said that there has seldom been a film of such assured technical brilliance" *Der Tagesspiegel*

THE FRENCH CONNECTION

1971 - USA - 104 MIN. - POLICE FILM

DIRECTOR WILLIAM FRIEDKIN (*1939)
SCREENPLAY ERNEST TIDYMAN, based on a work of non-fiction by ROBIN MOORE DIRECTOR OF PHOTOGRAPHY OWEN ROIZMAN
EDITING GERALD B. GREENBERG MUSIC DON ELLIS PRODUCTION PHILIP D'ANTONI for D'ANTONI PRODUCTIONS, 20TH CENTURY FOX FILM CORPORATION.

STARRING GENE HACKMAN (Detective Jimmy "Popeye" Doyle), ROY SCHEIDER (Detective Buddy "Cloudy" Russo), FERNANDO REY (Alain Charnier), TONY LO BIANCO (Sal Boca), MARCEL BOZZUFFI (Pierre Nicoli), FRÉDÉRIC DE PASQUALE (Henri Devereaux), BILL HICKMAN (Bill Mulderig), ANN REBBOT (Mrs. Marie Charnier), HAROLD GARY (Joel Weinstock), ARLENE FARBER (Angie Boca), EDDIE EGAN (Commander Walt Simonson), SONNY GROSSO (Bill Klein).

ACADEMY AWARDS 1971 OSCARS for BEST PICTURE (Philip D'Antoni), BEST DIRECTOR (William Friedkin), BEST ACTOR (Gene Hackman), BEST ADAPTED SCREENPLAY (Ernest Tidyman), and BEST FILM EDITING (Gerald B. Greenberg).

"It's like a desert full of junkies out there!"

"Today's world will brand him a racist," said director William Friedkin of the *French Connection's* singleminded protagonist, Jimmy "Popeye" Doyle (Gene Hackman). As it turned out, the Academy of Motion Picture Arts and Sciences was not only impressed with the then unknown Hackman, honoring his performance with an Oscar, but with the provocative Friedkin himself (*The Exorcist, 1973*). *The French Connection* swept the major categories of that year's award ceremonies, taking a total of five accolades, and making the then 32-year-old Friedkin the youngest person in Academy Award history to receive the Best Director Oscar, a distinction he still holds.

Even without a female lead in its cast, everything magically clicked into place for this picture. As the posters rightly said of its hero, "Doyle is bad news but a good cop." The role itself was based on New York police officer Eddie Egan, a detective in the narcotics bureau, whom the film promotes to Division Commander. In 1962, Egan and his partner Sonny Grosso (the Buddy Russo character played by Roy Scheider) stumbled onto the trail of an astounding 112-pound heroin sale and busted the deal after weeks of fieldwork. With this landmark victory in law enforcement, *The French Connection's* story was born.

Hanging out at an Eastside bar after work, "Popeye" and "Cloudy" notice suspiciously large sums of money being flashed by crooked playboy Sal Boca (Tony Lo Bianco), and on a long shot decide to tail him through the icy winter night. At about 7 o'clock in the morning, they witness a drug drop at a corner store that soon puts them in hot pursuit of French drug boss Alain Charnier (Fernando Rey). With the help of French actor Henri Devereaux (Frédéric de Pasquale), Charnier intends to flood the practically bone dry New York drug market – a plan Doyle and Russo will stop at nothing to foil.

No one is willing to believe the allegations of the two cops and with good reason. Not only does the fanatic Doyle have a reputation that precedes him among the city's scum, but his dubious crime fighting methods have also tarnished his name among fellow officers and superiors. This, however, all proves of no consequence when the two detectives locate Devereaux's car, which seems to be peculiarly overweight…

Despite or because of his do-or-die work ethic, the Popeye Doyle character presents a striking alternative to the orthodox police officer. He is cynical, brutal and utterly impetuous. In his fervor, he has been known to wage personal wars against corruption, even sacrificing the life of a fellow cop in the process.

In the spirit of Egan and Grosso's 'round the clock shadowing, director Friedkin relentlessly accompanied these two great policemen on their beat for several weeks. The dialog of the two leading actors stems in part from genuine cop conversations and slang. Even the legendary line, "Did you ever pick your feet in Poughkeepsie?" were the words the real life Egan uttered during his interrogation to get the suspect to give himself away.

Such fastidious details made for one of the bleakest, most deliciously pessimistic police capers of all time. The shoot took place on location during the harsh New York winter, forcing both cast and crew to battle against often sub-zero temperatures. Much of the energy that sparks the film to life is the result of brilliant improvisation. Cinematographer Owen Roizman went to

great lengths to ensure that the film would look 100% realistic and have an almost documentary feel. Actors and camera crew regularly rehearsed separately from one another to give the visuals an added sense of naturalism. The result is that the camera often seems to have been in the right place at the right time by pure coincidence.

To make the sequence underneath the tracks of the elevated train as convincing as possible (a scene many still consider the greatest cinematic car chase of all time), Friedkin and his team decided to violate traffic laws rather than prearrange to have the street blocked off. Thus the 90-mph visuals caught on film were actually shot in the middle of usual city traffic. Friedkin's ballsy bit of gambling certainly paid off, undeniably one upping the

3

4

"If you start counting 'movie moments' in *The French Connection*, you'll have to stop by about number eight – it's simply impossible to keep up." *steadycam*

1   Gene Hackman's Popeye Doyle is a bull on a rampage, whose ruthless and unconventional methods aggravate cops and underworld kings alike.

2   Tough as nails: with a bit of persistence and sheer luck, the two cops pick up on the trail of the drugs ring.

3   Doyle's partner Buddy Russo (Roy Scheider) is his last loyal ally. Both characters were based on real-life policemen.

4   No thinking cap no dice: Popeye Doyle seems naked without his pork-pie hat.

5   The law is down and dirty, while evil smells like a rose.

5

classic chase scene in *Bullitt* (1968) with Steve McQueen, which had held the "all time best" title before *The French Connection* hit the screen. While the film can still pride itself on the effectiveness of its intentionally raw look – the result of painstaking efforts to wipe all traces of artistry from the visuals – the piece surprisingly ends with an almost surreal sequence. We watch as a forlorn Doyle stumbles aimlessly into the darkness, until he disappears completely. A lone shot is suddenly heard, but we are left with no answers as to who plugged whom or why. It is an intriguingly obscure conclusion that even goes unexplained in the 1975 John Frankenheimer sequel *The French Connection II,* a piece that would prove to be yet another undisputed milestone in police drama.

SH

"Many things I experienced close up as a child went into *The French Connection*. I knew how policemen deal with one another." *William Friedkin*

6   The gangster (Fernando Rey) and his henchman (Marcel Bozzuffi) check out the lie of the land.

7   Stopped short: After the obligatory showdown, director William Friedkin surprises his audience with an abrupt ending.

8   Huffing and puffing: One of the most spectacular chases in film history leaves Doyle *a bout de souffle*. The words on the steps show Friedkin's instinct for irony.

7

**RUNNING ON EMPTY –
THE BIG SCREEN CHASE**

Movies are movement by definition. It is therefore only fitting that the so-called "chase" is one of the most beloved silver screen phenomena. Several films throughout cinematic history from *M* (1931), *The Sugarland Express* (1974) to *The Fugitive* (1993) and beyond are basically tributes to this device. The chase can be born out of escape, as in the case of *Vanishing Point* (1970), and quickly take the guise of a road movie. They seldom take place without the enlistment of a motor vehicle and often serve as the climax of thrillers and detective capers like *Bullitt* (1968), *The French Connection* (1971) and *To Live and Die in L.A.* (1985). Walter Hill's 1978 movie, *The Driver*, is in fact a non-stop car chase from start to finish. Over time, the four-wheel hunt eventually proved most suitable for TV crime series à la *Starsky & Hutch* (1975–79) or *Miami Vice* (1984–89). It did, however, continue to thrive in science fiction films and space odysseys. One need only be vaguely familiar with the *Star Wars* pictures (1977, 1980, 1983, 1999, 2002) to realize that they often consist of car chases transplanted into the outer reaches of the universe. Also worthy of mention are variations on the traditional chase like plane vs. pedestrian as in *North by Northwest* (1959), or pedestrian vs. motor scooter as in *Diva*, (1980), or even pedestrian and planes vs. locomotives as in *Silver Streak* (1976). Irrespective of the means of transport, the characters involved are often only loosely linked to the chase venue as far as the plot is concerned. It also seems to be less significant whether the quarry is caught than how well one can negotiate and command the terrain itself. Who is better at dealing with the given physical elements and recognizing the means of narrow escape? One rule almost always holds true, irrespective of plot detail: those who are chased are usually the chasers themselves.

PLAY IT AGAIN, SAM

1971 - USA - 85 MIN. - COMEDY

DIRECTOR HERBERT ROSS (1927–2001)

SCREENPLAY WOODY ALLEN, based on his play of the same name DIRECTOR OF PHOTOGRAPHY OWEN ROIZMAN EDITING MARION ROTHMAN
MUSIC BILLY GOLDENBERG, MAX STEINER PRODUCTION ARTHUR P. JACOBS for APJAC PRODUCTIONS, PARAMOUNT PICTURES.

STARRING WOODY ALLEN (Allan Felix), DIANE KEATON (Linda Christie), TONY ROBERTS (Dick Christie), JERRY LACY (Humphrey Bogart), SUSAN ANSPACH (Nancy Felix), JENNIFER SALT (Sharon), JOY BANG (Julie), VIVA (Jennifer), SUSANNE ZENOR (Girl at the Disco), DIANA DAVILA (Girl at the Museum).

"I won't take it personal, I'll just kill myself."

Movies are a treasured friend. They make our wildest dreams come true, allow us to take on perilous adventures and sometimes manage to reveal life's best kept secrets. Yet when the lights go up, the illusion comes to an end. We are abandoned in the aisles with our troubles and toil, and long to return to that world of silhouetted heroes. Film critic Allan Felix (Woody Allen) rejects this cold reality and succeeds in smuggling the celluloid magic back into his otherwise ordinary life.

Allan has been left by his wife Nancy (Susan Anspach). Her grounds for separation were Allan's passionate love affair with the cinema. "You like movies because you're one of life's great watchers. I'm not like that, I am a doer. I want to live." Nancy's biting commentary and action sends the forlorn neurotic into the deepest realms of depression. In a desperate search for comfort, Allan retreats into a world of Hollywood reveries populated by the classic characters of the silver screen. Allan's psyche employs Humphrey Bogart as his analyst, who assures the film fanatic that "The world is full of dames. All you got to do is whistle."

Lovely. Unfortunately, as the general mindset of the 1970s urban woman is pretty much at odds with that of the 1940s screen vamp, Allan's attempts at wooing the ladies fail miserably. Every time his real life friends Dick and Linda (Tony Roberts and Diane Keaton) introduce him to a woman, Allan goes into his bizarre rendition of Bogey. Instead of hat, trench coat and occasional swig of booze, the scrawny Casanova's trademarks include long

2

hair, glasses and a slight addiction to over-the-counter medication. Still, none of this prevents him from using pre-packed Hollywood lines like "I love the rain – it washes memories off the sidewalk of life," as if they were his own.

His unintentionally ludicrous inner Bogart doesn't do much to help him overcome his inferiority complex either. In fact, Allan's nervousness often gets the better of him. While out on a first date, he starts flailing his arms uncontrollably, throws vinyl records haphazardly through the air and somehow thinks he can impress the opposite sex by piling mounds of rice into his mouth at a Chinese restaurant. His love interest, understandably, has an allergic reaction to this sort of tomfoolery. In another scene, he is shunned by a self-proclaimed nymphomaniac when he begins to grunt like a wanton ape

"A poignant and hilarious ode to Humphrey Bogart films and physical comedy. Woody Allen's *Play It Again, Sam* is not only underrated but should even be considered a comedy masterpiece." *Apollo Guide*

1 "Why can't I be cool?" A pair of breasts is enough to drive film critic Allan Felix (Woody Allen) to distraction.

2 You must remember this… Classic one-liners take on a whole new meaning.

3 Allan's Chinese table manners will soon stifle the small talk.

4 Shrine to the almighty: Photos and posters of Bogart are plastered throughout Allan's apartment and help evoke his spirit when he is needed most.

4

in heat. Even the old reliable pickup at the disco standby proves an out and out bust. Focusing too hard on the rhythm, Allan can't string a sentence together for the life of him. Like an epileptic Buddhist at the junior prom, he lasciviously twitches while muttering some sort of personal mantra in a futile effort to suavely keep time with the music.

Linda, his best friend's wife, helps Allan deal with these painful mishaps. An explosive chain of events is set off when he ends up falling in love with her. In the end, Allan, with the help of his extensive film knowledge, is able to prove himself as great a hero as Bogey and, at the same time, discover his own real inner strength.

The movie's plot is based on Woody Allen's 1969 hit Broadway play of the same name, which marked his initial collaboration with enduring flame Diane Keaton. The piece bridges Allen's transition from lewd, irreverent comedies to truly touching pieces like *Annie Hall* (1977) and *Manhattan* (1979). *Play It Again, Sam* is also one of the rare "Woody Allen pictures" directed by Herbert Ross, who later enjoyed phenomenal box office success with the dance hit *Footloose* (1983) and the comedy *The Secret of My Succe$s* (1987). Ross masterfully interwove the sexual insecurity of an ordinary guy into one of the greatest Bogart tributes the big screen has to offer.

The result is an enchanting departure into the psyche of a film buff, both Allan's and our own. For, truth be told, there's a bit of that guy with two left feet in us all, who lets life imitate film and would readily tell Sam to play it again, if we ever had the chance.   OK

CINEMA CLASSICS   *Play It Again, Sam* (1972) is not only about a film buff, but also about his favorite film, *Casablanca* (1942). The latter is one of a select group of films collectively referred to as cinema classics. The term describes pictures that are serious pieces of art – and which are always able to present us with insights into life, no matter how much "time goes by." The brilliance of such films is that they successfully tell their stories through new modes of communication or rekindle the fire of familiar ones. It is for these reasons that the term "classic cinema" is, in fact, an ever-evolving concept, creating a gold standard against which the cineaste and movie critic alike can measure all productions to come.

For all this talk of classics, film is relatively young medium. Compared to music or literature, film has eluded a truly golden era of classics as each coming decade continues to produce its share. In this respect, Erich von Stroheim's *Greed* (1924) is as much a member of this elite as *2001: A Space Odyssey* (1968). The 1970s play a doubly important role in this discussion. For one thing, the decade produced one impeccable film after another: *A Clockwork Orange* (1971), *Taxi Driver* (1975) and *Apocalypse Now* (1979) are but the tip of iceberg. Simultaneously, the decade saw a resurgence of interest in the so-called Hollywood classics, which one might argue was at least partially inspired by the French *Nouvelle Vague* movement. The quintessential example is *Play It Again, Sam*, a film that goes as far as to recreate entire scenes from *Casablanca* and to appropriate its hero as its own.

5   A shameless schmoe: Allan fools around with his buddy Dick's (Tony Roberts) woman while he's away, and then innocently calls on him for spiritual counsel.

6   Travolta he's not: Allan goes through his grooming ritual before tripping the light fantastic… Yet, he need not rely on confidence and machismo to win over the ladies. As he puts it: "I'm short enough and ugly enough to succeed on my own."

"*Play It Again, Sam* is a mostly successful mix of one-liners, pathos and visual humor. Allen mixes his usual soup of anxious personalities, observations on the human condition and the difficulties of being a geek to fine effect." *Movie Reviews UK*

FELLINI'S ROMA
Roma

1971 - ITALY / FRANCE - 128 MIN. - GROTESQUE

DIRECTOR FEDERICO FELLINI (1920–1993)
SCREENPLAY FEDERICO FELLINI, BERNARDINO ZAPPONI DIRECTOR OF PHOTOGRAPHY GIUSEPPE ROTUNNO EDITING RUGGERO MASTROIANNI
MUSIC NINO ROTA PRODUCTION TURI VASILE for ULTRA FILM, LES PRODUCTIONS ARTISTES ASSOCIÉS, PRODUZIONI EUROPEE ASSOCIATI.

STARRING PETER GONZALES (Fellini as an 18-year-old), FIONA FLORENCE (Young Prostitute), PIA DE DOSES (Princess Domitilla), MARNE MAITLAND (Engineer) RENATO GIOVANNOLI (Cardinal Ottaviani), STEFANO MAYORE (Fellini as a Child), ELISA MAINARDI (Pharmacist's Wife), GALLIANO SBARRA (Compère), ANNA MAGNANI (Herself) GORE VIDAL (Himself).

"It's the stench of the ages!"

"The unusual, the mysterious, is right there before us. You only have to look closely to find the terror and beauty in everyday life." Thus spake Federico Fellini after completing his film *La dolce vita* (1959/60). The implication was clear: sedentary and immobile, he had no need to travel to distant countries in order to create exotic films. Ten years later, he furnished the proof: *Fellini's Roma* is an affectionate portrait of a city that's populated by the strangest of people – at least in Fellini's eyes. He sees Rome as a baroque construction where history, culture, religion and voluptuous life meet and mix unceasingly.

Fellini's Roma needs no dramatic storyline and has only one protagonist: Fellini himself. In a series of episodes, he tells how he dreamt as a child of the alluring city, and how he arrived there as a young man in 1939. He tells of his first evening in the metropolis, stepping off the train at Roma Termini, finding a seat in a crowded trattoria, standing in line at a shabby bordello. Fellini jumps to and fro between past and present, battles his way through the packed streets with a camera team in tow, visits a cacophonous wartime theater, hangs out with the hippies on the Spanish Steps, sits in an air-raid shelter and meets a German girl.

In Fellini's vision, Rome is an organic entity. At a dinner party, someone quotes a Roman proverb: "As you eat, so will you shit." The people are vulgar, obstreperous, argumentative, noisy. They smoke, they sweat, their children piss on the floor of the theater, and they only ever appear *en masse*: in the young Fellini's apartment house, there are an incredible number of subtenants; people push for room at the dinner table, gobbling snails and

tripe. The hippies, playing love games, practically tie themselves in knots. There's no such thing as privacy, everyone takes part in everyone else's life. The streets of Rome, says the narrator, are like corridors, and the public squares are living rooms.

The Rome we see here is so idealized that Fellini could find it only in the studio. Thus, he had an entire stretch of the Via Albalonga rebuilt in Cinecittà, including the trams. The real Rome appears only occasionally, above all at the end, as the camera accompanies a horde of bikers on their night journey through the city.

In one scene, the camera goes underground to film the building of the subway. Like a monstrous worm, the drill bores through the entrails of the city. The engineer explains that Rome was built in eight layers, and that a

"As Rome to Fellini, so Dublin to Joyce, Cologne to Heinrich Böll and Turin to Pavese ... but it's hard to think of another film director as close to a city, a country, an ever-present locus of lived experience, as Fellini is to Rome." *Frankfurter Rundschau*

1 Basking in the cinema: Country boy Fellini first discovered Rome at the movies.

2 Lining up for a rendezvous with the wife of the provincial pharmacist. "She's worse than Messalina," say the local men.

3 Puppy love: Young people on the Spanish Steps cast Fellini's mind back to the days when love was something shameful and furtive banished to brothels or public toilets.

4   Fellini's assembly of the weird and the wonderful. He had originally planned several more city scenes, including a soccer match between Lazio and AS Rome.

5   Running wild: Fellini said Rome was an ideal breeding ground for the imagination. Rome is the perfect mother, indifferent, "with too many children to waste time on you personally."

burial chamber has just been discovered in the fifth layer. Suddenly, they're up against another hollow space; the drill breaks through the wall to reveal an ancient Roman villa – there are mosaics in the untouched baths, and stunningly beautiful frescos. Abruptly, the paintings on the walls begin to fade and crumble to dust; they cannot survive contact with the air of the outside world. What fascinates Fellini is the clash of opposites in Rome: antiquity and modernity, the old and the new; how the past permeates the present, and how partial destruction is sometimes necessary to ensure the survival of the total organism called Rome.

Fellini cuts into the body of the city and takes a look beneath its surface; but he cannot grasp Rome as a whole. It never stops changing, said Fellini after filming: "This city is like a woman. You think you've had her, undressed her, heard her moan… but then you see her again a week later, and you see that she's nothing like the woman you thought you had possessed. In short, I still have the desire to make a film, another film, about Rome." Things turned out differently, though. In his next film, *Amarcord* (1973), Fellini revisited the scene of his childhood: Rimini.

NM

THE CITY IN FILM   As the modern city was undergoing radical change, thanks to electricity, tramlines and the separation of life and work, film was discovering its language: montage. The cut from one shot to another, the change of viewpoint and camera-angle – these resemble a streetcar journey through the city, with ever-changing views of narrow streets, tall buildings, strange faces, shop windows swooping past, and sudden, spacious squares. City and film are interdependent. In the early days of the medium, no one could understand an edited film unless he had experienced the city.

In the earliest films, the city was not merely a backdrop to the story; it was the story itself. The Berlin films made by the Brothers Skladanowsky in 1896 record the street life on Alexanderplatz or on the boulevard Unter den Linden. Since then, the image of the city in film has gone through several transformations. It has been shown as a brutal counterpart to the idyllic natural world, as in Friedrich Wilhelm Murnau's *City Girl* (1929/30), as a place of historical memory, as in Wim Wenders' *Wings of Desire* (*Der Himmel über Berlin / Les Ailes du désir*, 1987) or as a configuration of neon lights and shopping malls, as in *Fallen Angels* (*Duo luo tian shi*, 1995) by Wong Kar-wai. And – at regular intervals – there have been declarations of love to one city or another, as in *Manhattan* (1979) by Woody Allen or *Fellini's Roma* (*Roma*, 1971).

HAROLD AND MAUDE

1971 - USA - 91 MIN. - TRAGICOMEDY, SATIRE

DIRECTOR HAL ASHBY (1929–1988)
SCREENPLAY COLIN HIGGINS, based on his novel of the same name DIRECTOR OF PHOTOGRAPHY JOHN A. ALONZO EDITING WILLIAM A. SAWYER, EDWARD WARSCHILKA MUSIC CAT STEVENS PRODUCTION CHARLES MULVEHILL, COLIN HIGGINS, MILDRED LEWIS for PARAMOUNT PICTURES.

STARRING BUD CORT (Harold Chasen), RUTH GORDON (Maude), VIVIAN PICKLES (Mrs. Chasen), CYRIL CUSACK (Glaucus), CHARLES TYNER (Uncle Victor), ELLEN GEER (Sunshine Doré), ERIC CHRISTMAS (Priest), G. WOOD (Psychiatrist), JUDY ENGLES (Candy Gulf), SHARI SUMMERS (Edith Phern).

"What kind of flower would you like to be?"

When *Harold and Maude* hit American theaters in 1971, the off-beat love story about a stoic sixteen-year-old boy and an eighty-year-old woman flopped at the box office. It was not until 1979, when the picture was re-released, that it triumphed with audiences. Looking back, it makes perfect sense. How could a nation who had elected the staunchly conservative Nixon as its president embrace a tender, anarchic comedy, in which figures of authority like police officers, soldiers and members of the church get the proverbial "pie in the face," and where material wealth is not depicted as the pot of gold at the end of the rainbow. As Harold's home life shows us, money is arguably the root of spiritual barrenness. All the more reason why the movie spoke to so many individuals worldwide, capturing the hearts of younger audiences in particular, who felt so boxed in by the social conventions of the era. As Cat Steven's ballad inspiringly echoes throughout the film, "You can do what you want," and "If you want to be free, be free."

Yet *Harold and Maude* is much more than a love story. At heart, the film is also a social satire, a coming-of-age movie and a black comedy. Director Hal Ashby suavely negotiates the tightrope between the private and political arena, comedy and sentimentality, between the grotesque and the banal.

The story starts off macabre. Harold Chasen (Bud Cort), a young man from a wealthy family, turns on the phonograph, lights a candle, steps up onto a chair – and hangs himself. Moments later, his mother (Vivian Pickles) enters the room and seems completely unaffected by the event. She cancels an appointment at the hair dresser's and exits the room after informing Harold that dinner will be served promptly at eight.

Harold's staged "suicides" (there will be more of them to come as the film progresses) function as a sort of ritual, an utterly twisted and failed attempt at communicating with his mother. For the scenes between Harold and Mrs. Chasen all follow the same pattern. She throws an endless barrage of nonsense at Harold while he says stands there silently. When he does respond to her on occasion, it's simply water off a duck's back.

The Chasens live on a lavish estate, which director Hal Ashby plays up with long shots to accentuate its larger-than-life quality. Its rooms, on the other hand, are dark and oppressive and cage Harold in just as much as his wardrobe, exclusively made up of pressed suits and ties. Harold's body language is stiff and clumsy and his facial expressions appear to be frozen from ear to ear.

Harold and Maude is a poeticized slice of American life, in which automobile graveyards, garbage dumps, slums and junkyards are all awakened to new life. The film is a ballad, an allegory of life and death – in which life is ultimately triumphant." *Frankfurter Allgemeine Zeitung*

1 80 years old and still going strong: Maude (Ruth Gordon) is ready for anything.

2 Crying bloody murder: Harold's (Bud Cort) form of protest against his ice mama throws even house guests for a fatal loop.

3 A shared hobby: Visiting the funerals of strangers. Maude approaches Harold.

2

Harold is the polar opposite of Maude (Ruth Gordon). The two of them meet one day while partaking in their shared hobby. Both routinely attend the funerals of people they don't know. Brassy to the core and a fireball of energy, the eighty-year-old Maude is always on the move. She likes getting around by car, stealing one right after another and recklessly zooming around the bends.

Maude's youthfulness is so convincing (she puts the moves on Harold during a funeral service) that their putative misalliance never seems awkward. Indeed, the ones we want to shake our heads at are those who are so vehemently opposed to their relationship.

Harold awakens to life when Maude literally shoves him into motion. She encourages him to sing and dance, gives him a banjo and implores him to somersault whenever the spirit so moves him. After all, there's something new to be tried everyday, she insists.

Another saying Maude lives by is that you should never stop moving. Never commit to anything too long because you just might get stuck in a rut. In the end, it is the living world that she no longer wants to commit to and resolutely brings her own life to a close on her eightieth birthday. Harold is left, yet again, without someone to share his thoughts with, but he has learned from Maude's example. Ashby revisits the suicide theme one last time in the film's closing sequence as we watch Harold's Jaguar, which he has converted into a hearse, race along the coast and plummet off a cliff. With an upward swoop of the camera we see Harold still atop the hill exuding life and playing that banjo Maude gave him.   LF

RUTH GORDON
When Ruth Gordon won an Oscar at the age of 72 for her delightfully sinister supporting performance in *Rosemary's Baby* (1968), her amusing remark "I can't tell you how encouraging a thing like this is" nicely summed up the energy and optimism she displayed over a then 50-year career, which had begun with a 1915 stage debut as Peter Pan. The legendary actress soon landed bit parts in silent movies, but remained true to the stage for the next 25 years. Reaching the upper echelons of Broadway fame, she first made her way to Hollywood in the early 1940s. Tinseltown readily supplied Gordon with character and supporting roles in films like *Dr. Ehrlich's Magic Bullet / The Story of Dr. Ehrlich's Magic Bullet* (1939/40) and the celebrated wartime drama *Action in the North Atlantic* (1943).

Her career quickly took a new turn after she entered into her second marriage in 1942 with actor/director Garson Kanin. Together with Kanin, she wrote screenplays, many of which were filmed by George Cukor. These included the Katharine Hepburn/Spencer Tracy comedies *Adam's Rib* (1949) and *Pat and Mike* (1952), as well as the Judy Holliday films *The Marrying Kind* (1952) and *It Should Happen to You* (1954). Gordon's script for *The Actress* (1953) was based on her autobiographical stage play "Years Ago" and deals with her years as an adolescent when she decided to work in the theater despite her father's vehement disapproval. Her career experienced a miraculous renaissance in the mid-1960s: she won the above-mentioned Oscar, became a cult icon with *Harold and Maude* (1971) and proceeded to work right up to the end of her life in film and television. In 1985, the world said goodbye to the great Ruth Gordon.

THE LAST PICTURE SHOW

1971 - USA - 118 MIN. - DRAMA

DIRECTOR PETER BOGDANOVICH (*1939)
SCREENPLAY LARRY MCMURTRY, PETER BOGDANOVICH, based on the novel of the same name by LARRY MCMURTRY
DIRECTOR OF PHOTOGRAPHY ROBERT SURTEES **EDITING** DONN CAMBERN **MUSIC** Songs by EDDIE ARNOLD, HANK WILLIAMS, TONY BENNETT, FRANKIE LAINE, JOHNNY RAY, HAY STARR **PRODUCTION** STEPHEN J. FRIEDMAN for BBS PRODUCTIONS, COLUMBIA PICTURES CORPORATION.

STARRING TIMOTHY BOTTOMS (Sonny Crawford), JEFF BRIDGES (Duane Moore), CYBILL SHEPHERD (Jacy Farrow), BEN JOHNSON (Sam the Lion), CLORIS LEACHMAN (Ruth Popper), ELLEN BURSTYN (Lois Farrow), EILEEN BRENNAN (Genevieve), SAM BOTTOMS (Billy), JOHN HILLERMAN (School Teacher), RANDY QUAID (Lester Marlow).

ACADEMY AWARDS 1971 OSCARS for BEST SUPPORTING ACTRESS (Cloris Leachman), and BEST SUPPORTING ACTOR (Ben Johnson).

"Sam the Lion is dead!"

Anarene, Texas 1951. A Podunk dust-bowl where nothing's changed much in years, and there isn't a whole lot to discover. The "Royal," an old movie house, stands at the end of Main Street, just a few feet from Sam's pool hall. The place boasts two game tables, an adjoining diner run by Genevieve and a fully functioning juke box in the corner. That pretty much sums up the town sights. If the pickups didn't have radios, people might inadvertently forget that time really does march onward.

Not exactly the most exciting spot on the map if you're young and have your whole life ahead of you. Disenchanted dreamer Sonny (Timothy Bottoms), local star athlete Duane (Jeff Bridges) and transparently manipulative village beauty Jacy (Cybill Shepherd) are all feeling the burn of small town life. They're each about to graduate from high school, but that doesn't mean a heck of a lot in Anarene. The only thing the local adult population really cares about in terms of high school is whether or not the football team wins the title. In fact, the grown-ups treat the teenage boys like dirt when their last

game of the season ends in defeat. The nickelodeon offers the local teens their only solace and taste of intimacy. They nestle in the comfort of the back row, where they can be with each other for a few stolen moments. In these shadows, the kids seek oblivion from the world around them.

The Last Picture Show (1971) was Peter Bogdanovich's first major critical and box-office sensation. His next two projects (*What's Up Doc?*, 1972 and *Paper Moon*, 1973), which followed immediately, also enjoyed similar critical and public acclaim. *Picture Show* examines the lives of three teenagers confronted with a dilemma. They are young, pure of heart and yet their future seems to have been carved in stone on the day they were born. The film's black and white photography, a conscious choice on the part of Bogdanovich that went against New Hollywood's preference for color photography, accentuates the monotony of the characters' lives. The majestic skies above shine the only ray of light on Anarene's rigidity. The movie is a 1970s masterpiece reveling in a flawlessly recreated 1950s universe. It not only

"With his second feature, Director Bogdanovich, 31, has achieved a tactile sense of time and place. More, he has performed that most difficult of all cinematic feats: he has made ennui fascinating. Together, that is enough to herald him as the most exciting new director in America today." *Time Magazine*

JEFF BRIDGES

Son of actor Lloyd Bridges (1913–1998), Jeff Bridges (born 1949 in Los Angeles) made his screen debut when he was still sucking away at his pacifier. A baby was needed for *The Company She Keeps* (1950), and father Lloyd was willing to supply the services of his six-month-old son. Funnily enough, for years Jeff Bridges wanted to be a musician, and never saw himself as an actor. At the age of eight, he appeared in various TV series with his brother Beau. Jeff Bridges' breakthrough came in 1971 with *The Last Picture Show*, which earned him an Oscar nod. The sky was the limit after that. Bridges quickly put his musical ambitions on hold, although he was able to live them out years later in *The Fabulous Baker Boys* (1989). Initially, he gravitated toward doomed heroes, who audiences loved with because they could see their inevitable end from miles away. He was a class act as the hobbling car thief in Michael Cimino's *Thunderbolt and Lightfoot* (1974). Who would have guessed that behind a winning smile and bum leg lay a slick professional felon? Many parts such as in *Fearless* (1993), *The Big Lebowski* (1998), *Tron* (1982) and *Heaven's Gate* (1980) were hailed by only select audiences. Bridges also starred in *Texasville* (1990), the sequel to *The Last Picture Show*, featuring Duane as a middle-aged oil baron and married father of four, who still holds a candle for Jacy. In 2002, *Premiere* magazine elected Bridges America's most underrated actor. Praise worthy not only of a fine actor capable of achieving the presidency in front of the camera, *The Contender* (2000), but also of the true humanitarian who co-founded the "Hunger Network."

3

1 Breaking the mold: The classic Western always ends with a duel. But here the duelists are school friends on the brink of adulthood: Sonny (Timothy Bottoms) and Duane (Jeff Bridges).

2 The last cowboy: To the audience, Sam the Lion (Ben Johnson) is a grand relic of a bygone era. To Sonny and backward Billy (Sam Bottoms) he is both father figure and role model.

3 Fighting for a future, trying to wrest something from his surroundings, and struggling to find himself – to Sonny, Anarene is just one big Dead End.

reconstructs a bygone era, but also reclaims the cinematic conventions of the day, revealing its world in long, drawn-out, motionless shots that are seldom interrupted by rapid cuts. The cinematography is elegantly simple. There are noticeably few stagy close ups. Instead, the film's look is set by long shots and the search for the eternal salvation of the heavens, two characteristics normally associated with the Western. Bogdanovich glorifies his personal heroes like Howard Hawks, John Ford and Alfred Hitchcock in this work. Each moment in the film is driven by a clear objective, and Bogdanovich leaves nothing to chance. Country and easy listening tunes by Eddie Arnold, Hank Williams and Tony Bennett plink out of the ubiquitous radio sets, following the characters through the story like the haunting echoes of an off-key lullaby. Equally surreal is how the laws of time don't seem to apply here. We experience the lives of the protagonists in individual days often separated by weeks on end; yet we are made to believe that nothing has taken place in the off-screen downtime.

Of the salient episodes that prove that there is indeed life in this barren wasteland, the most poignant takes place between Sonny and the forlorn wife of his gym teacher, Ruth (Cloris Leachman). Their first romantic encounter is a microcosm of the disturbing social repression that surrounds them. Bogdanovich directs a seduction scene that wins the two actors our

sincerest compassion as we watch them grovel in their shame, afraid to risk looking at one another while they proceed to undress. Even once under the sheets, something lingers in the atmosphere that tells us Ruth and Sonny will never be able to block out their inexorable, external world. We are left to endure the squeaking of the bedsprings and thumping of the backboard.

We do, however, see hope afloat in these dismal seas in the character of Sam the Lion (Ben Johnson). He owns the movie house and is the moral role model for the kids, and for Sonny in particular. Sam's values stem from a time when striving to achieve ideals still meant something. The man is like a cowboy who survived the Old West, and it is no coincidence that former western star Johnson plays the role. When a heart attack claims the middle-aged Sam's life, it appears that the entire future of the Anarene's youth population has died with him. Almost in a stupor, Sonny and Duane head over to the Royal for their last picture show. The popularity of television is causing the place itself to shut down. The movie showing is Hawks' *Red River* (1948), and we watch as cowboys prepare to drive a herd of cattle to Montana, with John Wayne calling them to exuberant action. When the lights come up again, Sonny too, will feel called to action. Reinventing his preordained small-town ending, he will step into the Lion's shoes and take a stand against the insidious black and white complacency of his small-minded world. SB

4

5

"This is not merely the best American movie of a rather dreary year; it is the most impressive work by a young American director since *Citizen Kane.*" *Newsweek*

4   Without the jukebox in Genevieve's little diner, there'd be nothing to listen to in Anarene – only the tireless wind blowing over the dusty road where the occasional truck thunders by.

5   Too young, too rich, too pretty… Jacy (Cybill Shepherd), the daughter of a wealthy oilman, is looking for a little appreciation – and a man for life.

6   Lovers and other strangers: At the end, Sonny is a shadow of his former self, as is his former lover Ruth (Cloris Leachman). Two sad, lonely people against a rough, bleak background – an exemplary scene.

DELIVERANCE

1972 - USA - 105 MIN. - ACTION FILM, THRILLER

DIRECTOR JOHN BOORMAN (*1933)
SCREENPLAY JAMES DICKEY, based on his novel of the same name DIRECTOR OF PHOTOGRAPHY VILMOS ZSIGMOND EDITING TOM PRIESTLEY
MUSIC ERIC WEISSBERG, STEVE MANDEL PRODUCTION JOHN BOORMAN for ELMER PRODUCTIONS, WARNER BROS.

STARRING JON VOIGHT (Ed Gentry), BURT REYNOLDS (Lewis Medlock), NED BEATTY (Bobby Trippe), RONNY COX (Drew Ballinger), ED RAMEY (Old Man), BILLY REDDEN (Lonny), SEAMON GLASS (First Griner), RANDALL DEAL (Second Griner), BILL MCKINNEY (Mountain Man), HERBERT "COWBOY" COWARD (Toothless Man), LEWIS CRONE (First Deputy), JAMES DICKEY (Sheriff Bullard).

"That's the game, survival."

A river winds softly through a pristine landscape of craggy cliffs and dense virgin forest. Four men from the city are here to relax while exploring the area by canoe. Lewis (Burt Reynolds), Ed (Jon Voight), Bobby (Ned Beatty) and Drew (Ronny Cox), are paddling downriver in two fragile boats. They've paid some farmers to drive their cars to the final destination, which they expect to reach two days later; but this is an adventure holiday that will turn into pure terror.

The first day is idyllic, a boy-scouts' paradise for four grown men: paddling boats, pitching tents, fishing with bows and arrows, and playing guitar round the campfire. On the second day, the horror begins. Ed and Bobby have gone on ahead in their canoe, and a welcoming-party is waiting for them: two of the farmers, ugly rednecks with very bad teeth. After tying Ed to a tree, they beat, rape and humiliate Bobby. As they turn their attentions to Ed, one

of them keels over, pierced by an arrow; Lewis and Drew have caught up with their friends. The other attacker flees, and the four friends bury the corpse. They're sick of adventures and hungry for home, and the canoes are their only means of transport. But down on the river, between the sheer cliffs, they're as open to predators as a hamburger on a plate...

With its breathtaking journeys through whitewater rapids and overwhelming images of natural splendor, *Deliverance* is a wonderful action and adventure film. Director John Boorman, his editor Tom Priestley (both of whom received Oscar nominations) and the cameraman Vilmos Zsigmond (who got an Oscar for *Close Encounters of the Third Kind*, 1977) created a visual language of great beauty, combining careful composition with a directness and immediacy that pulls the audience right into the story. The

1 Hell bent over: Ed (Jon Voight) gets a close-up view of prison in the wild.	2 "The voyage down the river echoes the journey of Conrad's demonic Mr. Kurtz to the Congo's heart of darkness." (*The New York Times*)	3 A grassroots movement: Ed hunts his attackers with a bow and arrow.

"A repugnant but fascinating portrait of human beings out of their environment, forced to defend themselves where the laws of civilization no longer apply." *Motion Picture Guide*

immensity and indifference of the natural world and the threat of sudden attack are almost physically present. Boorman also demonstrates a fine feeling for effective but inconspicuous symbolism: In a famous scene, early on in the film, Drew and a retarded farmer's boy begin a tentative musical dialog on guitar and banjo. The game of question-and-answer develops into a regular duet – or duel – in which the city-dweller is eventually defeated by the sheer speed and skill of the hillbilly kid. In a beautifully understated manner, this joyful encounter anticipates the deadly power struggle to come.

The film's surface is brilliant, and the depths below it are multi-layered and hard to fathom. With a screenplay by the poet James Dickey, who adapted it from his own novel of the same name (1970), the film resists any easy interpretation. "Man Against Nature" won't do, for the dumb-but-crafty hill-

"It's the best film I've ever done. It's a picture that just picks you up and sends you crashing against the rocks. You feel everything and just crawl out of the theater."

Burt Reynolds, in: Motion Picture Guide

4   Bobby (Ned Beatty), Lewis (Burt Reynolds), Drew (Ronny Cox) and Ed are looking forward to some male bonding – two days in virgin nature.

5   Sneak attack: Ed resorts to archery.

6   The men park their cars in a tiny hamlet – and sacrifice a link to civilization.

5

billies can hardly be seen as symbols for a state of unspoilt nature. "Arrogant City-Slickers versus Disadvantaged Rural Population" is an equally unusable model, for neither the canoeists nor their antagonists can be reduced to this kind of cliché. What remains is the story of four men in an alien environment, defending their lives with alien methods; solid citizens far from civilization, struggling to survive with the aid of bows and arrows. Events take their course inexorably, and we are granted no comforting explanations. Lewis, the fittest of the four, is quickly incapacitated by an injury, while the cerebral pipe-smoking Ed is forced to kill in self-defense. When the survivors finally reach safety, they're still far from peace; the Sheriff (author James Dickey in a guest appearance) is a highly skeptical interrogator, and their dreams will long be haunted by memories of their hellish ordeal.   HJK

6

JOHN BOORMAN

Civilized human beings forced to come to terms with barbarism: this is as good a summary of *Deliverance* (1972) as any, and it's also the groundplan for many of John Boorman's films. In the SF movie *Zardoz* (1973/74) Sean Connery struggles against a terroristic slave system; in *The Emerald Forest* (1985), the son of an engineer (Boorman's own son, Charley) falls into the hands of an archaic forest-dwelling tribe.

England's John Boorman (*1933) has made highly idiosyncratic films in a wide range of standard genres. In *Hope and Glory* (1987), he called on his own childhood memories to tell the story of the war from a boy's perspective. The gangster in *The General* (1998) behaves like the gangsters he's seen in the movies. And in *The Tailor of Panama* (2001), Boorman portrays his "hero" (sex symbol and 007 Pierce Brosnan) as a deeply repellent character. Boorman made his cinema debut in 1965 with the Dave Clark Five pop vehicle *Catch Us If You Can* (*Having a Wild Weekend*). The big break came in 1967 with his second film, the gangster drama *Point Blank*.

7 Concealing evidence: Lewis hides the corpse of a redneck he's just neutralized. The men think their nightmare is over, but it's only just begun.

7

1972 - USA - 124 MIN. - LITERARY ADAPTATION, DRAMA, MUSICAL

DIRECTOR BOB FOSSE (1927–1987)

SCREENPLAY JAY PRESSON ALLEN, based on the Broadway musical of the same name by JOE MASTEROFF, JOHN KANDER and FRED EBB, the drama *I AM A CAMERA* by JOHN VAN DRUTEN, and the collection of short stories *THE BERLIN STORIES* by CHRISTOPHER ISHERWOOD **DIRECTOR OF PHOTOGRAPHY** GEOFFREY UNSWORTH **EDITING** DAVID BRETHERTON **MUSIC** JOHN KANDER, RALPH BURNS **PRODUCTION** CY FEUER for ABC CIRCLE FILMS, AMERICAN BROADCASTING COMPANY.

STARRING LIZA MINNELLI (Sally Bowles), MICHAEL YORK (Brian Roberts), HELMUT GRIEM (Maximilian von Heune), JOEL GREY (Master of Ceremonies), FRITZ WEPPER (Fritz Wendel), MARISA BERENSON (Natalia Landauer), ELISABETH NEUMANN-VIERTEL (Fräulein Schneider), HELEN VITA (Fräulein Kost), SIGRID VON RICHTHOFEN (Fräulein Mayr), GERD VESPERMANN (Bobby).

ACADEMY AWARDS 1972 OSCARS for BEST DIRECTOR (Bob Fosse), BEST ACTRESS (Liza Minnelli), BEST SUPPORTING ACTOR (Joel Grey), BEST CINEMATOGRAPHY (Geoffrey Unsworth), BEST MUSIC (Ralph Burns), BEST FILM EDITING (David Bretherton), BEST ART DIRECTION (Rolf Zehetbauer, Hans Jürgen Keibach, Herbert Strabel), and BEST SOUND (Robert Knudson).

"Divine decadence, darling!"

Berlin 1931. Despite a severe economic crisis, the German metropolis is determinedly cosmopolitan and exudes sensuality. Leave your worries at the door and come on into the Kit Kat Club, a dazzling night club where evening after evening an enthusiastic emcee greets you in three languages: "Willkommen, Bienvenue, Welcome!" His diabolically painted white face is reflected on the shimmering stage. And like a funhouse mirror, the film presents the cabaret to movie audiences as a caricature of the outside world. "Life is a cabaret!" exclaims Liza Minelli in an unforgettable song that is meant to be taken at face value.

Like so many other foreigners, British student Brian (Michael York) feels drawn to this thriving urban center. Arriving at a boarding house, he quickly makes the acquaintance of American Sally Bowles (Liza Minnelli), who works as a singer at the Kit Kat Club and dreams of making it big one day as a movie star. She's not only willing to capitalize on her charisma to get there, but will

readily exploit her body too if need be. Sexually uninhibited with a taste for luxury, Sally is a hedonistic modern whose deep-seated, hidden desire is to find true happiness. Beneath her decadent exterior we are shown more and more of the childish, vulnerable woman she really is. Brian, who at first seems immune to her erotic advances, eventually falls madly in love with her. It is a happy romance until the wealthy, young and rather attractive Baron Max von Heune (Helmut Griem) enters their world. Sally, mesmerized by his charms and riches, becomes more impractically minded with each passing day. Brian is jealous and turned on at the same time. Their love triangle is only spoken of in jest initially, but it soon becomes reality. Both of them have slept with the affluent Baron, and Sally, it turns out, is pregnant. While Sally and Brian are busy tackling their personal catastrophes, the Nazis take to the streets of Berlin in preparation for their rise to power. It seems the couple's lifestyle is doomed, for the epidemic of fascism spreading throughout the

"*Cabaret* is dance routines and hit songs. It's a murky tale inspired by the novels of Christopher Isherwood. It's the myth of 30s Berlin. And above all, it's Bob Fosse. He has a marvelous grasp of the world of cabaret, its pathos and its poetry: fleeting, illusory and poignantly authentic."

Le Monde

ation seeks to extinguish all that is urban and modern. In its place, the Nazi movement prescribes conservative and provincial values for the German people. Brian decides to return to England. Sally, however, stays on in Berlin to try her luck at acting.

Cabaret was one of last great Hollywood musicals. (Eat your heart out *Chicago*! [2002]) It was awarded an astounding eight Oscars at the Academy Awards. The movie version was based on John Kander and Fred Ebb's Broadway musical, which premiered in 1966. This, likewise, drew heavily from the short stories "The Last of Mr. Morris" and "Goodbye to Berlin" by Christopher Isherwood, which were published in a volume entitled *The Berlin Stories*. Unlike the majority of Hollywood musicals, such as *An Ameri-*

can in Paris (1951) or *Singin' in the Rain* (1952) there is nothing anachronistic about *Cabaret* even today. This is due to its songs, as popular as those of Kurt Weill's *Three Penny Opera* (*Dreigroschenoper*), and to the then 25-year-old Liza Minnelli, whose image is more intrinsically linked to *Cabaret* than almost any other actress' has ever been to a single production. Yet above all else, it is the film's narrative structure that plays the decisive role in its timelessness. Deviating from the traditional Hollywood musical format, *Cabaret* markedly separates its musical numbers from its plot. In other words, none of the characters in the film burst into song for no given reason. Instead, director and choreographer Bob Fosse brilliantly lets the stage acts at the nightclub serve as commentary on both the surrounding political situation

1   Cigarette, lipstick and a voice that won't quit: The role of Sally Bowles made Liza Minelli an international superstar.

2   "Life is a cabaret:" The stage as a world of entertainment and politics.

3   A pink-tinted love triangle: Only later does Sally discover that Brian (Michael York) and Maximilian (Helmut Griem) have been playing house.

4   Babe in the woods: When Brian comes to Berlin, he's a shy young writer. Sally's attempts to seduce him are initially unsuccessful.

"*Cabaret* may make a star out of Miss Minnelli, but it will be remembered as a chilling mosaic of another era's frightening life-style." Films in Review

LIZA MINNELLI

The extent to which her image was shaped by one single film is itself a Hollywood phenomenon. Her belting voice and touching yet extravagant flair breathed so much life into *Cabaret's* (1972) nightclub singer Sally Bowles that from then on world audiences viewed Liza Minnelli as virtually inseparable from the role she had played. The daughter of Hollywood legend Judy Garland and director Vincente Minnelli was literally born into show business in 1946. She made her first appearance in front of a Hollywood camera when she was just two years old. Be it on Broadway, in film, in TV movies or in the music industry, her work has always met with instant success. She received a Tony in 1965 for her performance in the Broadway musical *Flora, the Red Menace*. Her first Oscar nomination came for her portrayal of the eccentric Pookie in *The Sterile Cuckoo* (1969). Another nomination followed in 1970 for Otto Preminger's *Tell Me That You Love Me, Junie Moon*, and in 1973 she won the Best Actress Academy Award for *Cabaret*. She became more popular with audiences than ever before, and in 1972, NBC aired the award winning television special *Liza with A Z*. Liza Minnelli, who describes herself as both "hopeful and cynical," is a star to this day, even though not all her films are smash hits. She collaborated with her father Vincente Minnelli on *A Matter of Time / Nina* (1976). Images of her superstar mother, who died in 1969, pop up in many of her movies, including Stanley Donen's *Lucky Lady* (1975) and most prominently in Martin Scorsese's musical drama *New York, New York* (1977). She experienced one of her greatest commercial successes in 1981 with *Arthur*. Shortly thereafter, her film career started to dry up. She disappeared completely from the public eye for several years. Alcohol and prescription drug addictions contributed to her personal downfall. In 1984 she sought professional help. She staged a comeback in 1985 in the form of an NBC made for TV movie *A Time to Live*, winning the Golden Globe for her performance. She then went on a star-studded tour at the end of the 80s with Frank Sinatra and Sammy Davis Jr. and even recorded a single with the Pet Shop Boys entitled "Losing My Mind" that reached number six on the U.K. charts. In 1997, Liza Minnelli was celebrated on Broadway in Blake Edwards' "Victor/Victoria," yet another great comeback after a twelve-year absence.

5   Tomorrow belongs to… whom? It remains unclear how fascism will change Sally's wild and extravagant lifestyle.

6   Mirror, mirror on the wall, *Cabaret* was Liza's best picture of all.

5

and the lives of characters themselves. In particular, the stage appearances of the emcee (Joel Grey), whose character doesn't exist within the framework of the plot outside the nightclub, do a poignant job of this. Plot elements and musical numbers are occasionally brought together through the ironic use of parallel montage. Such is the case when a scene of a staged Bavarian folk-dance is cut between rapidly appearing images of Nazis brutally beating up the Kit Kat's manager elsewhere. This sequence feeds violence into the musical number and choreography into the street fight. *Cabaret*, with its strikingly dark palette, is highly reminiscent of the 1920s, as is the music inspired by Kurt Weill and Fosse's stylized dance numbers, which clearly draw from that era's expressionist tradition. Commendably, it does this with-out trying to ignore the cinematic conventions of the 1970s. The overall im-

pact of the film is born out of its song and dance sequences which, with one exception, all take place on stage. The only time we witness music outside the cabaret setting is when a young blond boy begins to sing what is meant to sound like a traditional German folk song at a beer garden. We just see his face at first, but soon the camera pulls back to show us his swastika arm-band. One beer garden patron after the next joins in his chant. The rhythm of the piece transforms into a military march and by the end, all have their hands extended in a Hitler salute. It may sound ludicrous, but at the time of the picture's European premiere, this scene was to be cut out for German audiences. Only after a number of critics were up in arms about the decision, was the sequence restored.

KK

THE GODFATHER

1972 - USA - 175 MIN. - GANGSTER FILM, DRAMA

DIRECTOR FRANCIS FORD COPPOLA (*1939)
SCREENPLAY FRANCIS FORD COPPOLA, MARIO PUZO, based on his novel of the same name **DIRECTOR OF PHOTOGRAPHY** GORDON WILLIS
EDITING MARC LAUB, BARBARA MARKS, WILLIAM REYNOLDS, MURRAY SOLOMON, PETER ZINNER **MUSIC** NINO ROTA
PRODUCTION ALBERT S. RUDDY for PARAMOUNT PICTURES.

STARRING MARLON BRANDO (Don Vito Corleone), AL PACINO (Michael Corleone), DIANE KEATON (Kay Adams), ROBERT DUVALL (Tom Hagen), JAMES CAAN (Santino "Sonny" Corleone), JOHN CAZALE (Frederico "Fredo" Corleone), RICHARD S. CASTELLANO (Peter Clemenza), STERLING HAYDEN (Captain McCluskey), TALIA SHIRE (Constanzia "Connie" Corleone-Rizzi), JOHN MARLEY (Jack Woltz), RICHARD CONTE (Don Emilio Barzini), AL LETTIERI (Virgil Sollozzo), AL MARTINO (Johnny Fantane), GIANNI RUSSO (Carlo Rizzi), SIMONETTA STEFANELLI (Appollonia Vitelli-Corleone).

ACADEMY AWARDS 1972 OSCARS for BEST FILM (Albert S. Ruddy), BEST ACTOR (Marlon Brando), and BEST SCREENPLAY (Mario Puzo, Francis Ford Coppola).

"I'll make him an offer he can't refuse."

The unmentionable words are never heard. No one dares speak of the "Mafia" or the "Cosa Nostra" in this film, despite the fact that it tells a tale whose roots are at the heart of organized crime. The contents are categorized by another word: family. "It's a novel about a family, and not about crime," said its author, Mario Puzo. Francis Ford Coppola initially rejected the offer to direct the film after reading the book over-hastily and dismissing it as just another Mafia-vehicle. He eventually changed his mind for a number of reasons, principally because he discovered the family aspect of the story and was fascinated by it.

It is no coincidence that the film begins and ends with traditional family celebrations – a wedding and a baptism. The marriage of Connie Corleone (Talia Shire) and Carlo Rizzi (Gianni Russo) is the occasion for an enchanting celebration. An orchestra plays in the Corleone's garden, filled with a mass of dancing guests. Feasting and joking, children run wild and glasses are repeatedly raised to toast the bride. During the festivities, FBI agents mill outside the gates of the villa and scrawl down license plate numbers of the guests. The father of the bride, Vito Corleone (Marlon Brando) is one of the five Dons of the Italian community in the New York area and the guest

"Like practically no other Hollywood film of recent years, the tale of the New York Mafia clan Corleone reflects the divisions, the compulsions and the fears afflicting American society. Damaged by Vietnam and shaken by a profound crisis of faith in the nation, America's hallowed norms of good and evil are looking more beleaguered than ever." *Kölner Stadt-Anzeiger*

2

ist is accordingly illustrious. According to old Sicilian tradition, the father of the bride cannot refuse any favor on his daughter's wedding day. Surrounded by his sons and confidants he aristocratically sits in his darkened reception room, glowing in a golden brown light, the perfect expression of dignity and power. He patronizingly receives the supplicants, listens to their dilemmas, accepts congratulations, and basks in the respect offered from all sides.

Like every scene with Marlon Brando in the role of the Godfather Vito Corleone, these scenes are filled with warmth. The colors fade when his son Michael (Al Pacino) flees to the family's ancestral home in sunny Sicily after committing two murders. Later Michael, who once strived for an honorable life and distanced himself from his family, will become the ringleader

of a blood bath: the images change with him, slowly acquiring a cold, bluish tinge.

The cause of the violent clash is Vito Corleone's decision to deny his backing to Virgil Sollozzo's (Al Lettieri) plans to branch out in the drug dealing business. Vito's temperamental son Sonny (James Caan) seems to disagree with his father, which inspires Sollozzo to try and topple the patriarch. Five shots bring Corleone down, but the old tiger survives. Michael, who to this point has held himself out of the family business, is shaken. His outsider role makes him seem unsuspicious, and he is therefore sent to the negotiation table. Michael promptly uses the opportunity to murder both Sollozzo and the corrupt police captain McCluskey (Sterling Hayden), and flees to Sicily. His unsuspecting girlfriend Kay (Diane Keaton) remains behind.

1   A man that won't take "no" for an answer: Marlon Brando takes life in stride as Don Corleone.

2   In sickness and in health: Making a deal with Don Corleone is more than a business transaction – it's a life-long bond.

3   One wedding for fifty funerals: *The Godfather* opens with the Corleone family renewing its vows, whilst Carlo (Gianni Russo) and Connie (Talia Shire) take theirs.

MARLON BRANDO   Among the many curiosities surrounding the legendary *The Godfather* (1972) is that its success sprung from a series of coincidences and imponderables. Mario Puzo was unhappy writing the screenplay, Francis Ford Coppola initially didn't want to direct the film, and the studio had problems with the choice of the male lead. At this time, Marlon Brando was at a low point in his career, which began in the 1940s in the theaters of New York City. In 1947, his portrayal of Stanley Kowalski in *A Streetcar Named Desire* was a triumph and in 1951 he played the character in Elia Kazan's film adaptation. Schooled in "method acting," Brando graduated to Hollywood big-time – four Oscar nominations in a row speak for themselves. Initially he was repeatedly cast as the youthful rebel, but he soon proved his versatility in costume films and musicals. In the 1960s, his notorious moodiness and a string of flops caused him to fall from grace with Hollywood producers. In 1972 he made his comeback with *The Godfather* and *The Last Tango in Paris* (*Ultimo tango a Parigi / Le Dernier Tango à Paris*), receiving Oscar nominations for both films. Though he was awarded the Oscar for his role as Vito Corleone in *The Godfather*, he refused to accept it for political reasons.

6

4 European vacation: A hunted man, Michael Corleone (Al Pacino) decides it's time to go back to his roots.

5 Like father like son: After some initial stumbling, Michael learns how to fill his father's shoes.

6 Deadlock: Michael Corleone and bride-to-be, Kate (Diane Keaton).

7 The emissary wore black: Michael holds out a Sicilian olive branch to Virgil Sollozzo (Al Lettieri).

8 When in Rome: During his time in Sicily, Michael fares the local cuisine and develops a taste for Appollonia (Simonetta Stefanelli).

"And all the while, we think we're watching a Mafia crime story; but we're actually watching one of the great American family melodramas." *The Austin Chronicle*

7

In Sicily, Michael's hardening process continues. He falls in love and – with old-fashioned etiquette – asks the bride's father permission for his daughter's hand. But the long arm of vengeance stretches to Italy – his young wife, Appollonia is killed in a car bomb that was meant for Michael. In New York, the war between the families rages on. Michael's brother Sonny is the next victim. The slowly recovering Vito Corleone is devastated, but forgoes his right to vengeance in an attempt to put an end to the killing. Michael returns to the United States. He marries Kay, who has become a teacher. Michael, whose eyes now have a cold, hard expression, knows that the old feud is not over. He plans a large liberating coup. While he is in church at his nephew's baptism, and is solemnly named as the child's godfather, the enemies of the Corleones are killed off one

8

9   Big brother: When Carlo makes putty of wife Connie, Sonny puts a little love in his heart.

10   Gone with the wind: Sonny Corleone (James Caan) walks into a trap and goes up in smoke.

11   Paying the piper: An attempt to rescue sister Connie from a violent marriage proves more dangerous than Sonny had imagined …

"Cast and designed to perfection, this epic pastiche of 40s and 50s crime movies is as rich in images of idyllic family life as it is in brutal effects."

Der Spiegel

by one. Among them is Connie's husband Carlo, who lured Sonny into a deadly trap.

Connie has become a nervous wreck and Kay begins to ask critical questions. Michael coldly denies responsibility and Kay is forced to experience her utter exclusion from the male circle. Before the doors close in front of her, she sees her husband, the new Don, Michael graciously receive the best wishes of his confidants and associates.

The film stands out for its clever dramatization of the balance of power enjoyed by Vito Corleone and his successor, Michael, as well as its scenes of heavy violence, such as the severed horse's head in film producer Jack Woltz's bed, Sonny's bullet-riddled body, or the gunshot through the lens of casino owner Moe Green's glasses. The brilliant finale has an Old Testament-like intensity about it. But these drastic images are mere moments compared

to the extensive family scenes. The business activities of the Corleones, which include murder and extortion, invariably take place outside the inner circle – they often follow car rides and trips, literally at a distance from the family core. This distance represents a lack of protection – the attempted hit on Vito Corleone occurs when he spontaneously stops to buy fruit from a street vendor, and hothead Sonny is killed when he leaves the family fortress with too great haste.

In a poignant reversal, Michael Corleone, the initially modern man, is unable to escape the chains of his family. Though he always considered himself an independent individual, he becomes a victim of the family tradition, a marionette whose strings are moved by the hands of fate, a metaphor the image on the book cover and film poster captures with perfection.

HK

FRENZY

1972 - GREAT BRITAIN / USA - 116 MIN. - PSYCHO THRILLER

DIRECTOR ALFRED HITCHCOCK (1899–1980)
SCREENPLAY ANTHONY SHAFFER, based on the novel *GOODBYE PICCADILLY, FAREWELL LEICESTER SQUARE* by ARTHUR LA BERN DIRECTOR OF PHOTOGRAPHY GILBERT TAYLOR EDITING JOHN JYMPSON MUSIC RON GOODWIN PRODUCTION ALFRED HITCHCOCK for UNIVERSAL PICTURES.

STARRING JON FINCH (Richard Blaney), BARRY FOSTER (Robert Rusk), BARBARA LEIGH-HUNT (Brenda Blaney), ANNA MASSEY (Babs Milligan), ALEC MCCOWEN (Chief Inspector Oxford), VIVIEN MERCHANT (Mrs. Oxford), MICHAEL BATES (Sergeant Spearman), BILLIE WHITELAW (Hetty Porter), BERNARD CRIBBINS (Felix Forsythe), JEAN MARSH (Monica Barling).

"Mr. Rusk, you're not wearing your tie."

In a manner reminiscent of *Psycho* (1960), Alfred Hitchcock's late work *Frenzy* begins with a long tracking shot across an urban skyline, before the camera descends inexorably into the nooks and crannies of everyday life. Like its legendary predecessor, *Frenzy* examines domestic spaces that conceal tiny misdemeanors and terrible crimes. The film begins with irony and horror. While a Parliament official extols the cleanliness of the Thames, a woman's corpse is discovered floating near the banks of the river. With typical narrative economy, Hitchcock introduces a virtuoso thriller that shows lust and violence lurking behind a façade of apparent normality. As usual, Hitchcock makes a cameo appearance, this time right at the start of the film; as the speech on water pollution draws to a close, he's the only listener not applauding.

Amid the hustle and bustle of Covent Garden, London's market area, a psychopathic greengrocer called Bob Rusk (Barry Foster) strangles female victims with neckties. Paradoxically, the very liveliness of his neighborhood seems to offer ideal conditions for his secretive dance with death. Thus, as so often in Hitchcock's psycho-thrillers, all the clues point in the wrong direction, and the police are on the trail of the wrong man. Their main suspect is Richard Blaney (Jon Finch), a friend of the murderer and a one-time navy pilot who has lost both his job and his wife and is now struggling to scrape a meager living. While Scotland Yard's finest grope around in the dark, the audience quickly realizes that the hapless Blaney is a red herring. In one of the most grueling rape scenes in film history, we are immediate witnesses of Bob Rusk's sexual sickness: an unsparing montage of

1   Brenda Blaney (Barbara Leigh-Hunt) is strangled
    with a necktie by charming Bob Rusk.

2   The director on location: Hitchcock loved his
    cameos.

3   Divided we stand: For his ex-wife (Barbara Leigh-
    Hunt), Richard Blaney (Jon Finch) is now *persona
    non grata.*

4   Down by love: Richard, too, will not enjoy his
    newfound love for long.

5   Fighting for justice: Friendly fellow-prisoners
    help Blaney flee the prison hospital.

tight shots and close-ups culminates in the murder of Blaney's ex-wife Brenda (Barbara Leigh-Hunt). The scene takes place on the premises of Brenda's matrimonial agency, whose services Rusk had sought – in vain – under a false name.

The strangling of Brenda Blaney cannot fail to evoke the stabbing of Marion Crane (Janet Leigh) in the shower scene in *Psycho.* It takes Rusk an almost unbearable amount of time to kill her, and we are left in no doubt of the sheer physical effort required to extinguish a life. In *Torn Curtain* (1966), Hitchcock had already made much of this fact. (A curious detail in passing: until very recently, the bizarre and almost endless murder of the Stasi officer Gromek was always cut from the versions of *Torn Curtain* shown on German TV.) Yet Hitchcock was fully aware that horror has much to do with the things we're *not* permitted to see. When Bob Rusk invites Blaney's girlfriend Barbara (Anna Massey) into his apartment, the camera creeps slowly back down the staircase to the busy street, leaving the viewer's imagination to conjure up the details of the murder that is taking place.

While Rusk continues to kill without hindrance, "wrong man" Richard Blaney is becoming more and more desperate in his attempts to escape the police. There seems to be no way out. Even when Rusk loses his mono-grammed tie-pin in the stiffening hand of Blaney's dead mistress Barbara, it still doesn't lead to his arrest; after a grotesque nocturnal search for the right sack in a lorryload of potatoes, he manages to find the body and dispose of the tell-tale pin.

The subplots are equally well seasoned with this jet black humor. In-spector Oxford's wife has fallen victim to French cuisine, and his desperate attempts to escape her cooking can only be described as delicious. (She has a particular talent for unidentifiable sea creatures in suspiciously slippery sauces.) This kind of thing certainly constitutes a disturbing peculiarity in the late work of a director so secure in himself and his cinematic style; and in *Frenzy*, above all, Hitchcock risks some very sharp contrasts between moments of extreme shock and grim humor.

Frenzy was also evidence of the film industry's gradual self-liberation from its strict norms governing the representation of sex and violence. But however radical Hitchcock's break with the taboos of the production code, the end of the film sees the noose of police investigations tightening relentlessly around the neck of the murderer.   BR

"Right from the start, *Frenzy* communicates a sense of enjoyment, as if Hitchcock knew he was back on form again."

Film Comment

4

CAMEO A brief guest appearance by a well-known actor, sometimes not named in the cast list and often unpaid. The term "cameo appearance" acquired particular currency after the release of *Around the World in Eighty Days* (1956), featuring (to name but a few) Buster Keaton, Charles Boyer, Fernandel, Frank Sinatra, Marlene Dietrich, Peter Lorre and John Gielgud, none of whom were identified explicitly in the credits. Moviegoers had huge fun spotting all the stars. Alfred Hitchcock's walk-on roles in his own films soon became his trademark. In his very first feature film *The Lodger* (1926), the director is to be found twice: once in a reading room, and later as a member of a crowd watching an arrest take place; in *Psycho* (1960), he is to be seen after four minutes through the window of Marion Crane's office – wearing a cowboy hat; in *The Birds* (1963), Hitchcock can be spotted leaving a pet shop with two white terriers as the main character Melanie Daniels (Tippi Hedren) arrives; in *North by Northwest* (1959), he misses a bus during the opening sequence; and so on. This game of cinematic hide-and-seek is often funny and sometimes ironic in its effect, and certainly adds to the films' entertainment value. Occasionally, however, a cameo appearance can constitute a moment of real critical self-examination; for example, when Francis Ford Coppola appears as a documentary filmmaker in his own war film *Apocalypse Now* (1979). His subject? War.

5

THE GETAWAY

1972 - USA - 122 MIN. - GANGSTER FILM

DIRECTOR SAM PECKINPAH (1925–1984)
SCREENPLAY WALTER HILL, based on the novel of the same name by JIM THOMPSON **DIRECTOR OF PHOTOGRAPHY** LUCIEN BALLARD
EDITING ROBERT L. WOLFE **MUSIC** QUINCY JONES **PRODUCTION** MITCHELL BROWER, DAVID FOSTER for SOLAR PRODUCTIONS, DAVID FOSTER PRODUCTIONS, FIRST ARTISTS, NATIONAL GENERAL PICTURES.

STARRING STEVE MCQUEEN (Carter "Doc" McCoy), ALI MACGRAW (Carol Ainsley McCoy), BEN JOHNSON (Jack Benyon), SALLY STRUTHERS (Fran Clinton), AL LETTIERI (Rudy Butler), SLIM PICKENS (Cowboy), RICHARD BRIGHT (Thief), BO HOPKINS (Frank Jackson), JACK DODSON (Harold Clinton), DUB TAYLOR (Laughlin).

"Only in God I trust."

Carter "Doc" McCoy (Steve McQueen) is about as tough as they come. A criminal as unscrupulous as he is intelligent, Doc enters into an illegal bargain with his lawyer Benyon (Ben Johnson) as a means of getting released early from his ten year sentence in a maximum security Texas penitentiary. Benyon, it so happens, is the head of a mafia-like organization in Texas and agrees to get McCoy out on the condition that he pulls off a bank robbery for him. Only after the deed has been done, does McCoy discover that Benyon's brother is the chairman of the board at the target bank, and that the heist was staged to cover up an embezzlement scheme.

Aided by two accomplices, McCoy makes the final preparations for the robbery. His wife Carol (Ali MacGraw) will drive the getaway car. Little does he know that Carol agreed to let Benyon have his way with her as part of the deal to get McCoy out of prison. The three men pull off the robbery, but then quickly attempt to do away with each other, leaving one of the accomplices dead. Doc and Carol manage to make their way to Benyon and plan on giving him his share of the loot. However, as Benyon insinuates to McCoy that Carol was also part of the booty he was entitled to, Carol snaps and blows the crooked attorney away. With a bang, the couple start on a race across Texas. To survive, they'll not only have to dodge the authorities, but Benyon's bloodhounds and the accomplice who's still alive.

This sordid band of bounty hunters gets closer and closer to Doc and Carol with each minute that passes. On numerous occasions, the couple rely on daredevil driving maneuvers and split-second decision making to escape the clutches of the police. They finally make it to their destination, a hotel they believe to be safe in El Paso just north of the Mexican border. Unfortunately, the ex-accomplice is already there, and Benyon's henchmen arrive shortly afterwards. In an extended action sequence, there is a frenetic exchange of shots between all the characters in the hotel rooms and along the corridors. McCoy and his wife escape unscathed and, at gunpoint, convince an unpleasant-looking junk collector to drive them across the border in his beat-up truck. Once there, McCoy buys the vehicle from its owner, and disappears into the Mexican sunset with wife and cash.

The Getaway was the first movie released by the newly established production company First Artists, a group founded that same year by Steve

McQueen, Paul Newman, Sidney Poitier, Barbra Streisand and Dustin Hoffman. The film portrays urban institutions such as state penitentiaries, bars and factories, as bloody, amoral and anarchic set-ups. The film depicts the flip side of the extreme mobility of American society, and the impact of modern-day violence on the individual. Sam Peckinpah's unmistakable signature has divided audiences into two camps since *The Wild Bunch* (1969) and *Straw Dogs* (1971). There are those who cheer him on and those who are appalled. This was also the case with *The Getaway*. Although the director shows restraint in the images of violence by using a slow-motion camera and operatic choreography, his characters are quite the contrary, they have no limits whatsoever. All social interactions and ties, right down to the most intimate, are dictated by power plays of one sort or another. It is a corrupt world, with no system of justice. The film's message is not, however, a direct commentary on Nixon's Watergate, and its plot culminates in a classic knock'em down style, a saloon shootout complete with plenty of bullets, smashed furniture and a wagonload of casualties.

As always, Steve McQueen plays the morally ambivalent gangster to a tee. He is, on the one hand, in full control, impenetrable, a veritable rock. On the other hand, he is a sensitive, no-nonsense kind of guy, who wears his short cut prison do like a wound that begins to heal with the taste of freedom. Only at the film's conclusion does the "every man for himself" mentality begin to disappear. We witness the change only briefly in the promised land of Mexico, as Doc McCoy spares the life of the old cowboy in the pickup and does his first square deal of the film: exchanging goods for money.   RV

"*Getaway* is pure action, exhilarating and wonderfully sure-footed, a wild but controlled dance amidst a hail of bullets."

Süddeutsche Zeitung

STEVE MCQUEEN   The definition of an actor's job means different things at different times. Today, two styles dominate the U.S. cinema. Thespians like Dustin Hoffman, Robert De Niro and Al Pacino belong to the first school characterized by an ability to slip into a wide range of roles and to take on traits foreign to their actual personality. The second school of thought believes that the actor is a mirror of the current zeitgeist, trends, and desires prevalent in society. Entertainers like Michael Douglas readily fall into this category. One could even make the distinction between "actor" and "performer" down these lines. Steve McQueen was certainly among the greatest of these Hollywood "performers." He was the quintessential adventuresome playboy, the rugged rebel, the fighter. Defeat could look him straight in the eye and McQueen still wouldn't give up. His stoicism seems almost philosophical. His performances certainly benefited from his real-life actions. The man was an avid racecar driver, pilot and an ardent individualist. Born Terence Steven McQueen in 1930 in a suburb of Indianapolis – home of the Indianapolis 500 – he was the son of a "Top Gun" military pilot. He worked a number of odd jobs as a teenager until John Sturges, famous for directing Westerns, discovered McQueen and cast him in *The Magnificent Seven* (1960) and *The Great Escape* (1963). Both pictures were smash hits at the box office. Further roles in films like *The Cincinnati Kid* (1965) and *Bullitt* (1968) made him one of the most popular screen personalities of all time. It was during the shooting of *The Getaway* (1972), that the strong, silent, competitive McQueen met his wife-to-be, Ali MacGraw. In 1980, Steve McQueen died of cancer. He was just 50 years old.

1   Sharp eyes and sharp shooting: Steve McQueen as Carter "Doc" McCoy.

2   Great balls of fire: Action movies are primarily concerned with extreme situations.

3 & 4   Love and death in Texas: The stars' on-screen marriage proved almost as complicated as their real-life one.

DIRTY MONEY
Un Flic

1972 - FRANCE / ITALY - 99 MIN. - GANGSTER FILM

DIRECTOR JEAN-PIERRE MELVILLE (1917–1973)
SCREENPLAY JEAN-PIERRE MELVILLE DIRECTOR OF PHOTOGRAPHY ANDRÉ DOMAGE, WALTER WOTTITZ EDITING PATRICIA NÉNY
MUSIC MICHEL COLOMBIER PRODUCTION ROBERT DORFMANN for CORONA, EURO INTERNATIONAL FILM, OCEANIA PRODUZIONI INTERNAZIONALI CINEMATOGRAFICHE.

STARRING ALAIN DELON (Edouard Coleman), CATHERINE DENEUVE (Cathy), RICHARD CRENNA (Simon), RICCARDO CUCCIOLLA (Paul Weber), SIMONE VALÈRE (Simon's Wife), PAUL CRAUCHET (Morand), ANDRÉ POUSSE (Marc Albouis), JEAN DESAILLY (Gentleman in Train), VALÉRIE WILSON (Gaby), LÉON MINISINI (Mathieu la Valise).

"Nobody can arrest a corpse."

Edouard Coleman (Alain Delon) is a *flic*, a French cop. To be precise, he's a Parisian police commissioner: tight-lipped, hard-boiled, quick-witted, and emotionally untouchable. Whether he's faced with the body of a beautiful dead prostitute or forced to kill in self-defense, his expression never changes. When small-time crooks try to shake him off their trail, he's frankly unimpressed; and when he needs to make it clear where he stands and what he stands for, he's not averse to slapping a face. The point is taken, by the slapped and the audience alike. This man is cool, a classic Melville hero who follows his own rules simply because he's obviously predestined to do so. Coleman is the kind of character that's familiar from the *noir* movies of Howard Hawks, Robert Wise or William Wyler; but as he insists on equating cynicism with realism, his take on the world is bound to be a little undiffer-

entiated. As he explains to the audience, "When faced with a human being, a policeman feels only distrust and disdain."

In the Melville cosmos, rigorous formalism and aesthetic force go hand-in-hand with uninterrupted suspense. Like his protagonists, Melville's films are driven by contradictions. Opposites clash, vying for the upper hand, but they also splinter and fuse, giving rise to new contradictions, new concepts and new characters. A Melville protagonist who embodies Good is not necessarily someone the audience can identify with; just as little, in fact, as the bad guy who wins out in the end. In Germany, this film carried a nicely ambiguous title: *Der Chef* = The Boss. For it's hard to say which boss is being referred to – is the hero of the movie the police chief or the gang leader?

3

1   Is a happy Melville hero imaginable? Alain Delon as Inspector Edouard Coleman.

2   Film Noir in color: Blond turns to gold, love becomes betrayal, and Cathy (Catherine Deneuve) turns into an ice-cold angel of death.

3   Greed, brutality, and a love of perfection all pave the way to crime.

4   Triple play: Cathy has to choose between Inspector Coleman, the nightclub owner and master criminal Simon.

5   "Car 5 here, who's speaking?" Coleman and his assistant: Another day, another crime.

"It's not the tough storyline that makes Melville's film so breathtaking. He's not the slightest bit interested in the caveman type of action movie, which boils down to little more than brute violence." *Frankfurter Rundschau*

Commissioner Coleman's adversary is Simon (Richard Crenna), a cultivated, well-groomed and highly intelligent nightclub owner, who also happens to be the leader of a criminal gang. Besides Simon, the select, four-man team includes a solid bourgeois bank manager (unemployed), a technology and transportation expert, and a faithful follower with a predictably criminal past. Once masked, these men become archetypal bankrobbers. The heist at the start of the film is calculated in its effects but a thrill to watch, with the gang driving up in a big black '62 Plymouth, each of them wearing a trench coat, dark glasses and a fedora pulled down low. Their second coup is

peerless in its laconic precision, with Simon abseiling from a helicopter to rob a drugs courier on a fast-moving train, a unique combination of real and animated effects.

A female figure completes the ensemble and sets up the connections between the lawmen and the crooks: Cathy (Catherine Deneuve) is the wife of Simon and the lover of Commissar Coleman. She's a blonde angel, a Film Noir dream who brings love, longing and destruction. Cathy is the embodiment of unattainable beauty; and when circumstances require, she can deal out death without batting an eyelid. In one scene, Melville's heroine – dress ed in a snow-white nurse's uniform and bathed in an icy pale-blue light – administers a deadly injection to a defenseless man. A pair of intently watchful dark-brown eyes, an exquisitely delicate complexion, a brief, surreptitious nibble of the lower lip – and death has visited the sickroom. Each tiny element in this scene – as indeed in the film as a whole – is consciously planned and executed, and a thoroughly minimalist acting style achieves maximum visceral effect. Cathy controls the fate of Coleman and Simon, two rivals who, could they but work together, might be capable of managing the perfect crime – or, for that matter, of devising the perfect law.

Cathy is the decisive factor in this story. It's she who determines the ending of the film, the denouement of the plot, and it is she who presides like a goddess over good and evil, love and betrayal, chill reality and hopeless illusion.　　　SR

JEAN-PIERRE MELVILLE Those whom the gods love die young. When Jean-Pierre Melville (1917–1973) succumbed to a heart attack in a restaurant, he had made only 13 films, many of which he had also scripted and produced. He liked to call himself a "créateur de cinema," which he felt to be a suitably resonant and imposing designation. The phrase also implies a creative impulse that goes beyond mere directing, and this we can confidently allow him. Melville gives the *form* of his movies more attention than the story alone would demand; his films are carefully constructed pictorial choreographies crafted onto suspense-laden plots. He had a far greater influence on the new French cinema than is generally recognized. One might say that he prepared the ground for the changes in the production system that enabled the *Nouvelle Vague*.

Born Jean-Pierre Grumbach, he adopted his new name in honor of his artistic idol, American novelist Hermann Melville, the author of *Moby Dick* and *Billy Budd*. In fact, this French filmmaker was much taken with American archetypes and role models. His films frequently reflect the Hollywood movies of the 1930s; and, off-duty, he sported a magnificent Stetson while tooling round Paris by night in a giant Ford Galaxy, constantly in search of new locations and breathtaking motifs. He enjoyed his greatest successes when working with Jean-Paul Belmondo (*The Finger Man / Le Doulos / Lo spione*, 1962) or Alain Delon (*The Samurai / Le Samouraï*, 1967; *Second Breath / Le deuxième souffle*, 1966). He made an unforgettable appearance in Godard's *Breathless* (*À bout de souffle*, 1959), as the writer Parvulesco who is interviewed by the Jean Seberg character. When asked to name his dearest desire, he replies: "To become immortal and then die." A statement straight from the heart of a Melville film.

THE DISCREET CHARM OF THE BOURGEOISIE

Le Charme discret de la bourgeoisie

1972 - FRANCE - 102 MIN. - SOCIAL GROTESQUE

DIRECTOR LUIS BUÑUEL (1900–1983)
SCREENPLAY LUIS BUÑUEL, JEAN-CLAUDE CARRIÈRE DIRECTOR OF PHOTOGRAPHY EDMOND RICHARD EDITING HÉLÈNE PLEMIANNIKOV
MUSIC GUY VILLETTE PRODUCTION SERGE SILBERMAN for GREENWICH FILM PRODUCTIONS.

STARRING FERNANDO REY (Rafaele Costa, Ambassador of Miranda), PAUL FRANKEUR (Monsieur Thévenot), DELPHINE SEYRIG (Madame Thévenot), BULLE OGIER (Florence), STÉPHANE AUDRAN (Madame Sénéchal), JEAN-PIERRE CASSEL (Monsieur Sénéchal), MILENA VUKOTIC (Ines, the Maid), JULIEN BERTHEAU (Bishop Dufour), CLAUDE PIÉPLU (Colonel), MICHEL PICCOLI (Minister).

ACADEMY AWARDS 1972 OSCAR for BEST FOREIGN FILM.

"There's nothing like a martini, especially when it's dry!"

An anecdote from Oscars Night, 1972, encapsulates the spirit of this film. When Luis Buñuel's movie was officially nominated, the 72-year-old Surrealist and scourge of the bourgeoisie made a statement to Mexican journalists: he was quite sure, he announced, that he would indeed be awarded the Oscar; after all, he insisted, he'd forked out the 25,000 dollars demanded for the prize – and though Americans might have their faults, they could always be relied on to keep their word... The story hit the press, and all hell broke loose in Hollywood. Buñuel's producer, Serge Silbermann, had his work cut out pouring oil on the troubled waters. When *The Discreet Charm of the Bourgeoisie* actually went on to win the Academy Award for the Best Foreign Film, Buñuel smugly told anyone who'd listen: "The Americans

may have their faults – but you can always count on them to keep their word."

In his last film but three, the Old Master unleashed the beast of surrealism once more. This time, however, the result was less visually disturbing than the early masterpiece *An Andalusian Dog* (*Un chien andalou*, 1929), made in collaboration with Salvador Dali. After years of struggle and exile, in his hard-boiled but still vital old age, Buñuel no longer had any need to prove his credentials as an anarchic, subversive, and unconventional artist. And though one might complain that the film has no plot, that its characters are as lifeless as marionettes, or that they're forced to caper through an all-too-theatrical set, this kind of criticism simply fails to recognize the film's truly

1 The Mirandan ambassador (Fernando Rey) is a connoisseur of good food. Madame Thévenot (Delphine Seyrig) admires his excellent taste.

2 The more unattainable the goal, the more authoritative the moral law, the more unsuspecting the husband… the more desire grows.

3 Everybody's nightmare: Suddenly on stage without a line in your head.

revolutionary quality, as a grotesque cinematic carnival of bourgeois ideals, values and clichés.

The story is easily summarized: six *grands bourgeois* are doing their damnedest to meet for an exquisitely cultivated evening meal – but something or other keeps stopping them from doing so. Either they mysteriously get the dates mixed up, or they're inconvenienced by a sudden death in the restaurant. So they try again; and this time, a squad of paratroopers burst into the house in order to carry out a maneuver. The would-be diners persist undeterred; and just as they've all taken their places and lifted their

cutlery, they realize they're on a theater stage; the chicken is made of rubber, the audience are booing, and the actors appear to have forgotten their lines…

This last scene is not the only one that turns out to have been dreamt by one of the protagonists. Various other nightmares disturb the diners, whose faultlessly polite but utterly trivial activity seems destined to peter out in one dead end after another. On one occasion, a dream within a dream leads to yet another dream. As the film proceeds, it becomes increasingly clear to the audience that they can rely on nothing they are shown. Reality

The title's complacent *grandezza* not only characterizes the bourgeoisie itself, but the visual style of the film, and Bunuel's analytical approach. No other director treats his characters with such distance and apparent passivity (or indifference); and none grants them such unconditional freedom to act according to the milieu or the atmosphere they happen to inhabit – to be new and different in each scene." *Die Zeit*

3

FERNANDO REY

He turned up in so many films that almost everyone must have seen him sometime – possibly without even noticing it, for his appearances were sometimes fleeting (though always worthwhile). In the 80s, he appeared in so many movies that one critic dared call him "a prop." His filmography comprises around 200 films.

Yet for all that, the Spaniard Fernando Rey (1917–1994) is best known and best loved for his performances in a handful of films by his friend Luis Buñuel, as well as for his major roles in *The French Connection I* and *II* (1971/1975). In the latter movies, he played a sophisticated French drugs czar who's pursued obsessively by a tough, streetwise New York detective (Gene Hackman). The chase scene in the subway is unforgettable: when Rey, the man with the elegant walking-stick and the perfectly-manicured beard, waves nonchalantly as his train draws away from his frustrated nemesis on the platform, it's surely one of the great moments in movie history. Only Rey could have embodied this figure in all its rich ambiguity: gallant and decadent, cultivated and greedy – a memorably nuanced characterization.

His great career with the exiled Spaniard Buñuel began in Mexico with *Viridiana* (1961). There followed *Tristana* (1969/70), *The Discreet Charm of the Bourgeoisie* (*Le Charme discret de la bourgeoisie*, 1972) and *That Obscure Object of Desire* (*Cet obscur objet du désir*, 1977), Buñuel's last film. Though it may be hard to believe, Buñuel discovered Rey when he was playing the part of a corpse; the director was simply blown away by the actor's "expressive power." An encounter of crucial – indeed vital – importance to both...

and illusion dissolve and merge into a new actuality, a surreal cinematic universe. Yet however bizarre the events that invade their lives, these six ladies and gentlemen never lose their cool, persevering heroically with their cultivated poses and their gestures of hypocritical friendliness. Quite literally, they never lose face; for when all they have is a succession of masks for every social eventuality, there's no face left to lose.

However elegantly the table is set, it's a uniquely hot, dry and spicy meal that Buñuel serves up to his audience, and it's not for tender palates (though he does include an excellent recipe for an extra dry Martini). In fact, the guests at this dinner table are so wonderfully adroit in their blasé bitchiness that it's hard not to end up liking them a little. The subtle pleasure of *schadenfreude* is something one could quite easily acquire a taste for.   SR

"You may note that I haven't really tried to say what the film is about, what it means. And the reason for that is that I don't know. But, I don't really care, either. A poem should not mean, but be, said someone, and if there was a film poem, this is it."

Guardian Weekly

4   Opportunity grabs: While the party is hiding from terrorists, the ambassador gets what he can.

5   Topsy-turvy: The dead hold a wake while the living sleep. Buñuel adopted and adapted the principles of Carnival.

6   Absolution: A bishop with a shotgun (Julien Bertheau) executes his father's murderer during Confession.

SOLARIS
Solyaris

1972 - USSR - 167 MIN. - SCIENCE FICTION

DIRECTOR ANDREI TARKOVSKY (1932–1986)
SCREENPLAY FRIEDRICH GORENSTEIN, ANDREI TARKOVSKY, based on the novel of the same name by STANISLAW LEM
DIRECTOR OF PHOTOGRAPHY VADIM YUSOV EDITING LJUDMILA FEYGINOVA MUSIC EDWARD ARTEMYEV, JOHANN SEBASTIAN BACH
PRODUCTION VIACHESLAV TARASOV for MOSFILM.

STARRING NATALYA BONDARCHUK (Hari), DONATAS BANIONIS (Kris Kelvin), NIKOLAI GRINKO (Kris's Father), YURI JÄRVET (Snaut), ANATOLI SOLONITSYN (Sartorius), VLADISLAV DVORZHETSKI (Berton), SOS SARKISSIAN (Gibarjan), OLGA BARNET (Kris's Mother), TAMARA OGORODNIKOVA (Aunt Anna), YULIAN SEMYONOV (Chairman at Scientific Conference).

IFF CANNES 1972 GRAND PRIZE OF THE JURY (Andrei Tarkovsky).

"We are dealing with the limits of human understanding."

Based on a novel by Stanislaw Lem, this is a film that takes on some very big issues: the nature of self-awareness, knowledge and perception. In an era of space epics that were strong on special effects but weak on content – from *Star Wars* (1977) to *Star Wars: Episode V – The Empire Strikes Back* (1980) – *Solaris* reminds us that the science-fiction genre has its roots in philosophical speculation. And the film begins like a poetic alternative to its high-tech rivals.

Its opening shots are long and slow, idyllic images of the natural world: grass waving softly in the waters of a lake, trees, fog, a solitary horse. In the background, we hear birdsong, frogs croaking, and the soft rustle of flowing water. From beginning to end, *Solaris* maintains this meditative tempo, and it's one of the film's great strengths. With a confidently minimalist use of cinematic means, Tarkovsky presents a maximum of disturbing effects. The world he creates is a kind of Utopia; highly idiosyncratic, familiar and yet strange. But Tarkovsky is in any case only marginally interested in doing justice to the conventions of the SF film. Indeed, his almost provocative refusal to serve up the special effects expected of the genre gives him more space to follow the development of the characters as they travel in search of themselves. Their story is told with the greatest of care.

The center of attention is the psychologist Kris Kelvin (Donatas Banionis). His task is to examine the crew of a space station in orbit around the planet Solaris, and to find out the reasons for their strange behavior. Before he departs from the Earth, however, he has to order his personal affairs, which means, above all, his relationship with his father (Nikolai Grinko).

This is a subject Tarkovsky returns to in each of his films. Kelvin's melancholy farewell is overshadowed by the still-raw memory of his wife Hari, who took her own life.

Against this background, the voyage to the space station seems like a welcome departure to a new life. On arriving, Kelvin finds the two astronauts Snaut (Yuri Järvet) and Sartorius (Anatoli Solonitsyn) in a strangely nervous and preoccupied state. Their peculiar behavior appears to have something to do with the ocean of Solaris, whose biostreams are somehow affecting the psychic wellbeing of the crew. It becomes apparent that the planet itself is capable of turning private thoughts and wishes into three-dimensional reality. Kelvin himself is not spared the experience. Soon, he is faced with a materialized copy of his wife Hari (Natalya Bondarchuk). He is drawn into

"The seething planet, turbulent metaphor as much for an imperfect deity as for the psychoanalyst's couch, provides what the men come to recognize as a mirror of themselves, reflecting with inescapable clarity the faults which caused the errors now incarnate before them." *Sight and Sound*

1 In bed with the blues: Color symbolism and religious imagery brighten up the ether of *Solaris*.

2 Scent of a woman: "Humanized" memory Hari (Natalya Bondartschuk) proves little more than a hatful of hollow.

3 Always on my mind: Despite all attempts to stifle the memories of his mistress, Hari lives on.

4   Through the looking glass: Hari realizes that her
    identity is a sham.

5   Mind scrambler: Snaut (Juri Järvet) and Sartorius
    have already grasped Hari's implications for future
    galactic travelers.

a series of mysterious encounters with this phantom creature – and confronted with the power of his own memories.

Like the astronaut Bowman in Stanley Kubrick's *2001: A Space Odyssey* (1968), Kelvin in *Solaris* ultimately attains a new level of consciousness. In many science fiction movies, outer space is the scene of conquest, of battles for new territory. In *2001* and *Solaris*, by contrast, infinite and apparently empty space provides anj144

 opportunity for evolution, for a growth in knowledge and self-awareness. Vast, obscure and barely explored, space is also a metaphor for the human race, a stranger to itself and to its own history, despite all the progress of technology. Thematically, however, *2001* takes a broader view,

examining the development of humankind as a whole; in *Solaris*, Tarkovsky is interested primarily in the individual, his unique subjectivity and personal history. The form chosen is a kind of filmic contemplation that forgoes fast cutting in favor of poetic images, long takes, and faces absorbed in thought, thus granting us some deep insights into the characters' mental states and private spiritual landscapes. What we see is the process of reflection given cinematic form; and, above all, given time to develop. If the methods seem unusual for a science fiction film, they are more than adequate to the director's theme. The film is powerfully poetic, and its melancholy atmosphere of loneliness and silence constitutes an invitation to the spectator: to follow Kris Kelvin on his Utopian search for the unknown self.   BR

SCIENCE FICTION Since the 20s, the term has served as a collective name for films and books that speculate on technological developments in fantastic future worlds. The first science fiction film appeared as early as 1902: Georges Méliès' *Journey to the Moon* (*Le Voyage dans la lune*), based on motifs from Jules Verne and H. G. Wells. While the set design and visual aesthetics of Fritz Lang's *Metropolis* (1926) formed a kind of stylistic prototype still imitated today, science fiction only achieved real popularity in the 50s, with films such as *The Thing From Another World* (1951) and *The War of the Worlds* (1953). The SF film appears to have no difficulty in formulating social and technical utopias, even when these are very far removed from the moviegoers' daily experience. A number of different strategies are available: the *Star Wars* saga (five episodes between 1977 and 2002) was just one example of an elaborate spectacle driven by special-effects technology; the *Alien* series (1979–97) showed how horror elements could be integrated; and *Blade Runner* (1982) picked up on the tradition of 40s Film Noir. As a rule, all these variants combine a vision of the human future with a scenario of existential threat. The philosophical content varies. In recent times, the genre has experienced a revival, with the satirical *Men in Black* (1997) and *The Matrix* (1999), which owes a lot to comics. The dramatic development of digital animation technology has produced a new "somatic cinema," whose sensuous and physical qualities could barely have been imagined even a few years ago. Films like *Solaris* (*Solyaris*, 1972) however, make it painfully clear that these technical advances have so far only been possible at the expense of real content.

LAST TANGO IN PARIS

Ultimo tango a Parigi / Le Dernier Tango à Paris

972 - ITALY / FRANCE - 136 MIN. - DRAMA

DIRECTOR BERNARDO BERTOLUCCI (*1941)
SCREENPLAY BERNARDO BERTOLUCCI, FRANCO ARCALLI DIRECTOR OF PHOTOGRAPHY VITTORIO STORARO EDITING FRANCO ARCALLI, ROBERTO PERPIGNANI MUSIC GATO BARBIERI PRODUCTION ALBERTO GRIMALDI for LES PRODUCTIONS ARTISTES ASSOCIÉS, PRODUZIONI EUROPEE ASSOCIATI.

STARRING MARLON BRANDO (Paul), MARIA SCHNEIDER (Jeanne), JEAN-PIERRE LÉAUD (Tom), MASSIMO GIROTTI (Marcel), VERONICA LAZAR (Rosa), MARIA MICHI (Rosa's Mother), GIOVANNA GALLETTI (Prostitute), GITT MAGRINI (Jeanne's Mother), CATHERINE ALLÉGRET (Catherine), CATHERINE BREILLAT (Mouchette).

"How do you like your hero? Over easy or sunny side up?"

The camera swoops down on a man, before encircling him with the fast, aggressive movements of a tango dancer. The man (Marlon Brando) is standing under a métro bridge in Paris, and he's screaming. His name is Paul and his wife has just committed suicide. In the distance, we see the shadowy figure of a young woman (Maria Schneider). She approaches, passes Paul, and turns to look at him once more. These two will meet again. In an empty apartment, their first sexual contact takes place within minutes – no holds barred. The couple are in flight from themselves. Estranged from their lives, enclosed in a barely furnished room and surrounded by diffuse sunlight, they meet to adopt the original male and female roles: Adam and Eve. Neither knows the other's name nor anything of their life outside the apartment, for what goes on beyond these walls is of no significance. Their relationship can only exist in the hermetic world of the apartment, in which all social links are erased. Paul is a hotelier and a vagabond, whose life has fallen apart since the death of his wife. It's he who makes the rules, though his bourgeois 20-year-old lover Jeanne adopts them with increasing alacrity. In the end, though, it's Paul who shatters this artificial unity against Jeanne's will. He moves out of the flat and announces his desire to marry her; but Jeanne cannot countenance a bourgeois alliance with the man she refers to, disrespectfully as *maître d'hôtel*. The iron rule remains: no names. As events draw towards the climax, he bursts into her apartment and demands to know her name. She's holding a gun in her hand, in self-defense; and as she fulfills his request, the gun goes off. It's impossible to say what killed him – the weapon or the word.

In the early 70s, few films aroused as much attention as Bertolucci's *Last Tango in Paris*. In New York, Pauline Kael celebrated *Last Tango* as a work that had "altered the face of an art form;" in Italy, the movie caused uproar. Bertolucci was only 32 when he made *Last Tango*, and it was already his sixth film. Though he had become world-famous with *1900* (*Novecento*) his epic of the Italian century, *Ultimo tango a Parigi* was eventually banned in his home country. It was the graphic sex scenes that caused all the trouble, for they went far beyond anything ever seen in mainstream cinema and were accused of being pornographic. Yet the censors felt provoked not only by the copulating couple (who are, incidentally, never seen naked) and the spectacular body of Maria Schneider (at that time, a young and unknown actress). They were equally offended by the film's fundamentally nihilistic attitude and its openly stated fantasies of degradation. The movie was a product of its period: without the climate of sexual liberation at the start of the 70s, a film like *Last Tango in Paris* would have been as unthinkable as Liliana Cavani's *The Night Porter* (*Il portiere di notte*, 1974) or Pasolini's

Arabian Nights (*Il fiore delle mille e una notte*, 1974). Since the 70s, we have grown accustomed to provocation as an artistic principle. It's the film's aesthetic qualities that impress us today. The pictorial composition, the light, the camerawork and the editing create a wholly unique atmosphere and provide the actors with the framework they require – especially Marlon Brando. Bertolucci's cameraman Vittorio Storaro had a huge influence on the director's visual style. The artfully lit interiors, the variations in focal depth and the precisely calculated camera movements combine to evoke the atmosphere that made the film so famous: a continual oscillation between sexual tension, power fantasies and sheer hopelessness. This effect is reinforced by Franco Arcalli's montage, with its often bewildering suspension of spatial logic, and the music of Gato Barbieri, till then known only as a composer for B-movies.

With admirable skill, Bertolucci weaves together three narrative threads. There's the story of Paul, mourning his dead wife and hunting for the traces of her suicide in his strange, labyrinthine hotel. There's the story of Jeanne, whose life we see filtered through the camera of her fiancé Tom (Jean-Pierre Léaud) as material for a TV documentary entitled "The Portrait of a Young Girl." This film-within-the-film is a parody of *cinéma vérité*; while Tom believes he's portraying the real Jeanne, all he can produce is a string of tired clichés. And finally we have the story of Paul *and* Jeanne, another manifestation of the old dream of innocence regained, of a new self beyond economic status, culture or civilization. The scene in which the couple sit naked on the bed has since become famous. Their bodies are bathed in warm, yellow light, and they converse only in sounds, in a series of grunts and chirrups. For

1 Alone at last: After his wife's suicide, Paul (Marlon Brando) escapes to the confines of an empty apartment. Jeanne (Maria Schneider) soon follows suit.

2 It takes two to tango… Paul and Jeanne dance to a different tune.

3 If only they knew the real me: The spectator can only see Jeanne through her fiancé's camera.

4 Sex among strangers: A desperate attempt to return to the arms of innocence.

"**This must be the most powerfully erotic movie ever made, and it may turn out to be the most liberating movie ever made, and so it's probably only natural that an audience, anticipating a voluptuous feast from the man who made** *The Conformist* **and confronted with the unexpected sexuality, and the new realism it requires of the actors, should go into shock. Bertolucci and Brando have altered the face of an art form. Who was prepared for that?**" *Pauline Kael*

language is civilization, words petrify social relationships, and these are the very things the two deeply different protagonists are seeking to escape in the secret world of the apartment. Yet this Garden of Eden, as a refuge from civilization, is also a place in which the rules of civilized behavior seem to have lost their normative force. Here, violence, raw sex and obscene fantasies can achieve expression, as putative manifestations of a non-social way of being.

The film is permeated by an existential despair that evokes the world of Francis Bacon. Not only does the film open with two Bacon paintings; Bertolucci also imitates the colors and compositional techniques of the artist, with shots framed in arches and faces filmed through a sheet of glass, shift-ing and dissolving their contours.

KK

5

"*Tango's* explosive impact will demonstrate to a wide public what many film buffs already know: that Bertolucci, 31, is Italy's most gifted director in the generation after Fellini and Antonioni, and one of the most gifted younger directors on the world scene." *Time Magazine*

BERNARDO BERTOLUCCI Alongside Godard, Antonioni and Chabrol, the Italian director Bernardo Bertolucci is regarded as one of the last survivors of the European film avant-garde. He alone, however, managed to introduce the aesthetics of the *cinéma des auteurs* into the cinematic mainstream. Indeed, his films were often astonishingly popular, not least the multiple Oscar-winner *The Last Emperor* (1987). Influenced by the theories of Freud and Marx as well as by artists as diverse as Francis Bacon and Giuseppe Verdi, Bertolucci is a great political filmmaker *and* an outstanding visual stylist. His best film is widely agreed to be *The Conformist* (*Il conformista / Le Conformiste*, 1970), a tale of guilt and political entanglement in the fascist Italy of the 1930s. The film was adapted from a novel by Alberto Moravia.

Bertolucci was born in Parma in 1941, and made his directing debut at the age of 21 with *La Commare secca*, based on a short story by Pier Paolo Pasolini. He went on to work with Pasolini as an assistant director on *Accattone* (1961), before achieving international recognition with his own film,

5 *A Streetcar Named Desire* (revisited): Domestic violence behind closed doors.

6 Empty chairs and empty tables: Vittorio Storaro's camera captures the character's inner isolation.

Before the Revolution (*Prima della rivoluzione*, 1963–64). Other works of the 60s include *the new yorker* (*Love and Anger*, 1969) and *Partner* (1968*)*, a homage to the French *Nouvelle Vague*. The scandal caused by *Last Tango in Paris* (*Ultimo tango a Parigi / Le Dernier Tango à Paris*) brought him unheard-of success, but the film was banned in Italy and the country's authorities even stripped the director of his right to vote.

Bertolucci's cinematic trademarks include a highly developed epic narrative style and a sophisticated delight in visual imagery. In the 70s, he consolidated his reputation as a director of high-quality films with *1900* (*Novecento*, 1975/76) and *La Luna* (1979). With *Stealing Beauty* (*Io ballo da sola / Beauté volée*), a film set in Tuscany, he made his cinematic return to Italy; but only since *Besieged / L'assedio* (1998), the story of an Englishman and an African woman in Rome, has he been fully accepted back in his native land. He made *Paradiso e inferno* in 1999 before his latest film in English, *Heaven and Hell* (2001).

WHAT'S UP, DOC?

1972 - USA - 94 MIN. - SCREWBALL COMEDY

DIRECTOR PETER BOGDANOVICH (*1939)
SCREENPLAY BUCK HENRY, DAVID NEWMAN, ROBERT BENTON, based on a story by PETER BOGDANOVICH **DIRECTOR OF PHOTOGRAPHY** LÁSZLÓ KOVÁCS **EDITING** VERNA FIELDS **MUSIC** ARTIE BUTLER **PRODUCTION** PETER BOGDANOVICH for SATICOY PRODUCTIONS.

STARRING BARBRA STREISAND (Judy Maxwell), RYAN O'NEAL (Professor Howard Bannister), MADELINE KAHN (Eunice Burns), AUSTIN PENDLETON (Frederick Larrabee), MABEL ALBERTSON (Mrs. Van Hoskins), SORRELL BOOKE (Harry the Detective), STEFAN GIERASCH (Fritz), KENNETH MARS (Hugh Simon), PHILIP ROTH (Mr. Jones), LIAM DUNN (Judge Maxwell).

"Once upon a time, there was a plaid overnight case..."

A delicate hand opens a red leather-bound volume with a Warner Bros. insignia on its cover, and we instantly know what Peter Bogdanovich's second feature film has in store for us. As if fondly glimpsing into a cherished children's storybook or family photo album, we watch pages containing the film credits turn to the tinkering of a music-box and Barbra Streisand's unmistakable singing. A hand, presumably hers, glides across the parchment, gesturing both lovingly and flippantly to the names of cast and crew that appear on screen. This introduction sequence greets the audience with a wink and a smile. Just like the film's title itself, it is a spoof on the classic animated shorts featuring Bugs Bunny, Tex Avery's fast-talking, carrot-munching "wascally wabbit." The 33-year-old Bogdanovich had already earned himself a reputation for being a well-versed chronicler of international and, even more so, American film history. This project, according to the movie's tagline, was to be his very own nostalgic twist on the screwball comedy. Remember them?

What's Up, Doc? gets (and gives) its kicks by poking fun at the icons of Hollywood entertainment. Bogdanovich proudly pays tribute to greats like Hawks, Hitchcock, the Marx Brothers and Buster Keaton. He steals enough of their material and gags to be tried for grand theft larceny a thousand times over. Not that we mind, for the picture's magic is wrapped up in the hidden and overt references to the Golden Age of Hollywood found in each character, scene, as well as in its flow and choreography. When a very svelte Barbra hangs onto a 33rd story window ledge for dear life, wearing nothing but a towel, we are reminded of Harold Lloyd's bombastic shot of the New York City skyscraper clock from Safety Last (1923), and that's just the tip of the iceberg. We watch as 90 minutes of non-stop nyuk nyuk jokes, complete with pies in the face and off-the-wall physical comedy explode onto the screen. There are even traces of the cinematic avant-garde when Bogdanovich humorously resorts to the "subjective camera" and thrusts his audience into the shoes of a homicidal maniac. Here, an outstretched arm points a pistol at petrified party guests, who stare directly into the camera (and at us) as if down the barrel of a gun.

What's Up, Doc? is a laugh attack compilation of film references and visual aesthetics. There are parodies jumping out at every corner, and the roller-coaster pace supplied by the three screenwriters is enough to make you dizzy. Conversations resemble ping-pong tournaments where the spectators are forced do one double take after another in order to keep score. It's a veritable shell game, and to win the audience must concentrate on all the visuals, from rapid cuts and over-the-top facial expressions, to tiny setdressing and costume details. Then, of course, there are the "shells" themselves – the four plaid overnight cases sought by a sordid cast of characters for the most diverse of reasons. As luck would have it, these four indistinguishable pieces of baggage "just happen" to land in four hotel rooms all on the same floor of one hotel, separated only by a hallway and a matter of feet. Doors fly open and shut, as those who have the suitcases are chased by those who'll stop at nothing to get them.

Five rooms, four bags, about a dozen eccentric characters and one unassuming elevator at the end of the hall – that is the winning recipe behind What's Up, Doc?, the Bogdanovich screwball that just won't quit. A virtual

2

1   The look of love? Barbra Streisand as zany Judy Maxwell.

2   High-speed bloopers and practical jokes: The twelve-minute "roller-coaster ride" through the streets of San Francisco took four weeks to film.

3   Twists and turns, thrills and spills: Once a screwball comedy gets into gear anything goes.

study in relentlessness, its crowning achievement is a hare-brained spin on the classic chase scene *à la* Peter Yates' *Bullitt* (1968), packed with shoots and ladders antics, Buster Keaton style window panes being transported across moving traffic and Chinese dragons. By the end, there's just nowhere else left for its mayhem to go except maybe smack into the middle of the San Francisco Bay or to a court of law where you never know just who you'll meet… Not to worry, it all ends happily, proving the age-old adage about love

healing all wounds – and occasionally even scrapes and bruises. This time, the lovers are irresistible home-wrecker Barbra Streisand and bungling straight man Ryan O'Neal, as Howard Bannister, professor of musicology. The academic bears a striking similarity to anthropologist David Huxley (Cary Grant) from Howard Hawks' *Bringing Up Baby* (1938), a picture that provided the foundation for *What's Up, Doc?*, undoubtedly Bogdanovich's greatest cinematic dissertation.   SR

BARBRA STREISAND

Her own mother didn't think she'd make it as a singer and actress. After all, what chance did a kooky Brooklyn kid with skinny legs, a crooked nose and slightly crossed eyes stand against all the attractive young women out there who were determined to make it big? And so, the Jewish girl born Barbara Joan Streisand (born 1942, Brooklyn, New York) started out small. She worked as a cleaning lady at a theater, an usher, a telephone operator – anything that would get her closer to realizing her dream. She persistently sung, acted and hummed her way to the front of the stage until audiences could not help but notice her. Her Broadway debut came with the 1962 musical "I Can Get It For You Wholesale" in the role of Ms. Marmelstein. Against the wish of those auditioning her, she performed the entire number while seated in a rolling chair. Barbra's tactic won out and audiences couldn't get enough of her. She quickly became the toast of the town, and landed the lead in Jule Styne's Broadway musical sensation "Funny Girl." Streisand's "Hello Gorgeous!" quickly went from being a New York catch phrase to a national one when she reprised the role of Fanny Brice for the 1968 Hollywood film adaptation of *Funny Girl*, a debut performance that won her the Best Actress Oscar in a vote to vote tie with Katherine Hepburn. Further comedies like *The Owl and the Pussycat* (1970) and *What's Up, Doc?* (1972) quickly followed, as did a Best Original Song Oscar for *A Star is Born* (1976). Yet Barbra, who did in fact drop the original second "a" from her first name when her manager requested that she adopt a new one, wanted more out of life than just comedy, song, stage and glamour – she wanted to play serious roles and to direct.
Both wishes came true with the 1983 film *Yentl* (1983), for which she also served as co-screenwriter and producer. Nonetheless, her "ugly duckling" persona had taken its toll. Barbra Streisand soon became known for her eccentricity, her stage fright and her megalomania. She began to purchase art and her gold records were soon eclipsed by the exclusive Art Deco and Jugendstil pieces that decorated her numerous residences. During the mid 1990s she took to the more minimalist functionality of modern art and auctioned off her painstakingly acquired collection. Many years after her divorce from actor Elliott Gould, the one-of-a-kind entertainer married movie and TV star James Brolin, to whom she is still wed.

"Bogdanovich is much too clever just to latch on to his role models. One might say he's trying to match up to them by reviewing the last few years of film history. In other words, his film is really an intelligent parody of recent box-office hits." *Frankfurter Rundschau*

4   Going my way? For Peter Bogdanovich, two escalators provide an ideal place to discuss the meaning of propriety.

5   Meeting of the minds: For a quiet tête-à-tête during a dinner party, what better place than under the table? But they won't be alone for long…

THE LEGEND OF PAUL AND PAULA
Die Legende von Paul und Paula

1973 - GDR - 105 MIN. - LOVE STORY, DRAMA

DIRECTOR HEINER CAROW (1929–1997)
SCREENPLAY ULRICH PLENZDORF, HEINER CAROW DIRECTOR OF PHOTOGRAPHY JÜRGEN BRAUER EDITING EVELYN CAROW MUSIC PETER GOTTHARDT PRODUCTION ERICH ALBRECHT for DEFA.

STARRING ANGELICA DOMRÖSE (Paula), WINFRIED GLATZEDER (Paul), HEIDEMARIE WENZEL (Paul's Wife), FRED DELMARE (Saft the Tyre Man), ROLF LUDWIG (Professor), DIETMAR RICHTER-REINICK (A Friend), FRANK SCHENK (Schmidt), JÜRGEN FROHRIEP (Blond Martin), PETER GOTTHARDT (A Musician).

"All or nothing."

In the spring of 1973, there were long queues at the East German movie theaters to see this unusual love story. Paula (Angelica Domröse) is an unmarried mother of two kids, and she works at a supermarket checkout. After an affair with a flute-playing hippie, she meets Paul (Winfried Glatzeder), a not-very-happily married state-employed bureaucrat with one child. Paula is a passionate woman who demands "all or nothing," but at first Paul is reluctant to get too deeply involved. Fearing for his status as an up-and-coming member of the East German elite, he feels compelled to keep up the appearance of a happy marriage, both at home and in the Ministry where he works. Then Paula loses one of her children in an accident and barricades herself in her apartment. Now Paul shows that love rules, even in a socialist society: he throws his career to the winds, stays off work, camps out in the stairwell of Paula's apartment house, and finally takes an axe to the door of her flat – as the neighbors stand round and applaud. East German theater audiences shared their feelings, and the film was an enormous hit. It provoked spontaneous ovations in the cinemas, something unheard of since the state production firm DEFA had commenced operations in 1945. Melodrama

was a genre that had previously not been tolerated by the East German cultural bureaucracy, but the public embraced it with open arms. Although Paul knows that another pregnancy could endanger Paula's life, she still wants a child from him… and dies after the child is born, just as a happy ending seems close enough to grasp.

After the Second World War, the German Democratic Republic was a determined attempt to sweep away everything old and discredited and to create a new society, to start again from scratch. This social program is evoked in the very first shot in *Paul and Paula*: a demolition ball tolls the death knell of Berlin's notorious slum tenements, clearing the way for spanking new apartment blocks. The conflict between old and new is one of the film's leitmotifs, and it demonstrates the attitude of the director and screenwriter towards their protagonists' pursuit of happiness: their desire for a better life is formulated, not in *opposition* to East German society, but *within* it. Paul is a member of his *Betriebskampfgruppe* – a works militia group, made up of workers under the leadership of the Party – and when he climbs into Paula's blossom-bedecked bed (she's crowned with flowers!), he has to take

"There's much more to this film than the tabloid love story. *The Legend of Paul and Paula* is a reflection on love in general, on conformity, on the dialectics of ideal and reality, and – *en passant* – on the cinema itself."

Der Tagesspiegel

off his uniform to do so. It's a scene that sent East German audiences wild with joy, and the film had found a perfect image for the tensions of the place and time. On the one hand, we see the strict regulation of everyday life under a communist regime (and the concurrent obligation to maintain a nervous high alertness). On the other, we have a relaxed presentation of the need for physical love, and recognition of the spirit of the age ("Flower Children"). At last it was possible for the East German cinema to deal with love, too, in a "modern" manner.

The Legend of Paul and Paula had a mixed reception in the West: either it was greeted with mild amusement (as a cultural "late-starter"), or it was praised, for ideological reasons, as a breakthrough for individualism in East German society. Yet, as a DEFA film, it has qualities that can only be recog-

nized when we understand the social and political context in which it was made. First, the characters are absolutely typical of the GDR: Paul is an academic for whom an encounter with a shopgirl is something more than a one-night stand. It should also be noted that Paula's "fatherless" children were no moral disgrace in East Germany. Second, (like many other DEFA films), this movie achieved credibility – and managed to capture a critical and skeptical audience – with many precise observations of everyday life. When we see the single mother Paula schlepping coal up to her third-floor apartment, the film's desire to demonstrate its own authenticity is almost palpable. In this sense, East German movies were always documentaries, too: records of how real people really lived, in their particular place and time.

RV

1   An East German epiphany: An ecstatic trip downriver on a barge (Angelica Domröse and Winfried Gletzeder).

2   Boat and bed are linked by rapid currents and violent storms.

3   Two hippies in the Eastern Bloc: She crowns him with flowers, as in some Polynesian paradise.

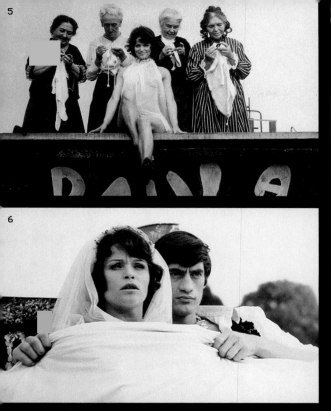

4 Instead of a yellowing family portrait, the oval frame shows the lovers themselves. This film's interest is the present.

5 The New Socialist Woman bids farewell to the old face of womanhood.

6 Facing reality: Dreams of a shared future won't solve the problems of today.

7 Sugar-coated: love is sublime, but it can end in kitsch.

"Sensational! The explosiveness of the subject matter and the frankness with which it's treated is – by East German standards – quite exceptional."

Stuttgarter Zeitung

FILM IN THE GDR

Unlike any country in the Western world, film production in the GDR (1949–1989) was *state-run*. This had its disadvantages, for both filmmakers and filmgoers. Movies were subject to state control: any scripts – or even completed films – that met with the disapproval of the responsible Party organs were put on ice or went into the archives unseen, and were known as "films for the shelf." The advantage for everyone working in East German film was that they enjoyed a secure existence as steady employees of DEFA or some similar body, even if their work was never shown in the cinema.

DEFA came into existence as a German-Soviet "joint enterprise" even before the GDR was founded. As the company was able to use the former UFA studios in Babelsberg (near Potsdam), it soon developed a reputation for productivity that extended far beyond East German borders. The very first postwar German film was made here: *The Murderers Are Among Us* (*Die Mörder sind unter uns*, 1946). DEFA also produced shorts, children's films, and weekly newsreels (*Der Augenzeuge*, "The Eyewitness"), as well as dubbing foreign films into German.

DEFA's central tasks were to convey the message of anti-fascism by cinematic means, and to show the problems and achievements of a Socialist society in the phase of construction. Genre films were extremely rare, and didn't reach the screens until the mid-60s: a sub-genre of the Western, for example, were the so-called "Indian Films" (Indianer-Filme). More and more, DEFA became a seismograph of everyday life under Socialism; and even today, after the demise of the GDR, it retains its historic importance as the powerhouse of a significant epoch in German film history.

SOYLENT GREEN

1973 - USA - 97 MIN. - SCIENCE FICTION, POLITICAL THRILLER

DIRECTOR RICHARD FLEISCHER (*1916)
SCREENPLAY STANLEY R. GREENBERG, based on the novel *MAKE ROOM! MAKE ROOM!* by HARRY HARRISON DIRECTOR OF
PHOTOGRAPHY RICHARD H. KLINE EDITING SAMUEL E. BREETLEY MUSIC FRED MYROW, EDVARD GRIEG ("PEER GYNT"),
PYOTR ILYCH TCHAIKOVSKY (6TH SYMPHONY), LUDWIG VAN BEETHOVEN (6TH SYMPHONY – "THE PASTORAL
SYMPHONY") PRODUCTION WALTER SELTZER, RUSSELL THACHER for MGM.

STARRING CHARLTON HESTON (Detective Robert Thorn), EDWARD G. ROBINSON (Sol Roth), CHUCK CONNORS (Tab Fielding),
LEIGH TAYLOR-YOUNG (Shirl), JOSEPH COTTEN (William R. Simonson), BROCK PETERS (Lieutenant "Chief" Hatcher),
PAULA KELLY (Martha), STEPHEN YOUNG (Gilbert), LINCOLN KILPATRICK (Priest), ROY JENSON (Donovan), WHIT BISSELL
(Governor Santini), LEONARD STONE (Charles).

"Ah, people were always lousy. But there was a world, once."

In the year 2022, New York City is a place no one would choose to visit. The city has 40 million inhabitants. Streets and apartment buildings are hopelessly overcrowded. Poverty and food shortages govern the lives of the people. To cap it all, a yellowish-green smog hangs over the city. The ecosystem has collapsed, and green plants are a thing of the past. In the midst of this chaos, there is only one guarantor of order: The New York City Police Department. Robert Thorn (Charlton Heston) is a detective in the homicide division, and he's been given the task of finding the killer of William Simonson

(Joseph Cotten), found dead in his luxury apartment and apparently murdered for his money.

Simonson had been CEO of the Soylent Corporation, a powerful organization with a near-monopoly on the production of food. Soylent produce a range of synthetic foodstuffs in handy chocolate-bar formats, distinguishable from each other only by their different colors. "Soylent Green," a natural product made of soy beans and plankton, is the most popular food around, for alternatives such as meat, fruit and vegetables can be afforded only by the

"Try all of Soylent's delicious flavors: Soylent red, Soylent yellow, and new, delicious, Soylent green. Made from the finest undersea growth."

Film quote: TV commercial

upper classes in their protected enclaves. Thorn is supported in his work by a man called Sol (Edward G. Robinson in his last role), a so-called "book," whose task is restricted to researching archives. Together, the two will uncover a shocking scandal, which the murder of Simonson was intended to conceal.

Soylent Green is a detective story, a political thriller, and a dark vision of ecological meltdown. Richard Fleischer's film evokes a world of crass dichotomies: in pursuit of his investigations, Thorn moves to and fro between the luxurious world of the rich and the hopeless squalor of the urban poor. He doesn't hesitate to enjoy the pleasures available in Simonson's stylish loft apartment: running hot water, a house bar, and Shirl (Leigh

Taylor-Young), an attractive girl who's just one more of the amenities. The greatest luxury of all, however, is space: the generous dimensions of Simonson's domicile stand in sharp contrast to the crammed housing blocks inhabited by the rest of the citizenry. When night falls, conditions are even more claustrophobic, with massed sleepers stacked in the stairways. As a policeman, Thorn is relatively privileged, but he still belongs to the world of the poor. He shares a tiny room with Sol, covers his nutritional requirements with Soylent Green, and has never eaten anything better. His place of work is no less dismal – the police station is a dilapidated hole, packed with irritable colleagues. Tough and cynical, Thorn shoulders his way through the daily routine of police work.

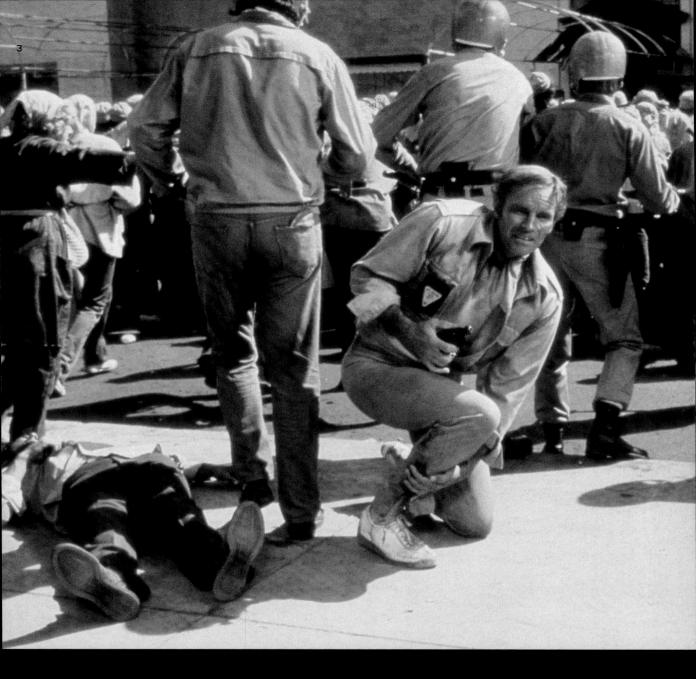

1   Close human contact is a scarce commodity in the year 2022.

2   Mass-produced food: Detective Thorn (Charlton Heston) has just found out what's in those little green bars…

3   In 2022, police brutality is a daily occurrence: Thorn is hurt, and his colleagues are still laying into the crowd.

"Director Richard Fleischer has created some shockingly effective scenes."

Die Welt

4

"It is too likely that such ecological chaos may occur, but there have been so many melodramatic warnings about it in essays and speculative fantasies such as this (*Soylent Green*) that urgency becomes blunted and worn through repetition." *Time Magazine*

Critics complained of this SF film's "unrealistically" contemporary look, for the early 70s are everywhere in evidence, from the style of the furniture to the flare in the jeans. These critics were missing the point. Director Richard Fleischer had no intention of emulating the timelessly futuristic ambience of films like *2001: A Space Odyssey* (1968); instead, he wanted to confront the audience of the time with the familiar city of New York grown suddenly nightmarish. The film's imagery is consequently shocking: thus we see the police deploy mechanical excavators to scoop up a group of angry protesters, before tipping them into containers and lugging them off like garbage. The message is clear, and chilling: in a world packed to overflowing, individual lives will lose all significance or value.

In the course of the film, this negative utopia is fleshed out with detail and acquires an almost documentary-like intensity. Fleischer succeeds in combining unpretentious realism with a grim yet spectacular vision of the world that awaits us. In this, *Soylent Green* is reminiscent of his previous film, the police drama *The New Centurions* (1972).

As foreshadowed in the impressively-edited title sequence, pollution is one of the film's main themes. In 1972, the publication of the Club of Rome report had sparked a broad public discussion on environmental protection, and the topic has become no less pressing in the last thirty years. Fleischer's Hollywood film was a timely and vigorous contribution to the debate, and he was clearly interested in taking a realistic stance: He employed Frank R. Bowerman, president of the American Academy for Environmental Protection, as an advisor on the film.

Soylent Green is a robust and uncompromising film, an unlikely, unusual and indubitable classic. Richard Fleischer presents an oppressively gripping scenario in the guise of a conventional thriller, and the film still has the power to disturb. It leaves us, to say the least, with a bitter taste in our mouths.   DG

4 The law of the jungle: *Soylent Green* offered Charlton Heston another chance to ooze testosterone.

5 Thorn checks the goods after Charles (Leonard Stone, right) has divided them up.

RICHARD FLEISCHER

Richard Fleischer was born in Brooklyn in 1916. His father was Max Fleischer, the man who invented Betty Boop. In 1942, Richard began his career in the newsreel section of RKO-Pathé in New York, before making his directing debut in RKO's B-movie department in Hollywood. In the early 50s, the new studio boss Howard Hughes discovered Fleischer's Film Noir classic *The Narrow Margin* (1952), after the film had spent two years gathering dust in the archives; Hughes was impressed, and promoted Fleischer to the A-list, though he was permitted only to re-shoot parts of the Robert Mitchum film *His Kind of Woman* (1951) and to add a new ending – anonymously. He acquired his reputation as a master of technically complex productions after making *20,000 Leagues Under the Sea* (1954), a classic of its genre. *The Vikings* (1958) brought further confirmation of his powers.

Elaborate widescreen compositions soon became one of his trademarks, as in his black-and-white movie *Compulsion* (1959). This film also demonstrated Fleischer's sure instinct when handling a sensitive theme: it featured Orson Welles as a lawyer who battles to save two young murderers from the electric chair. In Europe, Fleischer adapted a novel by the Swedish Nobel Prize winner Pär Lagerkvist (1951) for Dino De Laurentiis's production company: the biblical epic *Barabbas* (1962). In the 60s, he enjoyed his greatest successes with a series of films for Fox, including the SF spectacle *Fantastic Voyage* (1966), the Rex Harrison musical *Doctor Dolittle* (1967), and his masterpiece *The Boston Strangler* (1968), starring Henry Fonda and Tony Curtis. In 1970, he collaborated with Japanese filmmakers on the Pearl Harbor movie *Tora! Tora! Tora!*, and in the following decade he worked for a range of studios and independent production firms. The 80s again witnessed several collaborations between Fleischer and Dino De Laurentiis, including *Conan the Destroyer* (1984). Whatever the subject, most of Fleischer's films feature the use of documentary techniques in the service of greater realism, and his directing style is always clearly recognizable. His last film was the half-hour feature *Call From Space* (1989), which used the Showscan technique developed by SFX-master Douglas Trumbull. In 1993, Fleischer published his memoirs, entitled *Just Tell Me When to Cry*.

BADLANDS

1973 - USA - 95 MIN. - DRAMA

DIRECTOR TERRENCE MALICK (*1943)
SCREENPLAY TERRENCE MALICK DIRECTOR OF PHOTOGRAPHY BRIAN PROBYN, TAK FUJIMOTO, STEVAN LARNER EDITING ROBERT ESTRIN
MUSIC GEORGE ALICESON TIPTON, GUNILD KEETMAN, JAMES TAYLOR, CARL ORFF, NAT KING COLE, ERIK SATIE
PRODUCTION TERRENCE MALICK for PRESSMAN-WILLIAMS, BADLANDS COMPANY.

STARRING MARTIN SHEEN (Kit), SISSY SPACEK (Holly), WARREN OATES (Holly's Father), JOHN CARTER (Rich Man),
RAMON BIERI (Cato), ALAN VINT (Deputy), GARY LITTLEJOHN (Sheriff), BRYAN MONTGOMERY (Boy), GAIL
THRELKELD (Girl), CHARLES FITZPATRICK (Salesman).

"He wanted to die with me and I dreamed of being lost forever in his arms."

Fifteen-year-old Holly (Sissy Spacek) has grown up without a mother and whiles away the hours playing in her backyard. Kit (Martin Sheen) is 25 and works as a garbage man in Fort Dupree, a middle-of-nowhere town in South Dakota. When the two of them lay eyes on each other, it's love at first sight. Holly's father (Warren Oates) forbids her from associating with Kit, but to no avail. One thing leads to another and Kit ends up shooting Holly's father dead, sending the couple on an outlandish escapade in the great American frontier. They flee to the Montana Badlands, committing three more murders en route.

In their isolation, they revert to an archaic hunter-gatherer way of life, until they are finally discovered...

The work of filmmaker Terrence Malick is surrounded by legends. He directed two films in the 70s, Badlands and Days of Heaven (1978), and then disappeared from the scene until 1998 when he re-emerged behind the camera with the critically acclaimed The Thin Red Line. His first feature film, Badlands, marked an astounding debut. Malick's story of two star-crossed loners is a stunningly aesthetic ballad. From the sleepy town to the abandoned,

virtually endless expanses of land, right through the sanctuary of the wilderness, the scenes unfold in a blanket of golden sunlight. The film is a homage to the landscape of the region, showered in a melange of heat and dust. Malick employed the services of three cinematographers to realize his vision. His imagery is underscored, not by country music, but rather by the simple yet soothing xylophone sounds of Carl Orff's "Musica Poetica."

As luxuriously as the film exhibits its landscape, so it laconically tells the protagonists' story. *Badlands* is coldly distant in the depiction of its subject matter and avoids the psychological. The film is based on the true story

of "Mad Dog Killer" Charles Starkweather, a nineteen-year-old who alongside his fourteen-year-old girlfriend, Carol Ann Fugate, went on a killing rampage that left Carol's father and several others dead. Charles and Carol, according to the tale, were regular kids and not psychopaths. Malick's central characters too, are seemingly ordinary people, even when, for the most part, they appear apathetic and caught up in their own world, far from reality.

Holly looks like a little girl when we see her playing in the backyard wearing shorts and a T-shirt. Her one genuine interest is her love for movie magazines. We watch as she plows through one after the other. They infiltrate

1   Say say, oh, playmate: Volatile lovers Holly (Sissy Spacek) and Kit (Martin Sheen) are either a pair of innocents or a pair of fools.

2   Tess of the D'Urbervilles: "Holly is an unformed character, willing to be led in any direction, by anyone who pays attention to her." (*Guide for the Film Fanatic*)

3   Runaway train: He came from the wrong side of the tracks and decided to stay there.

"The couple has often been compared with Bonnie and Clyde, but Malick had something else in mind – these young rebels are too undeveloped, too emotionally immature to know how to approach each other sexually." *San Francisco Chronicle*

her language, as we hear in the off-camera narratives in which she tells us of her life with Kit. After her mother's death, her father even views her as the "little stranger he found in his house" and Kit as the kid from "the wrong side of the tracks."

To Holly, Kit is a projection of her own desires, an image come to life right out of her magazines. He is thin, muscular, wears white Ts, blue jeans and smokes. Naturally, she immediately sees him as James Dean. At one point, Kit actually takes on Dean's classic stance from *Giant* (1956), with a rifle mounted square across his shoulders. He and Holly are creatures who

know nothing of responsibility. They commit their bloody deeds as if they were a game, absent of emotion or compassion. The dead are no more real to Holly than the people she reads about in her Hollywood journals. She often appears more gruesome in her childlike inability to reflect than Kit, whose attempts at emulating James Dean are at times almost endearing. Simply stated, they are two overgrown children, who – for a while – are free to kill in cold blood. Who knows. Maybe it was the director's intention to paint an ironic portrait of the silver screen serial killer, a trend that took off in Holly-wood following this production.   HJK

TRUE CRIME DRAMAS   In the late fall of 1888, five prostitutes were slaughtered in London's East End. The case remains unsolved to this day and as recently as 2001, brothers Albert and Allan Hughes speculated whether the killings could have been the handiwork of Jack the Ripper in their film *From Hell*. From Hitchcock's *The Lodger* (1926) to the drama *From Hell*, Jack the Ripper, as well as gangsters like Bonnie and Clyde, Al Capone and Lucky Luciano have served as inspiration for many filmmakers. Real life criminals and crimes often make for good pictures. The added thrill of an act the spectator cannot dismiss as mere fiction and the sheer intrigue surrounding the perpetrators' motivations and psychology have always appealed to cinema auteurs. Other works of the genre including *M* (*M – Eine Stadt sucht einen Mörder*, 1931) about serial killer Peter Kürten (played by Peter Lorre), *The Sugarland Express* (1974) about jailbird Robert Samuel Dent and his wife as well as *The Deathmaker (Totmacher*, 1995), about the serial killer Fritz Haarmann have enriched the spectrum. Perhaps the most famous example is the 1959 case of a Kansas family killed *In Cold Blood* (1967). Director Richard Brooks brought Truman Capote's best-selling work of the same name to the big screen. With his story, Capote launched what he considered to be a new form of literature he called the non-fiction novel. True crime movies do not necessarily have to be about murders: the financial fraud committed by investor Nick Leeson inspired *Rogue Trader* (1999), yet another film that falls into this category.

"The more I looked at people the more I hated them, because I knowed there wasn't any place for me with the kind of people I knowed."

Motion Picture Guide

4 Living off the land: Kit and Holly return to primordial life in the Badlands of Montana.

5 End of the line: Taken into custody by the authorities, Kit and Holly learn that all good things must come to an end.

6 Field of dreams: *The Badlands* ballad celebrates the virgin frontier.

ENTER THE DRAGON

1973 - USA / HONG KONG - 99 MIN. - EASTERN, MARTIAL ARTS FILM, ACTION FILM

DIRECTOR ROBERT CLOUSE (1928–1997)
SCREENPLAY MICHAEL ALLIN DIRECTOR OF PHOTOGRAPHY GIL HUBBS EDITING KURT HIRSCHLER, GEORGE WATTERS MUSIC LALO SCHIFRIN
PRODUCTION FRED WEINTRAUB, PAUL M. HELLER, LEONARDO HO, BRUCE LEE for WARNER BROS., CONCORDE PRODUCTIONS INC., SEQUOIA PRODUCTIONS.

STARRING BRUCE LEE (Lee), JOHN SAXON (Roper), SHIH KIEN (Han), JIM KELLY (Williams), AHNA CAPRI (Tania), BOB WALL (Oharra), YANG SZE (Bolo), ANGELA MAO YING (Su Lin), BETTY CHUNG (Mei Ling), PETER ARCHER (Parsons).

"You have offended my family, and you have offended a Shaolin temple."

Lee (Bruce Lee) is a Shaolin Monk and a masterful kung fu fighter. A British secret agent comes to him with a mission: Lee is to enter a martial arts tournament held every three years by a man named Han (Shih Kien). Han deals in drugs and girls and lives on an island in the middle of the Chinese Sea that he has converted into a fortress. Entering the tournament is the only way to gain access to the island, and Lee has to use this opportunity to gather evidence against the gangster. He has a personal interest in the matter – Han's sidekick Oharra (Bob Wall) caused the death of Lee's sister.

Cornered by Oharra, she committed suicide to prevent herself from being raped. Lee accepts the mission. Among the men accompanying Lee to the tournament are two Americans: white trash gambler Roper (John Saxon), and a black playboy named Williams (Jim Kelly). Both men are first-rate fighters.

Enter the Dragon was the fourth and final completed film starring Bruce Lee, who died in 1973. It was also the first Hollywood film to feature a protagonist of Chinese origin. Producer Fred Weintraub saw Bruce Lee in Hong

1 The man of Shaolin: A master of mental and physical discipline, Lee (Bruce Lee) is a monk, kung fu fighter and irresistible sex symbol.

2 Hugh Hefner of Hong Kong: With an unlimited supply of drugs and human sex toys, Han lives like a king on his own island paradise.

3 The main event: From his island fortress in the Chinese Sea, the treacherous Han dreams up a tournament to determine the world's best fighter.

"Unlike his rivals, Lee, the actor, exploits his sexuality, stripping off his shirt to reveal his rippling muscles, posing for battle with legs spread."

Guide for the Film Fanatic

BRUCE LEE

It could be said that Bruce Lee (*1940 in San Francisco) inherited his success. Or at least that it was written in his birth certificate: Lee Jun Fan, his Chinese name, means "achieves success abroad." His success story did begin away from America – in Hong Kong. Lee initially appeared in a handful of U.S. television series like *The Green Hornet* (1966–67). The international breakthrough – his ascendancy from martial arts instructor and philosophy student to cult star was only achieved upon his return to Hong Kong. There he took over the lead role in martial arts films like *The Big Boss* (*Tang shan da xiong*, 1971) and *Fist of Fury* (*Jing wu men*, 1972). After differences of opinion with director Lo Wei, Lee began to direct himself. With *Way of the Dragon* (*Meng long guojiang*, 1972) he purposely set his sights on the world market. He switched the setting of the story from Hong Kong to Rome and chose the American martial arts sportsman and future action film star Chuck Norris as his opponent. Lee's next directorial project was to be *Game of Death*, but the postponed filming of *Enter the Dragon* (1973) caused a conflict, and his sudden death prevented the film from being finished. Four years after Lee's death, a film was made and subsequently released using a body double and the ten minutes of fight footage from *Game of Death* (*Si wang you ju*, 1977). After his death, copycats sought to profit from Lee's success, producing films with such no-names as Bruce Li or Bruce Le, none of whom came anywhere close to the style and flair of the icon they imitated.

3

4 Last rites: African-American Williams (Jim Kelly) is lynched soon after discovering the villain's secret lair.

5 Get those legs up there! Han (Shih Kien), with a prosthetic right hand, and kung fu legend Lee (left) fight to the death in the final battle.

6 She comes with the room: Upon their arrival, contestants of the Han's island "World's Greatest Fighter Showdown" will receive a complimentary fruit basket and a voucher for a 15-min. warm welcome.

"During a fight scene, Lee performed a flying kick so fast it couldn't be captured on film at 24 frames a second. The cameraman had to film the sequence in slow motion to get it look like it wasn't faked." *Motion Picture Guide*

Kong and was so impressed he immediately decided to produce a film with Lee in the United States. Bruce Lee was the unquestionable star of the film, choreographing the fight sequences and supposedly also revising the script. *Enter the Dragon* is a true Bruce Lee film – a star vehicle for the action virtuoso. The film is full of the ingredients of the American films of its time: cool chick-magnets who drink and gamble, a funky seventies soundtrack by Lalo Schifrin, which sometimes sounds like the title theme of the television series *Mission: Impossible* (1966–1973), and a plot that employs all the successful concepts and themes of the spy movie genre.

The rudiments of the story are strongly reminiscent of *Dr. No* (1962), the first Bond film, with a megalomaniac gangster who has barricaded himself in a fortress-like island full of underground corridors and laboratories.

ofeld, 007's adversary, the villain Han even has a white long-haired
t the charm of the film lies less in the story than in the fight se-
s. It begins with a battle in Lee's monastery (his sparring partner is
re director and actor Sammo Hung, a companion of Jackie Chan, who
worked as a stuntman in the film). The additional fights – with Roper,
s, and Lee – occur on the island and each fight trumps the previous
choreographic spectaculars. Adhering to the rules of the genre, the
ncludes with the fight between the main adversaries, Lee and Han. The
end all fights is made all the more astonishing by Han's prosthetic
and, fitted with sharp blades in place of fingers. The showdown is a
of martial acrobatics and is unrivaled for its visual ingenuity, not least
e it is staged in a house of mirrors.

Lee and Han are not only fighting against one another. Both are hard-
pressed to actually locate their adversary, and are required to separate the
physical opponent from his mirror image, adding a game of perception to
the dazzling fight choreography. This final scene and its theme – true and
illusory enemies – echoes a scene early on in the film where a priest explains
to Lee, "The enemy is only an illusion; the real enemy lies within oneself."
Supposedly Bruce Lee wrote this scene himself, but unfortunately it is absent
from the international version of the film, and only preserved in the Chinese
version. *Enter the Dragon* was released in the summer of 1973 in the United
States, and in Hong Kong in October of the same year. Bruce Lee did not live
to see the premiere, dying on July 20, 1973 from the effects of a brain edema
whose cause to this day remains a mystery.   HJK

DAY FOR NIGHT
La Nuit américaine

†

1973 - FRANCE / ITALY - 115 MIN. - TRAGICOMEDY, DRAMA

DIRECTOR FRANÇOIS TRUFFAUT (1932–1984)
SCREENPLAY JEAN-LOUIS RICHARD, SUZANNE SCHIFFMAN, FRANÇOIS TRUFFAUT DIRECTOR OF PHOTOGRAPHY PIERRE-WILLIAM GLENN
MUSIC GEORGES DELERUE EDITING MARTINE BARRAQUÉ, YANN DEDET PRODUCTION MARCEL BERBERT for LES FILMS DU CARROSSE, PECF, PIC.

STARRING JACQUELINE BISSET (Julie), VALENTINA CORTESE (Severine), DANI (Liliane), ALEXANDRA STEWART (Stacey), JEAN-PIERRE AUMONT (Alexandre), JEAN CHAMPION (Bertrand), JEAN-PIERRE LÉAUD (Alphonse), FRANÇOIS TRUFFAUT (Ferrand), NIKE ARRIGHI (Odile), NATHALIE BAYE (Joelle).

ACADEMY AWARDS 1973 OSCAR for BEST FOREIGN FILM (François Truffaut).

> *"Making a film is like driving a coach and horses through the Wild West; when you set off, you're looking forward to a nice trip, but very soon you're wondering if you'll ever reach your destination."*

In the studios in Nice, a French film team starts shooting "Je vous présente Paméla," the melodramatic tale of a young man (Jean-Pierre Léaud), whose wife (Jacqueline Bisset) falls in love with his father (Jean-Pierre Aumont) and runs away with him. The work is frequently hindered by technical difficulties and human problems. When one of the leading actors dies in a car accident, the project seems doomed to failure; but the team rallies round and improvises, enabling the director Ferrand (François Truffaut) to bring the work to a successful close.

"La nuit américaine" is the French expression for the process of filming scenes by daylight through a special filter that makes them look as if they had been filmed by night. A technical term, then: yet it also seems to express delight in the ability to create an artificial cinematic reality, and it sounds like the title of an exciting story. Indeed, it's a wonderful title for a declaration of love – a cineast's love of film, filmmaking and life. For François Truffaut, the three are in any case inseparable, and in this film they meet and mix with fascinating ease. *Day for Night* is an intelligent meditation on illusion and reality.

1 French flair: In François Truffaut's homage to filmmaking, sideline shenanigans matter as much as the actual movie. Here, script girl (Nathalie Baye) seduces the props master (Bernard Menez).

2 Don't mix business and pleasure: Everything grinds to a halt when the star, Julie Baker, locks herself in her dressing room.

3 Sugar and spice and everything nice: Alphonse (Jean-Pierre Léaud) and Bernard (Bernard Menez) never tire of discussing what little girls are made of.

> "*Day for Night*, François Truffaut's heartfelt homage to the joy and pain of making movies, is just as bracing (yet touching) as it was when it was first released. It inevitably reminds us of the loss movie-lovers suffered when Truffaut died at 52 in 1984." *Los Angeles Times*

The occasion of this unconditional homage is a pretty banal, old-fashioned studio melodrama. This alone is enough to show that *Day for Night* is certainly not an accurate depiction of Truffaut's own working methods, even if he does take on the role of the director, Ferrand. Rather, Truffaut weaves a complex fiction out of countless disparate elements: self-referential moments, friendly nods to the directors he admires, and general reflections on filmmaking. This is an ensemble film, in which the script girl and the production designer seem just as important as the director or the stars. In as much *Day for Night* is also a homage to all the colleagues who never see the limelight but who are indispensable to the realization of a film.

This is why Truffaut called his film "democratic," and it is so in more ways than one: it's a film that appeals as much to a broad public as it does

"In *Day for Night*, I show a director who's very happy in his work. But there are also directors who are at least as interesting because their films are difficult and painful births. I know a few colleagues who should really make their own *Day for Night*." François Truffaut

the critics and intellectuals. Truffaut has collected some of the imponderables that can arise in the course of a film production – from an aging Diva's alcohol problem to the chaotic love-life of an unstable star, from the pregnancy of an actress to the death of an actor – and made a charming, highly amusing and sometimes melancholy film-within-a-film.

Although it enjoyed a generally euphoric reception when first released, *Day for Night* was also harshly rejected by some, not least by Truffaut's former companion-in-arms Jean-Luc Godard. It was at this time that Truffaut finally broke with Godard. At the time, especially in France, many intellectuals were demanding a more political cinema, and some accused Truffaut of

wasting his affections on the wrong object – the making of a conventional studio film. One critic wrote that Truffaut had "allowed himself to be bought by the system," and he presumably felt vindicated when *Day for Night* won the Oscar for Best Foreign Film. Truffaut himself never saw it as *the* definitive film about filmmaking. The personal dimension of *Day for Night* is particularly apparent in the words spoken by Truffaut to Jean-Pierre Léaud, the actor who embodied his alter ego in the Antoine Doinel cycle of films: "You know very well that people like you and I can only be happy when we're working, when we're working for the cinema."

"*Day for Night* has grace, wit and affection enough to be one of fondest compliments the movies have ever been paid — a tribute to all dream spinners by one of the best." *Time Magazine*

4 Art imitates life: "Alphonse is similar in every detail to the Léaud of the early 70s." (De Baecque / Toubiana, in: *Truffaut – Biografie.* Cologne, 1999).

5 The many shades of gray: In Truffaut's cinematic cosmos, there's no clear distinction between fiction and reality. The relationship between Alphonse and Julie (Jean-Pierre Léaud and Jacqueline Bisset) is troubled – on-screen and off.

6 Not a publicity stunt: Truffaut casts light on the otherwise obscure aspects of filmmaking.

6

JEAN-PIERRE LÉAUD   Jean-Pierre Léaud was born in Paris on May 5, 1944, the son of a screenwriter and an actress. At the age of 15 he became famous when François Truffaut chose him for the autobiographical role of Antoine Doinel in his first feature film, *The Four Hundred Blows* (*Les quatre cents coups*, 1958/59). From then on, Léaud's career was inseparably bound up with Truffaut's films. In the course of the next 30 years, he appeared as the director's melancholy and chaotic alter ego in all five films of the Doinel cycle, as well as in two other Truffaut movies: *Two English Girls* (*Les deux anglaises et le continent*, 1971) and *Day for Night* (*La Nuit américaine*, 1973). But Léaud also appeared in films by other well-known directors, such as Jean-Luc Godard: *Masculine-Feminine* (*Masculin – féminin*, 1965/66), *Pierrot le fou* (1965), *Made in USA* (1966), *La Chinoise* and *Week-End* (both 1967), *Joyful Wisdom* (*Le gai savoir*, 1968) and *Detective* (*Détective*, 1985). He also appeared in Jacques Rivette's *Out 1 – spectre* (1971) and as the film-crazy friend of Maria Schneider in Bernardo Bertolucci's *Last Tango in Paris* (*Ultimo tango a Parigi / Le Dernier Tango à Paris*, 1972). After Truffaut's death in 1984, Léaud, who had cultivated a highly individual, amateurish and slightly comical style, was to be seen almost only in supporting roles. One exception was Aki Kaurismäki's black comedy *I Hired a Contract Killer* (1990), in which he played a suicidal Frenchman in London. In 1996, he appeared in Olivier Assayas' excellent *Irma Vep* as the depressive director of a silent-film remake, who is replaced in mid-shoot by another director.

WESTWORLD

1973 - USA - 89 MIN. - SCIENCE FICTION

DIRECTOR MICHAEL CRICHTON (*1942)
SCREENPLAY MICHAEL CRICHTON DIRECTOR OF PHOTOGRAPHY GENE POLITO EDITING DAVID BRETHERTON MUSIC FRED KARLIN
PRODUCTION PAUL LAZARUS III for MGM.

STARRING YUL BRYNNER (Mechanical Gunslinger), RICHARD BENJAMIN (Peter Martin), JAMES BROLIN (John Blane),
NORMAN BARTOLD (Medieval Knight), ALAN OPPENHEIMER (Chief Engineer), VICTORIA SHAW (Medieval Queen),
DICK VAN PATTEN (Banker), LINDA GAYE SCOTT (Arlette), STEVE FRANKEN (Technician).

"The holidays of your life."

"The holidays of your life," is the promise made by the TV commercial for Delos, a vacation and theme park complex in the desert that is just like an adults-only Disneyland. For a thousand bucks a day, visitors can choose between any of three fantasy worlds: the ancient Roman Empire, life in medieval times, and Westworld, the world of the Wild West. The illusion is entirely created by state-of-the-art technology. Those tired of the discipline of everyday routines can dive into another time in Delos and "let it all hang out," using a sword or a Colt to kill without remorse. The playful rampage is made possible by the fact that the personnel of the three worlds are human

replicas – robots programmed to lose each and every duel. They are repaired overnight and stand ready for the next group of visitors to come and strike them down again.

Peter Martin (Richard Benjamin) and John Blane (James Brolin), two businessmen from Chicago, decide to go for a Westworld adventure. They amuse themselves in a saloon that has all the trappings of the classic Westerns. Peter soon sheds all inhibitions and guns down a black-clad gunslinger (Yul Brynner) – the Colt is loose in its holster and blood spouts like the proverbial ketchup. But with one last trace of insecurity, he asks "who can

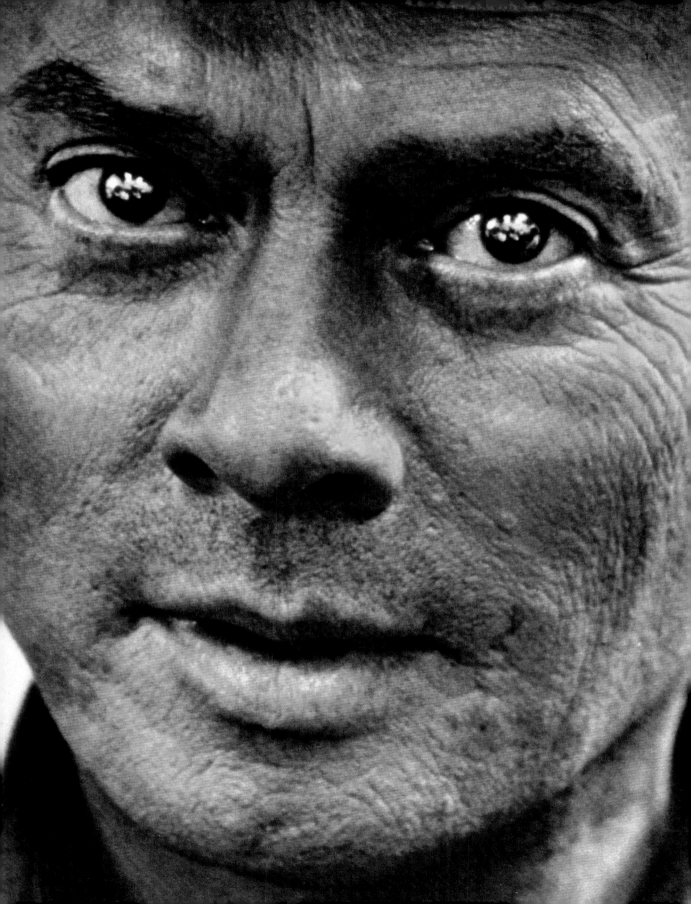

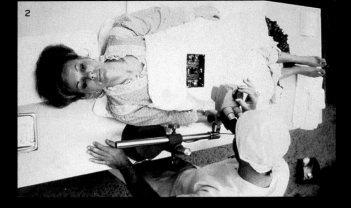

2

> # "Though casually enter-taining, the movie gives the smug, unimaginative feeling of having itself been programmed by a computer."
> *The Times*

MICHAEL CRICHTON   Novelist, screenwriter, and director Michael Crichton (*1942) is one of the most popular and valued authors of the film and television industry in the United States. Whether for science fiction (*The Andromeda Strain*, 1971), the technology thriller (*Rising Sun*, 1993), or the best of all current hospital series (*ER*, since 1994), Crichton gets at the cutting edge of scientific development, sleek technology politics and traditional morals, compressing them into exciting subject matter for film and television drama. Crichton began writing during his medical studies at Harvard (after earning a degree in Anthropology) but on a part-time basis (at the time he published a drug-dealer story with his brother Douglas under the now comical pseudonym Michael Douglas). He eventually decided to become a novelist after his exams were finished. In 1990, he picked up the theme of bio-engineering and wrote the script for Spielberg's *Jurassic Park* (1993) in 1992. Almost simultaneously, he worked on another book that was also filmed in 1992, *Rising Sun*, a high-tech thriller that combines the murder of a call girl with the Japanese technological offensive in the United States. The result was the birth of a new writer type in America – combining book and film as two separate forms of one theme. Crichton also wrote a biography of the American artist Jasper Johns, an important figure of abstract expressionism and a trail-blazing forerunner of Pop Art.

1   Human or cyborg? Even close-up, it's hard to tell
    (Yul Brynner as the mechanical gunslinger).

2   This won't hurt a bit: An automatic lady goes in
    for a routine check-up.

3   Entertainment value: For city slickers who've
    booked the Wild West program, a duel in a saloon
    is – usually – no sweat … (James Brolin, right)

4   … unless the dueling machine has a very human
    defect – the thirst for vengeance.

5   Falling to pieces: Artificial life en route to Nirvana.

guarantee I won't kill another guest by accident?" The answer to his question
seems simple: there is a safety sensor built into his weapon that prevents
objects with human body temperature from getting hit. The boys from Chicago spend the night comfortably in a Western brothel – with female robot
companions. They are awakened by the black-clad gunslinger, who – now
repaired – once again challenges Peter to an extensive duel. A frantic chase
leads through all three worlds of Delos, but now it is the robot that is pursuing Peter. The machine seems to have been wrongly re-programmed and
behaves like his creator, refusing to die, returning fire, and killing with live
ammunition. The other robots also revolt and incite a bloodbath, slaughtering
the visitors. Delos becomes tyrannized by its electronic beings until Peter
succeeds in setting fire to the machines. In the end he is the lone survivor in
a mass of dead bodies.

The first film of the now world-famous Michael Crichton offers yet
another variation on the story of artificial humans. It is the tale of parallel
humans or the once useful machine that develops into a threat. The superior
invasion machines of an external enemy, a favorite storyline of the 1950s,
no longer occupy the core of the science fiction film. Their place in combat is

taken by human-parallel machine constructions. The monster is no longer
simply a creation cranked up in a secret laboratory, but rather a part of everyday leisure time, an expression of the prevalent greed for pleasure and longing for perfection. Thus *Westworld* marks a new stage in the portrayal of
the robot in the history of film – that of subjectivity. We as an audience are
supposed to be shaken and punished. In the 70s, the robot becomes a tool
of social criticism, an uncontrollable creation that hounds its arrogant creator
– a theme Crichton continued and varied in the 1990s for Steven Spielberg's
Jurassic Park (1993).

Though Yul Brynner's black denim costume is a prop from John
Sturges' Western *The Magnificent Seven* (1960) – where he plays the gunman Chris who organizes the liberation of a Mexican village terrorized by
bandits – *Westworld* does not criticize film as part of the macabre entertainment industry. On the contrary, the beginning of the film points to television
as a temptation and threat to mankind. *Futureworld*, the sequel by Richard
T. Heffron was released in 1976. It combines the science fiction theme of the
rebellious human clones with a political conspiracy.

LIVE AND LET DIE

1973 - GREAT BRITAIN - 121 MIN. - SPY FILM

DIRECTOR GUY HAMILTON (*1922)
SCREENPLAY TOM MANKIEWICZ, based on characters appearing in IAN FLEMING'S JAMES BOND NOVELS DIRECTOR OF PHOTOGRAPHY
TED MOORE EDITING BERT BATES, RAYMOND POULTON, JOHN SHIRLEY MUSIC GEORGE MARTIN, PAUL and LINDA
MCCARTNEY (Theme Song) PRODUCTION ALBERT R. BROCCOLI, HARRY SALTZMAN for DANJAQ PRODUCTIONS, EON
PRODUCTIONS LTD.

STARRING ROGER MOORE (James Bond), YAPHET KOTTO (Kananga / Mr. Big), JANE SEYMOUR (Solitaire), CLIFTON JAMES
(Sheriff J. W. Pepper), JULIUS HARRIS (Tee Hee), GEOFFREY HOLDER (Baron Samedi), DAVID HEDISON (Felix Leiter),
GLORIA HENDRY (Rosie Carver), BERNARD LEE (M), LOIS MAXWELL (Miss Moneypenny), TOMMY LANE (Adam),
EARL JOLLY BROWN (Whisper).

"My name is..."
"Names is for tombstones, baby."

This gruff exchange spoils James Bond's trademark introduction. A doubly ironic remark at that, as it not only plays on the title of the eighth Bond Film *Live and Let Die*, but also makes reference to the big-name actors who lost out on the chance to replace original Bond legend, Sean Connery. After completing *Diamonds Are Forever,* Connery made it clear that he would "never" do another Bond picture, thus theoretically leaving the role of her Majesty's favorite secret agent open to Hollywood stars such as Burt Reynolds, Steve McQueen, Paul Newman and Robert Redford. However, Albert R. Broccoli and Harry Saltzman insisted that the role be played by a Brit and wholeheartedly agreed on Roger Moore.

Yaphet Kotto plays opposite Moore. His role is that of black diplomat Kananga, alias underworld lord Mr. Big, a man who wants to run the drug cartel of the entire western world from a small Caribbean island. To ensure success, he'll resort to modern crime tactics as well as ancient voodoo cult practices. The story begins shortly after the brutal murders of three British government agents, when James Bond is assigned to the case. The killer's trail first takes him to New York and then to the island of San Monique. He enlists the help of Kananga's prophetess and tarot card reader, Solitaire (Jane Seymour), by surreptitiously stacking a deck of her mystical cards. After a night with 007, Solitaire loses her virginity and with it her gift for telling the future. Now useless to Kananga, she flees the island with the secret agent. In their mad dash for escape, Bond sends a bus and nearly half an airport to high heaven. It is only back in New Orleans that Kananga is able to capture the British spy, intending to do away with him once and for all at a crocodile

farm on the Louisiana bayou. Bond, however, manages to foil his nemesis, sprinting to safety across the snouts of the crocs and racing away in a motorboat. Kananga's henchmen set off in hot pursuit of 007, but he succeeds in escaping their clutches thanks to a daredevil chase scene full of screwball antics. The final confrontation between Bond and Kananga will have to be postponed until they meet again on San Monique...

It goes without saying that 007 completes his eighth big screen mission as suavely and ingeniously as ever. Despite this, the image the "new" Bond shaped for himself went against many of the standards set by Sean Connery. Roger Moore relied on his pretty-boy elegance to take the audience and villains by storm, rather than on unabated masculinity like his predecessor. His

Bond had a wry sense of humor, was an impeccable dresser and nonchalant almost to the point of indifference. It made for an impression that was poles apart from Connery's hirsute virility and raw charm. Following his death, it was revealed that Bond novelist and creator Ian Fleming had, in fact, wanted Moore to play the part from the very start. But it had proved impossible to cast the actor in the role because his hands were tied on account of his contract with the television show *The Saint* (1962–68). Here, in his third Bond film, veteran director Guy Hamilton leads Moore to a fast and furious initial performance as 007. While critics across the board contend that Moore really came into his own as Bond with *The Spy Who Loved Me* (1977), his third picture in the series, the astoundingly successful, and then forty-year-

1 Our Man in Havana: James Bond flicks ash in the face of adversity.

2 Left in the lurch: In *Live and Let Die*, 007 has to make do without the gadgets from Q's arsenal – but a simple spray can proves indispensable in a tight spot.

3 It's in the cards: Solitaire (Jane Seymour) will trade her clairvoyant powers for an evening with Bond.

4 007's Delilah: Bond had better keep his eye on fellow agent Rosie Carver (Gloria Hendry) if he hopes to see morning.

"The film is dominated by a single theme: James Bond versus the myth of 007."
Michael Scheingraber

old, small-screen actor famous for series like *Ivanhoe* (1958–59), *The Saint* and *The Persuaders!* (1971–72) became a movie star virtually overnight with *Live and Let Die*. Although more recent films clearly outstrip most of the action sequences, the classic 13-minute motorboat chase sequence across the bayou remains as gripping as ever. The scene is a bonanza of amphibious stunts, with airborne vehicles flying over streets and even zipping through a garden wedding. To this day, it remains one of the most masterfully executed action sequences of the entire Bond series.

Although *Live and Let Die* features a new actor playing Bond, on first viewing the piece itself appears to follow the classic formula. In truth, however, the film breaks from several of the traditions established by its fore-

"In his third Bond film, Guy Hamilton deploys the technology so playfully and with such perfection that Bond seems little more than an excuse for a non-stop spectacle on land, at sea and in the air."
film-dienst

MAURICE BINDER

A white circle wanders across the screen and we're looking through the barrel of a gun. A man walks into its field of target. A shot is fired, and blood stains the screen red. The trademark James Bond opening sequence is truly unmistakable. The man who created it, Maurice Binder, was born in New York City on December 4th, 1925 and, after completing his formal education, started his professional career as a designer for Macy's department store.

His entry into the film world came with his involvement on marketing campaigns, for which he designed signs, posters and billboards. Before long, director Stanley Donen asked him to design the title sequence and trailer for the films *Indiscreet* (1958) and later *Charade* (1963).

Harry Saltzman got wind of his talent and, in 1962, James Bond walked onto the screen for the very first time in Binder's sequence at the top of *Dr. No* (1962). The Bond title song tableaux, most often featuring silhouetted women swimming in psychedelic seas, are as beloved as the shot down the gun barrel. Excluding *From Russia with Love* (1963) and *Goldfinger* (1964), Maurice Binder was responsible for all of the opening credit montages from 1962 until his death in 1991. In the case of *Live and Let Die* (1973) Binder's vision for the credits served as a source of inspiration for Paul McCartney's title. "I described the ideas that I had for voodoo sequences with painted bodies, flames and skeletons. I told Paul, I wanted a mix of slow and fast drum beats, which is pretty much how he ended up writing the song." Since Binder's death, Englishman Daniel Kleinman has been responsible for following in the footsteps of the great master.

runners. The hero no longer combats the forces of KGB agents, the international crime ring SPECTRE or villains with diabolical plans of taking over the world, but is faced instead with a high-ranking drug dealer. The task demands that Bond set foot on unfamiliar terrain. The case takes him to the streets of Harlem (where his snobbish air further punctuates his status as a bizarre foreign presence in the black community) and to the voodoo cults of the Caribbean. Conversely, the Kananga character is more in line with the traditional enemies Bond has confronted in the past. Much like the series' first super villain, Dr. No, an Asian scientist with two metal hands, Kananga stems from a racial minority and his cohorts like Tee Hee (Julius Harris) exhibit physical anomalies.

Uncannily reminiscent of Dr. No, Tee Hee has a metal claw with a deadly grip in place of a hand. The occult aspect of *Live and Let Die*, manifested in the voodoo witch doctor, Baron Samedi (Geoffrey Holder) and the seer Solitaire, add deliberately exotic overtones. At the time of its release, many movie magazines condemned the film's all black cast of villains as overt racism. What this observation seems to discount is that *Live and Let Die* was following a prevalent trend of the era brought on by the blaxploitation pictures of the early 1970s. By playing leading roles, stars like Richard Roundtree as *Shaft* (1971) and Pam Grier as *Coffy* (1973) had endowed African Americans with a new image and long overdue exposure in Hollywood. But then Bond always did have a certain gift for innovation.   ES

5   Saint Bond: Roger Moore played Her Majesty's
    Secret Servant with amiable nonchalance and
    more than a hint of irony.

6   Skin deep: On land, Moore may look less formid-
    able than predecessor Connery, but he was a
    regular shark when it came to underwater exploits.

7   Surf's up: Director Guy Hamilton made a splash
    debut with his chase through the Louisiana bayou.

7

PAPILLON

1973 - USA - 150 MIN. - PRISON FILM, LITERARY ADAPTATION

DIRECTOR FRANKLIN J. SCHAFFNER (1920–1989)
SCREENPLAY DALTON TRUMBO, LORENZO SEMPLE JR., based on the novel of the same name by HENRI CHARRIÈRE
DIRECTOR OF PHOTOGRAPHY FRED J. KOENEKAMP EDITING ROBERT SWINK MUSIC JERRY GOLDSMITH PRODUCTION ROBERT DORFMANN,
FRANKLIN J. SCHAFFNER for ALLIED ARTISTS PICTURES CORPORATION, CORONA-GENERAL, SOLAR PRODUCTIONS.

STARRING STEVE MCQUEEN (Papillon), DUSTIN HOFFMAN (Louis Dega), DON GORDON (Julot), ANTHONY ZERBE (Toussaint),
ROBERT DEMAN (Maturette), VICTOR JORY (Aboriginal Chief), WOODROW PARFREY (Clusiot), BILL MUMY (Lariot),
GEORGE COULOURIS (Doktor Chatal), BARBARA MORRISON (Oberin).

"If I stay here in this place, I'll die."

Henri Charrière's autobiographical novel *Papillon* appeared in 1968 and became an international bestseller. It describes the experiences of a man who succeeds in escaping from a prison colony in French Guyana. Because of the book's numerous contradictions and inconsistencies, many critics immediately cast doubt on the authenticity of the events it describes. Eyewitnesses confirmed that it gave a truthful representation of the cruel methods used in the colony (which no longer exists), but they criticized the way Charrière had taken the experiences of other prisoners and presented them as his own. Nonetheless, the book's gripping descriptions of desperate escape attempts and sheer density of detail were a goldmine for a Hollywood scriptwriter. The result was a box-office smash, a prison film in an exotic setting with two mega-stars in the leading roles.

Papillon (Steve McQueen), a French safecracker, acquired his nickname thanks to the butterfly tattooed on his chest. In 1931, despite being innocent of the murder he was accused of, he was sentenced to life imprisonment on Devil's Island. Among the others sent down is the weedy accountant and counterfeiter Dega (Dustin Hoffman). During their passage to South America, Dega fears for his life. He has a small fortune in cash concealed in his own back passage, and he has good reason to fear he'll be butchered for the money. Papillon makes a deal with Dega: he'll protect him, and in return Dega will finance his escape. On their arrival in the colony, the two prisoners are assigned to work in the swamps. After Papillon prevents a warder from beating his friend to death, Dega feels deeply indebted to the hard-bitten jailbird. But "Papi's" hasty escape attempt ends in failure: quickly recaptured, he is sentenced to two years in solitary confinement. Even in his isolation, however, he still retains tenuous contact to Dega. The latter has bribed his way into a more pleasant job in prison administration, and he provides Papillon with a secret supply of coconuts – an essential supplement to the foul prison rations, which barely ensure survival. When this illegal food bonus is discovered, Papillon's punishment is draconian: he is placed on half-rations and confined for years to a darkened cell. Yet he still holds his tongue and refuses to betray Dega. Years later, the two meet once again in the prison colony; on Papillon's next escape attempt, Dega will accompany him.

"We're something, aren't we? The only animals that shove things up their ass for survival."

Film quote: Papillon

1   Do not pass go: Forger Louis Dega (Dustin Hoffman) has seen better days. The prison camp in French Guayana is hell on earth.

2   Iron will: Even half rations and total isolation can't break his spirit: Papillon (Steve McQueen).

3   Breaking out of solitary: Though known for playing loners and individualists – in *Papillon*, Hoffman's brilliance lies in his on-screen friendship with Steve McQueen.

DALTON TRUMBO

"France has written you off – so forget France and get your clothes on." In the opening sequence of *Papillon* (1973), these words are spoken by an army commander to a group of naked prisoners lined up before him, shortly before they board the ship for French Guyana. The old officer is played by Dalton Trumbo (1905–1976), co-author of the film. This cameo appearance is a bitterly ironic commentary on the many years spent by Trumbo on Hollywood's notorious blacklist – "written off" by his own country as an alleged Communist. For his refusal to name names before McCarthy's "House Un-American Activities Committee," he had himself spent time in jail.

After his release, Trumbo moved to Mexico, where he wrote scripts for Hollywood under a series of pseudonyms. He had already received an Oscar nomination for *Kitty Foyle* (1940), as well as working with Joseph H. Lewis and others (*Deadly Is the Female / Gun Crazy*, 1949). In 1956, the Oscar for Best Screenplay was awarded to one Robert Rich for *The Brave One*. This led to a scandal, for Mr. Rich was none other than Dalton Trumbo himself. Trumbo endured years as a non-person before his real name finally appeared again in the opening credits to *Exodus* (1960; produced and directed by Otto Preminger). In 1971, Trumbo directed the film version of *Johnny Got His Gun*, his own world-famous, pacifist novel. He died of a heart attack in 1976. Sixteen years later, he received a posthumous Oscar for the screenplay to *Roman Holiday* (1953), a popular romance starring Audrey Hepburn and Gregory Peck. The film won three Oscars in total.

Papillon inevitably refers us to old movies rather than to reality. Audiences whose expectations do not exceed their grasp will find it a much more comfortable vehicle for escape than any that McQueen & Co. discover on location." *Time Magazine*

4 No girls allowed: Homosexuality is another theme examined in this "men's film." *Papillon* features only two small speaking parts for women.

5 Epic grandeur: Director Franklin J. Schaffner demonstrates the same masterful ease with crowd scenes and intimate dialogues alike.

Papillon tells the story of an unusual male friendship, marked by kindness and strong fellow feeling. More than once, Dega uses the following words to Papillon: "My thoughts are with you." It's an expression of deeply felt sympathy that sums up their remarkable bond.

Director Franklin J. Schaffner had already enjoyed success with *Planet of the Apes* (1968) and the Oscar-winning *Patton* (1969). In *Papillon*, he accomplishes a delicate balancing act, combining a realistic portrayal of monstrous prison conditions with some very funny moments. When Dega and "Papi" are sent off to retrieve a shot crocodile from the swamp, we witness a slapstick scene, for it turns out that the animal is still far from dead. Even their escape constitutes a kind of comic relief: while the prison orchestra plays marching tunes for the ladies and gents of the French colony, the two

jailbirds struggle like Keystone Cops to scale a very high wall. Gallows humor indeed, bitter and funny in equal measure.

The film derives its power from many unforgettable moments that demonstrate the leading character's impressive will to survive. We see him stave off starvation in his darkened cell by catching centipedes and roaches; taking a draw from the cigar of a leper who could help him escape from the island; and leaping into the sea from the clifftops – a tiny figure against a huge background, an individual victorious against an inhuman, implacable system.

Despite all the sadistic warders and the fugitives wading through swamps, *Papillon* has more to offer than the usual prison-film clichés. Schaffner had always been interested in connecting the history of cinema

itself to the historical and political events depicted in his films. In his study of the last Russian royal family, for example (*Nicholas and Alexandra*, 1971), his treatment of the crowd scenes draws on techniques of montage deployed by Sergej M. Eisenstein in *Strike* (*Statschka*, 1924) and *October* (*Oktjabr*, 1927). In *Papillon*, the characterization of the main figure constitutes an equally artful symbiosis between film history and history *per se*. It's no accident, for example, that "Papi," who spends 14 years in jail, bears more than a passing resemblance to another famous cinematic jailbird. In *A Man Escaped* (*Un condamné à mort s'est échappé / Le vent souffle où il veut*, 1956), Robert Bresson depicts the captivity and flight of a resistance fighter in occupied France during WW II. This film was also based on factual reports; and like Papillon, Bresson's protagonist is obsessed with escaping. Both characters

are driven by a yearning for freedom that expresses itself in untiring resistance, and each of them is prepared to risk death rather than submit to oppression. Schaffner's composer Jerry Goldsmith reinforced this link by taking his inspiration from the French music of the period. Papillon's "French" leitmotif dominates the film's soundscape, and we hear it for the last time after his successful flight: a musical bond between the exiled hero and his distant home country. The despised prisoner of Devil's Island and the heroes of the French resistance share more than their nationality. Thus the music in Schaffner's film is not a merely decorative "quotation;" it adds a dimension beyond Charrière's book and provides an original and illuminating insight into cinematic history.

DG

ANDY WARHOL'S FRANKENSTEIN
aka Flesh for Frankenstein / Carne per Frankenstein

1973 - USA / ITALY / FRANCE - 95 MIN. - HORROR FILM

DIRECTOR PAUL MORRISSEY (*1938), ANTONIO MARGHERITI (*1930)
SCREENPLAY TONINO GUERRA, PAUL MORRISSEY **DIRECTOR OF PHOTOGRAPHY** LUIGI KUVEILLER **EDITING** JED JOHNSON, FRANCA SILVI
MUSIC CLAUDIO GIZZI **PRODUCTION** ANDREW BRAUNSBERG, CARLO PONTI, ANDY WARHOL for BRAUNSBERG PRODUCTIONS, CARLO PONTI CINEMATOGRAFICA, RASSAM PRODUCTIONS, YANNE ET RASSAM.

STARRING JOE DALLESANDRO (Nicholas), MONIQUE VAN VOOREN (Baroness Katrin Frankenstein), UDO KIER (Baron Frankenstein), ARNO JUERGING (Otto), DALILA DI LAZZARO (Female Monster), SRDJAN ZELENOVIC (Sasha / Male Monster), NICOLETTA ELMI (Monica), MARCO LIOFREDI (Erik), LIU BOSISIO (Olga), CRISTINA GAIONI (Nicholas' girlfriend).

"Otto, look at this! Finally we find the right head with the perfect nasum! For my male zombie..."

The opening credits to *Andy Warhol's Frankenstein* might have been made by Charles Addams: two children, a boy and a girl, dissect a doll before beheading it with a miniature guillotine.

Baron Frankenstein (Udo Kier with a strong German accent) wants to create not just one human being but a couple, who will conceive and bear the representatives of a new race. In this he is assisted by his henchman Otto (Arno Juerging). Only one body part is lacking, for the male half of the couple: not the brain, as we might expect, but the perfect "Serbian" nose; for the Baron's racist ideology will accept nothing less. In order to secure the propagation of the race, Frankenstein and Otto head off to the village brothel in search of a suitable victim. This turns out to be Sasha (Srdjan Zelenovic),

whom they promptly kill, not realizing that he is in fact homosexual. His friend Nicholas (Joe Dallesandro), a farm laborer and servant to the Baroness, rushes to Sasha's aid, but too late: Sasha's head already adorns another man's body. In a bloody showdown, almost everyone ends up dead: Sasha murders both the Baroness and his creator Frankenstein, before killing himself. The only survivors are the Frankenstein children, who have witnessed everything, and who now calmly step up to accept their inheritance – much to the horror of the bound and helpless Nicholas.

Flesh for Frankenstein and the project that followed on its heels, *Andy Warhol's Dracula (Blood for Dracula / Dracula vuole vivere: cerca sangue di vergine!*, 1973) were low-budget projects, filmed entirely in the Factory in a

1 Modern day Salomé? Baron Frankenstein (Udo
   Kier) with his heart's desire – the head of a young
   man with the perfect nose.

2 Lo and behold! Henchman Otto (Arno Juerging)
   presents the female prototype (Dalila Di Lazzaro).

3 A new man: Frankenstein's guest Sasha (Srdjan
   Zelenovic) after his successful head transplant.

single seven-week period. Both were produced by Warhol himself. According to the director Paul Morrissey, the actors were given their lines on a daily basis. Viewers of this spectacle are disappointed all along the line, and this is by no means unintentional: if the title misleads anyone into expecting some creepy entertainment or even a faithful adaptation of Mary Wollstonecraft Shelley's novel, what they're given instead is a set of protagonists who are thoroughly bored, blasé or just plain beat. Not that the film isn't pretty much "in your face;" indeed, thanks to the film version's 3-D effects, it's quite often all over your clothes. Lopped limbs and entrails are sometimes close enough to taste.

Flesh for Frankenstein owes much to two genres: splatter and soft porn. Other versions of the story have seen Frankenstein's bodybuilding as a subtle compensation for his repressed sexual needs, and Warhol's Baron is certainly no high-minded Prometheus, no genius of the arts or sciences. He awakens his creatures to life by means of bloody penetration and a variety of necrophiliac activities. While the late 60s had hailed the coming of the sexual revolution, sexuality in this film offers no liberation from the constraints of society. On the contrary, desire is either unfulfilled or can only find expression through exploitation and rape. The plot is dominated by the protagonists' decadence and narcissism; little is to be seen, for example, of the normally

ANDY WARHOL'S FACTORY From 1963 onwards, the Pop artist Andy Warhol (1928–1987) produced hundreds of films in his Factory, a meeting place for artists, writers, dancers, transvestites, musicians, exhibition-makers and exhibitionists. These movies were often collective efforts, made in collaboration with avant-garde filmmakers such as Jonas Mekas and Jack Smith. In the initial phase, Warhol was clearly influenced by experimental films of the time: *Empire* (1964), for example, is an eight-hour shot of the Empire State Building, filmed with a static camera and without a single cut. Other works, such as *Chelsea Girls* (1966), were provocative in different ways, featuring endless improvisations, a gritty documentary feel, or pornographic scenes, often explicitly homoerotic. Most of Warhol's actors were amateurs, but he called them "superstars" in line with his credo that in the age of the mass media anyone can be a star. In 1968, he began to produce more commercially oriented films, directed by Paul Morrissey. Although smartened up in appearance by conventional post-production, the imagery, sound and narrative structure of these films are still a very long way from Hollywood. Besides *Andy Warhol's Frankenstein* (*Flesh for Frankenstein / Carne per Frankenstein*, 1973) and *Andy Warhol's Dracula* (*Blood for Dracula / Dracula vuole vivere: cerca sangue di vergine!*, 1973), his best-known films are: *Flesh* (1968), in which Morrissey's protagonist-of-choice Joe Dallesandro played a male prostitute, *Trash* (1970), and *Andy Warhol's Women* (*Women in Revolt*, 1971).

"*Warhol's Frankenstein* is no biting satire, but a gruesome burlesque. One only hopes that anyone who sees it will have enjoyed a vegetarian meal beforehand." Frankfurter Rundschau

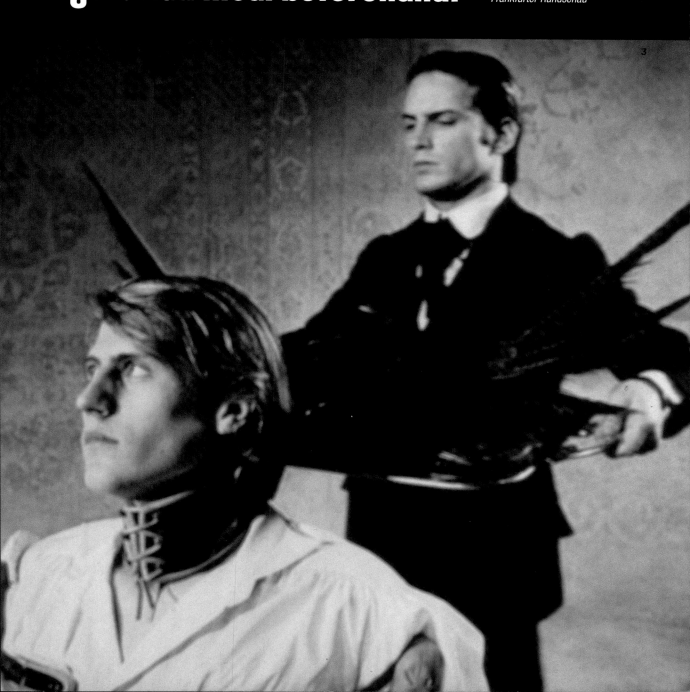

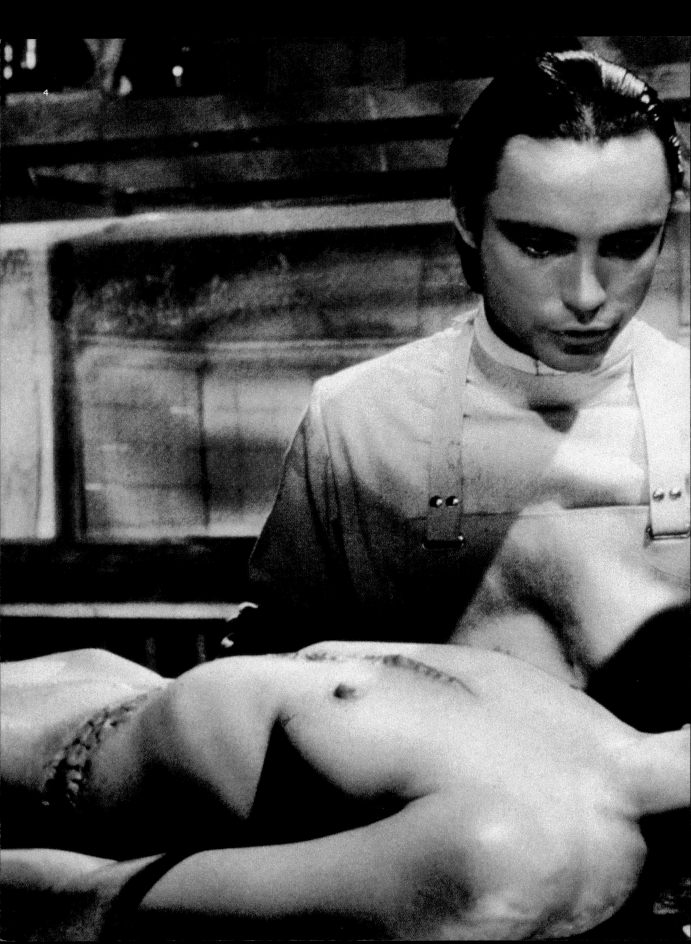

4 Doctor Frankenstein's anatomy lesson.

5 No cliché too cheap: The insatiable Baroness Katrin Frankenstein (Monique Van Vooren) seduces her willing servants.

6 Bottoms up: Sasha remains indifferent to the charms of the fairer sex.

7 Walking the straight and narrow: Warhol cast Joe Dallesandro, gay underground star, as Nicholas. Here, he takes a trip to the village brothel.

"Each night I'd think of what further absurdity might logically follow from where I began."

Paul Morrissey, in: Maurice Yacowar, The Films of Paul Morrissey

6

obligatory villagers, often portrayed as a revolutionary counterforce to the French aristocracy. Nor is it the holy family of bourgeois mythology that triumphs over the Baron and his monster, revealing the hubris of those who would dare emulate God. Nicholas does manage to expose Frankenstein's doings; but he ends up helpless in the hands of the children – incestuous siblings like their parents before them – who will simply carry on where the older generation left off. The monstrous Frankenstein family structure remains unscathed, an artificial and hermetically closed system.

Frankenstein is no mere parody: Morrissey dwells exclusively on the negative aspects of the tale, like the misogynistic episodes, Frankenstein's fascist ideas and the children's icy lack of feeling. And faced with this grim lack of alternatives, we soon find the laughter sticking in our throats.   PLB

PAT GARRETT AND BILLY THE KID

1973 - USA - 106 MIN. / 122 MIN. (restored version) - WESTERN

DIRECTOR SAM PECKINPAH (1925–1984)
SCREENPLAY RUDY WURLITZER DIRECTOR OF PHOTOGRAPHY JOHN COQUILLON EDITING ROGER SPOTTISWOODE, GARTH CRAVEN, ROBERT L. WOLFE, RICHARD HALSEY, DAVID BERLATSKY, TONY DE ZARRAGA MUSIC BOB DYLAN PRODUCTION GORDON CARROLL for MGM.

STARRING JAMES COBURN (Sheriff Patrick J. Garrett), KRIS KRISTOFFERSON (William H. "Billy the Kid" Bonney), BOB DYLAN (Alias), SLIM PICKENS (Sheriff Baker), KATY JURADO (Mrs. Baker), JASON ROBARDS (Governor Lew Wallace), RICHARD JAECKEL (Sheriff Kip McKinney), CHILL WILLS (Lemuel), JOHN BECK (John W. Poe), RITA COOLIDGE (Maria).

"It feels like times have changed."

New Mexico, 1881. The days of the Wild West are numbered. Although Billy the Kid (Kris Kristofferson) is still living the life of an outlaw, his one-time trusted partner in crime Pat Garrett (James Coburn) has changed sides. He has been elected sheriff of Lincoln County and the cattle barons want Billy out of their hair. Garrett sees no alternative but to advise his compadre to relocate to Mexico. Billy cannot be persuaded. Shortly after their talk, Garrett sets a trap for him. Gunfire breaks out and two of Billy's pals bite the dust. He himself is placed under arrest, but soon spots an opportune moment to fly the coop and Lincoln County while Garrett is away. He fatally wounds two deputies in the process, forcing Garrett to do away with Billy once and for all. And so begins a deadly game of cat and mouse.

Like almost all of Sam Peckinpah's Westerns, *Pat Garrett and Billy the Kid* is about the disappearance of the legendary Wild West. The land has been divvied up, and the settlers have staked their claims. Capital makes its way into the county and the dubious definition of law and order accompanies it, seeming to provide mainly property owners with a world of opportunity. There is no place left for outlaws. This has become glaringly clear to Garrett and he tries to fit the mold. Billy, on the other hand, has held onto his principles, although the fact is they offer him no chance of survival. Although Peckinpah never tries to brush over the fact that Billy is a killer, he clearly sympathizes with him, a man who's on the "wrong side of the law." For despite all his brutality and self-righteousness, Billy not only embodies qualities like bravery

> **"The changes ordered by the studio are mostly stupid but not disastrous. Even in the maimed state in which it has been released, *Pat Garrett and Billy the Kid* is the richest, most exciting American film so far this year. There are moments and whole sequences here that stand among the best Peckinpah has ever achieved."** *Time Magazine*

2

1   Double indemnity: As musician and actor, Bob Dylan chronicles the last days of legendary Western hero, Billy the Kid.

2   A man of principle: While Billy's violence seems inseparable from his passion for freedom, his opponents are often just sneaky and brutal.

3   Laying down the law: For James Coburn, Pat Garrett was the role of a lifetime.

nd integrity, but also exhibits free will. All the director's works code these raits as virtues inextricably linked to the great American frontier. The tone of he film is dominated by a sense of mourning for the extinct notion of pioneer ountry and for the long forgotten promise of "liberty and justice for all," on which the United States of America was founded. In its ballad-like structure, he film reads like an extended love letter to the West. The melancholy sound-rack by Bob Dylan, who also plays the role of the story's narrator, the young lias, further emphasizes this. Dylan's songs are a perfect complement to the

film's slow rhythm and its softly flowing, dimly lit, broad shots. Here, however, the technique lacks the optimism and sense of excitement about the future that filled the classic imagery of this genre.

Peckinpah's picture does not deal with the expansion or acquisition of the territory, but rather with the violent death of an anachronistic way of life. By taking this angle, he turns the traditional cinematic perspective of the classic Western on its head and sees the genre through to its inevitable conclusion.

JAMES COBURN James Coburn (born August 31, 1928 in Laurel, Nebraska, died November 18, 2002 in Los Angeles) was among the few American actors who personified the specific brand of raw masculinity dominant in Hollywood westerns well after their heyday had officially ended. His debut came with Budd Boetticher's Randolph Scott western *Ride Lonesome* (1958/59), at a time when the genre was still very much alive. His breakthrough came a year later when he played the taciturn sniper in John Sturges' *The Magnificent Seven* (1960). In 1963, he rejoined forces with Sturges for *The Great Escape*, a world-class breakout caper with an all-star cast.

He first collaborated with Sam Peckinpah on the military Western *Major Dundee* (1964/65), and Coburn quickly became the swashbuckling director's favorite son. Wildly popular were Coburn's James Bond spoofs *Our Man Flint* (1965) and *In Like Flint* (1967), in which he starred as the title character and displayed his knack for comedy. Further departures from the world of cowboys and Stetsons followed, including the sex-comedy *Candy / Candy e il suo pazzo mondo* (1968) and the film adaptation of Tennessee Williams' *Last of the Mobile Hot Shots* (1969).

James Coburn will remain eternally etched in our memories as the tough-as-nails man's man, a persona he continued to embody throughout the 1970s in movies like Sergio Leone's *Giù la testa / Duck, You Sucker* (1971) and Peckinpah's *Pat Garrett and Billy the Kid* (1973). After 20 years of very limited appearances due to severe arthritis, Coburn illuminated the screen yet again with a bravado comeback in Paul Schrader's family drama *Affliction* (1997), his only performance to win him the Oscar.

Peckinpah's *Pat Garrett and Billy the Kid* was heavily censored by the film studio, and this recurrent experience led him to direct his next project in Mexico. His original director's cut, which Roger Spottiswoode restored to a great extent in the early 1990s, includes a prolog missing from the studio release. The sequence shows hired guns of the influential ranchers murdering Garrett about thirty years after he killed Billy at their request. It also makes clear that Garrett had purchased land, and was therefore tied up with the cattle barons. These bits of information not only change the nature of his relationship to Billy, but also put a different spin on his character and make

Garrett the picture's actual tragic hero. Though he attempts to adapt to the signs of the times, and as he puts it at the top of the film, "grow old with the land," deep down he is a man anchored in days gone by. He goes against his principles, assassinates his best friend and, in the end, never attains his goals. In both the history of the American West and the Hollywood Western, Pat Garrett was a legendary sheriff who enforced the law with all his might. To Peckinpah he is someone who betrayed both himself and the old West. Billy the Kid may be dead by the film's end, but Pat Garrett gave up the ghost even before the curtains open.   JH

5

4 Free Love in the Old West: Kris Kristofferson's Billy the Kid embodied the ideals of the hippie era.

5 Hang him high: In Peckinpah's post-Western, civilization often looks a world away.

6 Lonesome Doves: For the aging men of the West, even women no longer offer a safe refuge. Time has left them high and dry.

"The link to contemporary America is clearer than ever before in Peckinpah's Western œuvre, thanks to the relaxed performance of folk-rock star, Kris Kristofferson. His Billy the Kid is a hero that fits none of the genre's jaded clichés. What we have instead is an affable, high-spirited Easy Horserider." *Die Zeit*

THE EXORCIST

1973 - USA - 122 MIN. - HORROR FILM

DIRECTOR WILLIAM FRIEDKIN (*1939)
SCREENPLAY WILLIAM PETER BLATTY, based on his novel of the same name DIRECTOR OF PHOTOGRAPHY OWEN ROIZMAN, BILLY WILLIAMS
MUSIC JACK NITZSCHE, KRZYSZTOF PENDERECKI EDITING NORMAN GAY, EVAN LOTTMAN, BUD SMITH PRODUCTION WILLIAM
PETER BLATTY for WARNER BROS., HOYA PRODUCTIONS.

STARRING ELLEN BURSTYN (Chris MacNeil), MAX VON SYDOW (Father Merrin), LEE J. COBB (Lieutenant Kinderman), LINDA
BLAIR (Regan MacNeil), KITTY WINN (Sharon Spencer), JASON MILLER (Father Damien Karras), JACK MACGOWRAN
(Burke Dennings), REVEREND WILLIAM O'MALLEY (Father Dyer), BARTON HEYMAN (Dr. Klein), PETER MASTERSON
(Barringer).

ACADEMY AWARDS 1973 OSCARS for BEST ADAPTED SCREENPLAY (William Peter Blatty), and BEST SOUND (Robert Knudson,
Christopher Newman).

"What an excellent day for an exorcism."

Evil neither stems from a dark abyss nor from a cosmic realm. It neither limits its dominion to dark shadows and blind alleys, nor does it attack in the form of a werewolf that can be slain with a silver bullet. When we are struck by the fear that without warning, something horrific could infiltrate our lives and turn our precious little worlds on their heads, perhaps we are tuning into something very real and tangible. Maybe evil has already made a nest for itself, where we'd least expect it. Namely, in our most intimate surroundings.

Although this is the central topic of the story involving American actress Chris MacNeil (Ellen Burstyn), whose twelve-year-old daughter Regan (Linda Blair) is transformed into the Antichrist before her very eyes, *The Exorcist* director William Friedkin opens his film with far off images of the Middle East. It is on an archaeological dig in Iraq that Father Merrin (Max von Sydow) unearths several ancient artifacts that send him into a state of panic, including decapitated statue heads and a most unnerving amulet.

The ensuing scenes, in which pure evil appears to take possession of Merrin's entire environment, are among the picture's most powerful. The vacant and yet piercing stares of the locals, the hammering of the blacksmiths that Merrin confuses with the sound of his own racing heart and a clock that stops cold are just a few of the images that contribute to the audience's visceral incorporation of the imminent danger.

When, at the end of this sequence, Merrin sits directly across from a statue of an ominous demon with rabid dogs running rampant at its feet, the

essence of the story becomes clear. According to the director, the film is "a Christian parable about the eternal struggle between good and evil."

Cut to "Georgetown." The on-screen caption and the bird's eye view of the city evoke a deceptive picture of order and distanced safety. Friedkin referred to the fade-in technique he often used as the "Means of luring the audience onto the wrong track." Nonetheless, the peace of Georgetown's idyllic autumn and the illusion of the stable family unit fall like a house of cards after one of the Jesuit priests from the university, Father Karras (Jason Miller) breaks down and admits that he has "lost faith." With these words something wicked this way comes.

It comes in the form of an appalling, disfigured little girl spewing out profanities and blaspheming uncontrollably. Wretched displays of gasping, choking and shrieking are let loose on the audio track, accompanied by a visual deluge of regurgitated green mucus. Never before and never since, for that matter, has a director been so intent on terrorizing his audience. At the time of its release, screenings often had spectators vomiting in the aisles, fainting and breaking into hysterics. This highly provocative work even made movie critic Roger Ebert question his faith in humanity, asking whether "people (are) so numb that they need movies of this intensity in order to feel anything at all?"

The intoxicating shock value of the gore can make one overlook the masterful web of allusions, contrasts, analogies and sociopolitical arguments

3

Friedkin has woven here. One example of this intricate layering can be witnessed when Regan forms a clay model of a bird with wings that recall those of the demonic statue in the Iraq sequence. Later on, Lieutenant Kinderman (Lee J. Cobb), assigned to investigate the mysterious death of Chris' close friend, finds yet another clay object at the scene of the crime. It is the pagan counterpart to the crucifix, which Chris recently discovered in her daughter's bed.

The way in which the film attempts to diagnose the cause of Regan's possession is also worthy of close examination. The arrogance of the doctors, Chris' outbursts of rage, her friend Burke's alcoholism, the burden of guilt Father Karras feels towards his dead mother are all signs that the source of

evil could be human. Karras' work as a psychologist for the university's Jesuit community makes him doubt God's existence, providing the audience with another possible clue to the origin of Regan's infection. Other events, including the Jesuit priest who comes across a defiled statue in the chapel, but doesn't acknowledge the Madonna as he enters, also point to lack of faith as a contributory.

All these factors are devices Friedkin uses to vary the film's underlying principle mentioned in the opening paragraph. Namely, that evil lurks in everyday life and even in our very hearts. In this respect, it is not a battle with the devil that Carras ends up winning. It's a battle with his own self. SH

"*The Exorcist* makes no sense, but if you want to be shaken, it will scare the hell out of you."

The New Republic

1 That little devil: Regan (Linda Blair) is about to have a religious experience.

2 Satanic verses: The Prince of Darkness moves in mysterious ways.

3 Who's been sleeping in my bed? Father Damien Karras (Jason Miller) suppresses his doubts and aids Father Merrin (Max von Sydow) in the ancient exorcism.

4 That thing upstairs is not my daughter: Actress Chris MacNeil (Ellen Burstyn) wants to be a good mother to Regan, but Dr. Spock never said anything about spitting up pea soup.

SUBLIMINAL MESSAGES At the speed of 24 frames per second in film and 30 NTSC frames per second in television, subliminal messages are usually only visible for less than the blink of an eye, and certainly not long enough to leave an imprint on the human retina. The term itself comes from the Latin "sub limen," 'below the threshold.'

The theory that even an image which people are not capable of consciously perceiving can still impact their minds is an age-old concept. In particular, the advertising industry has tried countless times to make use of scientifically and ethically disputed techniques of visual manipulation. "Invisible advertising" was tested in New Jersey in 1957 during the screening of *Picnic* (1955). The results, which contended that the several spliced in, split-second-long frames showing popcorn and Coca Cola caused sales to sky rocket, turned out to be falsified. Be that as it may, as recently as the U. S. presidential race in 2000, President George W. Bush ran a smear ad in which the word "rats" appeared in conjunction with a prescription drug proposal put together by his opponent, Al Gore. Strictly speaking, subliminal messages have only had a limited impact on the cinema directly. Filmmakers who experiment with them, like David Lynch, tend to implement montage sequences of image snippets. These, however, can be perceived by the naked eye of an alert viewer. In *The Exorcist: The Version You Haven't Seen Yet* (1973/2000) such a device was used briefly to show Satan's face – yet another attempt on the part of the director to petrify his audience.

AMERICAN GRAFFITI

1973 - USA - 110 MIN. - COMEDY

DIRECTOR GEORGE LUCAS (*1944)
SCREENPLAY GEORGE LUCAS, GLORIA KATZ, WILLARD HUYCK DIRECTOR OF PHOTOGRAPHY RON EVESLAGE, JAN D'ALQUEN
EDITING VERNA FIELDS, MARCIA LUCAS MUSIC BUDDY HOLLY, CHUCK BERRY, BOOKER T. JONES PRODUCTION FRANCIS FORD
COPPOLA for THE COPPOLA COMPANY, LUCASFILM LTD., UNIVERSAL PICTURES.

STARRING RICHARD DREYFUSS (Curt Henderson), RON HOWARD (Steve Bolander), PAUL LE MAT (John Milner),
CHARLES MARTIN SMITH (Terry Fields), CINDY WILLIAMS (Laurie Henderson), CANDY CLARK (Debbie Dunham),
MACKENZIE PHILLIPS (Carol), WOLFMAN JACK (XERB Disc Jockey), HARRISON FORD (Bob Falfa), BO HOPKINS
(Joe Young).

"Hey, is this what they call copping a feel?"

Not on your life, sister! The only reason John (Paul Le Mat), the reigning king of the road this side of the Sierra Nevada, presses Carol's (Mackenzie Phillips) face into his lap is out of sheer embarrassment to be seen with a thirteen-year-old while cruising the streets. As far as he's concerned, the kid just got into his roadster by mistake. Be that as it may, young Carol's somewhat naive question pricelessly captures the spirit of 1962, the year in which George Lucas' bittersweet adolescent comedy takes place. *American Graffiti* tells of the last days of teenage innocence, both for the protagonists, who are fresh out of high school and uncertain about what to do next, as well as for the era's way of life in general. For within the coming two years, American president John F. Kennedy will be assassinated and the nation will enter the Vietnam War.

The film tells the story of one night in the life of four adolescents growing up in sleepy Modesto, California. Curt (Richard Dreyfuss) and Steve (Ron Howard) have both won college scholarships and are scheduled to leave in the morning. Steve is starry-eyed and hopeful for the future, while Curt is still contemplating whether he'd be better off spending another year in his comfortable surroundings. Terry (Charles Martin Smith) is younger than the other two. A clutzy dork, he wears a pair of two-inch thick, horn-rimmed glasses, trying his damnedest to emulate the older guys where women and booze are concerned, but failing miserably. John is a bit older than the rest of the troop and drives around town in a suped-up 1932 Ford Deuce coupe. As far as cars go, John is the undisputed cock of the walk, although the "cool rider" title is beginning to sound a little stale. He eventually admits being jealous of Curt for being able to escape their hometown, a chance he'll never get...

American Graffiti was produced with a budget of 750 thousand dollars and raked in a total of 55 million at the box office. Its enormous appeal then, as now, was its ability to reconstruct a beloved era in recent American his-

1   Everything is copasetic: Drive-in restaurants and bubbly car hops light up main street.

2   Out of my dreams and into my car: Candy Clark as Debbie Dunham, impressed by an Impala.

3   American Bandstand: Live rock 'n' roll at the high school ball.

4   Speed demon: John Milner (Paul Le Mat) sets off on the open road to nowhere.

"This superb and singular film catches not only the charm and tribal energy of the teen-age 1950s but also the listlessness and the resignation that underscored it all, like an incessant bass line in one of the rock-'n'-roll songs of the period." *Time Magazine*

tory. It was a time of carefree better days, of gigantic street intersections, drive-in restaurants with carhops, jacked up hot rods in illegal drag races, school dances where bands still performed live and radio disc jockey Wolfman Jack's legendary rock 'n' roll broadcast.

Nonetheless, as nostalgic as the story reads, its episodic structure is rooted in the cinematic techniques of the 1970s. Without the use of transitions, director Lucas, who said most of the story was autobiographically inspired, flips back and forth between the separate storylines of the protagonists. Lucas blends comedy and suspense with melodrama, capturing that

interplay of boredom and forced excitement that characterized small tow America. Curt frantically searches for a dreamy blonde woman (most likely prostitute) he saw at a traffic light driving past him in a Thunderbird and get mixed up with a group of punks known as the "Pharaohs." The gang of ruffi ans seem to pose a real danger at first, but what starts off threatening has a undeniably humorous outcome. Steve, on the other hand, fights with his girl friend Laurie (Cindy Williams) the entire evening about his going away. Terr who was lent Steve's 1958 Impala, picks up cute blonde Debbie (Cand Clark), and takes her on a scenic trip full of ludicrous mishaps. Then there'

John, who just can't seem to rid himself of that pesky Carol. Not that he minds as much as he claims. When it comes down to it, he kind of likes the little chatterbox. Intentionally directionless, the plot never reaches a clear climax (even John's drag race against Falfa (Harrison Ford) is just one of many episodes), mirroring the characters' own disorientation. These are, after all, kids who don't really know what they want yet. The film concludes with Curt going away to college and Steve remaining home. Captions, serving as the movie's epilog, inform us of what destiny has in store for these boys later in life. Curt becomes a writer and Steve an insurance salesman. John dies in a car accident at the hands of a drunk driver and Terry is killed in Vietnam. And thus the age of innocence, when everything was copasetic, has come to an irreversible close. LP

GEORGE LUCAS

George Lucas is among the most commercially successful filmmakers alive today. His personal fortune alone is estimated at two billion dollars. In the grand scheme of things, Lucas' work as a director accounts for just a small part of his many diverse activities (over the last thirty years he has only actually directed five films himself). Primarily, Lucas has devoted himself to producing, writing and running his personal film "empire," which houses the well-known and phenomenally successful special effects company, Industrial Light and Magic (a part of Lucas Digital). After studying at the University of Southern California Film School and directing a wide range of short films, Lucas made the acquaintance of Francis Ford Coppola in 1967, and worked as his assistant for some time. It was Coppola, in fact, who helped Lucas produce his first full-length feature film, the sci-fi story *THX 1138* (1970). *American Graffiti* (1973), however, proved to be Lucas' first commercial success. He, of course, turned around significantly more profits in 1977 with the first installment of the *Star Wars* Saga (1977, 1980, 1983, 1999, 2002). Lucas directed this first picture in the series himself, but then the filmmaker loved and scorned for his perfectionism began to focus exclusively on writing and producing. In the mid 90s, the original *Star Wars* Trilogy was re-released in theaters, this time featuring new digital effects. Lucas reclaimed his seat in the director's chair for the long-awaited prequels *Star Wars: Episode I – The Phantom Menace* (1999) and *Star Wars: Episode II – Attack of the Clones* (2002), which followed shortly thereafter. Although both films were box-office sensations, they won the approval of few critics.

4

DON'T LOOK NOW

1973 - GREAT BRITAIN - 109 MIN. - HORROR FILM, DRAMA

DIRECTOR NICOLAS ROEG (*1928)
SCREENPLAY CHRIS BRYANT, ALLAN SCOTT, based on the story of the same name by DAPHNE DU MAURIER DIRECTOR OF PHOTOGRAPHY ANTHONY B. RICHMOND, NICOLAS ROEG EDITING GRAEME CLIFFORD MUSIC PINO DONAGGIO PRODUCTION PETER KATZ, FREDERICK MULLER, STEVE PREVIN for CASEY, ELDORADO FILMS.

STARRING JULIE CHRISTIE (Laura Baxter), DONALD SUTHERLAND (John Baxter), HILARY MASON (Heather), CLELIA MATANIA (Wendy), MASSIMO SERATO (Bishop Barbarrigo), RENATO SCARPA (Inspector Longhi), ANN RYE (Mandy Babbage), NICHOLAS SALTER (Johnny Baxter), SHARON WILLIAMS (Christine Baxter), BRUNO CATTANEO (Detective Sabbione), ADELINA POERIO (Dwarf).

"I have seen her... and she wants you to know that she is happy."

Two children frolic through the autumnal garden of a house in the English countryside. The children's parents, Laura and John Baxter (Julie Christie and Donald Sutherland), sit comfortably inside the house. While John looks over slides, Laura rests on the couch and reads. It is an idyll that is soon brutally shattered. Stirred by a dark premonition, John runs outside. But he is too late. His daughter Christine is already dead – drowned in the garden pond. To gain some distance from the horrible event, the couple travel to Venice, where John begins directing the restoration of a church. But when they meet two odd Scottish sisters (Hilary Mason and Clelia Matania) in a restaurant, their daughter's death catches up with them: one of the two old women is blind and presumably gifted with a supernatural talent. With a friendly laugh, she tells Laura that she has been in contact with Christine. Laura breaks down upon hearing this, but she then gains a new confidence from the stranger's vision and tries to convince John, who considers the entire story absurd, that their daughter is not yet lost.

Briton Nicolas Roeg began his career toward the end of the 1950s as a cameraman. He quickly became one of the most sought-after men in his field. In the 60s, he worked as director of photography for directorial icons such as Roger Corman, Richard Lester, John Schlesinger, and David Lean before making his long-overdue directorial debut alongside Donald Camme

"*Don't Look Now* is such a rich, complex and subtle experience that it demands more than one viewing. Roeg's insistence on the power of the image, his reliance on techniques of narrative that are peculiarly cinematic, remind us how undemanding and perfunctory so many movies still are. Roeg's is one of those rare talents that can effect a new way of seeing." *Time Magazine*

with *Performance* (1969), an extravagant gangster film that offered a reflection on the popular culture of the 60s. Roeg worked as director of photography on *Performance*, and again on his second film, *Walkabout* (1971). In *Don't Look Now*, he is also credited alongside Anthony B. Richmond as director of photography, unmistakable evidence that indicates just how important the visual aspect of filmmaking is for Roeg. Accordingly, *Don't Look Now*, like several Alfred Hitchcock films is based upon a Daphne du Maurier story, is a masterpiece of timeless beauty thanks to its visual qualities.

It's often the case in cinema that an unspecified, implicit threat produces a more lasting scare than any terror explicitly depicted on the screen. This is especially true for movies that convert human fears into a system of symbols, like horror films or thrillers. *Don't Look Now*, which effectively straddles these two genres, is a prime example. Even today, the film derives most of its extraordinarily disturbing effect and subtle horror from the tense atmosphere that Roeg evokes with his powerfully suggestive images, accentuated by a seemingly avant-garde montage technique, which almost anticipates the refined editing of Steven Soderbergh. From the very beginning, the film's time and reality planes are constantly interrupted by unsettlingly stark cuts, abrupt segues and enigmatic associations. A second, hidden meaning seems to lurk behind each image and the constant threat of something unexpected and inexplicable questions what has just been seen. As with the mosaics John reconstructs in the church, the truth is hidden behind a number of broken pieces in small symbols that seem to defy rational association, for which normal explanations simply do not suffice.

Roeg's suggestive coloration hugely intensifies the surreal, threatening atmosphere. The color red is given an especially significant meaning. At the beginning, little Christine runs around the garden in a radiant red raincoat.

"A modern Hitchcock. His film shows that he has already absorbed and reflected upon the turmoil of the 70s."

Kölner Stadt-Anzeiger

1   The end of innocence: In just minutes, the child
in the red raincoat will drown in the garden pond.
In Nicolas Roeg's film, each image holds multiple
meanings.

2   After the death of his daughter, John Baxter
(Donald Sutherland) experiences things in Venice
that threaten his rational worldview.

3   Dialing up the dead: Laura (Julie Christie) is
hoping two mysterious women will help her
contact her deceased child.

4   Indecent exposure: Tiny red details in gray, wintry
Venice recall the drowned girl at the start of the
film – Laura's shoulder bag, for example…

"... a haunting, beautiful labyrinth that gets inside your bones and stays there. *Don't Look Now* still has the power to frighten and disorient – to suggest a world that's perilous, cruel and out of control." *San Francisco Chronicle*

5 … and her boots.

6 The labyrinthine alleys of Venice reflect John's inner chaos.

The premonition that the girl is in danger comes to John as he discovers a figure clad in a red hooded jacket on the slide of a Venetian church and a red fluid – it is not clear if it's John's blood – subsequently spreads out on the screen. When later in Venice, Laura wears red boots or carries a red bag, it suggests that the Baxters are oppressed by thoughts of their daughter. It seems as if John is even visited by visions, as he repeatedly sees a mysterious small figure in a red raincoat scurrying away. The film appears to slowly but surely take over John's perspective, who in contrast to Laura is a committed rationalist and fights against his delusional visions, growing more and more bewildered as a result. Far from romantic glamour, wintry gray Venice, with its labyrinthine streets, becomes a mirror image of his inner chaos. In the end, the city exudes an almost gothic horror. It shockingly reveals itself to John as a kingdom of the dead.

The directorial projects of former cameramen are often plagued by a technical brilliance that renders films cold and sterile. The natural interaction between the leading actors, Julie Christie and Donald Sutherland, ensures that is not case here. Their wonderfully long love scene has passed into legend, its discrete sensuality all the more evident today, long after the scent of scandal has faded.

JH

THE STING

1973 - USA - 129 MIN. - GANGSTER FILM, COMEDY

DIRECTOR GEORGE ROY HILL (1922–2002)
SCREENPLAY DAVID S. WARD DIRECTOR OF PHOTOGRAPHY ROBERT SURTEES EDITING WILLIAM REYNOLDS MUSIC SCOTT JOPLIN, MARVIN HAMLISCH PRODUCTION TONY BILL, JULIA PHILLIPS, MICHAEL PHILLIPS, RICHARD D. ZANUCK for UNIVERSAL PICTURES.

STARRING PAUL NEWMAN (Henry Gondorff), ROBERT REDFORD (Johnny Hooker), ROBERT SHAW (Doyle Lonnegan), CHARLES DURNING (Lieutenant William Snyder), RAY WALSTON (J. J. Singleton), EILEEN BRENNAN (Billie), HAROLD GOULD (Kid Twist), JOHN HEFFERNAN (Eddie Niles), DANA ELCAR (F.B.I. Special Agent Polk), ROBERT EARL JONES (Luther Coleman).

ACADEMY AWARDS 1973 OSCARS for BEST FILM (Tony Bill, Julia Phillips, Michael Phillips), BEST DIRECTOR (George Roy Hill), BEST SCREENPLAY (David S. Ward), BEST FILM EDITING (William Reynolds), BEST MUSIC (Marvin Hamlisch), BEST ART DIRECTION (Henry Bumstead, James Payne), and BEST COSTUMES (Edith Head).

"What was I supposed to do – call him for cheating better than me?"

Joliet, Illinois, 1936. Con men Hooker (Robert Redford) and Luther (Robert Earl Jones) pull off a lucrative street swindle. But they don't suspect that the money they've stolen belongs to notorious gangster boss Doyle Lonnegan (Robert Shaw), who immediately sets a killer on the trail of the two crooks. After Luther is cold-bloodedly murdered, Hooker flees to Chicago, leaving behind the corrupt cop, Snyder (Charles Durning), who is also after him. He goes into hiding with Gondorff (Paul Newman), an old con man buddy of Luther's whose heyday is long past and who, in an attempt to stay out of trouble with the FBI, has settled down comfortably with brothel owner Billie (Eileen Brennan). But Hooker's determination to avenge Luther's death breathes new life into Gondorff. The two piece together a band of old associates and hatch a refined plan to swindle Lonnegan out of a half a million bucks.

The Sting is a phenomenon. A charmingly lightweight movie about gangsters and swindlers in 1930s Chicago, it was the clear winner at the Oscars and became one of the biggest box office smashes of the decade. Created by an independent production team, the film was a triumph for New Hollywood, though it showed that the methods of old Hollywood could still function provided well-known elements were rearranged. The producers built upon the successful trio from the Western Butch Cassidy and the Sundance Kid (1969), casting Robert Redford and Paul Newman in starring roles, and hiring George Roy Hill to direct the project. They also correctly guessed that film audiences of the 1970s would be very receptive to nostalgic films. Accordingly, the squalor of the Depression of the 1930s is hardly noticeable in The Sting. From the very beginning when the characters are introduced,

1   Shall I frisk ya? Although *The Sting* itself raked in a slew of Oscars, heartthrob Robert Redford only won the laurels of adoring fans.

2   "Reunited, and it feels so good!" Five years after riding off into the sunset, Butch and Sundance met up again in the Depression Era, striking box-office gold again.

3   Pick a card, any card... A tribute to con artistry that examines the tricks of the trade.

"Two of Hollywood's dream men form this genial marriage of criminal minds: Paul Newman, the mature senior partner, is unbeatably dashing; and in Robert Redford, the dream factory's latest young hero, he's found an ideal foil and accomplice."

Stuttgarter Zeitung

one realizes that what lies ahead is pure film fantasy, not an attempt at reconstructing the past. And sure enough, George Roy Hill's film is unadulterated and highly entertaining fiction, in which a perfect mix between historic and historicized set pieces is achieved: Scott Joplin's Ragtime piano, though from the 1920s, brings a sleight of hand and levity to the film that corresponds marvelously with the actions of the actors. Antique segment titles and the use of the fade-out further strengthen the tongue-in-cheek charm of the mischievous swindle. And the pleasant retro-look reminiscent of the color

films of the late 1940s, with which camera veteran Robert Surtees impressively refines the studio set, exudes the faded luster of the "good old times," a feeling that was not present in the harsh underworld dramas of the 1930s, the heyday of Warner Brothers' classic gangster films.

The Sting also mirrors the enthusiasm of filmmaking itself in the playful accentuation of its dramatization. It succeeds in reflecting the love of performance, deception and manipulation that drive the central characters and around which the entire plot revolves. No one can resist this virus

4

5

4 Blue eyes: Our, baby's got 'em and does he ever
   know it! Paul Newman has become as synonymous
   with Hollywood as that famous sign atop the hill.

5 The way we weren't: Redford makes misery and
   poverty look stylish and divine.

"How long has it been since you exited from a movie theatre smiling and just plain feeling good?" *Films in Review*

even the seemingly vice-free Lonnegan is ensnared by Gondorff in a round of poker. Needless to say, the cards are marked. As appropriate vengeance however, Gondorff & Co. find this action far too mundane. Instead, the plan is to get Lonnegan to place and subsequently lose a fortune on a horserace – in a fabricated betting office created just for this purpose. The action is without a doubt a masterpiece of deception and a challenge for true pros. Consequently, like in so many American films, the charm of *The Sting* lies in the pleasure of watching shrewd specialists at work. It is a pleasure that does not limit itself merely to the plot, but expands to the unmistakably brilliant performance of the entire film team – the actors, the cameraman, the art director, the author, and the director. *The Sting* is enthralling thanks to the professionalism of its entire crew. Hill's tour de force is a film by and about people who are clearly in supreme command of their craft – the craft of illusion.

JH

ROBERT SURTEES Robert Surtees (1906–1985) was one of the most famous of all American cameramen. He came to Hollywood in 1927, at the time of the introduction of the "talkie," and began his career as a camera assistant, initially at Universal and then later at both Warner Brothers and MGM. During these years, Surtees assisted Joseph Ruttenberg and Gregg Toland, the legendary master of focal depth, among others. Surtees graduated to head cameraman in the early 1940s and in subsequent years he developed into one of the most versatile and sought-after technicians in his field, as well as one of the most honored. Over the course of his 50-year career, Surtees was awarded an Academy Award on three separate occasions – for the color photography of *King Solomon's Mines* (1950) and *Ben-Hur* (1959), as well as for the black and white film *The Bad and the Beautiful* (1952). He received 13 further Oscar nominations, in 1967 and 1971 for two films simultaneously. Robert Surtees was one of the few camera virtuosos of the studio system who were also able to collaborate with young directors of New Hollywood, including Peter Bogdanovich in *The Last Picture Show* (1971) and Mike Nichols in *The Graduate* (1967). Surtees' son, Bruce, followed in the footsteps of his father. He is best known as Clint Eastwood's favorite director of photography.

MY NAME IS NOBODY
Il mio nome è Nessuno

1973 - ITALY / FRANCE / FGR - 117 MIN. - SPAGHETTI WESTERN, SPOOF

DIRECTOR TONINO VALERII (*1934)
SCREENPLAY SERGIO LEONE, ERNESTO GASTALDI, FULVIO MORSELLA DIRECTOR OF PHOTOGRAPHY ARMANDO NANNUZZI, GIUSEPPE RUZZOLINI EDITING NINO BARAGLI MUSIC ENNIO MORRICONE PRODUCTION FULVIO MORSELLA for RAFRAN CINEMATOGRAFICA, RIALTO FILM, LES PRODUCTIONS JACQUES LEITIENNE, LA SOCIETE IMP EX CI, LA SOCIETE ALCINTER.

STARRING TERENCE HILL (Nobody), HENRY FONDA (Jack Beauregard), JEAN MARTIN (Sullivan), REMUS PEETS (Biggun), PIERO LULLI (Sceriffo), GEOFFREY LEWIS (Band Leader), R. G. ARMSTRONG (John), NEIL SUMMERS (Squirrel), ULRICH MÜLLER (Dirty Joe), LEO GORDON (Red).

"A hero must die – it has to be so."

Three sinister figures ride into town. Dogs make themselves scarce and the townspeople stay in their houses. The trio make their way to the barber shop. They have no intention of harming the barber. They simply "borrow" his shop and his apron, posing as assistants in the hope of bumping off the next customer, gunslinger Jack Beauregard (Henry Fonda). But he smells a rat, shoves his revolver into an extremely sensitive spot of the fake barber's anatomy and survives the cut-throat razor. At the end of the film, the gunslinger's successor will also sit down in a barber's chair, and he too will know how to protect himself – just like Beauregard, but even more brazenly.

My Name is Nobody tells of a changing of the guard. With this brilliant prelude, an old gunslinger is introduced – a man who trusts his hunches and is quick with his pistol, but who's now tired and ready to hang up his gun. He's waiting for a ship to take him to Europe so he can retire. "Do you know anyone who can draw faster," asks the barber's son after Beauregard has done away with the three sinister characters. "Nobody," says the father. And Nobody (Terence Hill) soon appears. He is to become *the* new gunslinger.

He's just as quick on the draw as Beauregard, and just as cheeky. A fan of the old gunslinger, he can recount all of his "heroic deeds." Nobody wants Beauregard to retire into the history books so he can take his place. He helps matters along, by arranging a showdown between his idol and the so-called "Wild Bunch," a group of 150 men who are "as good as 1,000..."

The beginning of the film is pure "Leone" – a sweeping paraphrase of Sergio Leone's masterpiece *Once Upon a Time in the West* (*C'era una volta il West*, 1969). Just like in the old Leone Westerns, Ennio Morricone composed the music, and like in *Once Upon a Time in the West*, each character gets a personal melody. Nobody gets the cheerful title song; the "Wild Bunch" get a piece with more than a passing resemblance to Wagner's "Ride of the Valkyrie." Sergio Leone was both executive producer and co-author, and his one-time assistant Tonino Valerii directed the film. *My Name is Nobody* pays its respects to the Spaghetti Western, and is packed with countless little homages to the Hollywood Western. The "Wild Bunch" is clearly named after Sam Peckinpah's classic, *The Wild Bunch*

2

(1969), and their appearance recalls the troops from Sam Fuller's *Fort Guns* (1957).

The film becomes a parody through the Terence Hill character, Nobody. He has a comedic streak and goes as far as to face his adversary on the fair ground. He is silly, perpetually cracks corny jokes, and has none of the tragic honor typical of the classic gunslinger. This aspect makes the film a kind of late Western – the time of the great tragic heroes is over and the new gunslinger is a clown. The film also tells of the ritual of legend building in the West. It depicts the writing of history, so to speak, while it is happening. While Beauregard shoots up the "Wild Bunch," the camera, in a kind of fast forward, continually blends book illustrations into the frame that capture the events and will finally turn the old gunslinger into a Western myth.   HJ

"For me, the interesting thing about *My Name is Nobody* was that it confronts a myth with the negation of a myth." *Sergio Leone*

1   Nobody knows the trouble I've seen: Rootin' tootin' gunslinger Nobody (Terence Hill) isn't afraid of anything, except maybe gingivitis.

2   This chilli ain't made in NYC: Scooping up a hearty portion of Western-style beans right out of the pan.

3   See no evil, see no nothin': Nobody has planned out the showdown for his true hero, Jack Beauregard (Henry Fonda, in the distance).

4   Before you can say Jack Robinson: Nobody's West may not be as wild as it once was, but it sure is as dangerous.

3

5 Basket of goodies: Jack Beauregard may be getting on in years, but he still ain't afraid of no big bad wolf. Is he?

6 Retirement community: Beauregard wants to quit while the going's still good...

7 ... but to no avail: As Nobody puts it "A good exit is sometimes trickier than a grand entrance."

TERENCE HILL Blond hair and bright blue eyes are the distinguishing characteristics of Terence Hill (*29.3.1939 in Venice). Toward the beginning of his career, however, he had dark hair and appeared under his given name, Mario Girotti. As a twelve-year-old he was discovered by director Dino Risi, and for years played supporting roles in countless films, among them such differing projects as the Karl May adaptation *Winnetou II* (*Vinetu II*, 1964) and Luchino Visconti's masterpiece, *The Leopard* (*Il gattopardo*, 1963). In 1967 he became the blond Terrence Hill and appeared for the first time with the colleague at whose side he was to become famous – Bud Spencer (née Carlo Pedersoli). With *Dio perdona... Io no!*, a long collaboration began, which was to make Spencer and Hill famous as the wisecracking pugnacious duo. Many of these films (for example *Lo chiamavano Trinita*, 1970) are parodies of Spaghetti Westerns and were more successful than Leone's serious films. "Leone deserved artistic revenge," commented *Nobody* director Tonino Valerii. "If Terence Hill poked fun at the Spaghetti Western, he should be given an appropriate punishment – he should be the adversary of the most legendary Western actor (Henry Fonda) and he should acknowledge his own nothingness, which is where the title, *My Name is Nobody* (*Il mio nome è Nessuno*, 1973), comes from." Terence Hill remained true to the Western parody later as well – at the beginning of the 1990s he appeared in film adaptations of the comic book cowboy, *Lucky Luke* (1990, 1991, 1992), several of which he also directed.

"He totes his saddle on his shoulder like a pair of wings, punching and shooting his way through the West right there with the best of 'em."

film-dienst

THE TOWERING INFERNO

1974 - USA - 165 MIN. - DISASTER MOVIE

DIRECTOR JOHN GUILLERMIN (*1925), IRWIN ALLEN (1916–1991) (Action Scenes)
SCREENPLAY STIRLING SILLIPHANT, based on the novels *THE TOWER* by RICHARD MARTIN STERN and *THE GLASS INFERNO* by THOMAS N. SCORTIA and FRANK M. ROBINSON **DIRECTOR OF PHOTOGRAPHY** FRED J. KOENEKAMP, JOSEPH F. BIROC **EDITING** HAROLD F. KRESS, CARL KRESS **MUSIC** JOHN WILLIAMS **PRODUCTION** IRWIN ALLEN for 20TH CENTURY FOX, WARNER BROS.

STARRING STEVE MCQUEEN (Fire Chief Michael O'Hallorhan), PAUL NEWMAN (Doug Roberts), WILLIAM HOLDEN (Jim Duncan), FAYE DUNAWAY (Susan Franklin), FRED ASTAIRE (Harlee Claiborne), RICHARD CHAMBERLAIN (Roger Simmons), JENNIFER JONES (Liselotte Mueller), O. J. SIMPSON (Chief Security Guard Harry Jernigan), ROBERT VAUGHN (Senator Gary Parker), ROBERT WAGNER (Dan Bigelow).

ACADEMY AWARDS 1974 OSCARS for BEST CINEMATOGRAPHY (Fred J. Koenecamp, Joseph F. Biroc), BEST FILM EDITING (Harold F. Kress, Carl Kress), and BEST SONG: "WE MAY NEVER LOVE LIKE THIS AGAIN" (Music: Joel Hirschhorn; Lyrics: Al Kasha).

"Now just how bad is it?"

San Francisco pops open the champagne as Duncan Enterprises throws a gala party to celebrate the opening of the world's tallest building. The festivities are to be held in the panoramic equinox lounge, on the 135th floor of the skyscraper's whopping 137 total. Company owner and head of construction Jim Duncan (William Holden) has invited everyone who's anyone to the occasion. The mayor, the director of urban projects, his daughter, her husband Roger Simmons (Richard Chamberlain) who oversaw the installation of the tower's electrical wiring, and, of course, the building's architect Doug Roberts (Paul Newman) are among the distinguished guests. Even before the evening has gotten underway, it is doomed to a disastrous end when the building's circuitry proves defective and an electrical mishap ensues. Unbeknownst to the arriving guests, a fire has broken out on the 81st floor and is already out of control by the time the party begins. Duncan wants to avoid a scene at any cost. He puts his confidence in the fire department to control the blaze and lets the celebration continue. However, as soon as fire chief Michael O'Hallorhan (Steve McQueen) enters the scene, he immediately attempts to evacuate the guests and Duncan must cooperate.

The film allows time for a suspenseful build-up before letting the action tear loose. First, we are introduced to all those who contributed to erecting the glass tower. Architect Doug Roberts is extremely competent in the field of skyscraper design. He is thorough, always thinks two steps ahead and has provided for state-of-the-art safety precautions in the building plans. Needless to say, Simmons, the negligent dandy, didn't execute these measures. Everyone blames this slippery character for the inferno and rightly so. Simmons is of low moral fiber and he will prove it during the rescue efforts. In addition to this group of people, we are also presented with the potential victims of the disaster such as the deaf-mute mother and her two children, the wealthy widow Liselotte Mueller (Jennifer Jones) who con-artist Harlee Claiborne (Fred Astaire) intends to dupe on this cursed evening.

The film is sophisticated in its approach, telling the catastrophic tale on two independent levels. The unifying, larger story deals with the blaze itself, extinguishing it and, above all else, helping the guests and residents trapped inside get to safe ground. These scenes make use of exterior shots that show the tower ablaze from the street. Roberts and O'Hallorhan are seen attempting to save as many people as possible from the deadly flames and rush-

1 Burn baby burn: Fire has broken out on the 81st floor, and the flames are making their way to the floors above.

2 Short circuit: Architect Doug Roberts (Paul Newman) warned that the sloppy wiring job was a fire hazard.

3 Spontaneous Combustion! "It's Grand Hotel in flames at last," wrote critic Pauline Kael.

4 A hanged man: Politician Senator Gary Parker (Robert Vaughn) helped the contractor realize his reckless plans.

5 Dousing the flames in sweat: Fire Chief O'Hallorhan (Steve McQueen) battles to contain the blaze.

6 Fighting fire with fire: O'Hallorhan lays his life on the line while saving those of others.

"Now, you know we don't have a sure way to fight a fire over the seventh floor, but you just keep building 'em higher and higher."
Film quote: Fire Chief Michael O'Hallorhan

them out of the building. At the same time, the film examines the various personal stories of the characters. Roberts rescues the deaf-mute mother's children, whereas Mueller and Claiborne get to know each other a little bit better...

By magnifying the large-scale catastrophe through touching individual tragedies, filmmaker John Guillermin and producer Irwin Allen, who directed all the action scenes, adhere to the golden rule of the disaster movie formula and intensify the film's impact. Interestingly enough, one can even draw parallels between *The Towering Inferno* and the countless tellings of one of the most popularly filmed calamities of all time, the sinking of the Titanic. In both stories there is an initial arrogance that dominates the situation – no one wants to believe that anything could possibly go wrong. Neglect is the

DISASTER MOVIES

The disaster movie is a hallmark film genre of the 1970s. In was in this decade that the term first came to be, its heyday featuring pictures like *Airport* (1970), *Earthquake* (1974) and, of course, *The Towering Inferno* (1974). Hollywood cranked them out one after the other. They usually featured an all-star cast as well as grand sweeping images of Armageddon. The majority of these pre-digital age films had masterful special effects that sent chills running down the spines of the audience. They were all, more or less, hits at the box office. Often the scenarios touched on ancient myths and visions of apocalypse. The Icarus myth can be seen behind the plane crash drama *Airport*, as can the Old Testament Tower of Babel story in *The Towering Inferno*. These movies also allow for nature to avenge human arrogance and put mankind in its place. It's no accident that a preacher is the one who rescues the passengers of a capsized luxury liner in *The Poseidon Adventure* (1972). The genre experienced a renaissance just prior to the turn of the millennium with films in which erupting volcanoes threatened to destroy entire cities such as *Dante's Peak* (1996) and *Volcano* (1997), not to mention films in which Earth-bound meteorites endanger the entire future of the planet such as *Armageddon* and *Deep Impact* (1998). James Cameron's 1997 colossal blockbuster even gave new steam to the *Titanic*. One could describe this particular story as an independent disaster movie sub-genre. The tale has been filmed a thousand times over starting with a silent production that dates back to 1915 (*Titanic*). Subsequent versions appeared in 1943 and 1953.

:ause of both cataclysms, and in each case the impending danger can be :een a mile away, yet those in charge steer right to it. The icing on the cake ; that both events take place at a "premiere happening," one at a gala open- ng and the other during the maiden voyage.

The Towering Inferno, filmed in two actual San Francisco skyscrapers, he Bank of America Building and the Hyatt Regency Hotel, provides spec- acular disaster imagery, which one just can't simply watch and write off fter 9/11. This and its star-studded cast, featuring Paul Newman and Steve /lcQueen, two of the quintessential stars of the 70s, as well as dance legend red Astaire, led the 14-million-dollar film to become the box office smash f 1974. Nominated for eight Oscars, the film took home three, including Best iong, Cinematography and Editing.   HJK

LACOMBE, LUCIEN

Lacombe Lucien

1974 - FRANCE / FRG / ITALY - 137 MIN. - DRAMA

DIRECTOR LOUIS MALLE (1932–1995)
SCREENPLAY LOUIS MALLE, PATRICK MODIANO **DIRECTOR OF PHOTOGRAPHY** TONINO DELLI COLLI **EDITING** SUZANNE BARON
MUSIC ANDRÉ CLAVEAU, IRÈNE DE TREBERT, DJANGO REINHARDT with the "QUINTETTE DU HOT CLUB DE FRANCE"
PRODUCTION LOUIS MALLE, CLAUDE NEDJAR for VIDES-FILM, NOUVELLES ÉDITIONS DE FILMS, UNIVERSAL PICTURES
FRANCE, HALLELUJAH FILMS, HESSISCHER RUNDFUNK.

STARRING PIERRE BLAISE (Lucien), AURORE CLÉMENT (France Horn), HOLGER LÖWENADLER (Albert Horn), THERESE
GIEHSE (Grandmother Horn), STÉPHANE BOUY (Jean-Bernard), LOUMI IACOBESCO (Betty Beaulieu), RENÉ BOULOC
(Faure), PIERRE DECAZES (Aubert, the Barman), JEAN ROUGERIE (Tonin), CÉCILE RICARD (Marie, the Chambermaid).

"It's very strange... I can't seem to hate you completely."

Louis Malle described this film as his most important work of the 70s, and its meaning is disturbingly hard to pin down. There's something magical, almost idyllic about these sun-drenched images from the south of France in the year 1944. At the same time, the tragedy of the 17-year-old farmer's boy Lucien Lacombe (Pierre Blaise), who becomes a collaborator out of ignorance and moral weakness, is a shockingly clear-eyed study of a fascist character – in all its ambivalence. It's a brilliantly composed portrait in which every sequence is a key scene, in which the director has left nothing to chance. Yet the entire impact of the main character is the work of the actor who plays him. Pierre Blaise, it seems, was made to embody Lucien. He doesn't have to play him; he *is* him, a cruel child of nature who's moved by a whim to sign up as a Gestapo henchman. In fact, Blaise had never acted before. He was a boy from the area in which the film takes place, Malle's adopted country, and the director obviously chose him with care: he's crude, clumsy, apathetic, sensitive, not inclined to worry about good and evil – and

quite prepared to kill. No one had to teach him how to catch hares or chop the heads off chickens.

As in other Louis Malle films, the way the protagonists treat animals reflects the way they treat each other. Right at the start, Lucien shoots a bird in a tree, just for fun. Later, he strokes a dead horse, as softly as he can. The viewer's incomprehension in the face of such scenes derives from a kind of reflection that contradicts Lucien's nature; a nature that lost its innocence even before the greater events related in the film. Rejected by the Resistance as too young, this bored and politically indifferent casual laborer joins the "German police" – a horde of displaced Frenchmen lodging in a run-down hotel. Equipped with a pistol and an ID card, Lucien enjoys his power. When he sets eyes on the beautiful daughter of the Jewish tailor Horn, it's the start of a terrible game ruled by love, fear, and dependency. Lucien worms his way into the family's hiding place, until France (Aurore Clément), in equal measure fascinated and repelled by his cloddishness, lets him have his way

"Lucien is beguiled by the style in which the police maintain themselves: an elegant château, sleek automobiles, well-cut clothes, good food and drink, compliant women. More than the luxury, though, he likes the taste of power." *Time Magazine*

1 Live to tell: The 76-year-old actress Therese Giehse fled Germany in 1933.

2 A stitch in time: The Jewish tailor Horn (Holger Löwenadler) is at the service of collaborator Lucien (Pierre Blaise).

3 Fascist victim: Lucien's shady friend Jean-Bernard (Stéphane Bouy) is felled by the French Resistance.

4 The hills are alive: The idyllic south of France, Louis Malle's chosen home, is haunted by terror.

5 The power of love versus the love of power: A subtle interplay of sympathy and hatred, sexual attraction and fascist ideology.

with her. Horn (Holger Löwenadler), who can no longer bear the humiliation, gives himself up to the police. Together with an SS man, Lucien is sent to arrest France and her grandmother (Therese Giehse). Instead, he shoots the SS man. Finally, the three of them find refuge in an abandoned farmhouse; it's a return to the rural idyll – and, for the first time, a smile appears on Lucien's face. A fade-in tells us that Lucien Lacombe was court-martialled by the Resistance in October 1944, sentenced to death, and executed.

In 1974, in France, there was much about this film that was controversial; for example, that the Resistance is embodied by an arrogant schoolteacher, or that the collaborators are bourgeois bohemians, profiteers without conscience, strangers to any ideology. Yet the most shocking thing of all is the tender mixture of love and hatred the audience feels for Lucien. We are in the same position as the elderly Horn, who feels forced to confess: "It's

very strange… I can't seem to hate you completely." Malle disturbs our clear conscience with the subtle beauty of his images, softens our hearts with France's piano-playing, and adds moments of comedy with the fabulous Therese Giehse, who haunts the apartment like a grumbling gnome, never mentioning the horror at work. In Pierre Blaise, he has a rough diamond of an actor. The story of his casting is the key to the real mystery of *Lacombe, Lucien*. Used to obeying, the stubborn boy only went to the audition because his mother told him to. At first, he took no pleasure at all in working with the intellectual film crew. It was only after Malle told the entire team to treat him like Delon or Belmondo that he loosened up and came alive. As if he had only been waiting to lead the life of Lucien, he enjoyed his importance like a little king and felt accepted as what he was. In 1975, two years after the film was made, Pierre Blaise died in a car crash.   PB

THERESE GIEHSE   "I've been watching you," said Therese Giehse (1898–1975) to Louis Malle, after making *Lacombe, Lucien* (1974). "I think you should make a film in which the people don't speak." This was the inspiration to Malle's surrealist masterpiece *Black Moon* (1975), the last film in which the gnarled old woman appeared. The legendary theater actress had always created her own roles in this way – for example Mother Courage in Bertolt Brecht's play. Brecht described her as "the greatest actress in Europe." For Friedrich Dürrenmatt's *The Physicists*, she rewrote entire scenes. Born in Munich into a Jewish family, she appeared on stage for the first time in 1920 – against the express wishes of her mother: "Look, Therese, this is all wrong for you. You're not the least bit beautiful, what do you expect from the theater?" But her uncompromising interpretations of proletarian roles soon brought Therese Giehse acclaim. Among her admirers were Thomas Mann and his family, with whom she had a lifelong friendship. In 1933, she formed a political cabaret with Klaus and Erika Mann: shortly after its formation, however, "Die Pfeffermühle" (The Peppermill) was forced into exile in Zürich. At the Schauspielhaus Theater in Zurich, Therese Giehse enjoyed her greatest successes. On screen, this born comedienne was mostly to be seen in lighter films after 1932, but she did frighten an entire generation as Frau Oberin in *Girls in Uniform* (*Mädchen in Uniform* / *Jeunes filles en uniforme*, 1958) alongside Romy Schneider. After celebrated appearances in Berlin and Munich, Therese Giehse died in her home town in 1975. In accordance with her own wishes, she was buried in Zurich.

LENNY

1974 - USA - 111 MIN. - DRAMA

DIRECTOR BOB FOSSE (1927–1987)
SCREENPLAY JULIAN BARRY, based on his play of the same name DIRECTOR OF PHOTOGRAPHY BRUCE SURTEES EDITING ALAN HEIM
MUSIC RALPH BURNS PRODUCTION MARVIN WORTH for MARVIN WORTH PRODUCTIONS, UNITED ARTISTS.

STARRING DUSTIN HOFFMAN (Lenny Bruce), VALERIE PERRINE (Honey Bruce), JAN MINER (Sally Marr), STANLEY BECK (Artie Silver), FRANKIE MAN (Baltimore Comedian), RASHEL NOVIKOFF (Aunt Mema), GARY MORTON (Sherman Hart), GUY RENNIE (Jack Goldstein), MICHELE YONGE (Nurse), MONROE MYERS (Judge).

IFF CANNES 1975 AWARD for BEST ACTRESS (Valerie Perrine).

"I really dig what they do with a homosexual in this country. They put him into a prison with a lot of other men. That's really good punishment."

The opening text says it best. "It is ironic that he was prosecuted and persecuted for acts and language which have become a part of today's life." The acts for which entertainer Lenny Bruce, the subject of this picture, was arrested countless times over included speaking openly about sexuality, racial discrimination and other taboos, topics that first became accepted topics of "polite conversation" during the 1970s. Lenny Bruce, aka Leonard Alfred Schneider, was a Jewish stand-up comedian who become a countercultural icon after his death in 1966. Books were written movies were made and Bob Dylan even wrote a song about him. Bob Fosse's film, *Lenny*, was also a part of the movement honoring him, which reached its height in the early 1970s and saw a resurgence in 1998 with Robert B. Weide's documentary *Lenny Bruce: Swear to Tell the Truth*. These examinations into the recent

and slightly more distant past of the 1950s and 60s cast light on a man who took the stage in the guise of a comic and vocalized his thoughts on the mendacity and bigotry of society.

Bob Fosse endows his film with unusual character by telling the story from three angles. The people who knew Lenny Bruce best – played masterfully by Dustin Hoffman – his wife (Valerie Perrine), his manager (Stanley Beck) and his mother (Jan Miner) talk about their relationships with him in taped interviews. Flashbacks illustrate the anecdotes we hear, until we finally see Lenny performing on stage, letting us in on details of his life. The film's visuals are luxuriously photographic. Shot in black and white, with low-key atmospheric lighting giving the piece an almost Film Noir look, the movie builds a bridge between the time in which Lenny lived and the 1970s. Before

1 From run-of-the-mill comic to living legend: Lenny Bruce (Dustin Hoffman) brought topics such as sex and race into his irreverent stand-up performances.

1 From run-of-the-mill comic to living legend: Lenny Bruce (Dustin Hoffman) brought topics such as sex and race into his irreverent stand-up performances.

2 Love me or leave me: Honey (Valerie Perrine) is a mother and a junkie, a whore and a saint.

3 Bringing down the house: Arrested for obscenity on stage, Lenny's struggle against the state begins.

"A technical masterpiece. The camerawork, the editing, and the use of light and shade make *Lenny* the best black-and-white film in recent years." *Die Zeit*

our eyes, this "true story" is pieced together like a mosaic. *Lenny* makes use of a complex narrative structure that draws on various forms of documentary-like actual interviews to bestow an added degree of credibility. These devices prove the point that it is often subjective accounts that make a story interesting.

The flashbacks start in 1951, just as Lenny makes the acquaintance of his wife-to-be, Honey, who works as a stripper at a night-club where she sticks out her tits for adoring male fans. At the time, Lenny is working a stand-up comedian, complete with jokes about mother-in-laws and cheap imitations that gets a few chuckles out of his audience. In an era when Doris Day was the model of female perfection, Lenny inhabited a shadow world of jazz artists and drugs. Honey recounts their relationship, their marriage and

the happy period that followed. We witness their duo act, Lenny's first heckler during a performance, the serious car accident, his infidelity and, above all else, Honey's drug addiction. When their child is born in 1955, Honey's habit prevents her from being able to care for the baby properly and becomes her undoing. Divorce seems inevitable, and, when she is charged with possession of illegal drugs, Lenny takes their daughter away from her. As Honey pays her dues behind bars, Lenny's fame grows. His stage appearances create sensations in the clubs he works. He is the first entertainer to openly discuss homosexuality and racial discrimination. Terms like "cock sucker," which were never before used in public, and whose use was even strictly prohibited by the government, can be heard in his acts. He is arrested an infinite number of times and placed before the court. Lenny is obscene, but

5

4 No smoke without fire: Lenny Bruce emerged as a counter-cultural icon of the 70s. Bob Fosse's film pays him tribute.

5 Just what the doctor ordered: After his wife's accident, Lenny has a brief fling with a nurse (Michelle Yonge).

6 While Honey serves jail time for possessing narcotics, Lenny's fame soars to new heights.

he uses obscenity like a weapon. The film recreates his live acts, incorporates many of his most famous lines and constantly casts an eye onto the audience, their almost ecstatic reactions – images which tell us much more about just how outrageous his language was at the time than his actual words themselves. Nonetheless, illness and detainment by the police and criminal justice system destroy his career. His fortune is lost in legal fees, medical costs and, of course, his addiction. In 1966, he dies of a heroin overdose.

Although the film depicts Lenny Bruce as a martyr for free speech and a man who led a political struggle for leftist values, it by no means glamorizes him. His often sadistic treatment of Honey, his drug abuse and taste for luxury are all at least referred to in the picture. Lenny Bruce had a thunderous impact on people because he was decidedly different, insane and uncompromising. He lived the life he talked about on stage. He also knew exactly what role he served in society. "You guys need chumps like me to tell you when you've gone too far."

KI

"Hoffman excels on the cinematic stage. Fueled by Bruce's material, he jumps into the character and takes off for the stars."

U.S. commercial for the movie

BOB FOSSE

Bob Fosse's film career was relatively short-lived. Though he only directed pictures between 1969 and 1983, the few that came about under his leadership made him known to a larger audience than that familiar with the work he produced in his actual medium, the stage. The dancer/choreographer achieved his greatest cinematic success with the movie musical *Cabaret* (1972). The film turned Liza Minnelli into an overnight sensation and made Oscar winners of them both. Fosse was famous for his distinct style of choreography. His numbers showcased relatively few dancers and moves that created the illusion of a slow motion collective. His routines made human bodies virtually vanish, replaced by individual appendages that seemed to take on lives of their own. Born the son of a vaudeville entertainer in 1927, Robert Louis Fosse went on tour with his own dance numbers at just thirteen years old. During high school, he appeared in smaller Chicago clubs as a tap dancer, sharing the stage with a female stripper and a stand up comedian. After the end of the Second World War he found work as a dancer on Broadway. It was at about this time that he got his start in the movie business. Nonetheless, after playing smaller roles in just three films, including *Kiss Me Kate* (1953), he had to accept that his Hollywood aspirations – "I had fantasies of becoming the next Fred Astaire" – were just a pipe dream. Working back on Broadway, he eventually got the chance to choreograph his own pieces. He was soon stomping out one hit after the next like *Damn Yankees*, *New Girl in Town* and *Sweet Charity*. In 1969, he turned this last production into a modestly successful film with Shirley MacLaine and Sammy Davis Jr. However, his real breakthrough in the movie industry came in 1972 with *Cabaret*. 1973 was the year that brought him most acclaim. He won an Oscar for *Cabaret*, the Tony for Best Broadway Musical for *Pippin* and an Emmy for the TV Special *Liza with A Z*. His astounding success afforded him the chance to direct his most personal project, *Lenny* (1974), a tribute to his friend Lenny Bruce. The autobiographical picture *All That Jazz* (1979) and *Star 80* (1983), the tragic story of the 1980 Playboy "Playmate of the Year," Dorothy Stratten, proved to be his last pictures. He withdrew from film and devoted himself exclusively to the stage. In 1987, Bob Fosse died of a heart attack.

6

THE GODFATHER – PART II

1974 - USA - 200 MIN. - GANGSTER FILM, DRAMA

DIRECTOR FRANCIS FORD COPPOLA (*1939)

SCREENPLAY FRANCIS FORD COPPOLA, MARIO PUZO, based on his novel *THE GODFATHER* **DIRECTOR OF PHOTOGRAPHY** GORDON WILLIS **EDITING** BARRY MALKIN, RICHARD MARKS, PETER ZINNER **MUSIC** NINO ROTA, CARMINE COPPOLA **PRODUCTION** FRANCIS FORD COPPOLA for THE COPPOLA COMPANY, PARAMOUNT PICTURES.

STARRING AL PACINO (Michael Corleone), ROBERT DUVALL (Tom Hagen), ROBERT DE NIRO (Vito Corleone), DIANE KEATON (Kay Adams-Corleone), JOHN CAZALE (Frederico "Fredo" Corleone), TALIA SHIRE (Constanzia "Connie" Corleone-Johnson), LEE STRASBERG (Hyman Roth), MICHAEL V. GAZZO (Frankie Pentangeli), G. D. SPRADLIN (Senator Pat Geary), RICHARD BRIGHT (Al Neri), ORESTE BALDINI (Young Vito Corleone), GASTONE MOSHIN (Don Fanucci).

ACADEMY AWARDS 1974 OSCARS for BEST FILM (Francis Ford Coppola, Gray Frederickson, Fred Roos), BEST DIRECTOR (Francis Ford Coppola), BEST SUPPORTING ACTOR (Robert De Niro), BEST ADAPTED SCREENPLAY (Francis Ford Coppola, Mario Puzo), BEST MUSIC (Nino Rota, Carmine Coppola), and BEST SET DESIGN (Dean Tavoularis, Angelo P. Graham, George R. Nelson).

"There are many things my father taught me here in this room. He taught me: keep your friends close, but your enemies closer."

Francis Ford Coppola's film epic *The Godfather – Part II* forms a narrative frame around its predecessor, *The Godfather* (1972), one of the most successful films of the 1970s. With part two of the story of the rise and fall of a New York Mafia family, Coppola achieved much more than just a continuation of the first film. He made a self-contained masterpiece that was awarded six Oscars and which, according to many critics, even surpassed its predecessor in several ways.

In *The Godfather – Part II*, two narrative strands unfold in parallel. The first strand begins in Sicily at the dawn of the twentieth century: the young Vito Andolini (Oreste Baldini) from the village Corleone is the only member of his family to survive the Mafia's wholesale extinction of his clan. Friends of the family place him on a boat to America – his only chance of survival. Arriving on Ellis Island in New York, Vito, whom the immigration officials have given the surname Corleone, looks at the Statue of Liberty through the barred window in the quarantine station. Shimmering in the sunlight, it embodies the American Dream shared by the immigrants. Years later, when the adult Vito (now played by Robert De Niro) has his own family, he initially tries to make his way with honorable jobs in New

"This is a bicentennial picture that doesn't insult the intelligence. It's an epic vision of the corruption of America. (...) Within a scene Coppola is controlled and unhurried, yet he has a gift for igniting narrative, and the exploding effects keep accumulating. About midway, I began to feel that the film was expanding in my head like a soft bullet." *The New Yorker*

York's immigrant quarter, Little Italy. But even there, the Mafia has already struck powerful roots. Vito's rise to "Godfather" only begins after he successfully defends himself against the money-hungry Don Fanucci (Gastone Moshin).

The second narrative level picks up the story in 1958, a few years after the end of the first film. Vito Corleone's son Michael (Al Pacino), who has run the family business since his father's death, now lives in Lake Tahoe, Nevada, where he is attempting to legitimize and legalize his activities in Las Vegas. He is also beginning to expand them to Miami and Cuba with the help of the gangster Hyman Roth (Lee Strasberg). Michael has adopted

the business principles of his father. One of them is "the family..." Another is "Keep your friends close..."

Family members and business partners assemble at a large celebration that Michael arranges for his son's Communion. While the guests celebrate outside, Michael holds court in his shadowy study and greets the members of "the family." Here it becomes apparent that Michael's enemies really do stand closer than he himself believed. Michael, consummate briber of high-profile politicians and head of a family business that "is more powerful than U.S. Steel," as he will later say, is forced to watch as his attempts to hold the family together do nothing but destroy it.

1. Put your head on my shoulder: The role of Michael Corleone turned Al Pacino (pictured here with John Cazale) into a Hollywood headliner, who was soon renowned for his bravado performances in the most unconventional of movies.

2. The UN security counsel: Except these guys have the power to make things happen.

3. The actor's studio: Still willing to hit below the belt, legendary acting coach Lee Strasberg (left) appears in *The Godfather – Part II* as gangster Hyman Roth.

4. Let's get one thing straight… Al Pacino doesn't have to beat a brilliant performance out of Robert Duvall.

5. Italian made and tailored: Michael Corleone stylishly epitomized the crassest side of American individuality.

At the end of the film – his wife, Kay (Diane Keaton) has long since left him – we see Michael Corleone sitting in the garden, alone with his memories and seething with hate. Moments before, during his mother's wake, he gave the order to kill his own brother, Fredo (John Cazale), who like so many others, has betrayed him. The autumn leaves fall from the trees, and through Al Pacino's eyes we stare directly into "the heart of darkness."

Coppola's sequel contrasts the personalities of father and son, weaving a tale of morals, trust, and loyalty, betrayal, and vengeance. Vito is a respectable "paisan" from Sicily whose surroundings force him to adapt to the criminal lifestyle. He becomes powerful by earning the respect and trust of his friends. His son Michael is born into the Mafia and as the Don, must learn how to deal with the responsibility that has been handed

6

down and the power that comes with it. He trusts no one and even makes enemies within the family. But different as the two men are, their stories resemble each other in the fact that both must discover what it means to be a gangster.

The Godfather – Part II is a modern classic. This is predominantly thanks to Francis Ford Coppola, who in continuing the saga accepted a difficult task and rose to the occasion. He was assisted by an eminent ensemble of actors led by Al Pacino and Robert De Niro. De Niro was awarded an Oscar for his performance. Al Pacino shows that the Michael Corleone of The Godfather has become an entirely different person – a self-righteous man who harshly and bitterly attempts to achieve his objectives. Robert De Niro on the other hand is a young embodiment of Marlon Brando, in everything from his manner to the coarse, subdued voice. The meandering story, with

its multiple tangents, also gives the other characters significant space. John Cazale in his Cain-role as Michael's humiliated brother, Talia Shire as Michael's sister, Connie, the black sheep of the family (she was also nominated for an Oscar), and Robert Duvall, who once again plays the loyal family attorney, Tom Hagen.

The historic décor and costumes are meticulously exact, and the camera work of Gordon Willis – who filmed both the first and later the last part of the trilogy – captures the transformation of the family by switching from sepia-colored tones (in the flashbacks) to more sinister hues for the present day. After the success of The Godfather, which he assumed as a commissioned work, Coppola was able to secure full control over the second film. And it shows: The Godfather – Part II is quieter, more emotional, and more sinister than the first part. It is more authentic. It is Coppola. APO

LEE STRASBERG An actor, director, theater director, and drama teacher, Lee Strasberg was born on November 17, 1901 in the Austro-Hungarian town of Budzanow, which is now in the Ukraine. In 1909 he came to New York with his parents. In 1930 he founded the Moscow Artist Theater which influenced the critical Group Theater with Harold Clurman and Clifford Odets. Here he began to realize his idea of theater acting, in which "emotional memory" plays a central role and the actors don't fake emotions, but rather identify with the character's emotions.

At the beginning of the 40s Strasberg traveled to Hollywood to learn the art of filmmaking. But he was unable to make it as a director, and was convinced by Elia Kazan in 1948 to assume the artistic direction of the Actors Studio in New York, which was founded in 1947. He served as artistic director from 1951 until his death in 1982. He is considered one of the most important acting teachers in the world, and his "method" is still taught at theater schools. The stars he taught include Marlon Brando, James Dean, Steve McQueen, Dustin Hoffman, Robert De Niro, Jack Nicholson, Jane Fonda, Anne Bancroft, Ellen Burstyn, Al Pacino, Harvey Keitel, Marilyn Monroe, and many others.

Strasberg gave acting lessons, but also appeared in film roles. His portrayal of Hyman Roth in Francis Ford Coppola's The Godfather – Part II (1974) earned him a 1975 Oscar Nomination as best supporting actor. Lee Strasberg died in February 1982.

"I don't feel I have to wipe everybody out, Tom. Just my enemies."

Film quote: Michael Corleone

6 A chicken in every pot and a car in every garage: On occasion, the all-American Corleone family also sports a horse in every bed.

7 Calling the shots: Michael Corleone can tell you firsthand, it doesn't matter how you walk as long as you carry a big stick.

THE TEXAS CHAIN SAW MASSACRE

1974 - USA - 84 MIN. - HORROR FILM

DIRECTOR TOBE HOOPER (*1943)
SCREENPLAY KIM HENKEL, TOBE HOOPER DIRECTOR OF PHOTOGRAPHY DANIEL PEARL EDITING LARRY CARROLL, SALLYE RICHARDSON
MUSIC TOBE HOOPER, WAYNE BELL PRODUCTION LOU PERAINO, TOBE HOOPER for VORTEX.

STARRING MARILYN BURNS (Sally Hardesty), ALLEN DANZIGER (Jerry), PAUL A. PARTAIN (Franklin Hardesty), WILLIAM VAIL (Kirk), TERI MCMINN (Pamela), EDWIN NEAL (Hitchhiker), JIM SIEDOW (Old Man), GUNNAR HANSEN (Leatherface), JOHN DUGAN (Grandfather), JOHN HENRY FAULK (Narrator), JOHN LARROQUETTE (Voice of Narrator).

"My old grandpa is the best killer there ever was."

The Texas Chain Saw Massacre begins like a documentary, creating a dense, claustrophobic atmosphere. A blend-in promises the disclosure of one of the most unbelievable crimes in American history and the ensuing sequence leaves no doubt. Darkness, a sinister electronic sound with intermittent hacking and panting sounds, illuminated by flashing images of decaying body parts – followed by a radio report on the desecration of a Texan cemetery. We know that the idyll that follows will end in disaster. Pamela (Teri McMinn), Kirk (William Vail), Sally (Marilyn Burns), and her wheelchair-bound brother Franklin (Paul A. Partain) drive through this area. Short on gas, the friends decide to spend the night in the old house of Sally's grandparents.

But next to the partially dilapidated building live multiple generations of an unemployed butcher family who have developed into cannibals to survive.

The youths fall victim to "Leatherface" (Gunnar Hansen) and his chainsaw and in the end it is only the heroine Sally Hardesty, who in a breathtaking showdown fights for her life and – covered in blood – is ultimately able to escape.

Despite New York's renowned Museum of Modern Art purchase of The Texas Chain Saw Massacre, the film still repeatedly falls victim to censors. Watch it for a second time, and it becomes surprisingly apparent that contrast to other works of the genre, dismembered body parts and organs of mutilations are often not seen directly, but rather disappear behind doors or out of the camera's sight. Nonetheless, Tobe Hooper was still able to depict violence and make it absolutely palpable. There is no psychological or sociological commentary to create distance from what is portrayed or offer an explanation for the overwhelming brutality. The last half hour is particularly

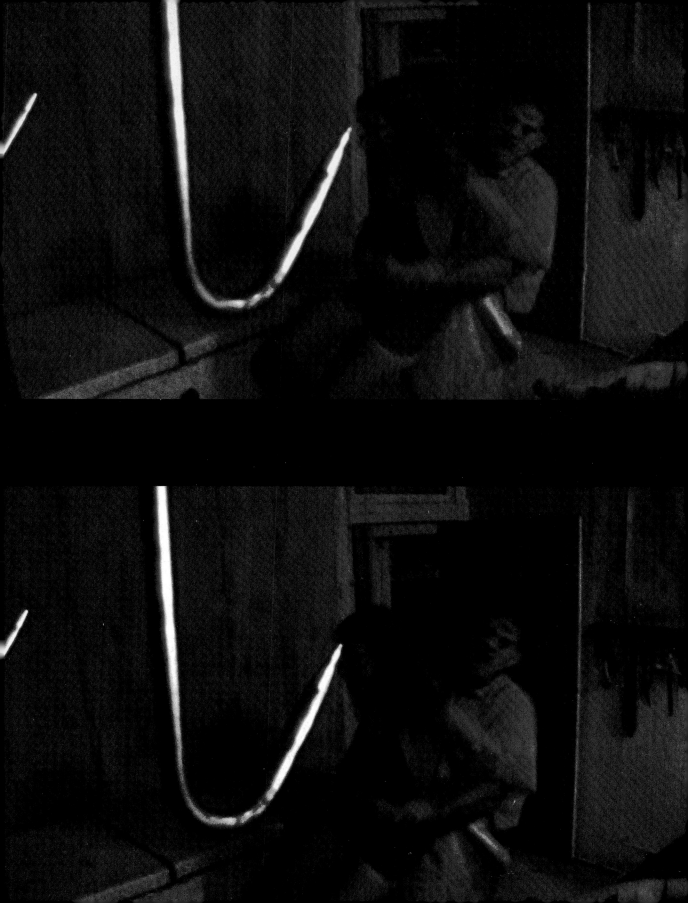

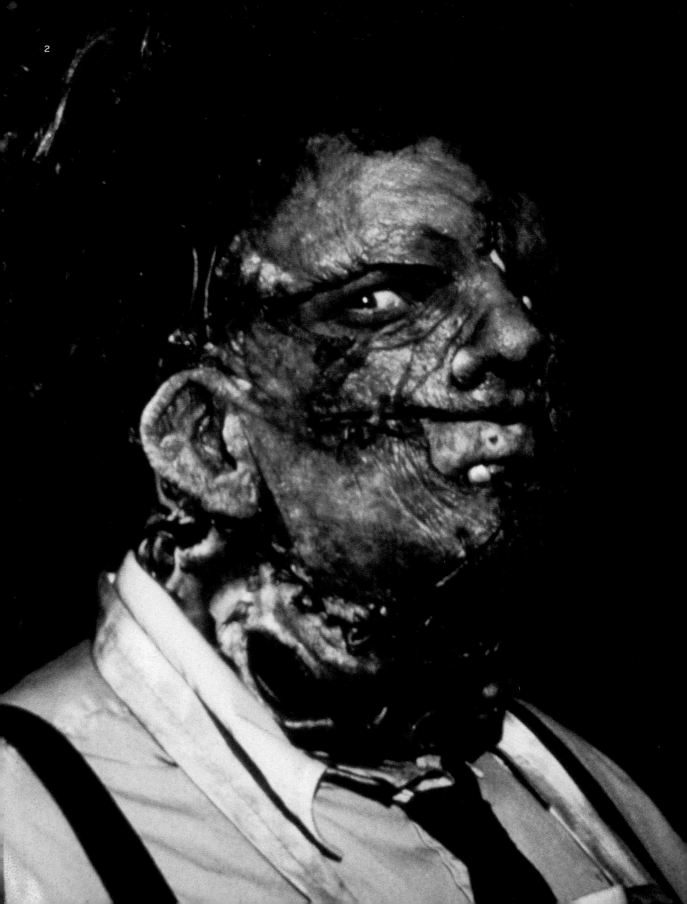

1   Cannibals' kitchen: The home as abattoir.   2   Leatherface (Gunnar Hansen) in one of his masks   3   When the chainsaw shrieks… be very afraid.
                                                    made of human skin.

"Rather than choosing violence as its theme, *The Texas Chain Saw Massacre* makes violence tangible. Tobe Hooper doesn't analyze the causes of violence. He shows us what it feels like to run right into it."

Ulrich von Berg

"The monster is the family, one of the great composite monsters of the American cinema." *Film Comment*

4 Family Values in the American South.   **5** Colder than the grave. Take a look in the freezer.   **6** Conflict management, country style.

LEATHERFACE – SERIAL KILLERS IN FILM

Fritz Lang hunted a serial killer in *M* (1931), but it wasn't until the 1970s that this theme gained an immense popularity. One of the most notorious characters is Leatherface, who hunts his victims wearing a roughly sewn mask of tanned human skin and a butcher's apron. In fact, he wears three different masks. Aside from the killing mask, one is of an old woman, and the other is of a made-up woman, worn when he cooks for the family in his mother role. Whereas in *The Silence of the Lambs* (1991), Jame Gumb also wanted to slip into another skin, patching together a female shell out of the remains of his victims, Leatherface's disguise indicates neither sexual fantasies nor the motive behind his murders. His identity remains a riddle and consequently "the evil" behind this spooky masquerade – as was the case of Michael Myers in *Halloween* (1978) – is not given a true face. Leatherface, who has long since advanced to an international cult figure, is on the one hand a projection surface for subconscious fears and – on the other hand – perfect for identification: in the film, parallels are suggested between the outsider of the group, Franklin, and Leatherface.

stark in its transgression of the boundaries of reason, as the violence is not, as is more usual, diluted with entertaining or aesthetic components. Instead, the audience is increasingly forced to identify with the victim.

When the film was released in America, it was immediately associated with the atrocities of the Vietnam War. Indeed, Tobe Hooper drastically deals with the collective trauma in America – touching on true events like the crimes of the serial killer Ed Gein or the "Manson Family." As in Wes Craven's *Last House on the Left* (1972), it is not monsters or supernatural beings, but rather humans who become cold-blooded murderers. Though Leatherface is surely one the most famous screen killers, the real monster on a metaphorical level is the American family.

Sally's grandparents' house, and that of their neighbors, is a haunted house with forbidden rooms that are not to be entered. As in a fairy tale, unintentionally breaking a rule results in death or sadistic tortures – tortures that often evoke memories of helplessness or nerve-wracking pranks from childhood or adolescence. Several surreal sequences have the structure of nightmares, for example when Sally flees from Leatherface into a large forest and, although she is much faster, she is unable to escape her pursuer. Though the Sally Hardesty character is a female long at the mercy of her sadistic tormentor, Hooper's dramatization avoids making her an object of sexual desire. When she tearfully offers to do anything the family ask of her, they respond with sinister cackling. Later, Sally displays an extraordinary strength. Twice she jumps through windowpanes Western-style, and ultimately succeeds in escaping the clutches of this most monstrous of families.

PLB

A WOMAN UNDER THE INFLUENCE

1974 - USA - 155 MIN. - DRAMA

DIRECTOR JOHN CASSAVETES (1929–1989)
SCREENPLAY JOHN CASSAVETES DIRECTOR OF PHOTOGRAPHY MITCH BREIT, CALEB DESCHANEL EDITING DAVID ARMSTRONG, TOM CORNWELL, ROBERT HEFFERNAN MUSIC BO HARWOOD PRODUCTION SAM SHAW for FACES.

STARRING PETER FALK (Nick Longhetti), GENA ROWLANDS (Mabel Longhetti), FRED DRAPER (George Mortensen), LADY ROWLANDS (Martha Mortensen), KATHERINE CASSAVETES (Mama Longhetti), MATTHEW LABORTEAUX (Angelo Longhetti), MATTHEW CASSEL (Tony Longhetti), CHRISTINA GRISANTI (Maria Longhetti), O. G. DUNN (Garson Cross), MARIO GALLO (Harold Jensen), EDDIE SHAW (Doctor Zepp).

> "Tell me what you want me to be.
> How you want me to be. I can be that.
> I can be anything. Just tell me, Nicky!"

Two adults try to play house and fail miserably. Two actors infuse their roles with every imaginable contour of human dignity and disgrace, taking their audience hostage for two-and-a-half hours as they unleash the demons of Pandora's box on their rocky marriage.

This was formula that led to one of the greatest cinematic triumphs for independent film-making icon John Cassavetes. In a riveting, powerhouse performance, Gena Rowlands plays a woman on the verge of a mental breakdown. For a long time now, there haven't been words to express what Mabel Longhetti has been feeling, and so she has substituted them with an arsenal of gesticulations and nervous ticks, mimicry and pantomime. She combats the stress of her daily life, which confines her like an iron chastity belt, with effective hand movements, eye rolls and jerking jaws. These are the mouthed screams of a desperate woman; they pound the audience with an utter devastation that is at times hysterically funny. Peter Falk plays Mabel's husband Nick, a simple blue-collar worker, who has as little control over his words as he does over his own body. He is someone who hollers. His gestures die before completion, often ending in an admonishing pointer finger, or, as on one occasion in the film, in physical abuse. Three children stand in the crossfire as man and wife frantically grasp at straws in the hopes of

pinpointing what originally made them fall in love. The couple are certain of their love for one another, yet they have no idea how to go about loving each other.

A Woman Under the Influence was originally conceived for the stage. The idea was scrapped because seasoned theater veteran Gena Rowlands didn't think she was capable of exerting such an extreme amount of emotional force night after night in front of a live audience. And so, with just a dialog script and no true screenplay, an intimate film was shot almost exclusively within the four walls of a small family residence. No shots were predetermined. The camera was free to roam at will, thus partially accounting for the piece's almost documentary feel. Of course, this atmospheric touch is more the result of Cassavetes' unique directing style, chiseled in diehard method acted techniques. This is illuminated in the film by an act of associative thought processes reflected in Mabel's behavior such as when she improvises the "dying swan" from *Swan Lake*. Here, she not only takes on Cassevetes' dual role of actor-director, but also that of prima ballerina and choreographer. In another scene, the oblivious Nick surprises her at the door with ten work buddies and she instantly transforms herself into a June Cleaver on amphetamines, whipping up a mess hall portion of spaghetti and

1

2

3

1   How much longer will Mabel Longhetti (Gena Rowlands) be able to ward off her nervous breakdown?

2   Loving you is easy 'cos you're beautiful… Mabel's children are her only sanctuary.

3   Was that lonely woman really me? Mabel drinks away her sorrows at a local bar…and falls into the arms of a total stranger.

4   Life of the party: Construction worker, Nick (Peter Falk) loves his wife, but is oblivious to her needs.

5   Big boys don't cry: But they have been known to beat their wives…

"Mabel's not crazy. She's unusual. She's not crazy, so don't say she's crazy!" *Film quote: Nick*

doing her best "hostess with the mostest" imitation. Mabel is emotionally electrified when one of the guys breaks into an aria and she implores yet another of the work crew to dance with her. She refuses to take no for an answer, prompting Nick to abruptly silence her. Her spirit and charm have, nonetheless, a miraculous impact on children. Yet upon seeing how the free-spirited Mabel allows the children to run naked through the house, one neighborhood father is convinced that she's off her rocker. Mabel, on the other hand, simply can't understand why he too doesn't just let loose and dance.

Observation of the pictures taken of Cassavetes on the set reveals the actor-director manifesting the same gestures as Mabel, from the ticking Cheshire Cat grin, to the chummy yet invasive hooking an arm around some-

one's shoulder while giving direction. The filmmaker readily encouraged his cast to search for authentic feelings and means of expression that often broke with Hollywood conventions. The product is a family drama and love story, whose tale itself also provides a map of the film's actual genesis.

Be that as it may, the real world is not run according to these rules; it adheres rather to the masculine leadership archetypes seen in Nick. Mabel, as well as all she represents, is too prone to the type of nervous breakdowns that Cassavetes often almost drove his team to. At one point, Nick just stands by and watches as his wife is institutionalized. Completely at a loss as a parent without her, he lets his children sip his beer on one of their family outings. When Mabel is released from the psychiatric hospital six months later, we see how all of his attempts to force his family into neat little roles have failed.

4

JOHN CASSAVETES

With his directorial debut, *Shadows* (1959), John Cassavetes (1929–1989) established himself as a permanent fixture in the world of indy-film-making. Today's independent director has him to thank for making it possible to shoot a movie without stepping into financial quicksand. Cassavetes was born in New York in 1929 to Greek immigrant parents. He used his acting to raise funds for his directing projects, appearing in front of the camera in such films as *The Killers* (1964), *The Dirty Dozen* (1967) and *Rosemary's Baby* (1968). Friends and family often played a dual role in Cassavetes' works. Despite the little he could pay them, the actor-director received a high degree of commitment and dedication. Thespians like Seymour Cassel, Peter Falk, Ben Gazzara as well as producer Al Ruban were on board for some of his most ambitious undertakings like *Husbands*, (1970), *Minnie and Moskowitz* (1971), *A Woman Under the Influence* (1974) and *The Killing of a Chinese Bookie* (1976). Gena Rowlands married Cassavetes in 1954 and portrayed the leading roles in many of his pictures such as in *Gloria* (1980). Although Cassavetes' pictures cover a wide range of genres, his constant themes remained individuality conveyed through unforgettable characters prone to double standards, the suffocating mechanisms of conventionality and the full expression of a given personality. Cassavetes is the idol of a long list of cutting-edge filmmakers like Larry Clark of *Kids* fame (1995), and *Happiness* director Todd Solondz (1998).

lick packs the house full of family and friends to welcome home his "healthy wife" in a gung ho effort to "have a party!" Not to be overlooked in this film is that Nick is not one ounce less out of his mind than Mabel. His relentless need to prove his masculinity leads to disaster time after time, and he appears incapable of recognizing this.

Nonetheless, Cassavetes has no intention of pinning the blame on either of them. The film's leitmotif is much more wrapped up in Nick's schizophrenic and seemingly impossible plea to "just be yourself!" – a philosophy that is possibly to blame for the break-up of his marriage. Cassavetes' own take on the matter shed a bit more light on the subject: "I don't believe that Mabel's collapse is a social problem. It is rooted in personal relationships. Someone can love you and still drive you insane."   PB

5

THE GREAT GATSBY

1974 - USA - 144 MIN. - LITERARY ADAPTATION, DRAMA

DIRECTOR JACK CLAYTON (1921–1995)
SCREENPLAY FRANCIS FORD COPPOLA, based on the novel of the same name by F. SCOTT FITZGERALD **DIRECTOR OF PHOTOGRAPHY** DOUGLAS SLOCOMBE **EDITING** TOM PRIESTLEY **MUSIC** NELSON RIDDLE **PRODUCTION** DAVID MERRICK for NEWDON PRODUCTIONS, PARAMOUNT PICTURES.

STARRING ROBERT REDFORD (Jay Gatsby), MIA FARROW (Daisy Buchanan), BRUCE DERN (Tom Buchanan), KAREN BLACK (Myrtle Wilson), SCOTT WILSON (George Wilson), SAM WATERSTON (Nick Carraway), LOIS CHILES (Jordan Baker), HOWARD DA SILVA (Wolfsheim), ROBERTS BLOSSOM (Mr. Gatz), EDWARD HERRMANN (Klipspringer).

ACADEMY AWARDS 1974 OSCAR for BEST MUSIC (Nelson Riddle), and BEST COSTUMES (Theoni V. Aldredge).

"Rich girls don't marry poor boys."

No one knows for sure who Jay Gatsby really is. Nick Carraway (Sam Waterston), a New York stockbroker, has been hearing the most incredible rumors about the new resident on the island of West Egg. Allegedly, he's earned his money on the black market and someone has even died at his hand. One thing's for sure: Gatsby (Robert Redford) has amassed an insurmountable fortune. He lives in a mansion that eclipses the rest of the affluent city's visible wealth, and has gone so far as to build a fun park on the grounds of his estate. Nick looks on as countless cars pull up for his extravagant parties night after night, where guests dance the Charleston, drink champagne and have a wild time until sunrise. We have arrived in the Roaring Twenties, the Jazz Age, an era wedged between the First World War and the onset of the Great Depression in 1929. British director Jack Clayton, whose previous films *Room at the Top* (1959) and *The Innocents* (1961) had met with success, pulled out all the stops to assure that his big screen interpretation of F. Scott Fitzgerald's 1925 classic novel, *The Great Gatsby*, would perfectly recapture the fashion, atmosphere and intricacies of the age. The pastel gowns are hypnotically elegant, and the classic roadsters a monument to bygone decadence. Riding the wave of 1970s period pieces, *The Great Gatsby* is a

full-fledged study in nostalgia. Despite this, a misleading advertising campaign that marketed the piece as a great romance meant that film's reception was disappointing. The screenplay, written by Francis Ford Coppola, wh enjoyed a tremendous triumph that same year with *The Godfather – Part* (1974), can also be cited as somewhat problematic. Although it large remained true to Fitzgerald's book, it proved impossible to bring his litera devices to life on screen. Thus, as with many adaptations of great works literature, there are moments that take on both a shallow and artificial ton Previous attempts to turn the book into a movie had met with a similar fat including a silent version from 1926 and a better-known 1949 movie wi Alan Ladd in the title role.

As in the novel, we are soon able to see past the alluring façade that Jay Gatsby to the broken man beyond. He is someone who has allowed a impossible dream to trap him in the past. Nick quickly discovers that Gatsb throws his parties for the sole purpose of winning the affections of Nick cousin Daisy (Mia Farrow), who has held his heart for years. She is married a man named Tom Buchanan (Bruce Dern), and the two of them live with the young daughter in the neighboring town of East Egg. Unlike West Egg, th

"The aim was to capture the spirit of the book, Fitzgerald's masterly evocation of the lifestyle of the rich and famous in the Roaring Twenties. And indeed, the formula romance + nostalgia + advertising campaign does seem to equal success." *Berliner Morgenpost*

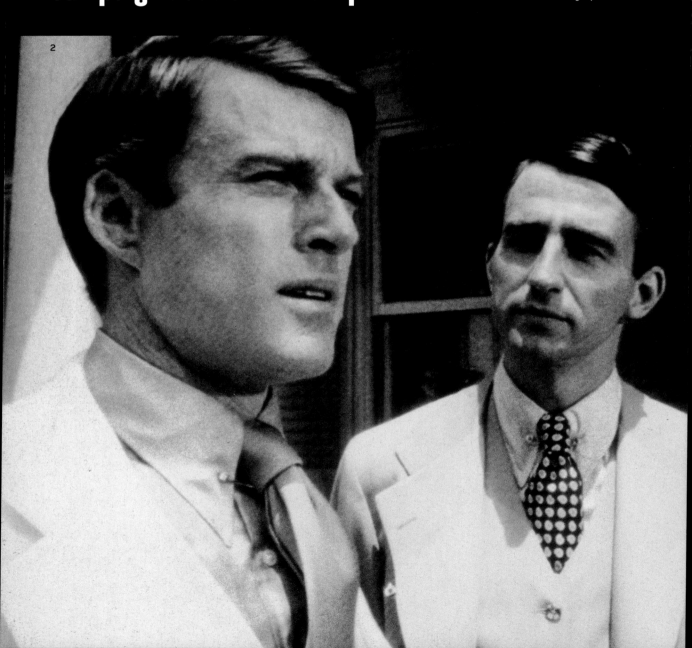

2

1 Bathtub gin and all that jazz: The film is a loving reconstruction of the fashions and frolics of the Roaring Twenties.

2 One-track mind: Jay Gatsby (Robert Redford) is haunted by the dream of winning back his first love.

3 Roses are red and Jordan is blue: Francis Ford Coppola's script stays true to the novel, but its depth is inevitably lost.

community represents old money and establishment. It has been eight years since Gatsby last saw Daisy; he was an army officer with no money at the time, and she was a poor little rich girl. His accumulated mountain of status and collateral exists for the sole purpose of sweeping Daisy off her feet and winning her back.

Everything seems to go according to plan. After an arranged rendezvous at Nick's residence, the two lovers get to know each other a bit better. Daisy is bowled over by the opulence of Gatsby's palatial manor, whose neoclassical grandeur seems incomprehensible even for the world of multi-millionaires. The plot soon unfolds into a love affair marked by exaggerated romantic conventions and "Vaseline lens" visuals, which prove as grating as Daisy's neurotic behavior. The audience is torn between wondering whether they are watching a farce or simply a world that is "genuinely" as far removed from the realities of ordinary life as is humanly imaginable. It is a dimension that appears even more sensational when compared to the downtrodden, suburban street where impecunious auto-body shop

MIA FARROW Many consider her to be one of the few great actresses of 1970s New Hollywood. Others see her as a frail crybaby. Perhaps a telling choice of words as actress Mia Farrow's rise to international stardom came with the 1968 picture *Rosemary's Baby*, about a child bride's devastating pregnancy. Farrow was born in 1945 in Los Angeles to actress Maureen O'Sullivan, famous for playing the role of Jane throughout the 1930s in the Tarzan movies, and director John Farrow. She began her acting career in the 1960s on the TV soap opera *Peyton Place* (1964–69). After the success of *Rosemary's Baby* she was offered a large number of promising roles, playing that same year in *Secret Ceremony*. In 1972, she appeared at the side of Jean-Paul Belmondo in *Docteur Popaul*. Other highlights include her 1974 performance opposite Robert Redford in *The Great Gatsby* and a 1978 all-star film adaptation of Agatha Christie's *Death on the Nile*.

A long-standing personal and professional relationship with Woody Allen burgeoned in 1982 when she was cast in his picture, *A Midsummer Night's Sex Comedy*. The once wife of both legendary entertainer Frank Sinatra and composer/conductor André Previn became Allen's favorite leading actress and companion of many years. Over the course of twelve years she performed exclusively in Allen's productions, playing the fragile yet sprightly woman in numerous pieces like *Zelig* (1983), *Broadway Danny Rose* (1983–84), *The Purple Rose of Cairo* (1985), considered by many to be Allen's masterpiece, *Hannah and Her Sisters*, (1985), *September* (1987) and *Alice* (1990). The couple split up in 1992 when it became clear that Allen was having an affair with Farrow's adopted Korean daughter, Soon Yi. After the mudslinging of the public scandal subsided, Farrow began to work again in film and television. In 1994 she stood before the camera in *Widows' Peak* and *Miami Rhapsody*. Mia Farrow is the mother of 13 children, nine of which she adopted. She is also the author of the 1997 autobiography *What Falls Away*.

"The film is faithful to the letter of F. Scott Fitzgerald's novel but entirely misses its spirit. Much of Fitzgerald's prose has been preserved, especially in Nick Carraway's narration, but it only gives the film a stilted, stuffy tone that is reinforced by the dialogue. Fitzgerald wrote dialogue to be read, not said; and the Coppola screenplay (much rejuggled by Director Clayton) treats Fitzgerald's lines with untoward reverence. When Daisy sighs, 'We were so close in our month of love,' she sounds like a kid in creative-writing course reading her first story loud." *Time Magazine*

4   Daisy, Daisy give me your answer do… Gatsby has found the love of his life (Mia Farrow) again.

5   Suddenly last summer: Gatsby shortly before his violent death.

6   A race to the finish: Gatsby's car symbolizes wealth and freedom, but in the end it costs him his life.

7   All that glitters is not gold: Mia Farrow and Robert Redford of *Butch Cassidy and the Sundance Kid* fame.

owner George Wilson (Scott Wilson) lives with his wife Myrtle (Karen Black). The ominous eyes of Dr. T. J. Eckleburg on a local billboard watch over this nowhere town and serve as one of the film's most evident symbols. This is a world sucked dry of color, providing a sharp contrast to the rainbow world of the two Eggs. Myrtle is Tom Buchanan's mistress and like Jay Gatsby, hopes to gain access to a new social stratum via her lucrative liaison. Both of these hopefuls are left hung out to dry. Not only does Tom soon find out that Gatsby has indeed, as accused, made a killing in the illegal alcohol trade, but it also becomes clear that Daisy has no intention of leaving her husband. Shortly after this shattering revelation, Myrtle meets an untimely demise when Gatsby unintentionally hits her with his car. In a wild act

of desperation, Wilson shoots Gatsby and then himself, leaving the two men dead.

Both the movie and the book equate Gatsby's personal desires with those inherent in the American Dream. Nevertheless, everything that Daisy represents to this social climber is rooted in the past. Likewise, the American Dream itself is deemed to be a concept that only exists in nostalgic reveries. Several generations separate the time between the mass European exodus to the western shores of the New World and the 1920s, and in *Gatsby*, we bear witness to an opposing trend within the United States. Here, characters from "western" cities like Detroit are returning to the East Coast. For Gatsby, the movement is a harrowing reverse that signals his undoing.   KK

THE PASSENGER
(AKA PROFESSION: REPORTER)
Professione: reporter / Profession: Reporter

1974 - ITALY / FRANCE / SPAIN / USA - 125 MIN. - DRAMA

DIRECTOR MICHELANGELO ANTONIONI (*1912)
SCREENPLAY MARK PEPLOE, PETER WOLLEN, MICHELANGELO ANTONIONI DIRECTOR OF PHOTOGRAPHY LUCIANO TOVOLI
EDITING MICHELANGELO ANTONIONI, FRANCO ARCALLI MUSIC IVAN VANDOR PRODUCTION CARLO PONTI for CIPI
CINEMATOGRAFICA S. A., COMPAGNIA CINEMATOGRAFICA CHAMPION, LES FILMS CONCORDIA, MGM.

STARRING JACK NICHOLSON (David Locke), MARIA SCHNEIDER (The Girl), IAN HENDRY (Martin Knight), JENNY
RUNACRE (Rachel Locke), CHUCK MULVEHILL (Robertson), STEVEN BERKOFF (Stephen), AMBROISE BIA (Achebe),
JOSÉ MARÍA CAFFAREL (Hotel Owner), ÁNGEL DEL POZO (Police Inspector), MANFRED SPIES (Stranger).

"People disappear every day." – "Every time they leave the room."

"No family, no friends – just a couple of obligations and a weak heart." This is how the arms dealer Robertson (Chuck Mulvehill) sums up his life. British journalist David Locke (Jack Nicholson) encounters his compatriot in a hotel in the middle of the Sahara desert, and a few hours later, he finds him dead in his room.

With hardly a second thought, Locke assumes the dead man's identity – partly for professional reasons, and partly (as the viewer gradually discovers) because he has become as estranged from his own life as from his profession as a war reporter. The ink isn't dry on the famous journalist's obituaries before Locke has arranged to meet with Robertson's contractors – a group of African freedom fighters. Clearly, Robertson had believed in what he was doing; and as conviction is precisely what Locke's life has been lacking, he uses the dead man's calendar to pick up where Robertson had left off.

It seems, at first, that the change of identity has gone off without a hitch. Soon, however, there's a bunch of people pursuing the imposter: Not just Robertson's business partners, but his enemies too; and – last, not least – the "widow" of David Locke... In flight from his own past and another man's future, the journalist is clearly in mortal danger.

Locke is joined by a young student (Maria Schneider), who is fascinated by his radical self-erasure and "rebirth." Yet he knows he'll have to come clean eventually, and his attempts to evade his pursuers are half-hearted. The journey ends in a Spanish no-man's-land, a kind of wilderness like the African desert in which it began.

For director Michelangelo Antonioni, the thriller plot of *The Passenger* is a vehicle for reflections on human identity. From the bits and pieces available to him, Locke tries desperately to reconstruct Robertson's life, but the attempt ends in failure. The arms dealer remains a phantom, for Robertson has no reality apart from the complex network of relationships that constituted his unique existence.

Even in his new identity, Locke falls victim to the contradictions inherent in his own profession. Antonioni shows us the journalist as a man doomed to passivity, even in his most active moments. Fragments of interviews from Locke's journalistic past reveal the roots of his crisis. Whether his

2

"I don't have anything to say but perhaps something to show."

Michelangelo Antonioni, in: The Architecture of Vision. Writings and Interviews on Cinema

MICHELANGELO ANTONIONI Antonioni was born in Ferrara in 1912. He began his career as a writer of short stories and as a contributor to the Italian film journal *Cinema*, the cradle of neorealism. After making several short documentaries, Antonioni retreated from the view that the cinema should serve a political agenda, and his first feature, *Story of a Love Affair* (*Cronaca di un amore*, 1950) broke with conventional narrative techniques. Until the mid-60s, Antonioni's great theme was "the sickness of feelings," depicted in films such as *The Night* (*La notte*, 1960), *The Eclipse* (*L'eclisse*, 1962) and *Red Desert* (*Il deserto rosso*, 1964). In his later works, *Blow Up* (1966), *Zabriskie Point* (1969) and *The Passenger* (*Professione: reporter / Profession: Reporter*, 1974), he examined the emotional and existential rootlessness of modern humanity. These films also express Antonioni's distrust of superficial appearances. To him, the essential nature of a thing is forever hidden beneath its visible surface, and no image or representation can alter this fact. In Antonioni's work, landscapes, buildings, gestures and sounds are the symbols of interior realities; he creates what has been termed a "dramaturgy of the fragmentary," where "the form swallows the content." (Thomas Christen in *du* Magazin 11/1995). At times, his style is almost mannered, perhaps too much in love with effects. Yet his considered use of technical means – like the slow-motion explosion in *Zabriskie Point* or the closing sequence of *The Passenger* – stands in striking contrast to his intuitive working methods, exemplified by his frequent changes to the dialog during filming. Unlike most of his Italian or American counterparts, Antonioni seems to approach his subjects tentatively, watchfully, as if waiting for an opening, a way into their deeper meaning. As he put it himself: "I know what I have to do. Not what I mean."

1 Lost for words: As gunrunner Robertson, David Locke (Jack Nicholson) loses his grip on reality.

2 Who did you say you were? Despite their unbridled intimacy, Locke and his nameless companion (Maria Schneider) never really get close.

3 One corpse and a fake ID: Locke is surprised how easy it is to become someone else.

4 Ticket to ride: On the road to nowhere, in flight from the unknown.

subject was a magician or a dictator, the actual person, the real significance, always remained hidden. What we see is what we get, but we only ever see what we want to see – or the little we're shown.

In a sense Locke is the director's alter ego, for he too is lumbered with perceivable reality, the only material available to him. As the plot dissolves into a plethora of locations and narrative levels, *The Passenger* emerges as a thesis on the possibility or impossibility of visual representation per se. A recurring metaphor: doors and windows that reveal only a portion of the past or the present. Whatever the image, the camera lingers a little longer than necessary, as if waiting for the magical moment when the visible world will finally yield up its secrets.

The seven-minute final sequence is a final reminder that we wait in vain for revelation. Locke is recumbent on his bed in a hotel room, but the camera-angle makes him invisible to the audience; through the window, we see the village square, and the bullring beyond it; a car drives past; a boy throws rocks at a beggar; and the girl converses with various people. In the midst of these barely decipherable details, the true drama remains hidden, indicated only by the vague sound of a single shot. The camera passes through the barred window, describes a broad curve around the square and comes back round to gaze through the window once more: At the end of his aimless journey, David Locke has arrived at the only inevitable destination. SH

DEATH WISH

1974 - USA - 93 MIN. - ACTION FILM, THRILLER

DIRECTOR MICHAEL WINNER (*1935)
SCREENPLAY WENDELL MAYES, based on the novel of the same name by BRIAN GARFIELD DIRECTOR OF PHOTOGRAPHY ARTHUR J. ORNITZ
EDITING BERNARD GRIBBLE MUSIC HERBIE HANCOCK PRODUCTION DINO DE LAURENTIIS, HAL LANDERS, BOBBY ROBERTS for
DINO DE LAURENTIIS PRODUCTIONS, PARAMOUNT PICTURES.

STARRING CHARLES BRONSON (Paul Kersey), HOPE LANGE (Joanna Kersey), VINCENT GARDENIA (Frank Ochoa), STEVEN
KEATS (Jack Toby), WILLIAM REDFIELD (Sam Kreutzer), STUART MARGOLIN (Ames Jainchill), STEPHEN ELLIOTT (Police
Commissioner), KATHLEEN TOLAN (Carol Toby), JACK WALLACE (Hank), FRED J. SCOLLAY (Prosecuting Attorney).

"A gun is just a tool, like a hammer or an axe."

It starts out picturesque. A blue sea, white sands and a woman posing in front of the camera as Marilyn Monroe might have. Joanna (Hope Lange) may not be as young or beautiful as the legendary pop icon, but architect Paul Kersey's (Charles Bronson) heart belongs to her just the same. She is, after all, his wife. However, by the time this snapshot has been developed, the reality of its idyllic imagery will have washed away with the tide. For Joanna is no more.

Shortly after her arrival in New York, underlined by the dissonant sounds of the Herbie Hancock score, Joanna and her daughter Carol (Kathleen Tolan) are battered in their apartment. Kicks and punches rob Joanna of her life. Carol is raped and beaten beyond repair, leaving her to live out her days as a vegetable at a mental health facility. Few other mainstream movies go to such violent extremes in their depiction of rape as Michael Winner's *Death Wish*. Even Stanley Kubrick's *A Clockwork Orange* (1971), which assumes

a similar stance to its delinquent perpetrators, is toned down by its hig stylized artificiality.

Death Wish, based on Brian Garfield's 1972 novel, examines the smu ness of middle class America. Kersey, like so many others of his generatic is a "bleeding-heart" liberal. But when his family is attacked, his comforta existence and values are turned upside down. Neither police investigate nor the criminal justice system have any intention of pursuing the ca and his son-in-law proves equally unwilling to help track down the a sailants. To Kersey, the city has come to represent a cesspool, where hoc lums and petty crooks known as "rats" terrorize upstanding citizens. A wo apart from Tucson, Arizona, a place Paul gets to know on a business trip. T initial images are an immediate indicator of the traditions rooted in t South-Western town. A tourist trap disguised as a Western sideshow, encounter a Tucson that not only conjures up the spirit of the frontier –

"In mobilizing primitive gut instincts, *Death Wish* encourages the meanest and most dangerous cravings for vengeance. This film might accurately be described as a time bomb." *Die Welt*

1 True colors: When his wife is murdered, bleeding heart liberal Paul (Charles Bronson) becomes judge, jury and executioner.

2 "I look like a rock quarry that someone has dynamited." Charles Bronson gives a reserved but intense performance as Paul Kersey.

3 Tunnel of lugs: In New York, crime lurks everywhere.

CHARLES BRONSON

In the 1970s, he was reportedly the most expensive actor alive. Charles Bronson became wildly popular after appearing as the mysterious harmonica player in Sergio Leone's *C'era una volta il West / Once Upon a Time in the West* (1969) and could command the meaty sum of 100,000 dollars a day from Hollywood studios. In 1972, the then 50-year-old was celebrated by the Golden Globes as "the world's most popular actor." His greatest success came in 1974 with the role of the lone avenger in *Death Wish*. Charles Bronson is an actor who will forever be associated with his angular features. "I guess I look like a rock quarry that someone has dynamited," he told reporters in a rare interview. Like the stone cold, impenetrable villains he plays in many of his pictures, Bronson himself is very much a publicity-shy outsider.

The son of a Lithuanian miner, he got a relatively late start in the movie industry. In 1951, still working under his given name, Charles Buchinsky, the actor landed his first role in the Gary Cooper vehicle *You're in the Navy Now*; he was 30 years old at the time. The headstrong actor, often cast as a Native American on account of his bone structure, made his first appearance as Charles Bronson in the 1954 film *Drum Beat*. He became a headliner in 1958 with the pictures *Gang War* and Roger Corman's *Machine-Gun Kelly* (1958) shortly thereafter. His first official fan club formed thanks to his role as adventuresome photographer Mike Kovac in the TV series *Man with a Camera* (1958–60). Bronson became a Western Maverick in 1960 with his performance in the John Sturges classic *The Magnificent Seven*, and in 1962 he appeared opposite Elvis Presley in *Kid Galahad*.

After only being offered supporting bad guy roles in Hollywood, he left for Europe in 1967 much like Clint Eastwood and Lee Van Cleef. It was here thanks to films like *La Bataille de San Sebastian / Guns for San Sebastian* (1968) and *Le Passager de la pluie / L'uomo venuto dalla pioggia* (1969) that he became an international superstar. Upon returning to the U.S., the man with the chiseled features and iron man body began to be seen as a sex symbol. In the early 1970s he continued to act in Westerns like Michael Winner's *Chato's Land* (1971) and Mafia movies like Terence Young's *The Valachi Papers / Le Dossier Valachi / Carteggio Valachi* (1971/72).

Bronson became an action icon in the 1980s as a result of the controversial though phenomenally profitable *Death Wish* series (1974, 1981, 1985, 1987, 1993). In particular his long-standing, 9-picture collaboration with director J. Lee Thompson helped establish this new image. Following the death of his wife, actress Jill Ireland, Bronson retreated from Hollywood in the 1990s and seldom agreed to do a movie. In 1991, he was cast in Sean Penn's directorial debut *The Indian Runner*. One of his most recent roles was as captain Wolf Larsen in *The Sea Wolf* (1993).

4   Emma Peel in support hose: Here an old lady
     finishes off her assailants with a hatpin.

5   The ratpack: a teenage street gang featuring Jeff
     Goldblum in his first role.

6   Sex on the beach: But following a brutal attack
     Joanna (Hope Lange) is found belly up.

battle between nature and civilization – but also glorifies the principles of vigilante justice.

The "philosophical" words of local construction company owner, Ames Jainchill (Stuart Margolin), best describe the prevailing sentiment: "A gun is just a tool, like a hammer or an axe." In Tucson, weapons are as holy as the Bible. Ames thus persuades the former draft dodger Paul to partake in a little target practice. Paul immediately hits the mark, earning the respect of the would-be cowboy, and suddenly regaining a long lost sense of self. For it just so happens that Paul has known how to handle a gun since he was a kid. His father was a firearms fanatic and died as a result of a hunting accident – an incident that led Paul to swear off weapons entirely. Before returning home, Jainchill gives him a pistol as a parting gift. Paul now knows what he must do. After dark, Paul seeks out places he knows are likely to be targeted by thugs and plugs the attackers full of lead without batting an eye.

His rampage awakens him out of his emotional stupor. Suddenly pulsing with life, he watches news reports of other citizens he has inspired to take the law into their own hands – one of whom is an elderly lady who wards off her assailant with a needle from her hat. From this point on, the audience is left asking itself just how serious the film is about the course of action it prescribes. Yet the film's ironic undertones are too weak to prevent

Death Wish from being interpreted as a vigilante justice thriller. Paul's deeds are applauded, not criticized. He becomes a heroic outlaw in whom the city dwellers can live out their dreams of vengeance. The traditional institutions responsible for upholding justice can't keep up with the anonymous crusader. They decide not to go after him and in doing so give him *carte blanche* in fighting the urban scum. Paul Kersey succeeds in becoming a New York City asset and is soon ready to embark on the road to new frontiers. The picture's final images show him heading for Los Angeles, where, rest assured, he will continue to bring crime to its knees.

Wrapped up in some of America's most compelling and problematic ideology, *Death Wish* was as controversial as it was effective. It was with good reason that the picture spawned several sequels in the 1980s. At the time of its release, virtually no movie, not even *Dirty Harry* (1971), had been so resolute in presenting a depiction of law and order that reflected the subconscious desire of the American people to simply annihilate anything perceived as a threat to society. The film presents them with a virtuous lone avenger, who, guided by the same simplistic principles that led countless mythical Hollywood cowboys to victory, effectively combats urban isolation, social injustice and violence. Seen outside the context of the film, Paul's development clearly maps the transition of an average citizen turned serial killer, whom public opinion makes into a modern day hero.

The Paul Kersey character relies heavily on mechanisms of audience identification, which makes it difficult to gain any objective distance. Nor does it help that the "rats" come across as somewhat comical. It is obvious that the film trivializes real inner city problems such as drug addiction and urban crime in its monochrome take on urban youth and subculture. Much like *First Blood* (1982) in the 1980s, *Death Wish* can be interpreted as an attempt to "solve" real life problems with film fantasies. Where *First Blood* sets out to reverse the outcome of the Vietnam War, *Death Wish* aims to combat urban crime. In either case, vigilante justice, which *Death Wish* finds in "Wild West" Tucson and matures on the streets of New York, is really nothing more than glorified violence. The picture could hardly present a more ambivalent message. KK

"Michael Winner has directed this absorbing melodrama so that attempted muggings have a chilling reality and the rough vigilante justice is presented with an ironic flip. Charles Bronson, too, leavens his portrayal of the half mad avenger with gruff, sardonic humor. In *Death Wish* headlines have been provocatively and vigorously dramatized in an excellent motion picture." *Herald Tribune*

THE CONVERSATION

1974 - USA - 113 MIN. - THRILLER

DIRECTOR FRANCIS FORD COPPOLA (*1939)
SCREENPLAY FRANCIS FORD COPPOLA   DIRECTOR OF PHOTOGRAPHY BILL BUTLER   EDITING RICHARD CHEW   MUSIC DAVID SHIRE
PRODUCTION FRANCIS FORD COPPOLA for AMERICAN ZOETROPE, THE COPPOLA COMPANY, THE DIRECTORS COMPANY, PARAMOUNT PICTURES.

STARRING GENE HACKMAN (Harry Caul), JOHN CAZALE (Stanley), ALLEN GARFIELD (Bernie Moran), FREDERIC FORREST (Mark), CINDY WILLIAMS (Ann), MICHAEL HIGGINS (Paul), ELIZABETH MACRAE (Meredith), TERI GARR (Amy), HARRISON FORD (Martin Stett), PHOEBE ALEXANDER (Lurleen).

IFF CANNES 1974 GOLDEN PALM for BEST FILM (Francis Ford Coppola).

"I don't care what they're talking about. All I want is a nice fat recording."

A bright, sunny day in downtown San Francisco. Union square is bursting with life. Passers-by soak up live jazz as a clown parades about the plaza, imitating the people he encounters. The initial camera shots observe the peaceful action from overhead, when, like a bolt from the blue, a disturbance shatters this blissful portrait. Static interference muffles every sound. Seconds later, the calm is fully restored, or so it seems. Yet as the camera moves in on the city dwellers and holds on an inconspicuous guy in a rain poncho, wearing a hearing device and carrying a shopping bag, we begin to see that there's more to this scene than meets the eye. Soon the clown approaches the mysterious man, who quickly turns away – all the while incessantly tailed by the camera.

Our xenophobic friend's name is Harry Caul (Gene Hackman), a professional audio surveillance expert and one of the best in the business. He and his expert team happen to be carrying out a routine assignment. They are to eavesdrop on the conversation of a young couple strolling guilelessly about the square. The jarring audio feedback we hear is caused by his hidden microphone. Much like the enlarged snapshots in Michelangelo Antonioni's

film *Blow Up* (1966), the reel-to-reel tape recordings of *The Conversation* also contain more information than intended. Caul goes over these tapes countless times. Something just isn't quite right about them. When the pieces at last seem to click into place, he is overcome with dread. Caul not only suspects that the couple could be in grave danger, but also that he has been made an accessory to murder. With this, the thriller begins.

Behind the veil of professional distance that this audio trapper exhibits towards his job and his human targets lies a deep-seated sense of shame. Years ago, Caul's stereo snooping was responsible for the deaths of several innocent people. To stop history from repeating itself, he puts his foot down and withholds the last reels from his client in the hopes of foiling a potential murder plot.

Francis Ford Coppola filmed *The Conversation* between the first two installments of his *Godfather* trilogy (1972, 1974, 1999). He had, in fact, been toying with the idea since the late 60s. Had *The Conversation* been made a few years earlier, it might have been written off as far-fetched hogwash by audiences and critics alike. Nonetheless, when the shoot began in November

1973, the Watergate scandal, which eventually led to the resignation of Presdent Nixon, had turned mere academic theory and speculation into blindin truth. Every U.S. American was confronted with the reality of a governmen not only capable of invading the private sphere by means of audio survei lance, but also not opposing it. Still *The Conversation* is much more than political thriller. It is as much a portrait of human fears as it is an intima drama about a police informant who cracks when he himself becomes th target of undercover surveillance.

Although the leading role was originally intended for Marlon Brando, n one could have delivered a more convincing performance as the scruff quirky and utterly alone audio-nark than Gene Hackman. His Harry Caul em bodies the average Joe more than he'd like to admit. He is someone wh

SOUND DESIGN & SOUND EDITING

By definition, sound design entails arranging an audio track made up of dialog, music and ambient sound. There is a long line of processes involved in its preparation for commercial film. The original recordings, also known as "raw sound," made during the shoot, are checked, selected for quality and synchronized to the picture. The sound is then finely edited at the post production level, allowing for sound effects and additional atmospheric touches to be introduced onto the audio track. Named after Jack Foley, the actual recording procedures of this additional material, which is later synchronized with absolute precision to the corresponding visual frames, are referred to as "foley taking" and "foley editing." Voices, dialog and lip-synched dubbings are re-recorded as well as mastered at the ADR taking and ADR editing phase (Automatic Dialog Replacement or Automated Dialog Recording) of the sound design process and are then later fused with the final visual cut. Music editing is (often) initially the responsibility of the composer, who creates clips of music that fit into the allotted visual material, stamped with a series of precise time codes, corresponding to the film's final cut. Working closely with the editor and the director, the music editor is the only member of the production team with a complete overview of all the music segments. The final mix is the product of all the processes described above.

1 Clogged reception? Harry Caul (Gene Hackman) will have things up and running in no time. Your crap may, however, be recorded for quality assurance purposes.

2 Bug extermination: In an act of emancipation, Caul rids himself of all hidden surveillance devices by destroying his own apartment.

3 Remixed and remastered: *The Conversation* understandably hit a nerve with post-Watergate America.

4   They're all crowding that other booth: Much like that year's Oscars, the cast of *The Conversation* sees someone else cashing in on the accolades.

Not to fret, as it was Coppola's other picture *The Godfather – Part II* that took home six golden statuettes.

"Wedded to secrecy as a moral principle, he's the kind of man who lies down to neck with his shoes on – an acutely repressed solitary who insists that he's not responsible for the outcome of his work." *Variety*

constantly intrudes on the privacy of others, but regards his quarry with a distanced abstraction: "I don't care what they're talking about. All I want is a nice fat recording." When the shoe's on the other foot, however, he freaks out like a wild animal that suddenly realizes it's been caged. Our first taste of this comes when his landlady drops off a birthday present in his well-secured apartment while Harry is out.

Walter Murch provided the audio mixes, essential to this film's subject matter. He first collaborated with Coppola on *The Rain People* (1969) and would work as his sound designer again on subsequent productions such as

The Godfather – Part II (1974) and *Apocalypse Now* (1979). In *The Conversation*, every manifestation of sound is more than just a means of underscoring the visuals. Here, the audio track becomes an autonomous entity that not only steers the plot but also generates a sinister smokescreen for the protagonist and spectators alike. We hear only that which Caul hears. Yet, as someone who exclusively focuses on sounds and background noise, making every effort to isolate each distinct thread, he loses sight of the *actual content* of the recorded dialog – what is really being said. *The Conversation* is a "talkie" at the highest level of introspection.   APO

CHINATOWN

1974 - USA - 131 MIN. - DETECTIVE FILM, DRAMA

DIRECTOR ROMAN POLANSKI (*1933)
SCREENPLAY ROBERT TOWNE **DIRECTOR OF PHOTOGRAPHY** JOHN A. ALONZO **EDITING** SAM O'STEEN **MUSIC** JERRY GOLDSMITH
PRODUCTION ROBERT EVANS for LONG ROAD, PENTHOUSE, PARAMOUNT PICTURES.

STARRING JACK NICHOLSON (J. J. "Jake" Gittes), FAYE DUNAWAY (Evelyn Cross Mulwray), JOHN HUSTON (Noah Cross), PERRY LOPEZ (LAPD Lieutenant Lou Escobar), JOHN HILLERMAN (Russ Yelburton), DARRELL ZWERLING (Hollis I. Mulwray), DIANE LADD (Ida Sessions), ROY JENSON (Claude Mulvihill), ROMAN POLANSKI (Man with the knife), RICHARD BAKALYAN (LAPD Detective Loach).

ACADEMY AWARDS 1974 OSCAR for BEST ORIGINAL SCREENPLAY (Robert Towne).

"I'm just a snoop."

Los Angeles, 1937. When private detective J.J. Gittes (Jack Nicholson) is hired to keep tabs on an unfaithful husband, he assumes it's going to be just another routine job. But the investigation takes an unexpected turn. The guy he's been keeping an eye on, a high-ranking official for the city's water and power department is bumped off. His attractive widow Evelyn (Faye Dunaway) retains Gittes' services to find out whodunit. Before he knows it, Gittes stumbles unexpectedly onto a foul smelling real estate scheme, and soon finds himself entangled in one sordid affair after another. Gittes has several bloody run-ins with thugs determined to put an end to his work on the case, and uncovers clues pointing to the involvement of influential power-players in the sinister dealings. Even Gittes' alluring employer Evelyn seems to know more about the matter than she's letting on...

Chinatown is considered by many film critics to be not only one of the greatest films of the 70s, but of all time. How the movie came to be illustrates, like so many other similar moments in Hollywood history, that masterpieces can still be born within the framework of the imperious big studios. Chinatown was simply one of those rare instances when the perfect combination of people came together at just the right time. Jack Nicholson who, at the time was not a solid "A list" star, brought prominent "script doctor" Robert Towne on board the project to write the screenplay. When he got wind of the project, Robert Evans, who was head of production at Paramount, wanted to try his hand at producing a film himself. He finalized an agreement with the writer and actor and secured Roman Polanski, with whom he had collaborated previously on Rosemary's Baby (1968), as the picture's director. (Understandably, Polanski had been working in his native Europe following the brutal death of his wife Sharon Tate [1943–1969] in their Los Angeles home.) When Faye Dunaway was cast as the female lead, yet another not quite famous personality was added to the mix. As one might expect, the shoot was not exactly plain sailing. Evans dubbed the verbal fireworks between Towne and Polanski, "World War III." The problem probably had something to do with the fact that this was first project Polanski directed without writing himself. The product was, nonetheless, an inter-

"*Chinatown* was seen as a Neo-Noir when it was released – an update on an old genre. Now years have passed and film history blurs a little, and it seems to settle easily beside the original noirs. That is a compliment." *Chicago Sun-Times*

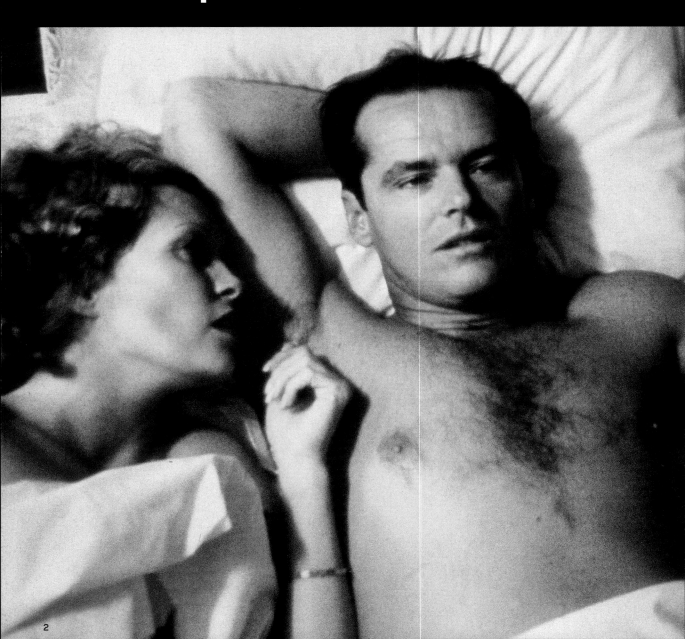

1　Portrait of a lady: Femme fatale Evelyn (Faye Dunaway) awakens men's dreams and inspires them to action.

2　In her clutches: The private eye (Jack Nicholson) has lost all professional distance from his seductive client.

3　Masterful execution: Veteran director John Huston plays a brutal patriarch who holds all the cards

4　Mack the knife: Polanski in a striking cameo as the "nose-slitter."

ational smash. *Chinatown* reeled in a total of eleven Oscar nominations, lthough Robert Towne was the sole person who ended up taking a statuette ome.

Yet what makes *Chinatown* truly fascinating, and the reason it attained its instant status as an uncontested masterpiece, is by and large the ilm's grace in evoking the Golden Age of 1930s–1940s Hollywood, without osing itself in the nostalgia of the era or turning the production into just nother stiffly stylized homage. Naturally, Polanski's film draws heavily on lassic Bogart characters like detective Philip Marlowe from Howard Hawks' *The Big Sleep* (1946) or his more cynical counterpart Sam Spade from *The Maltese Falcon* (1941), directed by Hollywood legend John Huston. Huston imself plays a pivotal role in *Chinatown* as a ruthless and sickeningly senti-

mental patriarch, who seems to be the key to the entire mystery. Unlike Bogart, Nicholson's character is only capable of being a limited hero. Although J. J. "Jake" Gittes is a likeable, small-time snoop, with a weakness for smutty jokes, the charming sheister fails miserably as a moralist and suffers terribly as a result. The scene featuring Polanski as a gangster who slits open Nicholson's nose is absolutely priceless. The Gittes character also lacks the romantic potential of a Bogart hero. Gittes doesn't embody desires, instead he falters on them. Yet his greatest weakness is Chinatown, the place where his career as a cop came to an end and a synonym for all the irresistible, exotic dangers of the urban jungle. This same sweet taboo seems to echo in Faye Dunaway's character. In the end, Chinatown presents Gittes with a double-edged defeat. Although Towne had originally written a happy

5   Just the facts Ma'am: *Chinatown* evokes classic Hollywood cinema without ever romanticizing t.

6   Still nosing around: J. J. Gittes (Jack Nicholson), bloody but unbowed.

ending, the film's final sequence, which just screams Polanski, sees Gittes inadvertently aiding the forces of evil and losing the love of his life at the same time.

Another great accomplishment of the piece is Polanski and cinematographer John A. Alonzo's triumph in achieving the impact of a black and white Film Noir piece with brilliant color photography. It is uncanny how little the city feels like a movie lot and how convincing the topography looks. Unlike in so many other so-called revisionist noir films, in *Chinatown,* L. A. is not a black, smoldering hell's kitchen but rather a vast, often sunny countryside metropolis still in the early stages of development. The imagery lets the viewer sense that the city and its surrounding valleys exist in spite of the imposing

desert. We are also made aware of the colossal pipeline, supplying the city with water, its artificial lifeblood. Water is, in fact, the major resource being manipulated in the story's diabolical real estate venture, a scandal with genuine historical roots in the region. Robert Towne based his screenplay on non-fictional accounts dating back to early 20th century Southern California. It was a time when the foundations for the future riches of the world's movie capital were in construction. The location was chosen primarily on account of the area's year-round sun, ideal for filming, and its affordable purchase price. The boom ushered in a wave of land speculators, corruption and violence. It is a grim bit of Earth that the City of Angels and Hollywood rests upon. A tale that unfolds in *Chinatown*.   JH

ROBERT EVANS

Robert Evans (born 1930 in New York), is one of New Hollywood's most illustrious personalities and got his start performing in film at the age of 14. His big break into the business came when actress Norma Shearer, widow of legendary Hollywood tycoon, Irving Thalberg, insisted that Evans play her husband in the *Man of a Thousand Faces* (1957). Dissatisfied with the state of his acting career, he began to work as a freelance producer, without ever producing a single picture, and eventually signed a contract with Paramount in 1965. In the blink of an eye, Evans climbed the rungs of the corporate ladder and emerged as the studio's head of production. He was able to bring the old "mountain" back to its state of former glory as a major studio by taking on a number of blockbuster projects such as *Rosemary's Baby* (1968), *Love Story* (1970), *The Godfather* (1972), *The Godfather – Part II* (1974) and *Chinatown* (1974).

Chinatown marked the first time Evans was able to realize his long harbored ambition of producing a film himself, which garnered him an Academy Award nomination for Best Picture. He left Paramount shortly thereafter to produce film independently, working on films like *Marathon Man* (1976) and *Black Sunday* (1977). These productions were, however, less popular at the box office. In 1984, Evans made headlines for his involvement in the *The Cotton Club* (1984), which not only bombed, but also entangled him in disastrous private scandals. As a result, Evans disappeared from the scene completely for several years. He returned to the business in 1990 with *The Two Jakes*, a further instalment of *Chinatown*, also starring Jack Nicholson. Evans published a book entitled *The Kid Stays in the Picture* (1994) about his personal life story, a constant target of media attention since his start in Hollywood. This gripping autobiography was made into a documentary film in 2002 under the same title.

YOUNG FRANKENSTEIN

1974 - USA - 106 MIN. - HORROR FILM, SPOOF

DIRECTOR MEL BROOKS (*1926)
SCREENPLAY GENE WILDER, MEL BROOKS, based on characters appearing in MARY WOLLSTONECRAFT SHELLEY'S novel *FRANKENSTEIN* DIRECTOR OF PHOTOGRAPHY GERALD HIRSCHFELD EDITING JOHN C. HOWARD MUSIC JOHN MORRIS PRODUCTION MICHAEL GRUSKOFF for GRUSKOFF / VENTURE FILMS, CROSSBOW PRODUCTIONS, JOUER LIMITED, 20TH CENTURY FOX.

STARRING GENE WILDER (Dr. Frederick Frankenstein), PETER BOYLE (Monster), MARTY FELDMAN (Igor), TERI GARR (Inga), MADELINE KAHN (Elizabeth), CLORIS LEACHMAN (Mrs. Blücher), KENNETH MARS (Inspector Kemp), RICHARD HAYDN (Mr. Falkstein), DANNY GOLDMAN (Medical Student), GENE HACKMAN (Blind Hermit).

"It's pronounced Frón-kon-steen."

It's not always easy being the offspring of a celebrity — especially if your famous ancestor made a habit of trying to reanimate bits and pieces of rotting cadavers. With this in mind, it's understandable that neurologist Frederick Frankenstein (Gene Wilder), whose grandfather took part in this peculiar pastime, tries to mask his familial roots by distorting the pronunciation of his surname.

But some origins just won't allow themselves to be brushed aside, and so Dr. "Froderick Fronkonsteen" is unexpectedly compelled to return to the family estate in Transylvania to retrieve the sketches of his grandfather's work. Igor (Marty Feldman), the indispensable family servant and Quasimodo-esque side-kick, alongside the gaunt housekeeper, Mrs. Blücher (Cloris Leachman), whose name causes wild horses to whinny and rear, succeed in getting the vain scientist to put his newly unearthed monster

assembly instruction manual into action. When it comes down to it, all you really need to reanimate a lifeless brain is "the instructions and a clear head."

Nonetheless, before the creature (Peter Boyle) can be let loose on mankind, the audience is going to have to stomach a hearty helping of screwball antics and lewd knee-slappers. Not that the hilarity is going to subside once the monster has been brought to life. After all, it's precisely this brand of humor we fork out good money to experience when we go to see a Mel Brooks movie.

Young Frankenstein thrives on the contrast between the rib-tickling absurdity of its plot and the austere attention to detail with which Brooks and his cinematographer Gerald Hirschfeld based the look of their film on the original horror classics. Primary sources were of course *Frankenstein* (1931

and the *Bride of Frankenstein* (1935), both of which were directed by James Whale, starring Boris Karloff as the monster. Brooks also helped himself to a handful of imagery from other legendary movies. The camera work of the opening sequence is an obvious spoof on *Citizen Kane* (1941). With affectionate irony, *Young Frankenstein* resorts to long-antiquated cinematic devices such as lap dissolves to indicate the passing of time.

In order to recreate the cinematic feel of the Frankenstein classics, Mel Brooks' picture was shot on the same site as the first Frankenstein movies, using the original props, set dressing, laboratory and all. Yet when Brooks toys with genre clichés, he takes them a step beyond, achieving a satiric sort of meta level. A case in point: as their coach approaches the castle in priceless Dracula style (the wolf howl care of the director him-

"You have to let this Mel Brooks comedy do everything for you, because that's the only way it works. If you accept the silly, zizzy obviousness, it can make you laugh helplessly." *Pauline Kael*

1 "Stay close to the candles:" Loyal assistant Inga (Teri Garr) helps her brilliant employer (Gene Wilder) get to the root of his family tree.

2 A mind for science: Frederick Frankenstein making a professional sacrifice.

3 Choking on Chihuahua: That's precisely what Frankenstein's Elizabeth (Madeline Kahn) will be

doing if Inga sees her mitts anywhere near the good doctor.

4 Baby mine, don't you cry: Gene Wilder assures the creature that there's nothing to be frightened of.

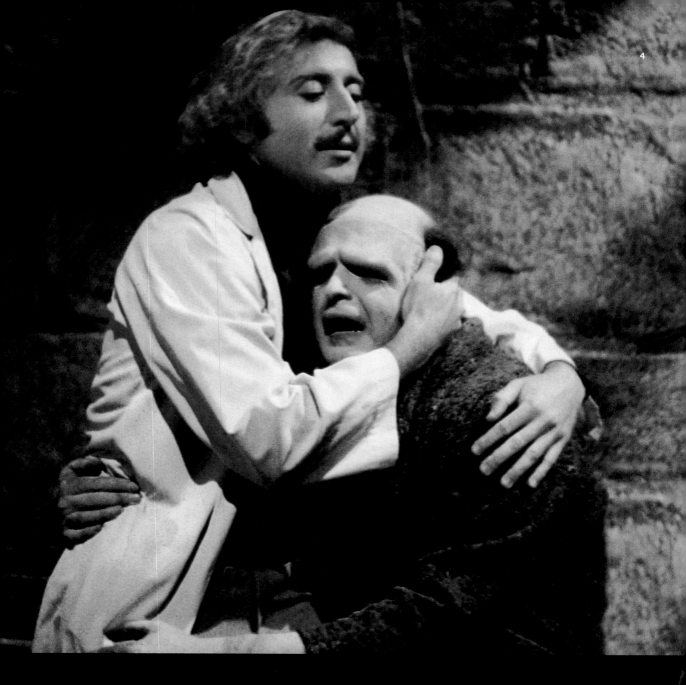

MEL BROOKS   Mel Brooks was never what one would describe as the silent type. Born Melvin Kaminsky in Brooklyn on June 28, 1926, he got his start in show business as a drummer with a hotel orchestra. Not surprisingly, his career proved to be anything but linear. After years as a gag writer, working on a Broadway musical, putting out a record and writing the script of *The Critic* (1963), an Oscar-winning animated short in which his voice can also be heard, Brooks directed *The Producers*, his first Hollywood film, in 1968. A satire about show business in which a has-been producer hits it big on Broadway with a wacky musical pageant about Hitler's life at Berchtesgaden, the film garnered Brooks an Oscar for Best Original Screenplay. Nonetheless, despite his success with crowd-pleasers like *Blazing Saddles* (1973) and *Young Frankenstein* (1974) he remains, for the most part, a Hollywood outsider. This could have something to do with his specific brand of irreverence. For instance, in 1983 he turned the Lubitsch classic *To Be or Not to Be* (1942) into a musical comedy without batting an eye. Then again maybe he is shunned as a result of his predilection for smutty wisecracks and tasteless humor. Of course, the reason could be that not all of his colleagues in the entertainment industry can laugh at his merciless parodies like *Spaceballs* (1987) or *Robin Hood: Men in Tights* (1993).

This is, however, not always the case as Burt Reynolds, James Caan, Paul Newman and Liza Minnelli proved in 1976 when this pack of stars appeared in *Silent Movie* and readily made fun of themselves. Even one of the biggest in the business, Alfred Hitchcock, was able to laugh at the Brook's *Vertigo* spoof *High Anxiety* (1977), a film Hitch is reported to have most thoroughly enjoyed.

"Hearts and kidneys are tinkertoys! I'm talking about the central nervous system!"

Film quote: Dr. Frederick Frankenstein

self), Igor and Freddy go into an Abbott and Costello style dialog. When the good doctor asks him why he's talking like that, Igor replies, "I thought you wanted to."

Brooks biographer Peter W. Jansen pointed out that his films often raise questions of lineage and father-son relationships. This also holds true for *Young Frankenstein*. How loyally Igor, the grandson of the original doctor's loyal servant, stands at "Fronkonsteen's" side, even if as he says, salaries have since improved. Of course, the father-son theme as it pertains to the

Frankenstein story gets a Brooks-style twist tacked onto it. To him, the monster is just a reflection of his master. As the doctor throws a temper tantrum despite his highfalutin, intellectual demeanor, the nonsense-babbling mammoth baby shoots us looks that let us know it is fully capable of understanding the absurdity of the situation. And this is how another scene, in which a blind hermit (Gene Hackman) obliviously scorches the monster with hot soup reaches poetic heights. As we empathize with monster, we key into the grand punchline: he's one of us.

SH

5 Brady bunch rejects: Igor (Marty Feldman) still can't get over losing the role to Ann B. Davis.

6 We'll have that Ovaltine after all: Loyal servant, Mrs. Blücher (Cloris Leachman, right) gets a taste of life when she tunes into Freddy and Inga's romantic interludes.

7 My master told me to pick the very best one…

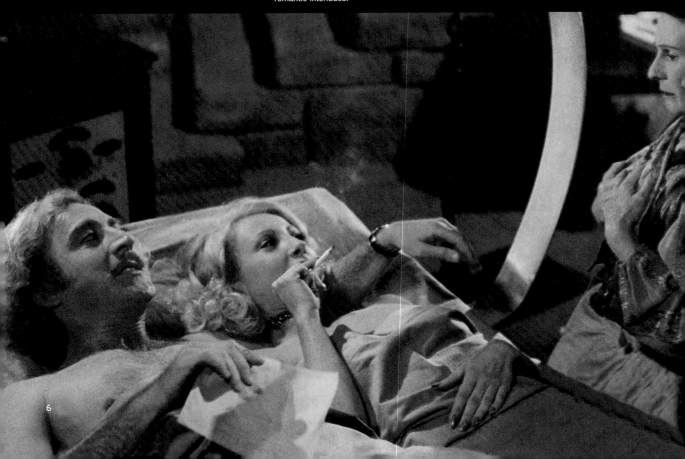

JAWS

1975 - USA - 124 MIN. - THRILLER, HORROR FILM

DIRECTOR STEVEN SPIELBERG (*1947)

SCREENPLAY CARL GOTTLIEB, PETER BENCHLEY, based on his novel of the same name **DIRECTOR OF PHOTOGRAPHY** BILL BUTLER **EDITING** VERNA FIELDS **MUSIC** JOHN WILLIAMS **PRODUCTION** RICHARD D. ZANUCK, DAVID BROWN for ZANUCK/BROWN PRODUCTIONS, UNIVERSAL PICTURES.

STARRING ROY SCHEIDER (Police Chief Martin Brody), ROBERT SHAW (Quint), RICHARD DREYFUSS (Matt Hooper), MURRAY HAMILTON (Mayor Larry Vaughn), LORRAINE GARY (Ellen Brody), CARL GOTTLIEB (Ben Meadows), JEFFREY KRAMER (Lenny Hendricks), SUSAN BACKLINIE (Chrissie), CHRIS REBELLO (Mike Brody), JAY MELLO (Sean Brody).

ACADEMY AWARDS 1975 OSCARS for BEST FILM EDITING (Verna Fields), BEST MUSIC (John Williams), and BEST SOUND (Robert L. Hoyt, Roger Herman Jr., Earl Mabery, John R. Carter).

"You're gonna need a bigger boat."

A hot summer night, a beach party, a little too much red wine, and some teenage sex is just the stuff Hollywood horror films are made of. While her drunken companion sleeps off his hangover on the beach, young Chrissie (Susan Backlinie) takes a midnight dip in the water and is torn to pieces by a shark. The fact that the monster with the dead eyes cynically emerges in innocent white from the depths of the water makes it all the more threatening. The shark – the fear and guilt in all of us – awakens our prehistoric terror of the incomprehensible, the truly wild. It is evil incarnate.

But in the small American beach town ironically named Amity, nobody wants to hear about the threat to a safe world and free market economy, least of all from the mouth of visiting New York cop Martin Brody (Roy Scheider), who, to cap it all, is afraid of the water.

Accordingly, the authorities, in the form of the mayor Larry Vaughn (Murray Hamilton), and the profit and pleasure-seeking public win out over Brody, who wants to close the beaches in light of the menacing danger. It comes as no surprise that the town has a new victim the very next day.

A reward of $3,000 for the capture of the shark incites hunting fever in Amity, and the gawking mob on the pier is duly presented with a dead shark. But it is quickly determined that the captured shark can't possibly be the feared killer: upon cutting open its stomach they find a few small fish, a tin can, and a license plate from Louisiana.

It is a motley trio that sets out to capture the beast – a water-shy policeman, a "rich college boy" named Matt Hooper (Richard Dreyfuss), and

"If *Jaws* was a kind of skeleton key to the angst of the 70s, from the puritanical fear of sex to the war in Vietnam, then its heroes were models of America's wounded masculinity, who meet and join to face a test of character." *Georg Seeßlen*

3

1   Baywatch: Police Chief Martin Brody (Roy Scheider) is fighting nature, the ignorance of those he's trying to protect and his own fears.

2   Beach, blanket, bloodbath: Beautiful Chrissie (Susan Backlinie) is the shark's first victim.

3   Smile for the camera: Three separate models, each seven yards long and weighing over a ton, brought the monster to life. The film crew dubbed the shark "Bruce" – after Steven Spielberg's lawyer.

shark hunting Vietnam veteran Quint (Robert Shaw), a modern Captain Ahab who unsuccessfully attempts to disguise a wounded psyche with a façade of disgust for everything around him. For each of the three men, the shark hunt also turns into a search for their true selves.

The unmistakably sexual aspect of the story of the unnamed monster – a terrifying mixture of phallus and vagina – which afflicts the home and the family has often been pointed out. But *Jaws* is also a film about human fears and character flaws, the overcoming of which gives birth to heroes. That

the story also tells of the capitalistic, self-endangering society, of patriotic America, of mass hysteria, guilt, atonement, and the sacrifice of the individual for the good of the whole is proof of Spielberg's ability to give a simple story plausible readings on multiple levels.

But let's not forget that *Jaws* is one of the most nerve-wracking thrillers of all time. When Spielberg explains that during the filming he felt as if he could direct the audience with an electric cattle prod, it speaks volumes about the cold precision with which, supported by an exceptionally sugges-

THE END OF ARTIFICIAL CREATURES
"Compressors, tanks, winches, pneumatic hoses, welding torches, blow lamps, rigging, generators, copper, iron, and steel wire, plastic material, electric motors, crammers, hydraulic presses" – just some of the trappings required to make "Bruce," as the film team christened the model of the white shark, come alive. In his book, "The Jaws Log," co-screenwriter Carl Gottlieb tells of the immense problems encountered trying to simulate real-life shark attacks with a life-sized model (because actually Bruce was made of three different models). Shooting was repeatedly interrupted by technical problems, most memorably when they first put Bruce in the water, only to see him sink like a stone. The hiring of long-retired Hollywood veteran Robert A. Mattey, creator of the special effects for Disney's *Marry Poppins* (1964) and countless other films, makes it clear that the mid-70s marked the end of conventionally created film monsters. "Bruce" was one of the last of his kind and craftsmen like Bob Mattey were increasingly relieved by computer programmers. Spielberg proved his ability to incorporate their work into his projects in 1981 with *Raiders of the Lost Ark*, in which entire sequences were created with the help of computer animation.

5

"If Spielberg's favorite location is the suburbs, *Jaws* shows suburbanites on vacation."

Chicago Sun-Times

...ive soundtrack, he was able to raise the tension and lower it again, all in ...eparation for the next dramatic highlight.

Just one example of Spielberg's virtuoso story-telling technique is the ...cene in which the men show one another their scars under deck. In the ...iddle of the scene, the audience is told the story of the *ISS Indianapolis*, ...e boat with which the Hiroshima bomb was transported to the Pacific. ...nder fire from Japanese submarines, the crew threw themselves into the ...cean and the majority of them were eaten by sharks.

During this sequence, which is actually quite humorous, Spielberg and his authors succeed in setting a counterpoint even before the appearance of the shark illustrates the terror of the story. Quint's tale contains a political dimension. Ultimately, this scene also reveals something about story-telling itself — reality catches you up in a flash. Right when Quint and Hooper attempt to stem their apprehension with loud song, Mr. Spielberg is right there with his electric shocker.

SH

4   Brody's scared of water, but he's about to undergo some shock therapy...

5   Rub a dub dub, three men in a tub: *Jaws* is also a parable about social conflicts in the USA.

6   Shark fin soup: Evil feeds on ignorance and Americans.

ONE FLEW OVER THE CUCKOO'S NEST

1975 - USA - 134 MIN. - DRAMA, LITERARY ADAPTATION

DIRECTOR MILOŠ FORMAN (*1932)
SCREENPLAY LAWRENCE HAUBEN, BO GOLDMAN, based on the novel of the same name by KEN KESEY and a play by DALE WASSERMAN DIRECTOR OF PHOTOGRAPHY HASKELL WEXLER, WILLIAM A. FRAKER, BILL BUTLER EDITING LYNZEE KLINGMAN, SHELDON KAHN, RICHARD CHEW (Supervising editor) MUSIC JACK NITZSCHE PRODUCTION SAUL ZAENTZ, MICHAEL DOUGLAS for FANTASY FILMS, N. V. ZVALUW.

STARRING JACK NICHOLSON (Randle Patrick McMurphy), LOUISE FLETCHER (Nurse Mildred Ratched), WILLIAM REDFIELD (Harding), BRAD DOURIF (Billy Bibbit), WILL SAMPSON (Chief Bromden), DANNY DEVITO (Martini), MICHAEL BERRYMAN (Ellis), PETER BROCCO (Colonel Matterson), DEAN R. BROOKS (Doctor John Spivey), ALONZO BROWN (Miller).

ACADEMY AWARDS 1975 OSCARS for BEST PICTURE (Saul Zaentz, Michael Douglas), BEST DIRECTOR (Miloš Forman), BEST ACTOR (Jack Nicholson), BEST ACTRESS (Louise Fletcher), and BEST ADAPTED SCREENPLAY (Lawrence Hauben, Bo Goldman).

"But I tried didn't I? Goddammit, at least I did that!"

The movie's opening shot evokes an image of paradise lost. Rolling hills are reflected in the glistening water by the rising sun, as a peaceful melody drifts through the air. The last shot is equally utopian. Chief Bromden (Will Sampson), a mountain of a man resident at the psychiatric rehabilitation facility tucked away in this picturesque countryside, wrenches a colossal marble bathroom fixture from its anchored position, hurls it through a window and embarks on the road to freedom. What director Miloš Forman manages to pack into the action that takes place between these two points is a mesmerizing parable about both the urge to capitulate and an ideological system that seeks to crush the individual at any cost. The tale is ingeniously coated in a tragicomic drama about life, death and the state of vegetative indifference exhibited by the residents of an insane asylum.

But all that is about the last thing assault and statutory rape convict, Randle P. McMurphy (Jack Nicholson) has on his mind when he first arrives at the sterile building with barred windows for clinical observation. To McMurphy, the facility serves as a promising alternative to the hard labo[r] he'd be subjected to at the state penitentiary. This is, of course, precisely wh[y] higher authorities suspect him of faking his mental ailments. It soon become[s] evident that McMurphy is the sole person at the institution still possessin[g] enough fantasy and initiative to combat the current reign of deadening bore[-]dom. His opposition comes in the form of the austere head nurse, Mildre[d] Ratched (Louise Fletcher), who has made it her life mission to suck th[e] marrow out of any bit of excitement within the ward in order to assure he[r] patients' eternal sedation. McMurphy, however, slowly undermines he[r] authority. He begins to question trivialities as well as the inalterable dai[ly] schedule by instigating "harmless" acts of defiance, even managing to g[et] the patients to sneak out of the clinic and treat them to a fishing trip. Althoug[h] McMurphy's actions infuse the sequestered men with newfound sel[f] esteem, Nurse Ratched's festering anger reveals her personal disdain fo[r] anything other than the prescribed routine. She, of course, defends th[e]

1   It's your move: Randle P. Murphy (Jack Nicholson) thinks he's in a game – and he thinks he can win.

2   Leading by example: Randle is the hero of the other patients in the psychiatric ward.

3   Shake, rattle and roll: Randle encourages his fellow patients to take control of their lives.

"*One flew over the Cuckoo's Nest* is a powerful, smashingly effective movie – not a great movie but one that will probably stir audiences' emotions and join the ranks of such pop-mythology films as *The Wild One, Rebel without a Cause* and *Easy Rider.*"

The New Yorker

prevailing order by enforcing a strict, borderline totalitarian regime rooted in pseudo-democratic doctrines.

To take the film as a critique of modern psychiatric medicine is to misinterpret it. Director Forman has clearly made an attempt at a more monumental allegory about the power structures at play in modern society. Among the poignant final scenes in *One Flew Over the Cuckoo's Nest* is the moment when we discover that the majority of patients at the clinic are there of their

own volition. In other words, they have all willingly acquiesced to the tyranny and perpetual humiliation. The counterpoint to this mentality manifests itself in McMurphy's reticence to resign himself to such blind compliance. One of the few actually incarcerated hospital inhabitants, the unforgettable words he utters, following his failed attempt at dislodging a marble bathroom fixture sum up the plea of Forman's picture: "But I tried didn't I? Goddammit, at least I did that!" Tragically, McMurphy never internalizes the extreme gravity

JACK NICHOLSON Wily, devious and even lecherous at times, Jack Nicholson still possesses all the qualities required to portray characters driven by animal instincts rather than intellect. His caustic mimicry, gestures and trademark sneer vitalize rebels (*One Flew Over the Cuckoo's Nest*, 1975), psychopaths (*The Shining*, 1980), career killers (*Prizzi's Honor*, 1985) and hardboiled P.I.s alike (*Chinatown*, 1974; *The Two Jakes*, 1990). Some might even regard the sinister, eternally grinning "Joker" in Tim Burton's *Batman* (1988) as the culminating fusion of his classic roles. Hard to believe that for many years it seemed that the movie star born in Neptune, New Jersey in 1937 was not destined to make it big as an actor. In the late 1950s, he joined the team of legendary exploitation film director/producer Roger Corman, performing bit roles in his horror flicks and wannabe rockumentaries, as well as writing screenplays. His screenwriting credits include Monte Hellman's Western *Ride in the Whirlwind* (1965) and Corman's exploration in LSD entitled *The Trip* (1967). The turning point in his career came with his role as a perpetually inebriated lawyer in *Easy Rider* (1969). Dennis Hopper's drama about the disappearance of the American Dream quickly attained cult status and earned Nicholson his first of many Oscar nods. His rise to superstardom reached its inevitable height in the 1970s. Among his many credits and honors, Nicholson has been awarded three Oscars, not to mention the projects he has directed himself. Still very much alive in the business, his more recent movies often feature him as stubborn, eccentric types. These parts attest to Nicholson's immense popularity and continuing role as one of Hollywood's all-time favorite actors.

3

4

his own predicament and continues to gamble in a poker game where no one can afford to bluff. At one point he is presented with a *deus ex machina* in the form of an open window offering escape. The camera holds its focus on McMurphy's face for some time before a cunning grin finally unfolds across his lips. He will stay and continue on with the "game."

Be that as it may, his tournament is over before he even realizes it. The burgeoning self-confidence and associated mental resilience demonstrated in the wisecracks of the patients cause the hospital staff to implement more drastic physical and psychological measures. The film concludes with a "pacified" McMurphy, who was subjected to a lobotomy, being put out of his misery by his friend, the chief. It is this character who continues what McMurphy has set into motion.

"**The 'cuckoo's nest' described by Forman is our very own nest. It's the world we poor lunatics live in, subjected to the bureaucratic rule of one set of oppressors and the economic pressure of another; forever chasing the promise of happiness, which here appears in the guise of liberty – but always obliged to swallow Miss Ratched's bitter little pills.**" *Le Monde*

5

4 First Lady of a mock-democracy: Nurse Ratched (Louise Fletcher) brings the patients to their knees.

5 Born free: "Chief" Bromden carries on the torch when he flies the coop.

6 Sex, drugs and fishing trips: There's nothing Dionysian Randle enjoys catching more than some female tail.

Miloš Forman earned his reputation in Hollywood as the most influential Czech "new wave" import in the 1960s with his sarcastic reflections on everyday life. Although Ken Kesey's novel, on which the screen adaptation is based, is told from the perspective of the mute Native American, McMurphy served as the perfect vehicle for Forman to express his personal cinematic interests and set of reccurring themes. The director transforms the story into a lighter satire, whose socio-political potential takes a slight backseat to the entertainment value, allowing the piece to soar to stunningly beautiful

heights. The actual directing in *One Flew Over the Cuckoo's Nest* is primarily evidenced in the world-class acting led by an energized Nicholson, his antithesis, the insidiously pleasant Louise Fletcher, and Will Sampson's gut-wrenching stoicism. Yet, it's not enough to speak of Sampson's Bromden character solely in these terms, for it is he who will undergo the most dramatic metamorphosis. From the ashes of his self-imposed silent retreat and symbolic emasculation arises a true warrior, who lets the eternal flame borne by McMurphy burn on inside him.

J.P.

THE YAKUZA
Yakuza

1975 - USA / JAPAN - 112 MIN. - GANGSTER FILM, DRAMA

DIRECTOR SYDNEY POLLACK (*1934)
SCREENPLAY LEONARD SCHRADER, PAUL SCHRADER, ROBERT TOWNE DIRECTOR OF PHOTOGRAPHY DUKE CALLAGHAN, KOZO OKAZAKI
EDITING DON GUIDICE, THOMAS STANFORD, FREDRIC STEINKAMP MUSIC DAVE GRUSIN PRODUCTION SYDNEY POLLACK for
TOEI CO. LTD., WARNER BROS.

STARRING ROBERT MITCHUM (Harry Kilmer), KEN TAKAKURA (Ken Tanaka), BRIAN KEITH (George Tanner), HERB EDELMAN
(Oliver Wheat), RICHARD JORDAN (Dusty), KEIKO KISHI (Eiko Tanaka), EIJI OKADA (Toshiro Tono), JAMES SHIGETA (Goro),
KYOSUKE MASHIDA (Jiro Kato), EIJI GO (Spider).

"Paint my eyes on my eyelids, man, and I'll walk through it."

The film opens with the following information: "The Japanese word 'Yakuza' is made up from the characters denoting the numbers 8, 9 and 3. When we add these together, the sum total is 20 – a losing number in Japanese gambling. Japan's outsiders have chosen their name with perverse pride. The Yakuza began life in Japan over 350 years ago as gamblers, con men and shady merchants at traveling fairs. They were also said to have protected the poor of the towns and countryside from bands of marauding noblemen. This, they apparently did with matchless skill and courage."

The Yakuza claim to be the descendents of Samurai warriors, and this is already enough to distinguish them from the Mafia. As Japan became increasingly centralized, westernized and militarized in the course of the 19th century, the Samurai were forbidden to carry their traditional longswords in public or to fight duels. Thus the Yakuza ethos is rooted in the choice between the loss of legality and the loss of pride. One of their rules states that a enemy may only be killed by means of the longsword. The Yakuza, howeve is no costume drama and no mere gangster film, but an examination – fror an American perspective – of the rules governing the Japanese world an underworld.

The daughter of a dubious American businessman resident in Japa has been kidnapped. His wheeling and dealing has not been well received i Yakuza circles. By holding his daughter hostage, they hope to force the unwelcome rival to abandon his crooked business practices. Instead of sub mitting, however, the American calls on the services of an old buddy from th years after WW II when Japan was still occupied by U.S. troops: enter the e> G.I. and detective Harry Kilmer – played by Robert Mitchum, an actor who no stranger to the gangster milieu. The man with the heaviest eyelids i

Hollywood will surely emerge from this underworld nightmare as lucki intact as a sleepwalker. But Tokyo is a jungle, an alien metropolis, and unlike most of the figures embodied by Mitchum, Kilmer has no hope of surviving here as a lone wolf. As a soldier during the occupation, he could afford to be indifferent to the moral framework of Japanese society; now, he finds himse obliged to study it. Solidarity is guaranteed by the social glue of the "giri," a ethos of personal obligation or duty that demands unconditional commitmen from all who serve it, and especially from members of the Yakuza: anyon who breaks ranks will pay with his life. It's a lot more persuasive than jus owing someone a favor…

The audience shares Kilmer's feelings as he studies the Japanese rule of conduct: the closer he looks, the stranger they seem. With this, *The Yakuz*

"At the end, the Yakuza is left contemplating a heap of ruins. He is a victim of the mythology he has subscribed to, a man who vanquished his enemies but lost the moral battle. This paradox embodies Pollack's basic and essential theme: the impossibility of reconciling myth with reality." *Deutsche Volkszeitung*

1   Eyes wide shut: Robert Mitchum as Harry Kilmer, a stranger in a strange land.

2   Don't make waves: In Japan, male bonding begins and occasionally ends at the pool (Herb Edelman, right).

3   Can I see some I.D.? Ken Tanaka (Ken Takakura) will eliminate the enemy at the drop of a hat.

4   Die by the sword: According to Yakuza, gunfighters
ignore sacred rites – and win.

eaves the standard formulae of the gangster film far behind. Kilmer has to operate between and across cultures, and he's faced with paradoxical situations. He meets a Japanese family who feel "giri" towards him, for he helped them to survive after the war and they are thus obliged to give him their unconditional support. With their help, he succeeds in forcing a showdown with the Yakuza gangsters and, in the battle between swords and handguns, technological progress carries the day. Kilmer survives, and from now on he owes one" to his helpers. He cuts off the little finger of his left hand and presents it to them as an IOU-note.

The Yakuza is of more than merely film-historical interest. For one thing, it's a convincing treatment of the conflict between the strict demands of a moral code and the messy ambivalence of everyday life. For another, it combines two very different film traditions: the American gangster movie and the Japanese Yakuza film, a highly popular genre in 60s Japan. Though Yakuza-film screenwriters included authors as serious and important as Yukio Mishima, Western critics and filmmakers never showed any interest in the genre. The only exception was the French director Jean-Pierre Melville: In *The Samurai* (*Le Samouraï,* 1967), the protagonist (Alain Delon) calmly accepts his own death as a simple matter of course, the logical consequence of his strict code of honor.

RV

ROBERT MITCHUM   Robert Mitchum (1917–1997) was one of the last great stars of the classic Hollywood cinema. He made his name in the Golden Age of the studio system that dominated the American film industry from the 20s until the late 50s. After the Second World War, a gem of a film brought Mitchum to the attention of a larger public: *Out of the Past* (1947) was originally a B-movie, but it established the archetypal Mitchum character, a man whose past will not leave him in peace.
Shortly afterwards, he spent a few weeks in jail for possession of marijuana; but he still developed into one of the most popular actors on screen. Mitchum was the ultimate tough guy. In films such as *River of No Return* (1954), *The Night of the Hunter* (1955), and *Cape Fear* (1962) he embodied loners and outsiders – laconically, with understated charm and a kind of nonchalant slothfulness that only increased with age. The characters he played might all have been created by Raymond Chandler; and in *Farewell, My Lovely* (1975), his dry and unflappable detective was the antithesis of the Humphrey Bogart figure. He fulfilled Raymond Chandler's definition of a hero: "… a complete man and a common man, and yet an unusual man."
Mitchum's legendary indifference to the art of acting is epitomized in his marginal note to the script of *El Dorado* (1967): NAR (= "no acting required"). His last film was Jim Jarmusch's *Dead Man* (1995), in which he performed alongside Johnny Depp.

THE LOST HONOR OF KATHARINA BLUM

Die verlorene Ehre der Katharina Blum

1975 - FRG - 106 MIN. - LITERARY ADAPTATION, THRILLER

DIRECTOR VOLKER SCHLÖNDORFF (*1939), MARGARETHE VON TROTTA (*1942)
SCREENPLAY VOLKER SCHLÖNDORFF, MARGARETHE VON TROTTA, based on the novella *DIE VERLORENE EHRE DER KATHARINA BLUM, ODER: WIE GEWALT ENTSTEHEN UND WOHIN SIE FÜHREN KANN* by HEINRICH BÖLL **DIRECTOR OF PHOTOGRAPHY** JOST VACANO
EDITING PETER PRZYGODDA **MUSIC** HANS WERNER HENZE **PRODUCTION** WILLI BENNINGER for BIOSKOP FILM, PARAMOUNT-ORION FILMPRODUKTION, WESTDEUTSCHER RUNDFUNK.

STARRING ANGELA WINKLER (Katharina Blum), MARIO ADORF (Commissar Beizmenne), DIETER LASER (Werner Tötges), JÜRGEN PROCHNOW (Ludwig Götten), HEINZ BENNENT (Doctor Blorna), HANNELORE HOGER (Trude Blorna), ROLF BECKE (State Prosecutor Hach), HARALD KUHLMANN (Moeding), HERBERT FUX (Weninger), REGINE LUTZ (Else Woltersheim), WERNER EICHHORN (Konrad Beiters), KARL HEINZ VOSGERAU (Alois Sträubeder).

"The thing is, my little blossom, you're famous now."

"It's dynamite – a German Watergate." These were the words of Volker Schlöndorff just before *The Lost Honor of Katharina Blum* reached the theaters. Expectations were almost unattainably high; but in the hothouse atmosphere of the 70s, with Germany divided by the terrorism debate, the film's impact was massive. It was a huge success at the box-office, highly praised by German and foreign critics alike, and showered with awards, including the German Film Prize for 1976. The film is based on a short novel by Heinrich Böll: *The Lost Honor of Katharina Blum, or How Violence Develops and Where It Can Lead*. It is both a gripping thriller and a painful dissection of contemporary German society. Böll himself collaborated on the script, and it was he who suggested casting Angela Winkler in the title role. A German star was born.

Angela Winkler embodies the young housekeeper Katharina Blum, thrown into conflict with the police and the tabloid press as a result of a casual acquaintance. Her performance is powerful and multifaceted, and the film casts a revealing light on the bigoted, divided West Germany of the 1970s. Heinrich Böll's labyrinthine narrative is transformed into a slim, no-nonsense movie. During the Cologne Carnival in 1975, Katharina meets

a young man at a party, with whom she falls instantly in love. It's Ludwig Götten (Jürgen Prochnow), a deserter from the West German army who under police surveillance. The audience doesn't learn much about Götten: merely that he's on the run, that police spies are following his every move, and that he is indeed eventually arrested. This scant information enough to evoke some real phenomena of the time: the hunt for Andrea Baader and Ulrike Meinhof, and what the foreign press described as "We German anarchist hysteria."

Katharina takes Götten home with her, spends the night with him, and gives him the key to the villa of a university professor called Sträubleder (Ka Heinz Vosgerau). Her motives are completely apolitical; but what she cal love, the police interpret as premeditated political action. The morning afte as Katherina makes coffee in her kitchen, a terrifying masked task force like something out of Terry Gilliam's *Brazil* (1984) – storms her apartmen armed to the teeth, under the command of Commissar Beizmenne (Mari Adorf). For Katharina, it's the start of a humiliating process. She is arreste and subjected to a series of interrogations, in which it's clear that the polic think they know the answers long before they've asked the questions. N

1   Carnival confetti: Katharina (Angela Winkler) falls
    in love with Ludwig (Jürgen Prochnow). He's
    deserted the German army, and the police are
    on his trail.

2   Calling the shots: Author, Heinrich Böll picked
    Angela Winkler for the role of Katharina Blum.

3   Look on in anger: Dr. Blorna (Heinz Bennent)
    and his wife (Hannelore Hoger) are appalled at
    the behavior of the police and the press.

one believes she's only just met Götten, nobody wants to know what really happened. It's not just the crass and dislikable Beizmenne who rushes to pronounce Blum guilty; the public mood is already aggressively vindictive, and the gutter press is happy to lead the pack. Worst of all is "Die Zeitung," clearly modelled on the *Bild-Zeitung,* Germany's most notorious popular tabloid.

Tötges (Dieter Laser), a slimy, unscrupulous reporter, scavenges around in Katharina's past in search of juicy details to add to the story he's already written. He invents statements from her desperately ill mother, for he knows

that "simple people require a little assistance in articulating their thoughts. What follows is a kind of witch hunt: Katharina is portrayed as a whore an a Communist sympathizer, and left to the tender mercies of an enraged pub lic. Day after day, she receives venomous letters and obscene phone calls Physically and psychically degraded, she can only hold on to her memories c Götten – until one night, she weakens and calls him. The police are listenin in, and Götten is arrested.

What happens next seems more a necessity than an act of revenge Katharina grants Tötges an exclusive interview, and invites him to her apart

> **"Schlöndorff has found a convincing solution to the dramaturgical problem of how to depict the course of events through the eyes of a young woman: allowing the spectator a naive, unmediated view of those events – while managing to keep his distance."** *Neue Zürcher Zeitung*

4   Witch hunt: To the cops and the tabloids, Katharina is a "left-wing slut" and has thus been stripped of her rights.

5   Search and seizure: Katharina Blum's arrest results in the shameless debasement of her private life.

The 70s were a period of political radicalization in Germany. At the heart of this development was the "Red Army Faction" (RAF), also known as the Baader-Meinhof gang, who have since remained a focus of interest for German filmmakers. Volker Schlöndorff's *The Lost Honor of Katharina Blum* (*Die verlorene Ehre der Katharina Blum*, 1975) was an early study of the German state's hysterical reaction to the perceived terrorist threat. The confrontation between the state and the RAF reached its climax in 1977, with the murder of the kidnapped employers' federation chief Hanns Martin Schleyer and the hijacking of the Lufthansa airliner "Landshut."

In the same year, eleven German directors – including Rainer Werner Fassbinder, Alexander Kluge and Edgar Reitz – collaborated on a direct and timely response to these very events: the film collage *Germany in Autumn* (*Deutschland im Herbst*, 1977/78). The social climate of the time led to the German government's deep distrust of the left-wing scene, which they believed to be riddled with terrorists or terrorist sympathizers. Reinhard Hauff's *Knife in the Head* (*Messer im Kopf*, 1978) is a subtle treatment of the theme. In 1981, Margarethe von Trotta made *The German Sisters*, aka *Marianne and Juliane* (*Die bleierne Zeit*), a film based on the life of Gudrun Ensslin, who had committed suicide along with Andreas Baader and Jan Carl Raspe in the Fall of '77 in Stuttgart's Stammheim prison. In 1985, Reinhard Hauff filmed the story of the Stammheim trial (*Stammheim*). Just over a decade later, Heinrich Breloer picked up on the events of fall '77 once more in his TV docudrama *Todesspiel – Teil 1 & 2* ("Deadly Game Parts 1 & 2," 1996–97). This film was accused of bias, for allegedly presenting only the viewpoint of the German state.

Since 2000, there has been a new cinematic discourse on the subject of terrorism. It began with Volker Schlöndorff's *The Legends of Rita* (*Die Stille nach dem Schuss*, 1999), a film based on the memoirs of Inge Viett, who went to live in East Germany after leaving the RAF. In 2001, Andreas Veie produced a documentary that won several prizes: *Black Box BRD*, a double portrait of the terrorist Wolfgang Grams and the Deutsche Bank's CEO Alfred Herrhausen, murdered by the RAF in 1989. Christopher Roth's *Baader* (2001) depicted the terrorist as a kind of pop star, while Christian Petzold's *The State I Am In*, aka *Internal Security* (*Die innere Sicherheit*, 2000) is one of the best films ever made on the subject; here, the former terrorists are lost souls, who can live neither inside nor outside society. The documentary *Starbuck – Holger Meins* (2002) is a personal portrait and a penetrating examination of the process of radicalization in Germany: director Gerd Conradt studied at the German Film and Television Academy in Berlin alongside Holger Meins, who later joined the RAF and died in prison on hunger strike at the age of 33.

> **"Worth seeing? Definitely. (...) It may not be a masterpiece, but it successfully examines the reality of modern life in West Germany in a way that is accessible to a wide public. That is no small achievement."** *Kölner Stadt-Anzeiger*

6 Critical condition: Tabloid hack Tötges (Dieter Laser) will do anything to get a quote, even if an elderly woman has to die as a result.

7 Guilty by default: Commissioner Beizmenne (Mario Adorf) never doubts his course of action.

"La Blum's" arrest is a pure demonstration of state power.

ment. In his cynicism and mendacity, he embodies everyone's night-mare of a tabloid hack. When he goes so far as to force his sexual attentions on her, Katharina shoots him dead.

The Lost Honor of Katharina Blum showed that the "New German Cinema" of the 70s could also be commercially successful. With its straight-forward narrative structure and the intense feelings it depicts and evokes – sadness, pity and rage – the film appealed both to cinephiles and a wider audience. Above all, it makes a powerful appeal to the emotions; this is a melodrama about a woman destroyed by society. Hans Werner Henze's disturbing music underscores the changes Katharina undergoes, from her initial incredulity at the accusations she's faced with to her final fury and despair. The camerawork by Jost Vacano (Das Boot, 1981; The Never Ending

Story, 1984) provides a visual realization of the tale's psychological dimen-sion. As viewers, we share in Katharina's ordeal. Yet the blatant collaboration of the police, the judiciary and the conservative, right-wing press impresses less as a political scandal than as the undeserved nemesis of a woman who's captured the audience's affections. Even at the time, critics accused the film of deploying the very methods it condemns: an undifferentiated black-and-white view of the world, and emotionalism instead of analysis. Yet the film has an undeniable and oppressive logic: those who are humiliated like Katha-rina Blum can only be expected to defend themselves. Thus the film can be seen above all as a depiction of the way in which state violence begets counter-violence in its turn.

KK

THE FRENCH CONNECTION II

1975 - USA - 119 MIN. - POLICE FILM

DIRECTOR JOHN FRANKENHEIMER (1930–2002)
SCREENPLAY ALEXANDER JACOBS, ROBERT DILLON, LAURIE DILLON DIRECTOR OF PHOTOGRAPHY CLAUDE RENOIR EDITING TOM ROLF
MUSIC DON ELLIS PRODUCTION ROBERT L. ROSEN for 20TH CENTURY FOX.

STARRING GENE HACKMAN (Jimmy "Popeye" Doyle), FERNANDO REY (Alain Charnier), BERNARD FRESSON (Inspector Henri Barthélémy), JEAN-PIERRE CASTALDI (Inspector Raoul Diron), CATHLEEN NESBITT (Old Lady at the Hotel), CHARLES MILLOT (Inspector Miletto), PIERRE COLLET (Old Pro), ANDRÉ PENVERN (Bistro Waiter), PHILIPPE LÉOTARD (Jacques, Drug Dealer).

"You bet your fuckin' ass it ain't New York!"

Popeye Doyle in Marseille! The guy with the pork pie hat amongst the "frogs," surviving in a culture where bartenders wear little white aprons and drink peppermint schnapps. Between the bouillabaisse and countless bistros, how will our bourbon-soaked ruffian ever get his bearings?

Given these new conditions, who could blame filmmaker John Franken-heimer for having little desire to direct a mere continuation of the maniac New York cop's brutal grudge match with the European drug baron. Instead, the film capitalizes on the French local color and plays up frivolous con-frontations between the tough-as-nails Popeye and the rather perplexed Frenchmen.

The plot itself imperceptibly eases its way into the amusing muddle. Doyle (Gene Hackman) has teamed up with the French police to get another chance to nab his nemesis Alain Charnier (Fernando Rey). Needless to say, the domestic official assigned to the case, inspector Barthélémy (Bernard Fresson), is familiar with Popeye's professional dossier and is far from

enthused by this collaboration. From his own specially designed desk locat-ed directly opposite the toilet, Doyle interrogates suspects who can't under-stand a word he says. Even abroad, Jimmy Doyle makes a conscious effo to get under the skin of everyone he encounters.

While aimlessly wandering about the city, he is discovered by Charnie kidnapped by his thugs and forced into becoming a heroin addict. Followin this torture, Doyle is thrown from a moving vehicle and deposited in fro of the police precinct. Partially as a means of covering up his own men incompetence and partially to spare the now junkie Doyle a discharge fro the force, Barthélémy sequesters him to an anonymous location, where h is mercilessly forced to quit his habit cold turkey. As it becomes clear to Doy that he was just bait to get Charnier to come out of hiding, he goes off on ballistic rampage.

The French Connection II dates from a time before movie sequels wer commonplace. Despite the rave reviews of the critics, it did not enjoy th

1   Come again? Popeye Doyle (Gene Hackman) doesn't know what to make of Marseille's peppermint liqueur and appalling lack of burgers. A Francophile he's not.

2   Budget cut: After surviving one of the most gripping chase scenes in movie history, Popeye is left to nab the bad guys on foot in the sequel. Is there no justice?

3   Connection casualties: France can be a killer.

4   Freedom fries with a side of spinach: Inspector Barthélémy (Bernard Fresson) and Popeye go together like heartburn and Alka-Seltzer.

same success as its predecessor. A misleading marketing campaign gave audiences the impression that the film was simply a newly released cut of the Friedkin original. Despite this, Frankenheimer's work still left a significant mark on cinematic history. For one thing, Gene Hackman, whom Friedkin had initial reservations about casting as the hardboiled police detective, takes the role to new heights, giving an absolutely impeccable performance highlighted by the excruciating detox sequence. Yet another great feat was that, despite all the parallels between the two movies, Franken-

heimer managed to create a completely independent work by depicting his Marseille in a faux documentary style similar to what Friedkin did with New York.

The city is the unbilled co-star and real opponent whom Doyle must combat against all odds in both installments of the saga. His cursing reveals how much he'd love to tear the place apart stone by stone, and he even attempts to burn down his former quarters of confinement. Whereas the inner realms of the narcotics underworld remained inaccessible to him on his ome turf despite all his street smarts, here we witness how he is taken risoner by the unspeakable horrors of its machinations. The crusade of the ndividual against his ominous surroundings and the all-powerful enemy is vhat Frankenheimer addresses in *The French Connection II* and throughout he entire body of his work.

Nonetheless, unlike Friedkin's sepulchral piece, Frankenheimer cuts he acidity of his characters with comedic elements. When asked by a bistro vaiter whether he'd like his whiskey "avec glace" Doyle replies "in a glass, eah," being sure to quickly snatch the glass away when the attendant eturns with *ice*. Nobody but nobody is going to water down his drink with ocks. Then again, what do you expect from a country where nobody even nows who Mickey Mantle is. SH

"Then we have the argument about whether form is more important than content. I can only say this — I don't think any director has ever made a great film with a bad script. But there have been many mediocre directors who have made very good films of very good scripts." *John Frankenheimer*

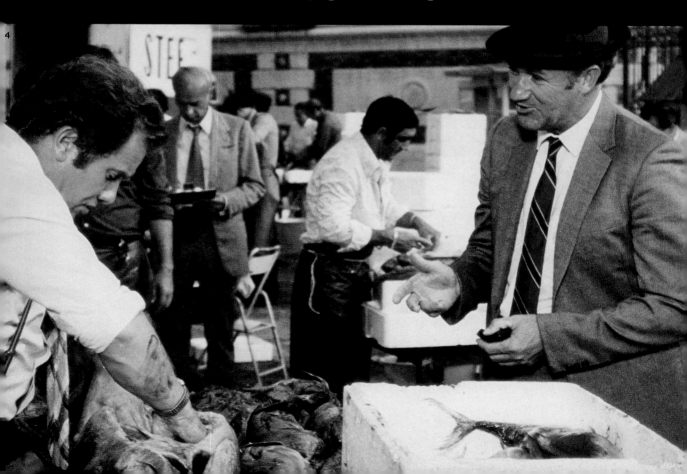

5

5   Oui, oui Madame! Membership does have its privileges…

6   A fire escape, at last! Doyle finds the first signs of intelligent life on the Côte d'Azur and makes a run for it.

"*The French Connection II* along with *The Godfather II* and *Aliens* will go down as one of movie history's most worthwhile sequels." *Inside Film Magazine*

JOHN FRANKENHEIMER   An undisputed master of the political thriller, an action aficionado and a technical wizard, John Frankenheimer met with success early in his career thanks to pieces like the *The Manchurian Candidate* (1962) and *Seven Days in May* (1963). The director would, nonetheless, wait until 1991's *Year of the Gun* before returning to the political thriller. Although the man born in Malba, New York in 1930 was always ready to instate action sequences for extra kicks, he was actually far more interested in the topic of the individual pitted against society and its institutions. This was a recurring theme in such works as *Birdman of Alcatraz* (1962), *The Train* (1964), *Black Sunday* (1977), *The Rainmaker* (1982) and *Against the Wall* (1994), and is revisited throughout his markedly diverse life's work.

Frankenheimer learned how to make pictures as a soldier with the U.S. Air Force and worked for many years in television. It is his mastery of the technical ins and outs of cinema that earned him his impeccable reputation. His predilection for live television can be seen in the piece *Grand Prix* (1966), whose race scene was filmed at an official racing event in Monte Carlo. Even after Frankenheimer became a widely acclaimed big screen director, he still voiced his disappointment at the downfall of live television. He is linked by his documentary style to other contemporary filmmakers of the age, who also started off in TV, like Sidney Lumet or Arthur Penn. He spiraled into an almost crippling crisis, following the assassination of his friend Robert Kennedy and battled for years with alcohol abuse. His later work was comprised of both flops like *The Island of Dr. Moreau* (1996) and masterpieces like *Ronin* (1998). He made a rather wry comment in an interview about the dilemma of selecting material for the screen. "You should oftentimes consider yourself lucky to be able to get a project off the ground (…) whether or not all the pieces fit into some neat canon or whether they turn out to be opportunities to develop yourself that much further is completely up to chance." His summarizing words are strikingly bitter: "Hollywood was never a place for artists. That is a great myth" (*steadycam*, 20/1991). What remains a fact is that when the 72-year-old Frankenheimer lost his life to complications resulting from a surgical operation in July 2002, the American cinema also lost one of its great craftsmen.

6

NASHVILLE

1975 - USA - 161 MIN. - DRAMA

DIRECTOR ROBERT ALTMAN (*1925)
SCREENPLAY JOAN TEWKESBURY **DIRECTOR OF PHOTOGRAPHY** PAUL LOHMANN **EDITING** SIDNEY LEVIN, DENNIS M. HILL **MUSIC** RICHARD BASKIN
PRODUCTION ROBERT ALTMAN for AMERICAN BROADCASTING COMPANY, PARAMOUNT PICTURES.

STARRING HENRY GIBSON (Haven Hamilton), LILY TOMLIN (Linnea Reese), BARBARA BAXLEY (Lady Pearl), NED BEATTY (Delbert Reese), KAREN BLACK (Connie White), RONEE BLAKLEY (Barbara Jean), TOMMY BROWN (Timothy Brown), KEITH CARRADINE (Tom Frank), GERALDINE CHAPLIN (Opal), SHELLEY DUVALL (L. A. Joan), SCOTT GLENN (Glenn Kelly), JEFF GOLDBLUM (Tricycle Man), BARBARA HARRIS (Albuquerque), MICHAEL MURPHY (John Triplette), GWEN WELLES (Sueleen Gay), KEENAN WYNN (Mr. Green).

ACADEMY AWARDS 1975 OSCAR for BEST ORIGINAL SONG: "I'M EASY" (Keith Carradine).

"Cut your hair. You don't belong in Nashville!"

"We must be doing something right to last 200 years," sings country music legend Haven Hamilton (Henry Gibson) as the band strikes up in *Nashville*. The picture is Robert Altman's opus, commemorating and investigating a country on the verge of its bicentennial. Rather than setting the film in the nation's capital, Altman travels to the Tennessee heartland where politics and country music are presented on the same ticket.

Music reverberates through this city swarming with singers and entertainment hopefuls. King of the scene is Haven Hamilton himself. The showman, a charismatic public speaker who radiates a political and evangelistic fervor, invariably appears in shimmering white suits. Nashville's reigning queen – also partial to white and curiously reminiscent of the great Loretta Lynn – is the mentally unstable Barbara Jean (Ronee Blakley), who returns to the city after a mourned absence only to collapse at her first public appearance. Other colorful characters among the performers we encounter include folk singer guitarist Tom Frank (Keith Carradine), as well as black country western star Tommy Brown (Timothy Brown), who some accuse of selling out to the white-run industry. We also meet an eclectic assortment of "undiscovered" talent like tone-deaf waitress Sueleen Gay (Gwen Welles), who is manipulated into putting on a strip tease for a drooling male voting contingent at an event promoting the fictitious third party presidential candidate Hal Phillip Walker.

Walker's booming campaign slogans and promises are as ubiquitous in this town as the deluge of country music. Despite the country music capital's traditional neutrality regarding partisan politics, the Walker team tries to win Haven's allegiance with the promise of a governor's seat. The candidate him-

self, who remains unseen throughout the entire film, spreads his gospel from the megaphone of his campaign, pitching a platform that swears to throw all lawyers out of congress and not allow tax-exemptions for churches. One of his most poignant slogans demands "new roots for the nation." These solutions appeal to the common man's sensibility concerning life, liberty and the pursuit of happiness. In this respect, they are not at all unlike the clichés proposed by country music. This backroads world seems, for the most part, to be dominated by surface appearances that allow it to block out all political realities. Yet there are instances where we witness characters like Haven's mistress and personal manager Lady Pearl (Barbara Baxley) contemplating some of the nation's all too fresh political wounds. Pearl, for one, harps on about the excruciating pain she still suffers as a result of the numerous tragedies associated with the democratic "Kennedy boys." Similar isolated sentiments throughout the film foretell an inevitable catastrophe – similar to the Kennedy assassinations – that will strike the crystal tower of country music.

Aside from this, political scandals like the Vietnam War and Watergate only subtly manifest themselves as an occasional song lyric or at most the lone soldier character just returned from the recently ended war. Ironically enough, Altman filmed the scene in the legendary Grand Ole Opry on the day President Nixon resigned from office.

Nashville is unique in that it offers no true main characters to its audience, presenting them instead with 24 more or less equally important human portraits. Of course, director Altman has proven himself time and again to be a master at negotiating this feat while still captivating his viewer

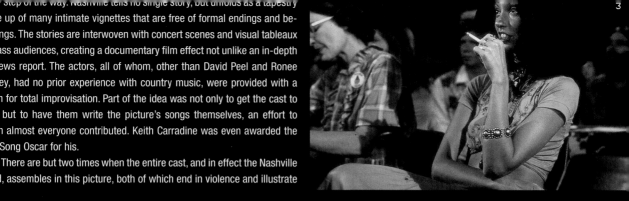

cry step of the way. Nashville tells no single story, but unfolds as a tapestry made up of many intimate vignettes that are free of formal endings and beginnings. The stories are interwoven with concert scenes and visual tableaux mass audiences, creating a documentary film effect not unlike an in-depth news report. The actors, all of whom, other than David Peel and Ronee akley, had no prior experience with country music, were provided with a rum for total improvisation. Part of the idea was not only to get the cast to ng, but to have them write the picture's songs themselves, an effort to hich almost everyone contributed. Keith Carradine was even awarded the est Song Oscar for his.

There are but two times when the entire cast, and in effect the Nashville orld, assembles in this picture, both of which end in violence and illustrate

"*Nashville* seems like a gigantic live broadcast, with 24 hidden cameras and a virtuoso at the control panel."

Peter W. Jansen and Wolfram Schütte

1 Press pass: Opal (Geraldine Chaplin) does some undercover investigating for what she claims is the BBC, but nobody seems interested in her professional credentials…

2 Let me entertain you! Waitress Sueleen Gay (Gwen Welles) wants to be a singer, but the presidential election just might strip her of her dreams.

3 Ain't never been grander! Joan (Shelley Duvall) enjoying a faerie tale theatre production of "Hee-Haw."

4 Harpo rides easy: There's just no telling where tha tricycle guy (Jeff Goldblum) and his bag of tricks will show up next.

4

"It is a musical, it is a political parable, it is a docudrama about the Nashville scene. But more than anything else, it is a tender poem to the wounded and the sad."

Chicago Sun-Times

5   Just a good ol' boy: Recording artist and country legend Haven Hamilton (Henry Gibson) belts out a ballad commemorating the nation's bicentennial.

6   Together in harmony: Nashville locals break out in song for any occasion, be it a weekend road-show

or the homecoming of country queen Barbara Jean.

7   I'm Easy: Singer, songwriter Tom Frank (Keith Carradine) spends significantly more time in bed than he does on stage.

8   Stars and Stripes Forever: Connie White (Karen Black) is sick of playing second fiddle to country queen Barbara Jean.

ROBERT ALTMAN   The engineer of the ensemble film deftly balanced 24 characters in *Nashville* (1975) and doubled that number for his next picture *A Wedding* (1978). Always innovative, Robert Altman (*1925) came up with a new mode of recording capable of picking up the overlapping dialog of his many protagonists. He furthered the brand of storytelling he coined in the 1970s with such works as the screen adaptation of Raymond Carver's *Short Cuts* (1993) and the British social drama/mystery *Gosford Park* (2001). These enormous ensemble productions are social portraitures that showcase specific cross-sections from literally all walks of life. Altman is a master of conveying the dreams, fears and propaganda of whichever group of people he chooses to examine, always breaking through their façades. In his scathing war comedy *M*A*S*H* (1969), he does his best to annihilate all romantic notions of combat. In *The Player* (1992), he makes out that the world of behind-the-scenes Hollywood is a veritable lion's den. Altman's career began in television, but he quickly switched to film. His projects have spanned an astoundingly wide range of genres and topics, including a wintertime Western (*McCabe & Mrs. Miller*, 1971), a political drama about Richard Nixon (*Secret Honor*, 1984), a comedy about haute couture (*Prêt-à-Porter*, 1994), a live action comic strip (*Popeye*, 1980), plays (*Fool for Love*, 1985) and even a John Grisham novel (*The Gingerbread Man*, 1997). The work of this great social satirist and critic is traditionally more widely hailed in Europe than in his United States homeland. A large number of his pictures have flopped in Hollywood and – despite numerous nominations – he has yet to win an Oscar. The flipside of this are the top European honors he has received such as the Golden Palm in Cannes for *M*A*S*H*, the Golden Lion in Venice for *Short Cuts* and the honorary lifetime achievement award at the Berlin International Film Festival in 2002.

---

ow twisted American values can be. The first instance follows a welcome ception for Barbara Jean where mass traffic spirals into a "Dukes of Hazrd" style freeway collision. None of the protagonists is wounded or incites ury. Yet their completely unfazed response, behaving as if they had simply en going for a ride on the bumper cars at the fair, is what is so disconcerting. The second occasion takes place during the finale at a packed concert d political rally for Walker that resembles a patriotic summer picnic. As rbara Jean is about to exit the stage, gunfire sounds and both she and

Haven are hit. We are led to believe that the queen of country music has been fatally injured, as the grazed Haven fanatically insists that the concert continue, handing the microphone to Albuquerque (Barbara Harris), a strung-out hopeful. By the grace of God, she is phenomenal and the crowd instantly forgets the blood bath they just witnessed, joining the new star in an uplifting yet ominous song, whose bittersweet words close the film: "You may say that I ain't free, but it don't worry me."

HJK

SUPERVIXENS

1975 - USA - 106 MIN. - SEX FILM

DIRECTOR RUSS MEYER (*1922)
SCREENPLAY RUSS MEYER DIRECTOR OF PHOTOGRAPHY RUSS MEYER EDITING RUSS MEYER MUSIC WILLIAM LOOSE PRODUCTION RUSS MEYER
for RM FILMS INTERNATIONAL, SEPTEMBER 19.

STARRING SHARI EUBANK (Super Angel Turner / Super Vixen), CHARLES PITTS (Clint Ramsey), USCHI DIGARD (Super Soul), HENRY ROWLAND (Martin Bormann), CHARLES NAPIER (Harry Sledge), Christy Hartburg (Super Lorna), SHARON KELLY (Super Cherry), JOHN LAZAR (Carl McKinny), STUART LANCASTER (Lute), DEBORAH MCGUIRE (Super Elua).

"I ask myself if the fucking he has is worth the fucking he gets."

They go by the names of Super Angel, Super Lorna, Super Soul and Super Cherry. The world they live in is a strange and mysterious place tucked away in the Arizona desert. If you saw them there you'd think you were looking at a Hustler magazine company picnic at the Duckberg junkyard. These blessed ladies have two striking traits in common. These would, of course, be their blinding set of knock-out melons and a bleeding thirst for good old-fashioned love making. Such a pity that the male element in Meyer's sexual Disneyland is either malevolent, as dumb as they come, or – brace yourselves ladies and gentlemen – cursed with impotence.

The big exception to these atypical archetypal masculine zeroes stomping about Meyer's playground is the simpleminded, honest Joe character that

takes the form of Clint Ramsey (Charles Pitts). He's the type of guy who war nothing more from life than a nice cold beer and a bit of peace and quiet. Cl also happens to possess the skills required to survive this starts with 'f' a rhymes with 'duck' fantasia. The man knows how to repair a car and carri around a monkey wrench you wouldn't want anywhere near your virg daughters. A guy like this doesn't really need anything more than a gas s tion, a burger joint and a fine woman like Super Angel (Shari Eubank) to ma him happy. She herself could personally while away the livelong day just bed, getting all revved up for her beau.

However, this missy is a she-devil, who isn't about to let anything, r even a man's career, stand between her and her incessant box-spring ma

2

"Russ Meyer was telling fairytales, in which voyeuristic pleasure was coupled with a cynical take on a seemingly atomized society." *Georg Seeßlen*

tress acrobatic act. One day, this conflict of interests causes things to get a little out of hand and the ensuing rampage sees a car pulverized to smithereens as well as the intervention of law enforcement officer Harry Sledge (Charles Napier), who steps in and beats some good sense into Clint with his nightstick.

Logically, this rough and tough Dirty Harry soon tries to fill the out of commission Clint's place in the sack with the relentless Angel. Harry, nonetheless, makes the mistake of working a double shift that nearly drives him over the edge. Angel reacts to his crude display of neglect by giving the cop a piece of her mind. He snaps and Angel meets with a gruesome demise. The murder is immediately pinned on Clint, who decides to make himself scarce and heads for the endless highway.

"Super Vixen – voluptuous, pure, good, totally giving, self-sacrificing." *Russ Meyer*

1   What beautiful eyes she has… and as long as the men are willing and able, the Supervixens keep smilin'.

2   It's a full moon tonight: Russ Meyer documents a solar eclipse.

3   Climb every mountain! Conquer every peak!

4   Let's get physical! Super Angel (Shari Eubank) puts poor Clint (Charles Pitts) to eternal booty camp.

5

What lies ahead are more filling stations, a whole new bunch of wacky characters and countless supervixens waiting to lure the sexually spent hitchhiker from one fiasco to the next. Along his road odyssey, he pulls into "Super Vixen's Oasis" and discovers a pit-stop paradise with a trusty gasoline pump, deluxe cheeseburgers and double-D cups. It would seem that the greater world order has been completely restored as, low and behold, Super Vixen is the spitting image of Super Vixen (Shari Eubank in a double role). Unfortunately, where there are angels, there are sure to be devils close by and that rotten ol' Harry is itching to stick sweet sucker Clint with a few logs of TNT.

Don't be fooled by the half baked plotline. Russ Meyer is no storyteller. His tempest of banged up lead, naked flesh and German military marches are visions of the apocalypse to an American audience. Yet while this Baroque surreal panorama is the distilled essence of bad taste, the raw worldview i presents is precisely what attests to the filmmaker's great love for his fellow man.

Russ Meyer's specialty is his knack for sexually charging every camera shot. Drawing liquid from a tap or even preparing eggs sunny side up suddenly becomes a blatantly obscene act. Perhaps it is therefore only fitting that this "culmination of all wet dreams" reads like a children's birthday party for grownups, as do all Meyer's productions.

Frequenters of the "Internet Movie Data Base" will find the most on target description of the legend that has become known as Russ Meyer. "(He) creates his own world in his movies and invites you to visit. And while I may not want to live there, I sure do like to visit!"   SH

"Too much for most men, too much for one movie."
U.S. commercial for the movie

RUSS MEYER   In the earlier years of his career, the Oakland, California native born in 1922, worked as a wartime reporter in Europe and a Playboy centerfold photographer for the magazine's initial issues. Clearly, these occupations served as preliminary training for the body of work filmmaker Russ Meyer would eventually produce. His directorial debut came in 1959 with his rather mild nudie *The Immoral Mr. Teas*. The picture netted over a million dollars for Meyer and provided him with a foundation for all his subsequent self-financed, self-produced, self-written and self-shot big screen flicks. As a German advertising slogan once put it, "there's always something to see in a Russ Meyer movie." Leading ladies with busts of intergalactic proportion became the calling card of his production company, RM Films International. For audiences seeking "a more classical Meyer aesthetic," the works of his black and white period including *Lorna* (1964), *Mudhoney*, (1965), *Motor Psycho* (1965) and *Faster, Pussycat! Kill! Kill!* (1966) are highly recommended. *Mudhoney* is by far the picture that the Fellini of the celluloid sex genre endowed with the most artistic merit. After the disproportionate success of *Vixen!* (1968), the bust sizes of his featured females underwent a dramatic inflation, the humor raunched up a notch and the film plots slimmed down significantly. *Megavixens / Cherry, Harry and Raquel!* (1969) was followed by *Beyond the Valley of the Dolls* (1970), *Supervixens* (1975) and his biggest commercial hit *Beneath the Valley of the Ultra-Vixens* (1979). The laurel wreaths won by the hardcore porn industry in the 1980s put an end to his career. The gregarious showman has produced both a film autobiography (*The Breast of Russ Meyer*) as well as a written one (*A Clean Breast*). Today, the pioneer of sexploitation's professional life consists primarily of actively promoting and reissuing his canon of work.

5   Old MacDonald had a ... Well, let's just say, here we see the benefits of the healthy farming life.

6   What's really behind door No. 3? A "Super Vixens Oasis" or "Bikini Car Wash?" You decide.

7   The Big Bang: Officer Sledge (Charles Napier) and his TNT prosthetic.

TAXI DRIVER

1975 - USA - 113 MIN. - DRAMA

DIRECTOR MARTIN SCORSESE (*1942)
SCREENPLAY PAUL SCHRADER DIRECTOR OF PHOTOGRAPHY MICHAEL CHAPMAN EDITING TOM ROLF, MELVIN SHAPIRO, MARCIA LUCAS (Editing Supervisor) MUSIC BERNARD HERRMANN PRODUCTION JULIA PHILLIPS, MICHAEL PHILLIPS for BILL/PHILLIPS, COLUMBIA PICTURES CORPORATION.

STARRING ROBERT DE NIRO (Travis Bickle), CYBILL SHEPHERD (Betsy), JODIE FOSTER (Iris), HARVEY KEITEL (Sport), ALBERT BROOKS (Tom), PETER BOYLE (Wizard), MARTIN SCORSESE (Passenger), STEVEN PRINCE (Andy the Gun Dealer), DIAHNNE ABBOTT (Candy Saleswoman), VICTOR ARGO (Melio).

IFF CANNES 1976 GOLDEN PALM for BEST FILM (Martin Scorsese).

"You talkin' to me?"

The restless, metallic strokes of the musical theme in the opening sequence say it all: this film is a threat. A rising steam cloud hangs over the street and covers the screen in white. As if out of nowhere, a yellow cab penetrates the eerie wall of steam and smoke, gliding through in slow motion. The background music abruptly ends atonally; the ethereal taxi disappears, the cloud closing up behind it. Two dark eyes appear in close up, accompanied by a gentle jazz theme. In the flickering light of the colorful street lamps they wander from side to side, as if observing the surroundings. They are the eyes of Travis Bickle (Robert De Niro), a New York taxi driver who will become an avenging angel.

Even at the premiere in 1976, *Taxi Driver* split the critics. Some saw the main character as a disturbed soul who revels in his role as savior of a young prostitute, for whom he kills three shady characters in an excessively bloody rampage, an act for which the press fetes him as a hero. Others looked more closely and detected a skillfully stylized film language in the melancholic images and a common urban sociopath behind the figure of the madman Travis Bickle: "On every street, in every city, there's a nobody who dreams of being somebody," reads one of the film posters.

Travis can't sleep at night. To earn a few cents he becomes a taxi driver. He'll drive anytime and anywhere, he says in his interview. He will even enter the neighborhoods his colleagues avoid at all costs – the districts with either too little or too much light, in which street gangs loiter around and teenage prostitutes wait for punters under bright neon lights. Travis is given the job. He and his taxi become one and the catastrophe takes its course.

Like Travis, the audience gazes out of the driving taxi into the night. Rarely was New York depicted as impressively. The camera style switches between half-documentary and subjective takes. Bernard Herrmann's sug-

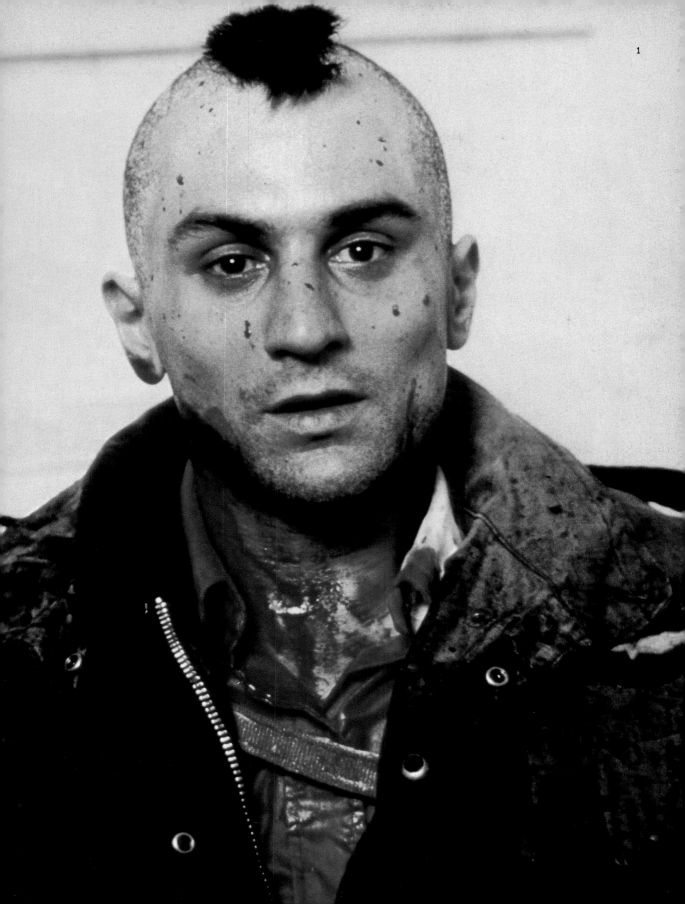

estive music, which accompanies the film, lends it an acoustic structure, creating a unique combination of image and sound. The taxi driving becomes nothing less than a metaphor of film.

Travis' attempt to build a romantic relationship with campaign assistant Betsy (Cybill Shepherd) fails. He can neither express himself, nor his feelings, which is why in the end he turns to the gun. Isolated and aimless, he wanders through the city. Travis' story resembles the yellow taxi cab that sliced through the cloud of smoke in the opening sequence. He too emerges out of nowhere, briefly appears in the night light of the city, and vanishes again into nothingness.

Travis is no hero, even if many applauded the brutal rampage at the premiere. Violence is naturally an important theme of the film, but the vio-

1   Robert De Niro in *The Last of the Mohicans?* Call central casting, quick!

2   Soldier of fortune at a buck a mile: Ex-Marine Travis Bickle, at war with New York.

3   Talk to the hand: Travis helps stamp out violent crime.

4   This screen ain't big enough for the two of us: Both pimp (Harvey Keitel) and taxi driver are used to getting their own way.

"Martin Scorsese's *Taxi Driver* is a homage to home from a homeless man; a New York Western, with a midnight cowboy cruising the canyons in a shabby yellow cab." *Der Spiegel*

"An utterly strange, disturbing, alarming and fascinating film. Syncretic and glamorous, it is a lurking reptile that changes color like a chameleon; a synthetic amalgam of conflicting influences, tendencies and meta-physical ambitions, raised to the power of a myth: comical, edgy, hysterical."

Frankfurter Rundschau

5   Jodie Foster as the child prostitute, Iris. Nonetheless, it was Foster's older sister who stood in as her body double for the more mature shots.

6   The facts of life: On tonight's episode, Mrs. Garrett tells Tootie what men really want.

7   Remember the Alamo: Election campaigner Betsy (Cybill Shepherd) is the object of Travis's desire.

BERNARD HERRMANN   He made a guest appearance in Hitchcock's *The Man Who Knew Too Much* (1956) as the conductor on the podium of the London Symphony, practically playing himself. He also wrote the music for the film. Born in New York on June 29, 1911, it was Bernard Herrmann who gave a number of film classics the final push towards immortality. He began working for radio, and then moved on to film, collaborating with Alfred Hitchcock, Orson Welles, François Truffaut, Brian De Palma, and Martin Scorsese to name but a few. He gave films like *Vertigo* (1958), *Psycho* (1960), *North by Northwest* (1959), *Citizen Kane* (1941), *The Magnificent Ambersons* (1942), *Fahrenheit 451* (1966), and *Taxi Driver* (1975) an unmistakable musical face, an aura of tonality. No one used the orchestra as eclectically Herrmann. He could make it sound conservative and classical, or send it into strange tonal regions in which the strings, accompanied by sonorous, dark horns, imitated the sounds of swinging metal wires.

Herrmann was fascinated by the sinister romantic literature of the Brontë sisters and by Melville's *Moby Dick*. The sea with its elemental force was an inspiration for the scores of his compositions. He could hear and compose the rising and falling of deep waters. Herrmann was not an affable man, perhaps because he was too much of an artist. He was known for his irascible and perverse behavior. He fell out of favor with Hitchcock during work on *Torn Curtain* (1966). He remained an artist through and through while working on his last soundtrack. He finished it on the day before his death on December 24, 1975. It was the music to *Taxi Driver*.

ence is not merely physical, but social. Travis embodies a person who has lost himself in the big city. Robert De Niro gave this type a face and an unmistakable body.

Scorsese is known for creating his films on paper. He draws them like sketches in a storyboard, and time and again he shows that images are his true language. The screenplay was the work of Paul Schrader, and marked the first close collaboration between two film-obsessed men. The scene in which Travis stands before the mirror shirtless, clutching his revolver and picks a fight with himself is unforgettable: "You talkin' to me? Well I'm the only one here. Who do you think you're talking to?" The scene has been cited over and over, but the original remains unattainable. It is a modern classic.

SR

6

BARRY LYNDON

1975 - GREAT BRITAIN - 184 MIN. - LITERARY ADAPTATION, HISTORICAL FILM

DIRECTOR STANLEY KUBRICK (1928–1999)
SCREENPLAY STANLEY KUBRICK, based on the novel of the same name by WILLIAM MAKEPEACE THACKERAY DIRECTOR OF PHOTOGRAPHY JOHN ALCOTT EDITING TONY LAWSON MUSIC LEONARD ROSENMAN, JOHANN SEBASTIAN BACH, WOLFGANG AMADEUS MOZART, FRANZ SCHUBERT, GEORG FRIEDRICH HÄNDEL, ANTONIO VIVALDI PRODUCTION STANLEY KUBRICK for HAWK FILMS, PEREGRINE.

STARRING RYAN O'NEAL (Barry Lyndon/Redmond Barry), MARISA BERENSON (Lady Lyndon), HARDY KRÜGER (Captain Potzdorf), PATRICK MAGEE (Chevalier de Balibari), STEVEN BERKOFF (Lord Ludd), GAY HAMILTON (Nora Brady), MARIE KEAN (Barry's Mother), DIANA KÖRNER (Lieschen), MURRAY MELVIN (Reverend Runt), FRANK MIDDLEMASS (Sir Charles Reginald Lyndon).

ACADEMY AWARDS 1975 OSCARS for BEST CINEMATOGRAPHY (John Alcott), BEST ADAPTED SCORE (Leonard Rosenman), BEST ART DIRECTION (Ken Adam, Roy Walker, Vernon Dixon), and BEST COSTUMES (Ulla-Britt Söderlund, Milena Canonero).

"It was in the reign of George III that the aforesaid personages lived and quarreled; good or bad, handsome or ugly, rich or poor, they are all equal now."

If Redmond Barry (Ryan O'Neal) hadn't fallen in love with his cousin (Gay Hamilton), his life might have been very different. As it happened, however, he had to fight a duel with an army officer who'd been promised the young lady's hand in marriage. And if Barry hadn't shot the officer, he wouldn't have had to flee his home village in Ireland; which is why he ended up fighting his way across Europe, first in the service of the British army, then for the Prussians. Barry's life is not in his own hands. Yet those who control him also help him, inadvertently, to climb the career ladder to a fairly dizzying height.

He has a talent for being in the right place at the right time. As a rewar for saving a high-ranking officer on the battlefield, he is given a position wit the Berlin police. Ordered to spy on an Irish aristocrat, he reveals the plot his compatriot – who repays the compliment by teaching him the tricks of h trade. Barry learns the craft of card playing and becomes a familiar face the royal courts of Europe. When he has acquired everything but a goo name and a wife, he meets Lady Lyndon (Marisa Berenson). The marriac brings him money, land and property, but he squanders it all. At the end of th

1 His troops go marching on: Kubrick based his film on the Thackeray novel, *The Luck of Barry Lyndon* (1844), but replaced the boastful first-person narrator with an omniscient commentator.

2 Take me, I'm yours: Barry Lyndon (Ryan O'Neil) enlists with the armed forces after losing his horse and his money.

"*Barry Lyndon* is not a warm film – Kubrick's never are – but it is so glorious to look at, so intelligent in its conception and execution, that one comes to respond to it on Kubrick's terms, which severely avoid obvious laughs and sentiment with the exception of two or three scenes." *The New York Times*

film, Barry is more or less back where he started: at a gambling table, but now minus his leg, his son, his wife, and his fortune.

We witness the rise and fall of an opportunist, filmed in breathtaking images. *Barry Lyndon* is a visual masterpiece, perhaps the most beautiful movie ever made. To see it in the cinema is like taking a walk through a gallery filled with works by Gainsborough and Reynolds. Few directors have ever composed a film with such care: each shot resembles an oil painting, and the colors are unparalleled in their intensity. The second half of the 18th

century has probably never been resurrected in such detail. *Barry Lyndon* the ultimate historical epic. In most costume dramas, the characters ca the cloaks and daggers of olden days, but their manners and morals a those of the 20th century. *Barry Lyndon* creates its own world: here, the pa is indeed another country, gone for ever yet still alive; and the first half of t film, especially, is notable for its quiet wit.

In creating a film that resembles a series of tableaux, Stanley Kubri has chosen a form that fits the content: superficiality and the power of t age in an ossified society. One of his main formal techniques is a gradually treating camera, a kind of reverse zoom effect, as if the viewer were observing a detail of the picture before walking back slowly to gain an impression of the whole. Only a few times does the camera actually move through e pictorial space: namely, whenever the film is dealing not with gestures d rituals, but with the naked struggle for existence. Examples include arry's boxing match with the strongest man in the unit, or the company's arch into the muzzle flash from the muskets of the French army.

In the final shot, the date "1789" appears. Before this time, the ideal individuality had not yet developed; clothing, for example, was merely indication of social status, and not an expression of personality. Like peacock spreading its tail, the army officer puts on his uniform: his rank

PAINTING AND FILM The beginnings of film are inseparable from the photography and literature of the 19th century. Yet the medium is most intimately related to painting. Even in the earliest days, filmmakers, like painters, frequently thematised their own work, the processes of creation, and the cinematic medium itself. The very first filmmakers, for example, appeared in front of their own cameras in slyly self-referential slapstick scenes.

Time and again, directors have taken their cue from painting, and not (as one might expect) from the more closely related medium of photography. In *Barry Lyndon* (1975), for example, Stanley Kubrick created scenes that seemed like paintings come alive, like *tableaux vivants*, an aristocratic pastime popular in the 18th century (described, for example, by Goethe in his novel *Elective Affinities*). In *Passion* (1982), Jean-Luc Godard made even more direct use of the Old Masters as an example and inspiration.

In turn, the invention of motion pictures had its effect on painting. First photography, then film robbed the medium of its previous task – or freed it from the burden – of providing a close approximation of external reality. The painters went on to develop new formal languages, such as Cubism and Futurism. Some film directors also paint: David Lynch, Federico Fellini and Akira Kurosawa are examples that come to mind.

3 Location scout: Kubrick found most of the untouched landscapes he needed in Ireland, but several scenes were shot in Great Britain and the East German city of Potsdam.

4 Going to great lengths: For Kubrick's painstaking reconstruction of the 18th century, the costumes alone took almost a year and a half. Bob Mackie was unfortunately unavailable.

"Kubrick's latest is, however, extremely beautiful. It is not only the superb photography that delights the eye. Most remarkable is the atmospheric composition of scene after scene, which reflects the golden glow and subtle moods of a Reynolds canvas. Eighteenth-century Ireland and Germany seem to live again." *Herald Tribune*

5   A discerning eye: Though Kubrick's film might appear cold and forbidding, Scorsese described it as one of the most soulful he had ever seen.

6   We have lift off! Kubrick filmed the interiors without artificial light, using a fast lens specially manufactured for NASA satellite photography.

Lady Lyndon's (Marisa Berenson) hairstylist demanded it.

and his wallet – is enough to ensure he will win the hand of Barry's cousin. From now on, Barry will single-mindedly pursue his goal: riches and reputation. Yet although he will eventually marry the beautiful Lady Lyndon, the off-screen narrator informs us that his wife was of no more importance to him than the carpets and paintings that formed the backdrop to his life.

A duel sends him on his way to wealth and fame, and a duel throws him back out of it again. At the end, Barry is standing in a barn, face-to-face with his own stepson. Kubrick devoted six minutes to this showdown, and it has the sober quality of a ritual. Yet we suddenly realize how terrified the stepson is, as he vomits for fear of his life. It's a moment of naked and public emotion that Barry would never permit himself. But his time has now passed: there's no place left in the world for fellows like him. He probably went back to Ireland, declares the narrator; but it's said he turned up in Europe again – as a gambler. This time, however, without success.

NM

DOG DAY AFTERNOON

1975 - USA - 124 MIN. - DRAMA

DIRECTOR SIDNEY LUMET (*1924)
SCREENPLAY FRANK PIERSON, based on a newspaper extract by P. F. KLUGE and THOMAS MOORE **DIRECTOR OF PHOTOGRAPHY** VICTOR J. KEMPER **EDITING** DEDE ALLEN **PRODUCTION** MARTIN BREGMAN, MARTIN ELFAND for ARTISTS ENTERTAINMENT COMPLEX.

STARRING AL PACINO (Sonny), PENELOPE ALLEN (Sylvia), JOHN CAZALE (Sal), SULLY BOYAR (Mulvaney), BEULAH GARRICK (Margaret), CAROL KANE (Jenny), CHARLES DURNING (Moretti), LANCE HENRIKSEN (Murphy), GARY SPRINGER (Stevie), JAMES BRODERICK (Sheldon), JOHN MARRIOTT (Howard), CHRIS SARANDON (Leon).

ACADEMY AWARDS 1975 OSCAR for BEST SCREENPLAY (Frank Pierson).

"The audience is interested in you, Sonny!" "Yeah! We're hot entertainment, right?"

An unbearably hot afternoon in Brooklyn. Those who don't have to work today are either catching a bit of shuteye at the park or indulging in an excursion to Coney Island. Stray dogs ransack the trash set out on the sidewalk, street laborers battle with heavy machinery in the middle of chaotic traffic, and security guard, Howard (John Marriott), is lowering the American flag in front of the First Brooklyn Savings Bank. Soon, it will be closing time, and only three more customers manage to squeeze their way through into the branch before its doors are locked up for the evening.

Well, "customers" is perhaps a poor choice of words, for Sonny (Al Pacino), Sal (John Cazale) and Stevie (Gary Springer) are three amateur crooks bent on emptying the bank's coffers. But moments after they set foot inside the building, things begin to go incredibly wrong. Stevie gets weak in the knees and tries to bolt. The tellers are all either making trips to the little girls' room or moaning about the heat. Worst of all, it turns out that the hot tip about the teller desks being full was way off the mark. There isn't more than 1,000 bucks to be found behind non-vaulted walls. Sonny manically attempts to salvage this bust of a predicament. He disables the security camera, scavenges what slim pickings he can and comforts the silently brooding Sal while simultaneously holding the increasingly blasé bank employees in check. Like a whirling dervish, he skates across the bank's slick floor. In just a matter of

seconds, the three guys will have successfully carried out the heist. Suddenly, the telephone jumps off the ringer. The call is for Sonny – Detective Moretti (Charles Durning), commanding officer of the special police squadron sent in to "neutralize" the criminals is on the other end of the line. It would appear that the three would-be hoodlums are bang in the middle of a sprung mousetrap.

A show business veteran, Sidney Lumet got his start in the industry at the tender age of four by acting in a radio show, and rapidly racked up a line of theatrical and live television credits. He opens *Dog Day Afternoon* with a twenty-minute sequence that flips back and forth between two plot lines and physical realms. On the one hand, Lumet shows us the mundane interior world of the bank, which plays like an intimate theater piece, featuring characters enslaved by spatial and temporal boundaries, which prevent them from dodging the mayhem of the imminent danger. Conversely, we are thrust outside to the sweltering hot streets, where the pressures of the inner world are given free expression, so to speak. Here, we are exposed to the details of everyday life, which Lumet sketches for us in the documentary-style opening credits. Although the city is still in a deep slumber, within minutes the general public will have transformed itself into a merciless beast fuelled by curiosity. Such is the case when the police show up on the scene and hunt

dreds of entertainment hungry spectators get as close to the blocked off action as they can. Helicopters hover over the street mob and camera crews in search of the perfect shot run around like headless chicken. What started off as a dilettantish, rookie job explodes into a full-fledged media extravaganza.

This twist of fate appears to initially act as a windfall to Sonny. As he conducts negotiations with Moretti on the street in front of the bank about procuring a getaway vehicle, he quickly wins the sympathies of the crowd. To them, he represents the abased common man, who stands up to the unjust system. Moretti can do nothing more than watch as Sonny taunts the rooftop snipers, throws wads of cash by the fistful to the cheering fans and inspires them to chant shouts of protest. It seems, Sonny has found his calling and readily takes the insanity to new heights: during a live TV news media interview, for instance, he's the one asking the questions – until the station cuts the coverage, that is. Nonetheless, the tide quickly turns on the apparent in-

undation of support, when Sonny makes public that he needs the loot to pa for his lover Leon's (Chris Sarandon) sex-change operation. Sonny's thievir bravado makes him a hero, but his sexual practices soon sever him fro grace and leave him branded a sodomite.

As it were, there's just no way to tune into the ins and outs of Sonny antics forever. Agent Sheldon (James Broderick), chief of the FBI, has bee following the chaotic chain of events with venomous eyes. When the getawa car that's supposed to transport Sonny, Sal and the hostages safely to th airport finally pulls up, robbers and bank employees alike believe that happy ending is in store for the Robin Hood-like crusaders. Of course, aft the TV crews have stopped rolling tape and the spectators have left th arena, the FBI agents show these clowns what they're really made of. The implement their assault at lightning speed, and Sonny's last glance at th camera lets us know that this is exactly what he'd been reckoning wi all along.

BIG SCREEN BANK ROBBERY The bank heist is a stock scenario with endless variations. This film genre lends itself to the most adrenaline-charged tales of cops and robbers crafty alarm systems and more often even wilier means of trickery. Criminals will risk landing behind bars for a chance at endless riches. Also because they don't swindle the "little guy," this brand of crook has been popularly deified as the crusader of the common man. *Bonnie and Clyde* the beloved gangster duo, who financed their romantic escapades with foolhardy robberies, are probably the most oft-cited example. In 1967, Arthu Penn paid cinematic homage to them with his brilliant film of the same name, starring Warren Beatty and Faye Dunaway in the title roles. In the end, however, the bank robber often proves to be no logistical genius. Both Robert De Niro in *Heat* (1995, directed by Michael Mann) and Jeremy Irons in the third *Die Hard* instalment, *Die Hard: With a Vengeance* (1995, directed by John McTiernan) fell victim to this flaw. The four Danish filmmakers Lars von Trier, Thomas Vinterberg, Søren Kragh-Jacobsen and Kristian Levring garnered much media attention for their New Year's Eve of 1999–2000 experiment entitled *D-dag – Instruktørene* (2000), in which four individual stories, broadcast simultaneously on four separate TV stations, wove a tale of bank robbery planned for the last night of the year. The viewer at home could change channels at will, thus enabling each spectator to become an amateur film editor.

"Pacino has an utterly pure and unspoiled talent, an absolute feeling for truth. He couldn't act badly if he tried." *steadycam*

1 Ready, aim, fire! The police, the FBI and the press have got the robbers surrounded and they'll shoot off their cameras and guns as soon as they get the chance.

2 Kicking and screaming: Moretti (Charles Durning) tries to persuade the gang to give up and leave peacefully.

3 Hell no, I won't go! Moretti fights to save all the hostages, but Sylvia (Penelope Allen) insists on staying with Sonny (Al Pacino) and "her girls."

4 Break the bank: Branch manager Mulvaney (Sully Boyar) had better watch himself because Sonny and Sal (John Cazale) are not about to compromise.

5 Inspiration for Norma Rae: Sylvia has the guts to stand up for her colleagues and tell Sonny to watch his mouth!

THREE DAYS OF THE CONDOR

1975 - USA - 117 MIN. - SPY FILM

DIRECTOR SYDNEY POLLACK (*1934)
SCREENPLAY LORENZO SEMPLE JR., DAVID RAYFIEL, based on the novel *SIX DAYS OF THE CONDOR* by JAMES GRADY DIRECTOR OF PHOTOGRAPHY OWEN ROIZMAN EDITING DON GUIDICE MUSIC DAVE GRUSIN PRODUCTION STANLEY SCHNEIDER for DINO DE LAURENTIIS CINEMATOGRAFICA, WILDWOOD ENTERPRISES, PARAMOUNT PICTURES.

STARRING ROBERT REDFORD (Joe Turner), FAYE DUNAWAY (Kathy Hale), CLIFF ROBERTSON (Higgins), MAX VON SYDOW (Joubert), JOHN HOUSEMAN (Mr. Wabash), ADDISON POWELL (Atwood), WALTER MCGINN (Sam Barber), TINA CHEN (Janice), MICHAEL KANE (S. W. Wicks), DON MCHENRY (Dr. Lappe).

"You guys are amazing.
You think not getting caught in a lie
is the same thing as telling the truth!"

The day starts off like any other at the New York "American Literary Historical Society." The small office staff sift through the details of the works they've been studying, run checks on the computers and discuss their findings. It's what you'd describe as a rather relaxed setting. The younger employees are chummy with one another and readily cover for co-worker, Joe Turner (Robert Redford), when a supervisor notices that he is running late for the umpteenth time.

A few hours later, a very different atmosphere will dominate this office. All of its staff will be dead, slaughtered by a sort of SWAT team who manage to gain entry into the facility despite all the hardnosed security measures. For this seemingly ordinary literary society was in fact a secret division of the CIA. Only Joe Turner, codename "Condor," escapes the massacre unscathed.

He's out picking up lunch for the entire office and, against regulations, he takes the shortcut through the back entrance and is thereby spared the awful fate of his team mates.

Upon his return, he discovers the gruesome bloodbath. Fearing for his life, the Condor grabs a gun hidden in a desk drawer and takes flight. Submerged in the crowd, he scans each and every face he sees out on the streets of New York, attempting to discern whether there's a psychopath among these pedestrians. At a public telephone booth he contacts CIA headquarters and informs them that his section has been hit. His superiors arrange to meet him at the Ansonia Hotel on Broadway. Turner is apprehensive and only agrees to show up when he is assured that his close friend and school chum, Sam Barber (Walter McGinn), will also be present. His ominous

FAYE DUNAWAY   A starlet beyond good and evil, Florida native Faye Dunaway has breathed life into some of Hollywood's most unforgettable female roles. Whether as the pensive, dissatisfied photographer Kathy Hale, who willingly jeopardizes the course her entire life for the Condor, the hard-as-nails insurance fraud investigator Vicki Anderson in *The Thomas Crown Affair* (1968) or Film Noir *femme fatale* Evelyn Mulwray in Roman Polanski's *Chinatown* (1974), Faye Dunaway has proven time and again that she is indeed worthy of the Best Actress Oscar she won for her role as the no-nonsense TV producer Diana Christensen in *Network* (1976).

Born in 1941, this military officer's daughter had already completed her theater studies and made numerous stage appearances before achieving big screen stardom. Her breakthrough came with her third film, *Bonnie and Clyde* (1967), Arthur Penn's study in glamor and violence about the Barrow gang. The picture earned Dunaway her first chance at Oscar. Another came in 1974 with Polanski's L. A. mystery *Chinatown*.

It's no secret that Dunaway has a volatile reputation that precedes her. At the time of filming, talk of Dunaway and Polanski's caustic disputes on the set of *Chinatown* was a Hollywood buzz topic.

While the majority of her roles have captured the attention of world audiences, not all of these are rated out-and-out triumphs. Her uncompromising and legendary portrayal of Joan Crawford in the unauthorized biography *Mommie Dearest* (1981) was savaged by the critics. After taking several second string roles in the 1980s, Dunaway won back much prestige with her work in pieces like *Arizona Dream* (1992) and *Don Juan De Marco* (1995). To this day, Faye Dunaway remains an undisputed star.

inⁱstinct is confirmed upon arriving at the spot where Sam is waiting. From ⁱt of nowhere, a second unidentified man opens fire on the two friends. ⁱrner shoots back, slightly "damaging" the perpetrator, who has mortally ⁱunded Sam. In an act of blind panic, the Condor kidnaps a random woman ⁱd manages to flee. Under duress, she drives him back to her apartment, ⁱich he uses as his hideout. Once there, he sees a report on the TV news ⁱout the incident at the Ansonia Hotel, but the media depiction distorts the ⁱtails of the crime. Turner now knows that he can rely on no one other than ⁱmself. Nonetheless, over their three days together, his hostage, photograⁱer Kathy Hale (Faye Dunaway), will prove to be an invaluable confidante.

In a 1975 interview with the magazine *Film Comment*, Sydney Pollack ⁱscribed his film *Three Days of Condor* as an examination of the destructive

"The director, Sydney Pollack, doesn't have a knack for action pulp; he gets some tension going in this expensive spy thriller, but there's no real fun in it." *The New Yorker*

1 Special delivery: After witnessing Turner (Robert Redford) bump off a postman, Kathy Hale (Faye Dunaway) succumbs to her kidnapper's steely charms.

2 To tell the truth: Joe Turner's tales may be larger than life, but before long Kathy will believe the CIA agent's every word.

3 Executive tricycle: Joe Turner, a man of the people, en route to the office.

4 Too close for comfort? Joe Turner doesn't need a gun to have his way with hostage Kathy.

potential of overblown mistrust. It's undeniably successful. As soon as the light-hearted kidder, Joe Turner (whose name is a tribute to one of John le Carré's novels) falls victim to the wave of paranoia brought on by the atrocities he's survived, the audience is glued to his side in what becomes an utterly suspenseful and action-packed production. Its intrigue lies in the killers' ability to disappear into the goings-on of everyday life. The woman with the stroller, the guy in the elevator or the mailman might all present a deadly menace – and two of them actually do. In a blind sea of millions of people, Joe Turner can't lower his guard. Even trusted work colleagues seem to present a threat to his life.

Cinematographer Owen Roizman depicts Turner's constant frenzy condensing the cinemascope format for exterior shots with a long focal length lens that deftly plays up the claustrophobia of the skyscrapers and imposing stationary objects. Turner appears to be visually caged in, and the sense of entrapment spills over unto the audience. Though the film's subtext screams "Watergate," the scandal was still to break when the shooting Condor began. According to director Pollack's own words, "we thought it was a really exaggerated idea until we started to read the newspaper headlines while we were in the middle of shooting."

5 A cold-blooded killer: Hitman Joubert (Max von Sydow) leaves his heart at home when he's on the job.

6 Official business: The masterminds of the literary society's massacre are top-ranking U.S. federal officers.

7 Help is on the way, but Joe Turner isn't sure it's the kind he wants.

8 The bitter taste of betrayal: Turner realizes who's behind the massacre

"Espionage drama about the parasite politics of the CIA, which sets spies to catch its own spies."

Sight and Sound

THE ROCKY HORROR PICTURE SHOW

1975 - USA - 100 MIN. - MUSICAL, SPOOF

DIRECTOR JIM SHARMAN (*1945)
SCREENPLAY RICHARD O'BRIEN, JIM SHARMAN, based on the stage play "THE ROCKY HORROR SHOW" by RICHARD O'BRIEN
DIRECTOR OF PHOTOGRAPHY PETER SUSCHITZKY EDITING GRAEME CLIFFORD MUSIC RICHARD O'BRIEN, RICHARD HARTLEY
PRODUCTION MICHAEL WHITE for 20TH CENTURY FOX.

STARRING TIM CURRY (Frank N. Furter), SUSAN SARANDON (Janet Weiss), BARRY BOSTWICK (Brad Majors), RICHARD O'BRIEN (Riff Raff), PATRICIA QUINN (Magenta), NELL CAMPBELL (Columbia), JONATHAN ADAMS (Doctor Everett Von Scott), PETER HINWOOD (Rocky), MEAT LOAF (Eddie), CHARLES GRAY (Criminologist).

"In just seven days, I can make you a man!"

If indeed the *Rocky Horror Picture Show* continues to glow in the minds of world audiences to this day, be assured that film critics of the time had little to do with lighting its eternal flame. Quite the contrary, my pretties. When the movie was beamed down to terrestrial theaters in 1975, the scathing verdict of these professional jurists was unanimous – the celluloid version was nothing more than a sorry adaptation of the London underground stage's surprise hit. According to the reviews, this fine specimen of big screen meningitis belly-flopped between gratuitous displays of histrionics and flawlessly unamusing musical numbers, which managed to completely obscure what little plot its 100 minutes had to offer. The outcome seemed clear. The film was doomed to the depths of oblivion in the vaulted hell of some dark, damp film archiving facility. At most, it would be a poor excuse for a footnote in camp and trash history.

Then something miraculous happened. During *Rocky's* midnight showing at the 8th Street Playhouse in New York, the owner of the movie house began to rant and rave at the screen (allegedly he shouted at Janet, "buy an umbrella, you cheap bitch!"). His words infected the audience and the ball was set rolling, with comments flowing like the downpour of rain. Spectators returned in droves armed with an ample supply of rice and water guns. This time, they were ready to take part in the wedding and the storm, dropping

their ironic commentary with increased fanaticism. The enthusiasm climaxe with moviegoers dressing up like their favorite characters, be it Frank I Furter, Riff Raff or Magenta. The complacent, passive undertaking of watch ing a film became an interactive black mass. The picture itself was tran formed into a blank canvas onto which both the uninhibited and party craze could project their most irreverent whims and fancies. Out of the reels of reproducible mass commodity, indistinguishable in both shape and conter a unique happening was born. No two showings of *The Rocky Horror Pictu Show* were fundamentally identical and no action set in stone. The hierarch cal fabric of active and passive parties, whether filmmaker and spectator, producer and consumer had begun to unravel.

The plot is indeed no more than a light and simple catalyst for th piece's music and spoof aesthetic. Newly engaged lovebirds Brad (Bar Bostwick) and Janet (Susan Sarandon) motor their way to the former's men tor, Dr. Scott (Jonathan Adams). The young killjoy is set on sharing his futu plans with the good doctor and getting his blessing. A flat tire and a thunde storm force the two wholesome (in the biblical sense) Midwesterners to see help at an old, ominous castle. What awaits them is a colorful cult of creep crawlies, who have all gathered to honor the groundbreaking achievemer of Dr. Frank N. Furter (Tim Curry), one very "sweet transvestite from tran

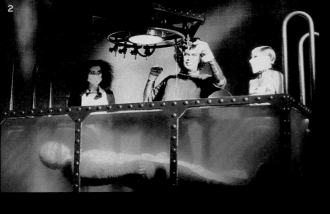

sexual Transylvania." A hunchback butler, a nymphomaniac chambermaid, an inorganically generated He-Man, a frozen solid rock star and even Dr Scott himself all serve as indicators that this may be an eclectic convention of intergalactic proportion. This proves to be the case when Brad and Jane realize that they have stumbled upon alien life forms who are avidly studying human sexual behavior.

This *Men in Black* style scenario under an altogether different astrological sign never strays from the universe of cinema and communicates its story through pointedly self-conscious movie references. As the sumptuous larger than life lips vocalize to us during the film's opening number *Science Fiction Double Feature*, the entire picture is little more than one colossal tribute to the horror and sci-fi classics of the 1950s. *Rocky* fills its loins with the

"Overall most of the jokes that might have seemed jolly fun on stage now appear obvious and even flat. The sparkle's gone." *Variety*

1   Full package and a strand of pearls: Tim Curry as the irreverent Dr. Frank N. Furter.

2   It's a boy! But in just seven days, Dr. Frankenfurter will make a man out of his well-endowed baby.

3   Heart attack: Frank N. Furter catches Rocky (Peter Hinwood) playing doctor with Janet Weiss (Susan Sarandon).

4   Dancing queens…

5   … go cool in the pool.

6

"But the greatest 'frisson' that *The Rocky Horror Picture Show* has to offer is that it was shot at Bray Studios, site of the decline and fall of Hammer horrors. It's ironically fitting that this bizarre, ill-conceived hybrid should be dancing on the grave of the real British B-movie tradition." *Monthly Film Bulletin*

6 Space oddity: When Metropolis meets King Kong at the film's conclusion, Magenta (Patricia Quinn) and brother Riff-Raff try to cut through the standing ovation.

7 Torn curtain: Furter and Brad sail to distant shores.

8 Blame it on the bossa nova: Riff Raff leads the castle guests in a most peculiar space conga line. Richard O'Brien, a writer of the stage version, joins in on the "Time Warp."

THE CULT CLASSIC The more often and more liberally a term is used, the harder it becomes to define. Its semantic essence diminishes with each extension of its meaning. The catchphrase, "cult film" fell victim to the grand mechanisms of movie marketing long ago. How else can one understand the unscrupulous efforts of distributors to deem *American Pie 2* (2001) and dozens of other pictures like it cult classics even prior to their initial release. Back when it was coined to refer to film, "cult" designated a specific audience reaction, which took the form of an actual "cult following" associated with the film. Whether *Blues Brothers* (1980) inspired costume parties, *Rocky Horror Picture Show* (1975) mayhem, or the *Once Upon a Time in the West* (*C'era una volta il West*, 1969) long duster coat fad, it was the audience's enthusiasm to integrate aspects of these pieces into their pop culture at large that made these pieces attain cult status.

The 1990s were particularly adroit at recognizing the promotional potential of a "cult classic" and proceeded to plant certain contrived elements in actual films and introduce lines of merchandise to accompany theatrical releases. Quentin Tarantino proved he had a remarkable knack for this sort of "cultification" by including some of the most memorable dialog from *Pulp Fiction* (1994) as bonus material on the film's soundtrack album. In no time flat, lines like "I love you, honeybunny, I love you, pumpkin," and "Zed's dead" were being chanted by addicted and adoring fans.

innuendoes and themes that once breathed life into the genre, managing to play up their original implications while making them relevant to the context of 1975. The film sends its own decade's sensibilities on a collision course with uptight, Cold War propriety. It thus paints a glaring portrait of revolution that has micromanaged its front to sexual fulfillment.

Taking all this into consideration, the film not only echoes in our hearts as a rich ode to bygone Hollywood with rock songs that have made history in their own right, but also marks the dawn of a new era in what an audience understands to be its role. Motion pictures ceased to solely exist as entities of passive consumption ever since. The door was now wide open to spectators getting up and playing along, reassessing the on-screen action and introducing elements of the piece into their own lives. MH

7

8

1900
NOVECENTO

1975/76 - FRANCE / ITALY / FRG - 318 MIN. - HISTORICAL FILM, EPIC

DIRECTOR BERNARDO BERTOLUCCI (*1941)
SCREENPLAY FRANCO ARCALLI, BERNARDO BERTOLUCCI, GIUSEPPE BERTOLUCCI DIRECTOR OF PHOTOGRAPHY VITTORIO STORARO
EDITING FRANCO ARCALLI MUSIC ENNIO MORRICONE PRODUCTION ALBERTO GRIMALDI for ARTÉMIS PRODUCTIONS, PRODUZIONI
EUROPEE ASSOCIATI, LES PRODUCTIONS ARTISTES ASSOCIÉS.

STARRING GÉRARD DEPARDIEU (Olmo Dalco), ROBERT DE NIRO (Alfredo Berlinghieri Jr.), BURT LANCASTER (Alfredo
Berlinghieri Sr.), STERLING HAYDEN (Leo Dalco), DOMINIQUE SANDA (Ada Fiastri Paulhan), DONALD SUTHERLAND
(Attila), LAURA BETTI (Regina), WERNER BRUHNS (Ottavio Berlinghieri), STEFANIA CASINI (Neve), ROMOLO VALLI
(Giovanni), ANNA HENKEL (Anita).

"There are no more masters."

Novecento – Twentieth Century – is the actual title of this mammoth pro-ject, an opulent epic covering five decades of Italian history, focusing on the lives of three generations whose tales are told in parallel. The year 1900 merely marks the connection to the previous century, which witnessed the emergence of one of the great modern ideas: that life in its totality might be encapsulated in a philosophical system or a work of art. It's an ambition shared by the film itself; and the theory of history as the story of class struggle and social conflict has clearly had a profound influence on Bernardo Bertolucci.

On a country estate in Emilia Romagna at the turn of the century, two baby boys are born on the same day: Alfredo, the grandson of the landowner Alfredo Berlinghieri (Burt Lancaster), is heir to the estate; Olmo, the fatherless grandson of the peasant Leo Dalco (Sterling Hayden), inherits the work. Hav-ing shared a childhood, they will grow up to confront one another as class enemies. Yet despite his clear sympathy for the oppressed workers, the artist

Bertolucci is no proponent of the primacy of politics. On the contrary: from th faces and landscapes of Northern Italy, he creates a panorama of rural lif assigning each of the four periods depicted – pre-Great War, postwar, fascism and liberation – to a season of the year: Summer, Fall, Winter, an Spring respectively. It's a subtle tribute to the composer Giuseppe Verdi, lik Bertolucci a native of the province of Parma, for despite the lamenting of th harlequin in the film's opening scenes, Italy's national composer is far fro dead. The film holds only superficially to the facts of recorded history, suc as the great land-laborers' strike of 1908: it impresses, above all, as a kin allegorical opera. Whether red flags are flying or fascist battalions marchir through the streets, the choreographed masses have the power of operat choirs, accompanied by Ennio Morricone's music and Bertolucci's Itali delight in pathos.

From beginning to end, the symbolic imagery of this baroque magnu opus is dominated not only by the colors of the earth and the changing lig

2

"This $8 million epic, Bertolucci's first effort since *Last Tango in Paris*, is a fabulous wreck. Abundantly flawed, maddeningly simple-minded, *1900* nonetheless possesses more brute force than any other film since Coppola's similarly operatic *Godfather II*. If Bertolucci irritates as much as he dazzles, he never bores: his extravagant failure has greater staying power than most other directors' triumphs." *Time Magazine*

1 Animal attraction: The beautiful and unconventional Ada (Dominique Sanda) is married to young Alfredo. But then what's fidelity if you can have Olmo?

2 Gone to the dogs: Padrone Alfredo Berlinghieri (Burt Lancaster) is an Italian landowner of the old school – and now, he's an anachronism.

3 A finger in every pie: The meddlesome schoolteacher Anita (Anna Henkel) becomes Olmo's wife.

4 The Age of Reason: The new master Giovanni Berlinghieri (Romolo Valli) organizes the estate on more economic lines.

"The land needs the people! The soil will rot without them! But who needs the *padrone*?"

Film quote: Voices from the crowd

f the sun, but also by blood, dung, and filth. There is nothing nostalgic in ertolucci's depiction of the merciless suppression of serfs by their masters. lfredo Sr. makes a quick departure: the Italian rural aristocracy, so splen-idly embodied by Burt Lancaster in Visconti's *The Leopard* (*Il gattopardo*, 963), expires in a cowstall. The old man's son employs the methods of a oodsucker to fight the demands of the nascent farmworkers' organization, nd ultimately calls on the help of the fascists. Salvation appears in the form the diabolical estate manager and blackshirt leader Attila (Donald Suther-nd). His brutal perversity is not just an expression of Bertolucci's desire present fascism as an embodiment of evil; he also shows these violent utbursts as a psychological consequence of the conflict between the bour-oisie and the proletariat. The sexual superiority of the working class is

manifested in the figure of Olmo (Gérard Depardieu), an eloquent and impassioned agitator. When the new *padrone* Alfredo Jr. (Robert De Niro) can't find his beautiful wife Ada (Dominique Sanda), he looks for her in Olmo's hovel. Not without reason. Even in their childhood years, Olmo had made him painfully aware of his weaknesses, making fun of his immaturity by challenging him to hair-raising tests of bravery. And now, in adulthood, he continues to laugh in his face. It's hardly possible to say how much irony is intended in this provocative amalgamation of sex and politics. For Bertolucci was himself a middle-class child, and his narrative mannerisms evince a great deal more ambivalence than his depiction of the characters. His mixed feelings are undoubtedly connected to the period in which the film was conceived and created, as is the victorious Olmo's appeal for a "histori-

"My son will study Law."
"My son will steal."

Film quotes: Alfredo Berlinghieri Sr. and Leo Dalco

5   Over my dead body: A moving manifestation of civil disobedience by peasant women, and just one example of Bertolucci's feminist perspective.

6   Learning by example: Leo Dalco (Sterling Hayden) is the role model for his grandson Olmo.

7   A little R & R: After preaching *revolution* at the workers' school, Anita *romances* Olmo (Gérard Depardieu).

8   Power trip: After a cocaine orgy at Uncle Ottavio's place, Alfredo has a rude awakening. Ada tells him his father is dead and he is the new padrone.

EPIC

The first cinematic epic appeared in the early years of the cinema: D. W. Griffith's *The Birth of a Nation* (1915). Yet the historical epic, a mirror of national destinies, is only one variety among many. There are science fiction epics such as the *Star Wars* films (1977, 1980, 1983, 1999, 2002), and contemporary social epics like *Nashville* (1975). Indeed, the Western, a form that need take no account of historical persons and events, was for a long time the epic form *par excellence*. For the subtext of this super-genre is the mythical, and myths are so infinitely interpretable that a definition of the term "epic" must finally be grounded in subjective perception. Factors such as the length of the film, the number of star actors, or the size of the budget are merely marketing arguments for "big pictures." What count are the high quality of the cinematic realization and the inner logic of the narrative, in which personal, cultural and universally human patterns of behavior are combined in such a way that they mean more than they tell. In this way, the epic acquires a transcendent quality, linking the most important areas of life and history, such as love, family and war.

Epic films depict people forced to contend with difficult, often tragic circumstances. It's interesting to see where the stress lies in different films: thus *Doctor Zhivago* (1965) and *Titanic* (1997) invoke an ideal of romantic love against the backdrop of a significant historical event. The *Godfather* trilogy (1972, 1974, 1990) confronts the American Dream with its relationship to violence and crime, with classical family structures playing an equally important role. Only one other genre can match the popular appeal of the epic, and it stands in almost irreconcilable opposition to this most serious of film forms: comedy.

ompromise." In 1975, the failed alliance between the Christian Democrats and the Communists was *the* political topic in crisis-torn Italy.

A betrayal of the class struggle? Or a transparent misuse of history in the interests of agitation, a pompous marriage between Hollywood and Socialist Realism? At the Cannes festival, Bertolucci's idiosyncratic interpretation of history caused an uproar. But Bertolucci had much more pressing problems ahead. Three U.S. production companies – United Artists, Paramount Pictures and 20th Century Fox – had borne equal shares of the production costs, which totaled six million dollars, and they objected to the "unmarketable" five-and-a-half-hour film delivered by Bertolucci. When the case reached the courts, a judge was forced to watch three versions of the film on three successive days. Besides the original version, there was a 4-hour-40-minute *1900* and a

"Long live the revolution! Long live the revolutionaries! Long live the General Strike!"

Film quote: Voices from the crowd

9 The lone white stallion: Ada and Alfredo are soon deeply estranged. Here she rides into the woods, to meet Olmo once again.

10 Brute force: Bailiff Attila builds a concentration camp on the estate. He and his henchmen murder at will. The peasants are powerless to resist.

11 Flags fly for freedom: Spring has come, the war is over, and the revolution is victorious – at least on the Berlinghieri estate. A People's Court puts landlord Alfredo on trial.

3-hour-15-minute version cut and pasted by Paramount themselves. A Bertolucci explained later: "The judge was dazed by an overdose of *Novecer to*," but he worked out a "historic" compromise between the filmmaker and the producers. For the American market, Bertolucci assembled a 4-hou version, which was prevented from reaching a large audience by the mach nations of the studios. Though the director had remarked that this slimmed down version was the best, he later retracted this statement. Even in its orig inal length, however, the film took a long time to reach Europe. On Bertolucci own suggestion, the film was divided into two parts, but only years after it was completed did *1900* achieve recognition as an impressive work of art and ga relative popularity as a cult film. The tattered history of the twentieth centu had acquired a cinematic memorial.   P

"The padrone is dead and Alfredo Berlinghieri is living proof of it."

Film quote: Olmo Dalco

12 Of mice and men: Class-conscious Olmo doesn't have much to say to intellectual Ada. But his sheer masculinity makes Alfredo pale in comparison.

13 Throw me a bone: Attila "the watchdog," seems devoted to his master. But soon, Alfredo's power-hungry stomach begins to growl…

14 Splendor in the grass: After the Liberation in 1945, Attila is hunted down. Rough justice for the fascist torturer, whose bloody end was anticipated at the beginning of Part 1.

13

"Bertolucci's film is a bucolic opera in the language of cinema, bursting with vitality, orgiastic fecundity and voluptuous urgency. He shows us an Italy without Riviera kitsch or Santa Lucia schmalz, choosing his images from a latifundium in the vast agrarian landscape of the Emilia: its endless wheat fields, its open barns with their brick colonnades, its canal-banks and dykes, its cattle stalls, its threshing floors, and its sparse forests of poplar." *Frankfurter Allgemeine Zeitung*

CARRIE

1976 - USA - 98 MIN. - HORROR FILM

DIRECTOR BRIAN DE PALMA (*1940)
SCREENPLAY LAWRENCE D. COHEN, based on the novel of the same name by STEPHEN KING DIRECTOR OF PHOTOGRAPHY MARIO TOSI
MUSIC PINO DONAGGIO EDITING PAUL HIRSCH PRODUCTION PAUL MONASH, BRIAN DE PALMA for REDBANK FILMS.

STARRING SISSY SPACEK (Carrie White), JOHN TRAVOLTA (Billy Nolan), PIPER LAURIE (Margaret White), AMY IRVING (Sue Snell)
WILLIAM KATT (Tommy Ross), NANCY ALLEN (Chris Hargenson), BETTY BUCKLEY (Miss Collins), P. J. SOLES (Norma
Watson), PRISCILLA POINTER (Mrs. Snell), SYDNEY LASSICK (Mr. Fromm).

"They're all gonna laugh at you!"

High school can be quite a blood bath. It's a world dominated by vanity, envy and petty fears. For those who don't fit the mold, teasing, sneering and even total ostracism can lie in store. But can't this clichéd view of the growing years be partly attributed to countless soap operas and teen flicks? Maybe so. Nevertheless, real reports of rampant violence repeatedly hit the headlines, a testament to the fact that the social microcosms within schools are no place for kids who journey the path less traveled.

Carrie White (Sissy Spacek) is one such person. She is the daughter of the mentally ill Margaret (Piper Laurie), who became a religious fanatic after Carrie's father left them. In her relentless crusade to protect Carrie from earthly sins, Margaret beats the word of God into her daughter. Thus, while showering in the girls' locker room, the innocent Carrie is horrified when she menstruates for the first time.

Only gym teacher Miss Collins (Betty Buckley) extends Carrie her support. Still, her efforts to discipline the malevolent, traumatizing girls present for the event only adds fuel to their sadistic fire. When one of the girls, Chris (Nancy Allen), is prohibited from attending the prom as a result of the embarrassing incident, she swears revenge on Carrie, which meets with disastrous consequences ...

For meanwhile Carrie has discovered that she possesses an extraordinary gift. She is a telepathic medium. When faced with the eternal callousness of her immediate environment, this seemingly mousy homebody turns into a ticking time bomb.

Even though the image forever engrained in the memories of world audiences is that of the young Sissy Spacek drenched in pig's blood, Carrie cannot be deemed a horror film in the classic sense. It is at its most gruesome when it shakes the audience with images of the true-to-life, spiteful machinations of the snide cliques led by John Travolta and De Palma's late wife Nancy Allen. Carrie is not, however, a scathing critique of American high schools. Above all else, the film is a heart-pounding thriller that keeps you on the edge of your seat even though the story's ending is clear from the start.

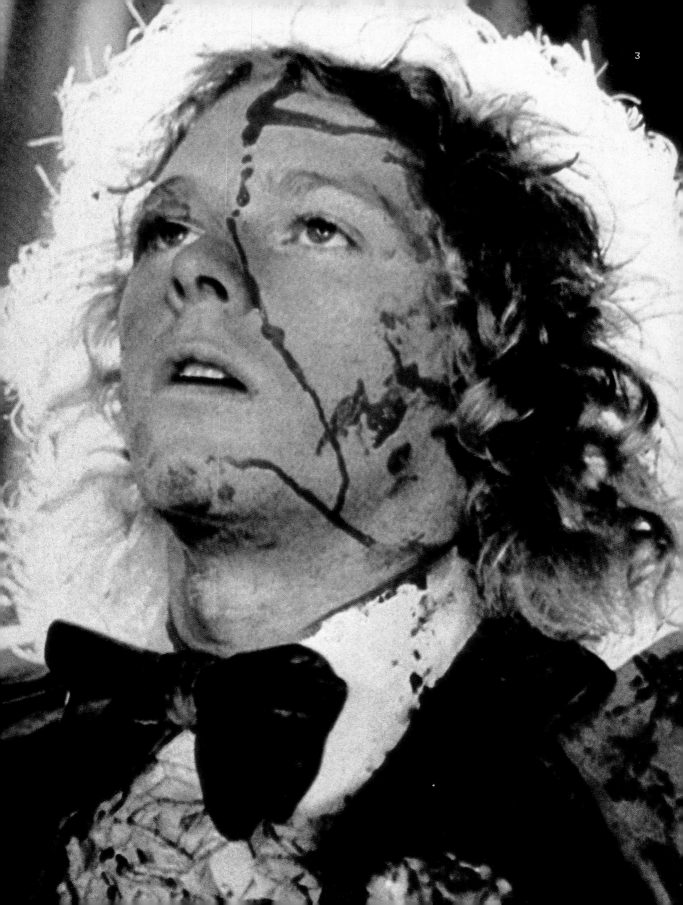

De Palma takes great pleasure in torturing his audience to the bitter end, manipulating its voyeuristic expectations and then tweaking the plot in such a way as to leave everyone hung out to dry. Which, according to Brian De Palma, is giving the audience their just desserts. For when it comes down to it, movie-goers are not that different from the on-screen juvenile brat pack, eager to put wise in Carrie's sails on prom night. With diabolic precision, he intensifies the audience's basic desire to put an end to the heroine's perpetual ridicule, by firing it up with the growing anticipation of the most climactic event of every high school girl's life – the prom. The dance's culmination is accompanied by the unleashing of an unstoppable act of apocalyptic wrath.

You could describe the last third of the film as pure mannerism. It's fireworks display, including the slow motion camera, split-screen action,

extreme close-ups and pointedly dramatic lighting. Though many a director would have shied away from a finale that could be branded as a cavalcade of cheap effects, De Palma implemented it flawlessly and turned its elements into his signature style.

What's more astonishing is that Carrie was shot on a spartan budget of just under two million dollars. The financial limitations forced De Palma to abstain from filming the total destruction of the town that takes place in the novel. Nevertheless, Carrie proved to be a milestone in the career of the then unknown director. The picture's popularity also most likely contributed to the acclaim of the story's author, Stephen King, who is considered today to be the most successful writer of all time.

SH

1 Baptized in blood: The poster image of Carrie White (Sissy Spacek) remains engrained in the minds of audiences to this very day.

2 & 3 Splitting images: De Palma's infernal ending was mannerist to say the least.

4 Just your average, ordinary schoolgirl: Carrie becomes a woman in the girl's locker room.

5 Instilling the fear of God: Margaret White (Piper Laurie) raises a hand to her heretic daughter.

6 Living the dream: For a few blissful minutes, Carrie and Tommy (William Katt) are the dream couple at the prom ball.

7 Coal Miner's Slaughter: The former country singer Sissy Spacek made her breakthrough in the role of poor, monstrous Carrie White.

"Combining Gothic Horror, offhand misogyny and an air of studied triviality, *Carrie* is De Palma's most enjoyable movie in a long while, and also his silliest." *Newsweek*

SISSY SPACEK The German newspaper *Die Zeit* once described Sissy Spacek, an actress born in Quitman, Texas in 1949, as "the phenomenology of backroads America captured in a single face." Spacek's America is one filled with characters from the nooks and crannies of small towns, like the awkward, intimidated schoolgirl, *Carrie,* and the birdhouse-building handicapped daughter in David Lynch's *The Straight Story* (1999). It is the America associated with romanticized hospitality that Spacek is most familiar with. At one time, this seemingly meek, homely-looking woman toured the nation's foothills as a country music singer, performing under the name "Rainbow" and relying on her fire and brimstone constitution to forge her way. After completing her acting studies with Lee Strasberg and winning critical acclaim for Terrence Malick's *Badlands* (1973), she cemented her career with her performance as *Carrie* (1976). Shortly thereafter, she was cast as country singer Loretta Lynn in *Coal Miner's Daughter* (1980), a role that must have fit like a glove, and was awarded the Best Actress Academy Award for her outstanding performance. The following year, Spacek received another Oscar nomination for her work opposite Jack Lemmon in *Missing* (1981). Oscar nodded twice more in her direction, for her portrayal of a farmer's wife in *The River* (1984) and most recently for her artistry *In the Bedroom* (2001), for which she won a Golden Globe.

MARATHON MAN

1976 - USA - 125 MIN. - POLITICAL THRILLER

DIRECTOR JOHN SCHLESINGER (*1926)
SCREENPLAY WILLIAM GOLDMAN, based on his novel of the same name DIRECTOR OF PHOTOGRAPHY CONRAD L. HALL EDITING JIM CLARK
MUSIC MICHAEL SMALL PRODUCTION ROBERT EVANS, SIDNEY BECKERMAN for PARAMOUNT PICTURES GELDERSE
MAATSCHAPPIJ N. V.

STARRING DUSTIN HOFFMAN (Babe Levy), LAURENCE OLIVIER (Dr. Szell), ROY SCHEIDER (Doc Levy), MARTHE KELLER
(Elsa Opel), WILLIAM DEVANE (Janeway), FRITZ WEAVER (Professor Biesenthal), RICHARD BRIGHT (Karl), MARC
LAWRENCE (Erhard), TITO GOYA (Melendez), BEN DOVA (Klaus Szell, Dr. Szell's Brother).

"Is it safe?"

It takes more than physical fitness to run a marathon. Equally important is the will to keep going even when the body is begging to stop. Babe Levy (Dustin Hoffman) is the Marathon Man, a small man with a big heart, and he'll spend most of this film running for his life. Out of the blue, Babe is drawn into a maelstrom of Secret Service machinations, with the elderly German Dr. Szell (Laurence Olivier) at the center of it all. A former concentration camp physician, Szell is now living in hiding in South America, from where he supplies the U.S. with information on the whereabouts of other fugitive top Nazis. In return, the so-called "Division" – a Secret Service unit somewhere between the CIA and the FBI – supplies Szell with the money he needs to survive i Uruguayan exile by paying cash for the diamonds he stole from inmates the camp. Babe's brother Doc (Roy Scheider) is a member of this mysteriou Division.

For a piece of Hollywood entertainment, this complex political thrille touches some pretty sensitive nerves. With its close proximity to real even of the recent past, coupled with a style that joins elements of French 60s cir ema to classic Film Noir conventions, Marathon Man is a film with a stron feeling for history and yet is still firmly rooted in its time. Reference is mad

to the anti-Communist witch hunts of the McCarthy era, which drove Babe['s] father to suicide. Demonstrations fill the background of many scenes; an[d] the fictitious figure of Dr. Szell cannot fail to evoke the all-too-real Dr. Jose[f] Mengele, who absconded to Argentina after the war and who was neve[r] found alive. The film is powerfully effective in its combination of nerve[-] wracking tension and elements that so closely mirror reality. The politicall[y] motivated Secret Service escapades are hardly less disturbing for bein[g] strictly fictional, and the film plays suggestively on our most basic and inad[-] missible fears, intensified by the deadly menace of a hidden and anonymou[s] force. Carefully timed eruptions of violence raise the tension to almost un[-] bearable levels, most dramatically in the sequences in the dentist's chair. D[r.] Szell calmly tortures Babe Levy, plucking and poking at nerves laid bare[.]

"In typical Hollywood fashion, Schlesinger shows us the oil truck first to allow us time to consider the implications of what we are seeing. For this, like the opening sequences of many Bergman and Fellini pictures, is the entire film in nucleo." *Literature / Film Quarterly*

1 Run for your life! Dustin Hoffman, one of the biggest names of New Hollywood, stars in the tense thriller *Marathon Man*.

2 An innocent looking face: But Elsa (Marthe Keller) can't be trusted.

3 All in the family: Babe's brother Doc (Roy Scheider) is a man with a dark secret.

4 Running on empty: Babe Levy (Dustin Hoffman), on a lonely, long-distance race to the truth about his brother's death.

while repeating the sinister and unanswerable question, "Is it safe?" Here and elsewhere, the film makes quite intentional use of shocking violence as an effective narrative device. The audience is never allowed to forget that the white-haired, bespectacled Szell is no harmless old gent but a monster of cynical cruelty. (After test runs of the film, this torture sequence had to be cut substantially.)

The plot is also quite something. For a long time, the audience is left in the dark as to exactly what's going on. Right at the start, we have a mysteri-ous race between two elderly motorists, trading insults until they crash. Then there's the enigmatic Elsa Opel (Marthe Keller), who steals the heart of Babe Levy. There's Babe's brother Doc, with his puzzling business in Paris; and we have deadly enemies posing as Babe's friends, like the shady Peter Janeway (William Devane). A long time passes before the various pieces of this com-plex puzzle can be made to fit together.

The narrative is fragmented, and our feelings are manipulated con-stantly by shocks, surprises and ironic twists. The audience is as confused

5   Babe turns the tables with a semi-automatic…

6   … and sadistic Nazi war criminal, Dr. Szell (Laurence Olivier), suddenly can't resist his powers of persuasion.

7   Nice work if you can get it: Doc cashes in on the secrets of Szell's merciless past.

5

"While the political implications are pushed further than they are able to go, the film runs into even more trouble when it attempts to work the loosely asserted personal elements deeper into the pattern." *Sight and Sound*

POLITICAL THRILLERS

In general, the word "thriller" denotes a cinema of fear and existential threat. Thrillers are tense tales of criminal misdeeds. As a rule, the viewer identifies with the heroic protagonists, who often don't know why they're being pursued or how they've suddenly landed in a terrible situation with no apparent way out. The thriller has many faces, depending on its thematic orientation and formal structure: there are psychothrillers, horror thrillers, erotic thrillers and political thrillers. As the name suggests, political thrillers derive their potential from fictional stories th enough to real political events to appear credible.

The political thriller tells of political corruption and only rarely refrains from commenting on history. One of the most important directors of political thrillers is the pugnacious Constantin Costa-Gavras. In films such as *Z* (1968) and *State of Siege* (*État de siège*, 1972), he did not merely deal with political themes, but also took up a clear political position. The great political scandals of world history are a particularly fruitful field. The murder of John F. Kennedy, for example, has been the subject of several films, most notably Oliver Stone's controversial *JFK* (1991). Oscars were showered on Alan J. Pakula's *All the President's Men* (1976), which dramatized the exposure of the Watergate scandal surrounding President Richard Nixon.

d disoriented as the protagonist. Throughout Babe's long flight, we never
ow more than he does. Near the end of his ordeal, he traps Szell in a reser-
ir building, where it becomes clear that the Nazi doctor is only interested in
e thing: his "life insurance," in the form of the diamonds he stole from his
urdered victims. They have financed his retirement very nicely so far, and
wants them to go on doing so. Once again, we see Szell's murderous cyni-
sm at work: he wants these jewels at all costs, and their inhuman price
irrelevant. As Babe forces Szell to eat the diamonds, the story takes one
al, unsettling twist: the torturer's victim tortures the torturer. Thus, even at
e end of this disturbing thriller-marathon, it's hard to breathe a simple sigh
relief.

BR

7

FELLINI'S CASANOVA
Il Casanova di Federico Fellini

1976 - ITALY - 154 MIN. - LITERARY ADAPTATION

DIRECTOR FEDERICO FELLINI (1920–1993)
SCREENPLAY FEDERICO FELLINI, BERNARDINO ZAPPONI, based on the memoirs *STORIA DELLA MIA VITA* by GIACOMO CASANOVA DIRECTOR OF PHOTOGRAPHY GIUSEPPE ROTUNNO EDITING RUGGERO MASTROIANNI MUSIC NINO ROTA PRODUCTION ALBERTO GRIMALDI for PRODUZIONI EUROPEE ASSOCIATI.

STARRING DONALD SUTHERLAND (Giacomo Casanova), TINA AUMONT (Henriette), CICELY BROWNE (Madame D'Urfe), CARMEN SCARPITTA (Madame Charpillon), CLARA ALGRANTI (Marcolina), CHESTY MORGAN (Barberina), MARGARET CLEMENTI (Maria Magdalena), SANDRA ELAINE ALLEN (Angelina the Giantess), CLARISSA MARY ROLL (Anna Maria), ADELE ANGELA LOJODICE (Mechanical Doll), OLIMPIA CARLISI (Isabella).

ACADEMY AWARDS 1976 OSCAR for BEST COSTUMES (Danilo Donati).

"Peace comes only with death."

With 600 wigs, more than 1,000 costumes, 186 actors – including a giant woman 2.38 meters tall weighing 270 kilos – 200 people working behind the scenes and 2,500 extras, this really was a monumental undertaking. No expense was spared in filming these episodes from the life of the Venetian Giacomo Girolamo Casanova (Chevalier de Seingalt, as he ennobled himself, 1725–1798), the epitome of the Rococo Age. Casanova's memoirs, although incomplete, are almost 4,000 pages long, and they remain a fascinating storehouse of detailed descriptions and observations. This uncompromising documentation allows us a close-up view of the century that was ended by the French Revolution.

Those who know these memoirs will barely recognize the figure created by Fellini. No frivolous adventurer, no salon lion here. Instead of the historical Casanova, we have a creature of artifice, a kind of human *objet d'art*;

instead of the gallant chevalier who allegedly "possessed" 1,000 women, melancholy Don Quixote. The Casanova we see here is not the master but the prisoner of his own sexuality. King Sex rules supreme.

Fellini cast the Canadian Donald Sutherland in the leading role, seeing him as an actor "with a vague, dissolved, watery face, reminiscent Venice." Sutherland's Venice-face had impressed Fellini in Nicholas Roeg's *Don't Look Now* (1973), a quiet horror film that takes place in the canal city. For the role of Casanova, the make-up department provided Sutherland with more than 100 different "faces" – the virtuoso of love as a hero of labor downtrodden slave to his own desperate vanity.

At regular intervals, we are shown Casanova pursuing his vocation, but any pornographic expectations are sadly disappointed. This is hard labor indeed. When we see the sweat streaming down his distorted face

"The birth of cinematic art from the spirit of Eros."

Der Spiegel

1 Come on baby, light my fire! Donald Sutherland as Casanova, with his flames guttering.

2 A real doll: The ideal woman for Fellini's Casanova...

3 ... she takes a licking and keeps on kicking.

4 Going through the motions: According to Fellini's, the legendary lover is a hollow man, and quite mechanical.

it's difficult to believe there's any kind of pleasure involved. To help him out, Fellini's Casanova takes an exquisite mechanical bird with him wherever he goes. When wound up, it functions as a kind of metronome, nodding its head and flapping its wings, setting out the rhythm of love (accompanied by Nino Rota's circus-like music) for Casanova to keep time to. And Casanova's lust is no less mechanical than the movements of the metal bird.

In the opening sequence of the film, Fellini had already shown us a kin of pleasure-machine: the Carnival in Venice, Europe's garden of earth delights. Having long since lost its military power, Venice is here seen feed ing off the remains of its accumulated wealth. The masked revelers come t a halt, the noisy crowd falls silent: the great Masque on the Grand Canal i just about to begin. Slowly, majestically, the head of an enormous woma emerges from the water, as the masked multitude cries in unison: "Blesse

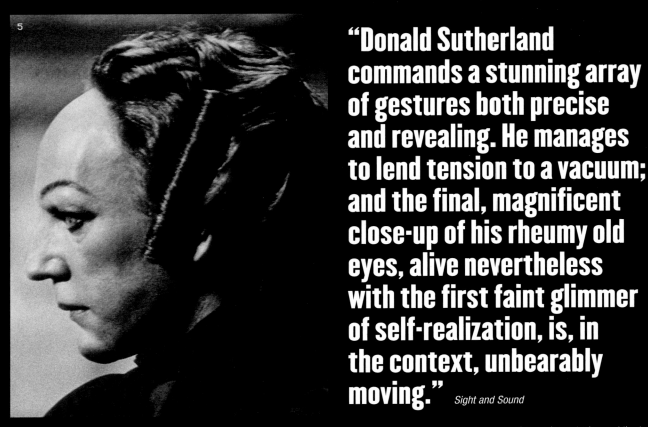

"Donald Sutherland commands a stunning array of gestures both precise and revealing. He manages to lend tension to a vacuum; and the final, magnificent close-up of his rheumy old eyes, alive nevertheless with the first faint glimmer of self-realization, is, in the context, unbearably moving." *Sight and Sound*

5 Blind sighted: Casanova can't see past his own mask.

6 Delusions of grandeur: As a guest at the royal courts of Europe, Casanova fails to recognize that

he is no more than a minor actor in a vast theater, a bit-part player in a cynical power game.

Venezia! Venezia is born!" … and then the ropes snap. The woman/Venice/ the Rococo age – all swallowed up by the sea. Thus the main motifs of the film are established early on: machines imitating life, or else the living made weirdly mechanical.

Only once, towards the end of these 10 episodes from the life of Casanova, does the Great Lover show any tenderness. He seems to have found his ideal woman: a life-sized doll, the perfect partner for the machine he has become. In the end, Casanova is all mask, pure artifice. The electri-fied human marionette with the erotic aura of a piston engine performs its last *danse macabre* on the icy surface of the Canale Grande; a Dance

of Death, in which all that's left of desire is the empty shell of mechanical motion.

Fellini's Casanova is the maestro's darkest and most pitiless film, an it's still a memorable settling of accounts with machismo, chauvinism, an the excesses of male ego. In the deliberately artificial settings of this film windows are either completely lacking or else they are "blind." There ar no prospects, no heavens, no horizon. In the 70s, the main reactions to th film were shock, bewilderment and point-blank rejection. Now, howeve one might venture an interpretation: while many films show us an artificia paradise, this one takes us to an artificial hell.   R

FEDERICO FELLINI   Federico Fellini was born and brought up in Rimini. In Italy, he became a national institution. When he diec in Rome in 1993 at the age of 73, the title pages of the Italian newspapers were printed with black borders, and news and politics made way for the obituaries. Six months previously, the "maestro" – who had never made a film outside Italy – had been given a special Oscar for his life's work. He was the first – so far – the only Italian to be so honored. Foreign distributors frequently added his name to the films' titles (e. g. *Fellini's Roma / Roma*, 1971; *Fellini's Amarcord / Amarcord*, 1973), and this is also unique in the hundred-year history of the cinema. Fellini began as an assistant to Roberto Rossellini, as he helped the Italian cinema make a new start immediately after the war: *Open City* (*Roma, città aperta*, 1945) and *Paisan* (*Paisà*, 1946). In 1954, Fellini attracted international attention as director of *La Strada*, featuring Anthony Quinn as the traveling fairground artiste Zampanò alongside Fellini's wife Giulietta Masina as the naive and passive Gelsomina. *La Strada* also won the Oscar as Best Foreign Film, but the film divided the Italian public into two camps, who carried on their struggle well into the 70s: the Communists, who swore by Visconti (*The Leopard, Il gattopardo*, 1963), and the Catholics, who swore by life, suffering and charity. Fellini himself, however, always claimed a third, independent position. His 22 films, half of them world-famous (e. g. *La Dolce Vita*, 1959/60), know neither enemies nor ideologies. Although Fellini's films lack any kind of traditional religious message, they are essentially "touching," for it is necessary to let oneself be touched, and to touch others, when the world is full of people who have to struggle through life and can't help themselves.

THE PINK PANTHER STRIKES AGAIN

1976 - GREAT BRITAIN - 103 MIN. - COMEDY

DIRECTOR BLAKE EDWARDS (*1922)

SCREENPLAY FRANK WALDMAN, BLAKE EDWARDS DIRECTOR OF PHOTOGRAPHY HARRY WAXMAN EDITING ALAN JONES MUSIC HENRY MANCINI PRODUCTION BLAKE EDWARDS for AMJO PRODUCTIONS.

STARRING PETER SELLERS (Chief Inspector Jacques Clouseau), HERBERT LOM (Ex-Chief Inspector Charles Dreyfus), LESLEY-ANNE DOWN (Olga), BURT KWOUK (Cato), COLIN BLAKELY (Alec Drummond), LEONARD ROSSITER (Inspector Quinlan), RICHARD VERNON (Doctor Fassbender), MICHAEL ROBBINS (Jarvis the Butler), VANDA GODSELL (Mrs. Leverlilly), BRIONY MCROBERTS (Margo Fassbender), OMAR SHARIF (Egyptian Agent).

"The mad are the only normal people I have ever met."

Two flabbergasted nuns watch a hunchback floating in the night sky above Paris. The lump is not a deformity but a cunning disguise, and the airborne Quasimodo is a policeman. His hump is filled with helium, and his inability to control the gas level has just saved his life: seconds before a bomb ripped through his apartment, the overfilled costume had lifted him gently out of the window. Having evaded certain death thanks to his inimitable incompetence, our hero drifts past the Sacre Cœur, letting out the gas to ensure a soft landing in the Seine. It's "Interpol's best man," Inspector Clouseau (Peter Sellers), as we know and love him.

His latest case begins with a visit to his former boss Charles Dreyfu (Herbert Lom) in a psychiatric clinic. Driven mad by Clouseau's stupidity, th former Chief Inspector is due to meet a commission of doctors who will de cide whether he has recovered sufficiently to be released. In an indescribab slapstick sequence involving Clouseau, a cricket ball, and a park benc Dreyfus takes a series of involuntary baths in the clinic lake – and succumt once again to his "insane" hatred of Clouseau.

A short time later, he escapes from the clinic, forms a criminal organ zation, and kidnaps the physicist Professor Fassbender (Richard Vernon) ar

his daughter Margo (Briony McRoberts). After bringing them to Castle Mond-schein in Bavaria, he forces the scientist to construct a deadly raygun. Thus armed, Dreyfus presents an ultimatum to the world: Clouseau must die – or Dreyfus will destroy the human race. The world's secret services don't have to be asked twice, and soon Clouseau is a fugitive. At the Oktoberfest in Munich, the hunt for Inspector Clouseau begins . . .

For Peter Sellers, Clouseau's imbecility was a blessing, and it made him an international star. Yet he only appeared in the first *Pink Panther* movie after Peter Ustinov had turned down the role at short notice. From then on, no other actor was imaginable as the world's most useless policeman: all

attempts to recast the role failed miserably, while the Sellers movies we big box-office hits. This was the third of his five *Pink Panther* films, and mar regard it as the best, thanks in no small part to Herbert Lom's excelle portrayal of the diabolical Dreyfus. Resplendent in a long black cape, he pla the organ in his creepy castle, a kind of latterday silent-film Dracula, b plagued with terrible teeth . . .

Director Blake Edwards' successes had included *Breakfast at Tiffany* (1961) before he made the *Pink Panther* series. *The Pink Panther Strike Again* is filled with references to the Hollywood classics, and not only the Castle Mondschein scenes. Even in the animated titles sequence, th

"The series hit its high point with its third film, *The Pink Panther Strikes Again*. The laughs simply don't relent."
At-A-Glance Film Reviews

Confessions of a dangerous mind: Peter Sellers often claimed that "there used to be a real me, but I had it surgically removed." Let's hope Inspector Clouseau can catch the witch doctor who performed the operation.

2   Martial arts: Interpol's best man – a serious match for Hong Kong Phooey.

3   Facial wrap: A bad injury or a cunning disguise?

4   Proof positive: The smoldering sleuth pursues his investigations in a gay bar.

5   Lost in translation: The French answer to Sherlock Holmes is a walking disaster area.

6

6 Riddle me this: "How can an idiot be a policeman?" The series' comic genius was born out of
Clouseau's deadpan conviction.

7 In a peaceful white room: Clouseau may be off
Charles Dreyfus' (Herbert Lom) payroll, but he's
still the cause of his mental anguish.

8 Kicking the habit: Dreyfus will stop at nothing
to free the world from the curse of Clouseau.

ISADORE "FRITZ" FRELENG One day in 1963, Isadore Freleng (1905–1995) saw pale red. Between 100 and 150 pink panthers lay before him, sketches for the animated titl
sequence to Blake Edwards' upcoming project, *The Pink Panther* (1964). In the film, the Panther is an enormous diamond; in the opening titles
Blake Edwards decided, it should be a big cat. Freleng and his cartoonist colleague Hawley Pratt developed a minimalist background world inhabite
by a slightly more complex Panther, an elegantly cool cat grooving to the cool jazz sax melody composed by Henry Mancini.
After the success of Saul Bass' closing titles to *Around the World in Eighty Days* (1956), many comedies of the 60s and 70s had featured animate
titles sequences. Freleng, however, actually succeeded in emancipating his cartoon creation from its lowly supporting role: in 1964, he was awarde
an Oscar for *The Pink Phink,* and the cartoon Panther went on to star in its own TV series.
Freleng, an autodidact, spent 33 years working for Warner Brothers, collaborating with great animators like Chuck Jones and Tex Avery. Three c
his films also received Oscars: *Speedy Gonzales* (1955), *Birds Anonymous* (1957) and *Knighty Knight Bugs* (1958). His creations included Yosemit
Sam and Sylvester, but no other cartoon figure shows his talent for combining animation with music so clearly as the Pink Panther.

...pector's hunt for the Pink Panther is a tour-de-force through movie his-...y, featuring such luminaries of the silver screen as Alfred Hitchcock, King ...ng, and Batman. And when Clouseau questions the Professor's servants ...er their employer's abduction, his bizarre interrogation is a parody of the Agatha Christie adaptations.

The rest of the somewhat loosely constructed plot consists of a series ...ketch-like episodes, including the now classic dog-bites-inspector dialog ...ouseau: "I thought you said your dog didn't bite?" Hotelier: "That is not my ...g."), and the cacophonous karate duel between Clouseau and his servant ...o (Burt Kwouk). In the end, it's Cato who manages to foul up the Bond-...le finale Clouseau fought so hard to achieve – with the help of a striptease. ...t then it would be strange to see Clouseau ever succeed at anything.   OK

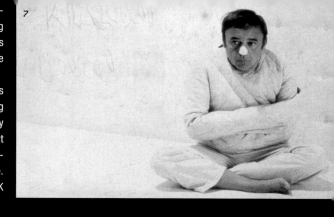

"There is a beautiful woman in my bed, and a dead man in my bath."

Film quote: Inspector Clouseau

Eureka! Far from bombing at the box office, the movie raked in 33 million dollars in the U.S. alone.

History showed that moviegoers would only accept one actor in the role of Inspector Clouseau.

THE TENANT
Le Locataire

1976 - FRANCE - 125 MIN. - PSYCHO DRAMA, LITERARY ADAPTATION

DIRECTOR ROMAN POLANSKI (*1933)
SCREENPLAY GÉRARD BRACH, ROMAN POLANSKI, based on the novel *LE LOCATAIRE CHIMÉRIQUE* by ROLAND TOPOR
DIRECTOR OF PHOTOGRAPHY SVEN NYKVIST EDITING FRANÇOISE BONNOT MUSIC PHILIPPE SARDE PRODUCTION ANDREW BRAUNSBERG for MARIANNA FILMS, MARIANNE PRODUCTIONS S. A.

STARRING ROMAN POLANSKI (Trelkovsky), ISABELLE ADJANI (Stella), MELVYN DOUGLAS (Monsieur Zy), JO VAN FLEET (Madame Dioz), BERNARD FRESSON (Scope), LILA KEDROVA (Madame Gaderian), CLAUDE PIÉPLU (Neighbor), RUFUS (Georges Badar), ROMAIN BOUTEILLE (Simon), JACQUES MONOD (Café Owner), DOMINIQUE POULANGE (Simone Choule), SHELLEY WINTERS (Concierge).

"I knew there was something wrong with him the first time I laid eyes on him!"

Since Hitchcock's *Rear Window* (1954), we have grown accustomed to the voyeuristic camera as the most self-explanatory of all cinematic motifs. In *The Tenant*, Roman Polanski submits himself to the pitiless gaze of his own camera, and the effect is hellish. He plays Trelkovsky, a submissive outsider in a shabby Parisian apartment house, who is driven mad by his nightmarish neighbors and by an apartment that seems to have a malignant life of its own.

Trelkovsky bears almost the entire weight of the camera's attention, and when it does look elsewhere for a moment, there is no relief: the people and the very walls are staring him down relentlessly. Gradually, neither he nor we can know with certainty where reality ends and hallucination begins. While the house and its terrifying inhabitants are a real threat, they are also a symbol of his inner life and a projection of his tortured mind. The apartment building itself is a collection of baffling fragments: the windows of the narrow back yard; the musty stairwell; the closed doors of the other apartments, whose inhabitants wait to pounce upon the timorous newcomer with the Polish accent. From the toilet opposite his apartment window, grotesque figures gaze steadily across at him, sometimes for hours on end. Are they really there, or are they a mere manifestation of his growing terror? We never know for sure; for even in the less horrible moments of his everyday life, there is an element of the ridiculous in this little man's struggle against a very cruel world. Every harmless sound he makes, every tiny proof of his mere existence, is cause for complaint. And when the neighbors protest by knock-

ing on his walls and ceiling, his pitiful anxiety to avoid giving offense is e[vi]dence of a painfully conformist spirit. The true horror lies in the inevitabilit[y] his fate: he will take on the life of his predecessor Simone Choule (Dominic Poulange) – and jump to his death, as she had done before him. On his v[ery] first visit to the apartment, the concierge had shown him, with a smirk, [the] canopy shattered by the young woman on her way from the window to [the] ground…

Polanski's use of horror-film conventions is economical and hig[hly] effective. In an early scene, Trelkovsky visits the dying Simone Choul[e in] hospital: bandaged like a mummy from head to foot, she suddenly em[its] a bloodcurdling scream. It seems like a cry from the grave. *The Tenant* is s[o] fused with a feeling of obsessive fear, an air of isolation and terri[ble] loneliness; and this is a dominant and very personal motif in many of Pola[n]ski's films. *Repulsion* (1965) and *Rosemary's Baby* (1968) also depicted p[eo]ple driven by desperation into the claustrophobic refuge of their own eg[o,] lost souls, brilliantly embodied by Catherine Deneuve and Mia Farrow.

Trelkovsky's apartment is filled with traces of the previous tenan[t's] existence: clothes, cosmetics, and even one of her teeth. The more he d[is]covers, the more Trelkovsky "becomes" Simone Choule. His ultimate tra[ns]vestism is merely the absurd and blackly funny nadir in his odyssey [of] humiliation. With shameless persistence, the landlord of the neighbor[ing] café insists on selling him the brand of cigarettes smoked by Simone Cho[ule] – whether Trelkovsky wants them or not is clearly beside the point. A[s]

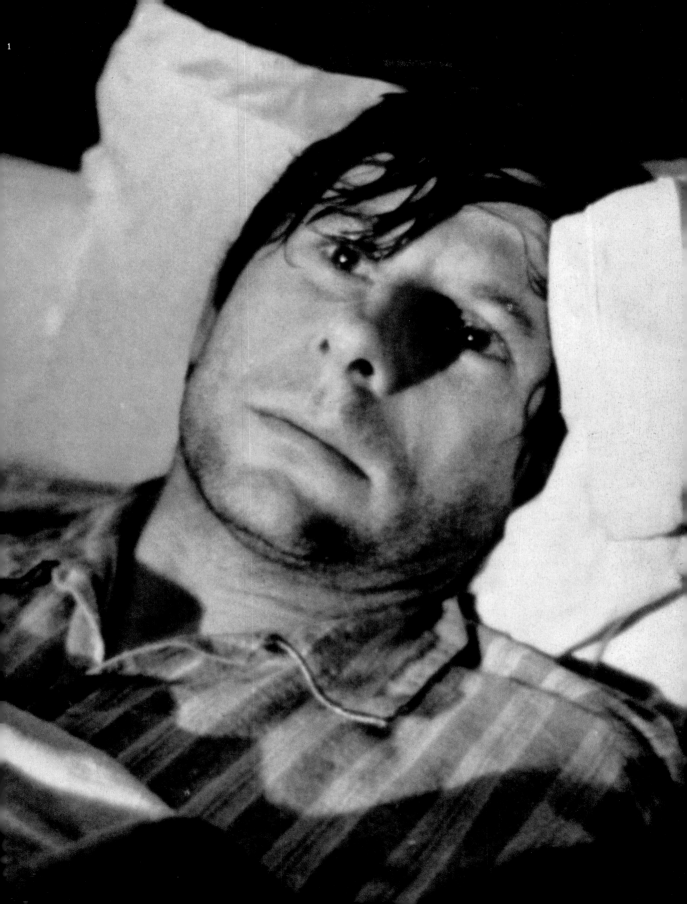

to demonstrate the tenant's feebleness, a visiting friend plays a loud recording of a military band; and there's not one word of complaint from Trelkovsky's ever-vigilant neighbors. The fiasco continues with his brave refusal to sign a petition against a poor family. Evicted nonetheless, the enraged mother leaves a pile of shit on every doormat in the building – with the sole exception of Trelkovsky's. In order to avert suspicion, he is obliged to finish her job himself… His struggle against the threat to his own existence is accompanied by feelings of embarrassment and shame, and these are reflected in the nameless terror that emanates from the house's communal latrine.

The apparent conspiracy against the tenant culminates in one of the most notorious suicides in the history of film. Having bought himself a wig to complete his transformation into Simone Choule, Trelkovsky prepares to take the leap. In his mind, the back court is now an opera house, and the neighbors are seated in their boxes, waiting expectantly for the show to begin. He will not disappoint them; indeed, he will entertain them with the spectacle of his self-immolation not once, but twice… The unparalleled grotesqueness of this climactic scene amounts to an exorcism of the director's own most personal ghosts. In *The Tenant*, the cosmopolitan Roman Polanski paints a disturbingly elegant portrait of Paris as a human sewer. Poor Trelkovsky is a soul in hell, and even Isabelle Adjani, as Simone's girlfriend Stella, can offer him no solace in his ordeal; the director has buried her beauty behind an enormous pair of sunglasses.

P

1 This property is condemned: The tenant Trelkovski (Roman Polanski), trapped in the crumbling edifice of his own ego.

2 The windmills of his mind: Actor-director Polanski subjected himself to the pitiless gaze of his own camera and reveals the workings of an overwhelmed subconscious.

3 Meeting the Neighbors from Hell: Trelkovski is by turns defiant and obsequious. Nothing can help him – and the latest blow to his dignity is more than he can bear…

4 Too little, too late: Not even the beautiful Stella (Isabelle Adjani) can stop Trelkovski from slipping into madness.

"Trelkovsky, the hero of Mr. Polanski's striking new horror film, *The Tenant*, is a character who might have been invented by an Edgar Allan Poe who'd had the opportunity to read about Raskolnikov and Josef K. He's a particularly Eastern European kind of late 19th-century outsider set down in contemporary Paris. He is also – by the end of the movie – something of a joke; but an entirely intentional one."

The New York Times

ACTOR-DIRECTORS   Among actor-directors, Hitchcock and Polanski can be seen as opposite poles. While the former enlivened his films by attaching his cursory personal logo – the jokey cameo appearance – the latter wished to preserve the initiative in every situation. Certainly, no more than a few people have made an equal name for themselves as both actors and directors; and the few who have done so have mainly been independent filmmakers such as Charlie Chaplin, Orson Welles, Woody Allen or John Cassavetes. When a director appears in his own film, his performance carries a special kind of authority and credibility. Actors who have taken up directing towards the end of their careers have generally had a harder time of it; Robert Redford and Kevin Costner, for example, have never really been able to free themselves from a certain aura of amateurism, despite having made some good films. For the star behind the camera always has to contend with the suspicion that he's only doing it to overcome the boredom of stardom, or to improve his position in the market, or to better his chances of acquiring that long-overdue Oscar nomination. That actor-directors need have nothing in common besides an apparently essential egotism is evidenced by Polanski's public criticism of John Cassavetes' appearance in *Rosemary's Baby* (1968): he complained that Cassavetes' excessively "authentic" performance was a crass misconstruction of the nature of the role.

4

ALL THE PRESIDENT'S MEN

1976 - USA - 132 MIN. - POLITICAL DRAMA

DIRECTOR ALAN J. PAKULA (1928–1998)
SCREENPLAY WILLIAM GOLDMAN, based on the factual reports of CARL BERNSTEIN and BOB WOODWARD DIRECTOR OF
PHOTOGRAPHY GORDON WILLIS EDITING ROBERT L. WOLFE MUSIC DAVID SHIRE PRODUCTION WALTER COBLENZ for WILDWOOD,
WARNER BROS.

STARRING DUSTIN HOFFMAN (Carl Bernstein), ROBERT REDFORD (Bob Woodward), JACK WARDEN (Harry Rosenfeld),
MARTIN BALSAM (Howard Simons), HAL HOLBROOK (Deep Throat), JASON ROBARDS (Ben Bradlee), JANE ALEXANDER
(Judy Hoback, Bookkeeper), MEREDITH BAXTER (Debbie Sloan), NED BEATTY (Dardis), STEPHEN COLLINS (Hugh W.
Sloan Jr.).

ACADEMY AWARDS 1976 OSCARS for BEST SUPPORTING ACTOR (Jason Robards), BEST ADAPTED SCREENPLAY (William Goldman),
BEST ART DIRECTION (George Jenkins, George Gaines), and BEST SOUND (Arthur Piantadosi, Les Fresholtz, Dick
Alexander, James E. Webb).

"Nothing's riding on this except the, uh, first amendment to the Constitution, freedom of the press, and maybe the future of the country."

Extreme close-up of a typewriter. A single date is hammered out onto the page and each keystroke rings out like a gunshot. The date is "June 17, 1972" and right from the first moment of the film one thing becomes vividly clear – the typewriter can be a lethal weapon.

Bob Woodward (Robert Redford) and Carl Bernstein (Dustin Hoffman) are two "hungry" young reporters working at the *Washington Post*. The two end up unmasking the scandal behind what will be forever known as Watergate. They work methodically, soberly and professionally, driven by a journalist's hunter instincts to trap a good story and their own thirst for success. Their goal is to be better, not to mention quicker, than their counterparts at the *New York Times* and they will let nothing stand in their way.

The picture tells the tale of "Woodstein," as the writing team quickly become dubbed by the rest of the reporting staff. We accompany the two on an expedition that will last approximately six months, starting on that ominous night of June 17, with the break in at Democratic headquarters (where the Republican party apparently paid to have bugging equipment planted)

up until the day when Nixon is sworn into office for a second term in January 1973. As inauguration day is upon them, it appears that the reporters have failed in their attempts to trace the scandal back to the highest White House officials. Nonetheless, the paper's chief editor Ben Bradlee (Jason Robards) offers them his unwavering support. The film's conclusion comes full circle as a television set placed prominently in the *Washington Post* newsroom shows us Nixon taking his presidential oath as well as the surrounding festivities full of pomp, circumstances and ceremonial gunfire while Bernstein and Woodward plug away at their typewriters. The chattering keys quickly drown out the sound of Nixon's fanfare. The film closes with a relentless news ticker that reports the concessions and sentencing of the case's principle suspects, concluding with President Nixon's resignation in August 1974.

Yet despite the subject matter, it's hard to call *All The President's Men* a political drama as the movie provides no forum for researching the causes of the Watergate affair or an analysis of its aftermath. We do, however, see

politicians in actual archived news footage from that year, which is seamlessly integrated into the story's fabric via television sets that appear throughout the film. Because its story unfolds through the eyes of the two investigative journalists, the political scandal seems to read like a detective caper. Although the outcome of the case is far from being a mystery, the path that leads there is what is of real interest. It is a relay race against time that consists of gathering evidence, making phone calls, meeting those involved, making more phone calls and conducting follow-up face to face interviews. We witness as a complex jigsaw puzzle compiled of dozens upon dozens of names, facts, appointments, organizations and secret monetary funds takes shape. This film, whose sights are as ambitious as those of its protagonists, demands our full attention and we gladly acquiesce.

The suspense of *All the President's Men* is born out of the story's authenticity and the impeccable acting. This first aspect is made evident by the film's loyalty to the historical facts and underscored by the Sisyphus-like efforts of the reporters, who screenwriter William Goldman does not even grant private lives. International mega-stars Redford and Hoffman must be credited for their artistic brilliance, which is absolutely electrifying as they cunningly win over tight-lipped individuals wrapped up in the affair. Silence suddenly speaks volumes. On one occasion, in a theatrical tour de force, the duo force the truth out of a witness by acting as if that which they only suspect is confirmed fact. Our eyes are glued to the screen as the wily Bernstein, much the opposite of the cautious, straight-edged Woodward, finesses his way into the home of an intimidated bookkeeper who worked for the "Com

3

"By simply sticking to the facts, Pakula and Redford pay tribute to a kind of journalism that has nothing in common with the prevalent clichés, the cheap and deliberate contempt often leveled at this profession."

Der Spiegel

ALAN J. PAKULA

Jane Fonda won an Oscar under his direction as call girl Bree Daniels in the detective caper *Klute* (1971), and a decade later he aided Meryl Streep in making a decision that won her the coveted golden statuette for her performance in the Holocaust drama *Sophie's Choice* (1982). Even his screenwriter for *All the President's Men* (1976), William Goldman, was bestowed with the Academy Award. Nonetheless, Alan J. Pakula (1928–1998), director of all these films and a two-time Oscar nominee, always remained the man behind the scenes. This could have to do with the fact that native New Yorker Pakula was never really viewed as a creative force but rather as an actor's director and meticulous craftsman as well as someone who was particularly gifted at helping others achieve their full potential. From 1957 to 1969, at the beginning of his career, he worked as a producer, collaborating on seven films with director Robert Mulligan. In 1969, while he and Liza Minnelli were on the lookout for a "fresh, new director" to take on *The Sterile Cuckoo*, Pakula suggested himself for the project and got his big break at fulfilling his greatest ambition. Much like Mulligan, Pakula had always been interested in political and sociological topics. His thrillers *Klute* (1971), *The Parallax View* (1974) and *All the President's Men*, which have become collectively known as the "paranoia trilogy," are considered exceptionally on-target studies of the political and social tenor of the Nixon era. Pakula further explored the conspiracy theory as a topic in later box-office triumphs like *Presumed Innocent* (1989) and *The Pelican Brief* (1993). In 1998, Pakula lost his life in a freak car accident.

1 Getting to the bottom of things: Reporters Carl Bernstein (Dustin Hoffman) and Bob Woodward (Robert Redford) investigate the Watergate break-in.

2 Out on a limb: Editor Ben Bradlee (Jason Robards Jr.) supports his journalists' detective work.

3 Working 9 to 5: It'll take thousands of phone-calls and hundreds of meetings before Carl Bernstein even has a clue as to what's really going on.

4 Turning cheap theatrics in big pay-offs: The Woodstein team devises a way to get witnesses to spill the beans.

> **"I found it brilliant and gripping. Even though the events and characters are familiar, the film has an understated and realistic quality that gives a completely fresh dramatic intensity to the crisis the United States went through so recently. Despite all the glamor of the actors (...) it is the unglamorous nature of newspaper work, even with such an assignment as trying to break open a government conspiracy that strikes home. The film breaks new ground in taking up a middle position between a documentary and a dramatization."** *The Times*

mittee to Re-elect the President," the organization whose coffers funded the break-in at Democratic headquarters. Using his savvy and charm, he gradually gains the trust of this "sacrificial lamb" and gets her to reveal everything she knows. The scene is parlor room drama at its finest.

The reporter as hero has a long tradition in the American cinema, often appearing as a clichéd "wise guy." Thankfully, director Alan J. Pakula was careful to avoid this stereotype and even spent several weeks observin the goings-on of the actual *Washington Post* newsroom prior to shooting While Pakula's film does indeed glorify the prevailing legend of an objective free press that is capable of bringing superpowers to their knees, one ca find but little reason to chide him for it. There are, after all, more problem atic myths. L

5   The first amendment as lethal weapon: The typewriter that brought down a president.

6   A date with Deep Throat: Bob Woodward has to take greater precautions in obtaining information.

5

ROCKY

1976 - USA - 119 MIN. - BOXING FILM

DIRECTOR JOHN G. AVILDSEN (*1935)
SCREENPLAY SYLVESTER STALLONE **DIRECTOR OF PHOTOGRAPHY** JAMES CRABE **EDITING** RICHARD HALSEY, SCOTT CONRAD **MUSIC** BILL CONT
PRODUCTION IRWIN WINKLER, ROBERT CHARTOFF for CHARTOFF-WINKLER PRODUCTIONS.

STARRING SYLVESTER STALLONE (Rocky Balboa), TALIA SHIRE (Adrian), BURT YOUNG (Paulie), BURGESS MEREDITH (Mickey Goldmill), CARL WEATHERS (Apollo Creed), THAYER DAVID (Miles Jergens), JOE SPINELL (Tom Gazzo), JIMMY GAMBINA (Mike), TONY BURTON (Duke, Apollo's Trainer), JOE FRAZIER (Himself).

ACADEMY AWARDS 1976 OSCARS for Best Film (Irwin Winkler, Robert Chartoff), BEST DIRECTOR (John G. Avildsen), and BEST FILM EDITING (Richard Halsey, Scott Conrad).

"That's your only chance!"

Philadelphia, December 1975, shortly after four in the morning. Continental winter and general depression reign. The city sleeps, illuminated by an electric half-light. There's not even a dog to be seen on the streets. It's bitterly cold. A newspaper deliveryman races through the banking district in his station wagon, distributing papers. Rocky appears behind him. Rocky is a powerfully built man with a broad, somewhat drooping face. He jogs through the city, the white bursts of his breath hanging in the cold air. He wears a baggy jogging suit, a wool cap, and a pair of worn Converse. This is what someone who comes from the bottom looks like. Rocky (Sylvester Stallone) is an unsuccessful boxer from the Italian neighborhood who can't survive on boxing alone and as a result, works as a money collector for a run-of-the-mill Mafioso. His jog leads him to the city art museum, which resembles the

Parthenon in Athens, up a wide set of stairs and onto a plateau with a m~ nificent view over the city. He boxes while he runs, and he runs whil~ shadowboxes. This is Rocky's first day of training, and it ends with pa~ cramps. But that doesn't matter – what does matter is taking the first ~ in conquering one's weaker self. Once that step is taken, one can ach~ anything.

Rocky has exactly six weeks to get himself into shape, at which p~ this third-class "Italian Stallion" is to step into the ring against Apollo C~ (Carl Weathers), a crafty, well-trained heavyweight champion. What R~ doesn't know is that the bout is a veiled showcase fight for the nation's 2~ birthday, an exhibition for the world champion billed as "black boxing ch~ pion gives white Italian-American the chance of a lifetime." The messa~

2

1   What doesn't kill you makes you stronger: Rocky, alias Sylvester Stallone, fighting his way to the top of the world.

2   A knock-out sensation: Rocky stands his ground against Apollo (Carl Weathers).

3   "I Want YOU:" Apollo Creed, reigning heavyweight champion, as Uncle Sam.

"Some day, *Rocky* will be seen as a key moment in cinematic history. It's the epitome of the feel-good movie."

Frankfurter Allgemeine Zeitung

simple: in America, the land of infinite possibilities, anyone can make it. What Apollo doesn't know is that Rocky is taking the fight more seriously than he'd ever imagine. Rocky has brains. The fight will last fifteen grueling rounds. And it will take place in a ring, especially in a cinematic ring where every fist, whether poor or rich, black or white, becomes a pounding sledgehammer. Rocky, the guy from next door, who up until this point has never had an even break, who is too good-natured to break the thumbs of the defaulting debtors, and the only man in the neighborhood interested in the shy, barely discernible Adrian (Talia Shire) – this guy shows everyone that you don't have to be a champion to discover yourself. "No revenge," stammers the exhausted Apollo after the fight. Eyes swollen and bloody, Rocky doesn't

want a rematch either. He just wants to get to his true love. Like a blinded Samson, he screams her name into the crowd: "Adrian!" She pushes her way through the masses. What happens then is a first in screen history: a woman steps into the ring and passionately kisses the sweaty loser.

Hollywood did not expect *Rocky* to be a success. Quite the reverse in fact – the film was deemed an ideal B-movie and given a $1 million production budget. Only the story's author, Sylvester Stallone, believed in the tale of the small man that makes it big. Rocky's story became Stallone's story, and Stallone's determined assertiveness was mirrored in Rocky's stamina. The Rocky character was tailor-made for Stallone and consequently he didn't want the role handed to Paul Newman or Burt Reynolds. He worked

SYLVESTER STALLONE Others would have given up ages earlier. Not him. When Sylvester Gardenzio Stallone (*6.7.1946, New York City) was born everything was already against him. An accident at birth disfigured his face and it was paralyzed on one side, which ironically made Stallone's characteristics in the film quite interesting. He was teased and called "Sylvie" in school because he was as thin and delicate as a girl. For a long time the son of an Italian hairdresser from a Philadelphia ghetto was nothing more than a marginal American afterthought. He was a pizza baker, a cinema attendant, a small-time actor in third-rate films, and even had a role in a porno.

Then the 30-year-old wrote the frustration from his soul with the script to *Rocky* (1976). At that point he already had a fantastic body he had trained hard to get and that he could display with pride. *Rocky* became his film, his career, and his life. And *Rocky* laid the groundwork for *Rambo* (1982, 1984, 1988). But those who have success as physical actors have trouble shedding the muscular role. What good is it that Stallone was proven to have an I. Q. of 141, that he collects modern art, and that he paints? "An image is an image is an image…"

He has attempted to break out of this typecasting several times: in the melodramatic *Over the Top* (1986), the ironic *Tango & Cash* (1989), the comic *Stop! Or My Mom Will Shoot* (1991), or the futuristic *Judge Dredd* (1995). For *Get Carter* (2000), he even grew a meticulous goatee. It didn't matter – Stallone remained and remains forever The Italian Stallion. This is how he wanted it – and the public accepted it. He is someone who doesn't give in, who gets knocked down but stands right back up, a man who struggles on because he doesn't have any other choice. He is a true *Cliffhanger* (1993), a cinematic Sisyphus.

thout a salary and negotiated a deal worth 10% of the profits. The film as a box office hit. After four months, it had earned $28 million and in the d it took home over $140 million. It won three Oscars. Stallone and the ung director John G. Avildsen suddenly found themselves at the top of e heap.

"Sometimes reality is crazier than all shit," says a Mafioso in Sergio one's *Once Upon a Time in America* (1983), the film about the ultimate nerican Dream. *Rocky* was a smash hit and Sylvester Stallone showed the orld that it was time to believe in the dream of the individual's rise once ore. Because the winnings were good for the victor in and out of the boxing ectacle, Rocky would step into the film ring four more times. "The Italian allion" from the gutters of Philadelphia had become a cult figure.   SR

"*Rocky* batters our emotions like almost no other movie before it. Stallone and his brilliant director John Avildsen play to the gallery so effectively that critical objections seem almost irrelevant." *Der Spiegel*

4 One man's future is another man's past: Rocky and his mentor Mickey (Burgess Meredith).

5 Down and out in Philadelphia: Paulie (Burt Young) needs a job – but Rocky, the debt collector, wouldn't recommend his own.

6 In this ring, I thee wed: Rocky and Adrian (Talia Shire) are ready to love each other to the bitter end.

NETWORK

♟♟♟

1976 - USA - 122 MIN. - DRAMA

DIRECTOR SIDNEY LUMET (*1924)
SCREENPLAY PADDY CHAYEFSKY DIRECTOR OF PHOTOGRAPHY OWEN ROIZMAN EDITING ALAN HEIM MUSIC ELLIOT LAWRENCE PRODUCTION HOWARD GOTTFRIED for MGM, UNITED ARTISTS.

STARRING FAYE DUNAWAY (Diana Christensen), PETER FINCH (Howard Beale), WILLIAM HOLDEN (Max Schumacher), ROBERT DUVALL (Frank Hackett), WESLEY ADDY (Nelson Chaney), NED BEATTY (Arthur Jensen), ARTHUR BURGHARDT (Ahmed Kahn), BILL BURROWS (TV Director), BEATRICE STRAIGHT (Louise Schumacher), KATHY CRONKITE (Mary Ann Gifford), CONCHATA FERRELL (Barbara Schlesinger).

ACADEMY AWARDS 1976 OSCARS for BEST ACTOR (Peter Finch), BEST ACTRESS (Faye Dunaway), BEST SUPPORTING ACTRESS (Beatrice Straight), and BEST ORIGINAL SCREENPLAY (Paddy Chayefsky).

"Who knows what shit will be peddled for truth on this network?"

The United States felt its impact as early as the Forties. In Europe it hit during the Fifties, and before long it had overtaken the world. At the speed of light, television, the "small screen," had claimed its throne as the supreme lord of the mass media, feeding culture and politics into homes worldwide. Between actual sales of sets, station programming and its unparalleled potential as an advertising platform, television quickly became a key factor in national economies. Time and again, the constant headway of the sector's audio-visual capabilities (VHS, DVD) has led to crises within the movie industry. This explains one of the many reasons why television is often presented in film as a medium rooted in competition, as in *The Truman Show* (1998) or *EDtv* (1999). Both of these pictures brand television as nothing more than a boob tube that feigns authenticity as it tries to pull the wool over the eyes of its viewers, which these films construe as uncritical and blind.

Network can be considered the first movie to open the investigation of television and take us behind the scenes to witness how its programming created. The three classic arguments, condemning television's potential manipulate, to encourage conformity and to commercialize at the expense its audience, are so crassly depicted here that, at times, we believe ourselve to be watching a documentary.

Howard Beale, played by Peter Finch (who died shortly after filming and was awarded the Oscar for Best Actor posthumously), is the first man television history to die on the air as a means of boosting ratings. This bizarre stunt is induced by the management of an American TV network. The exect

"With four Golden Globes and ten Oscar nominations, *Network* is one of the most highly-decorated films of the season. And for Hollywood, it's the perfect revenge on TV."

Berliner Morgenpost

...ion, scheduled to take place in front of running cameras as a part of regular programming, riles the spirits of citizens nationwide, who function as a sort of people's liberation army. In truth, it is Beales himself who opts for the dramatic sign off. Yet the network must be held at least partially accountable for inciting the incident.

Confronted with the alcoholic television commentator's long trend of low ratings, the station executives present Beale with his pink slip. Devastated, he responds to the news by announcing in front of a studio audience that for his upcoming final broadcast he will put a bullet through his head on live televi-

sion. Beale's fantastic and macabre promise skyrockets his popularity to new heights and prompts young, savvy Diana Christensen (Faye Dunaway), a ratings-hungry programming executive, to win the has-been a second chance.

Beale quickly becomes the voice of a fed-up America, sounding about the cumulative gripes of the nation into his microphone. Like a wrathful televangelist, he denounces decadence, corruption, egotism and the endless pack of lies facing modern-day society. "I'm mad as hell and I'm not going to take it anymore!" cries America's new favorite son, urging his viewers to run to their windows and scream their frustration at the top of their

1 Posthumous accolades: Peter Finch won the Oscar for his performance as TV news anchor Howard Beale.

2 Eye on America: William Holden as Howard's boss, news director Max Schumacher.

3 The clock is ticking: And time is running out for the "mad prophet of the airwaves."

HE BOOB TUBE
N THE BIG SCREEN

To this day, the prevailing impression of the relationship between film and television is one of rivalry. This feud between the two dominant forms of mass entertainment dates back to the 1950s, when television was still in its infancy. During this decade, the movies tended to write off television as a pesky little upstart, which could boast nothing better than a screen the size of a postage stamp.

Modern cinematic depictions devoted to "the second medium" more readily combine satire with cultural criticism. *The Truman Show* (1998), *EDtv* (1999) and *Pleasantville* (1998), for example, emphasize its artificiality as well as its potential to manipulate and enslave. All three assert that television programming seduces its audience by presenting an alluring candy-coated universe from which there is no need to escape. These films also argue that genuine fulfillment can be attained by those who manage to free themselves of the medium's grasp.

This ongoing dialog between film and TV took off in a whole new direction in the 1990s. New technological advances and forms of marketing made partners of the former arch-enemies. They began to work together in all imaginable types of production like the manufacture and distribution of videocassettes and DVD. The so-called "home theater" allowed for big screen blockbusters to be brought into the comfort of one's own home, while TV and film both made a small fortune. Today, television is far from being considered an intrusive medium intent on luring audiences away from the theaters in a ploy to bring the movie industry to its knees. Television and the movies have become trusted cohorts who rely on each other for survival.

> **"Television has revolutionized the world, but so gradually that we now take for granted what's simply unbelievable. This, for example: every day, millions of people around the world gather to stare at a wood-and-glass box."** *Frankfurter Allgemeine Zeitung*

lungs. From coast to coast, from Maine to Montana, the prophet's chant is echoed by countless U. S. citizens.

This almost utopian dialog between the television medium and its viewers is quickly silenced when Beale announces that the culprit behind the demise of culture and politics is none other than television itself. Soon the TV execs set the ball rolling for his last live presentation…

Network is rooted in the principle that television would go so far as to kill or undermine the foundations of human civilization like morality, social conscience and freedom of speech to attain its goals. As a result, the movi presents us with a much respected and widely spread critical take on po culture, a thesis which would be revisited ten years later by American autho Neil Postman in his provocative bestseller *Amusing Ourselves to Death*. Post man's exploration of infotainment, show business, and the visually reinforce world outlook prescribed by television is as pertinent today as when it wa first published. The same holds true for *Network,* a scathing satire abou television's demented "entertainment value."   R

4   Scheduling change: Diana Christensen (Faye
     Dunaway) makes Beale a national phenomenon.

5   That's a wrap! Robert Duvall and Faye Dunaway
     watch the ratings soar and the profits roll in.

6   Broadcast news: "Television is not the truth…
     We're in the boredom-killing business."

5

"You're beginning to believe the illusions we're spinning here, you're beginning to believe that the tube is reality and your own lives are unreal! You do! Why, whatever the tube tells you: you dress like the tube, you eat like the tube, you raise your children like the tube, you even think like the tube! This is mass madness, you maniacs! In God's name, you people are the real thing. WE are the illusion!" *Film quote: Howard Beale*

ASSAULT ON PRECINCT 13

1976 - USA - 91 MIN. - ACTION FILM

DIRECTOR JOHN CARPENTER (*1948)
SCREENPLAY JOHN CARPENTER DIRECTOR OF PHOTOGRAPHY DOUGLAS KNAPP EDITING JOHN T. CHANCE (= JOHN CARPENTER)
MUSIC JOHN CARPENTER PRODUCTION J. S. KAPLAN for TURTLE, CKK.

STARRING AUSTIN STOKER (Bishop), DARWIN JOSTON (Napoleon Wilson), LAURIE ZIMMER (Leigh), TONY BURTON (Wells), CHARLES CYPHERS (Special Officer Starker), NANCY LOOMIS (Julie), PETER BRUNI (Ice Cream Man), JOHN J. FOX (Warden), KIM RICHARDS (Kathy Lawson), MARTIN WEST (Lawson).

"It's a god-damn siege."

Damm-da-da-da-damm. A threateningly minimalist synthesizer theme brings terror, as a street gang lays siege to an isolated police precinct. A hail of bullets and countless dead bodies signify the arrival of the Wild West in the midst of the city.

The night had begun so quietly for police lieutenant Bishop (Austin Stoker), whose task it was to watch over an empty precinct during the last evening before its closure. This seemingly boring task takes him back to the district where he grew up: Anderson, a section of Los Angeles on the edge of anarchy. But the night turns out to be anything but boring. A bus full of prisoners stops at the precinct to unload an inmate who has fallen sick, and it just so happens that the members of a street gang have simultaneously come to the precinct to avenge the deaths of six of their comrades shot dur-

ing a police action the night before. A state of siege ensues – with scores of attackers thirsting for revenge, silencers on their weapons, and an apparently endless supply of ammunition on the outside, and a group of police officers and inmates inside the precinct who are unable to call for help. The electricity and phone lines have been cut, they're running out of ammunition, and they drop like flies until, aside from Bishop, only secretary Leigh (Laurie Zimmer), and two inmates, Napoleon Wilson (Darwin Joston) and Wells (Tony Burton), are left standing.

With his cleverly conceived but straightforward film, 28-year-old John Carpenter, who acted as director, author, editor and composer, accomplished a stroke of genius that is still a textbook example of how to create an impressive film with modest means. Assault on Precinct 13 (production cost

3

"A low-budget and taut update of the classic Howard Hawks western, *Rio Bravo.*"

Motion Picture Guide

1 Moving day: Napoleon Wilson (Darwin Joston) and other prisoners are transported to their new holding cells on death row…

2 … but when one of the prisoners falls ill, the inmates are re-routed to a non-operational precinct.

3 You'd best watch your back: The vengeful band of assassins is about to make its next move.

4 The emperor's new clothes: Ringleader Napoleon Wilson has nothing to lose. He's already scheduled for execution.

5 Calling all cars: "Carpenter cited three sources of inspiration: a newspaper clipping, the Western flick *Rio Bravo* and his own fear of random acts of violence." (*Cinema*)

4

JOHN CARPENTER

JOHN CARPENTER John Carpenter (*1948) gets a chapter all to himself in almost every book about fantastic cinema. As a student, Carpenter worked on the screenplay to the short film *The Resurrection of Bronco Billy* (1970), which won an Oscar. In 1974 he made his full-length film debut with *Dark Star*, a satire of the science fiction classic, *2001: A Space Odyssey* (1968). In 1978 he made the horror classic, *Halloween*, and three years later *Escape from New York* (1981), the prototype for all apocalyptic films. His effective use of cinematic methods (like the subjective camerawork in *Halloween*) and his familiarity with film history distinguish his films. In *Someone's Watching Me!* (1978), he paraphrased Hitchcock's *Rear Window* (1954). *The Thing* (1982) is a remake of the Howard Hawks classic of the same name (1951). In the 80s and 90s Carpenter made several more fantasy films, which were mostly uninteresting, with the exception of *Prince of Darkness* (1987), a kind of horror version of *Assault on Precinct 13* (1976) and the outstanding *In the Mouth of Madness* (1994).

!00,000) is both plain and overwhelmingly suggestive in its narration: few images of the shoot-out during which the gang members are killed d a single radio message suffice to reveal that the city is a powder keg just iiting to explode. Images of gangsters skulking through the neighborhood, !ws through a telescopic lens, and the horrible shooting of a small girl esta- sh the gang's total lack of scruples. Carpenter brilliantly constructs the !ge scenario. Though the precinct is in the city, it is completely cut off from ! rest of the world – no electricity, no telephone. The gangsters follow a rfidious strategy, clearing the streets after each attack so that neither rpses nor bullet-ridden cars indicate what has occurred.

A group of attackers surrounding a handful of captives is a scenario niliar from Westerns like Howard Hawks' *Rio Bravo* (1959) or George mero's horror classic, *Night of the Living Dead* (1968). Carpenter shifts ! setting from a lonely farmhouse in the Wild West directly into the heart of 'ilization – a modern city. The parallels to *Rio Bravo* go even further, as

the captives save themselves with explosives, just as John Wayne's sheriff did. Interestingly, Carpenter adopted Wayne's character name, John T. Chance, as a pseudonym for his work as film editor. Carpenter also pays homage to Alfred Hitchcock. The story Bishop tells his secretary toward the beginning of the film – how his father used to send him to the police precinct as a small boy – is an anecdote Hitchcock liked to tell about his own childhood.

Carpenter revealed himself to be a student of film history with *Assault on Precinct 13*, and the film itself became a model for countless others: various gang films and the "Blaxploitation" films of the 80s and 90s suggest his influence, and many action directors were inspired by his no-frills direction. The superb economy of the production is exemplified by Carpenter's soundtrack, which is comprised of merely two themes – the threatening synthesizer theme and an electrical piano melody that evokes sympathy. Both are entirely enthralling. HJK

AI NO CORRIDA (AKA IN THE REALM OF THE SENSES)

Ai no corrida / L'Empire des sens

1976 - JAPAN / FRANCE - 110 MIN. - EROTIC FILM

DIRECTOR NAGISA OSHIMA (*1932)
SCREENPLAY NAGISA OSHIMA **DIRECTOR OF PHOTOGRAPHY** HIDEO ITÔ **EDITING** KEIICHI URAOKA **MUSIC** MINORU MIKI **PRODUCTION** ANATOLE DAUMA for OSHIMA PRODUCTIONS, ARGOS FILMS, SHIBATA ORGANISATION INC.

STARRING TATSUYA FUJI (Kichizo), EIKO MATSUDA (Sada Abe), AOI NAKAJIMA (Toku, Kichizo's Wife), TAIJI TONOYAMA (Beggar), MEIKA SERI (Maid), KANAE KOBAYASHI (the old Geisha Kikuryû), YASUKO MATSUI (Tagawa Inn Manager), KYÔJI KOKONOE (Ômiya), NAOMI SHIRAISHI (Geisha Yaeji), SHINKICHI NODA (Old Man).

"Sada, don't let our pleasure ever end."

It begins like a harmless flirtation and ends in tragedy. In the tea-house managed by his wife (Aoi Nakajima), Kichizo (Tatsuya Fuji) discovers a beautiful new geisha named Sada (Eiko Matsuda). He pursues the young woman, joking, flirting, and generally making his intentions very clear. His wife, thinking this is just one more of his countless affairs, even offers her services as a go-between; and so the affair begins. Kichizo and Sada are soon seeing more and more of each other, and there's something obsessive about their relationship. They do nothing but make love, and they don't mind being watched while they do so. Their love-nest becomes a kind of cage or prison-cell, and the outside world practically ceases to exist for them. They drink to quench their thirst, and they eat nothing. Gradually, Sada becomes increasingly dominant and increasingly demanding. She wants Kichizo to sleep with her incessantly, grows ever more possessive, and insists he should no longer touch his wife. When Sada is forced to go to work again to earn money for herself and Kichizo, she hides his clothes to prevent him leaving while she's meeting her client. And she's the one who introduces ever more extreme practices into their loveplay: slapping, hitting, pinching, and finally choking...

Ai no corrida was a scandal. It showed sex organs in close-up, er penises and actual intercourse. Previously, such things had been seen only pornographic films, and never in a work with any claims to artistic legitima The director, Nagisa Oshima, worked under conditions of the utmost secre *Ai no corrida* was the first film made by his newly-formed production co pany. Filming took around 30 days, with Oshima and his cast and crew wo ing 15 hours a day in a strictly cordoned-off studio. After each day's work, sent the exposed film material to his producer Anatole Dauman in France was the only way to get the film made. Under Japan's strict censorship lav no laboratory in the country would have developed the film. Oshima a edited the movie in France.

In 1976, *Ai no corrida* was screened at the festival in Cannes, ami protests. The organizers of the Berlin film festival planned to show it in same year, but after sensationalized reports appeared in the tabloid pre the film was confiscated by the Public Prosecutor's Department on the s picion that it was pornographic. In Japan, where it is forbidden to show nal sex organs on screen, *Ai no corrida* reached the cinema only in a heavily ce

1

"The story of Sada and Kichizo unfolds like a Catholic Mass, till the final, inevitable, 'Ite missa est'."

Cinema

…ored form, with some parts cut and other parts concealed by strategically placed figleafs in the form of black bars. It came to a court case, which Oshima won in 1982.

Yet there's nothing titillating about the anatomical detail in this radical and disturbing film. Oshima tells the story of a sexual obsession, a love that consists entirely of physical desire, shutting out the whole world beyond the lovers' purview. This is a love that demands complete submission to the lover, a love that's indifferent to such epithets as "embarrassing" or "distasteful." With pitiless logic, Oshima takes the romantic idea of "belonging" to the loved one, and follows it through to its deadly conclusion. This love

story also acquires an almost subversive undertone when we consider that it's set in 1936, something that only becomes apparent in the few scenes that take place outdoors. This was the year that marked the birth of Japanese fascism. While the nation girds its loins for a megalomaniac imperialist campaign, Kichizo and Sada are interested in nothing but each other.

Ai no corrida was based on a true story. In 1936, a woman cut off her lover's penis and wandered around Tokyo with it for four days. Her obsessive passion aroused a wave of public sympathy, and she was sentenced to only six years in prison.

HJK

NAGISA OSHIMA   The problems involved in the making and showing of *Ai no corrida / L'Empire des sens*, (1976) were nothing new for Nagisa Oshima (*1932). He was already accustomed to difficulties. In 1960, his second film, *Night and Fog in Japan* (*Nihon no yoru to kiri*, 1960), was withdrawn from circulation by the production company after only four days. The film took an embittered look at the Japanese student movement; and Oshima's entire œuvre is characterized by its focus on the young generation, an interest in the asscciated topics of violence and sex, and a frequently angry confrontation with the traditional values of Japanese society. He became the central figure in the film renaissance of the 60s, which might be described as a Japanese *Nouvelle Vague*. In *Death by Hanging* (*Koshikei*, 1967/68) for example, he attacks the oppression of the Korean minority in Japan; in *Boy* (*Shonen*, 1969), he portrays greedy parents exploiting their son for their own criminal ends. Oshima's formal language is often brilliant: *The Cruel Story of Youth* (*Seishun zankoku monogatari*, 1960), for instance, tells the wild love story of a gangster couple – in candy colors, with a crazy handheld camera, and in widescreen cinemascope format. After *Ai no corrida*, Oshima achieved international fame one more time with the psychological war drama *Merry Christmas, Mr. Lawrence* (1983), starring David Bowie.

1 Love you to death: Thinking it's only another meaningless affair, teahouse proprietress Toku (Aoi Nakajima) aids Kichizo (Tatsuya Fuji) in making geisha Sada's acquaintance.

2 Miss Scarlet with the knife: "The case is still very much alive in the minds of the Japanese. It is thought of with reverence, as an eternal ode to the love sick." (*Frankfurter Allgemeine Zeitung*)

3 Dream weaver: Sada plants one on Kichizo.

3

L'AILE OU LA CUISSE
aka The Wing or the Leg

1976 - FRANCE - 104 MIN. - COMEDY

DIRECTOR CLAUDE ZIDI (*1934)
SCREENPLAY CLAUDE ZIDI, MICHEL FABRE **DIRECTOR OF PHOTOGRAPHY** CLAUDE RENOIR, WLADIMIR IVANOV **EDITING** MONIQUE ISNARDON, ROBERT ISNARDON **MUSIC** VLADIMIR COSMA **PRODUCTION** CHRISTIAN FECHNER for FILMS CHRISTIAN FECHNER.

STARRING LOUIS DE FUNÈS (Charles Duchemin), COLUCHE (= MICHEL COLUCCI) (Gérard Duchemin), JULIEN GUIOMAR (Jean Tricatel), ANN ZACHARIAS (Marguerite II.), CLAUDE GENSAC (Marguerite I.), RAYMOND BUSSIÈRES (Chauffeur Henri), DANIEL LANGLET (Lambert), MARCEL DALIO (The Tailor), PHILIPPE BOUVARD (Himself), VITTORIO CAPRIOLI (Vittorio).

"A loin of beef – Argentinian, three years old, southern slopes."

The delicate flavor and aroma of fine foods and wines makes life worth living for Duchemin (Louis de Funès), a man whose entire existence revolves around eating. Every day, he visits the best and most expensive restaurants in town with the reverence of a worshipper and the vigilance of a vestal virgin. To him, a prizewinning chef is a high priest of the palate, a privileged guardian of the Grail of good taste. Charles Duchemin is the most respected restaurant critic in France; and today and every day, he expects each cook to do his sacred duty.

He carries out his tests in a series of cunning disguises. One day he's an old lady, the next, he's an American, resplendent in a pink jacket and a Stetson. When he's sure no-one's watching, he checks the temperature of the schnitzel with his trusty thermometer, stores samples of the wine in the tanks in his tailor-made jacket, or tucks anything he can't face eating into a Tupperware box. The laboratory, and his tastebuds, decide how many stars a restaurant will be deemed to deserve. In this way, he and his colleagues banquet and burp their way through the restaurants of the nation, before publishing the verdicts in the *Guide Duchemin*: the gourmets' bible and a signpost to culinary Nirvana.

It's an achievement of national significance, and it's only fitting that Charles should be invited to join the hallowed ranks of the Académie française. But he's failed to reckon with his arch-enemy Jean Tricatel (Julien Guiomar), manufacturer of industrial grub and owner of a chain of junkfood restaurants. The scheming Tricatel, who is every bit as slimy as the food he produces, smuggles a spy into Duchemin's house to steal the names of the distinguished restaurants before the book is published. With the help of this list, he plans to buy up some of the best restaurants in the country and force them to accept his own inferior products. And by this somewhat roundabout route, he hopes to see his zero-quality fodder elevated to the rank of *haute cuisine*.

When Charles gets wind of this plot, he is understandably appalled. "I could give a restaurant two stars and this scoundrel would serve the customers dog food with tinned rice. On a saucer." The fanatical epicure resolves to save French cooking by putting Tricatel in his place: he will challenge his rival to a TV talkshow duel and show the world who's boss. But his culinary crusade ends in a trip to Gourmet Hell, for suddenly he's confronted by an irate gastronome whose business he ruined with a bad review. With a shot

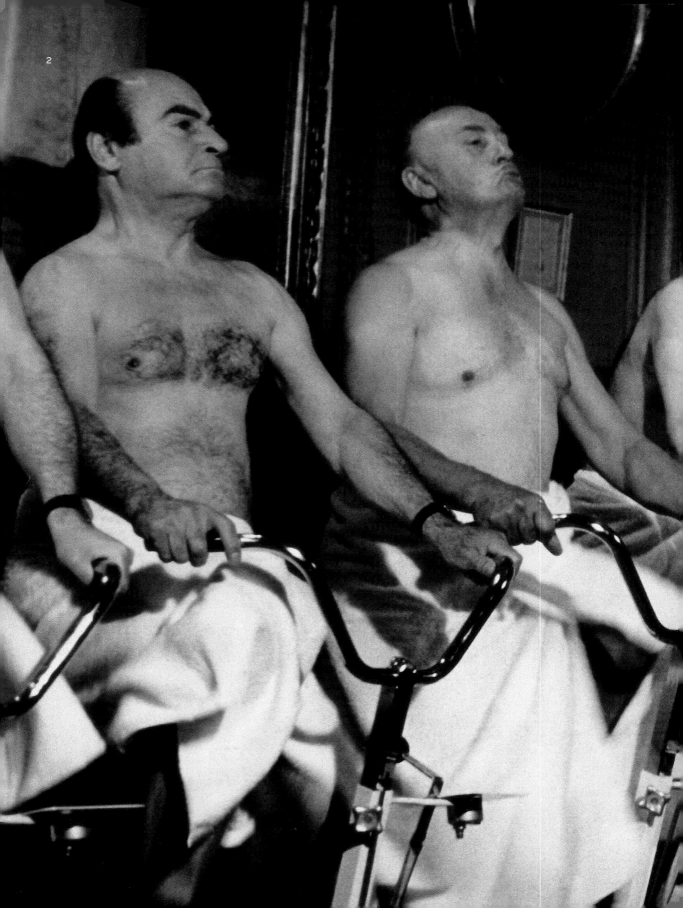

"Louis de Funès doesn't quite explode, but he certainly makes sparks fly, and his sheer comic energy is as powerful as ever." *Le Monde*

LOUIS DE FUNÈS

They called him Rumpelstiltskin, the Poison Dwarf, Mr. Hyperactive and Poltergeist: the small man with the big nose, the World Champ of hysterical rage. A typical de Funès character is the uptight *petit bourgeois* who despises his social inferiors, sucks up to his bosses, schemes to get ahead, and ultimately falls flat on his face.

(Carlos) Louis de Funès (De Galarza) was born in Courbevoie in 1914, the son of a Spanish diamond merchant. His trademark was his rubber face, which he could twist into the most incredible grimaces, combined with some truly wild body language. He was apparently able to increase the length of his nose in order to play it like a violin. While performing such esoteric practices, he occasionally lost the ability to speak his native language, resorting to bizarre onomatopoeic sounds said to be reminiscent of Donald Duck, to whom many of his film characters bore a striking resemblance. He learned a series of trades – furrier, decorator, bar pianist – before making his breakthrough at the advanced age of 50, in *Le Gendarme de Saint Tropez* (1964). After 20 years in supporting roles, he was suddenly a popular favorite, capable of making up to five films in a single year. Many of these were highly successful. Examples include the *Gendarme* series, the *Fantomas* films (1964, 1965, 1966) and *Oscar* (1967). His ascent marked the beginning of the comedy boom in France, and he won countless fans worldwide. They referred to him affectionately as "Fufu." De Funès died in 1983.

1 Frugal gourmet: When Charles Duchemin (Louis De Funès) partakes in France's national pastime, he turns up the heat on farce and tomfoolery.

2 Tour de France: Charles will stop at nothing to get his taste testers into prime physical condition.

3 A wolf in she's clothing: One false move and this black widow will spoil the soup with her poisoned pen. Here, food critic Charles moonlights as the happy homemaker.

4 Catch of the day: Duchemin and his staff close in on an unsavory intruder.

5 A night at Benihana's: This learned Teppan performance artist makes a laughing stock of the Cuisinart.

6 Pigs in a blanket: Keeping in line with his sugary menu, director Claude Zidi's recipe for success also calls for these little weenies to be honey glazed.

3

4

gun at his head, he's forced by his tormentor to eat a Tricatel menu… The expression on Charles' face as he swallows the snails is one of sheer horror, the elderly oysters bring him out in blotches, and the platter of slimy sauerkraut is more than he can bear.

After this culinary inferno, Charles is far from his normal self; more to the point, he's lost his sense of taste. Just 24 hours before his TV showdown with Tricatel, he can't tell the difference between a green bean and a wad of cotton wool. Rescue is at hand, however, in the shape of his son Gérard, played by De Funès' equally famous compatriot, the comedian Coluche; and soon this very odd couple – the father a French Foghorn Leghorn, the son as meek as a mouse – have entered the lion's den: Tricatel's food factory. In the surreal setting of the production halls, father and son only barely escape ending up as canned meat before uncovering the shameless tricks of Tricatel's trade: Among many other sins, he's been using the blessings of modern technology to pass off green bathing caps as lettuces.

L'Aile ou la cuisse is hardly a subtle comedy, but then it never tries to be. Its strength is in its snappy visual gags: a spell in hospital and the resetting of a broken leg are excuses for an orgy of slapstick. But the film also has its quiet moments. Take the scene in which Charles discovers that his son has been leading a double life as a clown: when the outraged father pours a bucket of foam over his son's head, the comedy is so bittersweet that the laughter sticks in our throats. *L'Aile ou la cuisse* is a choice morsel of a movie, and it's often deliciously funny.   OK

5

6

THE AMERICAN FRIEND

Der amerikanische Freund / L'Ami américain

1977 - FRG / FRANCE - 126 MIN. - GANGSTER FILM, LITERARY ADAPTATION, DRAMA

DIRECTOR WIM WENDERS (*1945)

SCREENPLAY WIM WENDERS, based on the novel *RIPLEY'S GAME* by PATRICIA HIGHSMITH **DIRECTOR OF PHOTOGRAPHY** ROBBY MÜLLER **EDITING** PETER PRZYGODDA, BARBARA VON WEITERSHAUSEN **MUSIC** JÜRGEN KNIEPER **PRODUCTION** WIM WENDERS for ROAD MOVIES FILMPRODUKTION, FILMVERLAG DER AUTOREN, MOLI FILMS, LES FILMS DU LOSANGE, WESTDEUTSCHER RUNDFUNK.

STARRING DENNIS HOPPER (Tom Ripley), BRUNO GANZ (Jonathan Zimmermann), LISA KREUZER (Marianne Zimmermann), GÉRARD BLAIN (Raoul Minot), NICHOLAS RAY (Derwatt), SAMUEL FULLER (Gangster), PETER LILIENTHAL (Marcangelo), DANIEL SCHMID (Igraham), RUDOLF SCHÜNDLER (Gantner), SANDY WHITELAW (Doctor in Paris).

"I don't know what to do."

In Wim Wenders' melancholy gangster film, based on a novel by Patricia Highsmith, no one really knows what to do any more. The two main characters are wandering in a kind of no-man's-land, bored, existentially desperate and in danger of losing their lives. On the one hand, we have the smart gangster Tom Ripley (Dennis Hopper), who commutes between New York and Hamburg, visiting auctions and buying expensive paintings by the forger Derwatt (Nicholas Ray), while cultivating his links to the underworld. And then we have the meek, unassuming picture-framer Jonathan Zimmermann, played by Bruno Ganz. Deliberately given the false impression that his illness is fatal – Jonathan is a hemophiliac – he is soon a compliant victim of criminal machinations, even becoming a contract killer to ensure the financial survival of his family after his death. Two men, two lives, and the contrasts could hardly be greater: one of them footloose and fancy-free, the other bound to his family and his tiny business – the globetrotting dandy Tom Ripley and the introspective framer in the bleak, depopulated docklands of Hamburg. The political graffiti on the grimly monotonous walls place the film firmly in 1970s Germany.

Ripley encounters Jonathan at an auction and hears about his treacherous illness. Devoid of scruples, Ripley sells the information to the French gangster Raoul Minot, who tempts Jonathan with a suggestion: he will put u the money to treat Jonathan's allegedly fatal hemophilia, if Jonathan carrie out a murder for him in return. And – how could it be otherwise? – Jonatha loses his moral integrity. After the first murder, he allows himself to be black mailed into committing another, this time in a Trans-Europe Express trail Just as things are going badly wrong on this second job, Ripley appears fror nowhere and helps Jonathan complete his deadly mission. Having begun to betraying Jonathan, Ripley seems suddenly to have befriended him: he's no Jonathan's dubious "American friend."

And yet they remain strangers. The audience can practically feel the spiritual isolation in the bleak images, half-suppressed movements and dis trustful glances, interior monologs and softly-whispered dialogs. A feelir of petrifaction spreads, telling of Jonathan's defenselessness and the rutl lessness of those who exploit him for their own criminal ends. Death for li and life for death: for Jonathan, there seems to be no way out of this viciou circle. Symbolically, he often holds a frame before his face, checking its qua ity, as if searching for an identity, a suitable frame for his own life.

In *The American Friend,* Wim Wenders created a little gem of a filr minutely detailed and without embellishment. Many critics read his work a

1

2

Essentially, the film is about colonization – or more specifically, about the need to resist the American colonization of the unconscious."

Literature / Film Quarterly

a parable on the "colonial" relationship between American and German culture, on the triumph of an aggressive, corrupt and bullying attitude that has no time for doubt or self-criticism. At the same time, Wenders delivered a contemporary reinterpretation of the social realism that has dominated gangster films since the earliest days of the genre, with protagonists who struggle to defend themselves even when all the political and economic odds are stacked against them. Wenders is part of this tradition, which he renews and updates. *The American Friend* is an intelligent thriller that easily combines great seriousness with a suspenseful plot. It's a complex film, not easily pigeonholed, in which almost all identities, relationships and motivations remain open. So too the friendship between Jonathan and Ripley. The film ends with a sequence of images almost surreal in their effect: Jonathan and Ripley, on a beach at the mouth of the river Elbe, set fire to an ambulance containing the bodies of two gangsters who had been pursuing them. But this final test of their friendship ends in failure: Jonathan flees with his wife, leaving Ripley behind him – alone.   BF

1   Flying paper dragons: Melancholy gangster Tom
    Ripley (Dennis Hopper) is holding all the strings.

2   Making quota: Monthly casualties keep business
    in the black.

3   His hands are tied: There's just no freeing himself
    of a criminal bind for Jonathan (Bruno Ganz).

4   Down and out in the underworld: Buddy Ripley
    gives Jonathan's morale a jump start.

3

WIM WENDERS

Wim Wenders was born in Düsseldorf in 1945. He took his first steps as a film director when his father gave him a Super-8 camera in 1954. From 1967 to 1970, he studied at the Film and Television Academy in Munich. During this period, he also made short films and wrote critical essays. In 1970, he made his first full-length film, *Summer in the City*. This was followed by a number of successful features, including *Alice in the Cities* (*Alice in den Städten*, 1974), *Kings of the Road* (*Im Lauf der Zeit*, 1975/76), *The American Friend* (*Der amerikanische Freund / L'Ami américain*, 1977), *Paris, Texas* (1984), *Wings of Desire* (*Der Himmel über Berlin / Les Ailes du désir*, 1987), *Faraway, So Close!* (*In weiter Ferne, so nah!*, 1993) and *Buena Vista Social Club* (1998/99).

These films made Wim Wenders one of the most internationally renowned German directors. His style is characterized by long, steady shots and careful cutting. We become aware of the camera as an observer, and we also have time to examine the pictures in detail. Wenders' narratives are correspondingly detailed. They focus on rootless characters and tight-lipped heroes incapable of making contact with their fellow human beings. In many of his films, Wenders uses this constellation to examine the influence of American culture on postwar Germany. At the same time, his poetic-philosophical filmmaking stands in sharp contrast to the fast-moving action-packed cinema of Hollywood, with its one-dimensional characters and transparent motivations. Although Wenders has produced fascinating new interpretations of Hollywood myths – especially in his road movies and gangster films – he advances the tradition in his own, specifically "European" way.

THAT OBSCURE OBJECT OF DESIRE
Cet obscur objet du désir / Ese oscuro objeto del deseo

1977 - FRANCE / SPAIN - 103 MIN. - DRAMA

DIRECTOR LUIS BUÑUEL (1900–1983)
SCREENPLAY JEAN-CLAUDE CARRIÈRE, LUIS BUÑUEL, based on the novel *LA FEMME ET LE PANTIN* by PIERRE LOUŸS
DIRECTOR OF PHOTOGRAPHY EDMOND RICHARD EDITING HÉLÈNE PLEMIANNIKOV, LUIS BUÑUEL MUSIC RICHARD WAGNER and others
PRODUCTION SERGE SILBERMAN for GREENWICH FILM PRODUCTIONS, LES FILMS GALAXIE, IN-CINE COMPAÑÍA INDUSTRIAL CINEMATOGRÁFICA S. A.

STARRING FERNANDO REY (Mathieu), CAROLE BOUQUET (Conchita), ANGELA MOLINA (Conchita), JULIEN BERTHEAU (Edouard the Judge), ANDRÉ WEBER (Martin), MILENA VUKOTIC (Train Passenger), BERNARD MUSSON (Police Inspector), MARÍA ASQUERINO (Conchita's Mother), DAVID ROCHA (El "Morenito"), MUNI (Concierge), ISABELLE SADOYAN (Gardener).

"You're not my father and you're not my lover!"

The great Luis Buñuel, hero of the Surrealist movement in the 1920s, was already 77 when he took the director's chair one last time to film the tale of the aging *grand bourgeois* Mathieu and his hopeless obsession with a young dancer from the lower orders. After only a few days, Buñuel broke off filming, dissatisfied with the performance of Maria Schneider (who had achieved fame five years previously in *Last Tango in Paris*) as the teasing temptress Conchita. In desperation, he suggested to the producer Serge Silberman that the role be recast – with two actresses. To his surprise, Silberman was delighted by this apparently absurd idea, so that Carole Bouquet, a classically cool French beauty with a Chanel face, shared the honors with Angela Molina, a sultry Spanish Carmen.

Film history will provide numerous examples of double roles – where an actor or actress plays two characters in the same film – but never before had two actresses shared a single role. Interpretations were not slow in coming: it was said that people always have several sides to their characters; or that

Mathieu is actually in love with two different women; or that Conchita embodies Woman As Such. Bullshit, said Buñuel, dismissing these philosophic pirouettes: it was simply the only solution he could think of, a decision arising out of sheer desperation. True to the spirit of Surrealism, Buñuel resists the rationalization of unconscious processes, adducing accidents and moments of inspiration whose meaning he himself cannot comprehend because there's simply nothing there to be understood. Surrealism had long tried to overcome the rational mind and its sly and stubborn self-censorship, using a range of techniques from automatic writing to the "exquisite cadaver" parlor game. In *That Obscure Object of Desire*, Buñuel carries this tendency to its limits once again, for here the apparently irrational is presented as if it were the most natural thing in the world.

What's astonishing is how quickly we forget that two actresses are sharing the same role, even though there's not the slightest resemblance between Bouquet and Molina. This merging of two individuals is facilitated

1 Human kindness is overflowing: Conchita relin-
quishes the key to her heart and falls flat on her
face.

2 Rear view vixen: Mirrors confirm that Conchita is
indeed "double trouble."

3 Gated: Is it people or his own emotions that
Mathieu (Fernando Rey) is blocking out?

4 Another kinky role-play: Carole Bouquet (4, 5)
shares the part of Conchita with Angela Molina
(1, 2, 6) without reason, without rhyme.

5 Feel your way: Director Luis Buñuel often cast
Fernando Rey as an imposing bourgeois trapped
by his own class.

6 Sheer elegance: She's clearly got legs, but
Mathieu is more interested in whether she can
handle a booty call.

"Different species of terrorism abound in the film, starting with the very evident sexual terrorism practiced by Conchita, and the less evident (except to Conchita who persistently resists being bought) financial terrorism practiced by Mathieu." *Monthly Film Bulletin*

the film's austere and businesslike style. For Buñuel, the Catholic atheist, th
iconoclastic lover of images, creates a world in which even bizarre occur
rences appear perfectly plausible. During a solemn conference in an elegar
office, a mousetrap snaps shut with a loud report; in the background c
another scene, a carbomb explodes and the characters seem utterly unfazec
Thus we are not merely presented with an abstract problem – the deadenin
effects of habit and convention – but are forced to experience our own grad
ual acceptance of the most absurd phenomena. The unexplained terrorism c
the "Revolutionary Army of the Infant Jesus" is as good an example of this a
the two faces of Conchita.

The film is based on Pierre Louÿs' novel *La Femme et le pantin*, whic
had already been filmed twice. In *The Devil Is a Woman (Der Teufel ist ei*

5

Luis Buñuel summed himself up with an immortal aphorism: "I'm still an atheist, thank God." Born in 1900 and educated by the Jesuits, he left Spain for Paris in 1925, accompanied by his extrovert friend Salvador Dalí. In 1929, they collaborated to create *An Andalusian Dog* (*Un chien andalou*), which was followed a year later by *The Golden Age* (*L'Âge d'or*); virulently anticlerical and sexually unabashed, each of the films became a *succès de scandale* for the Surrealist movement.

After a variety of activities in the course of the 30s, including the ironic ethnographical film document *Las Hurdes – Tierra sin pan* (1933), Buñuel was forced into emigration by the Second World War. In New York, he re-edited Leni Riefenstahl's *Triumph of the Will* (*Triumph des Willens*, 1935) for the Latin American market, transforming the Nazi propaganda into an antifascist statement. At the end of the 40s, he moved to Mexico, where he began his second directing career with a series of extravagant melodramas and adventure films.

His return to Spain was worthy of a Surrealist. While making *Viridiana* (1961), he succeeded in misleading Franco's censors as to the nature of the work in progress. Only when the pungently anticlerical film was shown at the Cannes festival (where it received the Golden Palm) did it become painfully clear to the Spaniards that Buñuel had taken perfidious revenge on the detested Franco regime. The Vatican protested to the Spanish government, which had a thoroughly deferential attitude towards the Church of Rome, and the Minister responsible was forced to resign. Buñuel, who had been heavily criticized for his apparent collaboration with the totalitarian regime, must have relished having the last laugh.

In his old age, Buñuel enjoyed the Olympian status of a great European *auteur*, and his films featured stars such as Catherine Deneuve, Franco Nero, Jeanne Moreau and Michel Piccoli. He died in 1983, in his adopted home country, Mexico.

au, 1935), Josef von Sternberg had cast Marlene Dietrich as the seductive ꞁnchita, another of his attempts to define the essence of femininity, man-ꞁy supported by the German diva. In Julien Duvivier's *La Femme et le Pan-* ꞁ *(1958,* aka *The Female* or *A Woman Like Satan*), Brigitte Bardot had been ꓒemon of sexual aggression under a mask of perfect naturalness. So this ꞁtically charged fable from the turn of the century served three times – ꓽ the 30s, the 50s, and the 70s – as an opportunity to get to grips with ꓒman (that impossible enigma…). In fact, these films supply little support ꓽ any theory of the Eternal Feminine; but – like the science fiction genre – ꓽy do tell us a lot about the mentality of their time and about changes in ꓽcial attitudes – not least towards actresses and the roles they are asked ꓽ embody. MH

6

STAR WARS

1977 - USA - 121 MIN. - SCIENCE FICTION

DIRECTOR GEORGE LUCAS (*1944)
SCREENPLAY GEORGE LUCAS **DIRECTOR OF PHOTOGRAPHY** GILBERT TAYLOR **EDITING** PAUL HIRSCH, MARCIA LUCAS, RICHARD CHEW
MUSIC JOHN WILLIAMS **PRODUCTION** GARY KURTZ for LUCASFILM LTD.

STARRING MARK HAMILL (Luke Skywalker), HARRISON FORD (Han Solo), CARRIE FISHER (Princess Leia Organa), ALEC GUINNESS (Ben "Obi-Wan" Kenobi), PETER CUSHING (Tarkin), DAVID PROWSE (Darth Vader), JAMES EARL JONES (Darth Vader's voice), KENNY BAKER (R2-D2), ANTHONY DANIELS (C-3PO), PETER MAYHEW (Chewbacca), PHIL BROWN (Owen Lars), SHELAGH FRASER (Beru Lars).

ACADEMY AWARDS 1977 OSCARS for BEST MUSIC (John Williams), BEST FILM EDITING (Paul Hirsch, Marcia Lucas, Richard Chew), BEST SET DESIGN (John Barry, Norman Reynolds, Leslie Dilley, Roger Christian), BEST COSTUMES (John Mollo), BEST SOUND (Don MacDougall, Ray West, Bob Minkler, Derek Ball), BEST SPECIAL EFFECTS (John Stears, John Dykstra, Richard Edlund, Grant McCune, Robert Blalack), and SPECIAL PRIZE FOR SOUND EFFECTS (voices of the aliens and robots, Ben Burtt).

"May the Force be with you!"

There's something rotten in the state of the galaxy. With the blessings of the Emperor, Grand Moff Tarkin (Peter Cushing) and the sinister Lord Vader (David Prowse/James Earl Jones) have been conquering and subjugating one planet system after the other in the old Republic. Tarkin commands a massive spaceship, whose firepower has the ability to annihilate entire planets. This "Deathstar" is the most dangerous weapon in the universe – perhaps with the exception of "The Force," a mysterious, all-pervading energy. Anyone who learns to master this force through years of ascetic training is possessed with superhuman powers. In the past, the Jedi Knights secured justice and kept the peace with the help of "The Force." But now Darth Vader, a renegade Jedi, is one of the last people with control of its powers, forming

with Tarkin an almost invincible alliance of evil in the once peaceful expan es of the universe.

Only a small group of rebels resist the might of the Empire and fight restore the old order. To achieve their aspirations, the construction plans the "Deathstar", which the rebels have acquired, could be of great ass tance. But the spaceship of Princess Leia (Carrie Fisher) is captured just she is returning to her home planet with the plans in hand. At the last mome she is able to save the blueprint of the "Death Star" inside the droid R2- (Kenny Baker). If this tiny robot can get the plans to the old Jedi Knight O Wan Kenobi (Alec Guinness) in time, there could still be a remote hope for t rebels' cause.

1   May the Force be with you: With a monk's habit and light sabre, Ben "Obi-Wan" Kenobi (Alec Guinness) links medieval mythology to a hi-tech future.

2   Iron lung of evil: Darth Vader (David Prowse) will stop at nothing to conquer the galaxy.

3   Man's best friend according to Lucas: Princess Leia (Carrie Fisher) confides in R2-D2 (Kenny Baker).

The journey of R2-D2 and his companion, the dithering and etiquette-conscious communication robot C-3PO (Anthony Daniels), takes them to the planet Tatooine, where they are purchased by farmer Owen Lars (Phil Brown). His nephew, Luke Skywalker (Mark Hamill) longs for a life more exciting than that of an agricultural worker. He would much rather fight with the rebels against the Empire – just as his father, a legendary Jedi whom he has never met, once did ...

Skywalker's dreams of adventure begin to become reality when the two droids meet Obi-Wan. Soon the imperial Storm Troopers are at their heels, and the old Jedi Knight is left with no other alternative but to travel with Luke and the droids to Alderaan, Leia's home planet, bringing the plans of the "Death Star" to help plan a counterattack.

They receive assistance from Han Solo (Harrison Ford) and old pro who, with his ship, the Millennium Falcon, manages to speed away from the fast-approaching imperial cruisers in the nick of time. Even so, they do not reach their destination: Tarkin and Darth Vader have already destroyed the planet Alderaan.

After our heroes free Princess Leia from the "Death Star," nothing stands in the way of the final battle between the Empire and the rebels in the Javin-System. The Achilles heel of the gigantic space station is a small ven-

tilation shaft, and in the end, after several intense battles, it is Luke who i able to hit the weak spot and destroy the "Death Star" in a powerful explo sion. Only Darth Vader escapes the blazing inferno. And while one battle ma have been won in this war in the stars, it won't be long before the Empir strikes back ...

George Lucas began working on his star-saga just as his teenag drama, *American Graffiti*, was poised to become the surprise hit of 1973 – success from which the director profited much less than the studios that pro duced the film. For Lucas, this experience was the driving motivation never t give control of one of his projects to anyone else again. *Star Wars* was pro duced entirely by his own company and the special effects were created b Industrial Light & Magic, also a Lucas company. Rounding out the deal was clause giving rights to merchandizing (toys, clothing, etc.) and the use of filr music to Lucas, initiating a new period in cinema in which the biggest pro ceeds of a film were no longer made at the box office. The blockbuster movi was born.

Real success always did depend on reaching the largest possible audi ence. Lucas stressed over and over that he wrote the screenplay with and 9-year-olds in mind. But in the end, the film was able to connect wit virtually every age group, primarily because with his "space opera," Luca

"I wanted to make a film for kids, something that would present them with a kind of elementary morality. Because nowadays nobody bothers to tell those kids, 'Hey, this is right and this is wrong.'"

George Lucas, interview with David Sheff

"A combination of past and future, Western and space odyssey, myth and dream world, *Star Wars* may be the most enduring piece of escapism ever put on film." *Sacramento Bee*

as neither attempting to depart from old genres, nor to enthusiastically reconstruct them. In fact, his goal was just the opposite. Like his colleague Steven Spielberg, Lucas pursued a higher path, which led him back to the classical narrative form, meeting the expectations of the public and employing the highest levels of technical mastery.

The subject matter of *Star Wars* is akin to a trip through the annals of cultural and film history. Lucas fused elements from the tales of knights and the myths of heroes with the high-tech world of spaceships, was inspired by German and Soviet military uniforms, based the Jedi religion on the Shaman cults of Central America, and created the Empire in the image of an Orwellian dictatorship. The android C-3PO is unmistakably based on the machine woman from Fritz Lang's *Metropolis* (1926), and the concluding hero-honoring ceremony is an obvious reference to Leni Riefenstahl's Nazi party film *The Triumph of the Will* (*Triumph des Willens*, 1935). In short, with *Star Wars* an inter-cultural super-cosmos was created, containing something for every audience member to recognize.

4 Rebels without a shave: Individualists Chewbacca (Peter Mayhew) and Han Solo (Harrison Ford) battle against the evil empire.

5 About face: The imperial storm troopers are trained and ruthless killers.

An overture: in the beginning of *Star Wars* (1977), a long block of text rolls up the screen, setting the stage and recounting the background story. What follows is no singular adventure; it is an entire universe. From the very beginning *Star Wars* was created as a multi-episode project. After the first episode came *Star Wars: Episode V – The Empire Strikes Back* (1980) and then *Star Wars: Episode VI – The Return of the Jedi* (1983). The pre-history of the saga was also conceptualized as a trilogy. Even during the first screenplay drafts, Lucas' Star-world was getting bigger and bigger. This is no exception in the fantasy and science fiction genre. Where new, exotic worlds are created, there will always be questions about how it all began. With the interest in both past and future, the plot possibilities are endless.

Serial science fiction stories were already prevalent and popular in the 1930s. Space heroes like *Flash Gordon* (1936) and *Buck Rogers* (1939) helped their comic forefathers to big screen success. Each 13-part series told of despotic rulers, beautiful women, and heroic men saving the universe; after 20 minutes the plot stopped at the most exciting moment – to be continued next week in this theater!

The *Star-Trek* Universe has been massively popular and has experienced considerable expansion. Since the first episode of the television series about the Starship Enterprise was broadcast in 1966, five spin-off series and ten films have been created, each piece of this long chain of individual stories adding to the colossal inventory of characters, events, time periods, and places that make up this fantastic world.

6 Budget getaway: Protocol droid C-3PO (Anthony Daniels) speaks millions of languages; but unlike brave little R2-D2, he's an exasperating penny-pincher.

7 Putting their lives on the line for a pleasant tomorrow: Princess Leia and Luke Skywalker (Mark Hamill).

8 Everyday life in the not-too-distant future: The furniture of the *Star Wars* universe is sometimes credibly and recognizably shabby.

"It's a terrifically entertaining war story, it has memorable characters and it is visually compelling. What more do we want in movies?" *San Francisco Chronicle*

The real highlight, however, was that Lucas' film, despite its complex plot, tells a story easily reduced to the battle of good versus evil. *Star Wars* is not a story of broken heroes. Lucas sends clearly defined characters into battle, and the audience are never left in doubt as to who will triumph in the end. The result is that the science fiction opus became an effortlessly digestible mixture of vignettes, whose charm lay not in complicated conceptual worlds, but rather in its fantastic moments and visual spectacles. It was these moments that made the film an ideal springboard for the budding entertainment industry of video and computer games. The space battles were replicated and prolonged on consoles and monitors all over the world, helping to reduce the time between episodes …

EP

8

ERASERHEAD

1974/77 - USA - 90 MIN. - HORROR FILM, PSYCHO DRAMA

DIRECTOR DAVID LYNCH (*1946)

SCREENPLAY DAVID LYNCH DIRECTOR OF PHOTOGRAPHY FREDERICK ELMES, HERBERT CARDWELL EDITING DAVID LYNCH MUSIC DAVID LYNCH, PETER IVERS (Songs), FATS WALLER PRODUCTION DAVID LYNCH for AMERICAN FILM INSTITUTE.

STARRING JACK NANCE (Henry Spencer), CHARLOTTE STEWART (Mary X), ALLEN JOSEPH (Mr. X), JEANNE BATES (Mrs. X), JACK FISK (Man in Planet), JUDITH ANNA ROBERTS (Beautiful Girl Across the Hall), LAUREL NEAR (Lady in the Radiator), JEAN LANGE (Grandmother), THOMAS COULSON (Boy), DARWIN JOSTON (Paul).

"In heaven everything is fine."

The man in space (Jack Fisk) is dreaming. His pockmarked face stares out the window as he works a lever, and a printer named Henry Spencer (Jack Nance) appears against the backdrop of a sad, hermetic, black-and-white world. We see a factory, pipes, courtyards, and one-room apartments – an industrial microcosm in which both the near and distant whine of machines and the buzz of menacing electric lines behind the wallpaper can be heard everywhere.

Henry hasn't heard form his girlfriend Mary (Charlotte Stewart) for ages. Suddenly, her parents invite him to a bizarre dinner. All the women in turn are shaken by nervous fits. Mary's father serves mini chickens whose legs twitc when they are cut, while something that looks like bloody bubbles pours ou over the plates. Then his girlfriend's lascivious mother tells Henry that he ha become a father.

But it remains questionable whether he is truly the progenitor of th tightly bandaged being that looks more like a sheared sheep than a baby. I any case, Mary moves in with him, only to leave during the first night to g back to her parents, irritated by the constant screaming. Henry remain alone. The monstrous "child" gets sick, an affair with the beautiful girl acros

2

1   Seeing is believing: Jack Nance as Henry Spencer
in *Eraserhead*. The film's admirers have included
directors as diverse as Stanley Kubrick, John
Waters and William Friedkin.

2   Headed for greatness: Henry is the eraser factory's
diamond in the rough.

3   All good things to those wait: Three years filming,
one year in post-production. To save money, the
impoverished director David Lynch actually lived
on the set of Henry's apartment for a while.

the hall (Judith Anna Roberts) ends in humiliation, and Henry dreams of an angelic, though horribly disfigured lady in the radiator (Laurel Near) and of a machine that transforms his head into an eraser. He ultimately kills the pitiful, reviled being and when he does so, his world dissolves into nothingness.

Despite the essentially linear plot, the story of *Eraserhead* evades explanation. Just as Henry seems to be merely a vision of the man in space shown at the beginning of the film, who at the end returns to the completely

surreal and unbelievable, the narrated story seems to be permanently put into question by the suggestive quality of the images, the menacing drone of the soundtrack, the surreal events of the subplots, the torturously slow movements, and the characters' strange speech. In the leaden atmosphere of this world, the half-hearted manifestations of life and helpless gestures of the humans have no permanence.

There are plenty of starting points for interpretation. The episode in which Henry's head – whose vertical hair is already highly suggestive –

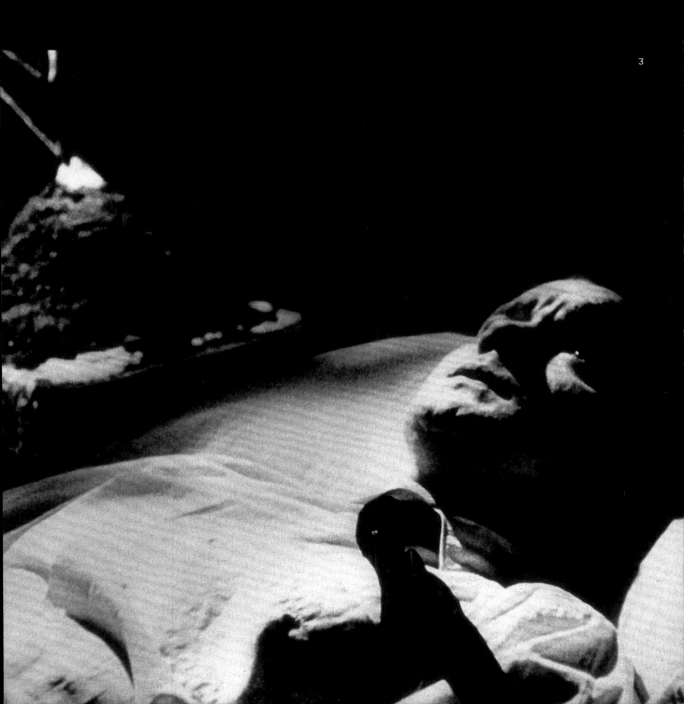

"The imagery of this eerie film is impossible to pin down, the sound is unnerving, the lighting is dreadful, the settings are execrable, and the characters are horrendous." *Cinema*

3

"The only artist I ever felt could be my brother was Kafka."

David Lynch, in: Chris Rodley (Ed.), Lynch on Lynch

used to make erasers for pencils can be read as a metaphor for oblivion and speechlessness. Lynch's daughter Jennifer Chambers Lynch saw herself as an infant in the portrayal of Henry's baby – as an unwanted child that prevented the artist from pursuing his actual vocation.

Confronted with such theses, Lynch routinely responded with such lines as "I don't want to talk about that," or "I can't answer that question." Lynch's anger regarding those who blurt out the technical and artistic secrets of film indicates that he views a glimpse behind the scenes, and one-dimensional interpretations in general, as attempts to demystify the cinematic art form, an intrusion into a fragile, opaque system of meanings, references, and associations that must be protected from outside influences. "No matter how weird

a story is," said Lynch, "as soon as you set foot inside it, you realize that this world has rules you have to follow."

For over four years, the young director worked with a small team on the film that Stanley Kubrick once called his favorite movie. Often on the brink of financial ruin, Lynch meticulously created each and every scene down to the smallest detail and despite warnings from family members and friends he was unable to put the project down – it was almost as if he could only free himself from Henry's claustrophobic artificial world by completing the film.

"I felt *Eraserhead*, I didn't think it up," explained the director. Similarly, the audience is asked to look, instead of trying to understand at all costs.

SH

4 Mary, mother of God!! Is Henry really the father of Mary's (Charlotte Stewart) monstrous child?

5 A living hell: In Henry's world, reality and nightmare are practically indistinguishable.

No art is as expensive as filmmaking. While the big Hollywood productions can easily eat up hundreds of millions of dollars, there have always been films that were realized on a financial minimum, so-called low or no budget productions. But necessity can become a virtue. The compulsory renunciation of personal and technical expenditure often contributes to a unique demonstration of a director's personal style. And so it can happen that films made without big studios and without huge budgets can recover their production costs and gross much more than they cost to make.

At the beginning of the 70s, a series of directors who now belong to Hollywood's crème de la crème succeeded in making low budget productions: Dennis Hopper with *Easy Rider* (1969), Sidney Lumet with *Serpico* (1973), or David Lynch with *Eraserhead* (1974/77). If minimal production expenditures are viewed almost as a prerequisite for artistic films – like for example the "Dogma" directors surrounding Lars von Trier (*Breaking the Waves*, 1996) – then the relationship to inexpensively produced B-movies illuminate the difference between art and trash, as with Russ Meyer's orgies of sex and violence (*Supervixens – Eruption, Supervixens*, 1975), the provocative cinema of John Waters (*Pink Flamingos*, 1972) or the in hindsight path-blazing horror masterpieces by George A. Romero (*Night of the Living Dead*, 1968) and Tobe Hooper (*The Texas Chain Saw Massacre*, 1974), whose influence is also evident in artistic productions like *Eraserhead*.

SATURDAY NIGHT FEVER

1977 - USA - 118 MIN. - DANCE FILM, DRAMA

DIRECTOR JOHN BADHAM (*1939)
SCREENPLAY NORMAN WEXLER, based on the magazine article "TRIBAL RITES OF THE NEW SATURDAY NIGHT" by NIK COHN
DIRECTOR OF PHOTOGRAPHY RALF D. BODE EDITING DAVID RAWLINS MUSIC BARRY GIBB, ROBIN GIBB, MAURICE GIBB, DAVID SHIRE
PRODUCTION MILT FELSEN, ROBERT STIGWOOD for ROBERT STIGWOOD ORGANIZATION, PARAMOUNT PICTURES.

STARRING JOHN TRAVOLTA (Tony Manero), KAREN LYNN GORNEY (Stephanie), BARRY MILLER (Bobby C.), JOSEPH CALI (Joey)
PAUL PAPE (Double J), DONNA PESCOW (Annette), BRUCE ORNSTEIN (Gus), JULIE BOVASSO (Flo), MARTIN SHAKAR (Frank)
SAM COPPOLA (Fusco).

"Nice move. Did you make that up?"

One movie embodies everything that disco stood for in the late 1970s, and all that it has continued to stand for in the years since its disappearance from the public eye. To this day, audiences around the world hear mention of John Travolta and his trademark white leisure suit and are instantly transported to the streets of Brooklyn and the world of *Saturday Night Fever!* The picture itself is not only a golden shrine to the nightlife of the era with the glamorous decadence of its disco dance palaces, but also to its prevailing fashions and zeitgeist. *Saturday Night Fever's* uncanny assessment of these trends is attested to by the waves of disco revivals, each of which has inevitably cited this film's semiotics in its act of tribute.

At the time of its 1977 release, Manhattan dance club Studio 54 was the throbbing hub of disco. The audience for what was known as dance music had by then branched out from non-Caucasians and homosexuals to include the white middle class. *Saturday Night Fever* played a decisive role in contributing to the extreme popularity of the disco movement. Overnight, it launched unknown 22-year-old John Travolta to superstardom. More than his fancy threads or even the beat-pumping Bee-Gees tunes, it was Travolta's sexy gyrations that set a precedent in popular music for all time to come. From that day on, Top 40 hits would be judged on the basis of how danceable they were.

The film itself tells the story of a group of twenty-somethings linke by the socio-economic stratum they have inherited, much like the protag nists of Martin Scorsese's *Mean Streets* (1973). Tony Manero (John Travolt comes from an Italian-American family and still lives with his parents, wh treat him more like a kid than a full grown adult. He works at a mundane jc selling paint and finds the recognition denied him at home on the dance flo Every Saturday night, he and his buddies head over to "2001," a disco with rainbow colored blinking floor and a fast-talking disk jockey who can alwa get the crowd moving. The sea of people parts when stallion Tony struts I way over to his table. Women worship him and his amassed following go wild when he takes the stage with his smooth-as-butter choreography. Tor is a tightly packaged macho stud and takes great care with his appearanc Each night before going out, he partakes in a meticulous ritual surrounded posters of his idols Al Pacino and Sylvester Stallone as Rocky. Transfixed his reflection, Tony slicks his hair, pulls on a dress shirt with flared collar a adorns himself with gold chains. He tops it off with a lascivious upward swi that slides the zipper of his hip-hugging slacks into place. Tony is the m with all the right moves and doesn't he know it. "I like the way you walk," r marks Annette (Donna Pescow) with girlish naivety and undying devotic Tony, however, is shamelessly hurtful toward this ordinary admirer. He clea

"John Badham's film is a snapshot of a period. Though born of a passing pop-cultural fashion, it has survived in the collective unconscious right up to the present day." *Frankfurter Allgemeine Zeitung*

2

1 Bright lights, big city: Tony Manero (John Travolta) with his goods on display in the legendary white leisure suit.

2 Music as the universal equalizer: But the disco ball's magic won't last forever.

3 "If I Can't Have You:" Annette (Donna Pescow) is in love with Tony, but the feeling isn't mutual.

as problems dealing with the female element and drops crude comments to rls who want to go bed with him, asking Annette whether she's "a nice girl a slut?" She responds by saying that maybe she's both, throwing the already twisted male logic of Tony and his crew into a loop. These guys think at women who engage in casual sex are filthy whores, while they seek out uch specimens night after night. Tony's small world revolves around work, mily, dancing and ladies. It is a lifestyle that lacks both goals and direction. ephanie (Karen Lynn Gorney), the girl of his dreams, lives in another universe altogether, although this wasn't always the case. She has made the uantum leap from Brooklyn to Manhattan, working at a swanky agency that fords her the luxury of looking back on her previous life with a degree of argance and disdain. To Tony, she comes across as a sexy, hardened woman the world, whose glamorous career requires her to consort with the rich nd famous on a daily basis.

It's no coincidence that *Saturday Night Fever* opens with the image of bridge. The device is both a physical link between Brooklyn and Manhattan well as a metaphoric link between a suffocating life of entrenched tradion and the opportunistic, self-determined escapism of modernity. Tony is an pert on everything there is to know about the Brooklyn Bridge, right down the exact amount of cement and steel contained in the architectural wonr. The bridge serves as a symbol of ultimate desire, which Tony and his clique pay homage to in adolescent initiation rituals and daredevil stunts, like scaling the mammoth structure. To the shy Bobby (Barry Miller), this foolhardy activity proves to be as deadly as the call of the ancient Sirens. His fall into the East River abyss is both a departure from a life that has nothing to offer him other than disco, cruising the streets and casual sex, as well as a convenient exit from dealing with the responsibilities brought on by his girlfriend's pregnancy. Although Tony manages to successfully cross the imposing barriers of the bridge, it remains unclear whether he will choose to live out his newfound adulthood in the Manhattan universe that lies beyond.

Making it in the big city has always been a central theme in American film. *Saturday Night Fever* takes an in-depth look at what this entails, subjecting its characters to dire hardships, and its eloquent message resonates to this day. The film triumphs precisely where attempted follow-ups like the sequel *Staying Alive* (1983), fall short. Martin Scorsese's 1968 picture *Who's That Knocking at My Door* told a similar story of an unquenchable thirst for Manhattan life and women trouble among male youth. Yet for all their similarities, *Saturday Night Fever* has the unique distinction of being the disco movie to end all others, forever reminding us that history is made at night!

KK

4

4   Shaking off the past: In the end, however, only Tony will manage to escape.

5   Prophet of the Disco Cult: As his brother, a priest, puts it, "When Tony hits the dance floor, the crowd parts like the Red Sea before Moses."

"Energetically directed and well acted (...), *Saturday Night Fever* succeeds in capturing the animal drive of disco music and the social rituals of the people who dance to its beat." *Time Magazine*

DANCE MOVIES

Dance is part of a grand Hollywood tradition. One of its earlier highs came in the 1930s and continued well on into the 1940s with great spectacles featuring Fred Astaire and Ginger Rogers such as *Shall We Dance* (1937), as well as with Eleanor Powell in pieces like *Broadway Melody of 1940* (1939–40). These marvels revolutionized the art form and instantly became living legends. Nonetheless, the dance film as we know it today, stems from a later cinematic movement that first became widely popular with the unstoppable disco drama, *Saturday Night Fever* (1977). The film turned dance into a metaphor for self-realization and a passion for life. For these reasons as well as for its intrinsic connection to current pop music, these films have historically spoken to a primarily younger audience and produced a large number of top 40 hit songs.

The 1980s took the genre to new heights with Adrian Lyne's *Flashdance* (1982). Arguably the greatest dance movie of all time, *Flashdance* took the crisp visual aesthetics of the 1980s music video age and magnified them with theatrical, stylized imagery. The film's title song "Flashdance... What A Feeling!" written by Irene Cara, Keith Forsey and Giorgio Moroder took home the Oscar for Best Original Song and the entire soundtrack has since gone triple-platinum. A supplementary instalment of *Saturday Night Fever* hit theaters at the peak of the boom in 1983. That same year, Herbert Ross' enormously successful *Footloose* made its appearance on the film scene. Similar to the 1978 sensation *Grease*, starring John Travolta and Olivia Newton-John, the nostalgic tribute took viewers back to the 1950s when modern pop music and teen culture were still in their infancy. Jennifer Grey and Patrick Swayze took 1987 by storm in *Dirty Dancing* (1987) and captured the hearts of countless young audiences with yet another picture whose story was set in this beloved bygone era. After lying more or less dormant for over an entire decade, Randa Haines' 1998 *Dance with Me*, about the Latin music star Chayanne, was received by an enthused audience and contributed to salsa's popularity at the movies. Two years later, *Cinema* magazine deemed Nicholas Hytner's *Center Stage* (2000) a new teen version of *Flashdance*. Other dance flicks that year included Thomas Carter's hybrid of ballet and hip hop *Save the Last Dance* (2000) and *The Dancer* (2000) about yet another girl who dreams of becoming a dance superstar. The latter movie's soundtrack included a star-studded soundtrack featuring The Prodigy, Fat Boy Slim and Neneh Cherry. The genre has recently expressed renewed interest in tap dancing as evidenced by diverse pieces such as Dein Perry's modern stomp the *Bootmen* (2000), which was also an appeal for social reform. Even more successful was Stephen Daldry's *Billy Elliot* (2000), both a great example of the aesthetic trends in current British cinema as well as a touching dance drama about a little boy whose family tries to pressure him into becoming a boxer, although his dreams are just of ballet.

CLOSE ENCOUNTERS OF THE THIRD KIND

1977 - USA - 135 MIN. - SCIENCE FICTION

DIRECTOR STEVEN SPIELBERG (*1947)
SCREENPLAY STEVEN SPIELBERG DIRECTOR OF PHOTOGRAPHY VILMOS ZSIGMOND EDITING MICHAEL KAHN MUSIC JOHN WILLIAMS
PRODUCTION JULIA PHILLIPS, MICHAEL PHILLIPS for COLUMBIA PICTURES CORPORATION.

STARRING RICHARD DREYFUSS (Roy Neary), FRANÇOIS TRUFFAUT (Claude Lacombe), TERI GARR (Ronnie Neary), MELINDA DILLON (Jillian Guiler), BOB BALABAN (David Laughlin), CARY GUFFEY (Barry Guiler), J. PATRICK MCNAMARA (Project Director), WARREN KEMMERLING (Wild Bill), ROBERTS BLOSSOM (Farmer), LANCE HENRIKSEN (Robert).

ACADEMY AWARDS 1977 OSCAR for BEST CINEMATOGRAPHY (Vilmos Zsigmond) and SPECIAL ACHIEVEMENT AWARD for BEST SOUND EFFECTS EDITING (Frank Warner).

"It's as big as a house!"

Suddenly, a gleaming light fills the sky. Car engines and radios go on the blink and the night is illuminated with brilliant colors. During a night-time procedure, electrical engineer Roy Neary has a strange experience: he sees aliens. But no one believes him. Consequently, he is fired by his company, continually made fun of, and totally misunderstood by his family. What Roy doesn't know is that his encounter is part of a string of strange phenomena that have been occurring around the world. Fighter bombers reported missing since 1945 suddenly appear in the desert of New Mexico, and the people of North India hear a melody coming from the sky.

Since his experience, Roy has been tortured by visions of an od formed mountain. He later sees the mountain again in a television program apparently it's the "Devil's Tower" in Wyoming. The report tells of an accide during which poisonous gas was released near the mountain. The entire ar is being immediately evacuated. It becomes clear to Roy that he must trave Wyoming. He begins his journey to the mountain with Jillian (Melinda Dillo a single mother who also had an encounter with aliens in the same night. F years later in E. T. – The Extra-Terrestrial (1982), director Steven Spielbe again portrayed a visit from outer space. But the earlier narration is mo

4   serious, more complex, and above all, more mature. Parallel to Roy's experiences, Spielberg depicts a worldwide UFO research team, led by Lacombe, a scientist from France (played by French director François Truffaut). The main plot of the film – an alien landing on the Earth – is accompanied by two subplots. One shows how Roy (excellently portrayed by Richard Dreyfuss) believes he is going mad and begins to doubt his own reason, ultimately causing his family to break apart. The other plot is a criticism of the media, which is still pertinent a quarter of a century later. The government, military and media collaborate to spread lies about a poisonous gas disaster that never occurred. Their aim is to evacuate people from the area where they are expecting the alien landing to take place. In so doing, they even anesthetize animals to make their fairy-tale appear more believable.

"I had such a yearning for the stars, such a longing for space travel. I wanted to take off and fly away from our planet. My childhood wasn't particularly happy, which is why I was always looking for ways to escape." *Steven Spielberg, in: Tony Crawley, The Steven Spielberg Story*

1   Mine eyes have seen the glory: Jillian Guiler (Melinda Dillon) has been touched by an angel, if that's what you want to call it.

2   An alien landing looks like that pot of gold at the end of the rainbow.

3   Star light, star bright: "Of all the UFO films ever made this is the most edifying – a wonder of superb special effects." (*Motion Picture Guide*)

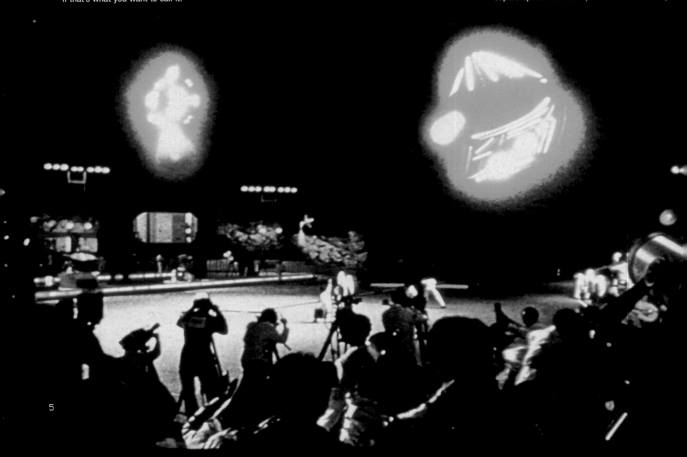

5

4 Group therapy: Roy (Richard Dreyfuss) had begun to question his own sanity until Jill shared her own out-of-this-world experience with him.

5 Spirits in the sky: Master technician Douglas Trumbull composed a forty-minute special effects extravaganza for the film's conclusion that left audiences in awe.

6 Keeping the faith: Electrical engineer Roy Neary is publicly ridiculed for his convictions and abandoned by his family.

The "main story" tells of the alien landing. As in *E. T.*, these aliens come to the Earth with peaceful intentions. The aliens, who appear only at the end of the film, are fragile, child-like figures who spread harmony, and with whom communication is only possible via music. They come to Earth as a kind of savior and their arrival is accompanied by unmistakably religious symbols, including celestial light and the mountain itself, which recalls Mount Sinai, where God gave the Ten Commandments to Moses. The almost forty-minute climax is an overwhelming orgy of special effects, with glowing spaceships of every size and shape, and a brilliant choreography of light in the sky. The effects were the work of Douglas Trumbull.

However, *Close Encounters* did not win the Oscar for special effects – the Oscar went to George Lucas' *Star Wars*, also released in 1977. Nonetheless, the film was a huge success at the box office. Both the production company and fans demanded a sequel. But Spielberg produced only a "Special Edition," which was eventually released in 1980. This version is three minutes shorter than the original – Spielberg cut 16 minutes and added 13 new minutes, including newly shot scenes (including a "stranded" ship in the Gobi desert) and initially unused material.

HJK

DOUGLAS TRUMBULL Special effects wizard Douglas Trumbull (*1942) began his career as a background illustrator for NASA promotional films. Stanley Kubrick saw one of these films and hired Trumbull as "special photographic effects supervisor" for his film, *2001: A Space Odyssey* (1968). Kubrick's masterpiece founded Trumbull's reputation as special effects magician and cleared the way for his directorial debut, the apocalyptic drama, *Silent Running* (1971). When afterwards, he was unable to realize further projects as a director, he started working as a trick specialist once again. He received Oscar nominations for his effects from *Close Encounters of the Third Kind* (1977), *Star Trek – The Motion Picture* (1979), and *Blade Runner* (1982).

For many of his films, Trumbull, son of an engineer, invented several technical devices, like the so-called Slit-Scan, a machine with which he captured the psychedelic color haze in the final sequence of *2001* (the flight through the star gate), or a zoom-microscope for *The Andromeda Strain* (1971). For his second film as director, *Brainstorm* (1983), he experimented with various film formats. He later developed the "Show-Scan" procedure. The film is projected at 60 frames per second instead of the normal 24, which results in a sharper image. But the format never caught on and was seldom used in the production of feature-length films.

ANNIE HALL

1977 - USA - 93 MIN. - COMEDY

DIRECTOR WOODY ALLEN (*1935)
SCREENPLAY WOODY ALLEN, MARSHALL BRICKMAN DIRECTOR OF PHOTOGRAPHY GORDON WILLIS EDITING RALPH ROSENBLUM, WENDY GREENE BRICMONT MUSIC CARMEN LOMBARDO, ISHAM JONES PRODUCTION CHARLES H. JOFFE, JACK ROLLINS for UNITED ARTISTS.

STARRING WOODY ALLEN (Alvy Singer), DIANE KEATON (Annie Hall), TONY ROBERTS (Rob), CAROL KANE (Allison), PAUL SIMON (Tony Lacey), COLLEEN DEWHURST (Mother Hall), JANET MARGOLIN (Robin), SHELLEY DUVALL (Pam), CHRISTOPHER WALKEN (Duane Hall), SIGOURNEY WEAVER (Alvy's Date), BEVERLY D'ANGELO (TV Actress).

ACADEMY AWARDS 1977 OSCARS for BEST PICTURE (Charles H. Joffe), BEST DIRECTOR (Woody Allen), BEST ACTRESS (Diane Keaton), and BEST ORIGINAL SCREENPLAY (Woody Allen, Marshall Brickman).

"You know, it's one thing about intellectuals, they prove that you can be absolutely brilliant and have no idea what's going on."

"There's an old joke. Two elderly women are at a Catskills mountain resort, and one of them says: 'Boy, the food at this place is really terrible.' The other one says, 'Yeah, I know, and such… small portions.' Well, that's essentially how I feel about life," says *Annie Hall's* actual protagonist, Alvy Singer (Woody Allen) at the top of the film. "(It's) full of loneliness and misery and suffering and unhappiness, and it's all over much too quickly."

Singer is a stand-up comedian, professional cynic and full-time misanthrope. When a big tall blond crew-cutted guy in a record store tells him that Wagner is on sale this week, Jewish Alvy knows exactly how to take it. He also despises Los Angeles for being a city whose only cultural advantage is that you can make a right turn on a red light. What ties this seemingly unrelated hodge-podge of scenes and sketches pieced together by editor Ralph Rosenblum from a heap of over 50,000 feet of film is Alvy's relationship to the movie's title character, Annie Hall.

We meet the couple after the two of them have called it quits for the very last time, and then take an endearing yet heart-breaking trip with them down memory lane to discover what led to the demise of their year-long romance. Annie (Diane Keaton) is the quintessential pseudo-intellectual, a caricature of the urban woman. Alvy brands her as eternally flawed for being born with original sin – she grew up in rural America. On the other hand Alvy's condemning remarks about everyone and everything (including himself) are just his way of concealing his own unique, neurotic blend of self-loathing, self-pity and self-worship, which not even 15 years of therapy could cure him of. As he explains in a TV interview he was deemed "four-P" by a personality assessment test: a hostage in the event of war.

Allen biographer Marion Meade rightly stated that *Annie Hall* could have just as easily been entitled *Alvy Singer* or even better, *Allan Konigsberg* Woody Allen's given name. The Alvy character is an unmistakable self-portrait of the director, who himself started out as a gag writer for stand-up comics. Up until three weeks before the premiere, Allen insisted that the film be called *Anhedonia* (the debilitating absence of pleasure or the ability to experience it). Arthur Krim, head of United Artists and Allen's paternal role model, allegedly threatened to throw himself out the window if he were through with it.

The almost non-existent cinematic structure of the piece allowed Allen to pack the movie full of amusing quips and snide remarks, more concisely

it supplied him with a vehicle for unabated hilarity. Nonetheless, *Annie Ha[ll]* remains a particularly significant work for two main reasons. The first bein[g] that the director makes a point of tweaking classic modes of cinemati[c] depictions of reality and storytelling. Whereas he filmed his 1969 piece *Tak[e] the Money and Run* (1969) in the style of a news exposé, *Annie Hall* is [a] veritable cornucopia of narrative conventions and even manages to weave i[n] an animated sequence. Time and again, Alvy directly addresses his audienc[e] sitting in the theater. Such is the case in a movie ticket line, when he wishe[s] to one-up and embarrass the wannabe film buff who loudly pontificates [&] claims to teach a course on TV, Media and Culture at Columbia Universit[y] and quotes extensively from influential Canadian media theorist Marsha[ll] McLuhan. Alvy quickly wins their debate by surreally calling upon McLuha[n]

"Personal as the story he is telling may be, what separates this film from Allen's own past work and most other recent comedy is its general believability. His central figures and all who cross their paths are recognizable contemporary types. Most of us have even shared a lot of their fantasies." *Time Magazine*

1 He'd never join a club that would have him as a member: Alvy Singer is Woody Allen's filmic alter ego.

2 A walk on the mild side: Neurotic New Yorkers Annie (Diane Keaton), Alvy and Dick (Dick Cavett) analyze life, art, and above all themselves.

3 New York is full of interesting, undiscovered places to hang out...

4

4   Uppers and downers: Alvy reveres European
     cinema – and especially Ingmar Bergman.

) personally step in and set matters straight. In another memorable se-
uence, Allen uses a split-screen to illustrate two incompatible worlds, as
lvy's New York Jewish family is compared in similar, juxtaposed dinner
cenes to Annie's family. On the left third of the screen is the brightly lit, af-
uent, politely gracious, aloof and sober Hall family discussing subjects such
s the Christmas play and the 4-H Club. On the right two-thirds of the screen
 a darkly lit, sloppy and informal, noisily argumentative, competitively bab-
ling Singer family talking about illness (diabetes, heart disease) and unem-
loyment (illustrating that Alvy's argumentative nature and fear of marriage
ere inherited from his family). The genius of the episode is born out of the

actual conversation of the two families that takes place *across* this divided
split-screen. This brand of narrative anarchy was both a liberating artistic
breakthrough and a triumph for Allen.

The second significant achievement for Allen that came out of *Annie
Hall* was the creation of his alter ego, which finally succeeded in distancing
him from his purely comic self. Since this picture, Allen's cosmopolitan neurotic has been a free-floating entity who can be readily integrated into the
context of more serious pieces like *Hannah and Her Sisters* (1985) and *Husbands and Wives* (1992), or just observe the action from the sidelines as in
his 1978 drama, *Interiors* (1978).   SH

DIANE KEATON   In a quirkily perfect performance that won her the Best Actress Oscar, Woody Allen's then flame Diane Keaton reveals Annie Hall's and her own zany
yet huggable nature through the character's stumbling, flailing gestures. These are reinforced by self-conscious, shyly banal statements, particularly
her self-effacing "La-dee-dah." The similarities between these two women include their over the top and "not quite with it" manner as well as their
taste in clothing, which according to Allen, includes an affinity for football jerseys matched to skirts, combat boots and mittens. Given all this, it
should come as no surprise that Keaton's original last name supplied the character with hers.
The actress born on January 5, 1946 in Los Angeles, met Allen in 1969 while acting with him in his Broadway play "Play it Again, Sam." A few years
later, she appeared for the first time in an often-overlooked performance at the side of Al Pacino in the role of Michael Corleone's wife in Francis
Ford Coppola's *Godfather* trilogy (1972, 1974, 1990).
She worked on numerous Woody Allen films, both before and after their relationship came to an end. In 1981, she collaborated with Warren Beatty,
with whom she was also romantically involved for some time, on the film *Reds*. Before long, Keaton proved she had what it took to join the male-
dominated world of directing and has been making pictures and TV shows, including an episode of the legendary TV show *Twin Peaks*, since the
1980s. Her 1995 work *Unstrung Heroes* is a little-known masterpiece in filmmaking. Her 1996 acting and comedic bravado in *The First Wives Club*
(1996) and dramatic eloquence in *Marvin's Room* (1996) reconfirmed her star appeal. Today, it is hard to imagine that this star in her own right was
once inextricably tied up with Allen.

PADRE PADRONE
Padre padrone

1977 - ITALY - 113 MIN. - DRAMA, LITERARY ADAPTATION

DIRECTOR PAOLO TAVIANI (*1931), VITTORIO TAVIANI (*1929)
SCREENPLAY PAOLO TAVIANI, VITTORIO TAVIANI, based on the novel of the same name by GAVINO LEDDA DIRECTOR OF PHOTOGRAPHY MARIO MASINI EDITING ROBERTO PERPIGNANI MUSIC EGISTO MACCHI PRODUCTION GIULIANI G. DE NEGRI for CINEMA SRL, RAI.

STARRING OMERO ANTONUTTI (Gavino's Father), SAVERIO MARCONI (Gavino), MARCELLA MICHELANGELI (Gavino's Mother), FABRIZIO FORTE (Gavino as a child), NANNI MORETTI (Cesare), GAVINO LEDDA (Himself), MARINO CENNA, PIERLUIGI ALVAU, PIETRO GIORDO, MARCO UNALI.

IFF CANNES 1977 GOLDEN PALM (Paolo and Vittorio Taviani).

"Today it was Gavino that got it – tomorrow it's your turn."

Padre Padrone was originally made for Italian television before being converted to cinema format and shown at the Cannes Film Festival in 1977, where it won the coveted Palme d'Or. Adapted from the autobiography of the Sardinian author Gavino Ledda, "Padre, padrone. L'educazione di un pastore" ("Padre Padrone. The Education of a Shepherd"), the film describes a boy's emancipation from his father (padre) and master (padrone). Yet it is less a psychogram of one young man in search of himself than the depiction of a cultural revolution. This is no tourist's-eye-view of a simple pre-industrial society fortunate enough to enjoy its own homemade bread, olive oil and cheese. The world inhabited by the shepherds of Sardinia is no pastoral idyll, and the indissoluble family bonds are primarily a guarantee of survival. In a world of unrelenting toil, the father begets his own workforce: serfs in the form of children.

The film begins by certifying its own authenticity: Ledda, the author of the book, assures the audience that this really is the story of his life. He hands the branch of a tree to a man with a face like granite, who carves it into a stick and storms off to the school, where he bursts into the classroom in mid-lesson. The children, no more than six to eight years old, are petrified, because unlike the audience, they know what's coming: "The boy belongs to me!" "Me" meaning the work of the family, and not of the state. Instead of

learning to read, write and count, Gavino (Fabrizio Forte) is destined to ten sheep.

Compulsory education, one of the elementary preconditions for the establishment of state control in the 19th century, was not yet enforced the island of Sardinia. In this wild rural environment, the ancient laws of the clan still apply. The father (Omero Antonutti) brings up his son as if he were training an animal. The boy is sent off into the desolate mountains to te the sheep. Day and night, these animals will be his only companions. If leaves his appointed station, he's beaten and sent back. He learns to under stand the innumerable languages of the natural world: the sounds of da break, the rustling of the oaks in the wind, the river's murmur and the snake hiss; and he learns the moods of the sheep, who shit in the bucket wh he's just finished milking, and who seem to snigger at his rage. He learn and he forgets. Silenced by loneliness, he loses the habit of speech. Wh other children suffer as he does, he's forbidden to have anything to do w them. The pastures and the sheep have to be guarded with a terrible p tience, and the enemies of the shepherd have been the same for millenn thieves, wild beasts, and sudden attacks of cold weather. In the distan the mournful tolling of a bell seems to announce a grim fate for a boy who life has barely begun.

1 Baa, baa black sheep: Not even his mother's love saves Gavino (Fabrizio Forte) from becoming a shepherd.

2 Picking on the little guy: "My father, the giant; the final instance," said Franz Kafka.

3 Sardinian dialysis: Cut your lips till they bleed.

"Class struggle in the countryside is the battle against the patriarchy."

Vittorio Taviani

At this point, the narrative leaps forward in time: the boy is now a 20-year-old (Saverio Marconi) – and he's still a shepherd. Once again, it's musical tones that herald his future: two traveling musicians, who seem to have lost their way in the wilderness, come over the mountains playing the accordion. The melody is familiar: the overture waltz from Richard Strauss' "Die Fledermaus." The young shepherd swaps two lambs for an accordion, and with music as his first foreign language, he seeks and finds a new world. He rebels against his father and labors endlessly to qualify for university, where he studies linguistics. The shepherd's emancipation begins with his recognition that language, too, can be a source of power – and speechlessness a kind of impotence. (That the language of Sardinia is a long way from standard Italian is a detail lost to those who see a dubbed version of the film.)

Padre Padrone combines an almost ethnographic camera with an extremely subjective soundtrack. Shots of a forbidding landscape are accompanied by a soundscape that underlines the feelings and perceptions of the protagonists: The father who has almost beaten his son to death cradles th unconscious boy in his arms and sings a Sardinian "Miserere" – and thoug only father and son are visible, we hear an overwhelming choral accompani ment. The function of the choir is as old as Greek tragedy: it anchors indivic ual suffering in the collective experience of humanity. Here, however, th heartrending lament seems almost to emerge from the desolate earth itsel Again: a religious procession winds through the valley, and Gavino is amon those bearing the statue of Jesus. The men talk of emigrating to German in the hope of escaping their poverty. Suddenly, one of them strikes up wit the first line of a German drinking song, "Trink, Brüderlein, trink" ("Drinl brother, drink"), and soon the valley echoes to the sound of the men singin beneath their burden: "Lass doch die Sorgen zuhaus!" ("Leave all your wor ries at home!") This is the principle that organizes the entire film: again an again, personal suffering is subsumed into collective experience, into share and universal dreams.

R

4 A smokeless cigarette: Take a drag the wrong way round, and your enemies can't see you in the dark.

5 Emasculated by age: The arm raised in anger by patriarch (Omero Antonutti) is now old and feeble.

6 Tinkle, tinkle little star: Even at school, Gavino is not safe from his father's looming authority.

COMING HOME

1978 - USA - 126 MIN. - DRAMA, VIETNAM FILM

REGIE HAL ASHBY (1929–1988)

SCREENPLAY NANCY DOWD, ROBERT C. JONES, WALDO SALT DIRECTOR OF PHOTOGRAPHY HASKELL WEXLER EDITING DON ZIMMERMAN MUSIC THE BEATLES, THE ROLLING STONES, BOB DYLAN, STEPPENWOLF and others PRODUCTION JEROME HELLMAN for JAYNE PRODUCTIONS, JEROME HELLMAN PRODUCTIONS.

STARRING JANE FONDA (Sally Hyde), JON VOIGHT (Luke Martin), BRUCE DERN (Captain Bob Hyde), PENELOPE MILFORD (Vi Munson), ROBERT CARRADINE (Bill Munson), ROBERT GINTY (Sergeant Dink Mobley), MARY GREGORY (Martha Vickery), KATHLEEN MILLER (Kathy Delise), BEESON CARROLL (Captain Carl Delise), WILLIE TYLER (Virgil).

ACADEMY AWARDS 1978 OSCARS for BEST ACTOR (Jon Voight), BEST ACTRESS (Jane Fonda), and BEST SCREENPLAY (Nancy Dowd, Robert C. Jones, Waldo Salt).

IFF CANNES 1978 AWARD for BEST ACTOR (Jon Voight).

"In my dreams I ain't sitting in a wheel chair. In my dreams I don't have one. I've got legs."

In 1968, a frenzy sweeps across the United States, dividing the nation. The federal government and the army stick to their guns about the legitimacy and necessity of their involvement in Vietnam. Week after week a number of enthusiastic young men join the service. Blinded by patriotism, they act as ammunition in an ongoing battle that sinks deeper into the quicksands with each passing day. Nevertheless, a vocal and undeniable peace movement has gained momentum. It is an age of hippies, flower power and doves.

In 1968, we meet Sally (Jane Fonda), a naïve, sheltered young woman. Married to Bob (Bruce Dern), an officer with the Marines who is preparing to depart for Vietnam, she lives in the cut-off world of the military base. Cries of dissonance and disgust regarding the atrocities of the battlefield rarely make there way here. Yet, when Bob is called to war, Sally too must abandon the dwelling they share in officers' quarters, and her way of life is about to change dramatically. She buys a convertible, moves into a house on the beach, and befriends the easy-going Vi (Penelope Milford). Suddenly Sally has a new, freer, and more self-determined lease of life. She even takes on a new job, volunteering at a veteran's hospital for injured soldiers, where they are rehabilitated in preparation for civilian life.

The pain of the soldiers goes beyond visible injuries. Other wounds lie deeper. Despair resulting from their own suffering or the suffering they inflicted on others dominates many of their lives. Possibly the worst blow th war has dealt is the bitter resignation that now fills their hearts where the patriotic spirit used to be. All the propaganda about becoming a war hero w just that. Vi's brother Bill (Robert Carradine), who eventually cracks as a res of his war experiences and sees no alternative but suicide, illustrates th point perfectly. Another veteran, Luke (Jon Voight), once the captain of t high school football team and apple of all the girls' eyes, now lives out h days as a vegetating paraplegic confined to a hospital gurney. Full of wra the cynical young man makes it his business to raise Cain amongst t stressed-out hospital orderlies — only to be regularly silenced by sedativ and handcuffed to his bed.

Sally recognizes Luke as an old schoolmate of hers and refuses be intimidated by his verbal attacks. With a bit of persistence, she is ab to break through his caustic exterior and sees him for who he really is – man with a vulnerable and wounded core. The two become fast frien and eventually lovers. The flame of their romance is doused when Sall husband Bob comes home from Nam. Yet Sally's infidelity is not the sour of Bob's woes. He wanted more than anything to be a war hero, only to e up shooting himself in the leg while taking a shower. Just moments af he is awarded a metal of honor for his bravery, he is overcome with desp

and takes his own life. He too becomes a victim of war, and many others will follow ...

Hal Ashby's film is a war drama set a million miles away from the grenade-riddled, napalm-scorched jungle battlefields. These are places from which one simply cannot return, for the memories remain. The film's title is also rather misleading. "Home," the bastion of normalcy where one can be revered a hero is proven to be an unattainable illusion. Values like "country," "honor" and "patriotism" have become nothing more than empty words without meaning. This realization usually comes too late, and for many is the true trauma of war. "I need to justify the fact that I'm crippled, that I've killed people. So I tell myself what I did was okay" – is how one of the veterans comes to terms with his past.

"An impressionistic meditation on the Vietnam War and the scars it has left on the bodies, minds, and souls of many soldiers and civilians." *Spirituality & Health*

1   People will say we're in love: The relationship of paraplegic veteran, Luke (Jon Voight), Sally (Jane Fonda) raises a few eyebrows.

2   Casualties of war: It's not only love that Bob (Bruce Dern) lost to Vietnam.

3   Making love, not war: It takes time for Luke and Sally to accept their feelings for each other.

4   Raising Lazarus: Vi (Penelope Milford) and Sally help Luke overcome his bitterness and cynicism.

Coming Home was filmed at a time when the socio-political climate in the U.S. allowed for rawer and more critical cinematic depictions of the Vietnam experience than in the immediately preceding years. *Alice's Restaurant* (1969) directed by Arthur Penn, Michelangelo Antonioni's *Zabriskie Point* (1969) and even George Lucas's *American Graffiti* (1973), presented Vietnam as a far-off topic somewhere on the horizon. But the late 70s could not ignore the nation's blatant wounds. A handful of exceptional films from this period stress the irrationality of war and brand all participants of war as victims. In its distance from direct representations of war, *Coming Home* distinguishes itself from other contemporaries like *The Deer Hunter* (1978, directed by Michael Cimino) and *Apocalypse Now* (1979, directed by Francis Ford Coppola). Both these pieces made fervent pleas against the madness of war, while confronting the viewer with gut-wrenching battlefield images of guerilla warfare.

Its gripping topic aside, *Coming Home* is a great example of world-class acting. Jane Fonda and Jon Voight both received the Oscar for "Best Performance in a Leading Role" (whereas the Oscars for Best Picture and Best Director went to the competing production, *The Deer Hunter*). The highlight of their performances is without a doubt the socially progressive love scene, in which the film went against an age-old taboo and showed a disabled man having sex. It is a cunning slap in the face that far exceeds a flat depiction of the "make love not war" slogan of the era.

The film's soundtrack, comprised of the pop songs of the late 1960s effectively summons the spirit of the time. The plea for a just world put forth by the Rolling Stones, the Beatles, Bob Dylan, Jimi Hendrix, Steppenwolf, Janis Joplin, Richie Havens, Jefferson Airplane, Simon and Garfunkel and many others who were against the military aggression in Vietnam does not fall on deaf ears.   EF

JON VOIGHT

Jon Voight, born the son of a golf pro in 1938, began his career in show business as a teenager and worked his way up the ranks on the Broadway stage. He first caught the public's eye in John Schlesinger's *Midnight Cowboy* (1969) for his portrayal of a naive young country-bumpkin turned gigolo, who dreams of striking it rich in the Big Apple. The performance also garnered Voight his first Oscar nod. He gained further recognition for his role as one of four city slickers in John Boorman's twisted backwater thriller *Deliverance* (1972); the four buddies embark on a canoe trip and end up fighting for their lives when a pack of inbred river settlers hunt the group down. Voight won international acclaim for *Coming Home* (1978), though he did not respond to his popularity by only accepting roles in prominent productions from then on. Another particularly noteworthy performance came with Andrei Konchalovsky's *Runaway Train* (1985), a pessimistic drama about escape from prison. The hefty number of supporting roles he continues to play show off his wide acting range. Such was the case when he played sports reporter Howard Cosell to a tee opposite Will Smith in Michael Mann's *Ali* (2001), and devised a plan of escape for Robert De Niro in yet another Michael Mann film, *Heat* (1995). This regular chameleon's list of golden cameos also includes assigning Tom Cruise with death defying tasks in Brian De Palma's *Mission: Impossible* (1996), responding to the Japanese attack as President Roosevelt in Michael Bay's *Pearl Harbor* (2001) and even standing alongside his daughter Angelina Jolie in Simon West's *Lara Croft: Tomb Raider* (2001) as her on-screen dad.

MIDNIGHT EXPRESS

1978 - GREAT BRITAIN / USA - 120 MIN. - PRISON FILM, DRAMA

DIRECTOR ALAN PARKER (*1944)
SCREENPLAY OLIVER STONE, based on the account of a personal experience by BILLY HAYES and WILLIAM HOFFER
DIRECTOR OF PHOTOGRAPHY MICHAEL SERESIN EDITING GERRY HAMBLING MUSIC GIORGIO MORODER PRODUCTION DAVID PUTTNAM, ALAN MARSHALL for CASABLANCA FILMWORKS.

STARRING BRAD DAVIS (Billy Hayes), JOHN HURT (Max), RANDY QUAID (Jimmy Booth), IRENE MIRACLE (Susan), NORBERT WEISSER (Erich), BO HOPKINS (Tex), PAUL SMITH (Hamidou), PAOLO BONACELLI (Rifki), MIKE KELLIN (Mr. Hayes), FRANCO DIOGENE (Yesil).

ACADEMY AWARDS 1978 OSCARS for BEST ADAPTED SREENPLAY (Oliver Stone), and BEST MUSIC (Giorgio Moroder).

"The best thing to do is to get your ass out of here."

It could be the most nerve-wracking panic attack in all of film history: on October 6, 1970, Billy Hayes (Brad Davis), an American student, attempts to leave Turkey with 2.2 kilograms of hash. Hayes is on the verge of a break-down upon eye contact with the first customs agent, but to his own surprise he is waved along. After the initial relief comes the shock: a dozer soldiers are waiting in front of the airplane. Hayes knows they're there for him and he tries to get rid of the treacherous package taped to his body. But it's too late. He's arrested before his girlfriend's eyes, and so begins a nightmare that is to last for years.

While awaiting trial, Hayes is repeatedly tortured. The devastating sentence is four years and two months in prison. Inside the prison, inhumane conditions are widespread – the violence of the inmates and the excessive force of the prison guards are part of the daily routine. But Hayes accepts his situation and befriends his cellmates Jimmy Booth (Randy Quaid) and Max (John Hurt). Max is the man who tells him of the only way out of the living hell – the "Midnight Express:" prison-speak for escape. While the drug-addicted Max has long since resigned himself to his situation, Jimmy Booth clings to the smallest of hopes that he might be able to escape.

1

2

"Parker magnificently depicts the claustro-phobic and irrational world of the prison, increased by the misanthropy and xenophobia of the authorities." *Edinburgh University Film Society*

Billy Hayes has just 53 days left to serve when the American Ambassador makes a terrible disclosure. At the instigation of the public prosecutor, the case against him is to be reopened and this time the authorities are seeking lifelong imprisonment. In a desperate courtroom statement, the accused finally seals his own fate. Ultimately the length of his sentence is set at 30 years. Hayes is now left with no other choice than to try to catch the "Midnight Express."

The film, whose screenplay was written by Oliver Stone and based on an authentic case, was a huge success at the box office. Alan Parker filmed the drama as a vividly image-laden picture, which held audiences spellbound from the very first minute. The actor Brad Davis, who died in 1991, gave a particularly impressive performance. But the film enraged a handful of

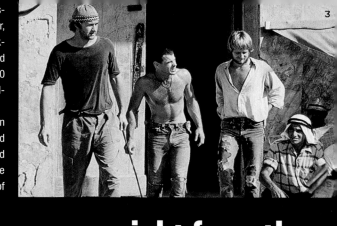

"Parker puts the squeeze on us right from the start. It's single-minded in its manipulation of the audience." *Pauline Kael*

1 Eyes on the prize: Billy Hayes (Brad Davis) knows that his only chance of freedom is escape.

2 Cry freedom: Billy's pleas for clemency fall on deaf ears.

3 Thick as thieves: Their shared fate makes Billy, Jimmy (Randy Quaid) and Max (John Hurt) inseparable.

4 Caught with his pants down: "There's a perfectly reasonable explanation for this, officer…"

critics. "Muted squalor with a disco beat in the background," was the harsh criticism of the New Yorker.

Indeed, the film leaves behind an inconsistent impression in more ways than one. Accordingly, one may ask whether the extremely aestheticized images of former advertising filmmaker Parker really suit the film's subject matter. Giorgio Moroder's pleasant electro-pop seems almost embarrassing in light of both today's perspective and the film's serious theme. Other critics were offended by the clearly homoerotic motif.

But screenwriter Oliver Stone was the main target of criticism for the racist undertones of the plot. Parker's dramatization was also criticized for its portrayal of Turkey as a backward, sinister, and threatening country. Stone later admitted that his picture of Turkey was too one-dimensional, though he chalked it up to both his youth and Alan Parker's humorless approach according to Stone, the director left out those elements in the script that aimed to establish some ironic distance.

Midnight Express almost sets a precedent for a film that resorts to manipulation for the sake of better effects. Even today, the film is cited as proof of Western resentment against Turkey. However, the fact remains that according to international human rights organizations like Amnesty International, torture in Turkish prisons and police stations is still a routine occurrence.

SH

5

5   So near and yet so far: Billy's father (Mike Kellin) would do anything to see his son free.

6   The scars of incarceration: Susan (Irene Miracle) hardly recognizes Billy after his prison ordeal.

"Walk into the incredible true experience of Billy Hayes, and bring all the courage you can!" *U.S. commercial for the movie*

PRISON FILMS   According to the Southampton Institute, the Center for Media and Justice, more than 300 prison films have been made since 1910. Nonetheless, the reason for which the prison film can hardly be called an independent genre lies primarily in the range of perspectives from which filmmakers have approached the theme. The material has been used to produce dramas, thrillers, comedies, and even musicals. Classification is made more difficult by the fact that a film does not necessarily have to play out in a prison in order to deal with the theme of imprisonment. Again, not all films that use the penal system as a set or as a plot element are automatically prison films. There are classic prison films like *Midnight Express* (1978), John Frankenheimer's *Birdman of Alcatraz* (1962), or Franklin J. Schaffner's *Papillon* (1973), and then pieces such as *The Hoose-Gow* (1929), with Stan Laurel and Oliver Hardy, produced by Hal Roach, or *Jailhouse Rock* (1957) with Elvis Presley, by Richard Thorpe, which stymie usual classification. There is an additional subcategory of films which, like 1932's *I am a Fugitive from a Chain Gang*, primarily deal with escape or flight. A more meaningful definition of prison films could be those that deal with the spatial and temporal conditions of imprisonment, or in a further sense, with the themes of guilt and atonement. Examples of films in this category are Lloyd Bacon's *San Quentin* (1937), Alan Clarke's *Scum* (1979), or Tim Robbins' *Dead Man Walking* (1995).

THE DEER HUNTER

1978 - USA - 183 MIN. - VIETNAM FILM

DIRECTOR MICHAEL CIMINO (*1943)
SCREENPLAY DERIC WASHBURN, MICHAEL CIMINO, LOUIS GARFINKLE, QUINN K. REDEKER **DIRECTOR OF PHOTOGRAPHY** VILMOS ZSIGMOND
EDITING PETER ZINNER **MUSIC** STANLEY MYERS **PRODUCTION** BARRY SPIKINGS, MICHAEL DEELEY, MICHAEL CIMINO, JOHN PEVERALL for EMI FILMS LTD., UNIVERSAL PICTURES.

STARRING ROBERT DE NIRO (Michael), JOHN CAZALE (Stan), JOHN SAVAGE (Steven), CHRISTOPHER WALKEN (Nick), MERYL STREEP (Linda), GEORGE DZUNDZA (John), CHUCK ASPEGREN (Axel), SHIRLEY STOLER (Steven's Mother), RUTANYA ALDA (Angela), PIERRE SEGUI (Julien).

ACADEMY AWARDS 1978 OSCARS for BEST FILM (Barry Spikings, Michael Deeley, Michael Cimino, John Peverall), BEST DIRECTOR (Michael Cimino), BEST SUPPORTING ACTOR (Christopher Walken), BEST FILM EDITING (Peter Zinner), and BEST SOUND (C. Darin Knight, Richard Portman, Aaron Rochin, William L. McCaughey).

"One shot is what it's all about. A deer has to be taken with one shot."

There are films that lose all their magic as soon as you know how they end; and there are others that keep their thrill even after several viewings. One of the cinema's undying magic moments is the scene at the end of *The Deer Hunter,* in which Nick (Christopher Walken) walks out of the back room of a Saigon gambling den with a red scarf round his head. His old friend Michael (Robert De Niro) steps towards him – he wants him to come home. But Nick can no longer recognize him; he's spent too long with his temple pressed to the barrel of a revolver with just one bullet in the chamber. He's gambled with his life so often, he can't believe it's still his. He moves towards the crowded gaming table with a bunch of banknotes in his hand. Michael tries in vain to persuade him to leave. And suddenly there's a flicker of recognition in Nick's eyes. He laughs, takes the gun, holds it to his head and pulls the trigger.

It's the end of the 60s. Michael, Nick and Steven (John Savage), three friends from a steel town in Pennsylvania, are sent to Vietnam. By coincidence, they meet again in the midst of war. And by misfortune, they end up in the hands of the Vietcong. The prisoners are forced to play Russian Roulette while their captors lay bets on the outcome. Finally, only Michael and Nick are left, face-to-face across the table. Michael demands three bullets instead of one, in order to raise the stakes. His ruse is successful: the two friends overcome the Vietcong guerillas, free Steven from the "tiger cage" (a half-submerged bamboo basket) and flee for their lives. But Michael is the only one who makes it home intact. Steven loses his legs, and Nick gets stuck in Saigon, making money with the game of death.

Only around one-third of this great epic takes place in Vietnam – the middle part. These are among the most impressive images of war ever filmed. The contempt for human life so typical of any war, the hatred, the powerlessness, the fear, and the pride: Michael Cimino brings all these together in a single symbolic action – Russian Roulette. Yet Cimino shows the Americans purely as victims of the Vietnam War, and this provoked a lot of protest, especially in Europe. The Americans, it was claimed, were much more guilty than their opponents of torturing POWs. The film was accused of being racist, and the controversy came to a head at the Berlin Film Festival in

War on the home front: Linda (Meryl Streep) and Michael (Robert DeNiro) tackle daily life and its many ghosts.

Birds of prey: Michael and Nick (Christopher Walken) on a hunting trip in the mountains.

3 Fun and games in Clairton, Pennsylvania. Cimino shot the Clairton scenes in eight separate locations to breathe life into the fictitious town.

4 Camerawork that is right on target. Cinematographer Vilmos Zsigmond went on to film *Heaven's Gate* (1980) for Cimino.

"There can be no quarrel about the acting. De Niro, Walken, John Savage, as another Clairton pal who goes to war, and Meryl Streep, as a woman left behind, are all top actors in extraordinary form."

Time Magazine

'9, as the Soviet Union, followed by the rest of the Eastern Bloc, withdrew its films in protest.

But Cimino is not even attempting to provide a political commentary to Vietnam War. Instead, his film tells the story of people uprooted from everything they used to call home, and it shows the destruction of everything t once made friendship possible. The first hour of the film is devoted to the als of the two friends, Michael and Nick. We see their last day in the elmill; we see them drinking with their buddies from the little community Vhite Russian immigrants; we see their wild celebrations at Steven's wedg reception, after the Russian Orthodox ceremony. One last time before tnam, the friends go hunting in the mountains of Pennsylvania, a pristine trast to the dirty steel town. Michael's hunting ambition, to kill a deer with

5 Celebrate good times: Steven's (John Savage, fourth from left) wedding marks the last joyous occasion of the boys' lives. Soon they'll be drafted to Vietnam.

6 Caught in the crossfire: Robert de Niro called this role "his toughest yet" after shooting was completed.

7 "One of the most frightening, unbearably tense sequences ever filmed – and the most violent excoriation of violence in screen history," wrote *Newsweek*.

8 Secret admirer: Back from the war, decorated soldier Michael visits the true love of his life – Nick's girl, Linda (Meryl Streep).

a single shot, will not survive his experiences in Vietnam. Indeed, when he returns in the third part of the film, he'll have difficulties even finding his home – because someone's missing, and he's made a promise. That's why he leaves once more, to search for Nick in Saigon.

At the end, the little group of mourners in the bar will strike up "God Bless America," but their rendition of the hymn is anything but triumphant.

These people are the walking wounded, and each of them has lost som thing: a friend, physical wholeness, trust in life, or hope for the future. Th fault lies with America; and yet America is their home, a part of their ve selves. In *The Deer Hunter*, Cimino shows us this painful contradiction, ar gives us a subtle, exact and outstandingly photographed portrait of Americ society after Vietnam.

N

"**Equally at ease in the lyrical and the realistic modes, a virtuoso of the shocking image who never loses sight of the whole, a consummate master of his technique, Michael Cimino is a supremely accomplished filmmaker.**" *Le Monde*

MICHAEL CIMINO

His films are always controversial: *The Deer Hunter* (1978) was showered with Oscars in Hollywood and condemned as a falsification of the Vietnam War in Europe. The epic Late Western *Heaven's Gate* (1980) was hailed as a masterpiece in Europe, and decried as a "catastrophe" in the USA. *Year of the Dragon* (1985), in which a sole cop takes on the Chinese mafia in New York, brought accusations of racism. *The Sicilian* (1987), an opulent biography of the Sicilian popular hero Salvatore Giuliano, was dismissed as historical kitsch.

Michael Cimino (*16.11.1943) came to filmmaking after studying architecture and painting. By the end of the 60s, he was making commercials. In 1973, he joined with John Milius to write the screenplay to *Magnum Force*, starring Clint Eastwood. Cimino's first feature film was *Thunderbolt and Lightfoot* (1974), a tragicomic thriller about a gangster in search of his money, with Eastwood and Jeff Bridges in the leading roles. The debut signaled some of the motifs that would be found throughout Cimino's work: male friendship, detailed milieu studies, and gorgeous landscape panoramas. His expensive obsession with authenticity drove United Artists to bankruptcy, and to this day, *Heaven's Gate* is a synonym for megaflops. Although his last film *The Sunchaser* (1996) was a fairly conventional effort, Michael Cimino is still regarded as one of the most visually brilliant directors in America.

8

SUPERMAN: THE MOVIE

1978 - GREAT BRITAIN - 143 MIN. - COMIC BOOK ADAPTATION, SCIENCE FICTION

DIRECTOR RICHARD DONNER (*1930)
SCREENPLAY MARIO PUZO, DAVID NEWMAN, LESLIE NEWMAN, ROBERT BENTON, TOM MANKIEWICZ, NORMAN ENFIELD, from the comics by JERRY SIEGEL and JOE SHUSTER DIRECTOR OF PHOTOGRAPHY GEOFFREY UNSWORTH EDITING STUART BAIRD, MICHAEL ELLIS MUSIC JOHN WILLIAMS PRODUCTION ALEXANDER SALKIND, PIERRE SPENGLER for DOVEMEAD FILMS, ALEXANDER SALKIND, FILM EXPORT A. G., INTERNATIONAL FILM PRODUCTION.

STARRING CHRISTOPHER REEVE (Superman / Clark Kent), GENE HACKMAN (Lex Luthor), MARLON BRANDO (Jor-El), MARGOT KIDDER (Lois Lane), NED BEATTY (Otis), JACKIE COOPER (Perry White), GLENN FORD (Pa Kent), TREVOR HOWARD (Senator), MARIA SCHELL (Vond-Ah), TERENCE STAMP (General Zod), VALERIE PERRINE (Eve Teschmacher).

ACADEMY AWARDS 1978 SPECIAL AWARD for SPECIAL EFFECTS (Les Bowie, Colin Chilvers, Denys N. Coop, Roy Field, Derek Meddings, Zoran Perisic).

"Look Ma – No Wires!"

The opening credits, an operatic overture of Wagnerian magnitude, indicate the dimensions of the tale that is to follow. A curtain slowly opens, the clattering of a projector is heard, and a date appears on the screen: "June, 1938." Aficionados understand – this was the month in which Superman made his debut in an issue of the comic series "Action Comics." And there on the screen is the comic book in question; a child's hand gently opens it and leafs through its pages.

The camera dives directly into the comic strip, showing the globe-crowned editorial building of the "Daily Planet." By means of a special effects blend-in, the comic image slowly transforms into a real life representation and the camera steadily wanders higher, focusing on the moon and then speeding past it. From the depths of outer space the first line of the opening credits zooms to the fore, jumping directly into the audience's face. The three words, "Alexander Salkind presents," grow bigger, bursting the borders

of the still visible theater stage and are ultimately emblazoned in the fu width of the scope format on the screen. And on we go, hurtling through th cosmos.

An opulent comic book opera like *Superman* must naturally begin dee in the realms of the heavens, and the authors take their time, opening wit the pre-story, which takes place on the crystal planet Krypton. Councilor Jo El (Marlon Brando) warns his people of a threatening catastrophe, but th remaining members of the planet's government sense defeatism in his warr ing and force him to swear that he will never leave Krypton. Jor-El remain true to his word, as does his wife, but they send their small son, Kal-El to wards the Earth in an escape pod. The boy is to be the last of his people, fo Krypton falls victim to destruction, just as Jor-El had prophesized. In th meantime Kal-El is taken in by adoptive parents on Earth and grows int Clark Kent, alias Superman (Christopher Reeve).

3

1 Clothes make the man: With the help of a suit, hat and pair of glasses, the Man of Steel assumes the identity of mild-mannered reporter, Clark Kent.

2 Leaping to new heights in a single bound: With a giant "S" across his chest, Superman (Christopher Reeve) fights for truth, justice and the American way.

3 X-ray vision: Somewhere under all that muscle and bravado lies the Daily Planet's most endearing dolt.

"… to commit the Crime of the Century, a man would just naturally have to face – the Challenge of the Century."

Film quote: Lex Luthor

4

Director Richard Donner regarded the Superman figure as an age-old American myth and dramatized it accordingly – in epic breadth, with numerous vignettes that highlight the irreproachable character of the boy wonder who falls from the sky. Contrary to Richard Lester, who in the two subsequent *Superman* films employed much more irony, Donner allowed his hero to be a child – a child who must take painful abuse from his peers, voluntarily doing without his superpowers because his mother and father forbade him to use them.

Retribution is granted to the Man of Steel in the last portion of the film when he gains the respect and gratitude of the earth's citizens after preventing a deadly inferno. And of course he wins the love of Lois Lane (Margot Kidder), a reward that surely made saving the world worthwhile.

"Richard Donner's direction is appropriately broad but not unnuanced; each segment of the film has its own mythic unity, related to various genres and movie types; and each has Superman developing not so much as a character but as the focus for different kinds of entertainment." *Monthly Film Bulletin*

5

4   The perfect illusion: neither a bird nor a plane, but Christopher Reeve as Superman.

5   Swept off her feet: Superman shows Lois Lane (Margot Kidder) the greatest sites Metropolis has to offer.

6   No way out: Armageddon is upon the crystal planet of Krypton.

7   Desperate times call for desperate measures: Jor-El (Marlon Brando) anticipates Krypton's catastrophic end and saves the life of his newborn son.

CHRISTOPHER REEVE   During the prolonged preparation phase for *Superman: The Movie* (1978), the search was on for the perfect leading actor. Several male stars of the time were considered, including Burt Reynolds, Sylvester Stallone, Clint Eastwood, and Charles Bronson. But the producers eventually decided upon Christopher Reeve (*1952), who had only appeared as an actor on Broadway. The decision was to prove correct, because as an unknown, Reeve was able to play Superman without eclipsing the new character by previous film roles.
He donned the Superman costume four times for the big screen, but rejected further action films like *The Running Man* (1987). He acted for the theater and appeared in television movies and in one-off screen roles, such as *The Remains of the Day* (1993). In May 1995 he had a severe riding accident and was paralyzed from the neck down. Nonetheless, Reeve remained active, writing his autobiography, *Still Me*, and several screenplays. He also produced and took on suitable roles, like that of the handicapped Jason Kemp in the Hitchcock remake, *Rear Window* (1998). Reeve devotes the majority of his time speaking on behalf of paraplegics; he collects donations and on May 3, 2002, together with his wife, he launched "The Christopher Reeve and Dana Reeve Paralysis Resource Center," which is dedicated to research and information.

Donner's dramatization isn't limited to a mere projection of the familiar themes of the *Superman* saga onto the big screen. He naturally knows where cinematography can surpass the static comic drawings, whose creators were limited to depicting movement with graphic tricks and onomatopoeia. Even well-versed fans of the Superman comics will enjoy watching Superman romping through the heavens like a dancer with Lois Lane in his arms, slinging missiles into outer space, or twisting himself into the Earth's core to prevent the separation of the coast of California.

Donner lays his trumps on the table right at the beginning of the film, focusing on an individual drawing and transcending its borders by making the camera zoom deeper and deeper into the flat surface of the illustration in dimensions that impressively burst the spatial relationships of the comic's story-telling formula, which must adhere to finite viewpoints. Here the film teaches yet another lesson, demonstratively switching from normal to scope format and flexing its technical muscles. The medium not only shows its capacity for monumental imagery but in the way in which the seemingly unbridled camera hurtles at light speed through space, announces its intention to take the audience along on a journey that can be offered nowhere else but in the cinema. For it is only here that Supermen can truly fly.

HK

LA CAGE AUX FOLLES
aka Birds of a Feather

1978 - FRANCE / ITALY - 91 MIN. - COMEDY

DIRECTOR ÉDOUARD MOLINARO (*1928)
SCREENPLAY MARCELLO DANON, ÉDOUARD MOLINARO, JEAN POIRET, FRANCIS VEBER, based on the play of the same name by JEAN POIRET DIRECTOR OF PHOTOGRAPHY ARMANDO NANNUZZI EDITING MONIQUE ISNARDON, ROBERT ISNARDON MUSIC ENNIO MORRICONE PRODUCTION MARCELLO DANON for DA MA PRODUZIONE, LES PRODUCTIONS ARTISTES ASSOCIÉS.

STARRING UGO TOGNAZZI (Renato Baldi), MICHEL SERRAULT (Albin Mougeotte / Zaza Napoli), CLAIRE MAURIER (Simone), RÉMI LAURENT (Laurent Baldi), CARMEN SCARPITTA (Louise Charrier), BENNY LUKE (Jacob), LUISA MANERI (Andrea Charrier), MICHEL GALABRU (Simon Charrier), VENANTINO VENANTINI (Chauffeur).

"What I am supposed to do? He's flying the coop."

What happens when an off-the-wall transvestite walks into a bar like a John Wayne impersonator, rolling her shoulders and standing tall? You guessed it, she is immediately ridiculed as a "faggot," forcing her other half to bravely confront the louse who made the remark and defend her honor. Even when the rogue suddenly reveals himself to be two heads taller than the gallant knight, and possibly a close relative of James Bond's nemesis, Jaws (*The Spy Who Loved Me,* 1977; *Moonraker,* 1979), that's no deterrent – honor is honor. Loved ones are not to be profaned with derogatory terms like that, especially when the person is question is not just an artiste but a star!

The drag-queen who has a whirl at playing cowboy is nightclub diva "Zaza Napoli," in a divine performance by Michel Serrault, who is both a "he" on stage and in life, even when his inner "she" bursts out on occasion with glistening mile-long lashes. Her significant other, the mature and dashing Renato Baldi (Ugo Tognazzi), who is forever sporting a white suit and trimmed moustache, is the owner of the "La Cage aux Folles," a club where, night after night, Zaza leads a high-pitched, high-heeled chorus line of silk-stockings and feather boas to victory. Renato and Zaza have been happily "wed for the last 20 years. Yet married life can have its ups and downs, like the pair of pumps that are hurled at Renato's head when he bursts into Zaza' flat without first proving his affection. Luckily he's used to such displays c affection and knows exactly when to duck. Just one day in the life of Balc and Zaza, who goes by the name of Albin Mougeotte during the dayligh hours.

This world of fun and games comes to a shuddering halt when Renato 20-year-old son Laurent (Rémi Laurent) announces his intention to marr Andrea (Luisa Maneri), the young daughter of Simon Charrier (Michel Gala bru), deputy general of the Tradition, Family and Morality Party. Unfortunately Andrea has told her bumptious dad that her father-in-law to be is the Italia consul in Nice. To make matters worse, the putative consul's apartment is fu of paraphernalia bound to create an uproar: vases shaped like comely rea

ends, pink frou-frou pillows, a plaster statue of the Greek Adonis and china with lewd kouros motifs. Not forgetting Jacob (Benny Luke), a black manservant who wiggles his way across their deep-pile rugs in a French maid's costume waving a feather duster. None of that would matter, were it not for the fact that the deputy general and his wife announce their imminent visit. The colorful members of this happy family had better put their heads together fast, or they might have one giant catastrophe on their hands…

In *La Cage aux Folles*, virtually every aspect of life is turned on its head. Each paradigm of social normality suddenly indicates its opposite. All that is off-kilter is transformed into the given norm, whereas norms are taboo and leave both the characters and spectators aghast. The film valiantly takes on a barrage of homosexual and effeminate stereotypes, and puts them through

2

"Édouard Molinaro's light touch ensures that *La Cage aux Folles* is never embarrassing, and he avoids any *faux pas* in dealing with the topic of love between men. This is a bubbly and highly enjoyable film with an unobtrusive moral." *Karlsruher Filmschau*

1   A little dab will do ya: Michel Serrault is a man – he's just a touch more charming, ostentatious and supple than average.

2   A father's worst nightmare: Not only must Renato (Ugo Tognazzi) embrace his son's heterosexuality; he also has to come to terms with his future daughter-in-law – who happens to be the offspring of Simon Charrier, deputy general of the "tradition, family and morality" party…

3   Charmed, I'm sure: The good-mannered Charrier (Michel Galabru) pays his respects to the alleged woman of the house (Michel Serrault).

4   Birds of a feather: Renato and Albin are storybook soulmates.

3

"Ugo Tognazzi's nonchalant virility constantly threatens to collapse into girlish affectation, and it harmonizes deliciously with the shamelessly exaggerated effeminacy of Michel Serrault."

Neue Zürcher Zeitung

5

MICHEL SERRAULT

Aged 50, and after countless supporting roles, Michel Serrault (born 1928) was finally offered a part that launched him to new heights. With the greatest of ease, the thespian slipped into the skin of *La Cage aux Folles'* Albin, a sensitive, highly-strung transvestite. In addition to his film portrayal, Serrault gave over 2000 stage performances as Albin in the play of the same name.

It was on the Paris stage that this gifted artist first flew his comedic colors. At the age of sixteen he received acting instruction from Bernard Blier. His film debut followed in 1954. Serrault was successful in moving on to other projects after the enormous public response to *La Cage aux Folles* and its two sequels (1980, 1985). He received the César for "Albin" and then abruptly switched gears from comedy to character acting. No-one could have played the double role of Biedermann and the arsonist better than Serrault. In both Chabrol's *Les Fantômes du chapelier* (*The Hatter's Ghost*, 1982), and Christian de Chalonge's *Dr. Petiot* (1990), he played perfidious, pathological serial killers masked by a façade of decorum and propriety. Simply clothed as an old man in a black hat with a well-trimmed moustache, he'd just tilt up his head, arch his eyebrows and purse his lips and it was instantly clear what sort of sinister intentions were actually harbored in the soul of this upstanding citizen. He played a downtrodden, fatherly private investigator, who combs Europe looking for young murderess Isabelle Adjani in Claude Miller's *Mortelle randonnée* (*Deadly Run*, 1982). He becomes more fixated by her with each passing mile, and is gradually convinced that the modern day Circe is the embodiment of innocence. "Don't laugh too quickly, and take your time before resorting to tears. The trick is to be sober and then wait." These were the words Serrault used on his 70th birthday to characterize what he considered to be the fundamentals of perfect acting.

5   They'll never notice: The grand inquisitor of propriety and morality, M Charrier, makes a graceful exit from the "Cage aux Folles" nightclub in three-inch pumps to dodge the paparazzi waiting at the door.

6   Basking in the limelight: Temperamental diva, Zaza (Michel Serrault), is less than delighted by her new supporting cast.

the wringer. The depiction of Charrier, the defender of propriety, is also hyperbolized. He and his wife sit twelve feet apart from one another at their grand banquet table, and the interior design of their not-so-humble abode is reminiscent of a medieval torture chamber.

Beyond the over-the-top antics and the hare-brained slapstick lies some genuine depth. This is evidenced in the moments of Albin's fragility, such as when he is to driven out of the house because he finds it impossible to act like anyone other than himself. He even makes a concerted effort to play along with the "charade" at one point, entering the living room, here re-

decorated in "good taste," in a black suit and tie. Without his makeup and cramped by a heavily starched dress shirt, he attempts to seat himself as masculinely as possible. His posture while lowering himself, not to mention the way in which he places his hand on the arm rest, immediately give him away. Yet it is precisely when Serrault succeeds in showing how Albin fails at getting outside his own skin that *La Cage aux Folles* is at its most brilliant. In the 1980s, two further installments of the saga rode on the coat-tails of the enormous success of this picture. But like the American remake *The Birdcage* (1996), they couldn't hold a candle to the original.   SR

DAYS OF HEAVEN

1978 - USA - 95 MIN. - MELODRAMA

DIRECTOR TERRENCE MALICK (*1943)
SCREENPLAY TERRENCE MALICK DIRECTOR OF PHOTOGRAPHY NÉSTOR ALMENDROS, HASKELL WEXLER EDITING BILLY WEBER
MUSIC ENNIO MORRICONE PRODUCTION BERT SCHNEIDER, HAROLD SCHNEIDER for PARAMOUNT PICTURES.

STARRING RICHARD GERE (Bill), BROOKE ADAMS (Abby), SAM SHEPARD (The Farmer), LINDA MANZ (Linda), ROBERT J. WILKE (Farm Foreman), JACKIE SHULTIS (Linda's Friend), GENE BELL (Dancer), DOUG KERSHAW (Fiddler), RICHARD LIBERTINI (Vaudeville Leader), JOHN WILKINSON (Preacher).

ACADEMY AWARDS 1978 OSCAR for BEST CINEMATOGRAPHY (Néstor Almendros).

IFF CANNES 1979 BEST DIRECTOR (Terrence Malick).

"It just used to be me and my brother. We used to do things together. We used to have fun. We used to roam the streets."

The film is a cinematic masterpiece, a veritable cascade of imagery all too seldom experienced on the silver screen. Packed with symbolism, Terrence Malick's drama relates the moving tale of a love triangle set in the social and political upheaval of the industrial revolution. A montage of the work of photographer Lewis Hine (1874–1940) gives us a first taste of this era of radical change. Stark pictures of the day, documenting the lives of the working class, reveal gigantic houses, narrow alleys, filthy inner courtyards and streets.

Most striking, however, are the nameless inhabitants we see peering at the camera with mournful stoicism.

These dramatically altered living conditions send young lovers Abby (Brooke Adams) and Bill (Richard Gere) to set sail for new shores. Together with Bill's kid sister Linda (Linda Manz), the vagabonds traipse across the countryside on the lookout for the next job that will provide them with a meal ticket. After much searching, they find work on a farm as seasonal

"The film, photographed by Néstor Almendros and Haskell Wexler, has a pictorialism, recalling at different moments the works of Corot, Millet, Seurat, Brueghel, Turner, and Murnau's American films."

Literature / Film Quarterly

1 Ouch, gerbils hurt! There's never a dull moment for Bill (Richard Gere). He rarely enjoys a moment of "inner peace."

2 A light in the attic: Abby (Brooke Adams) investigates life on the farm.

3 Catcher in the rye: Hard labor reaps golden rewards.

borers and help sort the harvest. Not suspecting that Bill and Abby, who ~ose as brother and sister, are actually romantically involved, the single and ~avely ill farmer David (Sam Shepard) falls in love with the radiant Abby. ~ is the basis for a melancholy love story that ends tragically for both male ~itors.

Yet the film is not just a tale of woebegone ties among three indi~duals. Malick's piece is far more than a patchwork of psychological impli~ations and well-ordered storylines. This is attested to by the non-linear ~ature of the plot, chronology and various interceding subplots. The piece ~so benefits tremendously from the poetry of its beautifully composed im~jes, often shot at twilight and dawn. A world apart from simplistic stereo~pes, the picture tells of the uprooted nature of its characters, the loss of ~meland, the intrusion of technology in the private sphere, and a journey into an uncertain future. The story and the characters do not just deal with individual destinies: they rise up to represent much larger concepts of humanity and cultural history. They are archetypes, symbolizing opposing worldviews locked in mortal combat. Their stories tell of love, jealousy and death, as well as the fundamental challenges and questions that arise when a new way of life replaces an existing one. The principles of modernity are championed by Bill, the hotheaded, aggressive go-getter, whereas tradition and the preservation of a soon-to-be-antiquated way of life are embodied by the reserved farmer, tied to the land.

The visual language of cinematographer Néstor Almendros reflects the polarized philosophies of this dialog in the juxtaposition of romantic and realistic imagery. The harsh, angular, filthy imagery of industrialization pervading the framing tale is a long way from the gracefully curved and

NÉSTOR ALMENDROS

Néstor Almendros was born in Barcelona in 1930. He started his academic studies in philosophy and literature in Havana, continued at the City College of New York and finished at the Centro Sperimentale di Cinematografia in Rome. It was during this time that he got to know avant-garde filmmakers Maya Deren and Jonas Mekas. Following Fidel Castro's rise to power, Almendros shot a considerable number of documentaries in Cuba from 1951–1961. After two of his films were banned by censors, he relocated to Paris in the early 1960s, where he found work in the media industries of television and short-film. Starting in the mid 1960s, Almendros became involved in the French *Nouvelle Vague* movement and collaborated with such greats as François Truffaut (*L'Enfant sauvage / The Wild Child*, 1969; *L'Histoire d'Adèle H. / The Story of Adèle H.,* 1975 etc.) and Eric Rohmer (*Le Genou de Claire / Claire's Knee*, 1970; *La Marquise d'O. / The Marquise of O.*, 1976). He gained prestige that won him international acclaim as a bright young cinematographer. With a predilection for natural light as well as the stark contrasts of black and white photography he played a prominent role in developing the *Nouvelle Vague's* definitive visual style. Upon his arrival in the United States in the late 1970s, he successfully transposed his trademark tendencies to color film. This impressive feat can be witnessed in films such as *Days of Heaven* (1978). Almendros wrote on his own professional life and the art of cinematography in many publications. His autobiographical reflection *Un homme à la camera* (A Man with a Camera) appeared in print in the 1980s. The multifaceted photographer extraordinaire also shot commercial spots for Giorgio Armani and Calvin Klein. In 1992, Néstor Almendros lost his life to AIDS.

outer lines of the main story, bathed in the magical twilight of the idyllic countryside.

Almendros goes so far as to implement apocalyptic religious symbols like a locust infestation, a torrential blaze, iridescent lanterns, gloom, smoke and screaming in the movie's climactic sequence. But the film takes no sides in the debate it poses. Instead, Malick is interested in the process surrounding cultural and social changes. He explores the mythical nature of life and evolution, while careful not to burden his investigation with rigid observations, leaving the film largely open to interpretation. Seen in this light, *Days of Heaven* presents us with nothing short of a true movie enthusiast's diehard philosophy: Life's truths do not lurk in any story, but are found in the beauty of an image. BR

"What Malick has done, however, is much more radical than supplying a child's-eye-view of some strange adult drama. His film is split between the much that we see and the little that we know." *Sight and Sound*

4   Needle in a haystack: American Gothic turns Rothko.

5   Oral tradition or just plain gossip: Young Linda (Linda Manz) narrates the tale of Abby and Bill.

6   Love on a pitchfork: Abby has given dying Dave a new lease on life.

THE MARRIAGE OF MARIA BRAUN
Die Ehe der Maria Braun

1978 - FRG - 120 MIN. - DRAMA

DIRECTOR RAINER WERNER FASSBINDER (1945–1982)
SCREENPLAY PETER MÄRTHESHEIMER, PEA FRÖHLICH **DIRECTOR OF PHOTOGRAPHY** MICHAEL BALLHAUS **EDITING** JULIANE LORENZ
MUSIC PEER RABEN **PRODUCTION** MICHAEL FENGLER for ALBATROS PRODUKTION, TRIO FILM, FILMVERLAG DER AUTOREN, TANGO FILM, FENGLER FILMS, WESTDEUTSCHER RUNDFUNK.

STARRING HANNA SCHYGULLA (Maria Braun), KLAUS LÖWITSCH (Hermann Braun), IVAN DESNY (Karl Oswald), GOTTFRIED JOHN (Willi Klenze), GISELA UHLEN (Maria's Mother), HARK BOHM (Senkenberg), ELISABETH TRISSENAAR (Betti Klenze), GEORGE BYRD (Bill), CLAUS HOLM (Physician), GÜNTER LAMPRECHT (Hans Wetzel).

IFF BERLIN 1978 SILVER BEAR for BEST ACTRESS (Hanna Schygulla), and BEST TECHNICAL CREW.

"I'd rather perform my own miracles than wait for them to happen."

It's 1943. Maria (Hanna Schygulla) and Hermann (Klaus Löwitsch) have been married for half a day and a single night when the war pulls them apart. Hermann is sent to fight on the Eastern Front, while Maria struggles to make a living on the black market. When the war ends, she's informed that her husband is dead. In the postwar period, everything's in short supply; so Maria ensures her material survival by doing something that can get a girl a bad name: she goes to work in a bar for American soldiers. But she soon makes the rules clear to her clientele: "I sell beer, not me." Maria is no man's property, and she takes what she needs: nylons, cigarettes, and above all warmth, which she finds in the arms of Bill (George Byrd), a black G.I. When the husband she had given up for dead appears in the door one day, there's one man too many in her bedroom. In the heat of the moment, Maria kills her naked lover with a blow from a bottle. Cameraman Michael Ballhaus films this scene in such a

distanced fashion that Maria's act of murder seems both unspectacular an wholly absurd. In court, Maria insists that while Bill only liked her, her hus band loves her. The judge is uncomprehending, but Hermann understands: h takes the rap for Maria and goes to jail. Maria, meanwhile, goes to work f the textiles manufacturer Karl Oswald (Ivan Desny). In the years that follo the young woman pursues a brilliant career as a businesswoman and as O wald's mistress. As she makes clear to the businessman, however, it's not h who's having an affair with her, but she with him. Maria may be calculatin but she's also emotionally honest. She really does like Oswald, but all the tim she's saving her money for the house she plans to build for herself and He mann. By now, Germany is looking tidier: the rubble of wartime has bee swept away, and Maria is a wealthy woman, the first member of her fam who can afford a house of her own. Suddenly Oswald dies of a heart attac

"With this cool melodrama full of strong emotions, Rainer Werner Fassbinder has created something exceptional: a densely concentrated film, lively, precise and witty. The dramaturgy is coherent, the dialogue tight, and the actors give highly discerning interpretations of their roles – especially Hanna Schygulla, who was crowned Best Actress at the Berlinale." *Kölner Stadt-Anzeiger*

1   The dragon lady of new Germany: Hanna Schygulla as radiant opportunist Maria Braun.

2   The price of capitalism: In the ruins of post-war Germany, Maria's man takes the fall for her dirty deeds and her career starts to soar.

and shortly thereafter Hermann is released from prison. While the radio transmits the legendary World Cup Final of 1954, the married couple in the big house try to get to know each other all over again. By the time the German soccer team have become World Champions, Maria and Hermann have inherited Oswald's considerable fortune – and they're dead. A gas explosion has destroyed the house and buried the two of them in its ruins.

The Marriage of Maria Braun was Fassbinder's first major international success. Like *The Merchant of Four Seasons* (*Händler der vier Jahreszeiten*, 1972), it paints a depressing and unprettified picture of the German "eco-nomic miracle." Maria's story reflects the rise of West Germany from the ruins of the lost war to a society in which money, possessions, and social standing count for more than human relationships. Maria Braun is a woman who takes charge of her own life, single-minded in her determination to build a career and accumulate wealth in order to achieve her dreams of happiness. Only when it's too late does she realize that she's lost the very thing she's been working for, that a shared life with Hermann is no longer possible. The film never makes it entirely clear whether the gas explosion was a tragic accident or an act of suicide.

3 The truth hurts: Maria is well aware that sexual relationships have both emotional and financial implications.

Maria begins as an embodiment of the strong women of postwar Germany, who shouldered the reconstruction of the country in the absence of their menfolk. Very soon, however, she's become a typical protagonist of the economic miracle. Hanna Schygulla, one of Fassbinder's favorite actresses, gives a performance of astonishing versatility: the young girl in the American bar is every bit as convincing as the cold and frustrated businesswoman. Yet *The Marriage of Maria Braun* offers no kitchen-sink realism. The narrative is concentrated, attenuated, and the characters are highly stylized.

Fassbinder creates a bizarre chronicle of the Adenauer era, in which fragments of superpower politics are strewn casually across the lives of the protagonists. The radio in the living room functions as a link between the private and the public spheres. We hear Adenauer making a speech on the rearmament of the Federal Republic; and a soccer commentary forms a counterpoint to the tragic deaths of Maria and Hermann, as it proclaims the rebirth of the nation in the field of sport. "Germany are World Champions!" indeed; but two of the country's minor players will never share in the celebrations. KK

4 They left her hanging: Hanna Schygulla was one
   of the great Fassbinder actresses. But in later
   years, her inflexible acting style made her little
   more than a monument to herself.

5 "Who knows Hermann Braun?" Their marriage was
   only a day and a night old when Hermann departed
   for the Russian front. When he returns, he'll find
   life with Maria is not what he bargained for.

"An ambiguous and solidly directed melodrama, *The Marriage of Maria Braun* is undoubtedly the director's best film to date" *Le Monde*

HANNA SCHYGULLA

Known as the *femme fatale* of the subculture, Hanna Schygulla was one of the great female icons of the German cinema in the 60s and 70s. It was above all her work with Rainer Werner Fassbinder that made her so instantly recognizable. In no less than 20 productions, she developed a consciously cool, understated style, and an image that made her a kind of anti-star. Born in Kattowitz (now Katowice in Poland) in 1943, she was a young drama student in Munich when she met Fassbinder, who introduced her to his experimental "action-theater" in 1967.

After roles in Danièle Huillet's and Jean-Marie Straub's short film *The Bridegroom, the Comedienne and the Pimp* (*Der Bräutigam, die Komödiantin und der Zuhälter*, 1968) and Peter Fleischmann's *Hunting Scenes from Bavaria* (*Jagdszenen aus Niederbayern*, 1969) she appeared in Fassbinder's *Love is Colder Than Death* (*Liebe ist kälter als der Tod,* 1969). Until 1974, she had roles in all of his subsequent films, including *Katzelmacher* (1969), *The Bitter Tears of Petra von Kant* (*Die bitteren Tränen der Petra von Kant,* 1972) and *The Merchant of Four Seasons* (*Händler der vier Jahreszeiten,* 1972). After *Effi Briest* (1974), there followed a temporary break with the *enfant terrible* of German filmmaking: as Hanna Schygulla explained to the *Berliner Zeitung* in 1994, "There came a time when I no longer wanted to see myself on screen. I felt like a doll, a puppet..." After a four-year pause, the two resumed their collaboration, on a film that achieved international success: *The Marriage of Maria Braun* (*Die Ehe der Maria Braun*, 1978).

In the intervening period, she had worked with other directors, on films including Wim Wenders' *The Wrong Move* aka *The Wrong Movement* or *False Move* (*Falsche Bewegung,* 1974) and Vojtech Jasny's adaptation of a Heinrich Böll story, *The Clown* (*Ansichten eines Clowns,* 1975). Hanna Schygulla cultivated an understated acting style, to such an extent that some of her later films made her look like a caricature of herself; examples include Fassbinder's *Lili Marleen* (1980) and Margarethe von Trotta's *Sheer Madness* (*Heller Wahn / L'Amie,* 1982). The latter film is regarded as a key work of the feminist movement. In *Passion* (1982), Jean-Luc Godard made subtly ironical use of her image: the character she plays is called Hanna, and her performance has a certain self-reflecting quality.

During the 80s and early 90s, Hanna Schygulla turned up more frequently in foreign films than in German productions. She appeared in Ettore Scola's *La Nuit de Varennes / Il mondo nuovo* (1982 – aka *That Night in Varennes*), in Andrej Wajda's *A Love in Germany* (*Un amour en Allemagne,* 1983), and in Kenneth Branagh's *Dead Again* (1991). In the years since then, she has concentrated on theater and concert appearances, often singing songs by the French film and theater composer Jean-Marie Sénia. Her relationship to Fassbinder is a subject she's struggled to come to terms with, and it continues to find expression in her art.

Wer kennt

HERMANN

BRAUN ?

Letzte Nachricht aus

dem Raum Smolensk

Fp.N. 16310-342

HALLOWEEN

1978 - USA - 91 MIN. - HORROR FILM

DIRECTOR JOHN CARPENTER (*1948)
SCREENPLAY JOHN CARPENTER, DEBRA HILL **DIRECTOR OF PHOTOGRAPHY** DEAN CUNDEY **EDITING** TOMMY LEE WALLACE, CHARLES BORNSTEIN **MUSIC** JOHN CARPENTER **PRODUCTION** JOHN CARPENTER, DEBRA HILL for COMPASS INTERNATIONAL PICTURES, FALCON FILMS.

STARRING DONALD PLEASENCE (Doctor Samuel Loomis), JAMIE LEE CURTIS (Laurie Strode), NANCY LOOMIS (Annie Brackett) P. J. SOLES (Lynda van der Klok), CHARLES CYPHERS (Sheriff Brackett), KYLE RICHARDS (Lindsey Wallace), BRIAN ANDREWS (Tommy Doyle), JOHN MICHAEL GRAHAM (Bob Simms), NANCY STEPHENS (Marion Chambers), TONY MORAN (Michael Myers, 21 years old), WILL SANDIN (Michael Myers, 6 years old).

"Was that the bogeyman?" – "As a matter of fact – it was!"

His eyes are the eyes of a devil. For 15 years, says psychiatrist Sam Loomis (Donald Pleasence), he has been trying to get a glimpse of what goes on behind those evil eyes, to make sense of what is going on inside that head. But all his efforts have been in vain. The boy seems to be driven by a single instinct: to kill. It was this heinous thirst for blood that propelled him back then, when he brutally stabbed his sister to death at the age of 6. Ever since that fateful day, Michael Myers has been under lock and key in an asylum. But now he's escaped. This dangerous beast is on the loose again and he begins stalking teenagers, returning to Haddonfield, the scene of his last homicidal rampage. And the timing of his escape couldn't be more threatening. It's Halloween, the most terrifying day of the year.

Halloween is a horror classic. Few films have made such a lasting mark on the genre. And this despite the fact that director John Carpenter did no-

thing to reinvent the art of filmmaking. The critics compared *Halloween* t Hitchcock's *Psycho* (1960), but felt that Hitch composed his murder scene much more deftly than the young Carpenter. Though they gave him credit fo mastering his craft, it was generally agreed that the film was shot far to conventionally.

Nevertheless, *Halloween* became one of the most successful independ ent films of all time. It cost $325,000 to make and grossed $100 million, per haps because its strength lies in its supposed weakness: the simplicity of th dramatization. With simple means he made no attempt to camouflage, Car penter aptly struck the public nerve. The eerie soundtrack hammers awa with its few incessantly repetitive notes. The vague images of the subjectiv camera conjure up an overwhelming insecurity, and excessively protracte tension slowly but surely escalates into naked fear.

1

2

"Replete with unobtrusive experiments, simple and clear in conception yet rich in internal links, *Halloween* is one of the finest horror films ever made. It's one of the reasons I'm in love with the cinema – and still go the movies all the time. And it's also one reason why I wanted to make movies myself." *Tom Tykwer, in: steadycam*

An arm reaches into the screen – our arm. A hand grabs a knife – our hand. The knife plunges into living flesh – we did it. The beginning of *Halloween* (1978) depicts the young Mike Myers as he butchers his sister. But the boy himself is not shown; we only see his action. The subjective camera assumes his perspective, through which the audience slips into the role of the protagonist and leaves its function as the omniscient and unnoticed observer. The subjective camera is able to create an atmosphere of insecurity or menacing danger because it gives the audience nothing more than the information that the film character also has.

The technique, however, seems to work best if used sparingly. Robert Montgomery failed with his Marlowe thriller *Lady in the Lake* (1947), which he filmed from the protagonist's point of view from beginning to end. Delmer Daves used the subjective camera much more adeptly in *Dark Passage* (1947): the audience only sees Humphrey Bogart's face a half an hour into the film after he undergoes a surgical operation – beforehand the action was filmed entirely from Bogart's perspective. Stanley Kubrick masterfully used the subjective perspective in his horror film *The Shining* (1980), continually leaving the audience in doubt as to whether the images are a part of the plot or just the fantasies of the characters.

This suspense-building quality is palpable when Laurie (Jamie Lee Curtis) ventures across the empty, dark, small town street to visit her school friends. She lives in a house across the way, and although the course of her path is filmed in standard time, the distance seems endless, because the audience knows something Laurie doesn't: Michael Myers (Tony Moran) is waiting for her on the other side of the street. A few minutes before, he sliced up three of her friends and is now cowering behind the dark window, eagerly sharpening his blade. Every footstep leads Laurie closer to the monster. She jiggles the knob on the front door – to no avail. She timidly makes her way to the back entrance – it is open. She stands in the kitchen, where just a few minutes earlier a knife plunged into the body of a young man. Moving to the stairs she tentatively begins to climb. Once upstairs she finds her friend lying peacefully in bed, but something is horribly wrong – her friend is dead. A second corpse falls from the closet at her feet, and suddenly the masked murderer is towering ominously behind her. Laurie runs. And she screams.

"Scream Queen" – Jamie Lee Curtis was bestowed this title after her first screen role. As Laurie Strode she manages to elude the lethal grasp of Michael Myers, thanks in large part to the psychiatrist Loomis, who empties an entire clip of bullets into the killer. The fact that Laurie is the one to survive, the outsider who prefers to babysit than make-out on the sly, proved ample ground to criticize the film for moral prudery. In self-defense,

1   A bloody encore: Michael Myers, the Bogeyman (Tony Moran). The mask, which was bought a costume shop, was first used in the horror film, *The Devil's Rain* (USA, 1975).

2   You were always on my mind: John Carpenter allegedly named his heroine Laurie Strode (Jamie Lee Curtis) after his first girlfriend.

3   Doctor death: Donald Pleasence was cast as the psychiatrist Samuel Loomis, after Peter Cushing and Christopher Lee had turned down the role.

3

Yet a lot of people seem to be convinced that *Halloween* is something special — a classic. Maybe when a horror film is stripped of everything but dumb scariness — when it isn't ashamed to revive the stalest device of the genre (the escaped lunatic) — it satisfies part of the audience in a more basic, childish way than sophisticated horror pictures do." *The New Yorker*

4

5

4 "An audacious hybrid of heterogeneous traditions. Held together by the fluid elegance of its camera-work, it conjures up an atmosphere of subtle terror." (*Die Zeit*)

5 Killer instinct: Donald Pleasence (left) also appeared in John Carpenter's *Escape from New York* (1981) and *Prince of Darkness* (1987).

6 Bedtime stories: Laurie tells Tommy that there's no such thing as the bogeyman, and the little boy discovers that adults really don't know everything.

7 The maxims of murder: Perverts will perish.

Carpenter declared that the psychology of the characters in *Halloween* was of little interest to him – he'd rattled off the screenplay in just two weeks with Debra Hill, who also produced his films *The Fog* (1979) and *Escape from New York* (1981).

Carpenter's aim was to deliver terror to the screen – unadulterated shock value and gruesome suspense. He hoped to make the true "psycho-path film," and he succeeded beyond his wildest dreams. Almost 25 years after his first appearance, Michael Myers continues to slaughter mercilessly on the big screen – he recently appeared in his 8th film. And Jamie Lee Curtis, alias Laurie Strode, is still the most prized victim of the sinister lunatic who seems immune to bullets, knife wounds, and electric shocks. To be continued – you can bet your life on it.   NM

6

7

THE LAST WALTZ

1978 - USA - 117 MIN. - CONCERT FILM

DIRECTOR MARTIN SCORSESE (*1942)
SCREENPLAY MARDIK MARTIN **DIRECTOR OF PHOTOGRAPHY** MICHAEL CHAPMAN, LASZLO KOVACS, VILMOS ZSIGMOND, DAVID MYERS, BOBBY BYRNE, MICHAEL W. WATKINS, HIRO NARITA **EDITING** YEU-BUN YEE, JAN ROBLEE, THELMA SCHOONMAKER
MUSIC THE BAND and many more **PRODUCTION** ROBBIE ROBERTSON for LAST WALTZ INC., FM PRODUCTIONS.

STARRING THE BAND (ROBBIE ROBERTSON, LEVON HELM, GARTH HUDSON, RICK DANKO, RICHARD MANUEL), RONNIE HAWKINS, DR. JOHN, NEIL YOUNG, THE STAPLES, NEIL DIAMOND, JONI MITCHELL, PAUL BUTTERFIELD, MUDDY WATERS, ERIC CLAPTON, EMMYLOU HARRIS, VAN MORRISON, BOB DYLAN, MICHAEL MCCLURE, LAWRENCE FERLINGHETTI.

"This Film Should Be Played Loud!"

They made a more serene and earthy rock music and reintroduced elements of blues, folk, and country into rock at a time when it had become louder and more psychedelic. The Band played as such from 1960 to 1976. Starting off as an accompanying band for Ronnie Hawkins (memorably described as a "second rate, reserve Elvis"), they rose to become Bob Dylan's band, and then ultimately went on to achieve success on their own. After 16 years on the road, The Band disbanded, holding a goodbye concert on Thanksgiving Day, 1976 at the Winterland Ballroom in San Francisco. Five thousand fans showed up – for $25 a pop, including turkey dinner – to a concert whose cinematic rendering by Martin Scorsese became a milestone of the "rocku-mentary" genre.

The Band was made up of Robbie Robertson (Guitar), Rick Danko (Bass), Levon Helm (Drums), Garth Hudson (Keyboards), and Richard Manuel (Piano). All told, they played 15 instruments and performed evergreens like "The Night They Drove Old Dixie Down," or "Up On The Cripple Creek." *Rolling Stone Magazine* called their first LP, "Music From Big Pink" (1968) a sensation. And the VIP guest list for the farewell concert gave their musical reputation its ultimate benediction: up on the bandwagon were rock legends such as Ronnie Hawkins and Bob Dylan, Neil Young, Joni Mitchell, and many many more. "We wanted it to be more than just a concert, we wanted it to be a celebration," said Robertson. And director Martin Scorsese made sure it would be just that.

The movie weaves together different narrative strands, including two authors (Michael McClure, Lawrence Ferlinghetti) reading their poetry, studio takes of The Band with the soul and gospel ensemble The Staples ("The Weight"), country music singer Emmylou Harris ("Evangeline"), and a series of brief interviews.

These interviews mostly consist of Robertson's stories from the band's past. Though every conceivable rock cliché is proffered ("more pussy than Sinatra"), wonderful anecdotes are also recounted, like that of keyboarder Garth Hudson, who joined The Band under one condition – that he could act as their "music teacher" and receive $10 a week from each of them for "lessons." Why? Hudson refused to tell his family that he was in a rock band.

"There is the whole pointless road warrior mystique, of hard-living men whose daily duty it is to play music and get wasted."

Chicago Sun-Times

MARTIN SCORSESE

A concert film (*The Last Waltz*, 1978), a musical (*New York, New York*, 1977), a gambling film (*The Color of Money*, 1986), a costume film (*The Age of Innocence*, 1993) – director Martin Scorsese never committed himself to a specific genre. Born on November 17, 1942, the son of Sicilian immigrants in New York, Scorsese grew up in the Catholic neighborhood of Little Italy and originally intended to join the priesthood. Although he dropped his ecclesiastical ambitions to begin studying at the New York University Film School, religious themes with stories of damnation and redemption run through many of his films. In *The Last Temptation of Christ* (1988) and the Buddhist film *Kundun* (1997) he directly addressed religious motifs.

Scorsese's personal style had already established itself by his third feature film. *Mean Streets* (1973) – a story about friendship, loyalty, repentance, and atonement – has a documentary-like touch, with Robert De Niro and Harvey Keitel in leading roles. Scorsese achieved his breakthrough with *Taxi Driver* (1975), a masterpiece about a psychopath (Robert De Niro) who feels he has been chosen to combat big city scum. De Niro became his most important leading actor, portraying Jake LaMotta in *Raging Bull* (1980) and dominating Scorsese's two epic Mafia films, *GoodFellas* (1990) and *Casino* (1995).

Key members of the Scorsese film clan include screenplay author Paul Schrader, editor Thelma Schoonmaker, and cameraman Michael Ballhaus. Scorsese is not only a gifted stylist, but also a profound student of film. He made two documentaries about the American and the Italian cinema: *A Personal Journey with Martin Scorsese Through American Movies* (1995) and *My Voyage to Italy* (*Il mio viaggio in Italia*, 1999), both of which are sweeping cinematic panoramas, as knowledgeable as they are passionate.

1 Rhinestone cowboy: Neil Diamond pours his heart into "Dry Your Eyes" and glides his way through *The Last Waltz*.

2 A man of many hats: To this day, the versatile Bob Dylan retains his title as the messiah of folk music. He is the only artist in the film who performs two numbers. Relatively few, considering the other musicians started life as his band.

3 I guess that's why they call it the blues: Muddy Waters (center) reminds audiences of rock's soulful roots.

4 Strike up the band! Guitarist Robbie Robertson (left) and bassist Rick Danko (center) sing alongside Van Morrison (3rd front left) and friends.

3

The bulk of *The Last Waltz* consists of the Winterland concert. Scorsese, editor of the legendary concert film *Woodstock* (1970) nine years earlier, worked with seven cameramen, including David Myers, one of the *Woodstock* cameramen, and the two men who had photographed his previous feature films: Michael Chapman (*Taxi Driver*, 1975) and Laszlo Kovacs (*New York, New York*, 1977), who chose fine-grain 35mm to capture the show. All songs, procedures, and camera movements were set to paper in a 300-page shooting script. The audience was barely shown, as the main focus was the action on stage, which was often shot in close-up. With a static camera and well-lit pictures, *The Last Waltz* turned into a concert film of feature quality, whose images offer us the irresistible opportunity to relish the youthful enthusiasm of Robbie Robertson, admire Blues legend Muddy Waters' remarkable gesticulations ("Mannish Boy"), and let Joni Mitchell's beautiful duet with Neil Young on "Helpless" send tingles down our spine. In his glittery pink suit, Van Morrison ("Caravan") initially cuts a weird if not ridiculous figure, but when he opens his mouth, he catapults straight from the clownish to the godlike. Jaws may drop at how beautifully schmaltz king, Neil Diamond ("Dry Your Eyes"), fits into the crown of this musical cosmos, and how pale the practically comatose Eric Clapton ("Further On Another Road") seems in contrast. And then there's that bizarre, gigantic white hat Bob Dylan's wearing – the only singer allowed two songs ("Forever Young," "Baby Let Me Follow You Down") – which must surely be one of the wilder sorts of mushroom. *The Last Waltz*: pure joy for movie buffs, ambrosia for rock fans.

HJK

4

5   Stage presence: Concert movies infuse their
    imagery with an air of authenticity.

6   A woman's touch: Country and western sweet-
    heart Emmylou Harris plays "Evangeline" in

one of two sequences that were edited into
the picture.

"Scorsese didn't let his experience working as a cameraman on Michael Wadleigh's *Woodstock* (1970) fall by the wayside."

San Francisco Examiner

NOSFERATU
Nosferatu – Phantom der Nacht / Nosferatu – Fantôme de la nuit

1978 - FRG / FRANCE - 107 MIN. - HORROR FILM, REMAKE

DIRECTOR WERNER HERZOG (*1942)
SCREENPLAY WERNER HERZOG, based on the novel *DRACULA* by BRAM STOKER, and on motifs from the film *NOSFERATU – EINE SYMPHONIE DES GRAUENS* (1922) by FRIEDRICH WILHELM MURNAU DIRECTOR OF PHOTOGRAPHY JÖRG SCHMIDT-REITWEIN
EDITING BEATE MAINKA-JELLINGHAUS MUSIC POPOL VUH, FLORIAN FRICKE PRODUCTION WERNER HERZOG, MICHAEL GRUSKOFF for WERNER HERZOG FILMPRODUKTION, GAUMONT.

STARRING KLAUS KINSKI (Count Dracula), ISABELLE ADJANI (Lucy Harker), BRUNO GANZ (Jonathan Harker), JACQUES DUFILHO (Captain), ROLAND TOPOR (Renfield), WALTER LADENGAST (Doctor Van Helsing), JAN GROTH (Harbormaster), CARSTEN BODINUS (Schrader), MARTJE GROHMANN (Mina), RIJK DE GOOYER (Official).

IFF BERLIN 1979 SILVER BEAR for BEST ART DIRECTION (Henning von Gierke).

"Your wife has a beautiful neck."

The camera crawls past a row of mummified corpses: to judge by their grimacing faces, most of these people died in terror. They look as if they had seen Death itself. Our flesh creeps to the funereal sounds of the German band Popol Vuh. Next image: a bat in slow-motion flight. Cut. A waxen-faced woman awakens with a start and releases a bloodcurdling scream.

Only dreaming...

Thus begins one of the most idiosyncratic vampire films of modern times. *Nosferatu* inhabits a world of dim, constricted spaces; extreme contrasts of light and dark give way to nearly monochrome images; long, static shots contrast with an almost hysterically unbridled handheld camera. The film is a cinematic homage to Murnau's dark and magical *Nosferatu – a Sym-*phony of Terror (*Nosferatu – Eine Symphonie des Grauens*, 1922), one of the earliest adaptations of Bram Stoker's *Dracula*.

In a dilapidated castle in the Carpathian Mountains, the sinister Count Dracula (Klaus Kinski) exists, or rather vegetates. Only Lucy (Isabelle Adjani), the beautiful wife of Jonathan Harker (Bruno Ganz) can free him from his terrible lethargy. The film begins with Lucy's nightmare, in which Dracula appears as a bat. She has a terrible foreboding that something dreadful is about to take its course, and that there's nothing she can do to stop it. Dracula has written to Renfield, a property agent, expressing his interest in an empty house in Wisborg, Lucy's hometown. It's the beginning of an inexorable courtship dance, which will end in the Count's demise.

2

3

"My head is one big garbage can where everything is jumbled around."

Klaus Kinski

Nosferatu is more than a skillful reworking of Murnau's film classic and Stoker's novel. Probably only Werner Herzog and his magnificent protagonist Klaus Kinski could have transformed this material into an apocalyptic vision of such unparalleled romantic intensity. Kinski's stylized interpretation of the vampire figure is an unforgettably powerful piece of acting. Take the scene when Dracula receives Jonathan Harker, who has been sent to the castle by Renfield to negotiate the sale of the house in Wisborg. Kinski is the first actor to show the terrifying melancholy at the heart of the Count's murderous obsession. Though the room is gloomy, lit only by candles, Dracula averts his deathly face as if in shame; yet his skinny fingers, with their claw-like nails, seem to reach out for Harker with a terrible life of their own. Jonathan soon falls victim to the undead Count, who can survive only by feeding on the blood of others.

Having placed Harker temporarily out of action, Dracula departs immediately for Wisborg – a pilgrimage to Lucy, from whom he hopes to acquire a new lease of life. He will arrive with an entourage of rats, bringing a plague epidemic to the solid and prosperous German town. In the delirium that follows, we are witness to an apocalyptic drama, a succession of grotesque and

1 The horrors of a bad manicure: Nosferatu (Klaus Kinski) is ready to scratch the eyes out of anyone who dare compare him to his predecessor, Max Schreck.

2 Bloodlust: Lucy (Isabelle Adjani) is precisely Nosferatu's taste.

3 Your kiss is on my list: Does Lucy have the courage to resist the touch of evil?

4 Struck down by the light of day: The Count cannot survive the sun's caress.

4

5   Lucy's premonition: Death is written in the wind.

6   The poetry of death: Nosferatu scuttles through the streets of a plagued city.

7   A man on a mission: Jonathan (Bruno Ganz) rides on to Wisborg.

"With this work, Herzog intended 'to forge a link to one of the great films of the German Expressionist era:' Fritz Murnau's 'symphony of horror,' made in 1921. Indeed, Herzog has laced his film with citations from this classic movie."

Frankfurter Allgemeine Zeitung

chilling scenes: an endless procession of coffins, choreographed like a dance of death; a table set for a feast among the rats, with the human guests vanishing in an instant by means of a simple cut. The horror that engulfs Wisborg could hardly be conveyed more poetically, or with a greater feeling for the sheer sadness of death. In the midst of this calamitous confusion, Lucy is the only person who knows what lies at the root of it all, and her nightmares are the source of her knowledge. But no-one will listen to her, not even Van Helsing, the local doctor, whose medical skills are no match for the mysterious powers he finds himself up against.

The film does a great deal more than simply quoting or imitating its predecessors. Herzog's *Nosferatu* casts an entirely new light on the old story. Aesthetically, the film is groundbreaking: the sparing use of dialog, the ethe-

real music, the strange images of the natural world and the claustrophobic treatment of space combine to create an eerie audio-visual *Gesamtkunstwerk* – a total work of art. In content, too, the film opens up new perspectives: unlike Murnau, Herzog depicts Lucy as an autonomous woman, sacrificing herself willingly to free Wisborg from Death's embrace. By pretending to find him attractive, she lures the Count to her bedroom, where she holds him at bay until dawn. The first rays of sunlight are enough to extinguish his life. In the end, however, Lucy's heroism is in vain; for Jonathan Harker, too, has struggled back to Wisborg – and he has become the new Dracula. In a symphony of hypnotic images and sounds, the film shows how the powers of darkness survive, as Jonathan rides towards the darkening horizon with his cloak billowing in the wind ... in search of new blood.

THE DRIVER

1978 - USA - 91 MIN. - ACTION FILM, THRILLER

DIRECTOR WALTER HILL (*1942)
SCREENPLAY WALTER HILL DIRECTOR OF PHOTOGRAPHY PHILIP H. LATHROP EDITING TINA HIRSCH, ROBERT K. LAMBERT MUSIC MICHAEL SMALL
PRODUCTION LAWRENCE GORDON for EMI FILMS LTD., 20TH CENTURY FOX.

STARRING RYAN O'NEAL (The Driver), BRUCE DERN (The Detective), ISABELLE ADJANI (The Player), RONEE BLAKELY
(The Agent), MATT CLARK (Red Plainclothesman), FELICE ORLANDI (Gold Plainclothesman), JOSEPH WALSH (Glasses),
RUDY RAMOS (Teeth), DENNY MACKO (Exchange Man), WILL WALKER (Fingers), SANDY BROWN WYETH (Split).

"I respect a man who's good at what he does. I'll tell you something else: I'm very good at what I do."

The streets and the garages are his turf. Director Walter Hill wastes no time in getting to the point in the very first scene of *The Driver*: cars are the calling of his hero – his manifest destiny. The Driver (Ryan O'Neal), an experienced getaway gangster, enters an underground parking garage. He inspects his surroundings, walks confidently to a car and jimmies the lock in a matter of seconds. After a quick look at the steering wheel, he starts the engine. The Driver was put on this Earth for one reason only: to drive. The audience need know no more about this man, and true enough we do effectively learn nothing else about him in the 90 min. still to come. He has no name, no past, and

carries no emotional baggage. He has found his place in life in the driver seat. He looks out of place in the cheap hotel rooms in which he disappea after his jobs. His nemesis, the Detective (Bruce Dern), remains equally i distinct. What connects the two men is the obsession with which they follo their goals. They seldom laugh, and are almost fanatically driven, a chara teristic that will unite them in the end.

The plot of *The Driver* is as minimalist as its characterization: th Driver commits crimes for which the Detective tries to nab him. The du that develops from this constellation, though it provides for several twis

1 Cloak and dagger: The detective (Bruce Dern) will catch the driver if it kills him, and it just may.

2 A game of cat and mouse: Poker-faced player (Isabelle Adjani) doesn't give anything away.

3 All revved up with nowhere to go: The driver (Ryan O'Neal) earns a living driving getaway cars.

nd turns, can be reduced to a game of cat and mouse between two men. This game is the springboard for the entire story – even extending to the mbiguous relationship both men have with the same woman (Isabelle djani). Nothing distracts from the game: the scenery – streets, garages, warehouses, and bars – almost all are set in the desolate, nocturnal me-opolis, and remain just as abstract as the characters. The dramatization enounces fancy camerawork and clever editing, and the spartan dia-logue matches the tight-mouthed style of its protagonists, who never waste or mince their words. During their encounters, the Detective calls the Driver a cowboy, a comparison that astutely picks up on the Western-like plot and style of this Walter Hill big city ballad. And true to the best of the West, the piece culminates in a classic showdown between the rival gun-slingers, as their two cars face off with one another before they race to the finish.

"By the end of *The Driver* you can almost smell the rubber burning."

Variety

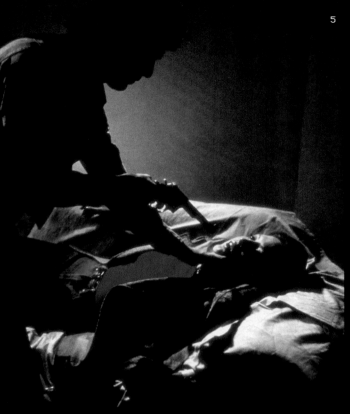

Hill skillfully combines these stylistic elements with components from Film Noir and the thriller – just as he would later do with *Streets of Fire* (1984) and *Last Man Standing* (1996): manipulation and bold tactical moves govern the game on both sides. The Driver understands the risks he takes. He is fully aware that the Detective will set a trap for him. That he ultimately agrees to the duel is a question of honor: the Detective openly challenges him: "If you win, you'll get some money. If I win, you'll get 15 years." To emerge victorious you not only have to be a real gambler, you've got to be in full command of the game.

Part of this game are the breathtaking chases: legions of faceless policemen appear on the street from nowhere and pursue the Driver, fail to match his driving skills, and vanish into nothingness. As a director's assistant or Peter Yates' *Bullitt* (1968), Walter Hill attentively peered over his shoulder and – together with stunt coordinator Everett Creach – used what he learned to choreograph several chase sequences in *The Driver*. These sequences heavily influenced the genre and are still cited today in movies like John Frankenheimer's *Ronin* (1998). Hill's stylistic and dramatic ambition is unmistakably present in films like *Vanishing Point* (1970) and *The Sugarland Express* (1974), where the spiritual home of the hero was always an automobile. But despite such sensational action sequences, and scattered eruptions of violence (which however are always necessary: the Driver kills only when he is left with no other choice), *The Driver* is a calm, easygoing film. The adversaries secretly observe one another, and the audience follows suit by observing how the characters are forced to react under extreme pressure. And as witnesses, the audience also becomes part of the game.   ES

4   Four eyes on the target: gangster Glasses
    (Joseph Walsh) arouses the driver's wrath.

5   A criminal constitution: Bullets provide an exit
    when there's no way out.

6   Recovery ward: Between jobs the driver recuperates in dreary motel rooms. And like a true outlaw he has no past, no friends and no home.

"There's a nightmarish thrill to the chase sequences and the claustrophobic underworld of subterranean parking lots." *film-dienst*

WALTER HILL   Walter Hill, born January 10, 1942 in Long Beach, California, is considered a solid craftsman among Hollywood's mainstream filmmakers. But this does director, author, and producer Walter Hill, only partial justice. Walter Hill belongs to the small group of action film virtuosos who made their mark on the genre in the 1970s and 1980s. After he got his foot in the film industry door, among other jobs as the second directorial assistant for *The Thomas Crown Affair* (1968), Hill wrote screenplays, including the script for Sam Peckinpah's *The Getaway* (1972). He made his directorial debut in 1975 with the action drama *Hard Times / The Streetfighter*. His two subsequent films, *The Driver* (1978) and the street gang drama *The Warriors* (1978) helped form his visual and narrative style. Hill straightforwardly dramatized his bitter stories of broken men with no frills. His characters are not big talkers, they are defined by their actions – a tradition from which he deviated only in buddy movies like *48 Hrs.* (1982), in which Nick Nolte doesn't shoot anywhere near as quickly as Eddie Murphy runs his mouth.

Otherwise Walter Hill dramatized brilliant, taciturn and brutal "guy movies" that only seldom offered women a main role: *Southern Comfort* (1981) is his answer to John Boorman's *Deliverance* (1972), *Streets of Fire* (1984) a fascinating symbiosis of Western myths and big city ballad, and *Extreme Prejudice* (1987) a macho Western in modern dress. Hill displayed his proclivity for the most American of all film genres in the Westerns *The Long Riders* (1980), *Geronimo: An American Legend* (1993), and *Wild Bill* (1995). And his final masterpiece, *Last Man Standing* (1996), a remake of Akira Kurosawa's *Yojimbo* (1961), also breathes the spirit of the stoic Western hero. In 1989 Walter Hill exhibited a much more humorous side for a television project: he was one of the producers of the self-consciously ironic horror series *Tales from the Crypt*.

AUTUMN SONATA
Höstsonaten

1978 - FRG / FRANCE / SWEDEN - 93 MIN. - DRAMA

DIRECTOR INGMAR BERGMAN (*1918)
SCREENPLAY INGMAR BERGMAN DIRECTOR OF PHOTOGRAPHY SVEN NYKVIST EDITING SYLVIA INGEMARSSON MUSIC JOHANN SEBASTIAN BACH, FRÉDÉRIC CHOPIN, GEORG FRIEDRICH HÄNDEL, ROBERT SCHUMANN PRODUCTION KATINKA FARAGÓ for PERSONAFILM, FILMÉDIS, SUEDE FILM.

STARRING INGRID BERGMAN (Charlotte), LIV ULLMANN (Eva), LENA NYMAN (Helena), HALVAR BJÖRK (Viktor), MARIANNE AMINOFF (Charlotte's Private Secretary), ARNE BANG-HANSEN (Uncle Otto), GEORG LØKKEBERG (Leonardo), ERLAND JOSEPHSON (Josef), LINN ULLMANN (Eva As A Child), GUNNAR BJÖRNSTRAND (Paul).

"Does one never stop hoping?"

When *Autumn Sonata* was first released, many reviewers spoke of the film as Ingmar Bergman's "homecoming." Though Bergman was at that time still exiled in Germany as the result of a tax dispute (*Autumn Sonata* was a German co-production made in Norway), the film did indeed mark a kind of artistic homecoming. For here – immediately after *The Serpent's Egg* (1977), his "big" movie on the rise of Nazism in 1920s Germany – Bergman returns to the form of the chamber piece, and to his "traditional" subject-matter: the spiritual plight of two individuals trapped in a deadly love-hate relationship.

Autumn Sonata tells the story of a mother-and-daughter reunion after a separation lasting seven years. Following the death of her companion, Leonardo (Georg Løkkeberg), the celebrated concert pianist Charlotte (Ingrid Bergman) is invited by her daughter Eva (Liv Ullmann) to spend a few weeks with her and her husband Viktor (Halvar Björk). Viktor is a pastor, and he and Eva live in a small parish in a remote region of Norway. There is little in the way of external action, and Bergman constructs the story like a three-act play: Act One: the arrival of the mother in the parsonage; Act Two: a protracted dispute between Eva and Charlotte, staged as a double monolog; Act

Three: a kind of cross-cut epilog, depicting the restoration of the women's original relationship: a phony peace based on lies and repression.

The film is a symphony of false notes. Even in the short prolog, in which Viktor talks of his wife and their life together, the pastor is forced to relativize his claim that they're happy and content. For Eva is incapable of love and mistrusts any expression of warmth. This dissonance continues in Eva's letter of invitation to her mother. Though she writes affectionately of her "dearest little mother," they've in fact spent years avoiding each other – and Eva wouldn't even have known of Leonardo's demise if someone else hadn't informed her of the fact. Finally, the lies culminate in an effusively cordial welcome, in which a torrent of words and gesticulations merely serves to conceal the fear and desolation at the heart of their relationship.

At first glance, mother and daughter could hardly be more different: Ingrid Bergman plays Charlotte as an elegant star in a stylish trouser-suit crowned with a hairdo that might be cast in concrete, she chatters airily of concert tours and meetings with the international jet set. Charlotte is always her own favorite topic of conversation, and some of her scenes are not with

2

1 Chopsticks: Chopin preludes in a country parsonage. Eva's (Liv Ullmann) uncertainty provokes a harsh reaction from her mother.

2 Music of the heart: Cool, masterly and perfect in every detail, Charlotte's (Ingrid Bergman) Chopin interpretations reflect her dealings with her daughter.

3 Etudes in black: Two monologues don't make a dialogue.

4 Mommie dearest: Eva's ruined childhood is a burden on her marriage to the parson Viktor (Halvar Björk).

"The intertwining of love and hate is the key to all intimate human relationships, perhaps most especially – for all sorts of mysterious primal reasons – the relationship between mother and daughter. No artist in any medium today has a greater genius for expressing that deepest human tension than Ingmar Bergman." *Newsweek*

out a certain wicked humor: thus she sashays up to the parsonage dinner-table in a red Yves-St.-Laurent dress, and lies awake in bed worrying where to invest her millions.

During the great nocturnal quarrel between Eva and Charlotte, the façade starts to show its cracks. Bergman and his cameraman Sven Nykvist shot this scene almost entirely in intense close-ups of the women's faces – in stark contrast to the distancing effect of the rigid long shots in the flash-backs to Eva's childhood. When Eva accuses her mother of lovelessness and egotism, Charlotte's sophistication gives way to increasing uncertainty. While she's forced to recognize that she's built her life on the illusion of being a good mother, she's angered that Eva would dare to place her in the wrong.

There's plenty of room for speculation about what motivates Eva, the frumpy parson's wife with the braided hair and the metal-rimmed spectacles. It's probably too much to say she invited her mother as a coolly planned act of revenge. Whenever she meets Charlotte, Eva involuntarily moves and talks like a timid child that yearns for recognition; yet at the same time, she provokes disappointment in order to have her hatred confirmed. In one superb scene, Eva plays some Chopin preludes on the piano – a little clumsily, almost as if she's challenging her mother to criticize her. Finally, Charlotte takes her place at the instrument, puts the music away, and plays to perfection – all the time lecturing her daughter on the difference between feeling and sentimentality.

Eva heaps blame on her mother, and her accusations are undoubtedly monstrous. In her view, Charlotte is responsible for practically everything bad that ever happened to her – or to her sister Helena (Lena Nyman), a handicapped girl who does little more than vegetate. Yet Eva's icy cruelty is ultimately no more than a mirror image of Charlotte's superficiality. Despite the differences, they share many fundamental similarities.

After Charlotte's departure, Eva sends her mother a conciliatory letter. Some critics have seen this as a sign of hope, a crumb of comfort from the director to his audience. Yet the tone of this missive recalls the invitation she had written at the start of the film. And all the while, we see her mother engaged, as ever, in trivial chitchat with her agent. At the very end, Bergman grants each of his protagonists a final close-up: the women's faces are so haggard as to seem almost destroyed. Clearly, nothing has changed.

LP

LIV ULLMANN In 1939, Liv Ullmann was born in Tokyo to Norwegian parents. From the mid-50s onwards, she enjoyed a successful career in the theater, starting work at the National Theater in Oslo in 1960. Her breakthrough as an international film star came in 1966, with the role of the silenced actress Elisabeth Vogler in Ingmar Bergman's classic psychodrama, *Persona*. In the years that followed, she became the Swedish director's favorite actress – and his real-life partner. For him, she created a series of highly complex portraits of modern women. In films such as *Hour of the Wolf* (*Vargtimmen*, 1967), *Shame* (*Skammen*, 1968), *The Passion of Anna* (*En Passion*, 1969), *Cries and Whispers* (*Viskningar och rop*, 1972), *Scenes From A Marriage* (*Scener ur ett äktenskap*, 1973) and *Face to Face* (*Ansikte mot ansikte*, 1976), she combined a disarming naturalness with a broad emotional spectrum. Thanks to the name she had made as a Bergman protagonist, the 70s saw her appear in several Hollywood productions – but mostly without great success. Her most notable roles in non-Bergman films were in collaboration with his fellow-Swede Jan Troell: in *The Emigrants* (*Utvandrarna*, 1971) and *The New Land* (*Nybyggarna*, 1971), she played a farmer's wife who moves to America. Besides her work in the cinema, Ullmann has always continued to pursue her theater career. She also writes books and screenplays. Since 1992, she has directed three movies and a film for TV, all of which were very well received.

DAWN OF THE DEAD / ZOMBIE: DAWN OF THE DEAD

1978 - USA / ITALY - 126 MIN. / 137 MIN. (Director's cut) - HORROR FILM

DIRECTOR GEORGE A. ROMERO (*1940)
SCREENPLAY GEORGE A. ROMERO, DARIO ARGENTO **DIRECTOR OF PHOTOGRAPHY** MICHAEL GORNICK **EDITING** GEORGE A. ROMERO
MUSIC DARIO ARGENTO, THE GOBLINS, AGOSTINO MARANGOLO, MASSIMO MORANTE, FABIO PIGNATELLI, GEORGE A. ROMERO (Director's Cut), CLAUDIO SIMONETTI **PRODUCTION** DARIO ARGENTO, RICHARD P. RUBINSTEIN for LAUREL GROUP.

STARRING DAVID EMGE (Stephen Andrews), KEN FOREE (Peter Washington), SCOTT H. REINIGER (Roger DeMarco), GAYLEN ROSS (Francine Parker), DAVID CRAWFORD (Doctor Foster), DAVID EARLY (Mr. Berman), RICHARD FRANCE (Doctor Milliard Rausch), HOWARD SMITH (TV Commentator), JESSE DEL GRE (Priest), FRED BAKER (Police Commander).

"Who the hell cares. Let's go shopping first."

Dawn of the Dead doesn't exactly go easy on its viewers. Terror immediately lunges into the opening shot, dominated by an unsteady camera and distorted voices. It is a portrait of disorientation, clearly indicating that a state of emergency has broken out in the USA. An epidemic is spreading like wildfire that turns humans into the living dead. When police squadrons storm a house in Puerto Rico, annihilating not only zombies but also massacring a large number of healthy humans in cold blood, there is no more denying it: America is at war.

Stephen (David Emge) and his girlfriend Francine (Gaylen Ross), both television station employees, have lost all faith in social cohesion and in the government's ability to uphold law and order. Along with SWAT team sharpshooter Peter (Ken Foree) and his friend Roger (Scott H. Reiniger), they make up their minds to flee the chaos of the city by helicopter, leaving their fellow citizens to fend for themselves. The zombies, however, are everywhere. The four take flight from this perished civilization not to hit ground in undiscovered country, but rather on the roof of a surrounded Pennsylvania shopping center. They quickly barricade themselves inside the mall and even

succeed in shutting out the entire contingency of living dead. The plentiful supply of goods within their citadel allows the human crusaders to maintain the illusions of the life they left behind them. That is, until Stephen and Roger fall prey to the undead, making antiheroes of the pregnant Francine and the African American Peter who quickly abort "Consumer Island" and head off in their helicopter towards an uncertain future.

Dawn of the Dead's gratuitous violence, something the critics couldn't stop talking about at the time of the movie's original release, is an unmistakable sign that the Age of Aquarius and its Utopian dreams were suddenly a thing of the past. In its place we find the jarring pessimism of the late 1970s, brought on to a great extent as a response to U.S. involvement in the Vietnam War. Romero's film expands on this American trauma of the last fifteen years. Tom Savini, who created the movie's special effects, worked as a battlefield photographer in Vietnam and drew from his endless experience with manifestations of violence. Nonetheless, the actual source of this piece's "horror" is the emotional numbness and egotism of its main characters.

Stephen, Francine, Peter and Roger block out all traces of the looming apocalypse upon them and help themselves to the shopping center's commodities. In doing so, they forge a pristine world, a veritable hedonistic wonderland, which they are willing to defend at all costs. Unlike many other works born out of this genre, the supernatural beings do not manifest themselves as the terrifying pawns of some greater power. Instead, they are intended to function primarily as an out-and-out critique on capitalism. The scenes in which the zombies mindlessly wander about the mall, as if commanded by remote control, hold up a mirror to the face of Middle America. Despite their insatiable hunger, the undead, who nourish themselves exclusively on human flesh, are remarkably passive and often do not appear to pose any physical danger. Additionally, these ungodly creatures represent the

"When the world is falling apart there are no heroes, only the need for self-preservation."

Films in Review

1 In your head: Stephen (David Emge) and Francine (Gaylen Ross) wonder where the zombies will turn up next...

2 Open for business. It's unclear whether the zombies are hungry for human flesh or mall merchandise.

3 Nowhere to run to: You can flee to the sales all you want – there's still nowhere to hide.

4

4 Breeding on a jet plane: As humanity's last
   remnants, Francine, Stephen and Roger

(Scott H. Reiniger) escape on a helicopter in
search of the undiscovered country.

5 Shop till you drop: Chain store bargains can't buy
   me love.

GEORGE A. ROMERO American director and screenwriter George A. Romero was born in the New York Bronx in 1940. He studied art, design and theater at Carnegie
Mellon University in Pittsburgh. His *Zombie Trilogy* (1968, 1978, 1985) turned him into a household name and sparked an onset of offspring by
other filmmakers. Romero's directorial debut, *Night of the Living Dead* (1968), was a radical departure from many of the established conventions
of Hollywood movies. In addition to its staunch critique on American politics, the film's underlying tone is one of pessimism and despair.
This was also the case for the sequels *Dawn of the Dead / Zombie: Dawn of the Dead* (1978) and *Day of the Dead* (1985). Romero's later works
included less remarkable stints in television, although he did collaborate with Stephen King in the 1980s on two projects. The first, *Creepshow*
(1982), was a horror movie anthology that lacked the sizzle of his earlier works, and the second was a rather high-profile production entitled *The
Dark Half* (1992/93). George A. Romero works from time to time as an actor and, despite breaking all the rules, follows in Hitchcock's tradition
of making cameo appearances in his own movies. In his zombie trilogy he played a reporter, the C.E.O. of a television station and a member of
the living dead, respectively.

army of the impoverished, who have not only been shut off from con-
sumerism, but have also been declared as inhuman so that they may be jus-
tifiably eliminated. Even Romero's first zombie movie, *Night of the Living
Dead* (1968), voiced strong social criticism against issues like racism in
American society. In that earlier picture, Ben, an African American serving as
the group's human leader, was the only one to survive the plague of the undead, only to be murdered by the white civilian army. *Dawn of the Dead* expands on this aspect and explores how readily people throw morality to the
wind when self-interest is at stake. The film is, therefore, significantly more
powerful than its predecessor in the assertion that "we must stop the killing
or lose the war."

5

MANHATTAN

1979 - USA - 96 MIN. - COMEDY

DIRECTOR WOODY ALLEN (*1935)
SCREENPLAY WOODY ALLEN, MARSHALL BRICKMAN DIRECTOR OF PHOTOGRAPHY GORDON WILLIS EDITING SUSAN E. MORSE MUSIC GEORGE GERSHWIN PRODUCTION CHARLES H. JOFFE for JACK ROLLINS & CHARLES H. JOFFE PRODUCTIONS.

STARRING WOODY ALLEN (Isaac Davis), DIANE KEATON (Mary Wilkie), MICHAEL MURPHY (Yale), MARIEL HEMINGWAY (Tracy), MERYL STREEP (Jill), ANNE BYRNE (Emily), KAREN LUDWIG (Connie), MICHAEL O'DONOGHUE (Dennis), WALLACE SHAWN (Jeremiah), KENNY VANCE (TV Producer).

"I think people should mate for life, like pigeons or Catholics."

Isaac (Woody Allen) and Tracy (Mariel Hemingway) are a couple. However, since she's only 17 and he's pushing 43, Isaac sees no future prospects for the two of them. "I want you to enjoy me, my wry sense of humor, and astonishing sexual technique, but don't forget you have your whole life in front of you." He dare not term what they have between them as love, instead insisting that it would be better if Tracy regarded him as more of a detour on the highway of her life.

At the end of the day, Isaac has enough problems of his own as it is. His second ex-wife, who left him for another woman, is in the process of writing a book about their failed marriage. Even his job as a comedy writer is anything but pleasurable as his true aspiration is to write a novel and establish himself as a serious artist. Acting on a rash impulse, Isaac resigns from his lucrative job in television, which in turn forces him to give up his apartment

and reduce the monthly income he allocates his parents. "This is going to kill my father. He's not going to have as good a seat at the synagogue. He'll have to sit at the back, away from God."

One of the few guiding lights that remain in the midst of Isaac's midlife crisis is his friend Yale (Michael Murphy), who surprisingly confides in the writer about his own infidelity. Isaac just can't come to terms with it, and especially not after he happens to run into Yale's mistress, Mary (Diane Keaton), at the Museum of Modern Art. The woman proceeds to praise a cluster of steel cubes to the skies, quite possibly the most revolting exhibition piece Isaac has ever laid eyes on. "To me it was really textural, it was perfectly integrated, and it had a marvelous sort of negative capability. The rest of the stuff downstairs was bullshit." This type of pseudo-intellectual mumbo jumbo is just the kind of crap Isaac can't stand – at least initially.

Anyone who thinks that first impressions are invariably correct clearly never met these two, for little by little romance blossoms between Mary and Isaac. The affair itself is afforded some of the film's most beautiful imagery, including the oft-cited sunrise scene, in which the two Manhattanites are taken aback by the majesty of the 58th St. Bridge and discuss their deep mutual affection for New York on the riverbank. The scene turns cosmic soon thereafter, when Isaac and Mary seek sanctuary from an incoming storm at the Hayden Planetarium; backlighting accompanied by black and white photography transform them to flirting silhouettes and floating celestial shadows, lifting these two loving souls to new levels of sublimity.

After Yale breaks off his affair with Mary, she turns to Isaac for comfort and succumbs to his charms. Before long, he calls it quits with

"Why is life worth living? It's a very good question. Um… Well, There are certain things I guess that make it worthwhile. Uh… like what… okay… um… For me, uh… ooh… I would say… what, Groucho Marx, to name one thing… uh… um… and Willie Mays… and um… the second movement of the Jupiter Symphony… and um… Louis Armstrong, recording of Potato Head Blues… um… Swedish movies, naturally… *A Sentimental Education* by Flaubert… uh… Marlon Brando, Frank Sinatra… um… those incredible apples and pears by Cezanne… uh… the crabs at Sam Wo's… uh… Tracy's face…" *Film quote: Isaac*

1 The May December romance: Sweet young Tracy (Mariel Hemingway) meets old curmudgeon Isaac (Woody Allen).

2 Mixed-up mother goose: Ex-wife Jill (Meryl Streep) is just about ready to break Isaac's crown.

3 Shadow selves: The characters' gestures and attitudes seem out of sync with the small talk.

4 Mary, Mary, quite contrary: Isaac is subject to extreme mood swings. In the midst of all the emotional turbulence, he can't be sure whether he loves or hates Mary (Diane Keaton).

NEW YORK AS A HOLLYWOOD BACKDROP

Be it *Ghostbusters* (1984), *Three Days of the Condor* (1975), *Sleepless in Seattle* (1993), John Carpenter's *Escape from New York* (1981) or Hitchcock's *Rear Window* (1954), the Big Apple plays an integral role in countless Hollywood films but has itself never been awarded the Oscar. The great U.S. metropolis served as the birthplace of the American cinema in 1896 when Thomas Edison unveiled his moving picture producing "vitascope" on the corner of 34th St. and 6th Avenue in front of Macy's department store. This new marvel of technology quickly attracted enthusiasts like Edwin S. Porter, who is deemed today to be the inventor of film editing and who shot such film hits as *The Great Train Robbery* (1903) with Edison's equipment. There is, however, no denying the film industry's 1914 mass exodus to California, where more space, better weather as well as the peace and quiet essential for the talkies that would come were in abundance. Nonetheless, a great deal of the production companies' administrative and executive offices could still be found in New York for years to come.

Ironically, its climb to fame in front of the camera accompanied the filmmakers' departure from the city. Many screenwriters of the day had resided in the East Coast magnet of urban life and began to produce scripts about the place they knew best. The 1930s saw Hollywood set designers recreating New York City streets, subway stations, bars and even the megalithic skyline whenever called for. The result gave rise to a larger than life image of the town perfumed by the futuristic allure of concepts like "Gotham" and "Metropolis." New York gradually gained mythical character. By many, it was regarded as a modern day Sodom and Gomorrah that would just as soon crush a man as crown him.

Following the end of the World War II, the camera began to return to its actual streets in search of an authenticity inspired by the documentary footage of wartime newsreels and European neorealism. Such was the case when Billy Wilder had Ray Milland walk down the real 3rd Avenue in his *Lost Weekend* (1945) instead of on an artificial Hollywood set. This "return to reality" reclaimed a stronghold on the Hudson River and allowed new film studios that lacked true movie lots of their own to appear on the scene. In particular, the New York based United Artists started to reap some of the sweetest harvests in its company's history. Yet somehow the negative stigma associated with the city lived on at the movies, even in comedies. In the large number of *Superman* and *King Kong* flicks, it continued to represent the bastion of human civilization; in Billy Wilder's classic, *The Apartment* (1960), it embodied isolation and anonymity, whereas *Serpico* (1973) and *Taxi Driver* (1975) branded it the hub of vice and corruption. When one stops to consider the directors who have shown the town's direct impact on their lives through film, the names Sidney Lumet, Martin Scorsese, Spike Lee and Woody Allen immediately come to mind. Of these, Allen stands alone in consistently painting an overwhelmingly positive portrait of the city that has never let go of his heart.

young Tracy and for the blink of an eye appears to have arrived victoriously in the winner's circle. His dreams are crushed before he even he has time to take it all in, as Mary brushes him off to try her luck once more with Yale.

The endearingly neurotic characters, led by Isaac, are like atomic particles buzzing about with their constant quips and puns, randomly encountering one another in restaurants or museums, only to lose each other again for no good reason. Adding some zing to the tune of these often off-beat paramours, director Allen zaps the television and film industry with a few volts of Jewish kvetching and deadpan. "Years ago I wrote a short story about my mother. It was called 'The Castrating Zionist'."Allen once stated in an interview that *Manhattan* was an attempt to blend the comedy of *Annie Hall*

"A masterpiece that has become a film of the ages by not seeking to become a film of the moment. The only true great film of the 1970s."

Andrew Sarris

5   The whole kit and caboodle: Sporting a wife and a
    perfect life, Yale (Michael Murphy) seems to be
    everything Isaac isn't.

6   All the wrong moves: Feigning seductive
    nonchalance on a romantic boat trip with Mary,
    Isaac lets his hand drift casually through the
    water – and it's soon dripping with something
    brown and slimy…

7   Showered with affection: From the MOMA to the
    Planetarium, every inch of Manhattan holds some
    sentimental value for Woody Allen.

1977) with the seriousness of *Interiors* (1978), his thoroughly unsuccessful
ribute to Ingmar Bergman. By abstaining from the forked-tongue satire and
iorn-honking yuck-yuck jokes that stole scenes in previous works like *Ba-
ianas* (1971) and *Everything You Always Wanted to Know About Sex – But
Were Afraid to Ask* (1972), the eternal neurotic and one-time stand-up comic
:reated a subdued yet amusing drama that contemplates the romantic
nelancholy surrounding 1970s urbanites.

As their appointed knight, Isaac battles the dragons of 60s free love and
the ensuing sexual indifference from behind a shield of self-pity and cynicism
on his infernally frustrating quest for true love. Yet when the over-the-hill
nebbish stands before Tracy like a schoolboy with a crush at the film's conclusion, we are struck by both the vulnerability and the heroic tragedy of his
character. It is this heartfelt truthfulness that continues to fill the spectator
with joy during each and every subsequent viewing.   APO

ALIEN

1979 - GREAT BRITAIN / USA - 117 MIN. - HORROR FILM, SCIENCE FICTION

DIRECTOR RIDLEY SCOTT (*1937)

SCREENPLAY DAN O'BANNON, RONALD SHUSETT DIRECTOR OF PHOTOGRAPHY DEREK VANLINT EDITING TERRY RAWLINGS, PETER WEATHERLEY MUSIC JERRY GOLDSMITH PRODUCTION GORDON CARROLL, DAVID GILER, WALTER HILL for 20TH CENTURY FOX, BRANDYWINE PRODUCTIONS LTD.

STARRING TOM SKERRITT (Dallas), SIGOURNEY WEAVER (Ripley), VERONICA CARTWRIGHT (Lambert), HARRY DEAN STANTON (Brett), JOHN HURT (Kane), IAN HOLM (Ash), YAPHET KOTTO (Parker), BOLAJI BEDEJO (Alien).

ACADEMY AWARDS 1979 OSCAR for BEST SPECIAL EFFECTS (H. R. Giger, Carlo Rambaldi, Brian Johnson, Nick Allder, Denys Ayling).

"In space no one can hear you scream."

The late 70s were overrun by the science fiction film, a trend that had begun with George Lucas' *Star Wars* (1977). Consequently, when Ridley Scott's *Alien* was released in theaters in 1979, the producers confidently expected the film to attract attention. But audiences were somewhat surprised: the film did not contain impressive space battles, but centered on the almost futile struggle of average, fallible humans against an eerie being, the like of which had never been seen before. *Alien* was pure horror set in outer space – the logical combination of two film genres.

The story takes place somewhere in the near future on the commercial trade space ship "Nostromo," which is on its way back to Earth filled with cargo. The seven-member crew, among them Captain Dallas (Tom Skerritt), his deputy, Ripley (Sigourney Weaver), and helmswoman Lambert (Veronica Cartwright), routinely go about their daily business. No one wastes a minute thinking about the dangers that might be hidden in outer space. But their routine is interrupted by an emergency signal from a planet previously thought to be uninhabited. There, Dallas, Kane (John Hurt) and Lambert find an empty space ship with a hold full of strange eggs. A ghastly being jumps from one of the eggs and attaches itself to Kane's face, wher it remains stuck, as though almost welded to his skin. Back on their ship the crew determine that the strange being can't be removed from the vic tim's face. But just a short time later it falls off by itself. The danger seems t have been averted. A deadly meal then ensues. As the crew sit down to ea we initially believe that Kane's hunger is a sign of his recovery, until a dis gusting beast pierces its way through his chest and disappears like ligh ning into the ventilation shafts of the Nostromo. Clearly the "Alien" trans forms its outer appearance during its development and the crew realize tha they are going to have to kill the monster before it gets them. One crew mem ber after the other falls victim to this mysterious being. When Captain Dalla is also killed, Ripley takes command of the ship. She learns the true reaso for their mission from the ship's computer, "Mother." Their corporation o Earth knowingly misled the crew in order to get their hands on one of th aliens.

Sigourney Weaver, who also played the main role in the three seque (1986, 1992, 1997) is initially an unsympathetic figure in *Alien*. Consequentl

1 All systems operational: Second officer Ripley performing a routine maintenance check.

2 Space bait: A member of the Nostromo investigates the alien distress signal and comes down with a case of indigestion.

3 Shoot the moon: Screenwriter Dan O'Bannon is the veritable bard of futuristic space voyages. In addition to working on *Alien 3 & 4*, he chartered the waters for *Screamers* (Canada/USA, 1995) and John Carpenter's cult classic *Dark Star* (USA, 1974).

4 Regaining consciousness: An alien distress signal leads Mother to wake up her Nostromo crew. Only when it is too late does Ripley realize that the "cry for help" is actually an ominous warning…

"When, as a director, you are offered a project like *Alien* – or any science-fiction-film, really – it is an offer to start with and becomes a confrontation afterwards." *Ridley Scott, in: American Cinematographer*

he camera depicts her from a slightly low angle during the first half of the ilm. She acts in a "manly" fashion and refuses to allow herself to be gov-erned by her emotions. She has no sense of humor and follows the rules y the book, while the other crew members behave helpfully and interact harmoniously. When she is left as the lone survivor, she attributes it to her udgment. In what is literally the last minute she finally manages to blow up he "Nostromo" and thereby destroy the alien.

Alien was Ridley Scott's second feature film after *The Duellists* (1977), nd its success instantly catapulted him into the first rank of Hollywood ilmmakers. Today his film is regarded as a milestone in the history of iorror, applauded with numerous imitations and frequent emulation over the ollowing decades. Scott's recipe for success is based on his preference for

5

H. R. GIGER The Swiss artist Hans Ruedi Giger was born on 5 February 1940 in Chur. Initially he worked for several years as a construction artist and began studying industrial design at the Zurich School of Arts and Crafts in 1962. After graduating in 1966, Geiger worked as a freelance artist, sculptor, and furniture designer for the renowned production company Knoll. In 1967 he met the actress Li Tober, with whom he lived until her suicide in 1975. In 1969 he designed his first "biomechanical" monsters for Fredi M. Murer's thirty-minute film *Swissmade – 2069*. Erotically sinister machine fantasies would soon become his trademark. At the end of 1977 Giger met his future wife, Mia, whom he divorced in 1982. After contacts with director Alejandro Jodorowsky, for whom he later created the world of the Harkonnen in David Lynch's *Dune* (1984), he was brought aboard the *Alien,* which won an Oscar for Best Special Effects in 1980.

 In addition to his work on other films, including David Fincher's *Alien 3* (1992), Roger Donaldson's *Species* (1995), Jean-Pierre Jeunet's *Alien: Resurrection* (1997), and Peter Medak's *Species II* (1998), Giger designed album covers for bands like Blondie, Emerson, Lake & Palmer, and Danzig. He has run the Giger-Bar in Zurich since 1992 for which he even designed the furniture himself. Giger has been together with Carmen Maria Scheifele y de Vega since 1996, and lives and works in Zurich.

subtle horror as opposed to roaring action scenes. In *Alien*, one can detect intimations of the dark, cyber-punk vision the director would demonstrate three years later with *Blade Runner* (1982). From the beginning of the film, Jerry Goldsmith's soundtrack, as rousing as it is oppressive, and Derek Vanlint's slow-motion-like camera movements through the spaceship create a sinister and torturous atmosphere, gradually compressing into pure claustrophobic terror in the last third of the film. The monstrous "Alien," created by H. R. Giger, combines the characteristics of a living organism and a machine – the organic and the inorganic. Blood does not flow through its veins, but corrosive acid. It is surely one of the most terrifying monsters in film history.

APO

"It's an old-fashioned scare movie about something that is not only implacably evil but prone to jumping at you when (the movie hopes) you least expect it." *The New York Times*

5 The A-Team's newest warrior: "Its structural perfection is matched only by its hostility."

6 Raising Cain: The baby alien hatches out of Kane's belly. Unfortunately, the proud mother dies during childbirth.

7 Lip locked: Defying Ripley's orders, Kane is brought back on board the Nostromo along with the alien object hugging his face. Interestingly, Walter Hill was originally signed to direct Alien, but soon passed the baton on to Ridley Scott.

7

THE TIN DRUM
Die Blechtrommel / Le Tambour

1979 - FRG / FRANCE / POLAND / YUGOSLAVIA - 145 MIN. - LITERARY ADAPTATION, DRAMA

DIRECTOR VOLKER SCHLÖNDORFF (*1939)
SCREENPLAY JEAN-CLAUDE CARRIÈRE, VOLKER SCHLÖNDORFF, FRANZ SEITZ, based on the novel of the same name by GÜNTER GRASS DIRECTOR OF PHOTOGRAPHY IGOR LUTHER EDITING SUZANNE BARON MUSIC MAURICE JARRE, FRIEDRICH MEYER PRODUCTION FRANZ SEITZ, ANATOLE DAUMAN for BIOSKOP FILM, ARTÉMIS PRODUCTIONS, ARGOS FILMS, HALLELUJAH FILMS.

STARRING DAVID BENNENT (Oskar Matzerath), ANGELA WINKLER (Agnes Matzerath), MARIO ADORF (Alfred Matzerath), DANIEL OLBRYCHSKI (Jan Bronski), KATHARINA THALBACH (Maria), HEINZ BENNENT (Greff), ANDRÉA FERRÉOL (Lina Greff), CHARLES AZNAVOUR (Sigismund Markus), MARIELLA OLIVERI (Roswitha), ILSE PAGÉ (Gretchen Scheffler), OTTO SANDER (The Musician Meyn).

ACADEMY AWARDS 1979 OSCAR for BEST FOREIGN FILM.

IFF CANNES 1979 GOLDEN PALM (Volker Schlöndorff).

"I first saw the light of the world in the form of a 60-watt bulb."

The film starts and ends in a field of potatoes. "I begin long before me," says the narrator, and describes the events that led to the conception of his mother. We see policemen pursuing a man, before a country girl grants him refuge under her voluminous skirts, where matters take their course. The begetting of Oskar, our narrator, is no less strange: his kindly mother Agnes (Angela Winkler) is married to the loudmouthed grocer Alfred Matzerath (Mario Adorf) and in love with the sensitive Pole, Jan Bronski (Daniel Olbrychski). Oskar is conceived "within this trinity." When he's born, hi mother promises him a tin drum; on his third birthday he gets it. And on th same day, already disgusted by the drunken, gluttonous, cacophonous worl of the adults around him, he makes an important decision: he's going to sta small. He throws himself down the cellar stairs and immediately stops grow ing. For the next 18 years, he'll go through life in the body of a three-year-ol with a tin drum hanging round his neck. And anyone who tries to take thi

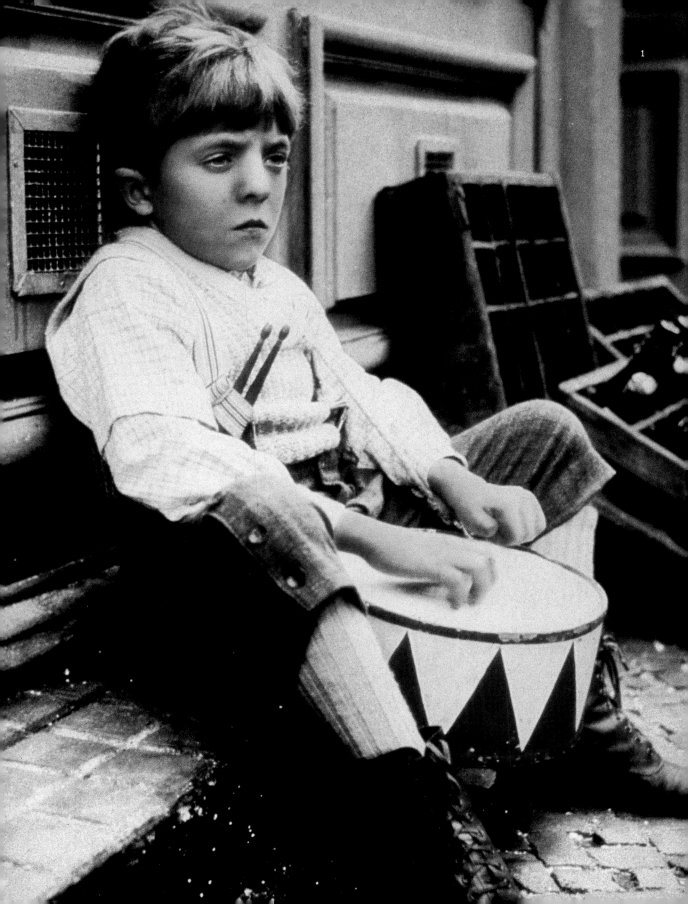

"Schlöndorff deliberately looked for a simpler narrative style. Whole fragments of the book were simply left out. Yet I still feel that he's succeeded in casting a new light on the whole story."

Günter Grass, in: Sequenz

1 Toy soldier: On his third birthday, Oskar Matzerath (David Bennent) is given a tin drum...

2 ... and, disgusted at the adult world, he resolves to stop growing immediately.

3 Sins of the fatherland: Oscar's father, grocer Matzerath (Mario Adorf), is a fervent fan of Adolf Hitler.

drum away from him will be subjected to little Oskar's unearthly glass-shattering scream.

Oskar is no normal child. From the day he's born, he can think and make decisions for himself; and his strangeness sets him apart. *The Tin Drum* is an opulent panorama of German-Polish history, seen through the eyes of an outsider. We are witness to the years between 1899 and 1945, from the peaceful co-existence of Germans and Poles in Danzig, to the German attack on the city, to Oskar's flight westwards as the war draws to a close. In the film's final image, the camera watches from the potato field as he fades into the distance. Tectonic shifts in politics are made visible in tiny details, as when Beethoven's portrait makes way for Hitler's. Oskar takes

no sides in all this; he remains an outsider. Once, however, his drumming causes chaos at a Nazi meeting. Oskar carries on drumming till everyone present is swaying happily to the strains of "The Blue Danube." It's reminiscent of the scene in *Casablanca* (1942), where the "Marseillaise" does battle with "Die Wacht am Rhein." On another occasion, Oskar lets the Nazis draw him in: he meets some kindred spirits at a circus, dwarves employed as clowns and later as "a tonic for the troops." Oskar joins them, and soon he too is wearing a Nazi uniform.

If the story is episodic and discontinuous, the cinematic style is a riot. Adapted from the novel by Nobel Prizewinner Günter Grass, the film is a kind of comical yarn, a burlesque bubbling over with ideas, by turns naturalistic

3

VOLKER SCHLÖNDORFF   The German weekly *Die Zeit* once had the following to say about Völker Schlöndorff: "Together with Fassbinder, he's undoubtedly the most skilled craftsman in German cinema; but he's not a director whose films can be said to add up to an inimitable style." Yet most of his films can be brought under a single heading: literary adaptations. So Volker Schlöndorff was perhaps an ideal director for *The Tin Drum* (*Die Blechtrommel / Le Tambour*, 1979).

He learned his trade in the Paris of the Existentialists and the *Nouvelle Vague*. He assisted Jean-Pierre Melville and Louis Malle before making *Young Toerless* (*Der junge Törless / Les Désarrois de l'élève Törless*) in 1966 – based on a story by Robert Musil. The works of other great writers would follow: Heinrich von Kleist (*Michael Kohlhaas – der Rebell*, 1969), Marcel Proust (*Swann in Love / Eine Liebe von Swann / Un amour de Swann*, 1983), and Arthur Miller (*Death of a Salesman*, 1985). In the 70s, he turned his attention to the contemporary political scene. Together with his then-wife Margarethe von Trotta, he made *The Lost Honor of Katharina Blum* (*Die verlorene Ehre der Katharina Blum*, 1975), based on a short novel by Heinrich Böll. He then took part in a collective project involving directors such as Alexander Kluge, Rainer Werner Fassbinder and others: *Germany in Autumn* (*Deutschland im Herbst*, 1977/78) described the atmosphere in the country after the abduction of Harns Martin Schleyer by the Red Army Faction, otherwise known as the Baader-Meinhof Group. In 1999, Schlöndorff returned to this theme, in the drama *Legends of Rita* (*Die Stille nach dem Schuss*), which tells the story of former terrorists gone to ground in East Germany.

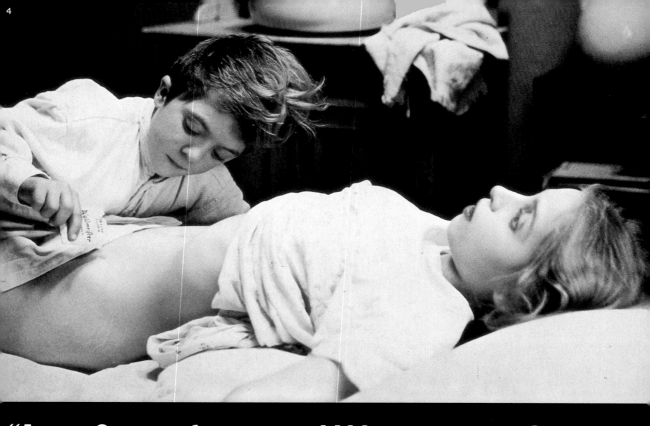

"A very German fresco: world history seen and experienced from below. Huge, spectacular images, held together by tiny Oskar." *Volker Schlöndorff*

4 Maid to order: A bellybutton full of sherbet marks Oskar's first sexual experience with servant Maria (Katharina Thalbach).

5 Marching band: Oskar's musical interludes disrupt his mother's regular Thursday rendezvous with Jan.

6 An officer and a gentleman: Oskar falls in love with the midget Roswitha (Mariella Oliveri).

7 The joker's wild: Gambler and ladies' man, Jan Bronski (Daniel Olbrychski), is also an anti-fascist.

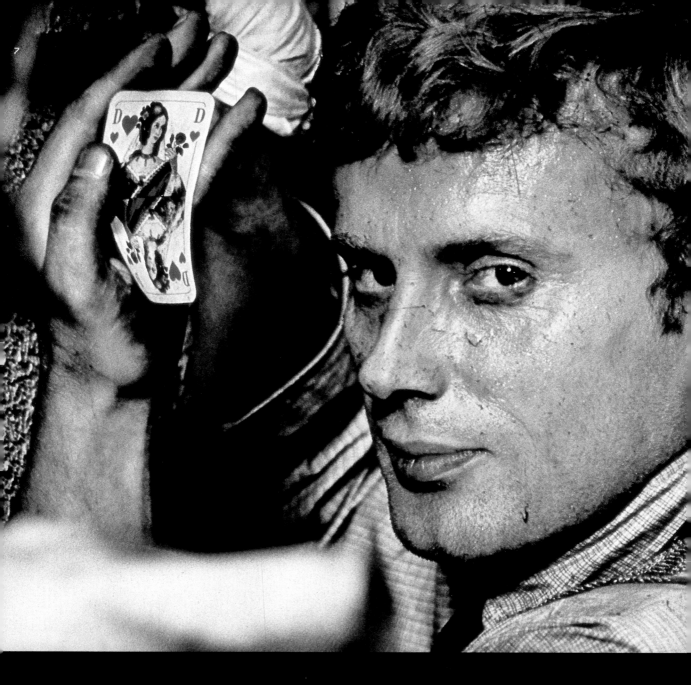

as in the unforgettable scene in which a horse's head is used to catch eels), grotesque (Oskar's view from the womb) or even slapstick (when Oskar's grandfather is chased across the field in a jumpy, flickering silent-film sequence). These disparate elements are held together by Oskar's precocious and knowing off-screen commentary. The actor who plays Oskar is perhaps the film's most fortunate find. While planning the filming of what the German weekly *Die Zeit* called "the most unfilmable novel ever written," Volker Schlöndorff's attention was drawn to the twelve-year-old David Bennent. The son of the well-known German actor Heinz Bennent, he suffers from a growth disorder. He brings a wonderful seriousness, depth and presence to the role

of Oskar. Schlöndorff was so delighted by David Bennent that he decided not to film the part of the book that takes place after 1945, when Oskar grows up – for he couldn't face replacing Bennent with another actor. In the 80s, Schlöndorff wrote the screenplay for a follow-up, but the film was never made.

In Cannes, *The Tin Drum* shared the Golden Palm with *Apocalypse Now* (1979). Later the same year, it won the Oscar as Best Foreign Film. And in 1997 came a suitably absurd epilogue: a judge in Oklahoma City had videos of *The Tin Drum* confiscated, saying the film was obscene because it showed a person under the age of 18 indulging in sexual intercourse.   H.JK

ESCAPE FROM ALCATRAZ

1979 - USA - 112 MIN. - PRISON FILM

DIRECTOR DON SIEGEL (1912–1991)
SCREENPLAY RICHARD TUGGLE, based on the report of the same name by J. CAMPBELL BRUCE DIRECTOR OF PHOTOGRAPHY BRUCE SURTEES EDITING FERRIS WEBSTER MUSIC JERRY FIELDING PRODUCTION DON SIEGEL for THE MALPASO COMPANY, PARAMOUNT PICTURES.

STARRING CLINT EASTWOOD (Frank Morris), PATRICK MCGOOHAN (Warden), ROBERTS BLOSSOM (Chester "Doc" Dalton), JACK THIBEAU (Clarance Anglin), FRED WARD (John Anglin), PAUL BENJAMIN (English), LARRY HANKIN (Charley Butts), BRUCE M. FISHER (Wolf), FRANK RONZIO (Litmus), FRED STUTHAM (Johnson).

"No one has ever escaped from Alcatraz."

January 18, 1960. The date at the beginning of the film verifies the authenticity of the events that are to follow. The camera pans over the Golden Gate Bridge. The name is a perfidious irony for a man like Frank Morris (Clint Eastwood), who is being moved to Alcatraz in this stormy, rainy night. Bound and chained, he stands on the deck of a small, storm-tossed ship and inspects the expansive rock island with its fortress-like compound, illuminated by intense searchlights.

The judges have decided he is to spend the rest of his life here, like hundreds of other inmates for whom a return to society is out of the question.

The Alcatraz prison is absolutely escape-proof. Even if a prisoner succeeded in escaping the heavily guarded fortress, he would assuredly meet his death in the treacherous currents below.

Frank slowly adjusts to everyday life in prison: single cells, no newspapers, and no relief from the harsh conditions. The program is strict, and the punishments hard. The inmates are led to eat in single file sections and speaking is forbidden. A giant of a man named Wolf (Bruce M. Fisher) makes unambiguous advances toward Frank. Frank gives him a beating, making an irreconcilable enemy. He doesn't have to wait long for the first attack, as Wolf

comes at him with a knife during a yard exercise. Frank is able to defend himself, but is punished with a stricter prison sentence. Frank is a notorious escapee. In Alcatraz he soon surveys the lay of the land, probing the possibilities of escape from the island. Charley Butts (Larry Hankin), a car thief and the brothers John (Fred Ward) and Clarence Anglin (Jack Thibeau) join him. Their plan is daring: with great effort they dig holes in the porous walls of their cells. Through the holes they have access to a ventilation shaft that leads out into the open.

In small increments, always in danger of being discovered by the watchful guards, the accomplices follow their plan and exhibit a tremendous inventiveness in the creation and production of the necessary tools and equipment. They patch together insets from papier-maché to disguise the

"*Alcatraz*'s cool, cinematic grace meshes ideally with the strengths of its star. At a time when Hollywood entertainments are more overblown than ever, Eastwood proves that less really can be more." *Time Magazine*

1   The Birdman of Alcatraz: Convicted criminal Frank Morris (Clint Eastwood) is itching to spread his wings again...

2   A fight to the finish: Wolf (Bruce M. Fisher) is just dying to cut Frank Morris to shreds.

3   Born free: Morris seeks the advice of an older inmate and analyzes possible means of escape.

4   The long and winding road: Frank enlists a fellow convict and a few spare parts in devising an escape.

5   Needing to vent: Two convicts on their way up in the world.

4

5

DON SIEGEL

It would almost be derogatory to reduce Don Siegel's directorial projects to their craftsman-like qualities. But his technical restraint and the concentration on the essential are consciously implemented stylistic means, and they form the signature of this director the renowned screenwriter Larry Gelbart once jokingly dubbed an "auteur".

The economical nature of his methods indicates that Siegel was schooled in documentary filmmaking. During World War II he worked as an editor in the newsreel department of Warner Studios. He won two Academy Awards with short films. His subsequent directorial projects however were initially limited to B movies. The breakthrough came with the prison film *Riot in Cell Block 11* (1953/54). Siegel was also successful in science fiction, creating a genre classic with *Invasion of the Body Snatchers* (1956). With 1960's *Flaming Star* he helped tease a respectable acting performance out of Elvis Presley.

The highlights of his work are the five films he made with Clint Eastwood. Siegel was able to successfully convert the Spaghetti Western image of the star returning from Europe into an American style, carefully crafting a new screen identity for Eastwood. He also became his mentor, for even as a TV actor, Eastwood yearned to direct. Eastwood's greatest artistic success, the Western *Unforgiven* (1992), is dedicated to Siegel and Sergio Leone.

holes they have dug. They also create life-sized skulls that are placed in their beds while they dig. A table fan is fashioned into a drill, and raincoats are sewn together to serve as an inflatable raft.

One day before Frank is to be relocated into another cell, they set their plan in motion. Butts' hesitation endangers the operation, and there looms the constant possibility that the zealous guards will discover the dummies in their beds, which can be seen from outside the cells. Ultimately Butts stays behind while the others climb over the roof and the outside wall, blow up their raft, and put it to water.

The real-life Frank Morris and the Anglin brothers were never found. Neither their bodies nor any other traces were discovered. The film ends with the blend-in: "Just a year later Alcatraz was shut down."

This true story was immediately of great interest to director Siegel and Clint Eastwood. Both had an infallible sense for fascinating material, proven once again by the resulting film. Siegel's laconic style of dramatization and Eastwood's callous minimalism made the film utterly believable. Siegel cleverly established the brittle nature of prison life, the basis for the gradually intensifying suspense that explodes in the breathtaking finale. The quietly droning, ethereal soundtrack by Jerry Fielding plays a great role in helping to create the film's stifling atmosphere.

Attentive viewers will discover two supporting characters among the inmates who would go on to attract attention with far greater roles: Carl Lumbly and Danny Glover.

HK

KRAMER VS. KRAMER

♟♟♟♟♟

1979 - USA - 105 MIN. - FAMILY DRAMA

DIRECTOR ROBERT BENTON (*1932)
SCREENPLAY ROBERT BENTON, based on the novel by the same name by AVERY CORMAN DIRECTOR OF PHOTOGRAPHY NÉSTOR ALMENDROS EDITING GERALD B. GREENBERG MUSIC HERB HARRIS, JOHN KANDER, HENRY PURCELL ("Sonata for Trumpet and Strings"), ANTONIO VIVALDI ("Concerto in C Major for Mandolin and Strings") PRODUCTION STANLEY R. JAFFE for COLUMBIA PICTURES CORPORATION.

STARRING DUSTIN HOFFMAN (Ted Kramer), MERYL STREEP (Joanna Kramer), JANE ALEXANDER (Margaret Phelps), JUSTIN HENRY (Billy Kramer), HOWARD DUFF (John Shaunessy), GEORGE COE (Jim O'Connor), BILL MOOR (Gressen), HOWLAND CHAMBERLAIN (Richter Atkins), JACK RAMAGE (Spencer), JESS OSUNA (Ackerman).

ACADEMY AWARDS 1979 OSCARS for BEST PICTURE (Stanley R. Jaffe), BEST DIRECTOR (Robert Benton), BEST ADAPTED SCREENPLAY (Robert Benton), BEST ACTOR (Dustin Hoffman), and BEST SUPPORTING ACTRESS (Meryl Streep).

"What law is it that says a woman is a better parent?"

Ted Kramer (Dustin Hoffman), a workaholic absorbed by his job as an advertising executive, is about to have his world ripped out from under him. No sooner does his boss O'Connor (George Coe) put him in charge of a million dollar account, than his wife Joanna (Meryl Streep), awaiting his arrival at home, informs him of her intention to abandon their family unit. As a result, he is left to take care of their five-year-old son, Billy (Justin Henry). Floored, Ted blurts out to friend and neighbor, Margaret (Jane Alexander), that this was supposed to be "one of the five best days of (his) whole life." Instead, it turns out to be the first day of his *new life* as a single father! It is an earth-shattering change for both Ted and Billy. It takes a while to make the adjustment, but somewhere down the line life's everyday hurdles like preparing meals, shopping for groceries, as well as taking Billy to school and picking him up, become part of an affectionate daily routine.

Their world is rocked yet again when Joanna turns up at their doorstep 18 months later. She has come with the clear intention of collecting Billy. Ted, however, isn't about to give up his son without a fight and abstain from the father-son relationship that has come to be. He'll even go to court if he has

to. The ensuing custody battle is just an additional stress on his already overloaded life, and his private affairs soon cause him to fall out of his boss' good graces. He continually shows up late to critical business meetings, and when he should be dedicating his full concentration to the project he's in charge of he worries too much about what's in his freezer for that night's dinner. It's not long before Ted's out of a job. But he's not down for the count just yet…

Robert Benton, director of *Places in the Heart* (1984), paints a riveting portrait of a burgeoning relationship between a father and son, which is, nonetheless, full of its share of ugly human emotions like rage and despair. Dustin Hoffman, alongside impressive child actor Justin Henry, pulls out all the stops in conveying a tender father-son tie founded on many ecstatic highs and heartbreaking lows. Their bumpy road towards gaining one another's respect is paved with incidents like spilling juice on dad's important business papers, worrying about illness and injury as well as disobeying parental rules. It is precisely moments like these that forge the touching bond between them. All the more reason why Joanna's attorney, Mr. Gressen (Bill Moor), pulls the audience's chain with his callous line of questioning

1   Facing facts: Billy (Justin Henry) can't get used to the idea that Mommy isn't coming home.

2   Three's a crowd: Ted Kramer (Dustin Hoffman) takes Billy to the park ...

3   ... where mother (Meryl Streep) and son are granted a short afternoon visit.

"What I'm trying to express in *Kramer vs. Kramer* is every man's longing to be a mother."

Dustin Hoffman in: Cinema

> "*Kramer vs. Kramer* is a rare movie that finds its tone, its focus und its poetry in its very first image. The image: a close-up of an anguished woman, her face surrounded by darkness. The shot is so intimate that the audience at first yearns for some relief. But the relief never really comes. *Kramer vs. Kramer* is composed almost entirely of actors' faces, of intense passions and of winter light. Since the actors are Dustin Hoffman and Meryl Streep, and since the suffering is real, the audience quickly finds that it is impossible to turn away. (...) *Kramer vs. Kramer* is the emotional bender of the year." *Time Magazine*

4   Growing pains: Ted Kramer and his son Billy.

5   One day at a time: Father and son gradually learn
    how to set rules and how to live with them.

MARITAL MAYHEM   The discovery of true love is often the cornerstone of a Hollywood happy ending. Nevertheless, there are also films that paint a more scathing picture of the grand emotion. In 1973, Swedish director Ingmar Bergman's *Scenes from a Marriage* (*Scener ur ett äktenskap*, 1973) took a thorough look at two people who had no idea their wedded life was on the rocks. Produced as a six-part TV miniseries, the three-hour film version accompanies a couple on the long and painful road to separation. One of the most extreme examples of marital malfeasance is Danny DeVito's black comedy *The War of the Roses* (1989), in which a couple literally tear each other's hair out. After 17 years of blissful marriage, husband and wife want to separate, but materialism causes them to turn their shared estate into a battlefield. Each is prepared to send the other to the grave for the finer things in life. The topic of marital instability was handled much more subtly in the 30s and 40s. During the golden age of the screwball comedy, Hollywood's beloved couples like Spencer Tracy and Katharine Hepburn in George Cukor's *Adam's Rib* (1949) or Clark Gable and Jean Harlow in Clarence Brown's *Wife vs. Secretary* (1936) mastered the art of verbal fencing. With *Mrs. Doubtfire* (1993), Chris Columbus served up a wild farce on the shattered marriage genre. After losing his kids in a custody battle, Daniel disguises himself as a loveable, middle-aged lady and deceives his ex-wife into hiring him as his own children's nanny so that he can be closer to them.

nd court room theatrics as he tries to prove that Ted is obviously an unfit arent.

Likewise, the trial is no walk in the park for Joanna. It is here in he courtroom, as allegations are lashed out at her, that she relates what an motional catastrophe the separation was for her as well. With her sensitive ortrayal of Joanna Kramer, Meryl Streep secured her position as an "A list" ctress. Streep evokes sympathy for her character as she explains how diffi-ult it was for her to break out of what had become a suffocating family fe that offered no prospects other than conceding to the role of wife and nother-in-waiting.

Joanna is granted custody at the end of the hearing. The verdict comes s a shock for both Ted and Billy. In a truly unforgettable scene, father and on sit in their kitchen and prepare French toast for the very last time. Billy's mpending departure weighs down each hand movement at breakfast. In

completely still at the table. The buzzer rings and Joanna lets him know tha she is waiting in the lobby. Yet, reminiscent of the film's opening, Joanna sur prises Ted once more with her decision. She can't bring herself to tear Bill away again from the parental trust that has shaped his world. She won't take Billy, even with the court's blessing.

With *Kramer vs. Kramer*, Benton creates a collage of emancipation ou of the patchwork of a failed marriage. At a time when new modes of living and freedoms were replacing traditional familial roles, the rights and respon-sibilities of men and women were beginning to change dramatically. By telling the story primarily from the perspective of the single father, Bentor provides his drama with an extra provocative punch that, in turn, accentuates the egocentric tendencies in Joanna's own self-realization. It is thus the im-peccable acting of the cast that makes us leave the film, not pointing finger at the characters, but rather full of respect and understanding for the entire

MAD MAX

1979 - AUSTRALIA - 93 MIN. - ACTION FILM, SCIENCE FICTION

DIRECTOR GEORGE MILLER (*1945)
SCREENPLAY JAMES MCCAUSLAND, GEORGE MILLER DIRECTOR OF PHOTOGRAPHY DAVID EGGBY EDITING TONY PATERSON, CLIFF HAYES
MUSIC BRIAN MAY PRODUCTION BYRON KENNEDY for MAD MAX FILMS, KENNEDY MILLER PRODUCTIONS, CROSSROADS.

STARRING MEL GIBSON (Max Rockatansky), JOANNE SAMUEL (Jessie Rockatansky), HUGH KEAYS-BYRNE (Toecutter), STEVE BISLEY (Jim Goose), ROGER WARD (Fifi Macaffee), TIM BURNS (Johnny), VINCENT GIL (Nightrider), GEOFF PARRY (Bubba Zanetti), DAVID BRACKS (Mudguts), PAUL JOHNSTONE (Cundalini).

"You've seen it! ... You've heard it! ... and you're still asking questions?"

He's simply trying to make sense of it all, policeman Max Rockatansky (Mel Gibson) explains to his wife Jessie (Joanne Samuel), after one of his colleagues is burned alive by a marauding gang of rockers. But he is unable to unearth any explanation.

Max is not alone in his helplessness. Indeed, Australian director George Miller's low-budget production also gives the audience no explanation for the openly waged "war" between cops and rockers. A blend-in at the beginning of the film succinctly identifies the time and location of the plot: "Somewhere in the near future." A street sign on a dusty highway specifies that "Anarchy Road" stretches from this point on, and another sign displays the number of people who have recently died in the area. Without further ado comes the spectacular car chase between the Nightrider (Vincent Gil), who has declared himself a gas-propelled suicide machine, and the custodians of the law, for whom the murderous race on the desolate country highways is apparently just as much fun as it is for the psychopathic rocker. After several spectacular stunts and half dozen crashes, he stalls — ultimately there is one obstacle too many on the highway.

Logic plays virtually no role in the story of the worn-down "Interceptor," Max, who turns into a merciless avenger after a band of bikers under the leadership of Toecutter (Hugh Keays-Byrne) murders his wife and child: although the adversaries never seek each other out, they continually meet.

1　Officer down: When the highway's a battlefield, there are bound to be some casualties.

2　A light breather: Max (Mel Gibson) will stop at nothing to avenge his murdered family.

3　Remodeling: A rocker practices for the demolition derby.

"*Mad Max* is a Western. It has the same story, but instead of riding horses they are riding motorcycles and cars. People say the Western's dead, but it's not; it's become the car-action film." *Cinema Papers*

Though the plot of *Mad Max* could have sprung directly from a vengeance Western of the 1950s, the scenery and the characters have a comic-like stylization; the protagonists speak in memorable bubbles, and they are motivated by the basic joy of movement.

In a way, *Mad Max* seems like the final stopover in a string of films like Dennis Hopper's *Easy Rider* (1969) and Richard C. Safarian's *Vanishing Point* (1970), which at the beginning of the decade raised the car and/or motorcycle into the consummate expression of individual freedom. But in *Two-Lane Blacktop* (1971) director Monte Hellman had already signified the motor-madness of his heroes as an element of their communication disorders. In *Mad Max*, all that is left for the protagonists is pointless violence.

But we should not label this as social criticism – the film is based on the commercial appeal of action and violence, and accentuates them as cleverly constructed highlights within the plot. Ultimately, it is an exploitative product.

Nonetheless, George Miller only seldom dramatizes the violence against people as the focal point of the images, with plot-related aspects remaining in the foreground (at one point a biker's arm is ripped off). Often the enormously violent and powerful impression of the film is a result of the dynamic montage. The most horrifying details are thus left to the viewer's imagination. In the scene in which the bikers kill Max's family, Jessie and the child run into the middle of the street while the rockers steadily approach on their bikes from the distance. After the edit, the bikers have already sped past the cam-

4   Car on the barbie: *Mad Max* has some grilling
     action scenes.

5   The bad boys of Melbourne: The future's tax
     collectors.

STUNTS   A film like *Mad Max* (1979) certainly doesn't belong to those cinematic masterpieces noted for their sleek character portraits or philosophical depths. But even virulent opponents of the film are forced to recognize director George Miller's sovereign command of cinematic forms of expression and the technical brilliance of the stunts coordinated by Grant Page. Presented as a visual attraction, the circus-like perfection of the stunts points to the inception of the cinema – the markets and vaudeville shows where nickelodeons and cinematographs served as entertainment for a wide public. In the early days of the industry (in American films at least), stuntmen were simply extras who realized their chances of employment would increase if they mastered skills not everyone could master. In the labor-divided world of film, a profession quickly developed out of this realization that soon included not only the implementation of actor doubles in dangerous situations, but also the coordination (and dramatization) of action sequences. A special sort of daring was not required, but the opposite: technical perfection and risk minimization are paramount for the stunt coordinator – ultimately a botched take can cost the production not only money, but more importantly, the lives of the stuntmen.

era and Jessie's fate is simply suggested by a stray shoe that tumbles to the side of the road. And when Max belatedly arrives on the scene, the camera retains a wide shot – one can see him sinking over the corpses on the highway in the distance.

Mel Gibson was a completely unknown actor when he made his debut in the role of Max, as a star could not and would not have taken the risk of participating in the production. But the film offers its hero an exceptionally interesting entrance: Miller combines takes of Max's boots, gloves, leather gear, and sunglasses to create the mythical image of the cool policeman. And when we finally get to see the cop's face, we're almost surprised to look into Gibson's still boyish features.   LP

5

MONTY PYTHON'S LIFE OF BRIAN

1979 - GREAT BRITAIN - 94 MIN. - COMEDY, SPOOF

DIRECTOR TERRY JONES (*1942)
SCREENPLAY GRAHAM CHAPMAN, JOHN CLEESE, TERRY GILLIAM, ERIC IDLE, TERRY JONES, MICHAEL PALIN DIRECTOR OF PHOTOGRAPHY
PETER BIZIOU EDITING JULIÁN DOYLE MUSIC GEOFFREY BURGON, MICHAEL PALIN ("Brian's Song"), ERIC IDLE ("Always Look on the Bright Side of Life") PRODUCTION JOHN GOLDSTONE for HANDMADE FILMS LTD., PYTHON (Monty) PICTURES LIMITED.

STARRING GRAHAM CHAPMAN (Brian and two other roles), JOHN CLEESE (Reg, Centurion and four other roles), TERRY GILLIAM (Jailor and three other roles), ERIC IDLE (Stan, Loretta and eight other roles), TERRY JONES (Brian's Mother, St. Simon and three other roles), MICHAEL PALIN (Francis, Prophet and six other roles), TERENCE BAYLER (Gregory), CAROL CLEVELAND (Mrs. Gregory), KENNETH COLLEY (Jesus), Sue Jones-Davies (Judith).

"Blessed are the cheese makers?"

The zeal of the righteous knew no limits: this film was banned even in isolated Scottish communities that didn't have a cinema. Yet offense should have been taken only where it was intended: by religious fanatics, who can tolerate opposition as little as they can take a joke. The humor of Monty Python is simply beyond these latter-day scribes and Pharisees. In fact, few of the film's opponents had actually seen the film; and even now, John Cleese and Terry Gilliam insist that their monumental epic has nothing whatsoever to do with the life of Jesus. It can't be denied, though, that the film raises doubts about his uniqueness as a religious founder, telling the tale of a parallel Passion endured by a simple man: Brian of Nazareth, a reluctant Messiah, born on the same day as Jesus and crucified under Pontius Pilate. We should probably count our blessings, for the revolutionary British comedy team had originally planned an alternative biography of the Man from Galilee. The title, proposed by Eric Idle: "Jesus Christ: Lust for Glory"… The real Jesus makes a brief and dignified appearance, but his Sermon on the Mount can barely be heard by most of the people in the massive crowd. ("Blessed are the Greek?")

Brian too, played by Graham Chapman, is sadly misunderstood; indeed, in his clumsiness, he achieves almost tragic stature. His central message

"You're all individuals," (The crowd: "We're all individuals!") brings him into fatal conflict with the merciless yearning for salvation so prevalent at the time. Though he asks his disciples to leave him in peace ("Piss off!"), they refuse to take the hint. A large part of the film's comic effect consists in its impressive attempt to sum up 2,000 years of world history in a very small number of characters; and what's more, they're all played by Pythons. Brian's selfless dedication to the cause of the People's Front of Judea reflects the eternal struggle against imperialism and the tortured history of the Holy Land. The movement of resistance against Roman occupation is crippled by internal divisions, and restricted almost entirely to the kind of revolutionary rhetoric to be heard at British universities in the 60s and 70s. Again and again, the film thwarts the audience's expectations of a historical epic, and the results are sometimes astonishing. When Brian scrawls graffiti on the palace walls, he's caught by a Roman centurion (John Cleese); but instead of arresting the culprit, he subjects him to a painful Latin lesson, in which the phrase "Romans go home" is reduced to a grammatical conundrum. This dialectic of form and content is at the root of several successful jokes, involving ex-lepers, proconsuls with speech defects, and women who disguise themselves with false beards in order to take part in a public stoning. The

1 "Larks' tongues! Otters' noses! Ocelot milk!" Brian (Graham Chapman) scrapes a living selling Roman delicacies in the Colosseum. But not for much longer…

2 If only they'd had Dolby Surround: In the Pythons' movie, as in several serious takes on the New Testament, Jesus is relegated to a marginal role.

3 That's all folks! "Always Look on the Bright Side of Life" was the ultimate hymn to optimism.

absurdity – the madness – only fully dawns on Brian as he's hanging on the cross, serenaded by Eric Idle and a host of crucified miscreants. Their advice? "Always look on the bright side of life."

Breaking with their usual practice, the sketch specialists worked long and hard on the internal unity of this fulminating late work. The short inter-mezzo with an alien spacecraft was an affectionate nod to Terry Gilliam's an-imated fillers, and as such, indispensable. The film owes its visual brilliance to the recycled sets of Franco Zeffirelli's TV mini-series *Jesus of Nazareth/ Gesù di Nazareth* (1977) – an elegant solution to the Pythons' permanent problems with money. The Tunisian locations lent further splendor to this parody of bombastic Biblical blockbusters, and additional help was provided by the former Beatle George Harrison, who rescued the project at the last minute by forming Handmade Films. He simply wanted to see one more Python movie. Later, he enabled them to realize projects like *Time Bandits* (1981) and *Monty Python Live at the Hollywood Bowl* (1982). In *The Life of Brian*, he makes a cameo appearance as Mr. Papadopolous, a man trying to sell his olive grove.

PB

CHRIST AT THE MOVIES OR THE NEW TESTAMENT IN FILM

Years before *Monty Python's Life of Brian* (1979) and Martin Scorsese's scandalous *The Last Temptation of Christ* (1988), an American-Israeli co-production delivered the most daring cinematic interpretation of the New Testament. *The Passover Plot* (1976) depicted Jesus as an opportunist who fakes his own resurrection as a clever propaganda trick in the struggle against Roman occupation. The churches' official image of Jesus was more closely approximated in Hollywood's Biblical epics. Cecil B. DeMille's silent classic *The King of Kings* (1927), the 1961 remake by Nicholas Ray (*King of Kings*), and George Stevens' *The Greatest Story Ever Told* (1964) all drew strongly on the visual tradition of Renaissance painting. Such films made no attempt to examine Jesus' personality, presenting him instead as a pious and passive victim of unavoidable events. In movies like *Barabbas* (1962), Biblical sidekicks acquired unexpected promotion, in an effort to accommodate armies of Hollywood stars. In the Stevens blockbuster, John Wayne made a cameo appearance as a Roman centurion at the foot of the Cross. His delivery of the line "Truly this man was the son of God" was indeed unforgettable.

The dilemma was: how could the epic structure of the material be reconciled with a humanized depiction of the central figure? Italian productions indicated a possible answer. Directors such as Franco Zeffirelli and Roberto Rossellini brought a realistic treatment of the historical context to the Bible's message of redemption. It was a self-confessed atheist, however, who came up with the most convincing cinematic solution: austere and evocative in its visual imagery, Pier Paolo Pasolini's *The Gospel According to St. Matthew* (*Il vangelo secondo Matteo,* 1964) places its trust in the poetic power of the Biblical texts. May we be pardoned for remarking that this film had a script made in Heaven.

5

"Just when you thought that the uproarious English comedy troupe had taken bad taste as far as it could go in *Monty Python and the Holy Grail*, along comes *Monty Python's Life of Brian* to demonstrate that it's possible to go even farther in delirious offensiveness. Bad taste of this order is rare but not yet dead." *The New York Times*

4   Hair-brained schemes: In first-century Judea, there's a booming market in loopy ideas. Michael Palin played a particularly furry prophet.

5   *Au naturel:* The Pythons have never been afraid to look ugly…

6   Cutting room execution: King Otto's suicide squad was axed from the picture before it had a fighting chance.

6

APOCALYPSE NOW

1979 - USA - 153 MIN. - WAR FILM

DIRECTOR FRANCIS FORD COPPOLA (*1939)
SCREENPLAY JOHN MILIUS, FRANCIS FORD COPPOLA, MICHAEL HERR (off-screen commentary), based on motifs from the novella *HEART OF DARKNESS* by JOSEPH CONRAD **DIRECTOR OF PHOTOGRAPHY** VITTORIO STORARO **EDITING** LISA FRUCHTMAN, GERALD B. GREENBERG, RICHARD MARKS, WALTER MURCH **MUSIC** CARMINE COPPOLA, FRANCIS FORD COPPOLA, THE DOORS (Song: "The End") **PRODUCTION** FRANCIS FORD COPPOLA for ZOETROPE CORPORATION, OMNI ZOETROPE.

STARRING MARLON BRANDO (Colonel Walter E. Kurtz), ROBERT DUVALL (Lieutenant Colonel William Kilgore), MARTIN SHEEN (Captain Benjamin L. Willard), FREDERIC FORREST ("Chef" Jay Hicks), ALBERT HALL (Chief Quartermaster Phillips), SAM BOTTOMS (Lance B. Johnson), LAURENCE FISHBURNE (Tyrone "Clean" Miller), DENNIS HOPPER (Photo-journalist), G. D. SPRADLIN (General R. Corman), HARRISON FORD (Colonel G. Lucas).

ACADEMY AWARDS 1979 OSCARS for BEST CINEMATOGRAPHY (Vittorio Storaro), and BEST SOUND (Walter Murch, Mark Berger, Richard Beggs, Nathan Boxer).

IFF CANNES 1979 GOLDEN PALM (Francis Ford Coppola).

"I love the smell of napalm in the morning."

Vietnam, 1969. Captain Willard (Martin Sheen) is on a top-secret mission to find Colonel Kurtz (Marlon Brando), a highly decorated U.S. Army officer. And when he's located the man, his next task will be to kill him; for Kurtz has clearly gone mad, is defying the control of his superior officers, and now commands a private army in the jungle beyond the Cambodian border. His soldiers are a mixed bag of indigenous people, South Vietnamese, and rogue G.Is, who he uses to his own unauthorized and murderous ends. Willard boards a patrol boat and heads upriver through the rainforest in search of Kurtz; and the further he penetrates into the jungle, the more intensely he and his four comrades experience the horror of war.

No other movie of the 70s received so much attention before it was even released. Francis Ford Coppola was the first director to risk making a big-budget film about the Vietnam War, and he did so with almost demonstrative independence. As his own production company American Zoetrope financed the film, *Apocalypse Now* could be made without the usual assistance – and interference – from the Pentagon. (Even today, such help is practically obligatory when a war film is made in the United States.) Coppola said later that he had originally aimed to make a lucrative action movie. Instead

the film became an unparalleled nightmare for the celebrated director of *The Godfather* (1972) – and not just in financial terms.

Coppola was looking for a country with a climate similar to Vietnam's, so he chose to film in the Philippines. As the necessary infrastructure was lacking, conditions were quite hair-raising from the word go. The military equipment, for instance, was the result of a deal with the dictatorial President Marcos, who was fighting a civil war against communist rebels while the film was being made. As a consequence, helicopters were sometimes requisitioned from the set at short notice and sent off by the military to take part in real battles. Conditions as tough as these made it hard to find stars willing to take part. Initially, the role of Willard was taken by Harvey Keitel, but he was replaced by the little-known Martin Sheen after only three weeks' filming, as his expressive acting was not to Coppola's taste, and he wanted a more passive protagonist. This was an expensive mistake, but harmless in comparison to the problems the director would later face. There was the deadly typhoon that destroyed the expensive sets; the almost fatal heart attack suffered by Martin Sheen; the difficulty of working with the grossly overweight Brando and above all, the trouble caused by the director's own constant departures

2

1   Tribal titan: Marlon Brando rocked the screen in his role as Colonel Kurtz although he only appeared at the end of the movie.

2   Battle of the Bulge: Captain Willard (Martin Sheen) and the photographer (Dennis Hopper) flesh out the fate of Colonel Kurtz.

3   Duty calls: Filmed on location in the Philippines, *Apocalypse Now's* helicopter was taken off the set and flown into the front lines of battle.

"My film is not a movie. My film is not about Vietnam. It is Vietnam. That's what it was really like. It was crazy." *Francis Ford Coppola, IFF Cannes*

from the script. As a result, work had to stop on several occasions, and the filming period expanded from four to 15 months. Soon, the 16 million dollar budget was exhausted, and Coppola – close to physical and mental collapse – was forced to mortgage his own property in order to raise the same sum all over again. The press could smell a disaster of previously unheard of proportions. But though two more years were taken up by post-production, the film ultimately became a box-office hit – despite mixed reviews, and the fact that other "Vietnam movies" had by then already reached the screen.

The legendary status of *Apocalypse Now* is inseparable from the spectacular circumstances of its making. Many people, including Coppola himself, have drawn an analogy between the Vietnam conflict itself and the agonized struggle to complete the film. It's all the more remarkable, then

that Coppola succeeded in freeing himself, gradually but radically, from the superficial realism that tends to typify the war-film genre. The Vietnam War has often been described as a psychedelic experience, but Coppola and his cameraman Vittorio Storaro created images that actually do justice to the description. Willard's trip upriver, inspired by Joseph Conrad's novella *Heart of Darkness*, is a journey into the darkness of his own heart, and so the various stages on his journey acquire an increasingly fantastic, dreamlike quality. At the beginning of his odyssey, Willard encounters the surfing fanatic Lieutenant Colonel Kilgore (Robert Duvall), who sends his squad of choppers in to obliterate a peasant village so that he can enjoy the perfect waves of the neighboring beach. Kilgore's insane euphoria is heightened by the musical accompaniment: Wagner's "Ride of the Valkyrie." At this point, Willard i

3

4

no more than a passive observer of a monstrous spectacle, which is ironically depicted by Coppola as a kind of hi-tech U.S. Cavalry. It's a grimly satirical scene, in which the director makes masterly use of aesthetic conventions
for his own purposes.

    Willard's journey terminates in a realm of the dead: Kurtz's bizarre and
bloody jungle kingdom, a garishly exotic and obscenely theatrical hell-on-
earth. As embodied by Marlon Brando, Kurtz has the quality of a perverted
Buddha. When he first receives Willard in his murky temple residence, both
men are sunk in the surrounding shadows. At the end of the line, in the heart
of darkness, good and evil have grown indistinguishable, and Willard has lost
what distance he ever had: Kurtz has become part of his very self. When

Willard finally kills him, the act – like an archaic ritual – is at once an exorcism and a manifestation of the darkness at the heart of mankind, a black
stain no civilization will ever erase. Ultimately, it's the cause and the irre-
ducible essence of war – whatever the epoch, and whatever the weapons
deployed.

    In 2001, Coppola brought out *Apocalypse Now Redux*, a director's cut
that was 49 minutes longer. It contains some sequences that had fallen
victim to the cutter's shears, and the director says it's the closest possible
approximation to his original intentions. Yet although the *Redux* version is
undoubtedly somewhat more complex than the original, it constitutes neither
a radical alteration to, nor a significant improvement on the original.

5

4 The river wild: Civilization on a voyage
   downstream.

5 The buck stops here: Having made it to the end of
   his journey, Willard is prepared to kill Colonel Kurtz.

"It is not so much an epic account of a grueling war as an incongruous, extravagant monument to artistic self-defeat."

Time Magazine

FRANCIS FORD COPPOLA Francis Ford Coppola (*7.4.1939 in Detroit) enjoyed a sheltered middle-class childhood in a suburb of New York. His father Carmine was a composer and musician who would later write the music to some of his son's films. Coppola at first studied theatre at the Hofstra University, then film at UCLA. While still a student, he worked as an assistant director to Roger Corman, who also produced his first feature film, *Dementia 13* (1963). Coppola made his breakthrough at the early age of 31, when his screenplay to *Patton* (1969) was awarded the Oscar.

A short time later, he was also world-famous as a director – and as the Boy Wonder of the New Hollywood: the Mafia saga *The Godfather* (1972) became one of the biggest hits in movie history and won three Oscars, including Best Film. Two years later, he topped even this: *The Godfather – Part II* (1974) scooped six Academy Awards – including Best Director. In the meantime, Coppola had also made an outstanding movie about an alienated surveillance expert: *The Conversation* (1974), which carried off the Golden Palm at the Cannes Festival.

In 1976, Coppola began work on the Vietnam film *Apocalypse Now* (1979), which he produced himself, and which came very close to ruining him. But after four years in production, that film also won the Golden Palm and two Oscars, and even recouped the huge sum that had been spent making it. Only two years later, however, the failure of the love story *One from the Heart* (1981) drove him into such horrendous debt that he was forced to sell his production company, American Zoetrope. Though he has since directed other films, such as *The Cotton Club* (1984) and *The Godfather – Part III* (1990), none have been as successful as his huge hits of the 70s.

THE CHINA SYNDROME

1979 - USA - 122 MIN. - POLITICAL THRILLER

DIRECTOR JAMES BRIDGES (1936–1993)
SCREENPLAY MIKE GRAY, T. S. COOK, JAMES BRIDGES DIRECTOR OF PHOTOGRAPHY JAMES CRABE EDITING DAVID RAWLINS MUSIC STEPHEN BISHOP (Title song "Somewhere In Between") PRODUCTION MICHAEL DOUGLAS for IPC FILMS.

STARRING JANE FONDA (Kimberly Wells), JACK LEMMON (Jack Godell), MICHAEL DOUGLAS (Richard Adams), SCOTT BRADY (Herman De Young), JAMES HAMPTON (Bill Gibson), PETER DONAT (Don Jacovich), WILFORD BRIMLEY (Ted Spindler), RICHARD HERD (Evan McCormack), Daniel Valdez (Hector Salas), Stan Bohrman (Pete Martin).

IFF CANNES 1979 AWARD for BEST ACTOR (Jack Lemmon).

"Hey! Hey! Is anybody listening to me?"

Perhaps no other science fiction film has ever come as close to reality: on March 28, 1979 a malfunction occurred at the atomic power plant in Harris-burg that was almost identical to the accident depicted in the film *The China Syndrome*, released just twelve days earlier. A realistic docu-drama un-expectedly sprang from a fictitious story that had been harshly criticized by the pro-nuclear faction. One party in particular benefited from this disastrous situation – the stock value of Columbia Pictures experienced a healthy upturn thanks to the masses of people that began streaming into cinemas.

Ironically enough, director and co-author James Bridges initially wa-tered down the critical statement before the film's release: "This is a monster movie and technology is the monster." Leading actress Jane Fonda spoke of a film about "greed," Michael Douglas simply about an "exciting story."

The audience is introduced to the story by a television reporter. Kimber-ly Wells (Jane Fonda) is the sort of reporter who normally covers events like birthdays at the zoo for a local television station. She would prefer to investi-gate more serious subjects, but according to the station's bosses, serious journalism and femininity do not mix. One day, however, Wells stumbles upon an explosive, scandalous story by chance. She puts together a report about energy supply in California with cameraman Richard Adams (Michael Dou-glas) and tours the Ventana atomic plant, where without a hint of criticism she repeats into her microphone exactly what the plant's glib PR manager Bill Gibson (James Hampton) tells her. They are on the visitor's platform to the switchboard area when the plant is shaken by a quiet quaking. An alarm signal rings, warning lights flash, and people become active in the sound and air-proof command center. Though prohibited, Adams surreptitiously contin-ues filming. Gibson's explanation that it is just a standard turbine failure is met with disbelief.

Wells wants to do a report about the unusual event, but her boss Jacovich (Peter Donat) refuses her request. Because it was shot without authorization, they won't use the filmed material. Richard Adams' hotheaded

"In the sense that it attacks big business and corporate morality, I suppose it is political; but it's essentially a gripping thriller which draws its strength from the very real anxiety about the safety of nuclear energy." *Encore Magazine*

1 Start spreadin' the news: Jack Godell (Jack Lemmon) is determined to tell the world what he knows.

2 Hazardous to your health: Contaminated material has caused an accident and the possible consequences are being studiously ignored.

3 Won't somebody listen! Desperate to prevent the looming catastrophe, Jack Godell tries to catch the eyes of the reporters.

reaction does not improve matters, and he puts Kimberly Wells into an uncomfortable position when he steals the controversial roll of film from the channel's archive and disappears.

While searching for Adams, Wells meets Jack Godell (Jack Lemmon), the head engineer of the atomic plant. He again claims that the situation they observed was not a malfunction. The next day Godell is to give testimony to an investigating committee whose findings ultimately exonerate the technicians – the plant's operators breathe a sigh of relief, as they are anxiously

awaiting a decision authorizing the construction of a new nuclear reactor. Every delay is a further financial disaster for the already debt-ridden undertaking.

Jack Godell is in fact worried, and he begins inspections of his own. He discovers that to save expenses, the construction firm forged several safety-related documents. His warnings are ignored and the reactor is to be reattached to the network as quickly as possible. In the meantime Kimberly Wells and Richard Adams have received information from independent experts

"A precise but appealingly ambivalent performance from Jane Fonda – as a media person who finds both a cause and a career boost in a nuclear energy crisis – centers this melodramatic account of how Harrisburg might have happened."

Sight and Sound

about the true nature of the secretly filmed malfunction. It turns out that t could have come to a melting of the reactor core, which inevitably would have released a large amount of radioactive material. The core could have even wound itself into the Earth's core – all the way to China ("China Syndrome"). They confront Godell with their information. Shaken, he tells of the construction firm's manipulation and promises the journalists hard evidence. The next morning he gives this evidence to a messenger, whose car is forced off the road. The messenger is found seriously injured and the documents have disappeared.

Hearing the news, Godell himself sets off. He too is followed, but escapes in the nick of time and reaches the power plant, where he realizes

with horror that the reactor is running at full capacity. Again his warnings have not been heeded. In a last moment of desperation he grabs a gun, forces the workers out of the command center and allows Kimberly Wells and Richard Adams to come and do a live report about what has occurred. While the necessary broadcast equipment is being delivered, unbeknownst to the journalists a special unit is attempting to get at Godell. When the cameras finally go live Godell's nervousness overwhelms him and he gets bogged down in technical details. The police force their way in before Godell can reveal his information. Godell is shot and the transmission cables are cut.

Outside, more and more television teams have assembled. Bill Gibson has already prepared a press release, in which he describes Godell as psy-

4 Hard pressed: Jack Godell finds an ally in TV reporter Kimberly Wells (Jane Fonda) – but her story is rejected.

5 Sabotage? Godell's messenger is badly hurt – and the documents he was carrying have disappeared…

6 Lying on her laurels: Jane Fonda's performance as Kimberly Wells earned her an Oscar nomination.

JAMES BRIDGES   In the original screenplay of *The China Syndrome* (1979), the leading character was a man. Richard Dreyfuss was briefly a candidate for the role. After the producers won Jane Fonda for the project, the script had to be accordingly revised. Fonda herself collaborated on the changes with James Bridges (*1936), who had been chosen to direct the film. Bridges had the best qualifications: he was originally an actor himself and played several television roles in the 1950s.

He simultaneously worked on a career as a screenwriter and made a breakthrough in the mid 60s with several genre films. He soon aroused attention with contemporary themes, which also drive his later directorial works. Included in Bridges' directorial projects are the Travolta films *Urban Cowboy* (1980) and *Perfect* (1985), and the film adaptation of Jay McInerney's *Bright Lights, Big City* (1988). His last project was the screenplay for Clint Eastwood's *White Hunter, Black Heart* (1990). Bridges died on June 6, 1993.

chologically disturbed. Kimberly Wells interrupts the reading and embarrasses Gibson with pointed questions. At Wells' insistence, Godell's colleague Ted Spindler (Wilford Brimley), who until that point had been strictly loyal to his employer, decides to break his silence. He refutes Gibson's statement and emphasizes that Jack Godell was not psychologically disturbed, but a hero.

The film, accompanied by music only during the title sequence, ends the same way it began: with images of the control center of the television station, where after the dramatic live transmission, the normally programmed entertainment is continued. The malfunction was an exception, a special case, and the medium that was briefly able to show its potential falls back into daily routine.   HK

BEING THERE

†

1979 - USA - 129 MIN. - SOCIAL SATIRE

DIRECTOR HAL ASHBY (1929–1988)

SCREENPLAY JERZY KOSINSKI, based on his novel of the same name DIRECTOR OF PHOTOGRAPHY CALEB DESCHANEL EDITING DON ZIMMERMAN MUSIC JOHNNY MANDEL PRODUCTION ANDREW BRAUNSBERG for LORIMAR FILM ENTERTAINMENT, NORTHSTAR, BSB, ENIGMA.

STARRING PETER SELLERS (Chance, the Gardener), SHIRLEY MACLAINE (Eve Rand), MELVYN DOUGLAS (Benjamin Rand), JACK WARDEN (The President), RICHARD A. DYSART (Doctor Robert Allenby), RICHARD BASEHART (Vladimir Skrapinov), RUTH ATTAWAY (Louise), DAVID CLENNON (Thomas Franklin), FRAN BRILL (Sally Hayes), DENISE DUBARRY (Johanna Franklin), OTEIL BURBRIDGE (Lolo).

ACADEMY AWARDS 1979 OSCAR for BEST SUPPORTING ACTOR (Melvyn Douglas).

"As long as the roots are not severed, all is well. And all will be well in the garden."

The main character, the film's protagonist and leitmotif, appears minutes after the picture has gotten underway. Surrounded by the mayhem of on-coming traffic, Mr. Chance (Peter Sellers) walks down Pennsylvania Avenue's center divider, utterly unperturbed. The spectator is overcome by the uncanny sensation that Chance has literally appeared out of nowhere. As the camera pans up, revealing the hub of the nation's legislature, the Capitol, it quickly becomes clear where destiny will lead him.

As it were, Mr. Chance is a man with no set goals. Since childhood, he has been the ward and faithful gardener of a wealthy eccentric, whose house-keeper saw to his upbringing. Chance has never left home, and the world that he knows is a collage of television images. A kind heart would deem him a pure soul, a more critical one brand him a "simple Simon" or a moron. He walks through life with a wide-eyed grin and, armed with his gardener's grab bag of fortune cookie philosophy, manages to take the world by storm.

When his lifelong employer dies and his estate liquidated, Chance must abandon the only home he has ever known. Utterly clueless, he embarks on new soil, awakening from his chronic lethargy when a video camera in an electronics store window forces him to come face to face with himself. Stunned, he absent-mindedly retreats into the path of a moving stretch lim-ousine, luckily incurring only minor injuries. The vehicle's owner, Eve Rand (Shirley MacLaine) takes him under her wing and brings him home to her mil-lionaire husband. A sound idea, as the terminally ill Mr. Rand has round the clock medical staff tending to him.

Many years Eve's senior, Benjamin Rand (Melvyn Douglas), knows his days are numbered. Impressed by the houseguest's reserved demeanor and the "profound" natural metaphors he uses to explain the world, the elderly gentleman immediately takes to him. It just so happens that Rand is not only rich but also an influential presidential advisor, and the head of state does, in fact, makes Chance's acquaintance when he comes round the house one day. The man is announced as "Chauncey Gardener," an innocent misunder-standing that Chance doesn't bother to correct.

Like the Rands, the president (Jack Warden) is electrified by the gar-dener's philosophic insight and quotes him during a public address. The win-dow of opportunity immediately opens up for the illiterate Chance, including

1 Like a virgin: Mr. Chance (Peter Sellers) is about to leave his familiar surroundings for the very first time.

2 No man's land: Chance wanders aimlessly through an alien world and stumbles upon the nerve center of political power.

3 Making friends: Chance turns his back on society and returns to Mother Nature.

4 Green fingers, black prospects: When his master dies, Chance is banished from the garden.

"*Being There*, directed by Hal Ashby, is a rare and subtle bird that finds its tone and stays with it."

Chicago Sun-Times

a silly attempt at seduction on the part of Eve Rand, and he soon emerges as a media sensation. The papers want to interview him. He even appears on a talk show and is offered a book deal so that he can share his views on life with the world.

When the wealthy benefactor passes away, Washington's elite assembles at the burial to pay recognition to their decorated comrade-in-arms. With the coffin still on their shoulders, the political movers and shakers convene to decide upon his successor and agree to appoint Chauncey Gardner to the position. His public appearances have won him the respect of the media and a large following among the people. Chance, however, seeks solitude and, while meandering through a grove, comes upon the bank of a lake, where he proceeds to walk on water without sinking.

4

5   Straight from the bush: With his homespun wisdom, Chance becomes a presidential advisor.

6   An innocent abroad: Eve Rand (Shirley MacLaine) is interested and the childlike Chance is flummoxed.

HAL ASHBY   Born in 1929, Hal Ashby received formal training in film editing at Republic Pictures back in the days of the old Hollywood studio system. Starting in 1953, he began to work as an assistant to editing master Robert Swink. 1965 marked the beginning of his career as head film editor and saw the dawn of a year-long collaboration with director Norman Jewison. Ashby won the Oscar for Best Film Editing for *In the Heat of the Night* (1967). He got his initial shot at directing pictures in 1970. His first film, *The Landlord*, about a hoity-toity white aristocrat who purchases a building in a black populated slum, earned him his reputation as a socially progressive satirist. Ashby remained loyal to the genre in the years that followed, directing films like *Harold and Maude* (1971) as well as *Shampoo* (1974), starring Warren Beatty as hairdresser to Beverly Hills' rich and famous. The film was set in 1968, on the eve of President Nixon's first victory. Further successes came with the film adaptation of the biography of folk music great, Woody Guthrie, entitled *Bound for Glory* (1976) as well as for his heartfelt reflection on Vietnam, *Coming Home* (1978). With *Being There* (1979), a satire about a mentally handicapped gardener, whom a twist of fate sends flying into important political circles and possibly into the Oval Office, Ashby struck it big once again – both commercially and artistically. Subsequent projects in the eighties fell short of his previous accomplishments. In 1988, at the age of fifty-nine, Hal Ashby died of cancer.

Peter Sellers, in the second to last performance of his life, consciously follows in the footsteps of his personal idol Stan Laurel. Much like Laurel's on screen persona, Chance the gardener has a childlike nature incapable of spite or malice. He is an oblivious soul who tries to rid himself of armed intruders by pointing the remote control at them and changing the channel. He is baffled when nothing happens as this puerile means of self-defense always functioned in the past.

His sophisticated attire – bits and pieces of his former employer's wardrobe – his introverted demeanor and his gardener's maxims all contribute to his astounding success in both social and political arenas. Un-

familiar with challenges, he takes each task asked of him with gratitude, expressing only concern and understanding for his fellow man. Indeed, Chance seems to be some saintly breed of fool.

Contrary to the original screenplay in which the film was supposed to close with a scene of Chance and Eve Rand on a stroll, director Hal Ashby inserted the scene just prior to the film's conclusion that shows Chance walking on water. The underlying message is not, however, that Chance is a saint or modern day messiah. Instead, it is an image rooted in logic: Chance doesn't sink, simply because he doesn't know he's supposed to.

HK

"*Harold and Maude* director Hal Ashby has created a wonderful satire full of sly humor. The brilliant Peter Sellers plays Mr. Chance with a stoicism reminiscent of Buster Keaton." *Cinema*

6

CRUISING

1980 - USA - 106 MIN. - PSYCHO THRILLER

DIRECTOR WILLIAM FRIEDKIN (*1939)
SCREENPLAY WILLIAM FRIEDKIN, based on the novel of the same name by GERALD WALKER DIRECTOR OF PHOTOGRAPHY JAMES A. CONTNER EDITING BUD SMITH MUSIC JACK NITZSCHE PRODUCTION JERRY WEINTRAUB for LORIMAR FILM ENTERTAINMENT, UNITED ARTISTS.

STARRING AL PACINO (Steve Burns), PAUL SORVINO (Captain Edelson), KAREN ALLEN (Nancy Gates), RICHARD COX (Stuart Richards), DON SCARDINO (Ted Bailey), JOE SPINELL (DiSimone), JAY ACOVONE (Skip Lea), RANDY JURGENSEN (Detective Lefronsky), BARTON HEYMAN (Doctor Rifkin), GENE DAVID (DaVici).

"There's a lot about me you don't know."

The clubs in Manhattan's seedy, red light haven, known as the Meat Packing District, comprise a world that plays by its own rules. Here on the West Side, the S & M constituents of the New York gay scene flaunt their taste for claustrophobically eerie catacombs, sweat-drenched human Ken dolls and hardcore leather daddies. Already a sleazy part of town, this parallel universe has been terrorized for some time now by a serial killer.

Because beat detective Steve Burns (Al Pacino), with his raven hair and coal-dark eyes, fits the physical profile of the victims, his superior, Captain Edelson (Paul Sorvino) sends him straight to the lion's den. Even Burns' fianceé Nancy (Karen Allen), who provides the picture with its only female role, must be kept in the dark about his double life. The mission causes Burns to spiral into an identity crisis, which soon jeopardizes his relationship. Unable to maintain his initial professional distance, the cop loses all grasp of previous life and embarks on a string of sexual adventures.

Like so many other aspects of this piece, just how far he goes is not explicitly spelled out. It is a film that works by insinuation, and even its conclusion is open to a number of interpretations.

Friedkin has explained his film's fragmentary nature as a means of responding to the extreme, government-imposed editing changes his piece suffered. An entire 40 minutes of material disappeared under the censors' shears, an attack the final version can hardly cover up. Still, these acts of censorship couldn't stifle the almost insane intensity of the microcosm that

"This film is not intended as an indictment of the homosexual world."

Note in the opening credits

Friedkin created. Imagery as strange and bizarre as that of a sci-fi movie, the brilliant and exceptionally well-integrated soundtrack, not to mention the spartan, often almost minimalist dialog, all blends smoothly to captivating, almost hypnotic effect.

Given this, it's relatively easy to imagine how unnerved the film's censors were when they saw *Cruising* in its raw version. There's something ironic about the fact that the New York gay community rushed to join the nation's moral enforcers to protest against the film. Homosexuals started

voicing their distress while filming was still underway, without having even seen any of the material.

As one might expect from this "shock therapy" director, Friedkin did indeed use every cinematic trick in the book to exploit his subject matter, but not in the manner that his accusers claimed. His motivation was not to get a mere rise out of his audience. He was very much indifferent to what was considered politically correct at the time and the graphic nature of the piece was driven primarily by his aesthetic principles. Following in the footsteps

1   Cruisin' for a bruisin': Cop Steve Burns (Al Pacino) takes a trip to a perilous parallel universe.

2   Sidewalk sirens: These sisters can turn a trick and hold their own.

3   The heat is on: As the corpses stockpile, Captain Edelstein (Paul Sorvino) is under increasing pressure to find the murderer.

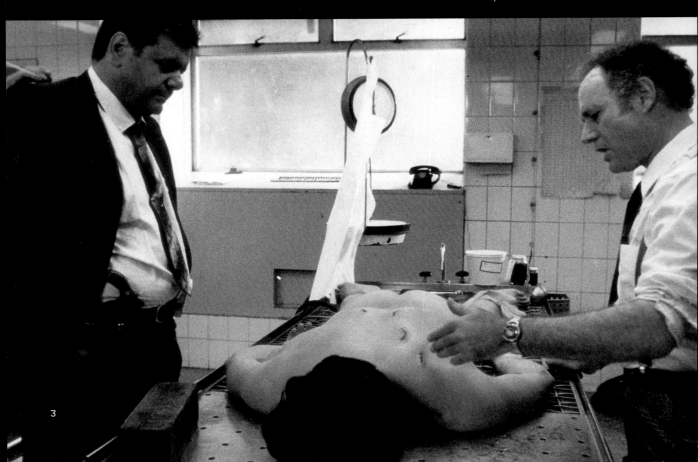

4   Loading zone: The Meatpacking District has just received a shipment. Come and get it!

5   Look into my eyes: Student Stuart Richards (Richard Cox) has a secret.

6   You scratch my butt, I'll scratch yours… Friedkin's hopes of mollifying the censors were dramatically misplaced. The responsible official was so shocked that he walked out of the preview.

7   Cap'n Crunch: Burns' disguise soon becomes a second skin.

8   "Come here often? What's a half-naked black guy like yourself doing in a police station?" Director William Friedkin just loves to unsettle his public.

"I thought it would be more interesting to make a thriller set in a milieu where sexually motivated role-changes and identity makeovers are common practice. It's a fascinating world."

William Friedkin, in: steadycam

of his film *The Exorcist* (1973), the director breaks down the walls between the spectators and the performers with surgical precision. Here, the means of deconstruction extends all way to the film's subversive audio track, filled with the ubiquitous, almost obscene squeaking of leather rubbing against itself.

In *Cruising*, Friedkin takes several avenues to explore a topic revisited time and time again in his work: the relativity of roles. We watch as police officers who despise transvestites readily have their way with them. We witness Steve Burns' transformation, see him keep his studded armband on while having sex with his girlfriend, and at the end, it is unclear as to what

extent he has implicated himself in the sickening crimes. Even Captain Edelson whispers to his despondent undercover agent "I need you" in a way that sounds like a confession of love.

Subculture and the governing body. Moral depravity and law and order. For Friedkin, these categories are just as unpredictable and fleeting as a realistic depiction of unfamiliar walks of life and their corresponding stereotypes. This becomes crystal clear when, on "precinct night," police uniforms and handcuffs become the sex toys of club patrons, a towering black man, wearing just a thong and cowboy hat, gets the suspects to talk. And is that really surprising? A uniform is, after all, just a uniform.

SH

7

X-RATING

In ancient Rome, children under the age of 10 were prohibited from entering the Coliseum. Supposedly, that's why the Motion Picture Association of America's (MPAA) usage of an "X" rating, indicating that youths are not allowed admission, is designated by the Roman numeral for "10." The MPAA has presided over the moral character of the material presented on U.S. movie screens since 1922. The American rating system, however, was first instated in 1968 by MPAA president Jack Valenti. It came about during a time when films like *Who's Afraid of Virginia Woolf?* (1966) and *Blow Up* (1966) began to subversively question social norms and propriety. An R-rated film restricts children under the age of 17 from viewing a film when not in the company of an adult. The austere "X" prohibits even that. It was officially renamed "NC-17" in 1990, because the "X" rating had been abused by less reputable productions that simply wanted publicity. Such a rating is often disastrous for non-pornographic productions because fewer than one hundred movie houses in the United States show these films. A similar fate befalls pictures that aren't ever reviewed by the MPAA. This is why filmmakers are often forced to enter into editing discussions that can lead to the butchering of a film. Still, this is the only way to avoid the stigma of an "X" rating. The sacrifices, as was the case for *Cruising* (1980), can compromise an entire project. Friedkin avenged this injustice by inserting pornographic imagery into several scenes, which can only be consciously perceived in the material's individual frames. Rumor has it that the Friedkin is currently working on a director's cut of the film.

William Friedkin's *Cruising* is a great film of the urban, North American night. His voyeuristic camera roams the streets that come alive with sexual promenades after sunset, and it lingers in noisy, jam-packed bars, watching men search for the man of their fantasies. *San Francisco Examiner*

8

STAR WARS: EPISODE V – THE EMPIRE STRIKES BACK

⬆⬆

1980 - USA - 125 MIN. - SCIENCE FICTION

DIRECTOR IRVIN KERSHNER (*1923)
SCREENPLAY LEIGH BRACKETT, LAWRENCE KASDAN DIRECTOR OF PHOTOGRAPHY PETER SUSCHITZKY EDITING PAUL HIRSCH MUSIC JOHN WILLIAMS PRODUCTION GARY KURTZ for LUCASFILM LTD.

STARRING MARK HAMILL (Luke Skywalker), HARRISON FORD (Han Solo), CARRIE FISHER (Princess Leia Organa), BILLY DEE WILLIAMS (Lando Calrissian), DAVID PROWSE (Darth Vader), JAMES EARL JONES (Darth Vader's voice), PETER MAYHEW (Chewbacca), ANTHONY DANIELS (C-3PO), KENNY BAKER (R2-D2), FRANK OZ (Yoda), ALEC GUINNESS (Ben "Obi-Wan" Kenobi).

ACADEMY AWARDS 1980 OSCAR for BEST SOUND (Bill Varney, Steve Maslow, Gregg Landaker, Peter Sutton), and SPECIAL PRIZE for VISUAL EFFECTS (Brian Johnson, Richard Edlund, Dennis Muren, Bruce Nicholson).

"Beware of the dark side."

The Empire Strikes Back is a suspenseful and engaging sequel to the extraordinarily successful first part of the Star Wars Trilogy, which has now expanded into a six-part saga. Luke Skywalker (Mark Hamill) and the rebels, who were able to snatch Princess Leia (Carrie Fisher) from the clutches of the evil Empire in the first episode, have been tracked down in their icy hideout on the planet Hoth by Darth Vader, the sinister, intergalactic villain in the service of the Emperor. With the help of their space adventurer friend Han Solo (Harrison Ford) and his companion Chewbacca (Peter Mayhew), they are just able to flee to the cloud city governed by their ally, Lando (Billy Dee Williams). But safety is merely an illusion. Darth Vader and his henchmen

have long since located the safe haven and have succeeded in forcing Lando to hand his guests over to the Empire. But the good side of the "Force," which accompanies Luke Skywalker and his friends, will not give up without a fight. In the final showdown between Good and Evil, Darth Vader reveals himself to be Luke Skywalker's father. But his attempt to pull Skywalker over to the dark side to help him triumph over the evil Emperor fails. Skywalker resists the temptations of the dark side of the Force and escapes with Princess Leia.

What this straightforward plot does not immediately divulge is the glut of fairy-tale themes, myths, and figures that come into play. Prime examples

1 Where there's a will there's a way: Luke Skywalker   2 Pretty as a princess: Carrie Fisher as Leia Organa.   3 Listen to your elders: The ancient Jedi Master wins
   (Mark Hamill) training with the Jedi Master, Yoda.   Luke's undying allegiance in the fight for good.

"From the first burst of John Williams' powerful score and the receding opening title crawl, we are back in pleasant surroundings and anxious for a good time – like walking through the front gate of Disneyland, where good and evil are never confused and the righteous will always win." *Monthly Film Bulletin*

are the fairy-tale-like Princess Leia, the chivalrous "space-age Robin Hood," Luke Skywalker, and his loyal sidekicks, Han Solo and Chewbacca. And of course there is the incarnation of Evil himself – Darth Vader, the masked, cloaked villain, as charismatic as he is asthmatic, whose ultimate lightsaber duel with Skywalker is reminiscent of the sword fights of the classic swash-bucklers. But the mythic elements do not end here. The new interpretation of the classic father-son conflict exposes the father as the ruthless perpetrator of the dark side of the force, while the white-clad, youthful Skywalker embodies the liberating, good side. Numerous components of the most disparate genres are simultaneously combined under the roof of science fiction. In addition to the aforementioned elements, pieces of fantasy, war, and action genres have most notably been borrowed. Battle robots that look like

outsize, fantastical, mechanical creatures, war scenes with classic battle formations, and risky stunts by the good heroes provide the proof. At the same time, the film affectionately and playfully deals with its own cinematic history: the two robots, R2-D2 and C-3PO wander aimlessly through the scenery like clownish relics of earlier science fiction films and repeatedly provide for laughs.

The Empire Strikes Back marks a further milestone on George Lucas' determined path to create a new, physical cinema of audiovisual effects targeting the audience's perceptive faculties. Computer-steered camera movements and the combination of idyllic calm and dramatic acceleration produced far more intense spatial impressions than any special effects seen before. The underlying scheme of employing extraordinary contrasts is a leit-

THE STAR WARS SAGA In the 1970s, no one could have predicted that George Lucas would lay the foundation for an unrivalled career in the film business with his epic fairy tale, *Star Wars* (1977). And to boot, he did so in a time in which science fiction films were decidedly unpopular. His ingenious idea of combining the developing special effects with a serialized blockbuster concept is still unparalleled. But Lucas simply built on the experience of contemporary special effects gurus and previous capital-intensive mega productions. He purchased long-forgotten technical machines, modified them with new electric steering capabilities, and devised a serial marketing concept that foresaw the dual capitalization possibilities provided by merchandizing articles. Lucas' modernization of existent production and marketing strategies proved in hindsight to be exceedingly successful and has often been copied (*Harry Potter and the Sorcerer's Stone*, 2001 or *The Lord of the Rings – The Fellowship of the Ring*, 2001).
The *Star Wars* saga includes six parts in total. It all began in 1977 with *Star Wars – Episode IV. Star Wars: Episode V – The Empire Strikes Back* followed in 1980, and *Star Wars: Episode VI – The Return of the Jedi* in 1983. In 1999 came *Star Wars: Episode I – The Phantom Menace*, and in 2002, *Star Wars: Episode II – Attack of the Clones*. The final part, *Episode III*, which sets the stage for *Star Wars* and has no title to date will be released in 2005. It is interesting to note that Lucas produced the last three chapters of the story first, while the first three episodes topped the box office at the end of the 1990s and early 2000s. The film industry is indebted to Lucas' special effects company, Industrial Light and Magic (ILM) for its innovative technical ideas and imagination which considerably advanced the development of special effects technology. The digitalization of film productions can be attributed almost solely to the popularity of the *Star Wars* saga.

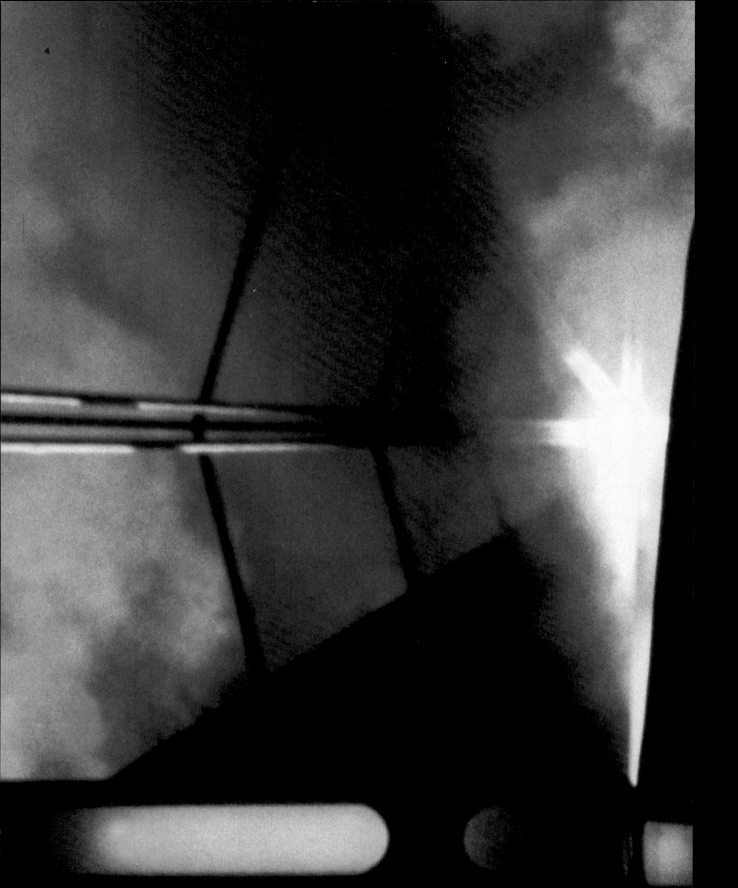

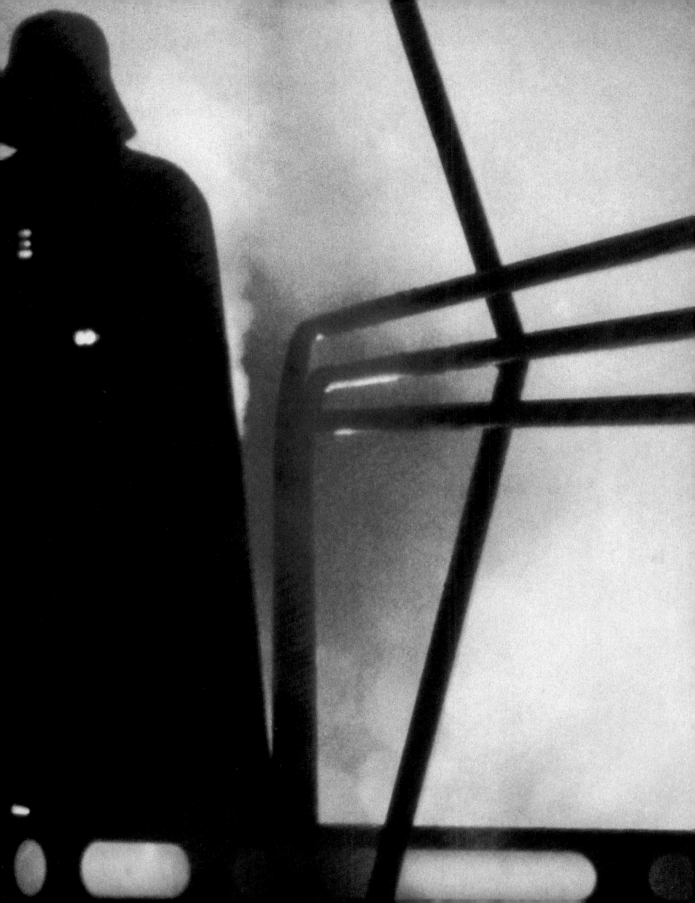

5

motif of the film, extending from the basic Good vs. Evil theme through to the explosive war in the icy expanses of the rebel refuge.

Above all, *The Empire Strikes Back* is an inventive children's film for adults, and all age groups can allow themselves to be enchanted by its naïve, cult-like charm. Its secret lies less in the never-ending story of the eternal spiritual conflict between elemental forces, its mix of childish and adult appeal, or the fabulously fantastic and the nightmarishly military. With the *Star Wars* saga (1977, 1980, 1983, 1999, 2002) George Lucas and his special effects team opened our eyes to the idea of a film that stretches far beyond the storyline: they revolutionized our perception of the optical and acoustic potential of the medium itself. *Star Wars* took off our blinkers, widened our horizons and gave us an innocent view into the future of filmmaking.   BR

"Ultimately, the success of this genre depends on the special effects. John Dykstra's special effects for *Star Wars* were some of the best in film history, and those in *Empire* (by Brian Johnson and Richard Edlund) are equally dazzling and impressive." *Films in Review*

4   The black death: A shadow fell upon the catacombs of modern day villains with the birth of Darth Vader (David Prowse).

5   Robots, beasts, and dinosaurs…Oh, my! *The Empire Strikes Back* is chock full of fantastic visuals and astounding effects.

6   Worth his weight in gold: Daft but endearing, C-3PO gives a human face to the intergalactic wars.

7   Hi-ho, Silver! *The Star Wars* series deftly reworks motifs from familiar genres.

6

THE ELEPHANT MAN

1980 - GREAT BRITAIN / USA - 123 MIN. - DRAMA

DIRECTOR DAVID LYNCH (*1946)
SCREENPLAY CHRISTOPHER DE VORE, ERIC BERGREN, DAVID LYNCH, based on the memoirs *THE ELEPHANT MAN AND OTHER REMINISCENCES* by SIR FREDERICK TREVES and the book *THE ELEPHANT MAN: A STUDY IN HUMAN DIGNITY* by ASHLEY MONTAGU DIRECTOR OF PHOTOGRAPHY Freddie FRANCIS EDITING ANNE V. COATES MUSIC JOHN MORRIS, SAMUEL BARBER ("Adagio for strings") PRODUCTION JONATHAN SANGER for BROOKSFILMS LTD.

STARRING ANTHONY HOPKINS (Dr. Frederick Treves), JOHN HURT (John Merrick), JOHN GIELGUD (Carr Gomm), ANNE BANCROFT (Mrs. Kendal), FREDDIE JONES (Bytes), WENDY HILLER (Mothershead), HANNAH GORDON (Anne Treves), MICHAEL ELPHICK (Night Watchman), JOHN STANDING (Dr. Fox), PHOEBE NICHOLLS (Merrick's Mother).

"I am not an animal! I am a human being! I am... a man!"

"Life is full of surprises. Ladies and gentleman, consider the fate of this creature's poor mother. In the fourth month of her maternal condition, she was struck down by a wild elephant. Struck down, if you take my meaning, on an uncharted African island. The result is plain to see, ladies and gentleman... THE TERRIBLE ELEPHANT MAN!" At a freak show in London, a shockingly deformed young man is served up for the delectation of the public. This shy and terrified creature is found, examined and adopted by the surgeon Dr. Frederick Treves (Anthony Hopkins), who discovers a sensitive and intelligent human being behind the monstrous façade. Not only can the "Elephant Man" think and speak; he loves conversation and literature, and creates exquisite paper sculptures with his undamaged left hand.

The Elephant Man is based on the true story of Joseph Carey Merrick, who was born in Leicester in 1862, suffering from multiple neurofibromatosis, a disease that engenders spongy growths on the victim's skin and bones. Frederick Treves discovered Merrick at a fairground. In 1923, the physician published his memoirs, *The Elephant Man and Other Reminiscences.* Together with Ashley Montagu's *The Elephant Man: A Study in Human Dignity,* Treves' book formed the basis for the film.

Director David Lynch (*Mulholland Drive,* 2001) portrays the deformed man with enormous empathy. In the first half-hour of the film, we see nothing of John Merrick's face, only the reactions of those who do so. By the time he is finally revealed to us, we have already become acquainted with a human being, and our reaction to his appearance is something other than shock. Treves rescues him from the freak show and takes him to hospital, but Merrick's martyrdom is still far from over. To the scientists of the Pathological Society, he is an object of research, a fascinating specimen; in London's better circles, it becomes *chic* to invite the monster to tea; and when Merrick is alone in his hospital bed, the night watchman opens his

1 Sandbagged: A sideshow attraction who proves himself a prince. John Hurt as the piteously deformed Elephant Man.

2 Step right up: Bytes (Freddie Jones) capitalizes on the star of his sidewalk circus.

3 Truncated: Surgeon Dr. Frederick Treves (Anthony Hopkins) "buys" the Elephant Man from Bytes.

"John Hurt gives a magnificent performance, masterfully conveying deep-felt emotions even while hampered by the inability to use his face or even much of his voice."

Motion Picture Guide

THE CINEMATOGRAPHER FREDDIE FRANCIS

The Elephant Man has a very particular, "historical" look to it. Despite the extreme contrasts between areas of light and dark, the light is soft, with backgrounds frequently lost in spaces permeated by a diffuse bloom. These images were created by the Director of Photography Freddie Francis (*22.12.1917), one of England's finest cameramen.

Freddie Francis was born in London. After learning his trade with the British army during the Second World War, he went on to work with some of the greatest directors in British cinema, including Joseph Losey and Karel Reisz. In 1960, he received an Oscar for his work on *Sons and Lovers* (Director: Jack Cardiff) – filmed, like *The Elephant Man*, in black-and-white and in widescreen Cinemascope format. Two years later, Francis took up directing; by 1975, he had made 20 horror films, none of them great works, but all finely crafted movies. For *The Elephant Man*, Francis accepted the job of cameraman for the first time since the early 60s, and he remained faithful to the visual style he had developed at that time. In the years that followed, Francis was increasingly active as a cameraman. He continued his collaboration with Lynch on *Dune* (1984) and – 15 years later – on *The Straight Story* (1999). In the intervening period, he worked with a variety of directors, among them Martin Scorsese (*Cape Fear*, 1991). For his work on *Glory* (1989), a drama of racial conflict at the time of the American Civil War, Freddie Francis was awarded his second Oscar.

4   Curiosity killed the cat: The clinic's night porter
    (Michael Elphick) displays the misshapen man to a
    paying customer.

5   PhDs at the freak show: Dr. Treves presents the
    Elephant Man to the members of the London
    Pathological Society.

"The point was to let the audience become familiar with the monster, so that the monster could disappear and the human being come into view."

David Lynch

door to hordes of drunks and streetwalkers hungry for a glimpse of his misery.

Lynch had only made one full-length film before this: the disturbing underground classic *Eraserhead* (1974/77). Though at first glance the two films may seem very different, *Eraserhead* can in fact be seen as a preliminary study to *The Elephant Man*. There are thematic and structural similarities: both movies tell the story of an outsider, and both are suffused with a nightmarish atmosphere. With its five-million-dollar budget, however, *The Elephant Man* was 250 times more expensive than Lynch's debut. Executive Producer Mel Brooks (whose wife Anne Bancroft appears in the film) had to fight to get Lynch accepted as director of the film. It was worth the struggle; the film is a masterpiece, both brilliantly constructed and deeply moving, and

it made Lynch's name worldwide. Apart from the visionary sequences that frame the film, and the nightmare in the middle, the film is thoroughly naturalistic, resurrecting Victorian London in a succession of atmospheric images. The cinematographer Freddie Francis and the costume and production designers achieved something exceptional here, and all were shortlisted for Academy Awards. Indeed, the film was nominated for eight Oscars in total, though, sadly, it received not a single one.

In *The Elephant Man*, Lynch also pays tribute to two great films with related themes: like Quasimodo in *The Hunchback of Notre Dame* (1939), Merrick lives in a belltower; and the scene in which he is freed from a cage by his fellow "monsters" is a reference to Tod Browning's classic *Freaks* (1932). HJK

THE LAST METRO
Die letzte Metro / Le dernier métro

1980 - FRANCE / FRG - 131 MIN. - DRAMA

DIRECTOR FRANÇOIS TRUFFAUT (1932–1984)
SCREENPLAY FRANÇOIS TRUFFAUT, SUZANNE SCHIFFMAN, JEAN-CLAUDE GRUMBERG DIRECTOR OF PHOTOGRAPHY NÉSTOR ALMENDROS
EDITING MARTINE BARRAQUÉ MUSIC GEORGES DELERUE PRODUCTION FRANÇOIS TRUFFAUT for LES FILMS DU CARROSSE,
SOCIÉTÉ FRANÇAISE DE PRODUCTION, SÉDIF PRODUCTIONS, TF1 FILMS PRODUCTIONS, MARAN-FILM.

STARRING CATHERINE DENEUVE (Marion Steiner), GÉRARD DEPARDIEU (Bernard Granger), JEAN POIRET (Jean-Loup Cottins),
HEINZ BENNENT (Lucas Steiner), ANDRÉA FERRÉOL (Arlette Guillaume), MAURICE RISCH (Raymond Boursier), PAULETTE
DUBOST (Germaine Fabre), JEAN-LOUIS RICHARD (Daxiat), SABINE HAUDEPIN (Nadine Marsac), JEAN-PIERRE KLEIN
(Christian Leglise).

"I love her –
I'm a glutton for punishment."

Paris, 1942. The city is under German occupation. Lucas Steiner (Heinz Bennent), the Jewish director of the Théâtre Montmartre, has gone into hiding; it's rumored he's left France. Since his disappearance, his wife Marion (Catherine Deneuve), the star of the ensemble, has been running the theater. Only she knows that Lucas is actually hiding in the cellar of the building, where a hole in the heating-pipes allows him to listen in on rehearsals. The play: "La Disparue"… Marion's task is made more difficult by the fact that Daxiat (Jean-Louis Richard), a critic who collaborates with the Nazis, is particularly interested in her theater, and she is thus forced to run a very tight

ship. The strictness of her regime is also felt by Bernard Granger (Gérard Depardieu), a talented young actor and notorious ladies' man. Though he's rehearsing the male lead at Marion's side, her interest in him seems purely professional.

For many years, François Truffaut had wanted to make a film about his memories of the Occupation. In The Last Metro, he combined this with a second ambition: to make a film set in a theater. For the one-time leader of the French Nouvelle Vague, it was an unusual project and, above all, a risky one. The Last Metro was Truffaut's most expensive film. As he hadn't had a box-

1 Love in the time of Catherine: Deneuve as a woman between two men – her husband (Heinz Bennent) and...

2 ... her young beau (Gérard Depardieu).

3 Star-struck: Truffaut's film is also a homage to Catherine Deneuve, the great icon of the French cinema.

2

"Deneuve, more beautiful than ever, displays a knowing humanity, and a sensuality she rarely shows in film, where she has been used more as icon than actress." *Time Magazine*

office success for years, a flop this time might well have jeopardized his independence. Yet despite the stars in the cast, there was no way of knowing whether the public would like the film. At that time, there had been little serious examination of the period of occupation in France. The few films that broached the topic were either burlesques or heroic epics. But Truffaut wanted to show everyday life in Paris under German occupation – and the result was a triumph. More than one million people saw the film on its first release in Paris alone. It received ten Césars, was nominated for an Oscar, and the critics were – almost – unanimous in their praise.

The Last Metro is almost classical in appearance. It was shot mainly in the grounds of an old factory, and this gives it a kind of "studio finish" unusual for Truffaut. Nonetheless, the film radiates vitality and authenticity. For one thing, enormous care was expended on getting the smallest details right, on everything from the music of the day to the radio programs of the time. Above all, despite the presence of two big stars, it is a wonderful ensemble film. It's full of utterly believable characters, whose function in the plot arises naturally from their role in the theater, and who give us an impression of the varied reactions of Parisians to everyday life under foreign occupation.

CATHERINE DENEUVE

For more than forty years now, Catherine Deneuve has been one of the biggest stars of European cinema. Born in Paris on October 22, 1943, she was only 19 when she made her breakthrough, in Jacques Demy's musical *The Umbrellas of Cherbourg* (*Les Parapluies de Cherbourg*, 1963). After this early success, she proved to be unusually demanding in her selection of roles, and this led to collaborations with some of the most interesting filmmakers in Europe. Controversial roles included a woman terrorised by her own aversion to sex, in Roman Polanski's *Repulsion* (1965), and a *grande bourgeoise* lady and occasional prostitute, in Luis Buñuel's *Belle de jour* (1966). From then on, Deneuve was stuck with the image of the icy, enigmatic blonde beauty. This image was reinforced by her second Buñuel-film *Tristana* (1969/70) and by François Truffaut's underrated *Mississippi Mermaid* (*La Sirène du Mississippi*, 1969). As a result, her qualities as an actress were long overlooked, although her popularity was huge. It was only with Truffaut's *The Last Metro* (*Le dernier métro*, 1980) that she finally got the recognition she deserved (she also received her first César for her performance in this film). Like very few female stars before her, she has been a lasting favorite with moviegoers, critics and directors alike. She also appeared in films such as André Téchiné's *Thieves* (*Les Voleurs*, 1996), Leos Carax' *Pola X* (1999) or – most recently – François Ozon's *8 Women* (*8 femmes*, 2001). In movies like these, she proved not only that she has the confidence to surprise her fans, but also that she can take a thoroughly ironical view of her status as *grande dame* of the French cinema.

3

4

> "*Le dernier metro* succeeds in making us forget the period and the setting, the symbolism and the morality. Instead, it allows us to share in the real actions of real people, as if we were watching them through a pane of glass."
>
> *Frankfurter Allgemeine Zeitung*

5

4 Hats off to Hitler: The German actor Heinz Bennent plays the Jewish theater director Lucas Steiner. A year before, he played a convincing Nazi in Schlöndorff's *The Tin Drum* (*Die Blechtrommel,* 1979).

5 The see-saw of collaboration and resistance: *The Last Metro* is a clear-headed and unglorified portrait of the French during WW II.

6 Air of authenticity: The production designers' endless attention to detail created a convincing image of everyday life in the 40s.

Truffaut shows us neither mere normality nor a permanent state of emergency. Instead, he presents a complex and detailed portrait of the time, with all the fine gradations between resistance and collaboration.

The film functions equally well as a dramatic love story set against a background of historical events; but typically, there's nothing stereotyped about Truffaut's use of this well-tried pattern. In his hands, it becomes a free-spirited and intimate study of a painful love triangle. As the film draws to a close, Deneuve, Depardieu and Bennent appear on stage – hand-in-hand.

Here, Truffaut is true to himself, and no closer to conventional morality than he was when he made *Jules and Jim* (*Jules et Jim*, 1961). The heart of this film is Catherine Deneuve, a woman torn between two men. This was her second collaboration with Truffaut, after *Mississippi Mermaid* (*La Sirène du Mississippi*, 1969). Now, in 1979, in the play-within-the-film, Truffaut asked her and Depardieu to repeat the wonderful closing dialog from the earlier movie. *The Last Metro*, then, is also a homage to the actress Deneuve, one of the great lovers in cinema history. JH

DRESSED TO KILL

1980 - USA - 106 MIN. - THRILLER

DIRECTOR BRIAN DE PALMA (*1940)
SCREENPLAY BRIAN DE PALMA DIRECTOR OF PHOTOGRAPHY RALF D. BODE EDITING GERALD B. GREENBERG MUSIC PINO DONAGGIO
PRODUCTION GEORGE LITTO for CINEMA 77 FILMS, FILMWAYS PICTURES, WARWICK ASSOCIATES.

STARRING ANGIE DICKINSON (Kate Miller), MICHAEL CAINE (Dr. Robert Elliott), NANCY ALLEN (Liz Blake), KEITH GORDON (Peter Miller), DENNIS FRANZ (Detective Marino), DAVID MARGULIES (Dr. Levy), KEN BAKER (Warren Lockman), SUSANNA CLEMM (Betty Luce), BRANDON MAGGART (Cleveland Sam), AMALIE COLLIER (Cleaning Woman).

"Do you have any sex that's not painful?"

How many psycho-thrillers start like this? A blonde woman gets off in the shower to the sound of violins and the rhythm of the slow-motion camera. Even as early as *Dressed to Kill's* opening sequence, Brian De Palma's imagery operates on multiple levels, making viewers stop to think for a second whether they've accidentally sat down to a soft-porn flick. Though as every versed Hitchcock fan knows, a shower can be a very hazardous location. Just moments into the erotic symphony, a shadowy figure rips Kate Miller (Angie Dickinson) out of her dream and into the waking world. Reality, however, provides no comfort. Kate is fed up with her stale marriage and wants out of her boring little life. Her son Peter (Keith Gordon), an electronic whiz-kid, is eternally engrossed in his high-tech projects, leaving Kate with no one to confide in other than her shrink, Dr. Elliott (Michael Caine).

The scenes that follow take place almost entirely without words. Kate encounters a handsome, dark stranger at the museum and embarks on a romantic adventure. Just before leaving his apartment, she finds a prescription that indicates she just may have contracted a venereal disease. Though the wind has been knocked out of her sails, an even more unthinkable doom awaits Kate in the building corridor. Having forgotten her wedding ring at her lover's apartment, she heads back there only to be brutally slashed to death by a razor blade in the elevator.

The only witness to the crime is paid escort Liz Blake (Nancy Allen). She quickly becomes the most interesting person involved on the case to police detective Marino (Dennis Franz), though he is not fully convinced by the call girl's story. Together with Peter Miller, the victim's son, Liz attempts to hunt down the murderess who is also apparently one of Dr. Elliott's patients.

With his deliciously brilliant direction of what can be deemed a fairly cut and dry plot, whose outcome always seems just one step out of reach, De Palma proves himself again to be a master of suspense. De Palma's previous

films had established his affinity with the uncontested master of the genre, who died three months prior to the picture's release. His tendency to borrow from these works was indeed so conspicuous in *Dressed to Kill* that it caused *Rolling Stone* to pose the following question in the October 16, 1980 issue: "Brian De Palma: the new Hitchcock or just another rip-off?"

Excluding the motifs of transsexuality and disguise, which are an out and out tribute to *Psycho* (1960), there are three major traits characteristic of De Palma's own cinematic roots and objectives as an artist.

First, he has a predilection for stylizing his pieces and allowing visuals to tell his story. Using devices like the split screen to play up the film's mannerism, De Palma significantly surpasses his mentor and proves that he'll implement chancy, avant-garde visual effects even at the risk of appearing trite.

"My films are very different from Hitchcock's, and I think anyone with a brain can see it."

Brian De Palma

1 Bored to shreds: A chance affair seals the fate of frustrated housewife Kate Miller (Angie Dickinson).

2 Silk stalkings: With a masked killer, blonde victim and distorted camera angles, De Palma gives Hitchcock's calling card his own personal signature.

3 Blind to the rules of the game: If only Liz Blake (Nancy Allen) woke up to the glaring dangers that await her.

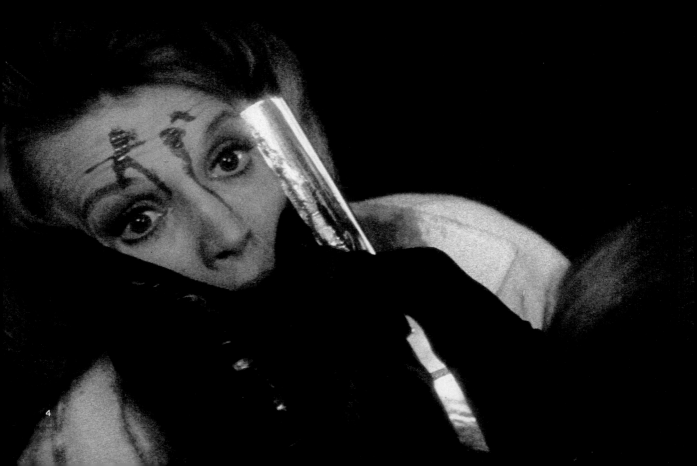

4 Eye opener: According to insiders, director De Palma just can't get enough of a good thing.

5 Doctor patient privileges: Kate confides her innermost secrets to Dr. Elliott (Michael Caine).

Also in the Hitchcockian vein, De Palma takes an ironically distant stance to his gruesome subject matter, but with a more satirical spin on his work than the British filmmaker. This turns up time and again, whether in the form of the cynical Detective Marino or the deplorable gang of armed hooligans in the New York subway. These flagrant caricatures of modern day city dwellers read a little like Americanised versions of some of Hitchcock's characters with their flair for subversive British irony.

Finally, De Palma's works are much more upfront and self-assured in their depiction of eroticism, something that the *Dressed to Kill* director was scorned for at the time. Interestingly enough, the film has its seed in Gerald Walker's novel *Cruising*. William Friedkin's film version of the book *Cruising* (1980), with Al Pacino in the leading role, was released just prior to *Dressed to Kill*. Friedkin had gay rights organizations up in arms over his picture, whereas De Palma, on the other hand, had to ward off feminist groups who saw the film as a "masterpiece of misogyny."

Friedkin's film got thoroughly tangled up in bureaucratic red tape and flopped at the box office. De Palma's *Dressed to Kill* was, at the time of its release, the greatest financial success of his career.   SH

CELLULOID PSYCHOPATHS Psychotic killers have served as stock characters in movies since the advent of the motion picture camera and are among the most reliable audience magnets. We could start with Robert Wiene's *The Cabinet of Dr. Caligari* (*Das Cabinet des Dr. Caligari*, 1919), where a homicidal maniac wreaks havoc on the world, causing a shroud of terror to descend upon society. This classic film illustrates just how suitable the device is to blur the borders between reality and the imagination, by visually externalizing the inner dialog of the protagonists. The condition in which the psychopath finds himself, at least on the big screen, usually involves dealing with a split personality comprised of a dark doppelganger hidden behind an unassuming façade. This lends itself nicely to narrative cinematic devices and allows for plenty of tricks and twists on audience expectations. One could argue that the prototype for the killer who lurks behind the mask of normality is the Norman Bates character (played by Anthony Perkins), from Alfred Hitchcock's *Psycho* (1960). Because all these individuals are dominated by bloodlust as they detach themselves from reality, wild eroticism pairs well with their antisocial behavior. Such was the case in Harold Becker's 1989 picture *Sea of Love*. Lastly, unsavories with eerily voyeuristic tendencies (as in Michael Powell's *Peeping Tom*, 1960) are often found among people who cannot distinguish between reality and fantasy. They might therefore be described as suitable counterparts to cinema spectators.

ORDINARY PEOPLE

1980 - USA - 124 MIN. - FAMILY DRAMA

DIRECTOR ROBERT REDFORD (*1937)
SCREENPLAY ALVIN SARGENT, based on the novel of the same name by JUDITH GUEST DIRECTOR OF PHOTOGRAPHY JOHN BAILEY
EDITING JEFF KANEW MUSIC MARVIN HAMLISCH, JOHANN PACHELBEL ("Canon in D") PRODUCTION RONALD L. SCHWARY for
PARAMOUNT PICTURES, WILDWOOD.

STARRING DONALD SUTHERLAND (Calvin Jarrett), MARY TYLER MOORE (Beth Jarrett), JUDD HIRSCH (Dr. Berger), TIMOTHY
HUTTON (Conrad Jarrett), M. EMMET WALSH (Coach Salan), ELIZABETH MCGOVERN (Jeannine Pratt), DINAH MANOFF
(Karen), FREDRIC LEHNE (Lazenby), JAMES B. SIKKING (Ray Hanley), BASIL HOFFMAN (Sloan), SCOTT DOEBLER (Jordan
"Buck" Jarrett).

ACADEMY AWARDS 1980 OSCARS for BEST FILM (Ronald L. Schwary), BEST DIRECTOR (Robert Redford), BEST SUPPORTING ACTOR
(Timothy Hutton), and BEST ADAPTED SCREENPLAY (Alvin Sargent).

"I'd like to be more in control."

After their elder son dies in a boating accident, Calvin and Beth Jarrett (Donald Sutherland and Mary Tyler Moore), a middle class couple from an uptight Chicago suburb, attempt to maintain the appearance of normalcy. While superficially successful in this endeavor, their younger son Conrad (Timothy Hutton) is overwhelmed by the weight of his traumatic memories. He feels responsible for the death of his big brother, and an extended stay at a psychiatric clinic after a suicide attempt does little to alter his feelings of guilt. He cannot shake the growing impression that his mother hates him and that his brother, the universally loved "Buck," meant everything to her.

Hollywood has always had its share of actors who crossed over into the director's chair. But it only became a normal occurrence after the end of the studio system. Robert Redford is a prime example of this trend of the late 60s and early 70s. *Ordinary People* was his directorial debut, and while the slow rhythm of its images, muted colors, and conspicuously minimalist soundtrack, make it seem a little affected today, it emanates an astounding maturity for a first film, principally evidenced in Redford's direction of the actors. Nonetheless, considering the strong competition from Martin Scorcese's *Raging Bull* (1980), the shower of Oscars it received seems

> **"Redford delineates these viciously suppressed and finally exploding feelings with considerable technical skill. He also directs his actors with impressive meticulousness – particularly Timothy Hutton, who delivers an outstanding performance. Yet in such an oppressive psychodrama, the directing style does seem a little misplaced – precisely because it so assiduously follows the rules of Hollywood filmmaking."** *Süddeutsche Zeitung*

to have more to do with its director – everybody's darling, Robert Redford – than the film itself.

As an actor, Redford already belonged to a small group of stars in the business whose political and sociological interests were mirrored in their films – a characteristic that earned him his reputation as a model Democrat. This critical conscience is also evident in his first directorial project. From the very beginning, Redford expands the family tragedy to a both subtle and mer-

ciless portrait of the advancing American middle class, the affluent WASPs who have always shaped the American value system. Redford depicts the clean white façades of their tidy homes, and the deeper his film delves into the family relationships of the Jarretts, the more these sterile structures become symbols of a prevalent emotional impoverishment. The Jarretts live in a milieu that apparently tolerates no deviation from the norm, where the people who count are the successful and self-controlled, those who have

2

3

1   Nothing more than feelings: Sutherland's multi-faceted manliness marked a clear break from the monolithic machismo of Bronson and McQueen.

2   Boy wonder: Timothy Hutton's (left) sensitive portrayal of a troubled teenager won him the Oscar for Best Supporting Actor. On the right, Elizabeth McGovern.

3   Where's the love? Some viewers were taken aback to see Mary Tyler Moore play an icy and unsympathetic mother.

conformed to the prescribed values. The duplicitous Beth, played marvelously by television star Mary Tyler Moore, is the perfect embodiment of this mechanism. Upon learning from her remarkably caring husband that Conrad is consulting the psychiatrist Dr. Berger (Judd Hirsch), she suspiciously asks if the doctor is a Jew or just a German. The veiled fear behind this statement is well-founded, as Berger, who immediately recognizes the price the Jarretts, and especially Conrad, are paying for their wholesome façade, ultimately succeeds in liberating the boy from his spiritual paralysis, triggering the family's collapse. But at the end, father and son reconcile with a newfound sincerity and tenderness. Despite this appeasing ending, *Ordinary People* ≤seems to be a farewell to the 1970s, anticipating the social stagnation of the Reagan Era. It appears as if the end of the 60s and 70s was never acknowledged in the clean white suburbs – or remained an intermezzo without sequel.

JH

DONALD SUTHERLAND   After acting studies in Toronto and London, and a few years on the road in Europe, Donald Sutherland (*17.7.1934, Saint John, New Brunswick, Canada) debuted in an Italian horror film in 1964. In the following years, the strikingly tall but plain actor appeared in numerous supporting roles in British and American productions, including Robert Aldrich's war film, *The Dirty Dozen* (1967), in which he played a psychopath. His role as a military surgeon in Robert Altman's war satire *M*A*S*H* (1969) ultimately made him famous, and his role in Alan J. Pakula's thriller, *Klute* (1971) fortified his star status. In the ensuing years he spoke out against American action in Vietnam alongside Jane Fonda and participated in *F.T.A.* (1972), an independent film critical of America. In 1973, Sutherland again caused a stir, this time because of his provocative sex scene with Julie Christie in Nicolas Roeg's horror film, *Don't Look Now*. Until the beginning of the 1980s, Sutherland, a very versatile actor with a disturbingly ambiguous aura, appeared in a string of remarkable films, including Bernardo Bertolucci's *1900* (*Novecento*, 1975/76), Fellini's *Casanova* (*Il Casanova di Federico Fellini*, 1976), Robert Redford's *Ordinary People* (1980), and Richard Marquand's *Eye of the Needle* (1981).

Things got quieter around Sutherland, perhaps because, in the era of muscular action heroes, he was offered fewer interesting roles, or because he increasingly lost interest in film: he supposedly rejected the main role in Atom Egoyan's excellent *The Sweet Hereafter* (1997) as the salary failed to meet his expectations. Donald Sutherland's son, Kiefer (*1966), also began a Hollywood career toward the beginning of the 1990s, though lately it appears to have come to a halt.

GLORIA

1980 - USA - 123 MIN. - GANGSTER FILM

DIRECTOR JOHN CASSAVETES (1929–1989)
SCREENPLAY JOHN CASSAVETES DIRECTOR OF PHOTOGRAPHY FRED SCHULER EDITING GEORGE C. VILLASEÑOR MUSIC BILL CONTI
PRODUCTION SAM SHAW for COLUMBIA PICTURES CORPORATION.

STARRING GENA ROWLANDS (Gloria Swenson), JULIE CARMEN (Jeri Dawn), JOHN ADAMES (Phil Dawn), BUCK HENRY (Jack Dawn), JESSICA CASTILLO (Joan Dawn), LUPE GARNICA (Margarita Vargas), BASILIO FRANCHINA (Tony Tanzini), TONY KNESICH (Gangster #1), TOM NOONAN (Gangster #2), RONALD MACCONE (Gangster #3).

IFF VENICE 1980 GOLDEN LION.

"I'm saving your life, stupid."

Gena Rowlands is Gloria, a tough talking dame ready to take on the world. A human tornado, she storms through New York by bus, subway, taxi or whatever means of transportation she can find. Her only peace is the occasional pit stop she makes at the odd small hotel to escape the strain. Armed with a shoulder bag containing a large caliber revolver she'll draw at the drop of a hat, this hell-raiser will go to lethal extremes to protect the small boy in her care from a motley bunch of gangsters. Gloria doesn't know why she does it, telling the boy's mother how she can't stand kids, just before his entire family is massacred. "I hate kids. Especially your kids." In this case, it's not exactly a surprise. Seven-year-old Phil (John Adames) is a brat, a pint-sized pain-in-the-ass, who harps on his Hispanic heritage. The audience would fully approve of her putting the kid on the next train to New Jersey with no return ticket. But against her better judgment, Gloria gives him cover and aids his escape. We don't doubt her strength for a second. Right at the beginning of this exercise in urban turmoil, the gangsters confront her openly on the street. Unfazed, she draws her pistol and sends the car-full of her former chums to Kingdom Come without so much as batting an eyelash. Her encore tops the act itself, as with a nonchalant wave of the hand and the magic word "Taxi," she casually hails a yellow limousine.

There is no reason to doubt that Gloria Swenson was indeed once a gangster bride, or "slut," as she puts it. We wouldn't believe her if she claimed the contrary. A living, breathing maelstrom, Gena Rowlands simply sweeps the audience away with the intoxicating presence of a true star. Gloria is swashbuckling, elegant, unpretentious, and capable of anything. In her husband John Cassavetes' other films, Rowlands had always portrayed women on the verge of a nervous breakdown, and these extraordinary

"I don't like kids. I hate kids. Especially your kids."

Film quote: Gloria

1 Legendary actress Gena Rowlands plays a chain-smoking, no nonsense momma in a one of a kind picture – Bonnie Parker, eat your heart out.

2 Don't cross Momma! Armed or not, Gloria's mere presence is enough to make mobsters quake with fear.

3 A friend in need: Jeri Dawn (Julie Carmen) turns to Gloria when the lives of her loved ones are at stake.

4 Ratifying the ERA: Gloria blasts the path clear for mini macho Phil (John Adames) and shows those suckers who's boss.

5 Cry baby cavalier: Seven year-old Phil may fancy himself a pint-sized Valentino, but he'd be more convincing if he'd just shut his trap.

6 Do not disturb: Gloria often grabs some shuteye at local hotels to stay fresh for the fight.

performances were a fair suggestion of what might happen were such a fireball ever to get her hands on a gun. An action film like this was most out of
character for Cassavetes. The unbridled camera, an expression of the inner
unrest of his protagonists, had previously been the trademark of all his projects in the cinema. Yet *Gloria* manages to burst with physical movement just
the same. It is not gangster movie conventions, but rather the individual fears
of regular people forced into conformity that drive both the narrative and this
"hard-boiled momma" to decisive action.

Cassavetes originally wrote the screenplay with the intention of selling
it to finance his more "difficult" films. This plan was quickly put to rest, however, when it turned out to be the perfect script for Gena Rowlands and
Columbia Pictures. Here, the great architect of "personal American film"
deals with subject matter existing entirely within the context of film and film
history. Subtle yet instantaneous, the image of Hollywood diva Gloria Swan-
son is evoked in the very name of the protagonist. We can see the affection
she eventually develops for her protégé Phil coming on from the very start of

the picture. The film's ending also draws from traditional motherly roles,
when the dead heroine appears in a fairy tale-like resurrection as loving
grandmother. "This is a dream," Gloria repeatedly tells the boy to make the
incomprehensible loss bearable. The deceptive realism of the grubby world
of tenement shafts and dirty subway tunnels is no exception.

The film developed into a true Cassavetes project in its depiction of the
subtle relationship between Gloria and Phil. The reversal of the gender roles
is anything but an ironic end in itself. Flouting convention, the two don't play
mother and child, but rather husband and wife. Phil is "one of the best guys
I've ever slept with," Gloria tells her ex-lover Mafia boss, expertly hitting him
where it hurts. She sees through the childish self-inflation in the macho lines
the wannabe mobster throws after his veritable Ma Baker. In *Gloria*, the great
indy filmmaker suavely unmasks the masculine hubris of the genre and its
gangsters, who seldom appear as ridiculous as they do here. He just sics his
wife on them. After all, Cassavetes always hated gangsters.

PB

GENA ROWLANDS "The way she lights a cigarette is a great argument for smoking," remarked actress Winona Ryder after working with Rowlands in Jim Jarmusch's
Night on Earth (1991). Gena Rowlands' performance as a burnt-out casting agent was her most important role since the death of her husband John
Cassavetes. The daughter of a Wisconsin senator, Rowlands stood at the side of the legendary filmmaker for a total of seven productions. No small
feat, but the admiration of many actresses – not to mention directors like Jim Jarmusch or actors like Sean Penn – goes far deeper. Rowlands'
sensitive, personal and always modern portrayals of off-the-wall women made her a symbol of female honesty and dignity at a time when the
sophistication of Hollywood *grandes dames* like Lauren Bacall and Bette Davis was a thing of the past. She received Oscar nominations for both
her hyperactive *tour de force* in *A Woman Under the Influence* (1974) and her extraordinary *Gloria* (1980). For her work in the film *Opening Night*
(1977), she was awarded the Best Actress Silver Bear at the International Film Festival in Berlin. Rowlands' most recent projects include
collaborations with Woody Allen, Terence Davies, and Peter Chelsom. She has even appeared in two films directed by her son, Nick Cassavetes.

RAGING BULL

⚜ ⚜

1980 - USA - 129 MIN. - BOXING FILM, BIOPIC, DRAMA

DIRECTOR MARTIN SCORSESE (*1942)
SCREENPLAY PAUL SCHRADER, MARDIK MARTIN from the autobiography of JAKE LA MOTTA together with JOSEPH CARTER and PETER SAVAGE **DIRECTOR OF PHOTOGRAPHY** MICHAEL CHAPMAN **EDITING** THELMA SCHOONMAKEr **MUSIC** PIETRO MASCAGNI ("Cavalleria Rusticana"), diverse songs arranged by ROBBIE ROBERTSON **PRODUCTION** ROBERT CHARTOFF, IRWIN WINKLER for CHARTOFF-WINKLER PRODUCTIONS, UNITED ARTISTS.

STARRING ROBERT DE NIRO (Jake La Motta), CATHY MORIARTY (Vickie La Motta), JOE PESCI (Joey La Motta), FRANK VINCENT (Salvy), NICHOLAS COLASANTO (Tommy Como), THERESA SALDANA (Lenore La Motta), MARIO GALLO (Mario), FRANK ADONIS (Patsy), JOSEPH BONO (Guido), FRANK TOPHAM (Toppy).

ACADEMY AWARDS 1980 OSCARS for BEST ACTOR (Robert De Niro), and BEST EDITING (Thelma Schoonmaker).

"You didn't get me down, Ray!"

It is the beginning of the 1940s and Jake La Motta (Robert De Niro) is one of the top middleweight boxers in the world. He's the "Raging Bull," famous for an almost inhuman ability to take a beating and notorious for his unpredictable attacks. He's not a stylist, he's a brutal puncher whose strength comes from a deep-seated aggression he is unable to control – inside or outside of the ring. The brunt of Jake's aggression is leveled at his wife, but his brother and manager Joey (Joe Pesci) are also forced to weather his temper. Even in his interaction with the Mafiosi from Little Italy, Jake is anything but diplomatic. This erratic behavior contributes to his continually being denied a title fight. He soon meets Vickie (Cathy Moriarty), a blonde beauty who is

already hanging out with the gangsters of Hell's Kitchen, despite being only 15 years old. Jake gets a divorce and marries her. But he is not calmed down. In fact, his jealous outbursts intensify and he terrorizes everyone around him. When he finally gets the chance to fight for the title in 1949, his predictable demise has been years in the making.

Robert De Niro had long dreamed of acting in a cinematic adaptation of Jake La Motta's autobiography. In the midst of shooting of *Alice Doesn't Live Here Anymore* (1974), he tried to convince Martin Scorsese to direct the project. Though initially unsuccessful, De Niro did not relent. He took another shot at it while Scorsese lay in a hospital bed, psychologically and physically

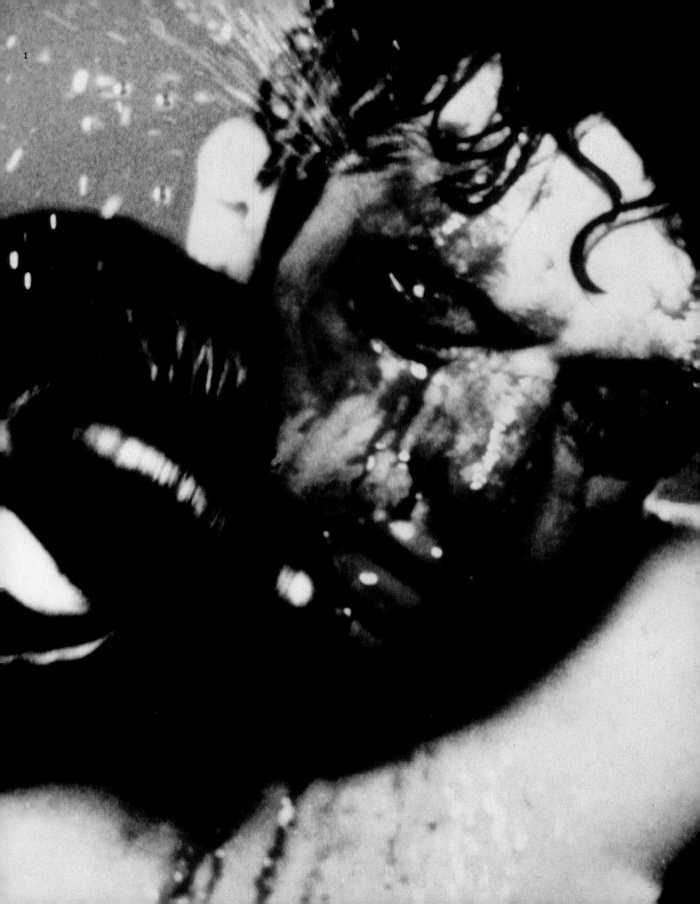

1

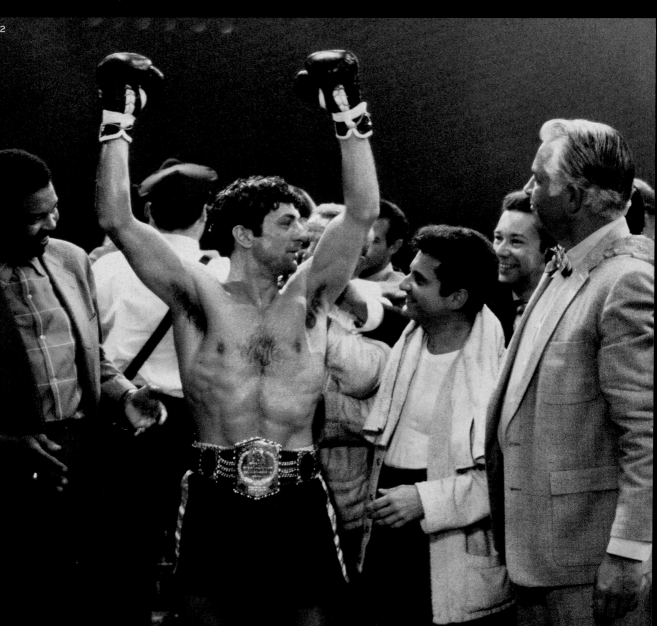

> "I put everything I knew and felt into this film, and I thought it would finish my career. I call it 'kamikaze', this way of making films: put all of yourself into it, then forget it and start a new life."
>
> *Martin Scorsese, in: Martin Scorsese, David Thompson, Ian Christie (Ed.), Scorsese on Scorsese*

1 Blood, sweat and tears: *Raging Bull* captures the sheer physicality of the fights in merciless close-up.

2 Method acting and a few black eyes: In order to give a convincing depiction of "The Bronx Bull," Robert De Niro spent months training as a boxer, and even fought some fights as an amateur. He was rewarded for his efforts with an Oscar.

3 Professional scene-stealer: Joe Pesci (left) worked alongside Robert De Niro in the Scorsese masterpieces *Goodfellas* (1989) and *Casino* (1995).

lacerated by the disaster of *New York, New York* (1977). This time around the director was fascinated by the subject matter, seizing on La Motta's self-destructive life story as a chance to exorcise his own demons. The film therefore focuses less on the boxer's career – the fight scenes are relatively brief – than the story of a man tortured by his own existence, a man who has only himself to blame for his downfall. The fact that La Motta grew up in the same milieu of Italian immigrants that Scorsese knew well from his own childhood intensified his identification with the subject matter.

Raging Bull was the challenge of a lifetime for De Niro. In the role of Jake La Motta, he radically explored the limits of his craft. The convincing physical presence De Niro lends to the violence La Motta turned on himself and others is as fascinating as it is terrifying. In order to make the fight scenes as believable as possible, he trained – partially under the guidance of La Motta – for months and on several occasions even fought a real bout. Legend has it that De Niro gained over fifty pounds to personify the aging La Motta, who traveled from night club to night club as a fat has-been entertainer.

The film's technical quality – its skilful sound design and editing – is just as extraordinary as De Niro's Oscar-winning performance, and the rest of the acting. Michael Chapman deserves a special mention for his excellent

MICHAEL CHAPMAN Michael Chapman (*21.11.1935 in New York) became one of the most sought-after American cameramen toward the middle of the 70s. He began by working as a camera operator for Gordon Willis, whose "classicism" became a major influence. The films he worked on during this period include Alan J. Pakula's thriller, *Klute* (1971) and Coppola's *The Godfather* (1972). In 1973, Chapman became director of photography for the first time in Hal Ashby's tragicomedy, *The Last Detail*, followed by the Arctic film *The White Dawn* (1974), the first of four collaborations with Philip Kaufman. Chapman worked as operator once again for Spielberg's *Jaws* (1975) before experiencing his real breakthrough with the legendary Scorsese film, *Taxi Driver* (1975), in which he beautifully transmitted the threatening atmosphere of a Film Noir into color images. Chapman proved his mastery of black-and-white photography with another Scorsese film, *Raging Bull* (1980), for which he received his first Oscar nomination, and later with Carl Reiner's lovely Film Noir homage, *Dead Men Don't Wear Plaid* (1981). Chapman built on his reputation in the years that followed, but only really hit the limelight again in 1993 when he received his second Oscar nomination for *The Fugitive*. Chapman repeatedly appears in small roles as an actor, and has been directing films himself since 1983, though without the impact he has had as a cameraman.

4 Sick with jealousy: Mindless violence soon
characterizes Jake's relationship with wife
Vicky (Cathy Moriarty).

5 & 6 A beached whale: De Niro put on fifty pounds
to depict Jake La Motta in his decline.

7 That's *amore*: Martin Scorsese, the son of Sicilian
immigrants, depicts the Italian milieu in 40s and
50s New York with a documentary filmmaker's
attention to detail.

black-and-white photography, which captures the private life of the boxer
with a merciless sobriety that recalls Italian neorealism and the "semi-docu-
mentaries" of the 40s. The camera often stands still and focuses on La
Motta's violent outbursts. Squeezed into the frame, he resembles an animal
caught in a cage, unable to come to terms with the lack of space and powerless to free himself from its constraints. Jake's torturous frustrations are so
painfully depicted in these images that the boxing matches begin to seem
like a necessary consequence of his life. The extent of his spiritual barrenness becomes clear during the fights. The camera zooms in on the action in
the ring, approaching La Motta's subjective perception. Fists pummel body
and face from close range, spraying blood and sweat, the images acoustic-
ally underscored by dull blows that sound as if they come from the inside out.
The violence exploding in these rapidly edited images have an edge of soothing intimacy. It appears that La Motta is only able to truly express himself
within the confines of the ring. He is a lonely man for whom punches are not
only a reward, but a means of communication. JH

"An American masterwork, a fusion of Hollywood genre with personal vision couched in images and sounds that are kinetic and visceral, and closer to poetry than pulp." *The Village Voice*

THE BLUES BROTHERS

1980 - USA - 133 MIN. - MUSIC FILM, COMEDY

DIRECTOR JOHN LANDIS (*1950)
SCREENPLAY DAN AYKROYD, JOHN LANDIS DIRECTOR OF PHOTOGRAPHY STEPHEN M. KATZ EDITING GEORGE FOLSEY JR.
MUSIC ELMER BERNSTEIN PRODUCTION ROBERT K. WEISS for UNIVERSAL PICTURES.

STARRING JOHN BELUSHI ("Joliet" Jake Blues), DAN AYKROYD (Elwood Blues), KATHLEEN FREEMAN (Sister Mary),
CAB CALLOWAY (Curtis), JAMES BROWN (Reverend Cleophus James), RAY CHARLES (Ray), ARETHA FRANKLIN
(Mrs. Murphy), CARRIE FISHER (Camille Ztdetelik), JOHN CANDY (Burton Mercer), ALAN RUBIN (Mr. Fabulous),
HENRY GIBSON (Nazi-Leader).

"We're on a mission from God!"

Strange that *The Blues Brothers* was initially a flop in the United States. The film has everything an action comedy could possibly require: two television comedy stars, break-neck chase sequences, laconically comic dialogues, and guest appearances by stars including James Brown, Aretha Franklin, John Lee Hooker, Ray Charles, and Cab Calloway. And naturally it has the Blues Brothers themselves, John Belushi and Dan Aykroyd, the most explosive duo since nitro and glycerin (at least that's how the advertising slogan billed them). *The Blues Brothers* first achieved cult status in Europe – and perhaps no other film has shown as often in program cinemas, university theaters, and drive-in theatres.

Why Americans initially gave the film the cold shoulder may also have been due to the abject contempt of the critics: "The massive scale of the production smacks of desperation. Faced with a script devoid of wit or invention, director Landis relies entirely on diversionary tactics – more cars, more extras, more crashes. Has anyone heard of more rewrites?" asked *Newsweek*. Were they looking at the same script? Take the Blues Brothers as they speed through a red light and promptly have a police cruiser hot on their heels:

Elwood Blues: "Shit!"
Jake Blues: "What?"

Elwood Blues: "Rollers."
Jake Blues: "No!"
Elwood Blues: "Yeah."
Jake Blues: "Shit!"

With their black suits, black hats, and dark sunglasses, the Blues Brothers are the essence of cool. Jake (John Belushi), just released from prison, and his brother Elwood (Dan Aykroyd), need to dig up $5,000 to save the Catholic orphanage in which they grew up. During a sermon by Reverend Cleophus James (James Brown), Jake has an epiphany: a tour with their old R&B band! Their first task is to gather together all the musicians. And they do this in their own style. Mr. Fabulous (Alan Rubin), one of their band mates, works in a high-class restaurant and has no intention of ever blowing his trumpet again. But a short visit from Jake and Elwood to "Chez Paul" soon puts an end to his hesitation: they burp, slurp champagne, and toss food into each another's mouths – he is left with no other alternative but to capitulate and come along.

The Blues Brothers implement any means necessary to fulfill their mission. The destruction left in their wake is irrelevant. They don't look back and don't look forward – they are pure present tense. The film could be viewed as

2

Elwood Blues: *"It's 106 miles to Chicago, we've got a full tank of gas,*
half a pack of cigarettes, it's dark and we're wearing sunglasses."
Jake Blues: *"Hit it!"* Film quote: Elwood Blues and "Joliet" Jake Blues

1   Hit the road, Jake: In the early summer of 1980, the Blues Brothers Band went on a 22 concert tour. It was one of the many "high" points of Belushi's (left) career. Right, Dan Aykroyd.

2   Shake Your Tailfeather: Ray Charles accompanies the Blues Brothers on the electric piano.

3   Wanted dead or insane: The police have been authorized to "use of unnecessary violence in the apprehension of the Blues Brothers."

4   Special guest from another star: Carrie Fisher also appeared on the hit TV series *Saturday Night Live* – birthplace of the Blues Brothers.

5   Heil, heil the gang's all here! Illinois Nazis in hot pursuit of the Blues Brothers. Soundtrack care of Richard Wagner.

3

He was small and fat, but he sure had a temper. Sometimes his energy almost burst out of him at the end of his sketches. John Belushi shot to the top, became a star but then crashed just as quickly as he had arrived. "It's better to burn out than to fade away" – the Neil Young line could have been written for Belushi.

The American comedy show *Saturday Night Live* began in 1975. John Belushi, 26 at the time, was soon to become a star. He appeared as a samurai, a killer bee, as Captain Kirk, and Marlon Brando's Godfather, and often in the company of brother James or Dan Aykroyd, with whom he invented the *Blues Brothers* characters.

In 1978 Belushi left television and took his chances on the big screen. He made his brief debut in Jack Nicholson's Western *Goin' South*. In the same year he played the lead role in *National Lampoon's Animal House* by *The Blues Brothers* director John Land s. He played the dirty, cross, offensive role once again in Steven Spielberg's *1941* (1979), after which came *The Blues Brothers* (1980). Then he tried his luck in Michael Apted's romantic comedy *Continental Divide* (1981). John Belushi died in 1982 from the effects of his excessive drug use. Contributing to his cult status was Bob Woodward's biography, *Wired. The Short Life and Fast Times of John Belushi*.

a subversive attack on the state and the white establishment: Jake and Elwood destroy a shopping center with their car, stir up a group of Nazis, and liven up a country bar with their soulful rendition of "Gimme Some Lovin'." When the cowboy hat and plaid shirt-wearing audience showers them with boos and beer bottles, they placate the enraged mob by singing "Rawhide," the title song of a Western television series starring redneck Clint Eastwood.

Right off the bat, the film caricatures state law and order, such as when Jake is given his worldly possessions with ridiculously exacting bureaucracy – he receives one condom, unused, and one condom, used. The Blues Brothers don't seem to be familiar with traffic rules – Elwood has 116 unpaid parking tickets and 56 additional tickets for other violations. In the end, numerous white police cars chase after the one black "Bluesmobile," and tanks drive into the building in which Jake and Elwood are just able to settle the

debts of the orphanage. It seems that the worst enemy does not threaten society from outside, but rather corrodes its values from within. And the state is forced to battle this cancer with the heaviest artillery available.

The joy of destruction, acerbic word play, and infectious music conspire to make *The Blues Brothers* a unique film experience. John Belushi became a legend in the role of Jake Blues. His most memorable scene is the moment when he takes off his sunglasses because an ex-girlfriend of his (Carrie Fisher) is blocking his way with an automatic rifle. Jake falls on his knees before her, begs her to spare his life, and twitches his eyebrows. She can't resist those eyes. She jumps into his arms and he promptly drops her into the mud. After all, Jake and Elwood are on a mission from God. And there are still 106 miles to Chicago – and many, many cars still need to be totaled during the final chase.

NM

EVERY MAN FOR HIMSELF (AKA SLOW MOTION)
Sauve qui peut (la vie)

1980 - FRANCE / SWITZERLAND / FRG / AUSTRIA - 88 MIN. - DRAMA

DIRECTOR JEAN-LUC GODARD (*1930)
SCREENPLAY JEAN-CLAUDE CARRIÈRE, ANNE-MARIE MIÉVILLE, JEAN-LUC GODARD DIRECTOR OF PHOTOGRAPHY WILLIAM LUBTCHANSKY, RENATO BERTA, JEAN-BERNARD MENOUD EDITING ANNE-MARIE MIÉVILLE, JEAN-LUC GODARD MUSIC GABRIEL YARED PRODUCTION ALAIN SARDE, JEAN-LUC GODARD for SONIMAGE, SARA FILMS, MK2 PRODUCTIONS, TÉLÉVISION SUISSE-ROMANDE, ZDF, ORF.

STARRING ISABELLE HUPPERT (Isabelle Rivière), JACQUES DUTRONC (Paul Godard), NATHALIE BAYE (Denise Rimbaud), ROLAND AMSTUTZ (Second Customer), ANNA BALDACCINI (Isabelle's Sister), FRED PERSONNE (First Customer), NICOLE JACQUET (Woman), DORE DE ROSA (Elevator Boy), MONIQUE BARSCHA (Opera Singer), CÉCILE TANNER (Paul's Daughter).

"If I had the strength, I'd do nothing."

Jean-Luc Godard called *Every Man For Himself* his "second first film," for it marked his return to "commercial" filmmaking, using 35-mm equipment and star actors. In the 60s, he had turned his back on the mainstream cinema with films such as *Weekend* (*Week-End*, 1967) and *One Plus One* / *Sympathy for the Devil* (1968). For years thereafter, he made Marxist-Maoist film tracts in collaboration with Jean-Pierre Gorin and the "Groupe Dziga Vertov." Sometime in the mid-70s, Godard then began to experiment with video, his last commercially distributed film being the 1972 piece *Everything's Fine* (*Tout va bien* / *Crepa padrone, tutto va bene*), a political drama starring Yves Montand and Jane Fonda. *Every Man For Himself* thus signified a new beginning. But although the film opens with a scrawled image of the figure "zero," Godard is – of course – not really starting from scratch: the movie, in fact, is a compendium of his ideas and techniques after 20 years of practice in the cinematic medium.

For one thing, *Every Man For Himself* comes across as an experimental collage of images (people, cities, landscapes) and sounds – which sometimes fit the image, yet often appear totally unrelated. Occasionally, indeed, there's no sound there at all, so that the viewer has to imagine what he ought to be hearing. The images, too, have an occasional tendency to "drift away:" in the middle of a dialog, the camera may suddenly turn its attention to other people who apparently have nothing to do with the matter at hand. Music plays an important role: in one scene, an accordionist competes with the composition on the soundtrack; and throughout, the protagonists are constantly enquiring about the music that accompanies their scenes – which only they seem to hear. (The opening credits contain the announcement: "Un film composé par Jean-Luc Godard.")

On top of all this, we have off-screen literary monologs, a homage to Marguerite Duras and her film *The Truck* (*Le Camion*, 1977), and various experiments with the depiction of motion. Certain sequences are slowed down or broken up into their component single frames. These passages are a direct result of Godard's work with the medium of video. He claimed it had allowed him to discover that girls move quite differently from boys, and that they also have a much larger repertoire of gestures and facial expressions. As such differences are imperceptible at the standard film speed of 24

images per second, he concluded that conventional male-dominated film technology had failed to do justice to the phenomena.

On the other hand, this film also marks Godard's return to non-linear narration. We are told the story of three people, who each represent a different "velocity." One "chapter" is devoted to each of them. Denise Rimbaud (Nathalie Baye) works in television but risks breaking out and making a fresh start: she ditches both her job and her boyfriend, TV director and producer Paul Godard (Jacques Dutronc), and moves out to the country, where she takes up farming and plans to write a novel. For Godard, Denise embodies "the Left, and what's left of it:" she travels everywhere by bicycle, but the faster she pedals, "the more slowly she progresses." Paul Godard would also like to change, but he doesn't have the nerve; his chapter is

"*Every Man For Himself* is a single seamless endeavor, a stunning, original work about which there is still a lot to say; but there's time. I trust it will outlive us all." *The New York Times*

1 "Got milk?" Isabelle's sister (Anna Baldaccini) is determined to go into dairy farming.

2 Leave no table unturned: Denise Rimbaud (Nathalie Baye) wants to change her life, but her partner Paul Godard (Jacques Dutronc) has more immediate concerns.

3 An ass in the cattle shed (Isabelle Huppert).

4 Director's chair: The character of Paul is loosely based on the director. The proof is in the pudding.

entitled "Fear." When Denise leaves him, Paul suffers a crisis. He meets up with his ex-wife and his 12-year-old daughter, but their relationship now consists solely of money and presents. Naturally, the bespectacled cigar-smoker Paul is in part Jean-Luc Godard himself. A quote from Duras functions as his motto: "I make movies to fill up my time. If I had the strength, I'd do nothing."

Isabelle Rivière (Isabelle Huppert) is a prostitute. She spends a night with Paul, and eventually moves in to the apartment abandoned by Denise. Isabelle is "a person of medium velocity" who goes about her business calmly and coolly. The exchange of sex for money is a subject that has always interested Godard, and prostitution has always been his favored metaphor for commercial filmmaking. It's no wonder, then, that Isabelle's relationships to

her clients are *staged* affairs, which in turn raise questions about the relationship of sound to image. A client who has just arranged the images of an orgy to his satisfaction concludes by creating the "sound track:" "Ay! Oh! Aaah!"

In *Every Man For Himself*, human relationships are characterized exclusively by violence or indifference. In the final chapter ("Music"), Paul is run over by a car; yet he can't believe he's really going to die, for his life hasn't yet passed before his eyes as it does in the movies. Paul's ex-wife and his daughter simply leave him lying where he is. As they walk away, they pass an orchestra stationed by the side of the road. At last, we know where that music's been coming from …

LP

ISABELLE HUPPERT Isabelle Huppert originally made her name playing frigid or inhibited characters. Born in Paris in 1955, she made her film debut in 1971, in *Faustine et le bel été*. Her international breakthrough came six years later in *The Lacemaker* (*La Dentellière*, 1977), directed by the Swiss filmmaker Claude Goretta, in which she played Pomme, a shy girl who falls in love with a student and is bitterly disappointed. In Cannes the following year, Huppert won the Golden Palm as Best Actress for her interpretation of the dead-hearted murderer of her own parents, in Claude Chabrol's *Violette Nozière* (1978). She went on to sustain a lengthy working relationship with Chabrol, appearing in films such as *The Story of Women* (*Une affaire de femmes*, 1988), *Madame Bovary* (1991), *La Cérémonie* (1995) and *Merci pour le chocolat* (2000).
Today, Huppert is one of the most important European film stars. In a career spanning three decades, she has worked with many major directors (Godard, Téchiné, Pialat, Jacquot, Assayas, Tavernier) without allowing herself to be pigeonholed in any particular genre. She has performed brilliantly in dramas and essayistic films, and she also has a fine feeling for comedy. In one of her more recent efforts, François Ozon's musical thriller *8 Women* (*8 femmes*, 2001), her performance as the bad-tempered spinster Aunt Augustine was a parody of her own enduring image.

HEAVEN'S GATE

1980 - USA - 219 MIN. - WESTERN, DRAMA

DIRECTOR MICHAEL CIMINO (*1943)
SCREENPLAY MICHAEL CIMINO DIRECTOR OF PHOTOGRAPHY VILMOS ZSIGMOND EDITING TOM ROLF, WILLIAM REYNOLDS, LISA FRUCHTMAN, GERALD B. GREENBERG MUSIC DAVID MANSFIELD PRODUCTION JOANN CARELLI for PARTISAN PRODUCTIONS, UNITED ARTISTS.

STARRING KRIS KRISTOFFERSON (Marshal James Averill), CHRISTOPHER WALKEN (Nathan D. Champion), JOHN HURT (Billy Irvine), SAM WATERSTON (Frank Canton), ISABELLE HUPPERT (Ella Watson), JOSEPH COTTEN (Reverend Sutton), ROSEANNE VELA (Pretty Girl), RICHARD MASUR (Cully), JEFF BRIDGES (John L. Bridges), RONNIE HAWKINS (Wolcott), BRAD DOURIF (Mr. Eggleston).

"It's getting dangerous to be poor in this country."

Heaven's Gate became notorious as the film that ruined United Artists, a distribution company with a long and proud history. Michael Cimino's late Western was originally budgeted at 7.5 million dollars, but by the time it was completed, the total production costs had risen to more than 40 million. In 1980, this was an unheard-of sum: even if the film had been a major success at the box-office, it wouldn't have put the producers and distributors back in the black. In any case, *Heaven's Gate* was anything but a success: the reviews in the States were unanimously scathing (the film was said to be confused, long-winded, and above all, anti-American), and the distributors withdrew Cimino's three-and-a-half-hour epic from circulation almost before it had reached the theaters. The director was allowed to rework the film, and he eventually produced a version that was only 149 minutes long – but this,

too, was a flop. In 1985, a longer version close to the director's original intentions was released in Europe alone – and *Heaven's Gate*, at very long last, was hailed as a masterpiece.

What happened? Cimino had picked up on an episode that had been relegated to the margins of American history: the "Johnson County War" of 1890–92, a conflict between WASP landowners and mainly Eastern European immigrants who had been assigned no land from the government. The clashes between rich and poor grew in frequency and violence, until finally the cattle-barons – with the connivance of the State Governor – hired a gang of killers to liquidate the settlers' leaders. The immigrants defended themselves, until the army intervened, saving the wealthy landowners and their henchmen.

1   Taxidermy.

2   These boots were made for walking: Gunslinger
    Nate Champion (Christopher Walken) is hoping
    to step up in society.

3   If you're happy and you know it, clap your hands!
    These impoverished immigrants sure know how
    to enjoy themselves.

Class struggle in Wyoming: Cimino demystifies both the American
Dream and the Western – a genre that had always celebrated the pioneer
spirit and the illusion of a big, free country. In *Heaven's Gate*, the immigrants'
hope of a better life comes to a sorry end, shattered by a corrupt caste in the
name of money. And, as the film makes clear, these newcomers are unwelcome not just because they're poor, but also because they speak a foreign
tongue and embody an alien culture.

Heaven's Gate follows the life story of a privileged man. James Averill
(Kris Kristofferson), an idealistic young fellow, graduates from Harvard in

1870 and begins the adventure of adult life. Twenty years later, we meet him
in Wyoming. Now a Marshal, he is expected to represent a law that has
no moral legitimacy. Averill takes the side of the people, while inevitably
remaining what he is: a wealthy man who doesn't belong. His antagonist is
Nate Champion (Christopher Walken), the gunman hired by the cattle-breed-
ers association. A strange friendship links the two men. For Nate, the Marshal
is a kind of role model, embodying the wealth, style and self-assurance to
which he has always aspired. At the same time, Averill and Nate are rivals for
the love of Ella (Isabelle Huppert), a strong and independent woman who runs

"I never want people to feel they've been watching something, to feel that they've just seen a movie; I want them to believe they've been somewhere."

Michael Cimino in: Frankfurter Rundschau

4   The sky's the limit! Grandiose sets, inflated costumes added several zeroes to production costs.

5   Riding the golden spike: The settlers end up covering the bill for the march of progress.

6 Horsemen of the apocalypse: When the settlers resist the cattle barons' murderous mercenaries, the U.S. Cavalry arrives to restore "order"…

7 Heart of gold or heart of glass: Whorehouse owner Ella (Isabelle Huppert) loves two men. She yearns for a well-ordered family life and two apartments.

8 A closed circle: The wealthy and fortunate dance to a trouble-free life.

a brothel. The fate of these three figures is another clear reflection of the film's moral trajectory. Both Nate and Ella are practically executed by the gang of killers; for the parvenu who stands up to his bosses, and the bourgeois whore who keeps her accounts so assiduously in order, there isn't a hope in hell. Averill, however, is treated a little differently: though he had "betrayed" his class by fighting on the side of the settlers, the landowners still consider him to be one of their own, and his life is spared.

The film meanders, following its characters down roundabout routes, telling of everyday life in the old West, granting even the immigrants faces and stories of their own. Again and again, Cimino shows images of circular movement, mostly dances expressing hope and the joy of living. At the end, however, the last battle is a Dance of Death. The film has a fascinating richness of detail, and the movie's exorbitant cost was due not least to the director's perfectionism: even the least of the extras wears an authentic hat. This material outlay is no mere bombast, but an artistic necessity. For Cimino, it's a way of creating a naturalistic background against which the characters and their story can unfold.

LP

9 Harvard class of 1870: Their education will last them 200 years.

10 Dunce cap: John L. Bridges (Jeff Bridges) may be a friend of the Marshal, but that's certainly no invitation to high society.

KRIS KRISTOFFERSON   Kris Kristofferson was born on 22.6.1936 in Brownsville, Texas, the son of an Air Force General. Before he became known as a country singer-songwriter, he had already seen a fair bit of life as a failed novelist and pop singer in London, and as an Air Force pilot and paratrooper in the States. In 1970, Johnny Cash topped the charts with a Kristofferson song, "Sunday Mornin' Comin' Down," and Janis Joplin's rendition of "Me and Bobby McGee" soon brought him even greater fame. While these successes helped Kristofferson to make his name as an unconventional country musician, the 70s also witnessed his breakthrough as a movie actor. He made his screen debut in Dennis Hopper's *The Last Movie* (1969/71), before Sam Peckinpah cast him as a legendary outlaw in *Pat Garrett and Billy the Kid* (1973). From then on, Kristofferson was destined to embody the virile and vital outsider with a sensitive soul. He played a supporting role in Peckinpah's next film, *Bring Me the Head of Alfredo Garcia* (1974), and the following year he appeared alongside Ellen Burstyn in Martin Scorsese's drama, *Alice Doesn't Live Here Anymore* (1974). In the Frank Pierson remake of *A Star Is Born* (1976), he played a self-destructive rock star. His own life may well have fuelled his interpretation of the role, for he too was dependent on alcohol at one time, although he managed to overcome his addiction.

In his third and last Peckinpah film, *Convoy* (1978), Kristofferson played the leader of a truckers' revolt. This was a highpoint in his acting career. After starring in the spectacular box-office disaster of *Heaven's Gate* (1980), Kristofferson was less often seen in the movies, though he remained a presence on TV and as a musician. In the 90s, things changed. Besides giving remarkable performances in John Sayles' present-day Western, *Lone Star* (1996), and James Ivory's *A Soldier's Daughter Never Cries* (1998), Kristofferson also acquired a new generation of younger fans, thanks to his roles in blockbusters such as *Blade* (1998) and *Planet of the Apes* (2001).

"*Heaven's Gate* is a magnificent opus. The images, sometimes tinged in sepia tones, have the realistic quality of period photographs. The directing itself is an essay on space, as in certain Anthony Mann Westerns, and on the 'field of history' as seen by Michael Cimino." *Le Monde*

KAGEMUSHA

1980 - JAPAN - 159 MIN. - HISTORICAL FILM, EPIC

DIRECTOR AKIRA KUROSAWA (1910–1998)
SCREENPLAY AKIRA KUROSAWA, MASATO IDE DIRECTOR OF PHOTOGRAPHY TAKAO SAITU, MASAHARU UEDA EDITING AKIRA KUROSAWA
MUSIC SHIN'ICHIRÔ IKEBE PRODUCTION AKIRA KUROSAWA, MASATO IDE for TOHO.

STARRING TATSUYA NAKADAI (Shingen Takeda / Kagemusha), TSUTOMU YAMAZAKI (Nobukado Takeda), KENICHI HAGIWARA (Katsuyori Takeda), DAISUKE RYU (Nobunaga Oda), MASAYUKI YUI (Ieyasu Tokugawa), KOTA YUI (Takemaru Takeda), SHUJI OTAKI (Masakage Yamagata), HIDEO MUROTA (Nobufusa Baba), TAKAYUKI SHIHO (Masatoyo Naito), SHUHEI SUGIMORI (Masanobu Kosaka).

IFF CANNES 1980 GOLDEN PALM (Akira Kurosawa).

"A shadow is a shadow and must remain a shadow."

Three men, identically dressed, are sitting in a spartanly furnished room: one on a podium; the second on the floor to his right, the third some distance away. The first man is Prince Shingen Takeda, the second is his brother and advisor, the third is a thief under sentence of death (both he and Shingen are played by Tatsuya Nakadai). The thief bears a striking resemblance to his lord and master, and is about to be employed as his double. This six-minute scene precedes the opening titles. Filmed with a static camera, it embodies the formal asceticism of the entire film and announces its essential themes: hierarchy and power, honor and betrayal.

It's 1573, and Japan is being torn apart by a bloody civil war. Shingen Takeda is engaged in a bitter struggle for mastery of the country with his two rivals Nobunaga Oda (Daisuke Ryu) and Ieyasu Tokugawa (Masayuki Yui). Besieging a castle, Shingen is wounded by a marksman and dies. His last will is that the campaign be abandoned and his death kept secret for three years.

Accordingly, the thief is installed as his double – or "shadow." Court society is not informed of the deception, nor are the concubines, nor even Shingen's grandson – chosen by Shingen to succeed him on the throne. The only people informed are the most important generals, among them Shingen's illegitimate son Katsuyori (Kenichi Hagiwara). Almost three years elapse before the trick comes to light. Then Katsuyori seizes power, goes to war, and loses the battle of Nagashino...

Kagemusha is based on real historical events. The film takes place before the Edo period, during the civil war in which several princes fought for control of the country. The Battle of Nagashino was the first to be decided by the use of firearms. In 1603, Ieyasu Tokugawa united the country under his rule. *Kagemusha's* basic constellation is historically accurate, as are some of the details (such as the use of doubles and the appearance of Jesuit monks in Japan). On this basis, Kurosawa created an overwhelming epic of war and

3

4

5

JAPAN AS FILM NATION When Akira Kurosawa's *Rashomon* (1950) won the Golden Lion at the Venice Film Festival, Japan suddenly appeared on the map of international cinematography. Although films have been made in Japan since 1899, this was the first time the West had really noticed Japan as a "film nation." Three artists became known above all: Kurosawa (1910–1998) was the all-round genius, who could handle both historical and contemporary material; Yasujirô Ozu (1903–1963) was the master of strict form, who found his great theme in the "family;" and Kenji Mizoguchi (1898–1956) became famous for his long uncut scenes and films that examined the place of women in society. All three made "art films," but there was also plenty of popular cinema – for example, the numerous Godzilla films from 1954 onwards. In the 60s, in parallel to the West, Japan produced its own kind of *Nouvelle Vague*, whose most outstanding representative was Nagisa Oshima (*Night and Fog in Japan / Nihon no yoru to kiri*, 1960). The 80s were dominated by "Young Turks" such as Sôgo Ishii (*Crazy Family / Gyakufunsha kazoku*, 1984), who demonstrated astonishing formal strengths and who often took a highly critical view of Japanese civilization. Katsuhiro Ôtomo's *Akira* (1988) was the first major film adaptation of a Japanese comic (manga) to achieve international success. A recent highpoint in the popularity of these "animes" was marked by Hayao Miyazaki's *Spirited Away* (*Sen to Chihiro no kamikakushi*, 2001), which won the Golden Bear at the IFF in Berlin in 2002.

"The century depicted in *Kagemusha* was distinguished by an aesthetic stance that also influenced the ritual of warfare. I wanted to document this martial aesthetic."

Akira Kurosawa, in: Le Monde

1 Charge!!! Nobunaga Oda (Daisuke Ryu, second from right) and his compatriots en route to pillage the village.

2 Chicken Katsuyori: Today's special includes Shingen's illegitimate son Katsuyori served over rice with fresh cabbage – compliments of chef Tokugawa.

3 Ghosts of the past: "I love the 16th century. In Japan, it was an age full of Shakespearean emotions." (Akira Kurosawa)

4 Wash that past right out of their mares: At the end of the 16th century, Japan was in the throes of a bloody civil war as three samurais battled for control of the entire land.

5 Life insurance: Samurai general Shingen Takeda (Tatsuya Nakadai, center) drafts a policy that will make sure his loved ones are provided for.

6 Looks like a tea ceremony, smells like a coup: Only the most select commanders are privy to the scam involving the dead general's double.

peace, a story told on several different levels. At one level, the film is a psychological drama, showing the ruses and deceptions employed by princes and generals in order to rule and conquer – and showing how the "shadow" Kagemusha comes to terms with his existence as a double. At another level, *Kagemusha* is a splendid battle picture with brilliantly choreographed crowd scenes. Again and again, stylized and very beautiful tableau-like images are inserted, for example the shot in which we see people before a lurid sunset. But however much Kurosawa aestheticizes the war, he never makes it look harmless; one never sees the butchery itself, but the horrible aftermath of corpses and mangled bodies.

As so often, Kurosawa had difficulty getting the film produced. Since his previous work *Dersu Uzala* (1975), he had developed three projects – among them *Kagemusha* – but found a production company for none of them. It was only when American directors Francis Ford Coppola and George Lucas persuaded Twentieth Century Fox to buy the foreign rights to *Kagemusha* for 1.5 million dollars that his regular production firm Toho decided to produce the film. With a budget of 9 million dollars, it was the most expensive Japanese film ever made; but with box-office takings of 10 million dollars, it also became the most successful. It received Oscar nominations for Best Art Direction and Best Foreign Film. HJK

ATLANTIC CITY

1980 - CANADA / USA / FRANCE - 105 MIN. - DRAMA

DIRECTOR LOUIS MALLE (1932–1995)
SCREENPLAY JOHN GUARE DIRECTOR OF PHOTOGRAPHY RICHARD CIUPKA EDITING SUZANNE BARON MUSIC MICHEL LEGRAND
PRODUCTION DENIS HÉROUX for CINE-NEIGHBOUR INC., SELTA FILMS, INTERNATIONAL CINEMA CORPORATION,
PARAMOUNT PICTURES, MERCHANT FILMS.

STARRING BURT LANCASTER (Lou Paschall), SUSAN SARANDON (Sally Matthews), KATE REID (Grace), ROBERT
JOY (Dave Matthews), MICHEL PICCOLI (Joseph), HOLLIS MCLAREN (Chrissie), AL WAXMAN (Alfie), MOSES
ZNAIMER (Felix), ANGUS MACINNES (Vinnie), WALLACE SHAWN (Waiter).

IFF VENICE 1980 GOLDEN LION.

"The world should be your oyster."

In some films, the true protagonist is the location. The laconic title of this Louis Malle movie certainly suggests it's true in this case. During the 1940s, this city on the east coast of the USA was an elegant watering hole. By the 1970s, though, Atlantic City had become a mere shadow of its former self: the hotels were crumbling, the promenade was decidedly undercrowded, and the people who lived here formed a panopticon of stranded souls.

There wasn't much life here, but suddenly there was hope: in 1979, gambling was legalized in New Jersey. The city awoke, threw away its crutches, and set out to make its fortune as a second Las Vegas. In Malle's film, which manages to combine a heavy heart with a light touch, this renaissance is marked, tellingly, by the demolition of the decrepit Grand Hotel.

Like the hotel, Lou Paschall (Burt Lancaster) is an embodiment and a leftover of the old days. For him, even the Atlantic is not what it used to be. Once he was a hood with ambitions, running messages for the Godfathers of big-time crime. Now, he's at the beck and call of Grace (Kate Reid), a dilapidated, hypochondriac diva, and her neurotic lapdogs. He's also a small-time

bookie on the side, raking in the cents from the little guys who hope Lady Luck might yet come through for them.

While Lou himself has no illusions that better times are just around the corner, Sally (Susan Sarandon) is training in her spare time to become a croupier. She already earns a living in the casino, behind the counter of a seafood buffet; when she gets home, she rubs herself down with fresh lemons to get rid of the stink of fish. Lou lives in the apartment opposite, and watches her perform this mysterious erotic ritual every evening.

One day, Sally gets an unexpected visit from a hippie couple: It's her long-lost husband Dave (Robert Joy) and the woman he ran away with – her sister Chrissie (Hollis McLaren). They have stolen a packet of cocaine from the Mafia, and now they need a place to lie low for a while. Lou agrees to help

them carry out a drugs deal. A short time later Dave is dead, so Lou carries on alone, quickly making enough money to take on the role of Sally's sugar daddy. Naturally, though, the Mob has already got its beady eye on him – and Lou soon has a real opportunity to prove he's a hero.

In 1981, *Atlantic City* was nominated for five Academy Awards – Best Film, Best Actor, Best Actress, Best Director, and Best Original Screenplay – and won none. Though the film has an American setting, it tells its story with a "European" tempo and rhythm, allowing its brilliant actors enough space to develop their characters. This includes even the supporting players, like Michel Piccoli in the role of Joseph, Sally's teacher and lover. It's one of Malle's greatest strengths that he passes no moral judgment on his characters, a stance reflected in Lou's attitude towards an old friend who now

"It takes Malle a little while to set up the crisscrossing of the ten or twelve major characters, but once he does, the film operates by its own laws in its own world, and it has a lovely fizziness." *The New Yorker*

1   Lucky in love? To hell with it! Sally (Susan Sarandon) and Lou (Burt Lancaster) would rather take their chances with the cards.

2   Crapping out: What happens to guys like Lou when they get mixed up in other people's business?

3   Full speed ahead: For Lou there's just no turning back.

3   4

works as a shoeshine boy in a restroom. Lou leaves the man guessing about his own situation, but always treats him with genuine and unpatronising respect.

It's the so-called little guys that interest Malle: those who are filled with the hope of a better life held out by the American Dream, though they can so easily end up as losers, washed up like driftwood on the edge of society. *Atlantic City* lays bare the divided heart of the United States: a country in which exorbitant wealth exists side-by-side with grim poverty, yet imbued with the naïve belief that anyone can make it if he really believes in himself. Maybe this film could only have been made by an outsider like Malle, so fascinated by America while remaining so thoroughly European as an artist.

SH

CASINOS IN THE MOVIES   Las Vegas, Reno and Atlantic City are the biggest casino towns in the USA, and they've also provided the backdrops to a range of very different films. Barry Levinson's *Bugsy* (1991) depicts the last years in the life of Bugsy Siegel, a mobster whose criminal energies played a decisive role in the rise of Vegas. Scorsese's *Casino* (1995) is another movie based on a true story, and it's also set in the Mafia milieu. Glamour, good-time girls and extravagant shows – the racy reputation of these dazzling cities was based on much more than mere gambling. In real-life Las Vegas, the legendary "Rat Pack" painted the town red: in one cinematic version of the gambler's paradise, Frank Sinatra, Dean Martin, Sammy Davis Jr., Peter Lawford, actually robbed a Vegas casino; their criminal caper *Ocean's Eleven* appeared in 1960, while Steven Soderbergh's remake came out in 2001. The latter also boasted an all-star ensemble, featuring George Clooney, Brad Pitt, and Julia Roberts. Casinos are often the locations of human tragedies, as in Karel Reisz's *The Gambler* (1974), starring James Caan, or Paul Thomas Anderson's remarkable feature-film debut, *Sydney,* aka *Hard Eight* (1995). In the noir classic *Gilda* (1946), a casino becomes the scene of a murky three-way relationship. The *crème de la crème* of the comedy scene has also discovered the casino as a movie location – see *Dirty Rotten Scoundrels* (1988), or *Vegas Vacation* (1996). Last but not least, a visit to a casino is obligatory for Agent 007. In *Dr. No* (1962), Sean Connery was positioned at a roulette table when he first uttered his most famous line: "My name is Bond... James Bond".

---

4   Don't talk to strangers: Sally hasn't the foggiest what these people want from her.

5   Game over. Please try again: Sophisticated Joseph (Michel Piccoli) breaks in new dealers and opens up a whole new world to Sally.

6   Beaten at his own game: After enlisting Lou to deliver drugs, Dave (Robert Joy) soon finds himself on the road to nowhere.

DIVA
Diva

1980 - FRANCE - 117 MIN. - THRILLER

DIRECTOR JEAN-JACQUES BEINEIX (*1946)
SCREENPLAY JEAN-JACQUES BEINEIX, JEAN VAN HAMME, based on the novel of the same name by DELACORTA
(= DANIEL ODIER) DIRECTOR OF PHOTOGRAPHY PHILIPPE ROUSSELOT EDITING MARIE-JOSÈPHE YOYOTTE, MONIQUE PRIM
MUSIC VLADIMIR COSMA PRODUCTION IRÈNE SILBERMAN for GREENWICH FILM PRODUCTIONS, FILMS A2, LES FILMS
GALAXIE.

STARRING FRÉDÉRIC ANDRÉI (Jules), WILHELMENIA WIGGINS-FERNANDEZ (Cynthia Hawkins), RICHARD BOHRINGER
(Gorodish), THUY AN LUU (Alba), JACQUES FABBRI (Jean Saporta), DOMINIQUE PINON (Le curé), GÉRARD DARMON
(L'Antillais), JEAN-JACQUES MOREAU (Krantz), ANNY ROMAND (Paula), CHANTAL DERUAZ (Nadja, an ex-prostitute).

"There is no such thing as innocent pleasure."

Jules (Frédéric Andréi), a young Parisian postman, loves opera with a passion. He is particularly devoted to the singer Cynthia Hawkins (Wilhelmenia Wiggins-Fernandez), a true Diva who flatly refuses to make records, much to the annoyance of her manager. When she gives a concert in Paris, Jules succeeds in making a top-quality bootleg recording of her performance. His achievement doesn't go unnoticed; from now on, the naive fan will be pursued everywhere he goes by two shady "businessmen" from the Taiwanese pirate-music mafia. As if the situation weren't dangerous enough, Jules is soon the hapless recipient of a second tape, bearing proof that the chief of

the Parisian police is also running a drugs-and-prostitution ring. In next to no time, a team of killers are hot on Jules' heels.

Like many a cult film, Diva flopped when first released. The French critics were decidedly sniffy about Jean-Jacques Beineix's directing debut, describing it as glossy but hollow, and moviegoers initially also showed little interest. Only after the film received an enthusiastic reception at American festivals did Diva begin to attract a mainly young audience in Europe. It gradually became one of the biggest hits of the 80s. Diva ran and ran... and what's more, its influence was considerable: it marked the beginning of

the French "neon cinema," an anti-intellectual counterblast to the dominant *cinema des auteurs* of the older generation. Beineix and Luc Besson were to be the leading lights of this brash new movement.

Diva is undeniably a film that likes to be looked at. It's a fairy-tale thriller that focuses entirely on overwhelming visual effects, at the expense of narrative and character-development. So while it's fair to say that Beineix's film is superficial, it cannot be denied that it also functions brilliantly at this surface level. For one thing, the film is edited so superbly that sheer tempo makes the holes in the plot seem negligible. Philippe Rousselot's camerawork is particularly outstanding. The artificiality of the film's imagery constitutes an all-but-independent cosmos, a synthetic parallel world consisting entirely of spectacular locations, and intersecting only tangentially with the

"A designer fairy tale, in which a decked out pad and Revox stereo are more significant than the protagonist's innermost thoughts." *Süddeutsche Zeitung*

1 Sleek and chic: Diva marked the advent of 1980s French Neon Cinema – a movement that basked in artificiality rather than the realism of the auteurs.

2 Skin-deep: Beineix's characters luxuriate in superficiality, but fail to fathom deeper waters.

3 Prima Wilhelmenia: A set of powerhouse pipes turned Wiggins-Fernandez into a screen icon.

4 Projection room: Lacklustre Jules' (Frédéric Andréi) voyeuristic fixation on the singer win him the hearts of the crowd.

5 Golden opportunity: From the wings of the supporting cast, dashing Bohemian Gorodish (Richard Bohringer) suddenly emerges as the film's true hero.

JEAN-JACQUES BEINEIX   Jean-Jacques Beineix (*1946 in Paris) originally studied medicine, before beginning his film career as an assistant to directors as famous as René Clément and Claude Berri. He was 34 by the time he came to make his first film, *Diva* (1980), which got off to a poor start in France before being enthusiastically received on the American festival circuit. Word spread back to Europe, and it eventually became one of the most successful films of the 80s, establishing Beineix's reputation as a cult director. The public enjoyed *Diva*'s visual brilliance and its characteristic fairytale atmosphere, qualities that also marked Beineix's later work and had a lasting influence on the "neon cinema" of the 80s. The critics, however, accused him of superficiality, and his subsequent films failed to mollify them. *The Moon in the Gutter* (*La Lune dans le caniveau*, 1983) was a naive love story about a longshoreman and a rich girl; *Betty Blue* (*37°2 le matin*, 1985) – Beineix's second big box-office hit – was a fashionable adaptation of Philippe Dijan's bestseller; and *Roselyne and the Lions* (*Roselyne et les lions*, 1989) was a somewhat unhappy circus film. After *IP 5* (*IP 5: L'île aux pachydermes*, 1992), noted mainly for the fact that Yves Montand died shortly after the film was completed, Beineix withdrew from the cinema, devoted his time to painting, and made a few documentary films. He attempted a comeback with the surrealistic thriller *Mortal Transfer* (*Mortel transfert*, 2000), but was unable to repeat the success he had enjoyed in the 80s.

real city of Paris. The slow-moving camera draws us in, as if we were dreaming Jules' dreams. And these are the daydreams of an overgrown boy who's built a fantastic playpen in his factory flat, complete with clapped-out luxury limousines, sultry Pop Art paintings and a hi-tech beast of a sound-system. Safe in this pubertal paradise, Jules can indulge in fantasies of a thrilling existence… until reality intervenes, forcing him to endure a series of perilous adventures before he can win the heart of his opera diva. The lady in question is played by Wilhelmenia Wiggins-Fernandez, and the scenes in which Jean-Jacques Beineix captures her wonderful voice are undoubtedly the highpoints of the film.

Jules, the gawky hero, would hardly have survived without the support of two guardian angels: Gorodish (Richard Bohringer), a master of the art of living, and his Vietnamese companion Alba (Thuy An Luu). At the time,

many felt that the eccentric Gorodish was the real hero of the film; not just because he freed Jules from every fine mess he got himself into, and kept his cool while doing so, but because he embodied the essential attitudes of the age. This was a generation that had turned its back on ideological struggle and accepted the fact that the world is corrupt. Thus the 80s witnessed a collective retreat from the public to the private sphere, and lifestyle became indistinguishable from life itself. Gorodish was equally at home in a loft or a lighthouse, and happy behind the wheel of a hoodlum's white Citroën; he could conjure up cars like Felix the Cat, and he smoked fine cigars to the music of the spheres while soaking in a free-standing bathtub. The man was almost heroic in his hedonism, and a perfect paragon of 80s style.

JH

THE SHINING

1980 - USA / GREAT BRITAIN - 144 MIN. / 119 MIN. (Europe and Australia) - HORROR FILM, LITERARY ADAPTATION

DIRECTOR STANLEY KUBRICK (1928–1999)

SCREENPLAY STANLEY KUBRICK, DIANE JOHNSON, based on the novel of the same name by STEPHEN KING **DIRECTOR OF PHOTOGRAPHY** JOHN ALCOTT **EDITING** RAY LOVEJOY **MUSIC** KRZYSZTOF PENDERECKI, GYÖRGY LIGETI, BÉLA BARTÓK, WENDY CARLOS **PRODUCTION** STANLEY KUBRICK, ROBERT FRYER, MARY LEA JOHNSON, MARTIN RICHARDS for HAWK FILMS, PRODUCERS CIRCLE, PEREGRINE, WARNER BROS.

STARRING JACK NICHOLSON (Jack Torrance), SHELLEY DUVALL (Wendy Torrance), DANNY LLOYD (Danny Torrance), BARRY NELSON (Stuart Ullman), SCATMAN CROTHERS (Dick Hallorann), PHILIP STONE (Delbert Grady), JOE TURKEL (Lloyd), ANNE JACKSON (Doctor), TONY BURTON (Larry Durkin), LIA BELDAM (Young Woman In Bathtub).

"Some places are like people: some shine and some don't."

Wendy (Shelley Duvall) slowly bends over the typewriter. Her jaw drops and her widening eyes move from left to right. "All work and no play makes Jack a dull boy." Wendy scrolls down the leaf of paper. The entire sheet is filled with this identical sentence. She looks next to the typewriter and flicks through the bulky manuscript. Line after line the same words, page after page the same sentence. Wendy immediately realizes that Jack (Jack Nicholson) has lost his mind. But it is too late, because in exactly this moment, her husband is standing behind her, resolved to kill her.

Perhaps the most frightening moment in *The Shining* is when Wendy understands she is at the mercy of a madman and cannot escape. For a month Wendy, Jack, and their son, Danny (Danny Torrance) have been looking after the large, empty Overlook Hotel, which lies secluded somewhere in the mountains. They activate the boiler to avoid frost damage from the long

winter and idly pass their time: Danny racing toy cars through the halls, Wendy in the kitchen, and Jack at his desk. He is a novelist and is trying to write a new manuscript. But he sinks into lethargy with the first snowfall. And he encounters people who couldn't possibly be present in the hotel: first a bartender who serves him a long-desired drink, then a naked woman who in his embrace transforms into a zombie-like creature. The ultimate hallucination is when an entire ballroom comes alive with party guests from the 1920s and a waiter convinces Jack to call his family to order — with drastic methods.

The Shining is a perfect symphony of horror, composed by Stanley Kubrick, the sublime master of all genres. With his obsessive love of detail, he re-shot some scenes as many as 120 times: one example is the scene in which Dick Hallorann (Scatman Crothers), the chef cook of the hotel, receives

2

1   It's too late, Baby… By the time Wendy Torrance (Shelley Duvall) acknowledges her marital problems, husband Jack is burning rubber on his hell ride.

2   Writer's block: Jack Torrance (Jack Nicholson) acts out when he can't get his ideas down on paper.

3   Jack the Ripper: "I'm not gonna hurt ya, Wendy. I'm just gonna rip your fuckin' heart out!"

a telepathic call for help from Danny. Like the old man, the boy possesses a special ability of the "Shining," which allows him to see traces of the past and images of the future. Halloran makes his way to the snowed-in hotel and becomes Wendy and Danny's last hope.

The terror in *The Shining* does not stem from shocking special effects, but the inexorable straightforwardness that leads to the deadly finale. Jack's path is predestined, steered by the Overlook Hotel. Like a magnet, it attracts the yellow Volkswagen Beetle as Jack drives through the mountains to interview for a job as caretaker. The hotel empowers him when he complains about his wife, and it frees him after Wendy zonks him with a baseball bat and locks him up. It is the location itself that comes alive – to assimilate and engulf the living.

Kubrick placed particular importance on the symmetrical construction of the images to intensify the feeling of imprisonment: the characters stick in

"Stanley Kubrick doesn't do anything by halves. What this diehard perfectionist has created, during the years of postproduction work that went on while tucked away in a British film studio, are exemplary pieces of artistic refinement: *2001, A Space Odyssey* was a masterpiece in science fiction, *Barry Lyndon* set a new standard for historical epics and *The Shining* redefined the meaning of horror altogether." *Der Spiegel*

3

Danny: "What about Room 237?"
Hallorann: "Room 237?"
Danny: "You're scared of Room 237, ain't ya?"
Hallorann: "No, I ain't."
Danny: "Mr. Hallorann, what is in Room 237?"
Hallorann: "Nothin'! There ain't nothin' in Room 237. But you ain't got no business goin' in there anyway. So stay out! You understand? Stay out!"

Film quote: Danny Torrance and Dick Hallorann

the middle of the rooms as if caught in the center of a spider web. In contrast to the film's literary forerunner, Kubrick scrapped the psychoanalysis of the family members, preferring to leave wide room for interpretation. And readings of the films were duly divergent. Some saw *The Shining* as a study of writer's block, while others interpreted the piece as a comment on the oppression of Native Americans by white settlers, because the hotel was constructed on an old Indian burial ground.

Stephen King, the author of the novel, made no secret of his dissatisfaction with the Kubrick version, particularly the finale in the labyrinth next to the hotel. But Kubrick's invention of the hedgerow labyrinth is nothing short of ingenious. To find their way out, they are going to have to lay breadcrumbs, says Wendy when she sees the enormous kitchen for the first time. The Overlook Hotel is a labyrinth of endless hallways, forbidden doors, and dead ends like the ballroom. The human brain also resembles a labyrinth. It offers endless possibilities – some paths lead in the wrong direction and one can sometimes get lost. There are ways out, but not everyone is able to find them. Some remain prisoners of their own labyrinth – like Jack.

NM

HORROR FILM   Shock, panic, terror – the horror flick feeds on fear and the passion for fear. The basic prerequisite is the audience's suspension of disbelief – the more they identify, the greater their fear for the wellbeing of the protagonists. And as horror movies seem to be a favorite among the younger generation – proved beyond doubt by John Carpenter's *Halloween* (1978) – younger actors generally take the leads in such cinematic enterprises. The roots of the horror genre lie in German silent film. Friedrich Wilhelm Murnau's *Nosferatu* (1922), *The Golem* (1914/15) by Paul Wegener and Henrik Galeen, as well as Robert Wiene's *The Cabinet of Dr. Caligari* (1919), establishes the stalwarts of the genre such as vampires, artificial creatures, and madmen. But the greatest terror reigns in the mind: films like Stellan Rye's *Der Student von Prag* (1913), Rouben Mamoulian's *Dr. Jekyll and Mr. Hyde* (1931), or Stanley Kubrick's *The Shining* (1980) beam a searchlight into the murky depths within ourselves.

Light and shadow are the basic ingredients of the genre and Jacques Tourneur most notably and masterfully played with these contrasts, as in his film *Cat People* (1942), a subtly metaphorical exploration of sexuality. It is precisely this reduction to the ABC of filmmaking that creates the best horror movies. Exceptional examples are George A. Romero's sinister social commentary *Night of the Living Dead* (1968) or *The Blair Witch Project* (1999), directed by Daniel Myrick and Eduardo Sánchez.

4   Victorian Age at the Overlook Hotel: All the interior scenes were shot at a British film studio.

5   Let it shine! Danny Torrance (Danny Lloyd) has a special power, a special friend and runs at the mention of "red rum."

6   All lines are down: Scatman Crothers picks up Danny's distress signal via mental telepathy.

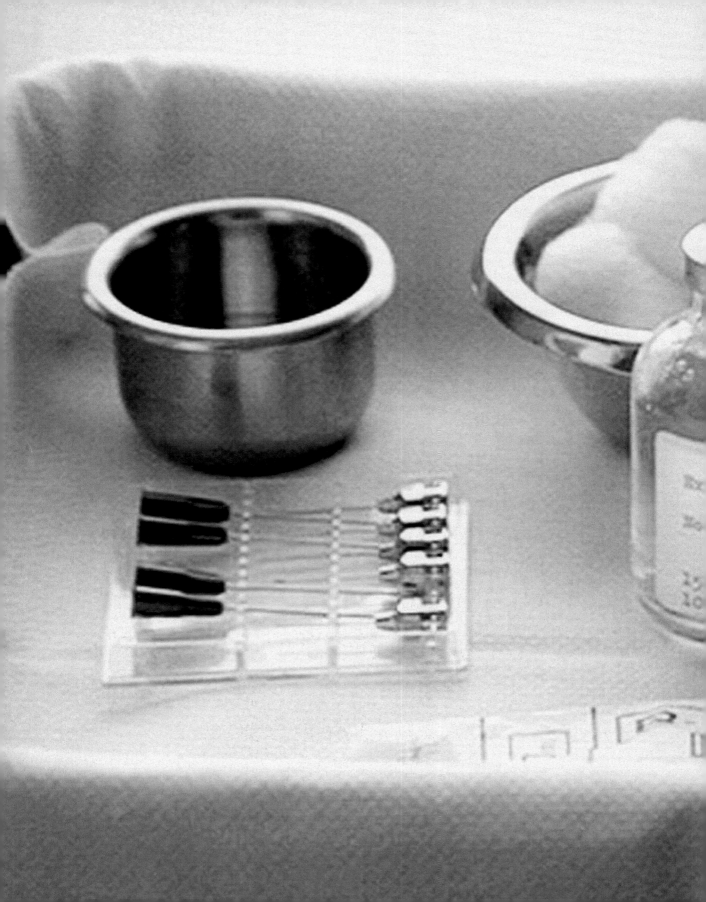

ACADEMY AWARDS *1971–1980*

1 Chase across the channel: *The French Connection*'s William Friedkin still holds the record as the youngest recipient of the Best Director Oscar.
2 Cashing in: Jane Fonda took home a little golden guy for her performance in *Klute*.

1971 OSCARS

BEST PICTURE	THE FRENCH CONNECTION (Philip D'Antoni)
BEST DIRECTOR	WILLIAM FRIEDKIN for *The French Connection*
BEST LEADING ACTRESS	JANE FONDA in *Klute*
BEST LEADING ACTOR	GENE HACKMAN in *The French Connection*
BEST SUPPORTING ACTRESS	CLORIS LEACHMAN in *The Last Picture Show*
BEST SUPPORTING ACTOR	BEN JOHNSON in *The Last Picture Show*
BEST ORIGINAL SCREENPLAY	PADDY CHAYEFSKY for *The Hospital*
BEST ADAPTED SCREENPLAY	ERNEST TIDYMAN for *The French Connection*
BEST FOREIGN LANGUAGE FILM	*The Garden of the Finzi-Continis* by VITTORIO DE SICA (Italy)
BEST CINEMATOGRAPHY	OSWALD MORRIS for *Fiddler on the Roof*
BEST ART DIRECTION	JOHN BOX, ERNEST ARCHER, JACK MAXSTED, GIL PARRONDO, VERNON DIXON for *Nikolaus and Alexandra*
BEST FILM EDITING	GERALD B. GREENBERG for *The French Connection*
BEST MUSIC	MICHAEL LEGRAND for *Summer of '42*
BEST SONG	ISAAC HAYES for "THEME FROM SHAFT" in *Shaft*
BEST COSTUMES	YVONNE BLAKE, ANTONIO CASTILLO for *Nikolaus and Alexandra*
BEST VISUAL EFFECTS	ALAN MALEY, EUSTACE LYCETT, DANNY LEE for *Bedknobs and Broomsticks*
BEST SOUND	GORDON K. MCCALLUM, DAVID HILDYARD for *Anatevka*
BEST SOUND EFFECTS EDITING	Not awarded

3 Capiche?!: Marlon Brando is *The Godfather*.
4 Showstopper: Liza Minnelli in *Cabaret*.

1972 OSCARS

BEST PICTURE	THE GODFATHER (Albert S. Ruddy)
BEST DIRECTOR	BOB FOSSE for *Cabaret*
BEST LEADING ACTRESS	LIZA MINNELLI in *Cabaret*
BEST LEADING ACTOR	MARLON BRANDO in *The Godfather* (the award was declined)
BEST SUPPORTING ACTRESS	EILEEN HECKART in *Butterflies Are Free*
BEST SUPPORTING ACTOR	JOEL GREY in *Cabaret*
BEST ORIGINAL SCREENPLAY	JEREMY LARNER for *The Candidate*
BEST ADAPTED SCREENPLAY	MARIO PUZO, FRANCIS FORD COPPOLA for *The Godfather*
BEST FOREIGN LANGUAGE FILM	*The Discreet Charm of the Bourgeoisie* by LUIS BUÑUEL (France)
BEST CINEMATOGRAPHY	GEOFFREY UNSWORTH for *Cabaret*
BEST ART DIRECTION	ROLF ZEHETBAUER, HANS JÜRGEN KIEBACH, HERBERT STRABEL for *Cabaret*
BEST FILM EDITING	DAVID BRETHERTON for *Cabaret*
BEST MUSIC	CHARLES CHAPLIN, RAY RASCH, LARRY RUSSELL for *Limelight*
BEST SONG	AL KASHA, JOEL HIRSCHHORN for "THE MORNING AFTER" in *The Poseidon Adventure*
BEST COSTUMES	ANTHONY POWELL for *Travels with My Aunt*
BEST VISUAL EFFECTS	L. B. ABBOTT, A. D. FLOWERS for *The Poseidon Adventure* (Special Achievement Award)
BEST SOUND	ROBERT KNUDSON, DAVID HILDYARD for *Cabaret*
BEST SOUND EFFECTS EDITING	Not awarded

1 Bitten by the Oscar bug: *Sting* director, George Roy Hill.
2 Little girl lost: Tatum O'Neal in *Paper Moon*.

1973 OSCARS

BEST PICTURE	THE STING (Tony Bill, Michael Phillips, Julia Phillips)
BEST DIRECTOR	GEORGE ROY HILL for *The Sting*
BEST LEADING ACTRESS	GLENDA JACKSON in *A Touch of Class*
BEST LEADING ACTOR	JACK LEMMON in *Save the Tiger*
BEST SUPPORTING ACTRESS	TATUM O'NEAL in *Paper Moon*
BEST SUPPORTING ACTOR	JOHN HOUSEMAN in *The Paper Chase*
BEST ORIGINAL SCREENPLAY	DAVID S. WARD for *The Sting*
BEST ADAPTED SCREENPLAY	WILLIAM PETER BLATTY for *The Exorcist*
BEST FOREIGN LANGUAGE FILM	*Day for Night* by FRANÇOIS TRUFFAUT (France)
BEST CINEMATOGRAPHY	SVEN NYKVIST for *Cries and Whispers*
BEST ART DIRECTION	HENRY BUMSTEAD, JAMES PAYNE for *The Sting*
BEST FILM EDITING	WILLIAM REYNOLDS for *The Sting*
BEST MUSIC	MARVIN HAMLISCH for *The Way We Were*
BEST SONG	MARVIN HAMLISCH (music), ALAN BERGMAN (text), MARILYN BERGMAN (text) for "THE WAY WE WERE" in *The Way We Were*
BEST COSTUMES	EDITH HEAD for *The Sting*
BEST VISUAL EFFECTS	NOT AWARDED
BEST SOUND	ROBERT KNUDSON, CHRISTOPHER NEWMAN for *The Exorcist*
BEST SOUND EFFECTS EDITING	Not awarded

3   A sequel beyond equal: Directing genius Francis Ford Coppola boldly trumped his own
ace with *The Godfather – Part II.*
4   Serving up excellence: Ellen Burstyn in *Alice Doesn't Live Here Anymore.*

1974 OSCARS

BEST PICTURE	THE GODFATHER – PART II (Francis Ford Coppola, Gray Frederickson, Fred Roos)
BEST DIRECTOR	FRANCIS FORD COPPOLA for *The Godfather – Part II*
BEST LEADING ACTRESS	ELLEN BURSTYN in *Alice Doesn't Live Here Anymore*
BEST LEADING ACTOR	ART CARNEY in *Harry and Tonto*
BEST SUPPORTING ACTRESS	INGRID BERGMAN in *Murder on the Orient Express*
BEST SUPPORTING ACTOR	ROBERT DE NIRO in *The Godfather – Part II*
BEST ORIGINAL SCREENPLAY	ROBERT TOWNE for *Chinatown*
BEST ADAPTED SCREENPLAY	FRANCIS FORD COPPOLA, MARIO PUZO for *The Godfather – Part II*
BEST FOREIGN LANGUAGE FILM	*Amarcord* by FEDERICO FELLINI (Italy)
BEST CINEMATOGRAPHY	FRED J. KOENEKAMP, JOSEPH F. BIROC for *The Towering Inferno*
BEST ART DIRECTION	DEAN TAVOULARIS, ANGELO P. GRAHAM, GEORGE R. NELSON for *The Godfather – Part II*
BEST FILM EDITING	HAROLD F. KRESS, CARL KRESS for *The Towering Inferno*
BEST MUSIC	NINO ROTA, CARMINE COPPOLA for *The Godfather – Part II*
BEST SONG	AL KASHA (text), JOEL HIRSCHHORN (music) for "WE MAY NEVER LOVE LIKE THIS AGAIN" in *The Towering Inferno*
BEST COSTUMES	THEONI V. ALDREDGE for *The Great Gatsby*
BEST VISUAL EFFECTS	FRANK BRENDEL, GLEN ROBINSON, ALBERT WHITLOCK for *Earthquake* (Special Achievement Award)
BEST SOUND	RONALD PIERCE, MELVIN M. METCALFE SR. for *Earthquake*
BEST SOUND EFFECTS EDITING	Not awarded

1 Speaking to deaf ears: Jack Nicholson has his mind set on neutralizing his nemesis...
2 ... but *Cuckoo Nest* queen, Nurse Ratched (Louise Fletcher) is the one giving the shots around here.

1975 OSCARS

BEST PICTURE	ONE FLEW OVER THE CUCKOO'S NEST (Saul Zaentz, Michael Douglas)
BEST DIRECTOR	MILOŠ FORMAN for *One Flew Over the Cuckoo's Nest*
BEST LEADING ACTRESS	LOUISE FLETCHER in *One Flew Over the Cuckoo's Nest*
BEST LEADING ACTOR	JACK NICHOLSON in *One Flew Over the Cuckoo's Nest*
BEST SUPPORTING ACTRESS	LEE GRANT in *Shampoo*
BEST SUPPORTING ACTOR	GEORGE BURNS in *The Sunshine Boys*
BEST ORIGINAL SCREENPLAY	FRANK PIERSON for *Dog Day Afternoon*
BEST ADAPTED SCREENPLAY	LAWRENCE HAUBEN, BO GOLDMAN for *One Flew Over the Cuckoo's Nest*
BEST FOREIGN LANGUAGE FILM	*Dersu Uzala* by AKIRA KUROSAWA (USSR)
BEST CINEMATOGRAPHY	JOHN ALCOTT for *Barry Lyndon*
BEST ART DIRECTION	KEN ADAM, ROY WALKER, VERNON DIXON for *Barry Lyndon*
BEST FILM EDITING	VERNA FIELDS for *Jaws*
BEST MUSIC	JOHN WILLIAMS for *Jaws*
BEST SONG	KEITH CARRADINE for "I'M EASY" in *Nashville*
BEST COSTUMES	ULLA-BRITT SÖDERLUND, MILENA CANONERO for *Barry Lyndon*
BEST VISUAL EFFECTS	ALBERT WHITLOCK, GLEN ROBINSON for *The Hindenburg* (Special Achievement Award)
BEST SOUND	ROBERT L. HOYT, ROGER HEMAN JR., EARL MABERY, JOHN R. CARTER for *Jaws*
BEST SOUND EFFECTS EDITING	PETER BERKOS for *The Hindenburg* (Special Achievement Award)

3 Sensuous dragon lady: Faye Dunaway in *Network*.
4 Persona non grata: Peter Finch (*Network*) was posthumously awarded the Oscar for Best Actor.

1976 OSCARS

BEST PICTURE	ROCKY (Irwin Winkler, Robert Chartoff)
BEST DIRECTOR	JOHN G. AVILDSEN for *Rocky*
BEST LEADING ACTRESS	FAYE DUNAWAY in *Network*
BEST LEADING ACTOR	PETER FINCH in *Network*
BEST SUPPORTING ACTRESS	BEATRICE STRAIGHT in *Network*
BEST SUPPORTING ACTOR	JASON ROBARDS in *All the President's Men*
BEST ORIGINAL SCREENPLAY	PADDY CHAYEFSKY for *Network*
BEST ADAPTED SCREENPLAY	WILLIAM GOLDMAN for *All the President's Men*
BEST FOREIGN LANGUAGE FILM	*Black and White in Color* by JEAN-JACQUES ANNAUD (Ivory Coast)
BEST CINEMATOGRAPHY	HASKELL WEXLER for *Bound for Glory*
BEST ART DIRECTION	GEORGE JENKINS, GEORGE GAINES for *All the President's Men*
BEST FILM EDITING	RICHARD HALSEY, SCOTT CONRAD for *Rocky*
BEST MUSIC	JERRY GOLDSMITH for *The Omen*
BEST SONG	BARBRA STREISAND (music), PAUL WILLIAMS (text) for "A WORLD THAT NEVER WAS" in *A Star Is Born*
BEST COSTUMES	DANILO DONATI for *Fellini's Casanova*
BEST VISUAL EFFECTS	CARLO RAMBALDI, GLEN ROBINSON, FRANK VAN DER VEER for *King Kong* (Special Achievement Award); L. B. ABBOTT, GLEN ROBINSON, MATTHEW YURICICH for *Logan's Run* (Special Achievement Award)
BEST SOUND	ARTHUR PIANTADOSI, LES FRESHOLTZ, RICK ALEXANDER, JAMES E. WEBB for *All the President's Men*
BEST SOUND EFFECTS EDITING	Not awarded

1 Footloose and fancy-free: Diane Keaton as Annie Hall.
2 A punim only mama could love! Woody Allen victimizes himself to a directing Oscar.

1977 OSCARS

BEST PICTURE	ANNIE HALL (Charles H. Joffe)
BEST DIRECTOR	WOODY ALLEN for *Annie Hall*
BEST LEADING ACTRESS	DIANE KEATON in *Annie Hall*
BEST LEADING ACTOR	RICHARD DREYFUSS in *The Goodbye Girl*
BEST SUPPORTING ACTRESS	VANESSA REDGRAVE in *Julia*
BEST SUPPORTING ACTOR	JASON ROBARDS in *Julia*
BEST ORIGINAL SCREENPLAY	WOODY ALLEN, MARSHALL BRICKMAN for *Annie Hall*
BEST ADAPTED SCREENPLAY	ALVIN SARGENT for *Julia*
BEST FOREIGN LANGUAGE FILM	*Madame Rosa* by MOSHÉ MIZRAHI (France)
BEST CINEMATOGRAPHY	VILMOS ZSIGMOND for *Close Encounters of the Third Kind*
BEST ART DIRECTION	JOHN BARRY, NORMAN REYNOLDS, LESLIE DILLEY, ROGER CHRISTIAN for *Star Wars*
BEST FILM EDITING	PAUL HIRSCH, MARCIA LUCAS, RICHARD CHEW for *Star Wars*
BEST MUSIC	JOHN WILLIAMS for *Star Wars*
BEST SONG	JOSEPH BROOKS for "YOU LIGHT UP MY LIFE" in *You Light Up My Life*
BEST COSTUMES	JOHN MOLLO for *Star Wars*
BEST VISUAL EFFECTS	JOHN STEARS, JOHN DYKSTRA, RICHARD EDLUND, GRANT MCCUNE, ROBERT BLALACK for *Star Wars*
BEST SOUND	DON MACDOUGALL, RAY WEST, ROB MINKLER, DEREK BALL for *Star Wars*
BEST SOUND EFFECTS EDITING	FRANK WARNER for *Close Encounters of the Third Kind* (Special Achievement Award); BEN BURTT for *Star Wars* (Special Achievement Award)

1978 OSCARS

BEST PICTURE	THE DEER HUNTER (Barry Spikings, Michael Deeley, Michael Cimino, John Peverall)
BEST DIRECTOR	MICHAEL CIMINO for *The Deer Hunter*
BEST LEADING ACTRESS	JANE FONDA in *Coming Home*
BEST LEADING ACTOR	JON VOIGHT in *Coming Home*
BEST SUPPORTING ACTRESS	MAGGIE SMITH in *California Suite*
BEST SUPPORTING ACTOR	CHRISTOPHER WALKEN in *The Deer Hunter*
BEST ORIGINAL SCREENPLAY	NANCY DOWD, WALDO SALT, ROBERT C. JONES for *Coming Home*
BEST ADAPTED SCREENPLAY	OLIVER STONE for *Midnight Express*
BEST FOREIGN LANGUAGE FILM	*Get Out Your Handkerchiefs* by BERTRAND BLIER (France)
BEST CINEMATOGRAPHY	NÉSTOR ALMENDROS for *Days of Heaven*
BEST ART DIRECTION	PAUL SYLBERT, EDWIN O'DONAVAN, GEORGE GAINES for *Heaven Can Wait*
BEST FILM EDITING	PETER ZINNER for *The Deer Hunter*
BEST MUSIC	GIORGIO MORODER for *Midnight Express*
BEST SONG	PAUL JABARA for "LAST DANCE" in *Thank God It's Friday*
BEST COSTUMES	ANTHONY POWELL for *Death on the Nile*
BEST VISUAL EFFECTS	LES BOWIE, COLIN CHILVERS, DENYS N. COOP, ROY FIELD, DEREK MEDDINGS, ZORAN PERISIC (Special Achievement Award) for *Superman*
BEST SOUND	RICHARD PORTMAN, WILLIAM L. MCCAUGHEY, AARON ROCHIN, C. DARIN KNIGHT for *The Deer Hunter*

1 Presiding over the divorce court: *Kramer vs. Kramer* director Robert Benton.
2 Strike back: Sally Field gets all worked up as Norma Rae.

1979 OSCARS

BEST PICTURE	KRAMER VS. KRAMER (Stanley R. Jaffe)
BEST DIRECTOR	ROBERT BENTON for *Kramer vs. Kramer*
BEST LEADING ACTRESS	SALLY FIELD in *Norma Rae*
BEST LEADING ACTOR	DUSTIN HOFFMAN in *Kramer vs. Kramer*
BEST SUPPORTING ACTRESS	MERYL STREEP in *Kramer vs. Kramer*
BEST SUPPORTING ACTOR	MELVYN DOUGLAS in *Being There*
BEST ORIGINAL SCREENPLAY	STEVE TESICH for *Breaking Away*
BEST ADAPTED SCREENPLAY	ROBERT BENTON for *Kramer vs. Kramer*
BEST FOREIGN LANGUAGE FILM	*The Tin Drum* by VOLKER SCHLÖNDORFF (FRG)
BEST CINEMATOGRAPHY	VITTORIO STORARO for *Apocalypse Now*
BEST ART DIRECTION	PHILIP ROSENBERG, TONY WALTON, EDWARD STEWART, GARY J. BRINK for *All That Jazz*
BEST FILM EDITING	ALAN HEIM for *All That Jazz*
BEST MUSIC	GEORGES DELERUE for "ICH LIEBE DICH – I LOVE YOU – JE T'AIME" in *A Little Romance*
BEST SONG	DAVID SHIRE (music), NORMAN GIMBEL (text) for "IT GOES LIKE IT GOES" for *Norma Rae*
BEST COSTUMES	ALBERT WOLSKY for *All That Jazz*
BEST VISUAL EFFECTS	H. R. GIGER, CARLO RAMBALDI, BRIAN JOHNSON, NICK ALLDER, DENYS AYLING for *Alien*
BEST SOUND	WALTER MURCH, MARK BERGER, RICHARD BEGGS, NATHAN BOXER for *Apocalypse Now*
BEST SOUND EFFECTS EDITING	ALAN SPLET for *The Black Stallion* (Special Achievement Award)

3   The man who would be king: It's lights, camera, Oscar for America's favorite son
    Robert Redford (r.).
4   Knock out! Robert De Niro sees red in *Raging Bull*.

1980 OSCARS

BEST PICTURE	ORDINARY PEOPLE (Ronald L. Schwary)
BEST DIRECTOR	ROBERT REDFORD for *Ordinary People*
BEST LEADING ACTRESS	SISSY SPACEK in *Coal Miner's Daughter*
BEST LEADING ACTOR	ROBERT DE NIRO in *Raging Bull*
BEST SUPPORTING ACTRESS	MARY STEENBURGEN in *Melvin and Howard*
BEST SUPPORTING ACTOR	TIMOTHY HUTTON in *Ordinary People*
BEST ORIGINAL SCREENPLAY	BO GOLDMAN for *Melvin and Howard*
BEST ADAPTED SCREENPLAY	ALVIN SARGENT for *Ordinary People*
BEST FOREIGN LANGUAGE FILM	*Moscow Does Not Believe in Tears* by WLADIMIR MENSCHOW (USSR)
BEST CINEMATOGRAPHY	GEOFFREY UNSWORTH, GHISLAIN CLOQUET for *Tess*
BEST ART DIRECTION	PIERRE GUFFROY, JACK STEPHENS for *Tess*
BEST FILM EDITING	THELMA SCHOONMAKER for *Raging Bull*
BEST MUSIC	MICHAEL GORE for *Fame*
BEST SONG	MICHAEL GORE (music), DEAN PITCHFORD (text) for "FAME" in *Fame*
BEST COSTUMES	ANTHONY POWELL for *Tess*
BEST VISUAL EFFECTS	BRIAN JOHNSON, RICHARD EDLUND, DENNIS MUREN, BRUCE NICHOLSON for *Star Wars: Episode V – The Empire Strikes Back* (Special Achievement Award)
BEST SOUND	BILL VARNEY, STEVE MASLOW, GREGG LANDAKER, PETER SUTTON for *Star Wars: Episode V – The Empire Strikes Back*
BEST SOUND EFFECTS EDITING	Not awarded

INDEX OF FILMS

INDEX OF FILMS

GENERAL INDEX

Production companies are listed in italics; film categories are preceded
by a dash; numbers in bold refer to a glossary text.

GENERAL INDEX

GENERAL INDEX

GENERAL INDEX

GENERAL INDEX

GENERAL INDEX

GENERAL INDEX

GENERAL INDEX

ABOUT THE AUTHORS

Philipp Bühler (PB), *1971, studied political science, history and British studies. Film journalist, writing for various regional German publications. Lives in Berlin.

David Gaertner (DG), *1978, studied film and art history. Freelances for the German film archives division of the Berlin Film Museum. Lives in Berlin.

Malte Hagener (MH), *1971, degree in Literature and Media Studies. Editor and author of numerous academic articles. Lecturer in Film History at Amsterdam University. Lives in Amsterdam and Berlin.

Steffen Haubner (SH), *1965, studied Art History and Sociology. Has written many academic and press articles. Collaborator on the science and research section of the *Hamburger Abendblatt*. Lives in Hamburg.

Jörn Hetebrügge (JH), *1971, studied German Literature. Author of many academic and press articles. Academic assistant at the Dresden Technical University Art and Music Institute since 2003. Lives in Berlin.

Harald Keller (HK), *1958, media journalist, works for national newspapers, essays and book publications on the history of film and television. Lives in Osnabrück.

Katja Kirste (KK), *1969, media journalist and academic. Author of numerous publications on film and related subjects. Lives in Munich.

Heinz-Jürgen Köhler (HJK), *1963, chief copy editor for *TV Today*. Author of many academic and press articles. Lives in Hamburg.

Oliver Küch (OK), *1972, studied English language and British history. Media and computer journalist; author of articles on film and television. Lives in Hamburg.

Petra Lange-Berndt (PLB), *1973, studied Art History and German Literature, doctoral candidate at the Department of Art History, University of Hamburg. Has authored numerous academic articles. Lives in Hamburg.

Nils Meyer (NM), *1971, studied German Literature and Politics. Has written many articles in various papers and magazines. Academic assistant at the Dresden Technical University Art and Music Institute since 2003. Lives in Dresden.

Eckhard Pabst (EP), *1965, film theorist, numerous publications as editor and author. Lives in Rendsburg near Kiel.

Lars Penning (LP), *1962, film journalist, works for numerous national newspapers, various articles and books on the history of film. Lives in Berlin.

Anne Pohl (APO), *1961, active as a journalist since 1987. Author of numerous academic articles. Lives in Berlin.

Stephan Reisner (SR), *1969, studied literature and philosophy in Hanover. Freelance journalist in Berlin, writing for *Edit, BELLAtriste, Glasklar* and the *Tagesspiegel*. 1st prize, Kritischer Salon-Preis 2001, Hanover; 2nd prize at the 2002 Vienna Studio Awards.

Burkhard Röwekamp (BR), *1965, researcher at the Institute for Contemporary German Literature and Media at the Philipps University in Marburg. Has taught numerous courses and published many articles on the aesthetics and theory of contemporary film. Lives in Marburg.

Eric Stahl (ES), *1965, studied German language and literature, focusing on communications. Film journalist; cultural editor of *Woman* magazine and freelance writer for other publications. Lives in Berlin.

Rainer Vowe (RV) *1954, historian, works for the EU Directorate General XII (audio-visual media) and the Institute for Film and Television Studies at the Ruhr University in Bochum. Numerous articles about the history of cinema and television. Lives in Bochum.

CREDITS

The publishers would like to thank the distributors, without whom many of these films would never have reached the big screen.

AFM, APOLLO, ARSENAL, ATLAS, BASIS, CINEMA INTERNATIONAL, COLUMBIA TRI STAR, CONCORDE, CONSTANTIN, FANTASIA, FIFIGE, FILMVERLAG DER AUTOREN UND FUTURA FILM, JUGENDFILM, DIE LUPE, MFA, MGM, NEF, NEUE VISIONEN, P.H.-KNIPP-FILM, PROGRESS, PROKINO, SCOTIA, SILVER CINE, TOBIS STUDIOCANAL, TWENTIETH CENTURY FOX, UIP – UNITED INTERNATIONAL PICTURES, UNITED ARTISTS, WARNER BROS., ZEPHIR, ZORRO, ZUKUNFT.

Academy Award® and Oscar® are the registered trademark and service mark of the Academy of Motion Picture Arts and Sciences.

If, despite our concerted efforts, a distributor has been unintentionally omitted, we apologise and will amend any such errors brought to the attention of the publishers in the next edition.

ACKNOWLEDGEMENTS

As the editor of this volume, I would like to thank all those who invested so much of their time, knowledge and energy into the making of this book. My special thanks to Thierry Nebois of TASCHEN for his coordination work and truly amazing ability to keep track of everything. Thanks also Birgit Reber and Andy Disl for their ingenious design concept that gives pride of place to the pictures, the true capital of any film book. My thanks to Philipp Berens and Thomas Dupont from defd and *Cinema*, and Hilary Tanner from the British Film Institute for their help in accessing the original stills. Then, of course, I am hugely indebted to the authors, whose keen analyses form the backbone of this volume. I would also like to thank David Gaertner for his meticulous technical editing, and Petra Lamers-Schütze, whose commitment and initiative got the project going. And last but not least, Benedikt Taschen, who not only agreed to produce and publish the series, but enthusiastically followed each volume's progress from start to finish. My personal thanks to him and everyone else mentioned here.

ABOUT THIS BOOK

The 120 films selected for this book represent a decade of cinema. It goes without saying this involved making a number of difficult choices, some of which may be contested. A note also on the stills from some of the earlier films: it is a regrettable but inevitable fact that the older the film, the more difficult it is to obtain images of the required technical quality.

Each film is presented by an essay, and accompanied by a glossary text devoted to one person or a cinematographic term. An index of films and a general index are provided at the back of the book to ensure optimal access.

As in the preceding volumes, the films are dated according to the year of production, not the year of release.

IMPRINT

ENDPAPERS / PAGES 1–19
AND PAGES 702–703

A CLOCKWORK ORANGE / Stanley Kubrick
WARNER BROS.

PAGE 20

EDWARD SCISSORHANDS / Tim Burton / 20TH CENTURY FOX

© 2003 TASCHEN GMBH
Hohenzollernring 53, D–50672 Köln
WWW.TASCHEN.COM

PHOTOGRAPHS

defd and CINEMA, Hamburg
BRITISH FILM INSTITUTE, London

PROJECT MANAGEMENT
EDITORIAL COORDINATION
DESIGN
TEXTS

PETRA LAMERS-SCHÜTZE, Cologne
STILISTICO and THIERRY NEBOIS, Cologne
SENSE/NET, ANDY DISL and BIRGIT REBER, Cologne
PHILIPP BÜHLER (PB), DAVID GAERTNER (DG), MALTE HAGENER (MH), STEFFEN HAUBNER (SH),
JÖRN HETEBRÜGGE (JH), HARALD KELLER (HK), KATJA KIRSTE (KK), HEINZ-JÜRGEN
KÖHLER (HJK), OLIVER KÜCH (OK), PETRA LANGE-BERNDT (PLB), NILS MEYER (NM),
ECKHARD PABST (EP), LARS PENNING (LP), ANNE POHL (APO), STEPHAN REISNER (SR),
BURKHARD RÖWEKAMP (BR), ERIC STAHL (ES) RAINER VOWE (RV)

TECHNICAL EDITING
ENGLISH TRANSLATION

DAVID GAERTNER, Berlin
DANIEL A. HUYSSEN (texts), PATRICK LANAGAN (introduction and texts), SHAUN SAMSON
(texts and captions) for ENGLISH EXPRESS, Berlin

EDITING

DANIELA KLEIN for ENGLISH EXPRESS, BERLIN and JONATHAN MURPHY, Brussels

PRODUCTION

UTE WACHENDORF, Cologne

PRINTED IN ITALY
ISBN 3–8228–2191–8